A study book for the

NEBOSH International General Certificate

in Occupational Health & Safety

rms

RMS Publishing Limited
Victoria House, Lower High Street, Stourbridge DY8 1TA

© ACT Associates Limited.
First Edition September 2007.

All rights reserved. No part of this publication may be stored in a retrieval system, reproduced, or transmitted in any form or by any means, electronic, mechanical, photocopying, recording or otherwise without either the prior written permission of the Publishers.

This book may not be lent, resold, hired out or otherwise disposed of by way of trade in any form or binding or cover other than that in which it is published, without the prior consent of the Publishers.

Whilst every effort is made to ensure the completeness and accuracy of the information contained herein, RMS/ACT can bear no liability for any omission or error.

Cover design by Graham Scriven.
Printed and bound in Great Britain by CPI Antony Rowe.

ISBN-13: 978-1-900420-90-7

Editor's Notes

Diagrams and photographs

A number of the diagrams included in the study book for the NEBOSH International General Certificate have been produced in hand-drawn format. In particular these are diagrams that students studying for NEBOSH examinations may be required, or find it helpful, to produce by hand at the time of examination. They are provided to help the student to get an impression of how to do similar drawings of their own. I hope that these diagrams show that such drawings are achievable by hand and also assist in illustrating a standard that might be expected in examination.

We have taken particular care to support the text with a significant number of photographs. They are illustrative of both good and bad working practices and should always be considered in context with supporting text. I am sure that students will find this a useful aid when trying to relate their background and experience to the broad based NEBOSH International General Certificate syllabus. They will give an insight into some of the technical areas of the syllabus that people have difficulty relating to when they do not have a strong technical background.

Where diagrams/text extracts are known to be drawn from other publications, a clear source reference is shown and RMS/ACT wish to emphasise that reproduction of such diagrams/text extracts within the study book is for educational purposes only and the original copyright has not been infringed.

Syllabus

Each element of the study book has an element overview that sets out the learning outcomes of the element, the content and any connected sources of reference. The study book reflects the order and content of the NEBOSH International General Certificate syllabus and in this way the student can be confident that the study book reflects the themes of the syllabus.

Acknowledgements

Managing Editor: Ian Coombes MIOSH - Managing Director, ACT; NEBOSH Advisory Committee and Board member; IOSH professional Affairs Committee member.

RMS Publishing and ACT Associates Ltd wish to acknowledge the following contributors and thank them for their assistance in the preparation of the International General Certificate study book: Nick Attwood, Sundeep Kaur Bagri, Roger Chance, Andrew Hayes, Dean Johnson, Geoff Littley, Janice McTiernan, Barrie Newell, Robert Sannwald, Clive Raybould, Richard Sherwood and Julie Skett.

NEBOSH Study Books also available from RMS:

Publication	Edition	10-digit ISBN	13-digit ISBN	EAN
The Study Book for the NEBOSH National General Certificate	Fourth	1 900420 87 2	978-1-900420-87-7	9781900420877
The Study Book for the NEBOSH Certificate in Fire Safety and Risk Management	Second	1 900420 88 0	978-1-900420-88-4	9781900420884
The Study Book for the NEBOSH National Certificate in Construction Safety and Health	Second	1 900420 89 9	978-1-900420-89-1	9781900420891
The Study Books for the NEBOSH National Diploma in Occupational Safety and Health:				
■ (Unit A) Managing Health and Safety	Second	1 900420 77 5	978-1-900420-77-8	9781900420778
■ (Unit B) Hazardous Agents in the Workplace	Second	1 900420 78 3	978-1-900420-78-5	9781900420785
■ (Unit C) Workplace and Work Equipment	Second Revised & Updated	1 900420 91 0	978-1-900420-91-4	9781900420914

Contents

ELEMENT   TITLE   PAGE NO.

UNIT IGC1 - MANAGEMENT OF INTERNATIONAL HEALTH AND SAFETY

Element	Title	Page
Element 1:	Foundations in health and safety	1
Element 2:	Policy	17
Element 3:	Organising for health and safety	23
Element 4:	Promoting a positive health and safety culture	31
Element 5:	Risk assessment	47
Element 6:	Principles of control	61
Element 7:	Monitoring, review and audit	79
Element 8:	Occupational incident and accident investigation, recording and reporting	89

UNIT IGC2 - CONTROL OF INTERNATIONAL WORKPLACE HAZARDS

Element	Title	Page
Element 1:	Movement of people and vehicles - hazards and control	99
Element 2:	Manual and mechanical handling - hazards and control	113
Element 3:	Work equipment - hazards and control	135
Element 4:	Electrical - hazards and control	159
Element 5:	Fire - hazards and control	171
Element 6:	Chemical and biological - health hazards and control	193
Element 7:	Physical and psychological - health hazards and control	221
Element 8:	Construction activities - hazards and control	243

Assessment   273

Figure List (including tables and quotes)

Figure Ref Title and Source *Page No.*

UNIT IGC1 - MANAGEMENT OF INTERNATIONAL HEALTH AND SAFETY

Element 1

1-1-1	Health definition. *Source: Occupational Safety and Health Convention (c155), ILO.*	3
1-1-2	Safety definition. *Source: OHSAS 18001:1999.*	3
1-1-3	Accident definition. *Source: OHSAS 18001:1999.*	4
1-1-4	Definition of a dangerous occurrence. *Source: ILO- RNOAD - Code of Practice.*	4
1-1-5	Definition of commuting accident. *Source: ILO- RNOAD - Code of Practice.*	4
1-1-6	Definition of hazard. *Source: OHSAS 18001:1999.*	4
1-1-7	Definition of risk. *Source: OHSAS 18001:1999.*	4
1-1-8	Sample costs of accidents. *Source: The costs of accidents at work, HSG96, HSE Books.*	6
1-1-9	Costs incurred by the main contractor (1:11) during the building of a supermarket. *Source: ACT / HSG96.*	7
1-1-10	Practicable. *Source: Corel Clipart.*	11
1-1-11	Key elements of successful health and safety management. *Source: ILO-OSH 2001, HSG65, HSE books.*	16

Element 3

1-3-3	Joint occupancy. *Source: ACT.*	28
1-3-4	Occupier's liability - to public. *Source: ACT.*	28

Element 4

1-4-1	Safety culture. *Source: NEBOSH Examiners Report.*	33
1-4-2	Observation made by chairman Mao Tse Tung. *Source: "Little Red Book".*	36
1-4-3	Maslow's hierarchy of needs. *Source: Maslow.*	37
1-4-4	Examples of perception images. *Source: Ambiguous.*	38
1-4-5	Model of perception. *Source: ACT.*	38
1-4-6	Human failures flow chart. *Source: HSG48.*	38
1-4-7	Safety notice board. *Source: ACT.*	43
1-4-8	Safety suggestion scheme. *Source: ACT.*	43

Element 5

1-5-1	Results of an accident. *Source: ACT.*	50
1-5-2	Accident ratio study. *Source: Frank Bird.*	51
1-5-3	Example of a job analysis sheet. *Source: ACT.*	53
1-5-4	Example of a job/task analysis. *Source: ACT.*	53
1-5-5	Risk assessment form. *Source: ACT.*	58

Element 6

1-6-1	Competence v supervision. *Source: ACT.*	64
1-6-2	Categories of safety signs. *Source: ACT.*	65
1-6-3	Prohibition signs. *Source: ACT.*	65
1-6-4	Warning and mandatory signs. *Source: ACT.*	65
1-6-5	Mandatory sign. *Source: ACT.*	65
1-6-6	Safe condition sign. *Source: ACT.*	65
1-6-7	Hazard identification - obstruction. *Source: ACT.*	66
1-6-8	Hazard identification - restricted width. *Source: ACT.*	66
1-6-9	PPE quote. *Source: Guidance on the Personal Protection Equipment Regulations 1992.*	67
1-6-10	Confined space - chamber. *Source: ACT.*	71
1-6-11	Confined space - sewer. *Source: ACT.*	71
1-6-12	Confined space - tank. *Source: ACT.*	71
1-6-13	Confined space - open tank. *Source: ACT.*	71
1-6-14	Entrance to a confined space. *Source: ACT.*	72
1-6-15	Access to a confined space. *Source: HSG150, HSE.*	72
1-6-16	Hot work permit - front of form. *Source: Lincsafe.*	75
1-6-17	Hot work permit - reverse of form. *Source: Lincsafe.*	75
1-6-18	Example of a permit to work for entry into confined spaces. *Source: HSE Guidance note on permits to work.*	76

Element 7

1-7-1	Accident statistics. *Source: ACT.*	82
1-7-2	Extract from Audit 123 Level 2 Vol 1 of 2 Auditor's Guidance [ISBN 1 900420 83 X]. *Source: RMS Publishing.*	85
1-7-3	Sampling - extract from Audit 123 Level 3 Section 1 Workbook [ISBN 1 900420 50 3] *Source: RMS Publishing.*	86
1-7-4	Policy statement abstract. *Source: Standard Wire Corporation circa. 1996.*	86
1-7-5	Extract from Audit 123 Level 3 Section 1 Auditor's Guidance [ISBN 1 900420 14 7]. *Source: RMS Publishing.*	87
1-7-6	Sample pages from the ACT / RMS Audit 123 system. *Source: ACT.*	88

Element 8

1-8-1	Definition of a dangerous occurrence. *Source: International Labour Office (ILO) - Recording and Notifying of Occupational Accidents and Diseases (RNOAD) - Code of Practice.*	91
1-8-2	Definition of an incident. *Source: International Labour Office (ILO).*	92
1-8-3	Domino theory of accident causation. *Source: Frank Bird.*	94

© ACT

UNIT IGC2 - CONTROL OF INTERNATIONAL WORKPLACE HAZARDS

Element 1

2-1-1	Trip hazards. *Source: ACT.*	101
2-1-2	Slip hazards. *Source: ACT.*	101
2-1-3	Falls from a height. *Source: ACT.*	101
2-1-4	Falls from a height - roof used for storage. *Source: ACT.*	101
2-1-5	Obstructed designated walkway. *Source: ACT.*	102
2-1-6	Falling materials i.e. unstable stack. *Source: ACT.*	102
2-1-7	Anti-slip flooring. *Source: ACT.*	103
2-1-8	Slip resistance surface on steps. *Source: ACT.*	103
2-1-9	Typical warehouse vehicle unloading / loading area showing separate pedestrian access. *Source: HSG76.*	104
2-1-10	Correct clothing and footwear. *Source: ACT.*	104
2-1-11	Vision panels in fire doors. *Source: ACT.*	105
2-1-12	Collision - lack of vehicle management. *Source: ACT.*	107
2-1-13	Risk of collision between people / vehicles. *Source: ACT.*	107
2-1-14	Roll bar and seat restraint. *Source: ACT.*	108
2-1-15	Falling materials. *Source: ACT.*	108
2-1-16	Segregating pedestrians and vehicles. *Source: ACT.*	109
2-1-17	No segregation - high visibility clothing. *Source: ACT.*	109
2-1-18	Control of vehicle movement. *Source: ACT.*	109
2-1-19	Barriers and marking. *Source: ACT.*	110
2-2-20	Visual warning on a dumper truck. *Source: ACT.*	110

Element 2

2-2-1	Manual handling - Spine. *Source: ACT.*	115
2-2-2	Sample manual handling risk assessment form. *Source: HSE Guidance L23.*	115
2-2-3	Manual handling. *Source: ACT.*	116
2-2-4	Reduction of handling capability as the hands move away from the central body area. *Source: HSE Guidance L23.*	116
2-2-5	Mechanical assistance. *Source: ACT.*	117
2-2-6	Frequently used objects should be stored in the 'A' zone. Source: www.comcare.gov.au.	118
2-2-7	Kinetic lifting - How not to do it! *Source: Ambiguous.*	118
2-2-8	Kinetic lifting - How not to do it! *Source: Manual handling, major workplace hazards, Government of South Australia.*	119
2-2-9	Work bench heights. *Source: www.comcare.gov.au.*	119
2-2-10	Work bench heights. *Source: www.comcare.gov.au*	119
2-2-11	Using a forklift to move a drum eliminates the Manual Handling required. *Source: www.comcare.gov.au.*	120
2-2-12	An electrically operated vacuum lifter eliminates the heavy lifting. The mechanical arm is guided by the employee. *Source: www.comcare.gov.au*	120
2-2-13	Ingredients can be put into a hopper then lifted by a hoist. *Source: www.comcare.gov.au*	120
2-2-14	Basic lifting principles. *Source: Ambiguous*	121
2-2-15	Industrial counter balance lift truck. *Source: HSE Guidance HSG6.*	123
2-2-16	Industrial reach truck. *Source: HSE Guidance HSG6.*	123
2-2-17	Rough-terrain counter balance lift truck. *Source: HSE Guidance HSG6.*	123
2-2-18	Telescopic materials handler. *Source: HSE Guidance HSG6.*	123
2-2-19	Side loading lift truck. *Source: HSE Guidance HSG6.*	124
2-2-20	Pedestrian controlled lift truck. *Source: HSE Guidance HSG6.*	124
2-2-21	Large lift truck. *Source: HSE Guidance HSG6*	124
2-2-22	Width of traffic route. *Source: ACT.*	125
2-2-23	Keys not secure. *Source: ACT.*	125
2-2-24	Hand operated pallet truck. *Source: ACT.*	126
2-2-25	Sack truck. *Source: ACT.*	126
2-2-26	Lift / hoist. *Source: HSG150, HSE books.*	126
2-2-27	Diagrammatic layout of belt conveyor showing in-running nips. *Source: J Ridley; Safety at Work; Fourth Edition.*	127
2-2-28	Preventing free running roller trap. *Source: J Ridley; Safety at Work; Fourth Edition - Courtesy HSE.*	127
2-2-29	Guards between alternative drive-rollers. *Source: J Ridley; Safety at Work; Fourth Edition - Courtesy HSE.*	127
2-2-30	Roller conveyor. *Source: ACT.*	127
2-2-31	Belt conveyor guard. *Source: ACT.*	127
2-2-32	Nip points on roller conveyor with belts. *Source: J Ridley; Safety at Work; Fourth Edition - Courtesy HSE.*	127
2-2-33	Screw conveyor guarding. *Source: J Ridley; Safety at Work; Fourth Edition - Courtesy HSE.*	127
2-2-34	Safety latch on hook. *Source: Corel Clipart.*	128
2-2-35	Lifting operation. *Source: ACT.*	129
2-2-36	Lifting points on load. *Source: ACT.*	129
2-2-37	Safety latch on hook. *Source: ACT.*	129
2-2-38	Accessories. *Source: ACT.*	129
2-2-39	Crane operation. *Source: ACT.*	130
2-2-40	Lifting operations. *Source: ACT.*	130
2-2-41	Lifting operations. *Source: ACT.*	130
2-2-42	Stability of cranes (hand drawn example). *Source: ACT.*	131
2-2-43	Danger zone - crane and fixed item viewed from above. *Source: ACT.*	132
2-2-44	Siting and stability. *Source: ACT.*	132

Element 3

2-3-1	Conveyor. *Source: ACT.*	139
2-3-2	Electrical isolator with hole for padlock. *Source: ACT.*	139
2-3-3	Inspection and examination. *Source: ACT.*	140
2-3-4	Air compressor. *Source: ACT.*	140
2-3-5	Air receiver. *Source: ACT.*	140
2-3-6	Controls and emergency stop. *Source: ACT.*	142

© ACT

2-3-7	Controls. *Source: ACT.*	142
2-3-8	Hammer shaft split with peg holding on head and very worn. hammer head. *Source: ACT.*	143
2-3-9	Mushroom shape head. *Source: ACT*	143
2-3-10	Piece of tube used as an extension. *Source: ACT.*	143
2-3-11	Broken file. *Source: ACT.*	143
2-3-12	Packing material used in spanner head. *Source: ACT.*	143
2-3-13	File used as a lever. *Source: ACT.*	143
2-3-14	Auger drill - entanglement. *Source: STIHL.*	144
2-3-15	Grinder - entanglement, eye injury & abrasion.. *Source: ACT.*	144
2-3-16	Chop saw - cutting. *Source: Speedy Hire plc.*	144
2-3-17	Abrasive wheel - abrasion. *Source: ACT.*	144
2-3-18	Nail gun - stabbing & puncture. Source: Speedy Hire plc.	145
2-3-19	Mobile elevated work platform - shear. *Source: ACT.*	145
2-3-20	Elevated work platform - crushing. *Source: ACT.*	145
2-3-21	Digger and dumper truck - impact. *Source: ACT.*	145
2-3-22	Lift mast - drawing-in. *Source: ACT.*	145
2-3-23	Lathe - ejection. *Source: ACT.*	145
2-3-24	Disc saw - ejection. *Source: Water Active, Nov 06.*	146
2-3-25	Fluid injection. *Source: ACT.*	146
2-3-26	Examples of mechanical machinery hazards (Questions). *Source: ACT.*	146
2-3-27	Abrasive wheel (grinder). *Source: ACT.*	147
2-3-28	Document shredder. *Source: www.axminster.co.uk.*	147
2-3-29	Bushcutter. *Source: www.kawasaki.co.uk*	148
2-3-30	Cement mixer. *Source: ACT.*	149
2-3-31	Bench cross-cut circular saw. *Source: ACT.*	149
2-3-32	Pedestal drill. *Source: ACT.*	149
2-3-33	Examples of mechanical machinery hazards (Answers). *Source: ACT.*	150
2-3-34	Fixed guard (hand drawn example). *Source: ACT.*	151
2-3-35	Total enclosure fixed guard. *Source: BS EN ISO 12100.*	151
2-3-36	Fixed guard - panel removed. *Source: ACT.*	151
2-3-37	Fixed guard over fan - mesh too big. *Source: ACT.*	151
2-3-38	Open and closed interlock guard. *Source: BS EN ISO 12100.*	152
2-3-39	Power press - interlock guard. *Source: BS EN ISO 12100.*	152
2-3-40	Automatic guard for a power press. *Source: BS EN ISO 12100.*	153
2-3-41	Trip device. *Source: BS EN ISO 12100.*	153
2-3-42	Trip device on radial drill. *Source: ACT.*	153
2-3-43	Adjustable (fixed) guard. *Source: BS EN ISO 12100.*	154
2-3-44	Self adjusting (fixed) guard. *Source: ACT.*	154
2-3-45	Two-Hand control device. *Source: BS EN ISO 12100..*	154
2-3-46	Fixed guard and push stick. *Source: Lincsafe.*	154
2-3-47	Information and instruction. *Source: ACT.*	155
2-3-48	PPE and supervision. *Source: ACT.*	155

Element 4

2-4-1	A basic electric circuit. *Source: ACT.*	161
2-4-2	An electric circuit under fault conditions showing resistance in the path of a fault current. *Source: R. Gilmour.*	161
2-4-3	Effects of current flowing in the human body. *Source: ACT.*	162
2-4-4	Risk of electric shock due to damage to cable. *Source: ACT.*	163
2-4-5	Work on live circuits. *Source: ACT.*	163
2-4-6	First aid sign. *Source: ACT.*	163
2-4-7	Used coiled up - risk of overheating. *Source: ACT.*	164
2-4-8	Max current capacity exceeded. *Source: ACT.*	164
2-4-9	Worn cable - risk of electrical fire. *Source: ACT.*	164
2-4-10	Evidence of overheating. *Source: ACT.*	164
2-4-11	Hazard - fused wired out. *Source: ACT.*	165
2-4-12	Continued use of defective equipment. *Source: ACT.*	165
2-4-13	Hazard - damaged cable. *Source: ACT.*	165
2-4-14	Hazard - taped joints. *Source: ACT.*	165
2-4-15	Plug - foil fuse no earth. *Source: ACT.*	166
2-4-16	Earthing. *Source: ACT.*	166
2-4-17	110V centre tapped earth transformer. *Source: ACT.*	167
2-4-18	Battery powered drill - 12V. *Source: ACT.*	167
2-4-19	110V powered drill. *Source: ACT.*	167
2-4-20	110V powered drill. *Source: ACT.*	167
2-4-21	Residual current device. *Source: ACT.*	168
2-4-22	Plug-in residual current device. *Source: ACT.*	168
2-4-23	Double insulated 240V drill. *Source: ACT.*	168
2-4-24	Double insulation symbol. *Source: HSG107.*	168
2-4-25	PAT labels. *Source: ACT.*	170

Element 5

2-5-1	Fire triangle. *Source: Corel.*	173
2-5-2	Smoking materials. *Source: ACT.*	173
2-5-3	Combustible materials - waste. *Source: ACT.*	173
2-5-4	Careless action - waste paper and smoking materials. *Source: ACT.*	175
2-5-5	Misusing equipment - overloaded electrical sockets. *Source: ACT.*	175
2-5-6	Defective electrical equipment. *Source: ACT.*	175
2-5-7	Potential for deliberate ignition. *Source: ACT.*	175
2-5-8	Compartment undermined - holes cut. *Source: ACT.*	176
2-5-9	Fire door held open. *Source: ACT.*	176
2-5-10	Materials inappropriately stored. *Source: ACT.*	176

2-5-11	Welding equipment. *Source: ACT.*	179
2-5-12	Control arson by external security. *Source: ACT.*	179
2-5-13	Control arson by internal security. *Source: ACT.*	179
2-5-14	Poor storage of flammable liquids. *Source: ACT.*	181
2-5-15	Storage of flammable materials. *Source: ACT.*	181
2-5-16	Gas cylinders for huts. *Source: ACT.*	182
2-5-17	Magnetic door holder linked to alarm. *Source: ACT.*	183
2-5-18	Door stop with automatic release. *Source: ACT.*	183
2-5-19	Smoke detector. *Source: ACT.*	184
2-5-20	Easy operation alarm call point. *Source: ACT.*	184
2-5-21	Alarm point identified & well located. *Source: ACT.*	184
2-5-22	Colour coding by label and sign. *Source: ACT.*	185
2-5-23	Types and use of fire extinguishers - summary. *Source: ACT.*	187
2-5-24	Fire extinguisher colour codes and classifications - Australia. *Source: www.wikipedia.org.*	187
2-5-25	Fire extinguisher colour codes and classifications - United Kingdom. *Source: www.wikipedia.org.*	187
2-5-26	Fire extinguisher symbols and classifications - United States. *Source: www.wikipedia.org*	188
2-5-27	Fire escape - hazard. *Source: ACT.*	189
2-5-28	Assembly point. *Source: ACT.*	189
2-5-29	Fire instruction notice. *Source: ACT.*	190

Element 6

2-6-1	Harmful, toxic. *Source: ACT.*	196
2-6-2	Respiratory system. *Source: BBC.*	199
2-6-3	Hand drawn respiratory system. *Source: ACT.*	199
2-6-4	Digestive system. *Source: STEM.*	199
2-6-5	Hand drawn digestive system. *Source: ACT.*	199
2-6-6	Skin layer. *Source: SHP.*	199
2-6-7	Hand drawn skin layer. *Source: ACT.*	199
2-6-8	Dermatitis. *Source: SHP.*	200
2-6-9	Detector tube example (hand drawn). *Source: ACT.*	204
2-6-10	Gas detector pump *Source: Drager.*	204
2-6-11	Personal sampling equipment. *Source: ROSPA OS&H Apr 98.*	205
2-6-12	Stain tube detector operating instructions. *Source: Reproduced by kind permission of Drager.*	206
2-6-13	Reduced exposure - bulk supply. *Source: ACT.*	209
2-6-14	Captor system on circular saw. Clearly shows the fixed captor hood, flexible hose and rigid duct. *Source: ACT.*	210
2-6-15	Shows the size of fan and motor required for industrial scale LEV. *Source: ACT.*	210
2-6-16	Flexible hose showing how captor hood can be repositioned to suit the work activity. *Source: ACT.*	210
2-6-17	Self contained unit which can be moved around the workplace. *Source: ACT.*	210
2-6-18	Components of a basic system (basic sketch). *Source: ACT.*	210
2-6-19	Paper filter respirator. *Source: Haxton Safety.*	211
2-6-20	3M disposable respirator. *Source: ACT.*	212
2-6-21	Full face canister respirator. *Source: Haxton Safety.*	212
2-6-22	Breathing apparatus. *Source: Haxton Safety.*	212
2-6-23	Mis-use of respirator. *Source: ACT.*	212
2-6-24	Eye and ear protection. *Source: Speedy Hire plc.*	213
2-6-25	Arc welding visor - UV reactive. *Source: ACT.*	213
2-6-26	Goggles. *Source: ACT.*	213
2-6-27	Spectacles. *Source: ACT.*	213
2-6-28	Gloves. *Source: Speedy Hire plc.*	214
2-6-29	Protective clothing - gloves. *Source: Haxton Safety.*	214
2-6-30	Personal Protective Equipment. *Source: ACT.*	214
2-6-31	Hazard label - environment. *Source: ACT.*	217
2-6-32	Environmental hazard oil spill. *Source: ACT.*	217

Element 7

2-7-1	Workstation design. *Source: ACT.*	223
2-7-2	Poor posture. *Source: Speedy Hire plc.*	224
2-7-3	Position of screen, reflective desk surface. *Source: ACT.*	225
2-7-4	Basic office chair, glare and space. *Source: ACT.*	225
2-7-5	Accommodation for clothing. *Source: ACT.*	227
2-7-6	Facilities for rest and to eat meals. *Source: ACT.*	227
2-7-7	Reflected light from window. *Source: ACT.*	228
2-7-8	Light from windows controlled by blinds. *Source: ACT.*	228
2-7-9	Inner ear diagram. *Source: www.echalk.co.uk.*	229
2-7-10	The ear (hand drawn). *Source: ACT.*	229
2-7-11	Rms and peak levels of a sound wave. *Source: ACT.*	229
2-7-12	Noise hazard sign. *Source: ACT.*	230
2-7-13	Mandatory signs. *Source: Stocksigns.*	230
2-7-14	Basic layout of the main control methods. *Source: ACT.*	232
2-7-15	Cover to reduce noise. *Source: ACT.*	232
2-7-16	Ear defenders. *Source: ACT.*	233
2-7-17	Disposable ear plugs. *Source: ACT.*	233
2-7-18	Use of road drill - vibration. *Source: ACT.*	234
2-7-19	Dumper truck seat. *Source: ACT.*	235
2-7-20	Workplace temperature. *Source: ACT.*	237
2-7-21	Ionising radiation. *Source: ACT.*	238
2-7-22	UV - from welding. *Source: Speedy Hire plc.*	239
2-7-23	Radio mast. *Source: ACT.*	239
2-7-24	Personal dose monitor. *Source: ACT.*	241
2-7-25	Contamination monitoring. *Source: ACT.*	241
2-7-26	Definition of work related violence. *Source: HSE.*	242

Element 8

2-8-1	Storage of materials. *Source: ACT.*	245
2-8-2	Poor storage of ladder and scaffold. *Source: ACT.*	245
2-8-3	Unauthorised access. *Source: ACT.*	246
2-8-4	Perimeter fencing and signs. *Source: ACT.*	246
2-8-5	Traffic passing beneath power lines. *Source: HSG144.*	247
2-8-6	Working near power lines. *Source: HSG144.*	247
2-8-7	Risk of falling objects. *Source: ACT.*	248
2-8-8	Risk of people falling. *Source: ACT.*	248
2-8-9	Ladder too long. *Source: ACT.*	248
2-8-10	Excavation hazards. *Source: ACT.*	248
2-8-11	Pre-demolition survey. *Source: ACT.*	249
2-8-12	Site Signs. *Source: ACT.*	249
2-8-13	Working above ground level. *Source: ACT.*	252
2-8-14	Ladder hoop. *Source: http://www.demuth.com*	254
2-8-15	Independent tied scaffold (hand drawn example). *Source: ACT.*	256
2-8-16	Independent tied scaffold. *Source: ACT.*	256
2-8-17	Independent tied scaffold. *Source: HSG150 Safety in Construction.*	256
2-8-18	Mobile tower scaffold. *Source: ACT.*	257
2-8-19	Tower scaffold. *Source: ACT.*	257
2-8-20	Base plates and sole boards. *Source: Lincsafe.*	257
2-8-21	Base plate and protection. *Source: ACT.*	257
2-8-22	Scaffold boards - some defective. *Source: ACT.*	258
2-8-23	Brick guards. *Source: HSG150 Safety in Construction.*	258
2-8-24	Tie through window. *Source: ACT.*	259
2-8-25	Ladder access. *Source: ACT.*	259
2-8-26	Side nets and sheets. *Source: ACT.*	259
2-8-27	Safety nets. *Source: ACT.*	259
2-8-28	Signs. *Source: ACT.*	260
2-8-29	Marking. *Source: ACT.*	260
2-8-30	Fans. *Source: ACT.*	260
2-8-31	Wheels with brakes. *Source: ACT.*	260
2-8-32	Mobile elevated work platform (MEWPs). *Source: ACT.*	260
2-8-33	Mobile elevated work platform (MEWPs). *Source: ACT.*	261
2-8-34	Use of harness with a MEWP. *Source: HSG150.*	261
2-8-35	Scissor lift. *Source: HSG150 ,HSE.*	261
2-8-36	Scissor lift. *Source: ACT.*	261
2-8-37	Ladder as access and workplace. *Source: ACT.*	262
2-8-38	Improper use. *Source: ACT.*	262
2-8-39	Poor storage. *Source: Lincsafe.*	263
2-8-40	Use of roof ladders. *Source: HSG150, HSE.*	263
2-8-41	Stepladder. *Source: ACT.*	263
2-8-42	Buried services. *Source: ACT.*	264
2-8-43	Excavation hazards. *Source: ACT.*	264
2-8-44	Battering. *Source: ACT.*	265
2-8-45	Trench box - for shoring. *Source: ACT.*	265
2-8-46	Close boarded excavation. *Source: BS6031.*	266
2-8-47	Open sheeting. *Source: BS6031.*	266
2-8-48	Close sheeting. *Source: ACT.*	266
2-8-49	Open sheeting. *Source: ACT.*	266
2-8-50	Marking of services. *Source: ACT.*	267
2-8-51	Materials storage. *Source: ACT.*	268
2-8-52	Preventing water ingress. *Source: ACT.*	268
2-8-53	This mans right leg had to be amputated owing to the severe burns he sustained from kneeling in wet cement for three hours. *Source: The Safety and Health Practitioner (Aug 2003).*	271

© ACT

List of abbreviations

GENERAL

AC	Alternating Current
ACOP	Approved Code of Practice
A&E	Accident & Emergency Services
APF	Assigned Protection Factor
BSI	British Standards Institution
CAT	Cable Avoidance Tool
CE	Conformité Européene
CEN	European Standards
CFCs	Chlorofluorocarbons
COP	Code of Practice
COSHH	Control of Substances Hazardous to Health
CPR	Cardio Pulmonary Resuscitation
CTS	Carpal Tunnel Syndrome
dB	Decibel
DC	Direct Current
DOSH	Department of Occupational Safety and Health
DSE	Display Screen Equipment
EEA	European Economic Area
ETA	Event Tree Analysis
EU	European Union
FLT	Forklift Truck
FMEA	Failure Mode and Effect Analysis
FTA	Fault Tree Analysis
GHS	Globally Harmonised System
HASAWA	Health and Safety at Work etc., Act 1974
HAVS	Hand-arm Vibration Syndrome
HAZOP	Hazard and Operability Studies
HSC	Health and Safety Commission
HSE	Health and Safety Executive
HSG	Health and Safety Guidance
Hz	Hertz
ICRP	International Commission on Radiological Protection
IEC	International Electrotechnical Commission
IEE	Institute of Electrical Engineers
ILO	International Labour Organisation
ILV	Indicative Limit Values
IOSH	Institute of Occupational Safety and Health
ISO	International Organisation for Standardization
IT	Information Technology
KPI	Key Performance Indicator
LEV	Local Exhaust Ventilation
LPG	Liquified Petroleum Gas
LTEL	Long Term Exposure Limit
mA	milliAmperes
mS	milliSeconds
MDI	Methylene Bisphenyl Di-isocyanate
MEWP	Mobile Elevated Work Platform
MSDS	Material Safety Data Sheets
MSW	Municipal Solid Wastes
OECD	Organisation for Economic and Cooperation and Development
OEL	Occupational Exposure Limit
OHS	Occupational Health Safety
OHSAS	Occupational Health and Safety Assessment Series
OSHA	Occupational Safety and Health
PAT	Portable Appliance Testing
PPE	Personal Protective Equipment
RCD	Residual Current Device
RCSs	Risk Control Systems
RNOAD	Recording and Notification of Occupational Accidents and Diseases
RPE	Respiratory Protective Equipment
SNR	Single Number Rating
STEL	Short Term Exposure Limit
SWL	Safe Working Load
TDI	Toluene Di-isocyanate
TWA	Time Weighted Average
UK	United Kingdom
URL	Unique Resource Locator

© ACT

USA	United States of America
UV	Ultra Violet
VWF	Vibration White Finger
WBV	Whole Body Vibration
WHO	World Health Organisation
WRULD	Work Related Upper Limb Disorder

Element 1

Foundations in health and safety

Learning outcomes

On completion of this element, candidates should be able to demonstrate understanding of the content through the application of knowledge to familiar and unfamiliar situations. In particular they should be able to:

1.1 Outline the scope and nature of occupational health and safety.

1.2 Explain briefly the moral, social and economic reasons for promoting good standards of health and safety.

1.3 Outline the role of national governments and international bodies in formulating a framework for the regulation of health and safety.

1.4 Identify the nature and key sources of health and safety information.

1.5 Outline the key elements of a health and safety management system.

Content

1.1 - The scope and nature of occupational health and safety 3
    The multi-disciplinary nature of health and safety 3
    Meanings of and distinctions between common terms..3
1.2 - The moral, social and economic reasons for maintaining and promoting health and safety.........................5
    General argument..5
    The size of the problem 5
    Health and safety requirements...5
    The business case for health and safety 6
1.3 - The role of national governments and international bodies in formulating a framework for regulation of
    health and safety 7
1.4 - Sources of information on health and safety 11
    Internal to the organisation 11
    External to the organisation 13
    Information provided by national and international agencies 14
1.5 - The key elements of a health and safety management system 15

Sources of reference

Guidelines on Occupational Safety and Health Management Systems (IL0-OSH 2001) ISBN 0-580-37805-5

ILOLEX (ILO database of International Law) http://www.ilo.org/ilolex/index.htm

Occupational Health and Safety Assessment Series (OHSAS 18000): Occupational Health and Safety Management Systems OHSAS 18001:1999 (ISBN-0-580-28298-8), OHSAS 18002:2000 (ISBN: 0-580-33123-7), BSI

Occupational Safety and Health Convention (C155), ILO

Occupational Safety and Health Recommendation (R164), ILO

1.1 - The scope and nature of occupational health and safety

The multi-disciplinary nature of health and safety

Health and safety is a fundamental aspect of managing an organisation as it impacts on all the functions within the organisation, just as quality might. Health and safety embraces a number of disciplines reflecting the scope of its influence, including finance, insurance, health, personnel, production, design, purchase and information technology (IT).

The barriers to success with health and safety are the same as with other business objectives, with an additional barrier being that the main operational requirements of the organisation will tend (unless the organisation has the balance correct) to take priority, whether this is construction, manufacture or health care. Organisations tend to focus on the immediate costs of implementing health and safety rather than the benefits that can be gained from doing so. The constant struggle to balance often complex, conflicting demands and behavioural issues with protecting profits (or those wanting to budget) by not spending unnecessarily is something that those wishing to improve health and safety face daily. The organisation may divert resources from health and safety needs to issues such as quality improvement.

Successful organisations are realising the need to take an inclusive approach to heath and safety that balances effort between the four primary issues - service, quality and health, safety and environment - by implementing technical, procedural and behavioural solutions.

Meanings of and distinctions between common terms

HEALTH, SAFETY, WELFARE AND ENVIRONMENTAL PROTECTION

Health

"a state of well being"

The term 'health' has been defined as a state of well being. It includes well being in a physiological and psychological sense. In occupational terms this would include not suffering from noise-induced deafness, mental fatigue or stress.

> "The term health, in relation to work, indicates not merely the absence of disease or infirmity; it also includes the physical and mental elements affecting health which are directly related to safety and hygiene at work".

Figure 1-1-1: Health - definition. *Source: Occupational Safety and Health Convention (c155), ILO.*

There is an element of overlap with the terms 'safety" and 'health'; for example, it would be clear that someone who has experienced a fall could sustain a physical injury such as a broken bone (a safety issue). In addition, it would not be a surprise if someone observed that the injured party had a 'poor state of health' for the period that the injury affected them. Maintaining health includes attention to the various health hazards (agents) in the working environment that can affect the worker and others, for example, chemical and biological agents.

Safety

"absence of danger of physical harm"

The term 'safety' is considered to be the absence of danger of physical harm to people. The term would extend to other things that could be harmed in the workplace such as equipment, structures and materials.

> "Freedom from unacceptable risk of harm".

Figure 1-1-2: Safety - definition. *Source: OHSAS 18001:1999.*

Attention to safety matters would typically deal with hazards such as fall from a height, fire, electricity, and moving plant, machinery and equipment.

Welfare

"facilities for workplace comfort"

The term 'welfare' relates to the provision of workplace facilities that maintain the basic well being and comfort of the worker, such as eating, washing, toilet facilities and first aid.

Environmental protection

"a measure used to prevent harm to the environment of the world"

The term 'environmental protection' relates to measures that are specifically focused on maintaining the general environment of the world. As such it focuses on such things as protection of plant life, animals, water, and land and air quality. Though the protection does not focus on the worker or other people directly by protecting the environment, people obtain a benefit.

OCCUPATIONAL ACCIDENTS, DANGEROUS OCCURRENCES, NEAR-MISSES AND WORK-RELATED ILL-HEALTH, COMMUTING ACCIDENTS

Occupational accidents

"an unplanned, uncontrolled event which led to, or could have led to loss"

The term 'accident' relates to the variety of events that occur which have, or might have, a detrimental effect in the workplace. The detrimental effect could be a physical injury to a person, equipment damage or one in which no material loss had occurred (near miss).

UNIT IGC1 - ELEMENT 1 - FOUNDATIONS IN HEALTH AND SAFETY

"an undesired event giving rise to death, ill health, injury, damage or other loss".

Figure 1-1-3: Accident - definition. *Source: OHSAS 18001:1999.*

The International Labour Office (ILO) Code of Practice for Recording and Notification of Occupational Accidents and Diseases: (RNOAD) defines an occupational accident as:

"An occurrence arising out of or in the course of work which results in:

(a) Fatal occupational injury. (b) Non-fatal occupational injury."

Dangerous occurrences

"an accident not resulting in personal injury reportable to the national competent authority"

"Readily identifiable event as defined under national laws and regulations, with potential to cause an injury or disease to persons at work or the public."

Figure 1-1-4: Definition of a dangerous occurrence. *Source: ILO- RNOAD - Code of Practice.*

Some countries list specific dangerous occurrences that are required to be reported by the employer to external agencies under national laws. Examples of dangerous occurrences are failure of lifting equipment, failure of a pressurised closed vessel and explosions.

Near-misses

"an accident that results in no apparent loss"

The term 'near-miss' refers to an event (accident) which did not result in personal injury, equipment damage or some other loss, but under slightly different circumstances could have done (e.g. a building block falling off a scaffold and landing on the floor). In terms of occupational health and safety performance, whether the accident resulted in actual loss or had the potential to (near-miss) is almost immaterial, as in both cases there would have been a failure to prevent danger of harm. Many management systems do not make a distinction between accidents and near-miss events, applying appropriate reporting and investigation techniques and resources to both.

Work related ill-health (physiological and psychological)

"harm to a worker's health caused by their work"

The term refers to harm to a worker's health caused by their work and will include harm to health in a physiological or psychological way. This would include ill-health in the form of asbestosis, noise-induced deafness and mental fatigue or stress. Some forms of ill health are specified by certain countries following ILO - RNOAD code of practice and are required to be reported to external agencies.

Commuting accidents

"A commuting accident is an accident occurring on the direct way between the place of work and

(a) The worker's principal or secondary residence.

(b) The place where the worker usually takes his or her meals.

(c) The place where he or she usually receives his or her remuneration.

And which results in death or personal injury involving loss of working time."

Figure 1-1-5: Definition of commuting accident. *Source: ILO- RNOAD - Code of Practice.*

In the majority of legal systems worldwide, commuting accidents are also included in the scope of cover of workers' compensation insurance and in most cases, it is the state monopoly systems that grant this extended cover.

HAZARD AND RISK

Hazard

"something that has the potential to cause harm (loss)"

"source or situation with a potential for harm in terms of injury or ill health, damage to property, damage to the workplace environment or a combination of these"

Figure 1-1-6: Definition of hazard. *Source: OHSAS 18001:1999.*

An example would be a substance, which could be a hazard in a particular way depending on the properties of the substance, e.g. a wet mixture of cement or concrete could present a chemical (alkaline) burn hazard.

Risk

"the likelihood of a given loss occurring in defined circumstances"

"combination of the likelihood and consequence(s) of a specified hazardous event occurring"

Figure 1-1-7: Definition of risk. *Source: OHSAS 18001:1999.*

For example, the risk from a substance is the likelihood that it will harm a person in the actual circumstances of use. This will depend upon:

a) The hazard presented by the substance.

b) How it is controlled.

c) Who is exposed, to how much and for how long, and what they are doing.

In the example of cement there is a risk that it may cause temporary harm, for example, contact dermatitis. But the level of risk will depend on the actual circumstances, including the susceptibility of the person, how much contact they have with the cement and the types of controls in place e.g. wearing protective gloves.

See also - Unit IGC1 - Element 5 - Risk Assessment.

1.2 - The moral, social and economic reasons for maintaining and promoting health and safety

General argument

There are three good reasons for preventing accidents in the workplace:

1) **Moral**

   Injury accidents result in a great deal of pain and suffering for those affected. A worker should not have to expect that by coming to work life or limb is at risk, nor should others be adversely affected by the worker's undertaking.

2) **Social**

   The moral reason to prevent harm is usually further reinforced in both civil law and criminal law, as without the potential for regulatory action or litigation, many employers would not act upon their implied obligation of protection. In many countries it is a specific legal requirement to safeguard the health and safety of workers and others that might be affected by the organisation's operations.

3) **Economic**

   Accidents at work cost a great deal of money, especially when we add in damage accidents (particularly when they interrupt production, downgrade the quality of our products or impair the environment). Many Governments realise that poor occupational health and safety performance gives rise to additional costs to the State (e.g. social security payments to the incapacitated and costs of medical treatment). Employers also sustain costs in the event of an accident at work (such as legal fees, fines, compensatory damages, investigation time and lost goodwill from the workforce, customers and wider community).

The size of the problem

The size of the problem internationally is difficult to fully quantify in terms of fatalities, injuries and incidence of work related ill health as data is reported in different ways in different countries. Globally, it is estimated that two million work-related deaths take place annually. Men suffer two thirds of those deaths. The biggest groups of work-related diseases are cancers, circulatory diseases and communicable diseases.

Some examples of the international experience of various regulatory agencies, drawn from a paper "Global estimates of fatal work-related diseases" by Päivi Hämäläinen, Jukka Takala,, Kaija Leena Saarela, is given below.

In the EU, the European Agency for Safety and Health at Work have identified that a worker is involved in a work-related accident at least every five seconds, and every two hours one worker dies in an accident at work.

The Association of Workers' Compensation Boards of Canada, states that 1,097 workplace fatalities were recorded in Canada in 2005, which on average equates to almost five work-related deaths per work day. In comparison in the same period, according to the USA's Bureau of Labour Statistics, 5,702 people suffered fatal injury and over 4,000,000 people were injured.

Every working day in Great Britain at least one person is killed and over 6,000 are injured at work. In the United Kingdom (UK) the Health and Safety Executive (HSE) statistics reveal that 212 workers were killed at work during the year 2005/06. Of the workers killed at work falls from height, being struck by a vehicle and being struck by a falling object account for 54% of all fatal injuries. Nearly 150,000 other injuries were reported under RIDDOR 1995 and, about 30,000,000 days where lost in total due to work related ill health and injury. Slipping and tripping accounts for 38% of all major injuries. The second most common type of major injuries is those sustained whilst lifting, handling or carrying. These types of injury account for 41% of all "3 day" injuries.

Irrespective of the country involved, the types of injuries arising from accidents tend to follow broad trends. Falling from height, being struck by a vehicle and being struck by a falling object are primary causes of fatal injuries, whereas manual handling and slips, trips and falls are significant causes of non-fatal injuries accounting for lost time.

Accidents and ill health are costly to workers and their families. They can also impact significantly on organisations because, in addition to costs of personal injuries, they may incur far greater costs from damage to property or equipment, and lost business time such as production.

Health and safety requirements

ILO - Occupational Health and Safety Convention C155 sets out broad requirements for member countries to follow to ensure health and safety requirements are set into national laws.

Article 16 requires:

1. Employers shall be required to ensure that, so far as is reasonably practicable, the workplaces, machinery, equipment and processes under their control are safe and without risk to health.

2. Employers shall be required to ensure that, so far as is reasonably practicable, the chemical, physical and biological substances and agents under their control are without risk to health when the appropriate measures of protection are taken.

A number of countries have established an employer's 'common law' duty of care which is owed to workers. This is a legal obligation imposed on an individual (including an employer) requiring that they exercise a reasonable standard of care while performing any acts that could foreseeably harm others. This duty of care could be considered as formalising the implicit responsibilities held by an individual towards another individual within society.

In the UK the employer's duty of care in common law has been established for some time and obligates the employer to take **'reasonable care of those that might foreseeably be affected by its acts or omissions'**. If the employer fails to meet this duty, they may be considered negligent. The duty extends to workers and to others (e.g. visitors) who might foreseeably be affected. It follows that workers have the right to work in a workplace and in a manner that provides reasonable protection from harm. Wilson's and Clyde Coal Co. Ltd v. English (1938) *(The NEBOSH International General Certificate does not require students to be able to quote case names)* is a notable legal precedent used to identify an employer's common law duties as the provision and maintenance of:

- A safe place of work.
- Safe appliances and equipment.
- A safe system of work.
- Competent and safety conscious personnel.

Common law constitutes the basis of the legal systems of: England and Wales, Northern Ireland, the Republic of Ireland, federal law in the United States and the states' laws (except Louisiana), federal law in Canada and the provinces' laws (except Quebec civil law), Australia (both federal and individual states), New Zealand, South Africa, India, Sri Lanka, Malaysia, Brunei, Pakistan, Singapore, Malta, Hong Kong, and many other generally English-speaking countries or Commonwealth countries. Essentially, every country which was colonised at some time by Britain uses common law except those that had been colonised by other nations, such as Quebec (which follows French law to some extent) and South Africa (which follows Roman Dutch law), where the prior civil law system was retained to respect the civil rights of the local people. India's system of common law is also a mixture of English law and the local Hindu law.

In addition to the common law duty of care many countries, including those of the European Union, have placed similar requirements to ensure health and safety is represented within common law and criminal law. Notably in the UK criminal law was introduced in 1974, the Health and Safety at Work etc Act 1974 set out specific legal requirements to provide a safe place of work, safe plant and equipment, safe systems of work, training and supervision. A number of countries have enacted similar legislation in more recent years.

The business case for health and safety

DIRECT AND INDIRECT COSTS OF ACCIDENTS AND ILL-HEALTH

The Occupational Safety and Health Administration (OSHA) of the USA found that the ratio of indirect costs to direct costs varies widely but for smaller claims of up to $3,000 they are often 4.5:1. OSHA also identified that workplace injuries alone cost USA businesses over $110 billion in 1993. Similarly, in 1993, in the UK the Health and Safety Executive (HSE) published a series of five case studies to illustrate just how much accidents at work could cost a company. The industries chosen were from a wide range of activities. The following table illustrates the losses identified.

		Total loss	Annualised loss	Representing
1	Construction site	£245,075	£700,000*	8.5% tender price
2	Creamery	£243,834	£975,336	1.4% operating costs
3	Transport company	£48,928	£195,712	1.8% of operating costs 37% of profits
4	Oil platform	£940,921	£3,763,684	14.2% of potential output

* represents length of contract.

Figure 1-1-8: Sample costs of accidents.

Source: The costs of accidents at work, HSG96, HSE Books.

Direct costs
- Lost time of injured worker and any continued payments to worker or family.
- Damage to the equipment, tools, property, plant or materials.
- Medical or first aid costs.
- Time and materials to clean up after the accident.
- Insurance, indemnity or compensation payments.
- Court costs.
- Fines.

Indirect costs
- Lost time by other workers who stop work or reduce performance.
  - Out of curiosity.
  - Out of sympathy.
  - Weakened morale.
- Lost time by supervisor or other managers.
  - Assisting injured worker.
  - Investigating the cause of the accident.
  - Arranging for the injured worker's production to be continued by some other employee.
  - Selecting or training a new worker to replace injured employee.
  - Preparing accident reports, attending hearings, inquests courts.
- Interference with production leading to failure to fill orders on time, loss of bonuses, penalty payments and similar causes.

INSURED AND UNINSURED COSTS

Some costs of accidents can have limited immediate impact on an organisation because they are offset by insurance arrangements, for example, compensation claims and medical costs. This can give the impression that there is no need to take interest in the costs of accidents.

In fact the larger part of accident costs are the uninsured costs such as time to investigate, first aid and the cost of damage or clean up. These costs are not only uninsured but are usually hidden costs relating to the accident. The UK HSE case studies shown above were used to identify the differences between insured costs and uninsured costs. It was shown that uninsured costs were between 8 and 36 times greater than the costs of insurance premiums. The following 'Accident Costs Iceberg' represents the ratio of insured to uninsured costs incurred by the main contractor (1:11) during the building of a supermarket. UK HSE studies found that uninsured costs outweighed insured costs by up to 36 times.

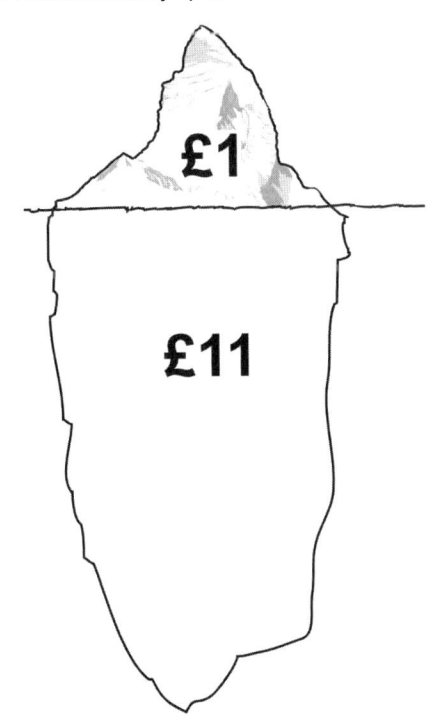

INSURED COSTS

- Employer's Liability
- Public / Third party liability
- Contractors all risks
- Plant and building damage
- Tool and equipment

UNINSURED COSTS

- Product and materials damage
- Emergency supplies
- Production delays
- Overtime and temporary labour
- Investigation time
- Supervisors' time diverted

Figure 1-1-9: Costs incurred by the main contractor (1:11) during the building of a supermarket.   Source: ACT / HSG96.

EMPLOYERS LIABILITY INSURANCE

The purpose of employers' liability insurance is to satisfy requirements for employers to carry appropriate insurance so that a worker, who is harmed due to the fault of their employer, is assured of receiving compensation even though the employer might have insufficient resources to pay compensation directly. This form of insurance enables organisations to meet the costs of compensation and legal fees. At a time where the number of claims and size of awards is increasing, and insurance premiums rise similarly, this type of insurance is exerting significant pressure on employers to improve their standards of health and safety.

Employers' liability insurance is designed to protect workers who have suffered a personal loss. Separate provision will need to be considered for the many costs associated with a workplace accident that may not, depending on the policies carried, be covered by insurance. Other costs that may be incurred relate to:

- Production delays.
- Damaged goods and equipment.
- Accident investigation.
- Loss of expertise or experience.
- Hiring and training replacement staff.
- Loss of goodwill and reputation.
- Clean-up operations.
- Possible fines and associated legal fees.

1.3 - The role of national governments and international bodies in formulating a framework for regulation of health and safety

The International Labour Organisation (ILO) sets out conventions, member states subscribing to the work of the ILO agree to be bound by conventions that they have ratified. Member states use the conventions to guide their approach to health and safety. This is particularly useful to emerging countries that have not gained experience of the issues to manage in complex industrialised countries. It saves them developing their own approach through their own experience, which would be both painful and costly in terms of human life. The ILO have set out a number of conventions and recommendations which relate to the management of health and safety, recording and notifying accidents, health and safety for the workplace and work equipment. ILO conventions set out what should be done by member countries at a national level and what should be done at employer level. Workers' rights and responsibilities are included within the conventions.

ILO - Occupational Health and Safety Convention C155 sets out broad requirements for member countries to follow to ensure health and safety requirements are set into national laws.

Article 8 requires - "Each Member shall, by laws or regulations or any other method consistent with national conditions and practice and in consultation with the representative organisations of employers and workers concerned, take such steps as may be necessary to give effect to Article 4 of this Convention. Article 4 requires "a coherent national policy on occupational safety, occupational health and the working environment".

National Governments set out law in a form that suits their culture and perspectives. In the past a lot of national legislation has been developed to deal with specific problems that have occurred in specific industries.

More recently national legislation is being introduced that reflects more the broad requirements in ILO - Occupational Health and Safety Convention C155, which is designed to make employers put in more arrangements to manage the health and safety risks without national legislation telling them what they must do for every risk. A good example of this would be the Malaysian Occupational Safety and Health Act 1994.

EMPLOYERS' RESPONSIBILITIES

According ILO Occupational Health and Safety Convention C155, employers have multiple responsibilities. These include ensuring that, so far as is reasonably practicable, the workplaces, machinery, equipment and processes under their control are safe and without risk to health. They must also ensure that, so far as is reasonably practicable, the chemical, physical and biological substances and agents under their control are without risk to health when the appropriate measures of protection are taken. This includes provision, where necessary, of adequate protective clothing and protective equipment to prevent, so far is reasonably practicable, risk of accidents or of adverse effects on health. Employers must also provide measures to deal with emergencies and accidents, including adequate first-aid arrangements.

Whenever two or more employers are engaged in activities simultaneously at one workplace, they must collaborate in applying the above requirements.

Some countries have set out employers' responsibilities in criminal law, for example in the United States of America (USA) the Occupational Safety and Health Act 1970:

"Section 5 - Duties

(a) Each employer

(1) shall furnish to each of his workers employment and a place of employment which are free from recognized hazards that are causing or are likely to cause death or serious physical harm to his workers;

(2) shall comply with occupational safety and health standards promulgated under this Act".

Similarly, in Malaysia general duties for employers and the self employed include:

"Section 15. General duties of employers and self-employed persons to their workers.

(1) It shall be the duty of every employer and every self-employed person to ensure, so far as is practicable, the safety, health and welfare at work of all his employees."

In common with a number of other countries Malaysia clarifies this general duty with specific duties which included:

(a) provision and maintenance of plant and systems of work

(b) safety and absence of risks to health in connection with the use or operation, handling, storage and transport of plant and substances

(c) information, instruction, training and supervision as is necessary

(d) place of work maintained in a condition that is safe and without risks to health and the provision and maintenance of the means of access to and egress

(e) provision and maintenance of a working environment and facilities for welfare at work".

WORKERS' RESPONSIBILITIES AND RIGHTS

Similarly, the ILO sets out workers' responsibilities to protect themselves and those around them from harm. They are expected to co-operate with their employer with regard to obligations placed upon the employer, including reporting any situation that presents imminent risk or serious danger. In order to achieve this, workers should receive adequate information and training on measures taken by the employer to secure occupational safety and health. They or their representatives should be consulted by the employer on all aspects of occupational safety and health associated with their work. Workers should not be made to work in situations of continuing imminent or serious danger, until the employer takes remedial action.

In the United States of America (USA) the Occupational Safety and Health Act 1970 sets out workers' duties in section 5:

"(b) Each employee shall comply with occupational safety and health standards and all rules, regulations, and orders issued pursuant to this Act which are applicable to his own actions and conduct".

Similarly, in Malaysia the Occupational Safety and Health Act 1994 sets out a number of duties of workers:

"Section 24. General duties of employees at work.

(1) It shall be the duty of every employee while at work:

(a) to take reasonable care for the safety and health of himself and of other persons who may be affected by his acts or omissions at work;

(b) to co-operate with his employer or any other person in the discharge of any duty or requirement imposed on the employer or that other person by this Act or any regulation made there under;

(c) to wear or use at all times any protective equipment or clothing provided by the employer for the purpose of preventing risks to his safety and health; and (d) to comply with any instruction or measure on occupational safety and health instituted by his employer or any other person by or under this Act or any regulation made hereunder.

(2) A person who contravenes the provisions of this section shall be guilty of an offence and shall, on conviction, be liable to a fine not exceeding one thousand ringgit or to imprisonment for a term not exceeding three months or to both.

Section 25. Duty not to interfere with or misuse things provided pursuant to certain provisions.

A person who intentionally, recklessly or negligently interferes with or misuses anything provided or done in the interests of safety, health and welfare in pursuance of this Act shall be guilty of an offence and shall, on conviction, be liable to a fine not exceeding twenty thousand ringgit or to imprisonment for a term not exceeding two years or to both.

Section 26. Duty not to charge employees for things done or provided.

No employer shall levy or permit to be levied on any employee of his any charge in respect of anything done or provided in pursuance of this Act or any regulation made hereunder.

Section 27. Discrimination against employee, etc.

(1) No employer shall dismiss an employee, injure him in his employment, or alter his position to his detriment by reason only that the employee-

(a) makes a complaint about a matter which he considers is not safe or is a risk to health;

(b) is a member of a safety and health committee established pursuant to this Act; or

(c) exercises any of his functions as a member of the safety and health committee.

(2) No trade union shall take any action on any of its members who, being an employee at a place of work-

(a) makes a complaint about a matter which he considers is not safe or is a risk to health;

(b) is a member of a safety and health committee established pursuant to this Act; or

(c) exercises any of his functions as a member of the safety and health committee.

(3) An employer who, or a trade union which, contravenes the provisions of this section shall be guilty of an offence and shall, on conviction, be liable to a fine not exceeding ten thousand ringgit or to a term of imprisonment not exceeding one year or to both.

(4) Notwithstanding any written law to the contrary, where a person is convicted of an offence under this section the Court may, in addition to imposing a penalty on the offender, make one or both of the following orders:

(a) an order that the offender pays within a specific period to the person against whom the offender has discriminated such damages as it thinks fit to compensate that person;

(b) an order that the employee be reinstated or re-employed in his former position or, where that position is not available, in a similar position".

See also - Unit IGC1 - Element 3 - Organising for health and safety.

ROLE OF ENFORCEMENT AGENCIES AND CONSEQUENCES OF NON-COMPLIANCE

ILO - Occupational Health and Safety Convention C155 sets out broad requirements for member countries to follow to ensure health and safety requirements are set into national laws and enforced. Member countries that ratify the convention are expected to set into place mechanisms to enforce the law and establish penalties for non-compliance. In order that the enforcement agencies can identify compliance or non-compliance the ILO convention expects the member countries to establish a system of inspection. In addition, the ILO convention expects employers to be provided with information and advice on compliance. The advisory part of the role may be set apart from the inspection and enforcement part of the role. The convention recognises that compliance with law will not happen without advice and information and that compliance has to be verified by inspection.

Convention C155 sets out the following requirements:

Article 9

"1. The enforcement of laws and regulations concerning occupational safety and health and the working environment shall be secured by an adequate and appropriate system of inspection.

2. The enforcement system shall provide for adequate penalties for violations of the laws and regulations.

Article 10

Measures shall be taken to provide guidance to employers and workers so as to help them to comply with legal obligations."

Different states take different approaches to legislation, regulation, and enforcement. In the European Union (EU), Member States have enforcing authorities to ensure that the basic legal requirements relating to occupational health and safety are met. In the UK, on behalf of the Government, the Health and Safety Commission (HSC) identify the need for legal requirements, arrange drafts and consultation. .Health and safety legislation is enforced by the Health and Safety Executive (HSE) and local authorities under powers provided by the Health and Safety at Work Act 1974. In the USA, OSHA, the Occupational Safety and Health Administration, has been regulating occupational health and safety since 1971.

In Malaysia, the Department of Occupational Safety and Health (DOSH) under the Ministry of Human Resource is responsible to ensure the safety, health and welfare of workers in both the public and private sector. DOSH enforces the Occupational Safety and Health Act 1994

Enforcing agencies may take a number of approaches to their role. A common approach would be, where possible, to take a monitoring and advisory role in the workplace but, where necessary, have a wide range of powers that enable them to enforce compliance. They will often set out requirements orally or in writing as they see fit. If a more formal approach is required they will usually issue some form of formal notice of non-compliance, an enforcement notice, or take steps to prosecute.

In order for enforcing agencies to carry out their role effectively they are often provided with powers, commonly this would include powers to:

- Enter premises at any reasonable time.
- Take a constable or some other authorised person if there is an obstruction in the execution of his duty.
- Examine and investigate.
- Direct that premises or part of premises remain undisturbed.
- Take photographs and measurements.
- Sample or retain unsafe articles and substances.
- Order the testing, dismantling and examination.
- Take possession of items.

UNIT IGC1 - ELEMENT 1 - FOUNDATIONS IN HEALTH AND SAFETY

- Require answers to questions with a signed statement, if necessary.
- Inspect and copy statutory books and documents or any other relevant documents.
- Assistance.
- Order a medical examination.
- Any other power.
- Serve:
    - Improvement notice / citation.
    - Prohibition notice.

INTERNATIONAL STANDARDS AND CONVENTIONS

The **International Organisation for Standardization (ISO)** is an international standard-setting body composed of representatives from various national standards bodies. Founded in 1947, the organisation produces world-wide industrial and commercial standards.

While the ISO defines itself as an Non-Governmental organization (NGO), its standards often become law, either through treaties or national standards. In practice, the ISO acts as a consortium with strong links to Governments. There are approximately 158 members of the ISO, each of which represents one country. ISO's main products are the international standards, but the ISO also creates technical reports, technical specifications, publicly available specifications, technical corrigenda (minor amendments to standards), and guides.

ISO international standards are not in any way binding on either Governments or industry merely by virtue of being international standards. This is to allow for situations where certain types of standards may conflict with social, cultural or legislative expectations and requirements. This also reflects the fact that national and international experts responsible for creating these standards do not always agree and not all proposals become standards by unanimous vote. The individual nations and their standards bodies remain the final arbiters. As yet ISO has not established an international standard for health and safety management systems.

The **International Labour Organisation (ILO)** is "devoted to advancing opportunities for women and men to obtain decent and productive work in conditions of freedom, equity, security and human dignity. Its main aims are to promote rights at work, encourage decent employment opportunities, enhance social protection and strengthen dialogue in handling work-related issues.

In promoting social justice and internationally recognized human and labour rights, the organization continues to pursue its founding mission that labour peace is essential to prosperity. Today, the ILO helps advance the creation of decent jobs and the kinds of economic and working conditions that give working people and business people a stake in lasting peace, prosperity and progress."

The ILO was founded in 1919. It is the only 'tripartite' United Nations agency in that it brings together representatives of governments, employers and workers to jointly shape policies and programmes. The ILO derives Conventions which members ratify, and when ratified they are expected to meet the requirements of the convention. It also produces recommendations, guidelines (Guidelines on Health and Safety Management Systems), codes of practice (Ambient Factors in the Workplace) and reports on issues that affect health and safety. In addition it produces a number of informative books, including the very useful health and safety encyclopaedia.

ABSOLUTE AND QUALIFIED REQUIREMENTS

The various organisations that set out requirements for health and safety at international and national level use terms to express the extent necessary to satisfy the requirement. These terms include:

    1. absolute   2. practicable   3. reasonably practicable   4. reasonable

Absolute statutory requirements

This duty does not allow choice and takes no allowance of how much effort is required to achieve it. Absolute requirements can be identified by the use of words such as 'shall' and 'must'. ILO - Occupational Health and Safety Convention C155 uses this term for requirements at national level, for example:

"Article 4

1. Each Member **shall**, in the light of national conditions and practice, and in consultation with the most representative organisations of employers and workers, formulate, implement and periodically review a coherent national policy on occupational safety."

Practicable requirements

Practicable requirements are those requirements carried out to the extent only limited by the current state of knowledge and invention. They have to be met even though implementation may be difficult, inconvenient and/or costly. For example, on a national level, the Malaysian Occupational Safety and Health Act 1994 sets out the requirement:

"Section 15

(1) It shall be the duty of every employer and every self-employed person to ensure, so far as is **practicable**, the safety, health and welfare at work of all his employees."

Reasonably practicable requirements

A requirement that has to be carried out 'as far as is reasonably practicable' is one where there is a risk/benefit trade off. An employer is entitled to balance costs of remedy against benefits in reduction of risk and if the benefit is minimal compared to the cost, he/she need not carry out the duty. "Reasonably practicable" is a narrower term than "physically possible" and implies that a computation must be made, in which the quantum of risk is placed on one scale and the sacrifices involved in the measures necessary for averting the risk (whether in money, time or trouble) is placed on the other, and that if it be shown that there is a gross disproportion between them, the defendants discharge the onus on them to take that measure. It should be remembered that this would not mean no action at all is taken, just that a less costly and less effective measure would be used instead.

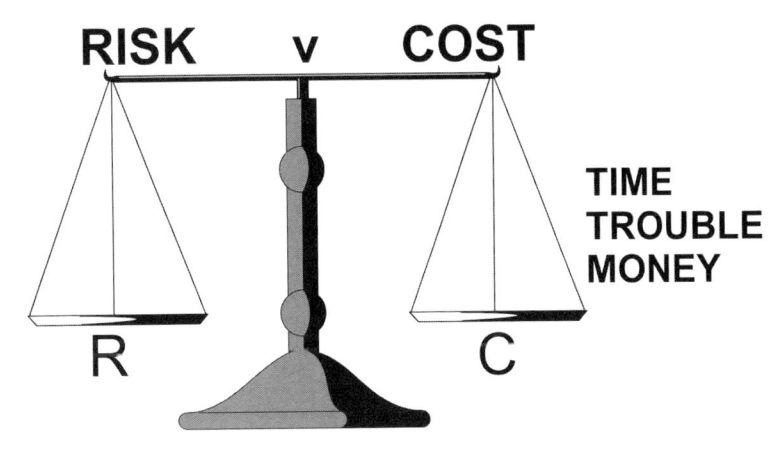

Figure 1-1-10: Reasonably practicable. *Source: Corel Clipart.*

ILO - Occupational Health and Safety Convention C155 uses this term for requirements at employer level, for example:

"Article 16

1. Employers shall be required to ensure that, so far as is **reasonably practicable**, the workplaces, machinery, equipment and processes under their control are safe and without risk to health."

Reasonable

Reasonable requirements are those requirements which might normally be expected of an average person taking care of what they are doing. For example, on a national level, the Malaysian Occupational Safety and Health Act 1994 sets out the requirement:

"Section 15

...duty of every employee while at work:

(a) to take **reasonable** care for the safety and health of himself and of other persons who may be affected by his acts or omissions at work."

1.4 - Sources of information on health and safety

Internal to the organisation

ACCIDENT/ILL-HEALTH AND ABSENCE DATA

Used properly, accident/ill-health and absence data allow comparisons to be made between different organisations and business sections by monitoring year on year performance. Analysis can be made to identify areas of possible concern and the overall effectiveness of any new control measures that may have been introduced. Data can be collected internally using accident records and report forms or from outside sources such as:

- The World Health Organisation (WHO).
- The International Labour Organisation (ILO).
- National records of the competent authorities.

There are several methods of presenting data for analysis and some of the more common ones are given below. Methods should not be mixed and figures should only be used to compare like with like. The multipliers used vary depending on whether the rates are derived at international, national or workplace organisation level. There is no formal structure as to what multipliers are used but the main purpose of the multiplier is to bring the numbers to a manageable size.

Accident/injury incidence rates

The typical national competent authority formula for calculating an annual injury incidence rate is:

$$\frac{\text{Number of injuries in a year} \times 100,000}{\text{Average number employed during year}}$$

This is the rate per 100,000 workers. It does not allow for part-time workers or overtime and should only be used for a comparison of an annual calculation. There must be an adjustment made if shorter periods are to be considered. The UK Government, as a competent authority, calculates national incidence rates using the 100,000 multiplier. When workplace organisations calculate their own incident rate the number employed and injuries will be far less and it is common practice to use a smaller multiplier, for example 1,000.

Accident/injury frequency rates

Some national competent authorities prefer to calculate injury frequency rates, often per million hours worked. Using the hours worked rather than the number of workers avoids the problem of part-time workers and overtime causing a distortion as it does in the incidence rate calculation. It should be noted that the International Labour Office uses 1,000,000 as a multiplier for the frequency rate, OSHA/ Bureau of Labour Statistics in USA use 200,000. As with incidence rates many workplace organisations use a smaller multiplier, for example, 100,000.

$$\frac{\text{Number of injuries in the period} \times 1,000,000}{\text{Total hours working during the period}}$$

Accident/injury severity rates

$$\frac{\text{Total number of days lost} \times 1{,}000}{\text{Total hours worked}}$$

The injury severity rate does not necessarily correlate well with the seriousness of the injury. The data may be affected by the propensity of people in different parts of the world and their ability to take time off after a particular injury.

Mean duration rate

$$\frac{\text{Total number of days lost}}{\text{Total number of accidents}}$$

Duration rate

$$\frac{\text{Number of hours worked}}{\text{Total number of accidents}}$$

Absence data

Why data should be analysed

Analysing absence data is critical for two reasons:

- The process enables an organisation to determine whether it has a work related absence problem.
- It can help the organisation to understand the causal effects of absenteeism.

Assessing the magnitude of absenteeism

'Days lost per employee' and 'percentage lost time' are the two measures used to gain an overall understanding of the magnitude of the problem.

$$\text{Days lost per employee} = \frac{\text{Total days lost}}{\text{Number of workers}}$$

$$\text{Percentage lost time} = \frac{\text{Number of days lost through absence} \times 100}{(\text{Number of workers}) \times (\text{Number working days})}$$

Technically, percentage lost time is the better overall measure of absenteeism. Days lost per employee, however, has an advantage in terms of simplicity of calculation. For this reason, it is the measure most commonly used by organisations to assess absenteeism.

RESULTS OF AUDITS / INSPECTIONS

The aim of audits and inspections is to give management a detailed picture regarding the standards of health and safety management within the organisation. Thus audits and inspection are, essentially, confirmatory exercises which demonstrate that the health and safety management system is effective. The level and detail of audits/inspections carried out will depend on the type of organisation and its confidence in the existing management system.

Information from audits and inspections enables both symptoms as well as the cause to be identified and appropriate action taken. It is critical to ensure that risk control measures provided by the organisation, including equipment and systems of work, are appropriate and that action is taken to establish and maintain good standards. Auditors will normally obtain information from three sources:

1. Interviewing individuals both about the operation of the health and safety management system and practices and their knowledge, understanding and perceptions of it.
2. Examining documentation for completeness, accuracy and reliability.
3. Visual observation of physical conditions and working practices to ensure conformity to legal and organisational standards.

Inspections generally rely on examination and observation of physical conditions in the workplace. Inspections can provide a perspective of the level of control of workplace hazards.

INVESTIGATION REPORTS

Any accident may result in a claim. It is essential that organisations anticipate this and at the earliest opportunity, assemble data necessary to consider whether a claim may be defended. Investigating accidents, and copying relevant data to a controlled document file, is normally part of the accident investigation process. Immediate and root (underlying) causes of accidents should be analysed and appropriate preventative measures identified and implemented.

MAINTENANCE RECORDS

If a system of planned maintenance is implemented then, by definition, any breakdown is likely to be accidental. Therefore, all breakdowns must be reported and investigated. Trends and patterns of failures can be analysed and the necessary preventative action taken. Equipment often fails to an unsafe condition, for example, the brakes on a car. Being able to predict, and therefore prevent these situations is an essential safety management tool.

COST AND OTHER AND MANAGEMENT PERFORMANCE DATA

Cost and management performance data is generated by nearly all organisations. This internal information is often relevant to the health and safety management system and should not be overlooked.

COMPLIANCE DATA

The results of compliance visits by enforcing authorities can sometimes give a limited view of an organisation's compliance with health and safety legislation. Enforcing authorities often have an aspect of their function which includes providing information on risks and controlling them. Some people are reluctant to seek advice from these sources as they do not wish to draw attention to themselves. The web sites of these organisations usually provide access to information without obligation or threat.

External to the organisation

MANUFACTURERS' DATA

ILO conventions set out an expectation that manufacturers make adequate information available to those they supply with machinery, articles or substances. The information should be sufficient to enable the person to use the machinery, article or substance safely and should cover reasonably foreseeable risks including those arising from disposal and dismantling. Information should be revised and supplied again if, as a result of testing or research, new hazards come to light. This is a very important and useful source of information which may give a perspective on risk and control measures.

LEGISLATION (E.G. DIRECTIVES, ACTS AND REGULATIONS)

These are prime sources of information which set out requirements that improve health and safety at an international and national level. For countries that do not have an established structure for health and safety it is possible to make use of legislation used in other countries as a 'good practice' approach. They are helpful to workplace organisations setting out requirements that can encourage an organisation to put systems in that ensure health and safety. They can be difficult to read without some legal understanding and it is also easy to miss changes and amendments unless an updating service is used.

GOOD PRACTICE AND GUIDANCE

Good practices are technical and/or practical documents prepared by a variety of interested parties, including labour inspectorates, social partners, accident insurance companies, industry associations, and practitioners' associations. They often demonstrate solutions to occupational health and safety issues. As these solutions can be transferred to other employers, or other countries, information on good practice provides a useful source of reference. They contribute to internal development of prevention policies and procedures, and savings of time, energy, and money.

Unlike regulatory standards, they are not drafted according to a specified format or procedure, and are generally not submitted to an approval procedure by officially recognised standards organisations. Due to this, good practice solutions and guidance are not considered legally binding, but are often used in the judicial process to demonstrate the expected level of health and safety performance required so that a preventive action can be achieved.

INTERNATIONAL

The International Labour Organisation (ILO) deals with labour standards, fundamental principles and rights at work. They have a website and a database listing all types of work-related information. It sets out conventions, recommendations and guidelines to assist countries and organisations to develop approaches that improve health and safety.

The World Health Organisation is the United Nation's specialised agency for health and was established in 1948. It has information on health, where good health is defined as a state of complete physical, mental and social well-being and not merely the absence of disease or infirmity.

EUROPEAN

The European Safety Agency was set up by the European Union (EU) to bring together the vast reservoir of knowledge and information on occupational health and safety related issues and preventive measures.

BRITISH

The British Standards Institute (BSI) provides some high quality advice which is usually above the legal minimum standard. There is a distinct trend towards linking British Standards with legislation, for example, with the Safety Signs Regulations and BS 5378 as described in the communications module.

There is also progressive harmonisation to European Standards (CEN) and the use of CE Marking. Of particular interest to health and safety is the BSI standard 18001:2007 Occupational Health and Safety Assessment Series. BS 18001 is intended to help organisations develop a framework for managing occupational health and safety so workers and others who may be affected by the organisation's activities are adequately protected.

IT SOURCES

There is an increasing amount of information available on-line using a computer, modem and an Internet service provider. The World Wide Web provides a consistent interface with which to access information using software known as web browsers. These browsers allow the user to navigate through the Internet using hypertext links to jump from one page of information to another.

Sites are found by the use of an 'address' known as an URL (unique resource locator). Many safety organisations have their own website - including the International Labour Office (ILO) (http://.www.ilo.org).

ENCYCLOPAEDIAS

The fourth edition of the ILO Encyclopaedia of Occupational Health and Safety is a widely respected comprehensive publication which is now available free of charge on the ILO website and also includes a leading OSH database. Reference books can be a useful reference but can quickly become out of date.

PROFESSIONAL BODIES

There are a number of safety related professional bodies such as the Institution of Occupational Safety and Health (IOSH). These provide local newsletters, regular meetings and a subscription to their magazine as part of the membership package. People who are interested in health and safety can join as affiliate members with no formal qualifications.

LAWYERS

Can provide expert legal advice but can be expensive and is rarely straightforward.

CONSULTANTS

These can be of variable quality and charge widely differing fees. As with selecting other types of contractor and service provider, health and safety consultants need to be chosen carefully.

TRAINING COURSES

In-house and external courses, seminars and exhibitions can prove a useful source of information about developments and trends, as well as single topic issues.

Information provided by national and international agencies

INTERNATIONAL LABOUR ORGANISATION (ILO)

The ILO makes available on its web site the conventions it derives from its work. Recommendations and guidelines, e.g. Guidelines on Health and Safety Management Systems are also available. Some of their codes of practice (e.g. Ambient Factors in the Workplace) and reports on issues that affect health and safety are readily available on the website. One of the most valuable items produced by the ILO, that is available for reference on their website, is their health and safety encyclopaedia.

OCCUPATIONAL SAFETY AND HEALTH ADMINISTRATION (USA)

The United States Occupational Safety and Health Administration (OSHA) is an agency of the United States Department of Labor. It was created under the Occupational Safety and Health Act 1970. Its mission is to prevent work-related injuries, illnesses, and deaths by issuing and enforcing rules (called standards) for workplace safety and health.

OSHA provides a wide range of information via their website - a database on chemicals, web based tools to help people identify problems, legal requirements and enforcement strategies, news items and information on health and safety topics such as biological agents and construction.

EUROPEAN AGENCY FOR SAFETY AND HEALTH AT WORK (EU-OSHA)

The Agency makes good practice information available covering a range of topics and sectors. These include good prevention practices, campaigns and an active publications programme producing everything from specialist information reports to:

- Fact sheets and covering a wide variety of OSH problems and translations.
- Collect and disseminate technical, scientific and economic information.
- Promote and support cooperation and exchange of information and experience amongst the Member States.
- Organise conferences and seminars and exchanges of experts.
- Supply the Community bodies and the Member States with the objective available technical, scientific and economic information they require to formulate and implement judicious and effective policies designed to protect the safety and health of workers.
- Provide the Commission in particular with the technical, scientific and economic information it requires to fulfill its tasks of identifying, preparing and evaluating legislation and measures in the area of the protection of the safety and health of workers, notably as regards the impact of legislation on enterprises, with particular reference to small and medium-sized enterprises.

HEALTH AND SAFETY EXECUTIVE (HSE) (UK)

The Health and Safety Commission is responsible for health and safety regulations in Great Britain. The Health and Safety Executive (HSE) and local Government are the enforcing authorities who work in support of the Commission. They look after health and safety in nuclear installations and mines, factories, farms, hospitals and schools, offshore gas and oil installations, the safety of the gas grid and the movement of dangerous goods and substances, and many other aspects for the protection both of workers and the public. Local authorities are responsible to HSC for enforcement in offices, shops and other parts of the services sector.

HSE provides an extensive range of information on their website - legislation, approved codes of practice, publications and translations, leaflets (some are free), research reports, HSE journals and operational guidance.

WORKSAFE (WESTERN AUSTRALIA)

WorkSafe WA is a division of the Department of Consumer and Employment Protection, the state government agency in Western Australia responsible for the administration of work safety and health laws. The other states and territory authorities, such as the Northern Territory and Tasmania have similar organisations. WorkSafe WA undertakes a wide range of regulatory activities as well as industry and community awareness programmes in its role to minimise the social and economic impact on workers with work-related injury or disease in order to achieve cost effectiveness for employers and the community.

Their website gives access to a range of useful information, such as farm safety information and initiatives, and information for small businesses.

1.5 - The key elements of a health and safety management system

Health and safety management systems may be structured in a number of ways, therefore the key elements may be described differently.

The British Standards Institute's (BSI) Occupational Health and Safety Assessment Series 18001 (OHSAS) has been developed in response to customer demand for a recognisable occupational health and safety management system which can be assessed and certified. It was developed to be compatible with quality (ISO 9001) and environmental (ISO 14001) management system standards to aid the combination of all these disciplines should an organisation wish to operate one integrated management system.

The ILO identified that the introduction of occupational safety and health management systems, such as OHSAS 18001 and others, into organisations has had a beneficial effect, both on the reduction of hazards and risks and on productivity. The ILO has developed voluntary guidelines on OSH management systems which reflect their values and instruments relevant to the protection of workers' safety and health. These practical recommendations are not legally binding and are not intended to replace national laws, regulations or accepted standards, and their application does not require certification.

The ILO - Guidelines on Occupational Safety and Health Management Systems (ILO-OSH 2001) follows a structure that uses the following key elements:

- Policy.
- Organising.
- Planning and implementation.
- Evaluation.
- Audit.
- Actions for improvement.

SETTING POLICY

Organisations that are successful in achieving high standards of health and safety have health and safety policies which contribute to their business performance, while meeting their responsibilities to people and the environment in a way which fulfils both the spirit and the letter of the law. In this way they satisfy the expectations of shareholders, workers, customers and society at large. Their policies are cost effective and aimed at achieving the preservation and development of physical and human resources and reductions in financial losses and liabilities. Their health and safety policies influence all their activities and decisions, including those to do with the selection of resources and information, the design and operation of working systems, the design and delivery of products and services, and the control and disposal of waste.

ORGANISING

Organisations that achieve high health and safety standards are structured and operated so as to put their health and safety policies into effective practice. This is helped by the creation of a positive culture that secures involvement and participation at all levels. It is sustained by effective communications and the promotion of competence that enables all workers to make a responsible and informed contribution to the health and safety effort. The visible and active leadership of senior managers is necessary to develop and maintain a culture supportive of health and safety management. Their aim is not simply to avoid accidents, but to motivate and empower people to work safely. The vision, values and beliefs of leaders become the shared 'common knowledge' of all.

PLANNING AND IMPLEMENTING

These successful organisations adopt a planned and systematic approach to policy implementation. Their aim is to minimise the risks created by work activities, products and services. They use risk assessment methods to decide priorities and set objectives for hazard elimination and risk reduction. Performance standards are established and performance is measured against them. Specific actions needed to promote a positive health and safety culture and to eliminate and control risks are identified. Wherever possible, risks are eliminated by the careful selection and design of facilities, equipment and processes or minimised by the use of physical control measures. Where this is not possible, provision of a safe system of work and personal protective equipment are used to control risks.

EVALUATION (MONITORING, REVIEW, MEASUREMENT, INVESTIGATION)

Procedures to monitor, measure and record health and safety performance on a regular basis should be developed, established and periodically reviewed. Responsibility, accountability and authority for monitoring at different levels in the management structure should be allocated. The selection of performance indicators should be according to the size and nature of activity of the organisation and the health and safety objectives. Performance monitoring and measuring should be used to determine the extent to which the policy and objectives have been met and risks controlled.

Health and safety performance in organisations that manage health and safety successfully is measured against pre-determined standards. These reveal when and where action is needed to improve performance. The success of action taken to control risks is assessed through active self-monitoring involving a range of techniques. This includes an examination of both hardware (premises, plant and substances) and software (people, procedures and systems), including individual behaviour. Failures to control risks are assessed through reactive monitoring which requires the thorough investigation of accidents, ill health or incidents with the potential to cause harm or loss. In both active and reactive monitoring, the objectives are not only to determine the immediate causes of sub-standard performance but, more importantly, to identify the underlying causes and the implications for the design and operation of the health and safety management system.

Learning from all relevant experience and applying the lessons learned are important elements in effective health and safety management. This needs to be done systematically through regular reviews of performance based on data both from monitoring activities and from audits of the whole or part of the health and safety management system. Review of the health and safety management system and its elements is an essential activity and provides a good basis for continuous improvement actions.

AUDITING

This formal process is specifically designed to determine the extent to which the health and safety management system, or elements of it, are compliant with standards (in place, adequate and effective). Internal auditing will confirm compliance with internal standards.

From time to time it is critical that the whole health and safety management system be audited by an independent organisation to determine the extent to which it complies with recognised health and safety management systems and appropriate legislation. An audit policy and programme should be developed, which includes auditor competency, the audit scope, the frequency of audits, audit methodology and reporting.

ACTION FOR IMPROVEMENT (PREVENTATIVE AND CORRECTIVE ACTION; CONTINUAL IMPROVEMENT)

Arrangements for *preventive and corrective action* resulting from health and safety management system performance monitoring and measurement, include health and safety management system audits and management reviews should be established to ensure that the management system continues to be effective. It is critical to take corrective action related to system non-conformities, particularly those that result in accidents/incidents, promptly. Corrective action is that action to deal with the issue where it happened and tends to deal with the immediate causes of the issue. Supporting this is the introduction of preventive action to deal with the underlying (root) causes of the issue. This type of action will reduce the likelihood of it re-occurring where it happened before and in other places.

Arrangements should also be established to aid the *continual improvement* of health and safety management system elements and the system as a whole, taking into account such areas as the health and safety objectives of the organisation, changes in national laws and regulations, voluntary programmes and collective agreements and any other new relevant information.

Commitment to continuous improvement involves the constant development of policies, approaches to implementation and techniques of risk control. These form the basis for self-regulation and improved standards of health and safety. Organisations which achieve high standards of health and safety assess their health and safety performance by internal reference to key performance indicators and by external comparison with the performance of business competitors. They often also record and account for their performance in their annual reports.

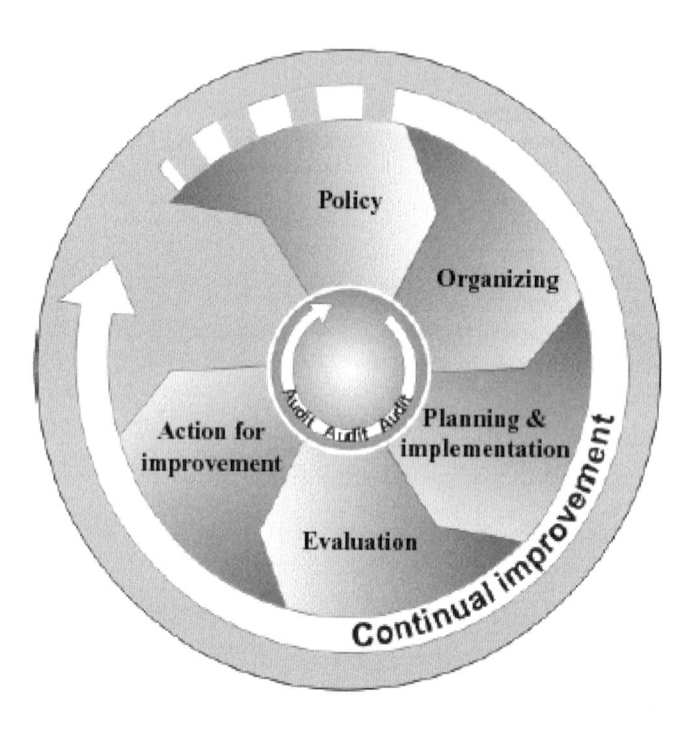

Figure 1-1-11: Key elements of successful health and safety management.   *Source: ILO-OSH 2001, HSG65, HSE books.*

Element 2

Policy

Learning outcomes

On completion of this element, candidates should be able to demonstrate understanding of the content through the application of knowledge to familiar and unfamiliar situations. In particular they should be able to:

2.1 Explain the purpose and importance of setting policy for health and safety.

2.2 Describe the key features and appropriate content of an effective health and safety policy.

Content

2.1 - The purpose and importance of setting policy for health and safety 19
    Role of the health and safety policy in decision making 19
    Aims, objectives and key elements of a health and safety policy 19
2.2 - The key features and appropriate content of an organisation's health and safety policy 20
    Setting targets 20
    Organising for health and safety 20
    Health and safety arrangements 20
    Reviewing the policy 21
    Standards and guidance relating to health and safety policy 21

Sources of reference

Guidelines on Occupational Safety and Health Management Systems (ILO-OSH 2001) ISBN-0-580-37805-5

Occupational Health and Safety Assessment Series (OHSAS 18000): Occupational Health and Safety Management Systems OHSAS 18001:1999 (ISBN-0-580-28298-8), OHSAS 18002:2000 (ISBN 0-580-33123-7), BSI

POLICY - ELEMENT 2 - UNIT IGC1

2.1 - The purpose and importance of setting policy for health and safety

Role of the health and safety policy in decision making

European Union and International Laws / Regulations set out an obligation to manage the risks that organisations create, and a cornerstone of this was seen to be the establishment of an active health and safety policy. This has been consistently misunderstood and underestimated by many over the years, especially in the United Kingdom (UK) since the introduction of the Health and Safety at Work etc. Act (HASAWA) 1974 came into force. Other Acts/Regulations have been introduced since then i.e. the Management of Health and Safety at Work Regulations (MHSWR) 1999 which has given this a new focus. When considering the international forum other guidelines have emerged in recent year such as the Guidelines on occupational safety and health management systems, ILO-OSH 2001 Geneva, International Labour Office, 2001 and the conversion of occupational health and safety management systems - requirements 18001, from a specification to a British Standard which will subsequently apply for European EN status and *International Organisation for Standardisation,* ISO status / recognition.

Without active management any attempt at organised accident prevention will be restricted and predominantly reactive. The overall intent of a policy will provide direction for an organisation, establishing a remit that will both guide the organisation to satisfy the goals set by it and to bind it so that it does not stray from the standards that it sets. This will influence the decisions made by an organisation, in that they will need to fall within the intent of the policy. Many employers are required to have a health and safety policy by the national or local legislation, and indeed it is a key element to any occupational safety and health management system, certified or voluntary. It is apparent that employers, in consultation with workers, must produce a clear statement of their overall health and safety objectives and a commitment to improving health and safety performance.

Organisations differ greatly in their goals, risks, structure and what they feel capable of committing themselves to. In the same way a policy is therefore a 'personal' thing setting out a particular organisation's position at that point in time. Guidance on effective OHS policies state that any policy must be appropriate to the size and nature of the employer's activities and the nature and scale of its OHS risks.

Aims, objectives and key elements of a health and safety policy

OVERALL AIMS

The aim of the policy of an organisation is to create a structure to its approach to health and safety.

Main elements of the Guidelines on occupational safety and health management systems, ILO-OSH 2001 Geneva, International Labour Office, 2001 are as follows:

The OSH policy should include, as a minimum, the following key principles and objectives to which the organisation is committed:

- To a policy which is specific to the *organisation* and appropriate to its size and the nature of its activities.
- To making the policy concise, clearly written, dated and made effective by the signature or endorsement of the employer or the most senior accountable person in the *organisation.*
- To ensure it is communicated to all persons working under the control of the organisation with the intent that they are made aware of their individual OSH obligations and that the policy is readily accessible to all persons at their place of work.
- To be reviewed for continuing suitability, and made available to relevant external interested parties, as appropriate.

Additional elements to consider as part of an occupational health and safety policy as taken from the occupational health and safety management systems - requirements 18001 are as follows:

- Protecting the safety and health of all members of the organisation by preventing work-related injuries, ill health, diseases and incidents.
- Complying with relevant OSH national/international laws and regulations, voluntary programmes, collective agreements on OSH and other requirements to which the organisation subscribes.
- Providing the framework for setting and reviewing OSH objectives.
- Ensuring that the policy is documented, implemented and maintained.
- Ensuring that workers and their representatives are consulted and encouraged to participate actively in all elements of the OSH management system.
- Continually improving the performance of the OSH management system.

Source: ILO - OSH 2001

The objectives are to ensure clear definition of the organisation's goals, set out responsibilities for health and safety matters and describe the arrangements in place to ensure health and safety is achieved.

HEALTH AND SAFETY ROLES AND RESPONSIBILITIES OF INDIVIDUALS WITHIN AN ORGANISATION

In order to achieve the policy objectives the employer must allocate responsibility, accountability and authority for the development, implementation and performance of the OSH management system. This will require the employer to establish OSH as a known and accepted line-management responsibility at all levels, and identify key roles with responsibility, accountability or authority for the identification, evaluation or control OSH hazards and risks. Specifically, the policy statement itself should be made effective by the dating and signature of the most senior accountable person, demonstrating commitment to the policy objective.

Worker participation is an essential element of the OSH management system in the organisation. The employer should ensure that workers and their safety and health representatives are consulted, informed and trained on all aspects of OSH, including emergency arrangements, associated with their work, and the employer should make arrangements for workers and their safety and health representatives to have the time and resources to actively participate.

UNIT IGC1 - ELEMENT 2 - POLICY

SPECIFYING THE ARRANGEMENTS FOR ACHIEVING GENERAL AND SPECIFIC AIMS

This involves the arrangements to control the risks, set the direction, scope and actions of an organisation to manage health and safety. This part of the policy document specifies the arrangements for achieving general and specific aims for health and safety.

To be effective the policy should be:

- In a number of formats.
- Effectively communicated.
- Revised as appropriate.
- Monitored through audits.

The effective communication of the policy is critical; all affected by it must understand it. In order to achieve this, a lot has to be done. Merely posting it or distributing a copy to workers is not enough. Training and briefings will be necessary, as a minimum, to ensure effective communication. For new workers this is often done as part of the induction process. The format, complexity and language used should be considered. Experience shows that no one form of document is adequate to meet everyone's needs; therefore the document is usually produced in at least a summary and a detailed format. If it is likely to be revised frequently, a loose-leaf scheme will be advisable for the detailed version. This is especially true when the names and contact telephone numbers of staff are included.

2.2 - The key features and appropriate content of an organisation's health and safety policy

Setting targets

A particularly effective way of demonstrating management commitment to health and safety is by communicating a policy **statement of intent**. It sets quantifiable organisational objectives for health and safety. In order to accentuate this commitment the statement should be **signed** and **dated** by the most senior member of the management team. A lack of firm management commitment of this kind leads to the perception that health and safety is not equal to other business objectives. The addition of a date to the statement will indicate the last time the statement was reviewed.

Organisations should translate their overall aims that are set out in the statement into **objectives** for the organisation, key parts of the organisation and key individuals. In line with other business objectives, health and safety objectives should be set out as **quantifiable targets**. An easily quantifiable item is the number of accidents occurring in an organisation. This is probably why workers are attracted to targets for accident reduction; however it is critical to look at the effect of such targets on accident reporting. Objectives should, ideally, be proactive; though it is not uncommon to have reactive objectives related to reduction in accidents as part of a group of objectives. Proactive objectives related to such things as manager training completed or risk assessments conducted are critical to maintain progress on health and safety. Many organisations seek to compare their performance against other organisations, sometimes called **'benchmarking'**. This is easiest done with performance indicators that are measurable, the most obvious of which are accident statistics. Though they are often unreliable for comparison in this way they are still used and limitations accepted. In more recent times organisations have compared other proactive factors such as the percentage of managers that have achieved a specified level of competence or training, such as holding a NEBOSH International / National General Certificate in Health and Safety.

Organising for health and safety

It is usual to express the organisation by showing an organisational chart, showing a reporting/communication structure and workers' functions/job descriptions to be depicted. Clear **allocation of responsibilities** for all levels of management, and duties of workers are necessary, as are the role and functions of health and safety professional workers. Part of organising for health and safety is to establish a clear perspective of the role and function of workers' representatives and committees, including clarification of the **communication lines** and **feedback loops**.

The active involvement of managers in achieving health and safety is critical for its success; this includes the **role of the line manager** in ensuring compliance with the policy. It is necessary for managers to ensure resource is in place and work is being carried out in a safe and healthy way. It is essential therefore that they **monitor the effectiveness** of the policy and the practices used to achieve it.

Health and safety arrangements

This section of the policy details the practical arrangements for planning, organising, and controlling hazards, as well as monitoring compliance with and **assessing the effectiveness** of the arrangements. The main headings of arrangements that could be detailed in the health and safety policy might include:

General arrangements:

- Allocation of finance for health and safety.
- Planning.
- Organising.
- Control of hazards - general e.g. risk assessments.
- Consultation.
- Communication.
- Competence.
- Accident and hazard reporting.
- Monitoring compliance.

Specific arrangements for hazards, such as those relating to:

- Fire.
- Electricity.
- Manual handling.
- Work at a height.

The specific style and scope of the policy needs to reflect that of the organisation. Though there will be some common elements, a policy from a construction company should be different to one for a charity that looks after dogs, as the risks they manage are different. Arrangements set out in a policy may not reflect well the circumstances of the workplace and as such may not be effective. It is essential that those affected by the arrangement be involved in its development.

In addition, arrangements that are made can quickly become outdated by changes in the way that things are done in the organisation; this can undermine their effectiveness. It is essential that systems be in place to monitor and assess this.

Because it is useful to plan for arrangements to change it is worth producing documents in such a way that it is easy to identify changes. This can involve highlighting the different changes on the document, explaining the reasons for change, having a controlled number of copies of the document issued and recording that the changes have been issued to those that hold copies.

Reviewing the policy

A number of circumstances may lead to a need to review the policy, for example, the passage of time, technological, organisational or legal changes, the results of monitoring or following a major accident or incident.

As *time* passes the arrangements for control of health and safety are influenced by workers finding different ways of doing the same thing. Arrangements as practised can therefore differ greatly from the original way it was set out in the policy.

Technological change is happening in the workplace all the time, and this can mean that arrangements may be set out against circumstances that do not exist anymore because equipment or substances have been altered. It might also be that the organisation has been able to take advantage of technological advantages in something, e.g. materials handling, yet the policy refers to the earlier way of working.

Changes in *organisation* have a specific bearing on the arrangements. For example, if reporting of accidents is set out in the policy and in relation to a certain worker's post, this may be influenced by a reorganisation that removes the position. Similarly, changes in work patterns e.g. shift working could influence arrangements that have been made.

Legislation changes periodically and it is fair to say it usually reflects a strengthening of society's expectations. This may mean that specific arrangements set out in the policy may no longer conform with the law, in that it may be incomplete or not to a satisfactory standard.

If *monitoring* methods are in place and are working they could identify a gap in a specific arrangement or that something is unclear or contradictory. This might be from enforcement action, professional advice such as an audit or following an accident or incident investigation.

Standards and guidance relating to health and safety policy

As provisionally mentioned earlier there are several recognised standards, guidelines that require employers to have a policy and provide guidance on how to comply with this requirement. For example, in UK, it is a mandatory requirement under the Health and Safety at Work etc. Act (HASAWA) 1974, that employers have a health and safety policy. In addition, information on policy requirements can be found within management system guidance such as OHSAS 18002: *Guidelines on occupational safety and health management systems, ILO-OSH 2001* Geneva, International Labour Office, 2001, which both provide a route plan for employers seeking to implement OHS management systems into their organisation.

This page is intentionally blank

Element 3

Organising for health and safety

Learning outcomes

On completion of this element, candidates should be able to demonstrate understanding of the content through the application of knowledge to familiar and unfamiliar situations. In particular they should be able to:

3.1 Outline the health and safety roles and responsibilities of employers, managers, supervisors, employees and other relevant parties.

3.2 Explain the importance and means of consulting with employees on health and safety issues and the means to achieve effective consultation.

Content

3.1 - Organisational health and safety roles and responsibilities..25
    The roles and responsibilities of: 25
3.2 - Consultation with employees 29
    Duties to consult 29
    The importance and means of consulting with workers on health and safety issues.....................29
    The distinction between 'informing' and 'consulting'...29

Sources of reference

Guidelines on Occupational Safety and Health Management Systems (ILO-OSH 2001) ISBN 0-580-37805-5

Occupational Health and Safety Assessment Series (OHSAS 18000): Occupational Health and Safety Management Systems OHSAS 18001:1999 (ISBN 0-580-28298-8), OHSAS 18002:2000 (ISBN: 0-580-33123-7), BSI

Occupational Safety and Health Convention (C155), ILO

Occupational Safety and Health Recommendation (R164), ILO

Other sources of reference

Occupational Safety and Health Act 1984 (OSHA 1984 Western Australia)

Occupational Safety and Health Act 1970 (USA)

3.1 - Organisational health and safety roles and responsibilities

The roles and responsibilities of:

THE EMPLOYER (CORPORATE AND NON-CORPORATE)

All employers whether self-employed, subcontractors, and visitors to places of employment, members of the public affected by the employer's activities, designers, suppliers, importer, workers, directors and managers, have a responsibility for those that might be affected by their undertaking. Depending upon local arrangements this provides enforcement powers to local, national and international authorities, whether they are charities, small company, a medium sized construction company, or multi-national organisation (plc), a local authority or a Government department. Depending on territories this may be a civil and criminal responsibility, depending on the local arrangements. The main responsibilities as defined in the International Labour Office (ILO) Occupational Health Safety (OHS) 2001 and Safety Convention and Recommendation 1981 are set out below.

For the health, safety and welfare of employees

Some of these obligations may include:

- Provision and maintenance of workplaces, machinery and equipment, the need to establish work methods, which are as safe and without risk to health as is reasonably practicable.
- Necessary instructions and training, taking account of the functions and capacities of different categories of workers.
- Provision of adequate supervision of work, of work practices and of application and use of occupational safety and health measures.
- Institute organisational arrangements regarding occupational safety and health and the working environment adapted to the size of the undertaking and the nature of its activities.
- Provide, without any cost to the worker, adequate personal protective clothing and equipment which are reasonably necessary when hazards cannot be otherwise prevented or controlled.
- Ensure that work organisation, particularly with respect to hours of work and rest breaks, does not adversely affect occupational safety and health.
- All reasonably practicable measures with a view to eliminating excessive physical and mental fatigue.
- Undertake studies and research or otherwise keep abreast of the scientific and technical knowledge necessary to comply with the foregoing clauses.

For others affected by work activities

In addition to the employer's responsibility to the workers, the employer has responsibilities to other people who are not workers. This covers a wide range of people including visitors, contractors, subcontractors and members of the public. The responsibility of the employer extends to others affected by their work activities. In so doing this will mean doing similar things to those that would keep workers healthy and safe. The responsibility extends to consideration of the fact that these people may not understand hazards they are exposed to or how they should be dealt with.

Visitors

Some of the practical steps that an organisation might take in order to satisfy its responsibility to ensure the health and safety of visitors to its premises are:

- Identify visitors by signing in and the provision of badges.
- Provide information regarding the risks present and the site rules and procedures to be followed, particularly in emergencies.
- Provide escorts to supervise visitors throughout the site and restrict access to areas where higher risk activities take place.

Many organisations issue badges to visitors. The main purpose of this is to ensure that visitors are clearly identified, but the issuing of badges may be combined with recording visitors and providing information on emergency procedures that can be included on the badge. In addition, badges may be used to identify regular contractors or people who may only have access to certain parts of the business, e.g. by differently coloured badges.

It is critical that badges are numbered and that at the end of the working day (or whenever) a note is made of outstanding badges to ensure that all are accounted for. Action should be taken to determine what has happened to the badge-holders. In organisations where it is common practice to issue badges to workers it is critical that visitors' badges are noticeably different (e.g. in style or colour). Badges for workers and regular contractors should have a photograph of the holder in order to aid identification.

Contractors

Contractors are used to perform a wide variety of tasks on behalf of employers. Whilst the contractor may have duties of their own, the employer often carries responsibility for the work done by contractors as part of the employer's undertaking. These responsibilities are both organisational and legal. In the organisational sense the employer commissions contractors to perform tasks on its behalf, and in doing this appropriately it is essential for good management that health and safety be included, along with provision of the service on time and with quality.

In addition, the employer may need to take reasonable care to control the work of contractors to discharge their duties related to, where applicable, common law and reasonably practicable steps to discharge its duty under international, national requirements or local regulations. These responsibilities work in harmony with the employer's responsibility to look after the contractor while the contractor is working in a workplace that the employer controls.

It is critical to conduct risk assessments with contractors in mind and clearly define the task of the contractor in a way that includes health and safety issues. In this way the risks to a contractor can be identified and controlled. For example, if an employer needs a contractor to work at a height above the entrance to an office building using a scaffold, it is necessary for the employer to control this work such that it is conducted safely for the protection of contractors working on the scaffold and anyone passing near the scaffold. The provision of toe boards, guard rails, and lighting and the siting of the scaffold are factors that affect contractors and others.

The Public

Employers need to be aware of the ways in which their work can affect the public and their responsibilities for control of these risks. The public may be visitors to the workplace by specific invitation or by straying into the workplace. The employer may invite and encourage the public into the workplace to enable them to purchase goods or services.

It is critical that the employer controls the exposure of the public to risks, such as slippery floors in shops, an unprotected excavation by the side of a pathway, operation of vehicle maintenance equipment in a garage, and a release of cement dust or dust from a demolition site to neighbouring houses.

DIRECTORS' AND SENIOR MANAGERS' RESPONSIBILITIES / IMPLEMENTATION

Directors and senior managers implement the employer's responsibilities and are accountable for ensuring health and safety is established. In practice this will include ensuring that an appropriate health and safety policy is in place and that it is worked to; failure to do so may render the director or senior manager personally accountable.

MIDDLE MANAGERS AND SUPERVISORS

In a similar way to senior managers, managers at all levels in an organisation are expected to ensure health and safety is effectively established in their area of control. If they fail to do this they could be held accountable for their failings. This may be seen as a separate accountability to that of senior managers or the employer. In some jurisdictions all will be accountable in law.

The supervisor plays a particularly critical role on behalf of the employer in that they provide the supervisory control that ensures immediate causes of accidents (hazards) are identified and controlled. If they fail to take reasonable care in their provision of supervision they could be held accountable. *See also - Employees' duties - later in this element.*

PERSONS WITH PRIMARY HEALTH AND SAFETY FUNCTIONS

A person with responsibility for primary health and safety functions (health and safety practitioner) should be appointed by the employer to provide advice and assistance in meeting the employer's responsibilities. The appointment of a practitioner does not remove line management responsibilities for health and safety but it provides support to line mangers in fulfilling these responsibilities.

The health and safety practitioner is an employee and has responsibilities to take reasonable care for their acts and omissions when conducting their work, for example, failure to provide advice or agreed service such as an inspection or inadequate advice or service could lead to their prosecution in some jurisdictions. This would apply equally to an occupational health nurse or fire specialist who did not discharge their duties.

WORKERS FOR THE HEALTH AND SAFETY OF THEMSELVES AND OTHERS WHO MAY BE AFFECTED BY THEIR ACTS OR OMISSIONS

The principles behind the term 'duty of care' (previously outlined in Unit IGC1 - Element 1) clearly requires workers to be also involved in the prevention of risk and not to solely rely on the actions of their employer. The requirements placed on workers, which are often interpreted at the local level in both civil and criminal law, ensure that they:

- Take reasonable care for their own safety and that of other persons who may be affected by their acts or omissions at work.
- Comply with instructions given for their own safety and health and those of others and with safety and health procedures.
- Use safety devices and protective equipment correctly and do not render them inoperative.
- Report forthwith to their immediate supervisor any situation which they have reason to believe could present a hazard and which they cannot themselves correct.
- Report any accident or injury to health which arises in the course of or in connection with work.

RESPONSIBILITIES OF PERSONS IN CONTROL OF PREMISES

Anyone in control of non-domestic premises or plant used by persons not in their employment should, so far as is reasonably practicable:

- Ensure safe access and egress to premises and plant.
- Ensure that plant or substances in the premises, or provided for their use, are safe and without risk to health.

This is a wide-ranging responsibility and extends to some logical areas where the public or other workers need protection, for example, a self service launderette, a multi-story car park, an office block being built, or industrial units rented to employers. In addition it would extend to students studying in a college / university, or outside contractors who go onto premises under someone else's control to install / repair machinery. The duty is not imposed on workers who may have day to day 'control' on behalf of the person in control, for example, a caretaker, security workers or supervisor. However, such people must fulfil their general duties as a worker.

There may be several employers operating within one workplace. It should be noted that whenever two or more undertakings engage in activities simultaneously at one workplace, they should collaborate in applying the provisions regarding occupational safety and health and the working environment, without prejudice to the responsibility of each undertaking for the health and safety of its workers.

THE RESPONSIBILITIES OF THE SELF-EMPLOYED

There are a great many self-employed workers at work today and they are frequently involved in work in other employers' (and the public's) premises. They carry a responsibility for the risks of their work that may affect those that work alongside them or the public. In addition, they are expected to take a responsibility for their own safety, for example, getting electrical equipment inspected and tested at intervals or making sure the ladder they use to access a scaffold platform is safe. The role of self-employed person is effectively that of employers and workers combined.

As self employed persons often work on host employer sites, a degree of collaboration as outlined above, will be required in applying the provisions regarding occupational safety and health and the working environment.

RESPONSIBILITIES OF SUPPLIERS, MANUFACTURERS AND DESIGNERS OF ARTICLES AND SUBSTANCES - "THE SUPPLY CHAIN"

It is essential that we recognise the importance of the influence of the supply chain on health and safety in the workplace. If a designer or manufacturer does not create articles that are safe by design or faults occur during manufacture they may easily pass down the supply chain and hazards will be introduced into the workplace.

Small companies have to place a high degree of reliance on the supply chain to provide suitable articles and substances. The best way to deal with hazards is at source, e.g. at design and manufacture. In the same way, if an article or substance has residual hazards that the employer needs to take account of when using it, it is appropriate that the supply chain provide information on the hazards and controls to deal with them. This would include the provision of substance data sheets and instructions for the safe use of equipment.

DUTIES OF SUPPLIERS, MANUFACTURERS AND DESIGNERS OF ARTICLES AND SUBSTANCES

Suppliers, manufacturers and designers often have specific duties placed on them to ensure that articles and substances for use at work are as safe and without risks as far is reasonably practicable. The responsibility relates to both new and second hand articles as well as all substances (including micro-organisms) supplied to workplaces. This includes:

- Safe design, installation and testing of articles (including fairground equipment).
- Substances are safe and without risks to health.
- Carry out or arrange for tests or examinations to ensure safe design and construction of articles and to ensure substances will be safe and without risk to health.
- Provision of information on use and conditions essential to health and safety, and information about new and serious risks which come to light is to be provided to those supplied.
- Carry out research to minimise risks.
- Erectors and installers of articles for use at work must ensure it does not make the article unsafe or a risk to health.

Importers and suppliers often carry the same duties as designers and manufacturers, although it would usually be enough for them to rely on the tests and examinations conducted by the manufacturer/designer. An importer would be expected to prove that the article had the same standard of health and safety protection as that of a local supplier.

There are several international standards organisations that identify required performance levels, such as the International Electrotechnical Commission (IEC) which deals with electrical, electronic and related technologies, and which is currently recognised in more than 130 countries. Also, the CE mark (officially CE marking) is a mandatory safety mark on many products placed on the single market in the European Economic Area (EEA). By affixing the CE marking, the manufacturer, or its representative, or the importer assures that the item meets all the essential requirements (including safety) of all applicable EU directives.

In North America Underwriters Laboratories (Inc.) is a well-known laboratory with headquarters in Northbrook, Illinois, that develops standards and test procedures for materials, components, assemblies, tools, equipment and procedures, chiefly dealing with product safety and utility. For a United Kingdom (UK) supplier, conformity with European harmonised standards would usually be sufficient.

THE RELATIONSHIP BETWEEN CLIENT AND CONTRACTOR AND THE DUTIES EACH HAS TO THE OTHER AND TO THE OTHER'S EMPLOYEES

The principal duties are expressed in the above sections and show that a client has duties towards a contractor and their workers as visitors to their workplace. In addition, when a client commissions a contractor to conduct work relating to the client's undertaking the client retains responsibility to see that it is conducted in a safe and healthy manner. Clearly this may benefit the contractor's workers, other contractors' workers, the public and the client's workers.

A contractor that agrees to a contract for service must provide appropriate health and safety standards when conducting the work - this will benefit all those that might be affected. It is the responsibility of both parties to build health and safety into the contract and work methods. To this end it is essential that they co-operate with each other, seeking to plan and co-ordinate activities.

Persons working in host employers' or self employed persons' undertakings

Host employers and self-employed people must ensure that workers carrying out work on their premises receive relevant information. If reliance is placed on the employer of the visiting workers providing information, a check should be made to ensure information has been passed on. The information should be enough to allow the employer of the visiting employee to comply with their responsibilities to the local acceptable standard or where appropriate laws and would address the risks arising from the host employer's undertaking.

In addition, information should identify people nominated by the host employer to help with emergency evacuation. Such workers would include those working under a contract of service and workers provided by temporary employment businesses under the control of a host employer.

Clients

Clients, as employers, are obliged both by national criminal and civil law in most countries to protect their workforce and others from health risks and personal injury and to conduct all undertakings in such a way as to ensure that members of the public around or entering their premises are likewise protected.

Clients contract operations for a wide range of situations, from activities such as window cleaning, catering or security to large-scale construction works, such as extensions to premises or the building of new premises on land not previously used. Consultation with contractors prior to a contract being signed, commencement of work and during the course of the work is of the utmost significance if a safe and healthy site is to be maintained.

Contractors

In the context of health and safety at work, the term contractor is commonly applied to those who visit the premises of others to conduct work. This is usually in connection with the repair, maintenance, refurbishment or installation of plant and equipment, or building alterations, and in this sense will be either an employer or self-employed person.

Contractors carrying out maintenance works are a significant cause of accidents in the workplace. In general, visiting contractors are less familiar with the workplace and associated risks than the indigenous workforce, yet often carry out more hazardous operations. In order to minimise the risk potential of such activities and to ensure that all concerned are made aware of their health and safety responsibilities, a detailed knowledge of relevant legislation / health and safety standards is essential, risks must be identified and effective control methods introduced.

EFFECTIVE PLANNING AND CO-ORDINATION OF CONTRACTED WORK

It is essential that all contracted work be planned and co-ordinated. Contracted work carries particular risks in that workers may be unfamiliar with the workplace and work may be organised such that activities conflict with each other putting contractors or workers at risk. It is essential that a risk assessment of work activities be made foreseeing how they interact with each other. This would, naturally, extend to contract work commissioned by the employer.

PROCEDURES FOR THE SELECTION OF CONTRACTORS

There are six main elements to a management strategy for selection of contractors. The extent to which each element is relevant will depend upon the degree of risk and nature of work to be contracted. The elements are:

1. Identification of suitable bidders (preferred list).
   - Insurance details.
   - Status and depth of implementation of health and safety policy.
   - Status of the competent person.
   - Previous accident record.
   - Details of any prosecutions.
   - Details of any Enforcement Notices.
   - Competence of workers.
   - References for previous clients.
2. Identification of hazards within the specification.
3. Checking of (health and safety aspects of) bids and selection of contractor.
4. Contractors' agreement to be subject to client's rules.
5. Management of the contractor on site.
6. Checking after completion of contract.

Adopting a strategy similar to that outlined above ensures that the employer has taken steps to plan, organise, control, monitor and review their arrangements for managing health and safety.

Figure 1-3-1: Joint occupancy. *Source: ACT.*

Figure 1-3-2: Occupier's liability - to public. *Source: ACT.*

SHARED RESPONSIBILITIES IN THE CASE OF JOINT OCCUPATION OF PREMISES

The occupier of premises often has duties regarding the state and condition of the premises. When contractors are working on a premise it could be argued that they are joint occupiers with an employer under these duties. Therefore both employer and the contractor have joint liabilities in 'common areas'. The occupier is not normally liable for dangers associated with the contractors' work activities, unless when selecting the contractor as far as reasonably practicable the occupiers has ensured competency, and is satisfied that the works are being carried out properly.

CO-OPERATION AND CO-ORDINATION

Employers who work together in a common workplace have a duty to co-operate in order to discharge their duties under good practice or where appropriate relevant statutory provisions. This will include consideration of each other when conducting risk assessments and provision of procedures for serious or imminent danger. For example, when establishing fire evacuation arrangements on a site with multiple occupancy, the whole of the site should be considered. Each occupant should co-operate with a co-ordinated response. It is necessary for all employers and self employed involved in situations where they have a common workplace to satisfy themselves that the arrangements are adequate. Employers should ensure that all relevant workers and in particular, competent workers appointed are aware and fully take part. They must also take all reasonable steps to inform other employers concerned of risks to their workers' health or safety that may arise out of their work.

3.2 - Consultation with employees

Duties to consult

The primary responsibility to consult employees is set out in national and international laws/regulations. This is further specified in regulations that express how this is done with regard to Trade Union Safety Representatives and other non-union employees.

The importance and means of consulting with workers on health and safety issues

The employer should ensure that workers and their safety and health representatives are consulted, informed and trained on all aspects of OSH, including emergency arrangements, associated with their work. The employer should make arrangements for workers and their safety and health representatives to have the time and resources to participate actively in the processes of organising, planning and implementation, evaluation and action for improvement of the OSH management system.

The employer should ensure, as appropriate, the establishment and efficient functioning of a safety and health committee and the recognition of workers' safety and health representatives, in accordance with national laws and practice. Workers' safety delegates, workers' safety and health committees, and joint safety and health committees or, as appropriate, other workers' representatives should:

- Be given adequate information on safety and health matters, enabled to examine factors affecting safety and health, and encouraged to propose measures on the subject.
- Be consulted when major new safety and health measures are envisaged and before they are carried out, and seek to obtain the support of the workers for such measures.
- Be consulted in planning alterations of work processes, work content or organisation of work, which may have safety or health implications for the workers.
- Be given protection from dismissal and other measures prejudicial to them while exercising their functions in the field of occupational safety and health as workers' representatives or as members of safety and health committees.
- Be able to contribute to the decision-making process at the level of the undertaking regarding matters of safety and health.
- Have access to all parts of the workplace and be able to communicate with the workers on safety and health matters during working hours at the workplace.
- Be free to contact labour inspectors.
- Be able to contribute to negotiations in the undertaking on occupational safety and health matters.
- Have reasonable time during paid working hours to exercise their safety and health functions and to receive training related to these functions.
- Have recourse to specialists to advise on particular safety and health problems.

The distinction between 'informing' and 'consulting'

A basic requirement for a successful consultation through the use of a safety committee is the desire of both employee and management to show honest commitment and a positive approach to a programme of accident prevention and the establishment of a safe and healthy environment and systems of work. For any committee to operate effectively, it is necessary to determine clear objectives and functions. It is critical to establish a committee that is balanced in representation of workers and management.

ILO-OSH: 2001 SECTION 3.6 COMMUNICATION

Arrangements and procedures should be established and maintained for: receiving, documenting and responding appropriately to internal and external communications related to OSH.; ensuring that the internal communication of OSH information between relevant levels and functions of the *organisation;* and ensuring that the concerns, ideas and inputs of workers and their representatives on OSH matters are received, considered and responded to.

REQUIREMENTS FOR EFFECTIVENESS

A basic requirement for a successful safety committee is the desire of both employee and management to show honest commitment and a positive approach to a programme of accident prevention and the establishment of a safe and healthy environment and systems of work. For any committee to operate effectively, it is necessary to determine clear objectives and functions. It is critical to establish a committee that is balanced in representation of workers and management.

Frequency of meetings

This would depend on the nature of the organisation's business, the risks involved, how active the health and safety programme is, items on the agenda and other local considerations such as a hierarchy of committees representing departments / locations / sites. Usually, meetings are held varying between once a month to every three months.

Minutes and agenda

The minutes must be circulated as soon as possible after the meeting. A suggested agenda is:

- Apologies for absence.
- Minutes of the previous meeting.
- Matters arising.
- Reports of health and safety practitioner.
- Other reports e.g. fire officer, nurse, and occupational hygienist.
- New items (and emergency items).
- Date of next meeting.

Reasons why safety committees are effective

- A clear management commitment.
- Clear objectives and functions.
- An even balance between management and employee representatives.
- Agenda agreed, distributed in advance and followed in meeting.
- Minutes or notes of the meetings being produced promptly and distributed in good time for actions to be taken before the next meeting.
- Personal copy of minutes provided to each member, each representative covered by the committee and the senior manager of the organisation.
- Effective publicity given to discussions and recommendations, including posting/displaying copies.
- Effective chairing of meeting enabling points to be raised but within the agenda; controlling points taken as any other business.
- Full participation by members.
- Access to the organisation's decision making processes through the chair and in that the committee's views are taken into account.
- Speedy decisions by management on recommendation promptly translated into action and effectively publicised.
- Regular meetings at a frequency that reflects the matters to be discussed.
- Meetings not cancelled or postponed except in very exceptional circumstances.
- Dates of meetings arranged well in advance and published to members, e.g. for a one year period.
- Appropriate topics.
- Access to health and safety expertise.
- Sub-committees established where there is a need to focus in detail on specifics and report back.

Element 4

Promoting a positive health and safety culture

Learning outcomes

On completion of this element, candidates should be able to demonstrate understanding of the content through the application of knowledge to familiar and unfamiliar situations. In particular they should be able to:

4.1 Describe the concept of health and safety culture and its significance in the management of health and safety in an organisation.

4.2 Identify indicators which could be used to assess the effectiveness of an organisation's health and safety culture and recognise factors that could cause a deterioration.

4.3 Identify the factors which influence safety related behaviour at work.

4.4 Identify methods which could be used to improve the health and safety culture of an organisation.

4.5 Outline the internal and external influences on an organisation's health and safety standards.

Content

4.1 - Concepts of safety culture 33
    Definition of 'health and safety culture'..33
    Correlation between health and safety culture and health and safety performance 33
4.2 - Factors influencing safety culture 33
    Tangible outputs or indicators of an organisation's or site's health and safety culture 33
    Factors promoting a negative health and safety culture..34
4.3 - Factors influencing safety related behaviour 34
    Individual, job and organisational factors 34
    Attitude, aptitude and motivation 36
    Perception of risk 37
    Errors and violations 38
    Effects of age and experience 39
    The influence of peers 39
4.4 - Improving health and safety culture..40
    Securing commitment of management..40
    Promoting health and safety standards by leadership and example...40
    Use of competent personnel with relevant knowledge, skills and work experience.........................40
    Effective communication within the organisation...41
    Training 43
4.5 - Internal and external influences on health and safety management standards 44
    Internal influences on health and safety 44
    External influences on health and safety...45

Sources of reference

Guidelines on Occupational Safety and Health Management Systems (ILO-OSH 2001) ISBN 0-580-37805-5

Occupational Health and Safety Assessment Series (OHSAS 18000): Occupational Health and Safety Management Systems OHSAS 18001:1999 (ISBN 0-580-28298-8), OHSAS 18002:2000 (ISBN 0-580-33123-7), BSI

Reducing Error and Influencing Behaviour (HSG48), HSE Books ISBN 0-7176-2452-8

4.1 - Concepts of safety culture

Definition of 'health and safety culture'

> "The safety culture of an organisation is the product of individual and group values, attitudes, perceptions, competencies, and patterns of behaviour that determine the commitment to, and the style and proficiency of, an organisation's health and safety management."

Figure 1-4-1: Safety culture.
Source: NEBOSH Examiners Report.

Correlation between health and safety culture and health and safety performance

The correlation between health and safety culture and health and safety performance can be illustrated by research that has been conducted.

For example, after the introduction of a safety programme in the range of forestry and logging organisations in Columbia, it was found by Painter and Smith (1986) that there were dramatic improvements in performance. The accident frequency rate was reduced by 75% and the workers' compensation costs were reduced by 62%. In further research, Lauriski and Guyman (1989) found that after a safety management programme had been introduced at the Utah Power and Light Company, lost time injury rates were reduced by 60% over a period of five years. From 1980 to 1988, the accident frequency rate was reduced from 40 to 8 per annum, while production more than doubled.

Research has shown that improvements in safety management are influential in achieving a positive safety culture. This leads to reduced accident rates, which is seen as a positive step forward, which is a further influence on the safety culture.

4.2 - Factors influencing safety culture

Tangible outputs or indicators of an organisation's or site's health and safety culture

Developing and promoting a positive safety culture is an important aspect of health and safety management. A safety culture is an intangible thing, which has tangible manifestations. These manifestations can be measured.

Effective communication

Effective communication is essential in achieving a positive safety culture; therefore effectiveness of communication can be used as a measurement. Considering a practical example: an organisation's safety policy must be communicated to the workers; therefore asking them about it will give an indication as to how well it has been communicated.

Leadership and commitment

Evidence of commitment by personnel at all levels of the organisation can be measured. The evidence can be shown by **the clear identification and acceptance of responsibility** for health and safety from the most senior. As Du Pont say: "The Chairman takes the role of Chief Safety Officer." Areas that can be considered are: membership of safety committee and attendance; responsibilities accepted and taken seriously - rules apply to everyone, for example the wearing of necessary personal protective equipment (PPE). Measurement of the level of organisational achievement compared to the standards that have been set in the safety policy can be done by **safety audit.** Any variances from the standards which are promptly corrected provide a clear indication of a positive safety culture.

Equal priority

Evidence that health and safety is treated as an equal partner alongside other critical business issues such as quality, finance, and production. The health and safety policy should be integrated with other corporate policies for, say, purchasing or training.

Incident (accident) investigation

Findings of incident (accident) investigations can be used as a measurement of a safety culture. Root cause incident investigation can show where things are going wrong, for example, by considering:

- Technical, procedural and behavioural aspects and Controls.
- Validity of management controls.
- Level of commitment to working safely.

The procedure for dealing with the findings of the incident investigation will indicate the level of safety culture through the recommendations for improvement and prevention. For example:

- People responsible for action should be named.
- Completion dates for each action.
- Follow up for actions not completed.
- Findings communicated to the workers.

Consultation

Proactive involvement of workers and/or their representatives in decision making, for example when selecting new equipment such as access equipment for work at height. Discussion with workers about work methods and conditions of work will result in fewer or no complaints.

SPECIFIC TANGIBLE OUTPUTS INDICATORS

Organisations developing a positive health should soon begin to see a significant reduction in the following areas:
- Accidents.
- Absenteeism.
- Sickness rates.
- Staff turnover.
- Complaints about working conditions.

The results of safety audits should then improve and show a greater level of compliance with health and safety rules and procedures.

Measurement of these specific indicators may be easily done with 'direct labour' workers, but this can present a greater challenge where workers are mainly contractors.

Factors promoting a negative health and safety culture

Just as a positive safety culture starts with commitment from the most senior manager, a negative safety culture will develop from lack of it. There are, however, other factors involved which may lead to a negative health and safety culture.

When a company is **reorganising**, it is a time of upheaval, personal as well as corporate. Individuals and groups tend to be resistant to change, especially when they are unsure of the need for it. Lack of proper communication can lead to rumours of closure, dismissal or changes in the company's structure. The resulting decrease in morale may lead to uncertainty in the company's commitment. Reorganisation can also lead to people changing their position in the company structure with more, fewer or different responsibilities than previously. Without proper communication and necessary training this can lead to **uncertainty** and a mistrust of the company and its aims and objectives.

The company may state the aims and objectives, but the achieve ability may be in doubt. The aims and objectives may state a commitment to health and safety, yet the changes in work patterns do not allow for safe working. This could be from the point of view that production is seen as all-important and safety must be secondary or an 'add on' done only if time allows for it.

A practical example would be if a company decided on a speed limit of five miles an hour for site vehicles as a control to prevent accidents, but then increased the overall amount of material a driver had to move in a work period. This would create a misunderstanding. On one hand, the company is showing commitment to safety by restricting the speed of the vehicles, but on the other, no one seems to care that the increased workload means that the drivers must break the speed limit to get their job done. The management and workers then have different aims and objectives and energy is exerted by each in conflict with the other. These **management decisions** prejudice mutual trust and lead to misunderstanding regarding commitment to health and safety. This promotes a negative safety culture.

In many countries organisations have a responsibility to set standards for health and safety performance when selecting potential contractors or suppliers to carry out work on their behalf. Any contracts entered into may represent or impose the equivalent requirements of a contract of service for workers. The system of awarding contracts, of itself, does not have a positive or negative influence on health and safety. Influence rather depends on the standards expected by the person that establishes the contract and those delivered by the contractor and finally by the level of monitoring / enforcement of the contract.

4.3 - Factors influencing safety related behaviour

Individual, job and organisational factors

INDIVIDUAL FACTORS

Individual differences

All individuals are different. These differences will influence patterns of work behaviour and may limit the effectiveness with which a worker carries out a job. They will also influence how safely the work tasks are carried out. These individual differences arise from an interaction between the 'inherited characteristics' (passed on from the parents) and the various 'life experiences' through which the individual passes from the moment of conception.

- Experiences in the womb.
- Birth trauma.
- Family influences.
- Geographical (cultural) location.
- Pre-education (school) influences.
- Education - opportunities, quality, support.
- Occupational factors - training and retraining.
- Individual pastimes and interests.
- Own family influences - marriage, children.
- Ageing.

Any, many or all of the above will create a unique person different from all other individuals. The ways in which people differ are many and various and it is critical to bear this in mind from the point of view of work effectiveness and safety. It is vital to know what a particular job entails (the job description) and to specify the characteristics required to enable a person to perform that job effectively (the personal specification). Physical differences will need to be considered carefully when establishing controls for work activities; some differences may limit or prohibit individuals from certain tasks.

Summary of individual differences

Physical	Mental
Gender - e.g. females not exposed to lead.	Attitude - e.g. all PPE is uncomfortable.
Build - e.g. may restrict movement in a confined space.	Motivation - e.g. risks v reward.
Health - e.g. colour blindness.	Perception - e.g. do not respond to alarms.
Capability/strength - e.g. manual handling.	Capability - e.g. ability to follow instructions.

The significance of individual factors

Workers bring to their job personal habits, attitudes, skills, personality and so on, which in relation to task demands may be strengths or weaknesses. Individual characteristics influence behaviour in complex and significant ways. Some characteristics, such as personality, are fixed and largely incapable of modification. Others such as skills and attitudes are amenable to modification or enhancement. The job should be matched to the worker.

Critical considerations within the personal factor category include the following.

a) **Thorough task analysis** (especially for critical jobs) which should enable a detailed job description to be generated. From this, a specification can be established to include such factors as age, physique, skill, qualifications and experience, aptitude, knowledge, intelligence and personality. Personnel selection policies and procedures should ensure the specifications are matched to the appropriate worker.

b) **Training** will produce a worker capable of the task without close supervision with confidence to take on responsibility and perform effectively, providing that initial selection is done properly. Training should be carried out from induction and throughout the career of the worker to reflect not only changes in the task, but to maintain, through refresher training, standards of performance. Self confidence and job satisfaction grow significantly when workers are trained to carry out the task correctly under both routine and emergency conditions. This will not only benefit workers themselves and fellow workers but greatly improve the achievement of organisational objectives. Training should aim to give all workers the skills to allow them to understand the risks and controls of plant and processes. Training should be on going and not regarded as a one off exercise since procedures and processes change and complex skills (particularly when underused) deteriorate. Refresher training significantly contributes to worker performance and safety.

c) **Monitoring of personal performance.** All work practices should be monitored through direct supervision. The degree of supervision or frequency will be risk based and will be influenced by many factors such as the experience or skill of the worker or the supervisor. Monitoring should not be at the task level only, but carried out by all of the management team, from the most senior down. This will ensure delegated tasks are performed correctly and ensure statutory requirements for health and safety are met.

d) **Fitness for work and health surveillance.** For certain jobs there may be specified medical standards for which pre-employment and/or periodic health surveillance of workers is necessary. These may relate to the functional requirements of the job or the impact of specified conditions on the ability to perform it adequately and safely. An example is the medical examination of divers. There may also be a need for routine surveillance of the effects of exposure to workplace hazards, both physical, such as the effects of acute heat stress: or chemical, for example, absorption of organic phosphorous insecticides which may impair ability to control a tractor or aircraft. Medical surveillance is not a substitute for proper control of the hazardous agent.

e) **Review of health on return to work from sickness absence.** The recognition of the purpose of counselling and provision of advice during periods of individual need, such as dealing with anxiety or stress related to failure to achieve work objectives, in this context alcohol or drug abuse and the possible adverse side effects of prescribed drugs may be relevant stressors. Access to specialist assistance may be appropriate with the possible need for temporary or permanent re-deployment.

JOB FACTORS

Tasks should be designed in accordance with ergonomic principles to take into account limitations in human performance and physical ability. Matching the job to the person will ensure that they are not overloaded and that they will make the most effective contributions to the work. Physical match includes not only the design of the equipment associated with the task, but the whole workplace and working environment. Mental match involves the individual's information and decision-making requirements, as well as their perception of the tasks. Mismatch between job requirements and workers' capabilities provide potential for human error.

The major considerations in the design of the job include the following.

a) Identification and comprehensive analysis of the critical (high risk) tasks expected of workers and appraisal of likely errors.

b) Evaluation of required worker decision making and the optimum balance between the human and automatic contributions to safety actions.

c) Application of ergonomic principles to the design of worker-machine interfaces, including displays of plant and process information, and suitable positioning, labelling of control devices and panel layouts.

d) Design and consistency of presentation of procedures and operating instructions.

e) Organisation and control of working environment, including the workspace, access for maintenance, lighting, noise and thermal conditions.

f) Provision of correct tools and equipment.

g) Scheduling of work patterns, including shift organisation, control of stressors such as noise or heat to reduce fatigue.

h) Arrangements to cover for absence and procedures for emergencies such as a fire.

i) Efficient and suitable communications, both immediate and over periods of time.

ORGANISATIONAL FACTORS

Organisations need to produce a climate that promotes worker commitment to health and safety and emphasises that deviation from corporate safety goals, at whatever level, is not acceptable.

Producing such a climate requires clear, visible, management commitment to safety from the most senior level in the organisation. The commitment should be not just a formal statement but be evident in the day-to-day activities of the company. This commitment must be known and understood by the worker. Workers may be reluctant to work safely if their decisions to do so are likely to be subject to unwarranted criticism from their superiors or their colleagues.

The attitude of a strong personality at a senior level within the organisation may have either a beneficial or an adverse effect on a safety climate. Inevitably, junior workers will be influenced by that person's example.

UNIT IGC1 - ELEMENT 4 - PROMOTING A POSITIVE HEALTH AND SAFETY CULTURE

Health and safety procedures soon fall into disuse if there is no system of ensuring that they are followed. Too often procedures lapse because of management neglect, or workers are discouraged from working to them by peer groups or other pressures, such as production targets. Where managers become aware of deficiencies in safety procedures but do not act to remedy them, the workforce readily perceive that such actions are condoned.

Workers may not understand the relevance of procedures or appreciate their significance in controlling risk. Sometimes procedures are faulty, irrelevant, or lacking in credibility. When accidents happen managers cannot blame workers for not following the correct work practice if such actions have been allowed to become routine. Managers are responsible for explaining the importance of safe working, and monitoring that work procedures are followed

To promote a proper working climate, it is essential to have an effective system for monitoring safety that identifies, investigates and corrects deviations. The introduction and operation of such systems requires considerable effort by managers and only by allocating adequate resources can they be confident that failures will be prevented or controlled.

In short, the organisation needs to provide:

- Clear and evident commitment, from the most senior management downwards, which promotes a climate for safety in which management's objectives and the need for appropriate standards are communicated and in which constructive exchange of information at all levels is positively encouraged.
- An analytical and imaginative approach identifying possible routes to human factor failure. This may well require access to specialist advice.
- Procedures and standards for all aspects of critical work and mechanisms for reviewing them.
- Effective monitoring systems to check the implementation of the procedures and standards.
- Incident investigation and the effective use of information drawn from such investigations.
- Adequate and effective supervision with the authority to remedy deficiencies when found.

Attitude, aptitude and motivation

ATTITUDE

"The tendency to respond in a particular way to a certain situation"

Attitudes are another set of factors that constitute ways in which individuals differ one from another. Attitudes are not directly observable and can only be assessed by observing behavioural expression (physical or verbal behaviour).

Clearly, a person's attitudes will govern the way in which an object or situation is viewed and it will dictate the resultant response or pattern of behaviour. This is obviously very critical when considering an individual's working patterns and any safety aspects associated with them. Attitudes, like other aspects of individual differences, are formed (not necessarily consciously) because of a lifetime of experiences and as such are not easily changed. A person's attitudes are not simply an aid to coping with their environment, but may determine how they wish to change what is there. Any attempts to change such a fundamental part of an individual's personality will be resisted. The individual will feel their very being is under threat. This is worth remembering in the context of safety propaganda (information) campaigns.

"People's attitudes and opinions that have been formed over decades of life cannot be changed by holding a few meetings or giving a few lectures".

Figure 1-4-2: Observation made by Chairman Mao Tse Tung. *Source: "Little Red Book".*

Examples of attitudes affecting safe working:

1) It will never happen to me.
2) We have never had an accident.
3) Its only the price of a plaster.
4) I know my limits.

Everyone at work should attempt to change their own and their colleague's attitudes to health and safety from - Work safely because -

I have to. ➔   I should. ➔   I want to. ➔   It is automatic.

Remedial action
- Train, and retrain when need for reinforcement is evident.
- Change by experience (involvement), e.g. selection of personal protective equipment (PPE).

Organisational factors that may cause a person to work unsafely even though they are competent include:

- Management or peer group pressure.
- A poor safety culture in the organisation.
- A lack of resources or equipment.
- A lack of clarity in roles and responsibilities.
- Inadequate supervision.
- Poor working conditions.

APTITUDE

"A tendency to be good at certain things"

Aptitude is closely linked to personality. Some people are particularly good at certain things, for example, an individual may be good at working with his hands, while another may say they *"could not change a light bulb"*.

Aptitude can be developed over time as a skill, but it is more likely to be part of that person's characteristics. This can be a factor when placing people in particular jobs. A person with no aptitude for precision work, but superb at felling trees is 'an accident waiting to happen' if given the job of soldering electronic components.

MOTIVATION

"The driving force behind the way a person acts in order to achieve a goal"

In the context of the working situation there have been many attempts to identify why people work. The earliest approach (by F. W. Taylor) was that people worked for money and fear of losing their livelihood. Financial reward was seen as the prime motivator. The more they were paid the harder they worked. This led to a new management philosophy:

- Payment by results.
- Incentive schemes.
- Piece work.
- Danger money.

From a health and safety management viewpoint, this theory is unsound since most bonus schemes encourage people to work **unsafely** by cutting corners, rushing to get the job done etc. with safe working practices being ignored or compromised. Money *is* critical but other factors are more critical, e.g. social belonging, acceptance by one's peers. With this in mind, motivating people to adopt safe working practices should include:

- Establishment of a positive health and safety culture where risk taking is frowned upon by all workers but especially supervisors and managers.
- Setting realistic objectives with regard to accident rates.
- Involvement in health and safety policy setting.
- Clarification of responsibilities.
- Developing a positive reward structure.
- Monitoring health and safety performance.
- Improving worker's knowledge of the consequences of not working safely (through information and training).
- Showing the commitment of the organisation to safety (by providing resources and a safe working environment).
- Involving workers in health and safety decisions (by consultation, team meetings, for example).
- Recognising and rewarding achievement.

Positive motivation (i.e. workers working safely because that is how they want to work) tends to be more effective than negative motivation (i.e. workers working safely for fear of disciplinary action), although both have a place.

Remedial action
- Establish positive health and safety culture.
- Positive reward structure.
- Set clear objectives e.g. accident statistics.

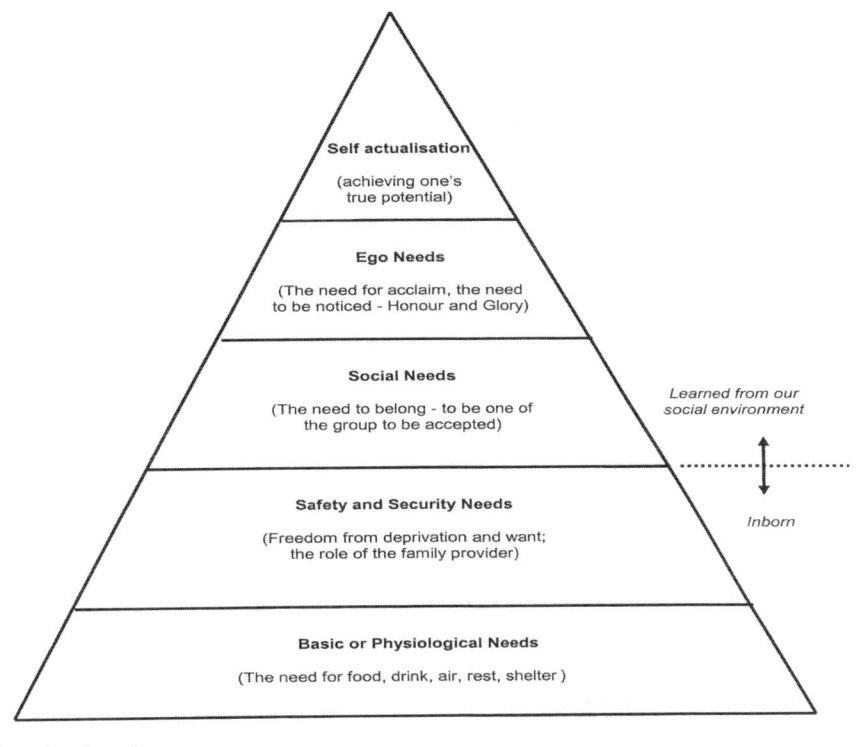

Figure 1-4-3: Maslow's hierarchy of needs.
Source: Maslow.

(The NEBOSH International General Certificate does not require detailed knowledge of Maslow's Hierarchy).

Perception of risk

"The way that a person views a situation"

Factors that influence the effectiveness are:

- A boring, repetitive job may result in 'day dreaming' which may result in a lowering of the impact of a stimulus.
- Warnings (or threats) may not be strong enough to get through the perceptual set.
- Patterns of behaviour and habits can be carried from one situation to another where they are no longer appropriate or safe (e.g. we tend to drive too quickly after leaving a motorway).
- Individuals can get 'used to' a stimulus and, if it is not reinforced, it ceases to command the attention and is ignored.
- Intense concentration on one task may make paying attention to another stimulus difficult or impossible.

Remember: **We do not see what is there!** **We do not see what we do not expect to be there!**
We see what we expect to be there! **We do not see what we do not want to be there!**

Figure 1-4-4: Examples of perception images.

Remedial Action
- Information.
- Training.
- Instruction.
- Drills.

Source: Ambiguous.

Process of perception

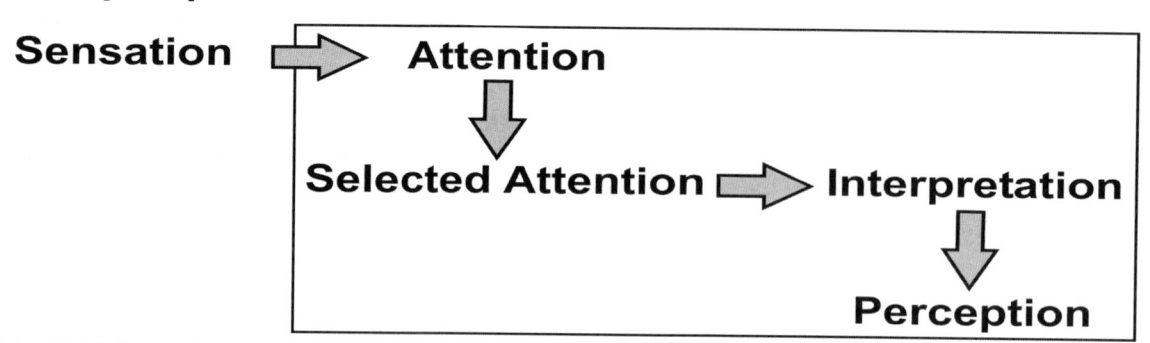

Figure 1-4-5: Model of perception. Source: ACT.

Within each individual, these processes of attention and interpretation are closely interlinked. The factors that influence these processes and the way in which they operate are often referred to as the "perceptual set" (the way we see things) of the individual.

Errors and violations

ERRORS

Errors fall into three categories:

1) Slips.
2) Lapses.
3) Mistakes.

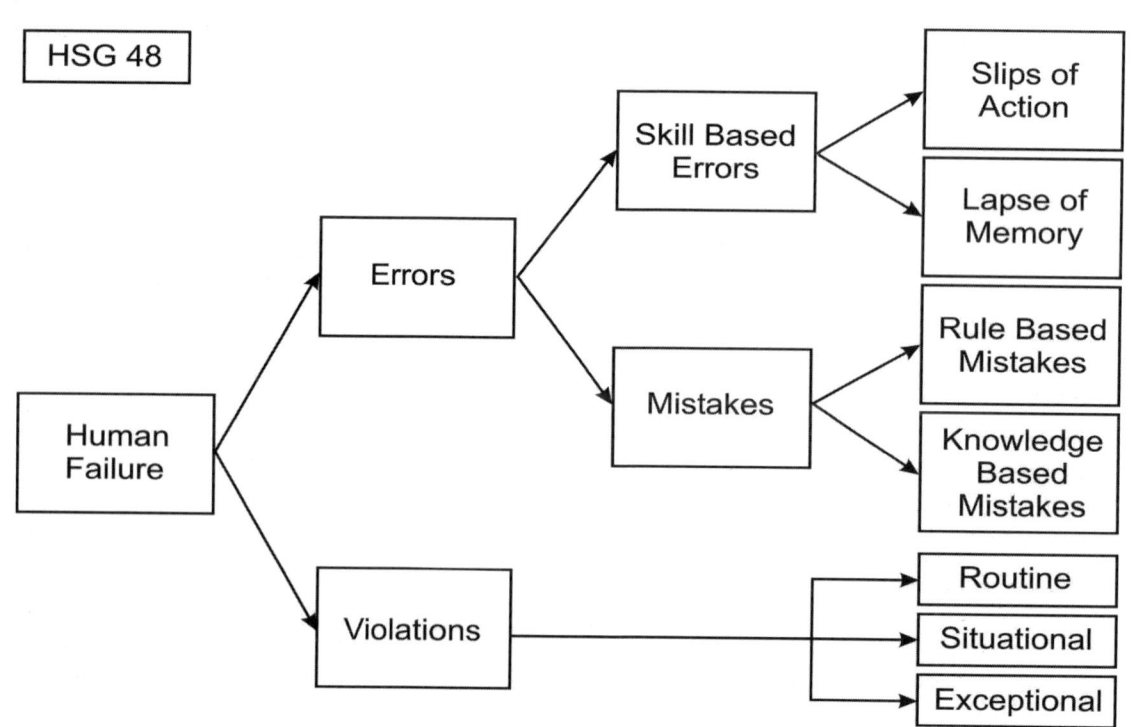

Figure 1-4-6: Human failures flow chart. Source: HSG48.

Slips and lapses

Once we have learned a skill, there is little need for much conscious thought about what we are doing. We can carry out a task without having to think too much about the next step. We learn to ride a bike or drive a car in this way. We need to pay attention to the road and the traffic, but we manipulate the pedals and change gear without thinking about it. If our attention is diverted, we may fail to carry out the next action of the task, or we could forget the next action or lose our place resulting in an error.

Mistakes

Mistakes are a little more complex than slips and lapses. We may do the wrong thing believing it to be also correct. We have a tendency to use familiar rules or procedures, often when they don't apply. The wrong application of a rule to a situation can result in an error e.g. use of a water based extinguisher on electrical equipment on fire.

In unfamiliar situations, we may have to apply knowledge-based reasoning. If this is miscalculated or the situation is misdiagnosed, then a mistake may occur.

These errors typically occur with trained, experienced people, but also occur with untrained and inexperienced people. The untrained and inexperienced may base their decisions on misunderstandings and a lack of perception of risk.

VIOLATIONS

These violations are rarely acts of vandalism or sabotage, but are often carried out in order to get the job done e.g. using a convenient ladder of insufficient length. Many accidents, injuries and cases of ill health come about because of violations.

Routine violations

Routine violations are where breaking the rules or procedure has become the normal way of working, for example, not removing work clothes when taking refreshment breaks in a canteen facility. New workers come in and learn the incorrect ways, not realising they are wrong. The incorrect method may have come about because it is a quicker way to work or because the rules are seen as too restrictive. In one company, it was felt that the work could not be finished on time if all of the rules were followed.

Situational violations

Situational violations may occur with pressures from the job: time pressure, extreme weather conditions, wrong equipment, for example. Roof work may continue without edge protection, because the correct equipment has not been provided.

Exceptional violations

Exceptional violations occur when something has gone wrong. A decision has to be made to solve the problem and that might involve breaking a rule and taking a risk, e.g. temporary repair to equipment hydraulic lines that become permanent. It is erroneously believed that the benefits outweigh the risk.

Effects of age and experience

EFFECTS OF AGE ON BEHAVIOUR AT WORK

The design of the human body is uniform, allowing for differences of sex. The spine, joints, tendons and muscles work in the same way and will suffer after the same abuse, although to a varying extent. Individuals, therefore, have different physical capabilities due to height, weight, age and levels of fitness. They also have different mental capabilities, memory retention and personalities.

The body will be affected, more or less, by tasks that involve bending, reaching, twisting, repetitive movements and poor posture. The aches, pains and fatigue suffered doing certain tasks will eventually impair the operator's ability and lead to degradation in performance. It is therefore essential to consider the task in order to match it to the individual so the level of general comfort is maximised. For example, when carrying out manual handling assessments it is critical to look at the relationship between the individual, the task, the load and the environment.

EFFECTS OF EXPERIENCE ON BEHAVIOUR AT WORK

The experienced worker will know the hazards in the workplace and can make a decision on the risk he can take based on past experience. The problem with this is that his accident-free past may well be down to luck and that may change at any time. He may no longer see the hazards because of familiarity with them. More than half the fatalities from electrocution involve competent people. The experienced worker will, however, be more aware of what can cause harm, unlike the inexperienced young person. It would be unethical to cause someone to have an accident in order to heighten their awareness of risk or so they could gain experience. Awareness must be heightened in other ways: training and education or simulation.

The influence of peers

Nearly all human beings need the company and social acceptance of their fellows. When we are in a group situation, it is very difficult to behave differently to others. The group will have established a norm for behaviour. The norm behaviour is what keeps the group together. There are two main groups, social and work.

The social group is formed out of individuals with common beliefs, interests expectations , for example Individuals in the social group will be under its influence most of their time. Within the workplace we have groups of individuals working together often with common skills, but not always common beliefs.

The work group is different to the social group; individual behaviour may be strongly influenced by their peers (others in the group) and personal choice may be changed by the peer pressure. This group behaviour is what sets the standard of performance and the method of achieving the particular work goal or situation. The observance of health and safety rules may strongly be influenced within a group. If the norm is to follow the rules, e.g. a pre flight equipment check on an aircraft before take off, then the rules will be obeyed. Conversely, if the norm is to flout the rules, e.g. failure to wear eye protection for a grinding operation, then the rules may well be disobeyed by an individual who may know the risks.

UNIT IGC1 - ELEMENT 4 - PROMOTING A POSITIVE HEALTH AND SAFETY CULTURE

SUMMARY OF HUMAN BEHAVIOUR

Human failures:

Errors
- Slips.
- Lapses.
- Mistakes.

Violations
- Routine.
- Situational.
- Exceptional.

Control measures:

Individual factors:
- Increase skill and competence levels.
- Select staff according to their capabilities.
- Provide health surveillance wherever necessary.
- Job rotation to prevent boredom.

Job factors:
- Correct ergonomic design of tools and equipment.
- Prevent disturbances and interruptions.
- Provide clear instructions.
- Maintain equipment to a suitable standard.
- Minimise exposure to unpleasant working conditions such as noise, heat, adverse weather, for example.

Organisational factors:
- Good work planning to avoid high work pressure.
- Adequate safety systems and barriers.
- Respond quickly to previous incidents.
- Consultation rather than information.
- Clear identification of responsibilities.
- Thorough management training.
- Create positive health and safety culture.

4.4 - Improving health and safety culture

Securing commitment of management

Organisations should identify key performance indicator (KPI) standards for heath and safety. The standards should be achievable and designed not to compete with other organisational performance standards such as those set for production / service or quality. The standards must be agreed at the highest level within the organisation and standards for establishing management control must be established. The management controls must be designed to send a clear signal, that health and safety is an equal partner to the other organisational objectives. Management controls may take many forms, but should include system checks, such as random examination of completed permits to work, observations of high risk work activities or periodic tours. It should not be assumed that those that manage projects and quality issues are skilled in managing health and safety. Their competence should be confirmed through formal training in health and safety management controls.

CONTROL

Control is achieved by:

- Getting the commitment of all workers to clear health and safety objectives.
- Managers taking full responsibility for controlling the factors that could lead to loss.
- Nominating a senior figure to monitor the policy implementation.
- Allocating responsibilities to line managers and safety specialists.
- Encouraging worker safety representatives to make a contribution.
- Setting performance standards.

The emphasis is on a collective effort to develop and maintain systems of control before the event - not on blaming individuals for failures afterwards.

Promoting health and safety standards by leadership and example

Management actions at all levels should send clear signals to staff and others within the workplace of the importance of observing the health and safety standards which have been set. Leadership through example will include such issues as correct use of personal protective equipment, observance of rules, which might require special skills or training and commitment by seniors to attending health and safety training identified for development of subordinate managers.

Use of competent personnel with relevant knowledge, skills and work experience

The organisation should identify the safety critical tasks and establish suitable controls. The task analysis should not only take account of engineering controls, such as guard design or fume extraction requirements, but the requirements of the personnel involved in the task. This will include ensuring that the relevant knowledge (of the risks associated with the activity), skill (application of appropriate practical experience) and work experience (history of working in an appropriate activity/environment) is established, before an individual is put to work. Factors such as individual aptitude, dexterity and physical ability / endurance may also be critical e.g. not everyone will be comfortable or able to work at height or in confined spaces. High-risk tasks may utilise simulation equipment to allow skill to be developed, at no risk to the individual or others, for example, the use of aircraft flight simulators. Similarly, it may be necessary for the trainee to be under close supervision (an instructor flies with a new pilot of an aircraft) until their skill can be demonstrated as appropriate through their displayed actions and ability.

COMPETENCE

- Assess the skills needed to carry out tasks safely.
- Provide the means to ensure that all workers, including temporary workers, are adequately instructed and trained.
- Ensure that workers on especially dangerous work have the necessary training and experience to carry out the work safely.
- Arrange and encourage access to sound advice and help.

Effective communication within the organisation

It is the job of the middle manager/supervisor to translate decisions from superiors into clearly understood actions and, at the same time, be aware of the needs, capabilities and expectations of subordinates in order to communicate them back to superiors. The ideal is increasingly seen to be that of giving information and explanation. The emphasis must be on participation of all levels in all decisions which affect health and safety.

MERITS AND LIMITATIONS OF DIFFERENT METHODS OF COMMUNICATION

General principles of communication

Communication is a two-way process where the needs of the receiver are equally as critical as the needs of the speaker. The speaker should not assume that the receiver has understood what has been said. To ensure the success of the communication:

- The message should be directed towards and reach the intended recipient.
- Communicated in a form capable of being understood by the recipient.
- Open ended questions should be used to ensure understanding.
- Closed questions which yield yes/no answers, should be used to confirm understanding.
- Avoid unclear or ambiguous terms.
- Be assertive but not aggressive.
- Keep content concise.
- Ensure the recipient understands.
- Check to ensure understanding.
- Budget time to encourage feedback.

Verbal communication

It is imperative that verbal communication is clear, concise and easily understood. However this is not always the case and the reasons listed below are some of the barriers to effective verbal communication:

- Noise - creating difficulty in understanding.
- Complexity of information.
- Language and/or dialect of the speaker.
- Sensory impairment (perhaps deafness).
- Ambiguity.
- Use of technical terminology.
- Mental - difficulty in understanding requirement.
- Inexperience on the part of the recipient.
- Communication indirect; passed through several individuals before it reaches the recipient.
- Inattention - distracted.

Some barriers to communication that may lead to workers failing to comply with safety instructions or procedures:

- Unrealistic or ill-considered procedures.
- Inadequate training.
- Lack of involvement in consultation.
- Peer group pressure.
- Risks not perceived.
- Mental and/or physical capabilities not taken into account.
- Poor safety culture in the organisation.
- Complacency or lack of motivation.
- Competing priorities and pressures.
- Fatigue and stress.

Written communication

The primary purpose of written information is to communicate. The writer should, therefore, always have the reader in mind when producing the text. The use of plain text avoiding confusion must be encouraged - this is particularly critical for safety related material. One useful vehicle for conveying information is the *report*. A simple structure is as follows:

- Introduction and background.
- Main body of the report.
- Recommendations.
- Conclusions.

Introduction and background This section includes the title page that should clearly identify the writer and the document. It should contain a brief explanation of the subject described in the document title and the reason for the document. Consider the aim of the report and inform the reader of the problems it intends to address.

Main body of the report This section deals with details, facts and findings. Keep the style simple and to the point. Avoid the use of sector specific terminology, unexplained abbreviations. Inaccuracy, inadequate or illogical organisation of the contents can distract the reader and reduce understanding.

Recommendations These should flow logically from the main body of the report. Recommendations should consist of a plain statement of action without repeating the arguments of the preceding section.

Conclusions This section should contain a summary of the main findings and inferences.

Graphic communication

Health and safety signs and other public signs rely heavily on information graphics, such as stylised human figures and emblems to represent concepts such as "personal protective equipment must be worn" and the direction of traffic flow on a construction site. They illustrate information that would be unwieldy in text form, and act as a visual representation for everyday concepts such as stop and go. There use is particularly critical where it is necessary to communicate risk to those who might have limited or no knowledge of the written language in their place of work

Technical manuals and work instructions make extensive use of diagrams and also common icons to highlight warnings, dangers, and standards certifications.

USE AND EFFECTIVENESS OF VARIOUS COMMUNICATION MEASURES

Notice boards

A traditional communication technique is to display safety information on notice boards. The advantage of this method is that the communication is available to everyone in a particular work area. Notice boards should only be used to make general statements or to keep workers aware of current information or proposed developments. Notice boards should not be used where the information must be up to date or completeness of the information impacts on safety critical issues.

The information must be kept up to date and maintained in a legible condition if it is to be effective. Notice board information relies on people's ability to read, understand and apply the information correctly. Information provided should be written in the language(s) relevant to the people in the workplace.

Safety propaganda

There are many forms of safety 'propaganda' which aim to sell the safety message. Their effectiveness in modifying human behaviour and attitudes has been the subject of much debate. Many professionals now view them to be of little value - however there is a marked reluctance to abandon them.

Films, videos, DVD's

Films and videos are often used to renew attention during periods of training. The visual impact is a strong stimulus on the delegate; the video enables the training to expand experience outside the training room or the experience of the trainees. Shock videos are sometimes used to illustrate what might happen if procedures are not followed. It has been found that their effect does not change attitude in the longer term. A common use for videos is at site induction, for both new workers and contract labour.

Poster campaigns

Posters displaying information are sometimes seen as a low cost and visible way of showing commitment to safety. This can be self-defeating if management places too much reliance on them. For example, the workforce can perceive this as an excuse for not providing appropriate training. To be effective messages must be:

Positive - posters exhorting people to 'be safe' or threatening severe injury if a particular action is not taken are rarely effective. People are not necessarily rational or logical - particularly in giving priority to safety. If the "normal work practice learned" is unsafe, in the absence of personal injury experience or training, workers will not perceive they are at risk and not change their unsafe behaviour. Messages should emphasise positive safety benefits.

Aimed at the correct audience - interest in safety posters is quickly lost. This is compounded when messages are seen as irrelevant. Information must be carefully targeted and posters positioned for those most affected by their content message. For example, a poster warning of the dangers of loose clothing being entangled in machinery should be sited close to the relevant machine.

Acceptable - messages should be relevant, practical and realistic.

Care must be taken to avoid offending or distracting your audience away from the message. Some male or female representations may be inappropriate or illegal in some countries. Similarly, pictures of horrific accidents can lead to a rejection of the message on the basis that it could not happen to them. Posters should be changed regularly to maintain attention.

Summary:

Advantages:
- Relatively low cost.
- Flexibility (allowing them to be displayed in the most apposite positions).
- Pictorial (allowing messages to be easily understood).
- Use in reinforcing verbal instructions or information and in providing a constant reminder of critical health and safety issues.
- The potential to allow workers to become involved in their selection and use.

Disadvantages:
- Need to change posters on a regular basis if they are to be noticed.
- They may become soiled, defaced and out-of-date.
- The possibility that they might be seen to trivialise serious matters.
- They might alienate people if inappropriate stereotypes (e.g. of the 'stupid worker') are used.
- No direct way of assessing whether the message has been understood.
- They may be perceived by unscrupulous employers as an easy, if not particularly effective, way of discharging their responsibility to provide health and safety information, and even of shifting the responsibility onto the workforce for any accidents that may occur.

Toolbox talks

Toolbox talks are often used in organisations which operate work on a continuous shift basis. The technique is very good for fast communication on specific subjects. It relies on the cascade of information from supervisors or team leaders to their worker group. Issues are normally kept to a minimum and two-way communication is very effective with individuals within the worker group. Issues raised may be current, such as warning of some concerns over equipment reliability, or recent good or poor safety trends i.e. accidents. Other, future issues may be raised, such as proposed changes in personal protective equipment or work practice(s).

Memos

Memos are often used to communicate on short-term issues. The memo is an easier and faster vehicle to use than the more formal document change procedure. Safety related issues may be concerned with person, job or hours worked or work patterns. Written communication is effective in that it states what is to change and from when, but again relies on individual interpretation and understanding. It is often one way, as proof of issue is not always proof of receipt. As with memos, e-mails have similar limitations. Software is available to check whether the recipient has opened the correspondence, but not that it has been read, understood or actioned.

Employee handbooks

Employee handbooks are often issued to new workers at induction. They are useful in communicating site rules and information such as accident, injury-reporting mechanism. Similarly, they will often contain information on site emergency arrangements such as fire and first aid. To be effective a mechanism needs to be established to recall and reissue the handbooks when changes occur. Some organisations operate a loose leaf folder design. Consideration needs to be given to where each employee keeps the information provided.

CO-OPERATION AND CONSULTATION WITH CONTRACTORS AND THE WORKFORCE

The employer should arrange to consult workers on matters of health and safety, in particular before any changes in arrangements are implemented. The employer may not have a duty to adopt any suggestions made by workers or their representatives. A grievance procedure should be in place to deal with any disputes or misunderstandings. In some territories grievances which cannot be resolved internally may be referred to a Government enforcement agency for resolution.

Co-operation

Pooling knowledge and experience through participation, commitment and involvement means that safety becomes everybody's business.

- Consultation with workers and their representatives.
- Involvement in planning and reviewing performances, writing procedures and solving problems.
- Share information on loss and experience with contractors.

Roles and benefits of worker participation, safety committees and employee feedback

Those organisations which recognise the importance of managing heath and safety have embraced the concept of good worker cooperation and participation at all stages of business development. This may be achieved through communication with worker's representatives or on a one-to-one basis. One of the benefits of using worker representatives is the extra time, which can be made available to representatives over individual workers. This will enable the representatives to get to know the business and issues of health and safety better through structured training. Representatives will also be able to contribute to forums with management, such as safety committees. The roles and communication lines must be determined and monitored for effectiveness. Care needs to be taken to ensure that the correct message is being communicated by the representatives to avoid the possibility that they might minimise or be selective in what they communicate.

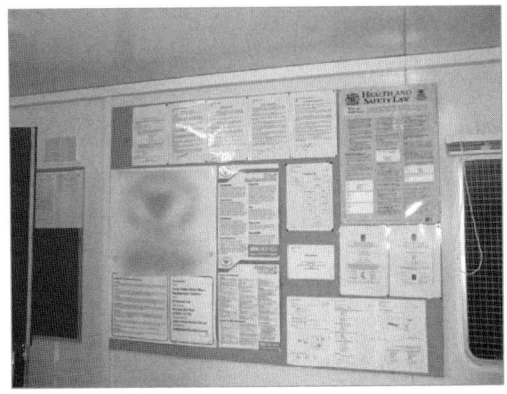

Figure 1-4-7: Safety notice board. *Source: ACT.*

Figure 1-4-8: Safety suggestion scheme. *Source: ACT.*

Training

THE EFFECT OF TRAINING ON HUMAN RELIABILITY

General points

Workers should be provided with adequate information, instruction, training and supervision, to ensure the health and safety of all at work. This requirement is not only essential to underpin health and safety standards, but may be made more specific in certain countries. Where appropriate those who employ others to carry out work may need to take into account the capabilities of their workers before entrusting tasks. This is necessary to ensure that they have adequate health and safety training and are capable enough at their jobs to avoid risk to themselves or others. To this end consideration must be given to procedures for recruitment including job orientation or when transferring workers between jobs and work departments. Training must also be provided when other factors, such as the introduction of new technology and new systems of work or work equipment arise.

Training must be repeated periodically, where appropriate, be adapted to take account of any new or changed risks to the health and safety of the workers concerned, and ideally take place during working hours. A safety-training programme should be instigated for all workers from director (most senior employer representative) level down. This should include:

- Specialist training.
- Internal and external courses.
- Formal and informal training.

All the training should be recorded and the employer needs to recognise the importance of further training at each stage of a person's career.

Effects and benefits of training

Benefits to employee
- Better understanding and involvement raises all workers morale / job satisfaction.
- Understanding of relevance of systems of work and controls reduces risk.
- Understanding of welfare arrangements aids health, safety and hygiene.
- Allows worker's to reach experienced worker standard more quickly.
- Increases flexibility of staff.

Benefits to employer
- Reduces accident frequency and severity.
- Reduces injury related absenteeism.
- Reduces claims and insurance premiums.
- Reduces the chance of prosecution.
- Increases profits/benefit.

OPPORTUNITIES AND NEED FOR TRAINING PROVISION

Induction training for new workers

Induction training is generally defined as the information, instruction and training given when a person starts a new job, task or process. Its purpose is to orientate the individual to his or her environment in order to maximise both productivity and safety. Thus, a workforce that is aware of the risks is familiar with procedures and systems of work, knows how to recognise and report unsafe conditions. This ensures that the worker shares a common commitment to health and safety which should contribute greatly to a safer workforce. Induction training for new workers should include:

- Review and discussion of the organisation's safety policy.
- Specific training requirements.
- Fire and emergency procedures.
- Welfare facilities.
- First aid procedures and facilities.
- Personal protective equipment (PPE) provisions - limitations, training, use and maintenance, for example.

Refresher training

As time passes a worker's approach to health and safety may change from that intended by the employer. This may simply be because they have forgotten, sometimes because of infrequent use, or because they prefer to have a different understanding or way of working. It is critical that regular refresher training be used to reinforce the employer's desired approach. A common refresher period used for lift truck operators is three years. This may be an acceptable interval for some tasks but the period may need to be shorter for others. Refresher training needs to be provided to managers as well as workers that need to apply health and safety skills.

Job change / process change

Required at appropriate intervals to update techniques and ensure awareness of correct methods. Training will include information and skills relevant to:

- Introduction of new substances/processes.
- Changes in working procedure.
- Changes in work patterns.
- Review of risk assessments.

This also assess the behaviour of the workforce and their attitude. In addition, further safety training may be required following an increase in accidents/incidents.

Introduction of new legislation

Employers have a duty to bring to the attention of workers specific changes in legislation which may have an effect on their safety or the safety of others. Changes that may affect personal safety include revisions of limits of exposure to noise and where a reduction in occupational exposure limits may cause workers to adopt more stringent exposure controls.

Introduction of new technology

The introduction of new technology will often require the adoption of new work practices. Such training will include developing skills to interpret equipment control layout and data display, e.g. the introduction of nets and airbag fall arresters, used in new builds.

4.5 - Internal and external influences on health and safety management standards

Internal influences on health and safety

GENERAL POINTS

Internal influences on health and safety will depend on the maturity of the organisation concerning health and safety. This maturity and how it is displayed may be described as the culture of the organisation. The culture may be positive or negatively disposed to safety initiatives, rules or safe working practices.

MANAGEMENT COMMITMENT

Management commitment to safety should be demonstrated through clear, visible actions and cascade down from the most senior level in the organisation. The commitment should not just be a formal statement, but more importantly, it should be evident in the day-to-day activities of the company. This commitment must be known and understood by workers at all levels within the organisation. The correct attitude of a dominant personality at a senior level within the organisation who leads by example, e.g. wearing a hard hat where required on site, will have a beneficial effect on a safety climate. Inevitably, junior workers will be favourably influenced by that person's example.

PRODUCTION DEMANDS

Production / service targets are an integral part of running an organisation. The setting of targets (objectives) is a positive way of influencing an organisation, provided they are realistic and achievable. They are only considered realistic and achievable if they can be met in a safe and healthy manner. It is not uncommon for workers (including managers) to dismiss health and safety by taking risks to achieve a work completion target/date. Analysis of the situation often reveals such things as ill communicated health and safety objectives whereas work completion targets are well defined. If senior management attention (monitoring) is singularly focused on work completion targets, health and safety will inevitably suffer. Individuals may choose to take risks to meet their personal production targets, e.g. when involved in work such as 'job finish go home', where an employee might work faster than is reasonable in an effort to leave work earlier.

COMMUNICATION

Communication of health and safety matters has a strong positive or negative influence on health and safety. If it is absent when needed it can lead to doubt and uncertainty; when communication takes place it may be mistimed or incomplete. Those affected by health and safety risks usually feel more confident in the risk controls around them if it is explained what they will or will not do to protect them. If problems with the controls arise those affected are most comfortable if they are informed of the problem and what is being done about it. It is essential to plan to communicate positives in the form of successes; often they are invisible in organisations and are unnecessarily overshadowed by negative situations that are over assertively communicated. A positive health and safety culture thrives on balanced communication of both positive and negative issues.

COMPETENCE

Every employer has a duty to ensure that workers at work are provided with competent and safe fellow workers and in order to achieve this, varying assessments and collation of evidence may be required to substantiate claims of competency. Competency can be defined as a balance of experience (not only of the type of work or job, but of the work area or location) and training. Information which may be held on file includes references, qualifications and records which chronologically demonstrate work experience. Competent workers improve health and safety working within the workplace and generate a culture of safety awareness.

EMPLOYEE REPRESENTATION

Internal influences of trade unions, where they exist in organisations, depend mainly on the views of the individuals that comprise the members, but in particular their representatives. In situations where appointed representatives deal with all union matters their efforts on health and safety may be diluted, particularly at times when pay is being reviewed and the representative is involved directly with collective bargaining. If the representative is appointed to deal with health and safety alone they will not be driven so much by payments as conditions of work e.g. negotiating more cash for potentially unhealthy work, rather than seeking better ways of working to reduce personal risk. Many employee representatives have received significant training on health and safety matters and therefore have an opportunity to influence health and safety through knowledge. In some organisations, employee representatives have received more training than managers. This can lead to misunderstanding and conflict with such managers who might not have receive equivalent training to enable them to carrying out their duties. How an organisation communicates with workers either directly or through employee representatives on safety will have a bearing on workers perspective on commitment to health and safety promotion.

External influences on health and safety

GENERAL POINTS

There are many external influences on an organisation. They will have a varying influence depending on the status of the management of health and safety in the organisation. The status of health and safety management may be observed to be in one of three broad stages: 'young', 'immature' and 'mature'.

The young organisation will tend to be driven by events that are occurring and the pressures put on it by external organisations such as the insurers or local enforcement where appropriate. The young organisation tends to see remedies as technical in nature and can be said to be operating at level one.

The immature organisation will tend to be driven by unplanned events, but is beginning to establish systems and practices in anticipation of events. The choice of preventive systems tends to be those required to comply with laws or regulation where appropriate or cost reduction, e.g. conducting risk assessments and to be procedural in nature and is therefore seen to be operating at level two.

The mature organisation has spent considerable resource establishing active systems and practices. Unplanned events that result in actual loss are infrequent. Enhanced systems and practices are being established as the organisation observes opportunities for continuous improvement. Attention is tending to be focused on preventive systems and practices that are behavioural in nature and is therefore seen to be operating at level three.

SOCIETAL EXPECTATIONS

Societal opinion tends to fall into two parts:

- Strategic influenced by the general mass of public concerning its tolerance of specific workplace hazards or situations (e.g. display screen equipment or major disasters).
- Local influences tend to surround acceptability or unacceptability of the practices of a specific organisation. This is most acute following an accident and has had the effect of causing closure of some organisations within a location.

LEGISLATION

More recently, the introduction of regulation in many countries has encouraged health and safety preventive action and self-development. For legislation to influence organisations either they must want to comply or there has to be a real prospect of punishment for non-compliance.

ENFORCEMENT

Many countries ensure health and safety regulations are enforced through the use of central enforcement agencies which establish local enforcement officers or inspectors. Enforcement agencies have a significant role in influencing an organisation's level of performance concerning health and safety. If the focus of the enforcement agency is on technical specifics then organisations will tend to follow this lead and deal with these issues. It is therefore critical that the enforcing agencies demonstrate the value of not only technical, but procedural and behavioural preventive measures. The relative influence of the enforcement agencies is highly dependent on them being sufficiently field active to contact a significant number of organisations. It would not be a balanced influence if the only time they were seen was following an accident. They should be seen by organisations before accidents occur to encourage planned preventive actions to be implemented.

INSURANCE COMPANIES

Insurance companies have become increasingly aware that they may have underestimated the risks related to some companies they are insuring. This has caused them to look again at the risks and the factors that lead to claims. A focus on the development of the management of health and safety in the organisation insured has been found to be a useful predictor of future loss. This approach has been seen to influence many organisations and cause them to minimise the risks in order to control their level of premium increase.

TRADE UNIONS

In many countries trade unions have had a significant influence on health and safety. In some countries following improved changes in socio economic development worker members within the national workforce have declined. Unions have always maintained a profile of member support in making claims from employers concerning injury at work. As claims consciousness increases their role and influence will increase in those countries where they are recognised.

STAKEHOLDERS

Stakeholders (owners) include Government's investment banks, co-operatives or shareholders of an organisation which have a financial investment in that particular business and as a result wish to see their investment grow. Generally, stakeholders are not directly interested or involved in the day to day operations or undertakings of the business, but more likely to be concerned with the company's financial accounts and personal investment reward. Focus tends to be on increasing profits, which more often than not includes reducing overheads or improving worker productivity. Additional pressures may be placed on the workforce following announcements of worker reduction or the need for profits to increase. Less resource may be available to undertake and fulfil a project safely or the workforce may feel under pressure to work faster, harder or longer in order to achieve profitability and gain job security. Some stakeholders recognise that poor health and safety will result in lower profitability; such organisations generally invest considerably in risk management and are very successful in the marketplace.

ECONOMICS

The state of prosperity of an organisation or the country as a whole falls into the subject of economics. An economic 'climate' can be prosperous or in 'recession'. Although possible to vary greatly, in a prosperous, ascending or stable economy, industry generally is busy and productive, unemployment decreases and morale improves. However, a declining economy can plunge into recession, resulting in closure of business, higher unemployment and the morale of the population weakened by the thought of personal loss (i.e. reduced earnings, job loss, and increased debt). The construction industry has historically suffered from changes in economic strength. The impact on struggling organisations may result in less time, effort and money spent on health and safety measures, thus creating less safe working conditions. This may cause individuals in the workplace to subject themselves to hazards and risks that they would not normally subject themselves to in an attempt to try and remain in work, resulting in workers performing unsafe acts.

Element 5

Risk assessment

Learning outcomes

On completion of this element, candidates should be able to demonstrate understanding of the content through the application of knowledge to familiar and unfamiliar situations. In particular they should be able to:

5.1 Explain the aims and objectives of risk assessment.

5.2 Identify hazards by means of workplace inspection and analysis of tasks.

5.3 Explain the principles and practice of risk assessment.

Content

5.1 - Aims and objectives 49
    Definitions of hazard and risk 49
    Objectives of risk assessment 49
    Outcomes of incidents 49
    Different types of incident 50
    Typical ratios of incident outcomes and their relevance 51
    Utility and limitations of accident ratios in accident prevention 51
5.2 - Identifying hazards 51
    Identifying hazards 51
    Accidents in terms of injury 54
    Health related hazards 55
5.3 - Principles and practice of risk assessment 55
    Identifying population at risk 55
    Identification of hazards 56
    Evaluating risk and adequacy of current controls 56
    Recording significant findings 58
    Reasons for reviewing 58
    Criteria for a 'suitable and sufficient' risk assessment 59
    Special case applications of risk assessment 59

Sources of reference

Guidelines on Occupational Safety and Health Management Systems (ILO-OSH 2001) ISBN 0-580-37805-5

Five Steps to Risk Assessment (INDG163), HSE Books ISBN 0-7176-1565-0

Occupational Health and Safety Assessment Series (OHSAS 18000): Occupational Health and Safety Management Systems OHSAS 18001:1999 + Amendment 1:2002 (ISBN 0-580-28298-8), OHSAS 18002:2000 + Amendment 1:2002 (ISBN 0-580-33123-7), BSI

5.1 - Aims and objectives

Definitions of hazard and risk

HAZARD

"Something that has the potential to cause harm"

For example, bleach in a sealed bottle. Following hazard identification, it is possible to establish that risks exist, that are or are not acceptable. In order to establish the presence of a risk it is necessary to identify the existence of hazards that may give rise to unplanned risk.

RISK

"A risk is the likelihood that a hazard will cause a specified harm to someone or something"

For example, bleach in use may come into contact with the hands and may result in dermatitis. The presence of hazards at a given level of risk may not be a cause for immediate concern. However, some situations may exist or arise where there is a significant danger of loss, which will require some prompt action to be taken to reduce the danger. The process of identification assessment is considered later.

Objectives of risk assessment

GENERAL POINTS

Definition of term "risk assessment"

"An identification of what within your work or workplace, which may have the potential to cause harm to people or workers, so that you can consider whether you have provided sufficient precautions or need to do more to prevent harm."

Objectives of risk assessment

Risk assessment involves:

1. The identification of the hazards at work.
2. The evaluation of the risks from the hazards.
3. Deciding how to control the risks.
4. Implementing a control strategy.

Most people undertake risk assessment as a normal part of their everyday lives. Routine activities, such as crossing the road and driving to work, routinely call for a complex analysis of the hazards and risks involved in order to avoid damage and injury. Most people are able to recognise hazards as they develop and take corrective action. People do, however, have widely different perceptions regarding risk and would find it difficult to apply their experience to the formal workplace risk assessments required to ensure safe working.

The aim of this unit is to introduce the basic principles of risk assessment techniques in order to carry out the systematic, structured assessments needed to fulfil the requirements of modern health and safety good practice. There may be a legal requirement within your country to complete specific risk assessments within other legislation, such as control of noise at work and manual handling operations applicable in the UK.

The risk assessment should be **suitable and sufficient** and should cover the whole undertaking; it should also be broad enough so that it remains valid for a reasonable period. Risks arising from the routine activities, associated with life in general, can usually be ignored **unless** the work activity compounds these risks.

Outcomes of incidents

The reasons why we need to work safely can be summarised in three main groups:

HUMAN HARM

Considerations should include the general well being of workers; the interaction with the general public who either live near the organisation's premises or come into contact with the organisation's operations - e.g. transportation, nuisance noise, effluent discharges etc.; the consumers of the organisation's products or services, who ultimately keep the organisation in business.

LEGAL

Considerations should include where relevant to your country possible consequences of failing to comply with health, safety and environmental legislation, approved codes of practice, guidance notes and accepted standards.

ECONOMIC

Considerations should include the financial impact on the organisation of the costs of accidents, the effect on insurance premiums, possible loss of production / service and the overall effect on the 'profitability' of the organisation. Costs may be direct and indirect.

Different types of incident

ILL-HEALTH

The health and well-being of individuals may be affected by a number of work-related factors. Ill health may develop over a long period of time; these are commonly called chronic diseases. Typical examples of work-related ill health are asbestosis, pneumoconiosis and silicosis, where the ill heath effects may take several years to develop. More recently ill health effects have been related to work load and stress.

INJURY ACCIDENT

Some injury effects will be acute in nature and recognised immediately, such as strains or sprains of muscles or ligaments caused by inappropriate lifting of heavy items. Other common injuries include cuts, burns, and bruises.

DANGEROUS OCCURRENCE

The definition of dangerous occurrences will differ depending on your country's enforcement reporting requirements. This term is used to describe significantly hazardous incidents, such as the collapse of, the overturning of, or the failure of any load-bearing part of any lift or hoist; mobile powered access platform; access cradle or window-cleaning cradle; excavator; pile-driving frame or rig having an overall height, when operating, of more than 7 metres; or fork lift truck; the collapse of a scaffold of more than five metres high.

NEAR-MISS

A near-miss is an incident with the potential to cause harm, but where there is no measurable injury / loss. A near-miss is classified under the term accident:

"An unplanned, uncontrolled event which led to, or could have led to injury / loss"

It is critical to analyse near-misses to assess the potential of the event, had circumstances been different. This will enable corrective action to be put in place to prevent a reoccurrence of the incident.

DAMAGE-ONLY

Substantial damage occurs to property and materials at work annually. Often the most significant losses are associated with workplace fires, when the workplace may be destroyed, although fortunately only rarely are people injured. The study of the incidence of damage and potential losses may be a useful predictive tool to identify scenarios which might result in person damage. For example, a series of collisions into scaffold on a site with poor access and lighting may be predictive of a vehicle failure / scaffold collapse leading to personal injury. Such considerations enable the employer to take corrective action before any worker loss occurs.

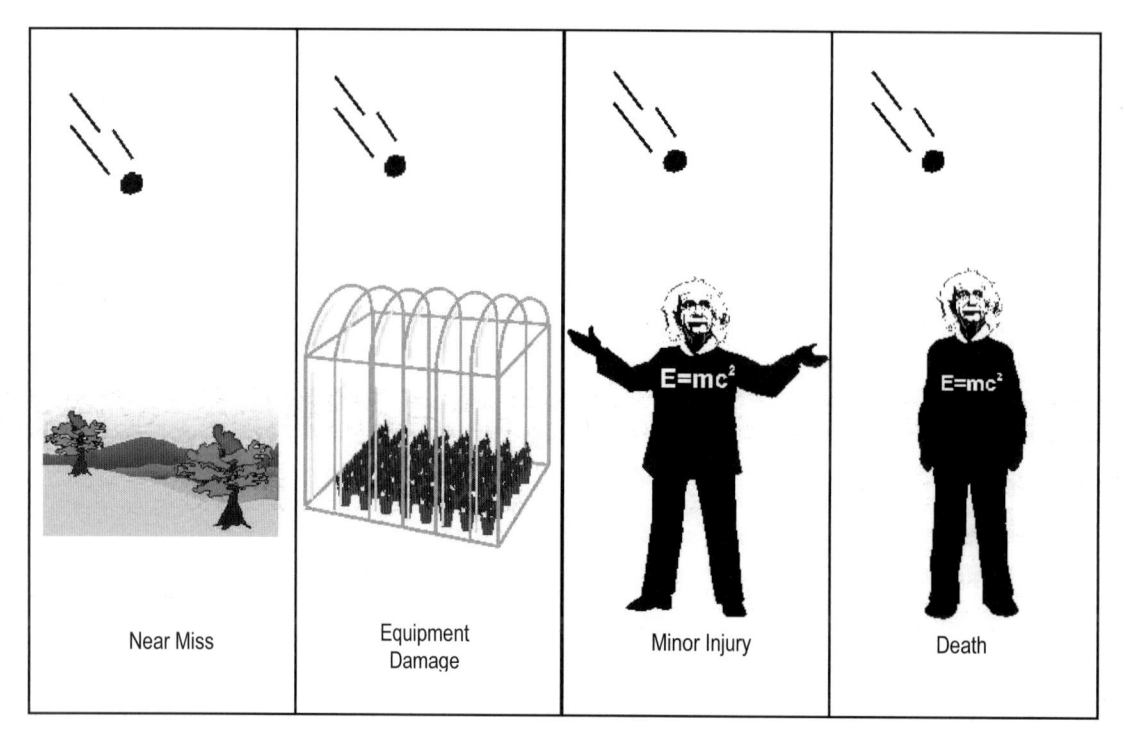

Figure 1-5-1: Results of an accident. Source: ACT.

THE DISTINCTION BETWEEN DIFFERENT INCIDENTS IN SUMMARY

An accident is an event which brings about a result. We must not think of injuries etc. as accidents, but rather as the *results* of accidents. In short, accidents result in *losses* of one kind or another: The following accident model is offered to illustrate the above statement. In a situation where a stone falls from a height the following could result:

- Falls into the ground and there is no damage or injury, *a near miss*.
- Hits a pane of glass, resulting in *damage*, but no injury.
- Hits a person causing cut and bruises to hand. **This is an injury accident.**
- If the person was working directly under the stone when it fell there could have been a fatality*, or fatal accident.*

This definition, therefore, includes "near-misses', i.e. where no injury or damage etc. occurs. The difference between a near-miss and a fatal accident in terms of time and distance can be very small indeed. It is therefore clear that the damage to persons or property is not the accident, but part of the effects of the accidents, the result or consequences of the accident.

An old adage says: "Never waste an accident". Apart from being unpleasant and perhaps very costly, every accident constitutes an opportunity to correct some problem. For this purpose, a near miss is just as valuable as a serious injury/damage, in fact even more valuable and an excellent opportunity not to be missed.

Typical ratios of incident outcomes and their relevance

Some years ago, a study in the USA of 1,750,000 accidents in 21 industries, led by Frank Bird, showed that there is a fixed ratio between losses of different severity and accidents where no loss occurred, i.e. near misses. This is illustrated in the pyramid model of incident outcomes - Frank Bird's accident ratio study.

Pyramid model of incident outcomes

```
        /\
       /1 \         Serious Or Disabling Injury
      /----\
     / 10   \       Minor Injuries
    /--------\
   /   30     \     Property Damage
  /------------\
 /    600       \   Near Misses
/----------------\
```

Figure 1-5-2: Accident ratio study.   Source: Frank Bird.

The principle applies equally to other situations. The organisation, site or department that has most accidents is therefore, likely to have the *most serious losses*.

Utility and limitations of accident ratios in accident prevention

For statistics derived to be of value their limitations have to be understood. Variables in work methods, hours of work, hazard controls and management system effort make it fundamentally difficult to make comparisons outside the organisation deriving the data. Ratios, such as these, are best suited to comparison of performance of the same organisation over similar periods of time, for example yearly.

5.2 - Identifying hazards

Identifying hazards

SOURCES AND FORM OF HARM

The first step is to identify the hazards. This can be done in many ways. The methods used will need to be assessed so all the hazards associated with a task can be identified and ranked in order of severity. For complex activities, it may be necessary to break the activity down into its component parts by, for example, job analysis.

For a large machine, this could mean looking at:

- Installation.
- Normal operation.
- Breakdown.
- Cleaning.
- Adjustment.
- Dismantling.

The hazards associated with each activity could then be identified more easily and thoroughly.

It is necessary to identify contingent hazard, which can arise from system, component, checking or maintenance failures, as well as continuing hazards, i.e. those present continuously, e.g.:

- Mechanical hazards.
- Electrical hazards.
- Thermal hazards.
- Noise and vibration.

- Radiation.
- Toxic materials.
- Ergonomic design.

Once the area/activity has been selected, the method(s) of hazard identification can be chosen. If a hazard is defined as being something with the potential to cause harm, then hazard identification can be carried out by observing the activity and noting the hazards as they occur in the actual work setting. This is seen to have advantages over carrying out a desktop exercise using the safety manual, for the use of a machine for example, as the operator may have developed their own method of working, contrary to instructions and training.

Another method of hazard identification may be a simple walk around an area, a tour, taking notes or using a checklist. Tours may be carried out daily, weekly or be ongoing. They may be formal or informal, but require a reporting and follow-up system in order to be effective. A further method is an inspection. This may be a random arrangement or a routine scheduled inspection and involve someone familiar with the task/area and someone not familiar with the normal work practices. It is more formal than a tour, takes place less often, and requires documenting.

Hazards may also be identified during accident investigation, especially if the accident was not foreseen. An accident will not be wasted if it highlights previously unforeseen hazards. Accident statistics, from internal and external sources, can also be used for hazard information. There are other hazard identification techniques, which form part of the advanced risk assessment techniques:

- Hazard and operability studies (HAZOP), which are much used by the chemical industry at the design stage of processes and equipment.
- Reliability analysis and Failure mode and effect analysis (FMEA), which are inductive techniques.
- Fault tree analysis (FTA) and Event tree analysis (ETA), which are deductive techniques.

ROLES OF INSPECTIONS

The obvious purpose of safety is to identify areas where improvements are needed. Inspections may also affect the organisational safety culture, particularly where employee's views are sought as part of the inspection. In this way, employer's commitment to health and safety can be demonstrated, ownership of health and safety can be shared and worker morale can be increased by simple improvements being implemented at the time of the inspection.

Inspections involve examination of the workplace or items of equipment in order to identify hazards and determine if they are effectively controlled. Four different types of inspection are common:

- General workplace inspections - carried out by local first-line managers and worker representatives.
- Technical inspections (thorough examination) of equipment, e.g. boilers, lifting equipment - by a specialist competent person.
- Preventive maintenance inspections of specific (critical) items - carried out by maintenance workers.
- Pre use 'checks' of equipment, e.g. vehicles, forklift trucks, access equipment - carried out by the user.

An important aid used by anyone carrying out an inspection is a checklist, i.e. a list of the standards of performance which should be achieved. When a work area or item of equipment fails this test, it is considered substandard and represents a hazard. Each substandard condition should be assessed and corrective action carried out and details recorded.

Issues to be considered when creating a checklist should include: substances or materials being used, condition of traffic routes and means of access and egress, work equipment, work practices (manual handling, etc.), work environment, electricity, fire precautions, welfare provision including first aid arrangements and workstation ergonomics.

JOB / TASK SAFETY ANALYSIS

Job / task analysis is the identification of all the accident prevention measures appropriate to a particular job or area of work activity, and the behavioural factors which most significantly influence whether or not these measures are taken. The approach is diagnostic as well as descriptive.

Analysis can be:

1) Job based: operators of plant, fork lift truck drivers.

2) Task based: manual handling activities, housekeeping.

The results can be used to correct existing analyses and to improve such things as emergency procedures, reporting of information and the layout of work areas. The process of job analysis needs to be carried out methodically through a series of steps and the whole analysis should be documented.

EXAMPLE JOB ANALYSIS SHEET

Job Title: Filling machine operator.
Department: Finishing.
Purpose: Filling beer bottles using automatic filler and capper.

Machinery and Equipment

Vickers Dawson rotary filler incorporating capping press.
Empty bottle conveyor, marshalling table and filled bottle conveyor.
Hand Tools - spanners, steel lever.

Materials

Empty bottles.

Protection

1) Clothing, one-piece overall and apron.
2) Safety shoes/Wellington boots as necessary.
3) Eye protection against bottle breakages.
4) Hair enclosed in combined drill cap and snood.
5) Heavy duty gloves.
6) Ear defenders.

Guards

Total enclosure of rotary filler and capping press; conveyor end adjacent to filler.

Figure 1-5-3: Example of a job analysis sheet. *Source: ACT.*

Intrinsic hazards

1. Hand contact with moving filler and capping press, and when changing cap supply.
2. Cuts to hand from removal of broken bottles from filler.
3. In-running trap hazard to conveyor.
4. Flying glass splinters due to occasional bottle explosions.
5. Broken glass on floor.
6. Noise - occupational deafness.
7. Slips and falls on wet floor.

Incidence of accidents

Four machines of this type are in regular use in the same department. The worker with least experience has been doing this job for 8 months; others have up to 20 years' experience. No recent accidents can be recalled although the risk of flying and broken glass is always present.

Work organisation

A bonus system is operated and the work is mainly repetitive. After setting-up, a large order could run for two or three days. On the other hand, a series of small orders are done occasionally which requires re-setting the machine after every 4 minute cycle when much more time would be spent setting than running the machine.

Operator and assistant are inter-changeable but the operator always does the adjustment to the flow control device to ensure even and smooth running. Little engineering work is required on the machine, which is very reliable. Typical repairs are replacing a driving belt and adjusting the brake which are straightforward operations occupying a short period.

Tasks

1. Setting up machine.
2. Regulating flow control device.
3. Controlling input of bottles to machine.
4. Removing broken bottles and caps, together with any broken glass present.

Example - Job/task analysis

	Task	Hazards	Good Skills	Influences on behaviour	Learning Method
1	Sharpening a knife using a steel	Cuts to hand, arms	Co-ordination of knife and steel movement	Sharpness of knife Condition of knife Space limitations Other people present Condition of floor	Demonstration of technique Repetitive practice until speed increases
2	Dispensing strong chemical compounds from 200 litre container	Burns to eyes, face and body Inhalation of fumes	Correct position of drum cradle, drip tray and container, use of tap Correct protection clothing, fitting and limitations	Strength of chemicals Type of fume Corrosive effects Illumination Ventilation	Demonstration of techniques Practice using PPE Hazards of spillage, splashing and fumes

Figure 1-5-4: Example of a job/task analysis. *Source: ACT.*

LEGISLATION

Information about hazards can be obtained by considering a range of organisation standards legislative documents such as ISO International Standards.

MANUFACTURERS' INFORMATION

Manufacturers should provide product equipment health and safety information. Information provided in relation to articles and substances must be relevant and kept up to date. Those that design, manufacture, supply or install should inform of any issues determined through research that may affect the users, including product liability aspects, safe operating and use of instructions. Manufacturers/suppliers of equipment should provide material safety data sheets that can then be considered when carrying out a risk assessment.

INCIDENT DATA

Statistics provide useful response information from past accident experience. Types include lost time, sickness absence, first aid records.

Accidents in terms of injury

The following are examples of hazards, together with some of the associated risks, which can occur in the workplace.

HAZARD	ASSOCIATED RISKS	SIGNIFICANCE
Slips/trips/falls	Fall of a person on the same level.	Statistics show that slips, trips and falls on the same level are the most common source of major injuries reported.
Falls from height; falling objects	Fall of a person, object/material.	Falls from height (usually more than 2m) are by far the most common cause of fatal injuries.
Collision with objects	Bumps and bruises. Striking the head on low beams.	Although minor injuries they are very painful and can result in poor morale amongst the workforce if they happen frequently.
Trapping/crushing under or between objects	Serious injury caused by loss of load from crane, collision with site vehicles.	Due to the nature of the machinery involved, death or serious injury is often the result of incidents such as the loss of load from a crane.
Manual handling	Back strains, cuts, injury to joints.	Back strains that occur during manual handling operations often result in absence from work.
Contact with machinery/hand tools	Parts being ejected from the machine. Trapping / crushing. Entanglement of clothing or hair.	All dangerous parts of machinery must be guarded so far as is practicable. Serious injury such as amputation can easily happen should contact with moving parts occur.
Electricity	Fire, shock, burns.	Static electricity or contact with live services can cause shock, burns and/or fire. Particular care should be taken during demolition activities to ensure that all services are disconnected.
Transport	Collision with people and/or property.	Only suitably trained and authorised people should be permitted to drive vehicles on site.
Contact with chemicals	Dermatitis, burns, poisoning.	It is very easy to underestimate the severity of diseases like dermatitis. Good personal hygiene is a must.
Asphyxiation / drowning	Asphyxiation.	Precautions must be taken when dealing with or entering confined spaces, gas fumes and chemical vapours must be taken into account (e.g. cellars).
	Drowning.	Strict precautions need to be taken to protect people who work above or around water. Rescue/resuscitation equipment may be required.
Fire and explosion	Static electrical sparks causing explosions in say flammable or dusty atmospheres.	Permits to work must be used to control non routine work such as grinding and welding.
Animals	Anthrax, leptospirosis, psittacosis caused by coming into contact with animal hides, etc.	Many construction workers regularly come into contact with animal-borne micro-organisms during demolition work and when working in or near water.
Violence	Unhappy customers/clients, criminals, patients in hospitals.	A common problem, particularly for workers who come into contact with the public and those who are responsible for site security.

Health related hazards

CHEMICAL HAZARDS

Examples include:
- Acids and alkalis - dermatitis and burns.
- Metals - lead and mercury poisoning.
- Non metals - arsenic and phosphorus poisoning.
- Gases - carbon monoxide poisoning, arsine poisoning.
- Organic compounds - occupational cancers e.g. bladder cancer.
- Dust - silicosis, coal worker's pneumoconiosis.

BIOLOGICAL HAZARDS

Examples include:
- Animal-borne - anthrax, brucellosis, leptospirosis.
- Human-borne - viral hepatitis.
- Vegetable-borne - aspergillosis (farmer's lung).
- Others (water/land) - legionella.

PHYSICAL HAZARDS

Examples include:
- Heat - heat cataract, heat stroke.
- Lighting - miner's nystagmus.
- Noise - noise induced hearing loss (occupational deafness).
- Vibration - vibration induced white finger.
- Radiation - radiation sickness (at ionising wavelengths), burns, arc eye.
- Pressure - decompression sickness.

PSYCHOLOGICAL HAZARDS

Examples include:
- Work pressure, bullying, - stress, alcohol / narcotic abuse.

5.3 - Principles and practice of risk assessment

Identifying population at risk

A suitable and sufficient risk assessment will identify all those at risk. When assessing numbers and types of people who might be affected it is critical to remember certain groups of workers who may work unusual hours (e.g. security, cleaners, etc.). High risk groups include young people, pregnant women or nursing mothers.

GENERAL GROUPS AT RISK

This category includes vulnerable people that might be at risk from a particular hazard. For example, women of childbearing age (or more particularly any unborn foetus they may be carrying) may be deemed to be at risk from exposure to the hazards presented by lead. Other at risk groups could be the public (because of their lack of knowledge of the hazard/risk), young persons (16-18 years), people with health conditions, workers that have come from other countries where language or work practices may be different. The 'at risk group' depends on the hazard and the circumstances.

SPECIFIC GROUPS AT RISK

Operatives / workers

Typically these are individuals engaged in production type activities where they have little control over their environment or work routine. Issues include repetitive strain, slips, trips and falls, together with a variety of equipment hazards. Consideration of the task and issues of fatigue and loss of concentration are usually significant.

Maintenance staff

Maintenance issues, which may result in injury, are usually associated with poor access and egress. Sometimes maintenance is infrequent and lack of familiarity can cause serious mistakes to be made. Injuries may be compounded by lone working and a system for checking the work of those who are alone or in remote workplaces should be established.

Cleaners

Cleaners may be at risk from the materials that they use or that which they clean. Often the turnover of cleaners is high and their competency in terms of issues, such as the correct use and health effects of the materials they use or remove, is low.

Contractors

Arrangements for contractors need to be clearly established; the work to be done and limitations must be understood by all involved and only controlled deviation allowed. Typical issues may include consideration of location of equipment or materials, welfare or first aid arrangements.

Visitors / public

Before visitors or members of the public are allowed into the workplace issues of access, use of facilities, arrangements for escort or accompaniment must be established. Other issues include arrangements for safe evacuation. Certain workplaces such as places of sport will present specific risks and may require appointment of fire wardens.

UNIT IGC1 - ELEMENT 5 - RISK ASSESSMENT

Identification of hazards

Identification of hazards requires the following practice:

- **Walk around** the workplace and look at what could reasonably be expected to cause harm.
- **Ask workers** or their representatives if they have specific concerns. They may have noticed things that are not immediately obvious.
- If you are a member of a **trade association**, contact them. Many produce very helpful guidance on workplace hazards/controls.
- **Check manufacturers' instructions** or data sheets for chemicals and equipment to determine hazards and precautions.
- **Accident and ill-health records** - these often help to identify the less obvious hazards.
- **Consider any tasks which may result in long-term hazards to health** e.g. high levels of noise or exposure to harmful substances as well as safety hazards.

Evaluating risk and adequacy of current controls

LIKELIHOOD OF HARM AND PROBABLE SEVERITY

After the hazards have been identified it is necessary to evaluate the risk. In order to do this, at least two areas must be considered - the consequence and the likelihood of harm. This requires a judgment for each hazard to decide, realistically, what is the most likely outcome and how likely is this to occur. It may be a matter of simple subjective judgement or it may require a more complex technique depending on the complexity of the situation.

1. **Consequence** - is there a risk of death, major injury, minor injury, damage to plant/equipment/product, or damage to the environment?
2. **Likelihood** - there is a danger present constantly, but there are in-built or applied safeguards. These may fail, be defeated or become inactive at various times. At these times, the hazard will be realised and the probability of this can be evaluated by such techniques as fault or probability tree analysis.

Factors affecting likelihood

In order to consider likelihood accurately, some or all of the following need to be considered:

- Competence of operators / workers.
- Levels and quality of supervision.
- Attitudes of operators and supervisors.
- Environmental conditions e.g. adverse weather.
- Frequency and duration of exposure.

QUALITATIVE AND SEMI-QUANTITATIVE RISK RANKING

Qualitative

Qualitative risk assessment considers the probability or likelihood of failure. This analysis relies on failure rates and typically would consider such information as manufacturer reliability information for its components. It is useful at the micro and macro level.

Semi-quantitative

Semi-quantitative considers the relative effects of workplace risks for common task or operation. It uses the technique of risk ranking. It is useful at the macro level.

Risk ranking

Here associated risks are ranked in order. This normally consists of assigning a numerical value for consequence and likelihood typically in the range 1-5. The product of each risk is then listed and of those which are the most significant, the ones with the highest risk ranking number, are addressed first.

The purpose of ranking risks is to prioritise the need for action and to consider whether or not further action is required. Everyone has their own perception of risk because their personal experiences and background. A method is therefore required in order to have a common approach and attempt to overcome individual differences. We can rate and therefore rank a risk according to the consequence and likelihood of any loss resulting from a hazard. Thus:

Risk rating = consequence x likelihood

Where the: Consequence   Is the degree or amount of any resultant loss.
Likelihood   Is how likely this loss will occur.
Risk rating   Is the severity of the remaining risk after current controls have been taken into account.

Consequence categories

The consequence can be assessed on a scale of 1 to 5.

5.	Major	Causing death to one or more people. Loss or damage is such that it could cause serious business disruption (e.g. major fire, explosion or structural damage). Loss/damage in excess of a financial value.
4.	High	Causing permanent disability (e.g. loss of limb, sight or hearing). Loss/damage in excess of a financial value.
3.	Medium	Causing temporary disability (e.g. fractures). Loss/damage in excess of a financial value.
2.	Low	Causing significant injuries (e.g. sprains, bruises, and lacerations). Loss/damage in excess of a financial value e.g. damage to fixtures and fittings.
1.	Minor	Causing minor injuries (e.g. cuts, scratches). No lost time likely other than for first aid treatment. Loss/damage in excess of a financial value e.g. superficial damage to interior decorations.

RISK ASSESSMENT - ELEMENT 5 - UNIT IGC1

The amounts in each of the above categories will depend on the size and type of organisation. Senior management in each case should decide these figures.

Likelihood categories

5.	Almost Certain	Absence of any management controls. If conditions remain unchanged there is almost a 100% certainty that an accident will happen (e.g. broken rung on a ladder, live exposed electrical conductor, and untrained personnel).
4.	High	Serious failures in management controls. The effects of human behaviour or other factors could cause an accident but is unlikely without this additional factor (e.g. ladder not secured properly, oil spilled on floor, poorly trained personnel).
3.	Medium	Insufficient or substandard controls in place. Loss is unlikely during normal operation, however it may occur in emergencies or non-routine conditions (e.g. keys left in forklift trucks; obstructed gangways; refresher training required).
2.	Low	The situation is generally well managed, however occasional lapses could occur. This also applies to situations where people are required to behave safely in order to protect themselves but are well trained.
1.	Improbable	Loss, accident or illness could only occur under exceptional conditions. The situation is well managed and all reasonable precautions have been taken. Ideally, this should be the normal state of the workplace.

Using the formula stated above (Risk Rating = Consequence x Likelihood) the risk rating can be calculated. It will fall into the range of 1 - 25. This risk rating is used to prioritise the observed risks.

The risk rating is then classified as follows:

Risk Rating   1 - 9   Low
Risk Rating   10 - 15   Medium
Risk Rating   16 - 25   High

Possible factors to consider in determining what further measures could be taken to reduce the risk include:

a) Can the hazard be enclosed/guarded/segregated from workers/people?
b) Is there a safe system of work/written procedures/ adequate supervision?
c) Is training required?
d) Have people been informed/consulted/instructed?
e) Is personal protective equipment required? Has it been provided?

RESIDUAL RISK

This is the risk which remains when controls have been decided; for example, whilst a fall from a height may be prevented by a guard rail, the potential to slip or trip may remain present.

ACCEPTABLE/TOLERABLE RISK LEVELS

Societal standards change and risk acceptability reduces each year. Successful organisations will reduce the level of risk as far as possible. This is often achieved through the use of new improvements in technology.

USE OF GUIDANCE

When making a judgement as to whether controls are adequate care has to be taken to consider relevant guidance. This can be in the form of guidance to legislation, official guidance documents, industry standard guidance and relevant International/local standards.

SOURCES AND EXAMPLES OF LEGISLATION

There are many sources of legislation available from Government, international organisations or manufacturer's websites. Legislation examples - the Occupational Safety and Health Management Systems (International Labour Organisation ILO-OSH 2001); Health and Safety Executive (HSE United Kingdom) Five Steps to Risk Assessment (INDG163); Occupational Health and Safety Management Systems OHSAS 18001:1999 (British Standards Institute).

APPLYING CONTROLS TO SPECIFIED HAZARDS

Controls will need to be identified and applied to specific hazards e.g. electrical, chemical, manual handling.

GENERAL CONTROL HIERARCHY

The principle is to address each risk in the following order of priority. Often a combination of measures will be used. The general control hierarchy is:

- **E** liminate - the substance or work practice.
- **R** educe - the use or frequency or substitute - for a lesser hazard or change the physical form (dust to pellets).
- **I** solation - glove box for handling hazardous biological agents.
- **C** ontrol - at source, i.e. fume dust extraction, totally enclose.
- **P** PE - a physical barrier between you and the risk.
- **D** iscipline - follow the rules, obey signs and instructions.

© ACT

UNIT IGC1 - ELEMENT 5 - RISK ASSESSMENT

PRIORITISATION BASED ON RISK

When risk potential has been identified prioritisation can be given to the order of work to mitigate the risk.

DISTINCTION BETWEEN PRIORITIES AND TIME SCALES

Often risks are of high priority, but the need to establish realistic time scales is also critical. Often it is possible to carry out some aspects in the short and medium term to reduce the likelihood of a loss and remove the need to give everything considered a high priority for completion.

Recording significant findings

FORMAT

Employers are required to record the **significant findings** of their risk assessments in writing.

It should be noted that there are many forms and systems designed for recording assessments and while these may differ in design, the methodology broadly remains the same.

INFORMATION TO BE RECORDED

The task/plant/process/activity together with the hazards involved, their associated risks and workers/persons affected by them together with existing control measures, should be recorded. The necessary actions required to further reduce the risk are then dealt with and are usually recorded separately.

Some items, particularly those with a high-risk rating, may require a more detailed explanation or there may be a series of alternative actions. Information on risk assessments and any controls must be brought to the attention of those assigned the task of work. Risk assessment information should be included in lesson plans to ensure items are not missed when staff are trained or retrained.

No.	Hazard Identification	Associated Risks	No. At Risk	Existing Controls	Consequence	Likelihood	Current Risk Rating	Comments

Figure 1-5-5: Risk assessment form.

Source: ACT.

Reasons for reviewing

Any significant changes to a workplace, process or task/activity, or the introduction of any new process, activity or operation, should be subject to risk assessment.

The risk assessment should be periodically reviewed and updated.

Examples of circumstances that would require the re-evaluation of the validity of a risk assessment are:

- When the results of monitoring (accidents, ill-health effects, environmental) are adversely not as expected.
- A change in process, work methods (introduction of shifts) or materials.
- Changes in the work force.
- Changes in legislation.
- The introduction of new plant or technology.
- New information becoming available.
- As time passes - the risk assessment should be periodically reviewed and updated. A common approach would be no longer than 5 years.

The risk assessment should be periodically reviewed and updated. This is best achieved through a combination of monitoring techniques such as:

- Preventive maintenance inspections.
- Safety representative/committee inspections.
- Statutory and maintenance scheme inspections, tests and examinations.
- Safety tours and inspections.
- Occupational health surveys.
- Air monitoring.
- Safety audits.

Routine analysis of accident and ill-health reports, damage accident reports, and 'near miss' reports can also provide a trigger to an earlier than planned review of risk assessments.

Criteria for a 'suitable and sufficient' risk assessment

The content of a training course for workers who are to assist in carrying out risk assessments should include:

- Legal requirements with respect to risk assessment.
- Process of identifying hazards and evaluating risks.
- Identification and selection of appropriate control measures.
- Awareness of the individual's own limitations and the occasions when specialist assistance might be required.
- Accessing sources of information such as organisational or legislation, Codes of Practice and in house information, including accident records.
- Report-writing skills.
- Interpretation of any local regulations and standards.
- Means available for communicating the outcomes of the assessment.

Special case applications of risk assessment

YOUNG PERSONS

Another specific group of people who must be considered in risk assessments are young people (under 18 years of age) and children. The employer must carry out risk assessments before young workers start work. These risk assessments must pay particular attention to the following risks:

- Work which is beyond their physical or psychological capacity.
- Work involving harmful exposure to agents which are toxic, carcinogenic or may cause heritable genetic damage, harm to the unborn child or other chronic health effect.
- Work involving harmful exposure to radiation.
- Work involving risk of accidents, which it may reasonably be assumed, cannot be recognised or avoided by young persons owing to their insufficient attention to safety or lack of experience or training.
- Work in which there is a risk to health from extreme cold or heat, noise or vibration.

Where children are involved, the significance of assessments must be communicated to the people who have parental responsibility.

Factors such as lack of knowledge, experience or training, the tendency of young persons to take risks such as over- enthusiasm and to respond more readily to peer pressure should also be taken into account when carrying out risk assessments.

EXPECTANT AND NURSING MOTHERS

There are many factors that may increase risks to women of a childbearing age, new or expectant mothers and pregnant workers in the workplace. These include: exposure to chemicals such as pesticides, lead and those causing intracellular changes (mutagens) or affecting the embryo (teratogens); biological exposures (e.g. hepatitis); exposure to physical agents such as ionising radiation and extremes of temperature; manual handling; ergonomic issues relating to prolonged standing or the adoption of awkward body movements; stress; and issues associated with the use and wearing of personal protective equipment.

DISABLED WORKERS

When a general risk assessment is conducted it is common for the assessor to principally have in mind the majority of the working population being considered. For most situations this will be people that are not disabled or otherwise vulnerable. It is essential that if this is the case and disabled workers are, or are going to be, involved in the work being considered that the risk assessment take full account of them. This may mean conducting a separate risk assessment for the disabled workers. As disabilities vary greatly it may be necessary to conduct separate risk assessments related to the specific disabilities that the workers have. In this way they are more likely to be both suitable and sufficient. Care should be taken to consider the particular disabilities in relation to the job when it is functioning normally, when problems arise from it and where emergencies may exist.

LONE WORKERS

Risk assessments that relate to people working alone are a special case in that special risks can arise from this work that are not present in other work. It should be remembered that work that is risk assessed on the basis of it normally being conducted whilst other people are around, in the main part of the day, can quickly become lone working when people work late, come in early or work weekends. Essentially the hazards from the work are often the same as those if the person was working with others but the additional risk control of having others at hand to provide routine assistance, for example to move something or hold something, are not available. Furthermore, lone working leads to the removal of another risk control - the ability of a co-worker to observe if another worker is suffering harm from the risks they are exposed to and the ability for the co-worker to respond or obtain assistance. When assessing the risks it is therefore essential to identify how the risks are controlled to take account of the lone working and whether this is adequate.

This page is intentionally blank

Element 6

Principles of control

Learning outcomes

On completion of this element, candidates should be able to demonstrate understanding of the content through the application of knowledge to familiar and unfamiliar situations. In particular they should be able to:

6.1 Describe the general principles of control and a basic hierarchy of risk reduction measures that encompass technical, behavioural and procedural controls.

6.2 Describe what factors should be considered when developing and implementing a safe system of work for general work activities and explain the key elements of a safe system applied to the particular situations of working in confined spaces and lone working.

6.3 Explain the role and function of a permit-to-work system.

6.4 Explain the need for emergency procedures and the arrangements for contacting emergency services.

6.5 Describe the requirements for, and effective provision of, first aid in the workplace.

Content

6.1 - General principles of controlling hazards and reducing risk	63
General principles of prevention (technical, behavioural and procedural controls)	63
General hierarchy of control	66
6.2 - Safe systems of work	67
Responsibility of the employer to provide safe system of work	67
The role of competent persons in the development of safe systems	68
Importance of involvement in the development of safe systems	68
Importance and relevance of written procedures	68
The distinction between technical, procedural and behavioural controls	69
Development of a safe system of work	69
Introducing controls and formulating procedures	70
Instruction and training in the operation of the system	70
Monitoring the system	70
Confined spaces	70
Lone working	73
6.3 - Permit to work systems	74
6.4 - Emergency procedures	76
6.5 - First aid	77

Sources of reference

First-Aid at Work (ACOP) (L74), HSE Books ISBN 0-7176-1050-0

Safe Work in Confined Spaces (ACOP) (L101), HSE Books ISBN 0-7176-1405-0

Permit-to-Work Systems (INDG98), HSE Books ISBN 0-7176-1331-3

Safety in the Global Village, IOSH Information Sheet, 1999

http://www.iosh.co.uk/index.cfm?go=technical.guidance

6.1 - General principles of controlling hazards and reducing risk

General principles of prevention (technical, behavioural and procedural controls)

In order to control the risks identified by risk assessments, workers and the self-employed need to introduce a risk control strategy of preventive and protective measures. To be effective a risk control strategy needs to consider technical, behavioural and procedural controls.

AVOIDING RISKS

If risks are avoided completely then they do not have to be either controlled or monitored. For example, not using pesticides or not working at height.

EVALUATING UNAVOIDABLE RISKS

Carry out a suitable and sufficient assessment of risks.

CONTROLLING HAZARDS AT SOURCE

Repairing a hole in the floor is safer than displaying a warning sign. Other examples are the use of local exhaust ventilation to remove a substance at source, the design of equipment so that mechanical movement is enclosed and does not create a hazard and the replacement of a defective bearing to control the hazard of noise at source.

ADAPTING WORK TO THE INDIVIDUAL

This emphasises the importance of human factors in modern control methods. If the well-being of the person is dealt with, there is less chance of the job causing ill-health and less chance of the person making mistakes which lead to accidents. Consideration should be given to the design of any equipment used, frequently used controls should be close to the operator, start buttons should be positioned to avoid inadvertent use, stop buttons should be close to the operator and easy to operate in an emergency. All equipment should be clearly labelled. Consideration should be given to minimisation of fatigue. Alleviating monotonous work by breaks or task rotation can help the individual to remain alert and pay attention to the task.

ADAPTING TO TECHNICAL PROGRESS

This can lead to improved, safer and healthier working conditions, for example the provision of new non-slip floor surfaces or the bringing into use of less hazardous equipment such as new sound proofed equipment to replace old noisy equipment. In recent years this has included the use of waste chutes for removal of materials from scaffolds and the use of lower vibration equipment.

REPLACING THE DANGEROUS BY THE LESS/NON-DANGEROUS

For example, using a battery operated drill rather than a mains (supply voltage) powered tool, providing compressed air at a lower pressure or providing water based chemicals instead of solvent based chemicals.

DEVELOPING A COHERENT PREVENTION POLICY

Taking a holistic stance to the control of risk, this involves consideration of the organisation through the establishing of risk / control identification systems, consideration of the job through the use of task analysis and selection of the people. Also, consideration of human factors that affect an individual such as mental and physical requirements.

GIVING PRIORITY TO COLLECTIVE PROTECTIVE MEASURES OVER INDIVIDUAL PROTECTIVE MEASURES

Organisations with a less developed approach to health and safety may mistakenly see the solution to risks is to provide individual protective measures such as warning people of hazards and provision of personal protective equipment - using the 'safe person' (and healthy person) strategy. A more developed and effective approach is to give priority, where possible, to collective measures that provide protection to all workers such as provisions of barriers around street works or cleaning up a slippery substance spill rather than putting signs to warn workers - using the 'safe place' (and healthy place) strategy. These two strategies are supported by a third strategy sometime called the 'safe system' (and healthy system) strategy. This strategy establishes the correct way to do things in the form of rules and procedures, for example, the rule that says 'clean up after you do work' in order that the place is left in a safe and healthy condition.

Reliance on only a safe/healthy person strategy is the weakest of controls. The preferred strategy is the safe/healthy place and priority must be given to using it where possible. By ensuring a safe/healthy place all people that find themselves in it will gain protection. This approach is reflected in the hierarchy used for safeguarding dangerous parts of equipment - our first priority is to provide guards around the dangerous parts (making it a safe place) and for the remainder that cannot be enclosed in this way we provide information, instruction and training to those that use the equipment (making the safe person).

In practice, the most successful organisations use a combination of the three strategies, with the emphasis on making the place safe/healthy, supporting this with systems of work (procedures) and paying attention to the person element so that they support rather than undermine the other strategies. Many organisations that feel they have invested effort in getting the place and procedures correct are taking a fresh look at the actions necessary to ensure the person is also correct. Studies have shown that this too is a critical aspect of effective management of health and safety.

PROVIDING APPROPRIATE TRAINING, INFORMATION AND SUPERVISION TO EMPLOYEES

It is essential to distinguish between: information, instruction, training and supervision. This will ensure clarity of purpose for each and suggest the best way to communicate each effectively.

Information

Purpose
To improve awareness about health and safety generally and in relation to specific hazards, their controls and management performance to bring about these controls. In itself passive, it relies on the recipient to interpret.

Subjects
Legislation.
Company policy statements.
Accident statistics.
General hazards and controls.
Names of appointed first aiders.

Means of communication
Bulletins and news sheets.
Notice boards, propaganda, films
Team briefing.
Written material for visitors.
Site signs and labels.

Instruction

Purpose
To control worker's, contractor's and visitor's behaviour with regard to general and specific health and safety arrangements. Typically one way, often no real check or understanding.

Subjects
Health and Safety rules.
Policy, arrangements and plans.
Use of PPE.
Specific hazards e.g. smoking.
Emergency procedures.
Reporting accidents.

Means of communicating
Formally using verbal, written and visual material, notice boards, induction and job training, direct issue of document, 'tool-box talks'.

Training

Purpose
To develop people, their attitudes, perception and motivation with regard to health and safety to ensure acceptable actions. Training should use two-way communication - information / instruction given and understanding checked. This may be by observation of a person's practical skill, for example, by driving a fork lift truck or using a simulator, and / or by written or verbal assessment.

Subjects
Accident investigation.
Conducting risk assessments.
Conducting inspections/audits.
How to comply with instructions.
How to set up your display screen workstation.
How to use work equipment e.g. rough terrain fork lift truck.
Use of personal protective equipment.
Manual handling techniques.
Emergency procedures.

Means of communicating
On/off the job.
Internal/external trainers.
Explanation, demonstration, discussion and practice.
One-to-one or group.
Written, oral and visual material.

Supervision

Supervision consists of the provision / re-enforcement of performance standards of workers to ensure health and safety. It includes monitoring that agreed work practices are followed and the use of motivation techniques such as involvement of the workforce in task design to help ensure compliance with the required actions.

The success of information instruction and training activities needs to be measured to enable updating to take place to cater for changes in the workplace. The supervisor has a crucial part to play in this monitoring process. It is critical to balance the amount and timing of supervision against the work being done. It is generally appropriate that the level of supervision necessary increases with the level of risk related to the work. It can be said that when considering supervision of individuals it is critical to take account of the competence of the person. In cases where a person has qualifications but has no experience and is therefore low in competence (e.g. a young person straight from college) then supervision must increase accordingly.

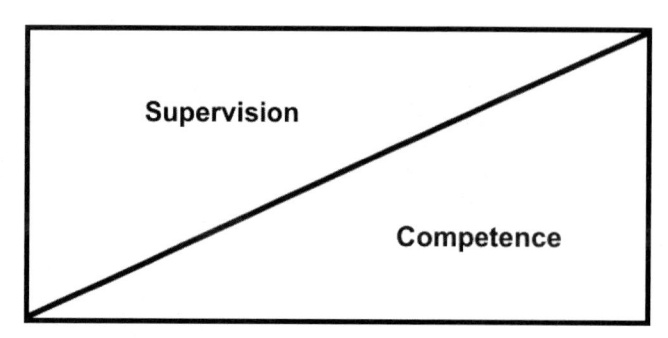

Figure 1-6-1: Competence v supervision.   Source: ACT.

CATEGORIES AND FEATURES OF SAFETY SIGNS

Signs are defined as those combining shape, colour and a pictorial symbol to provide specific health and safety information and instruction.

1)	PROHIBITION	Circular signs. Red and white. e.g. ■ No smoking. ■ No pedestrian access. ■ No children. ■ No unauthorised access.	Prohibition

PRINCIPLES OF CONTROL - ELEMENT 6 - UNIT IGC1

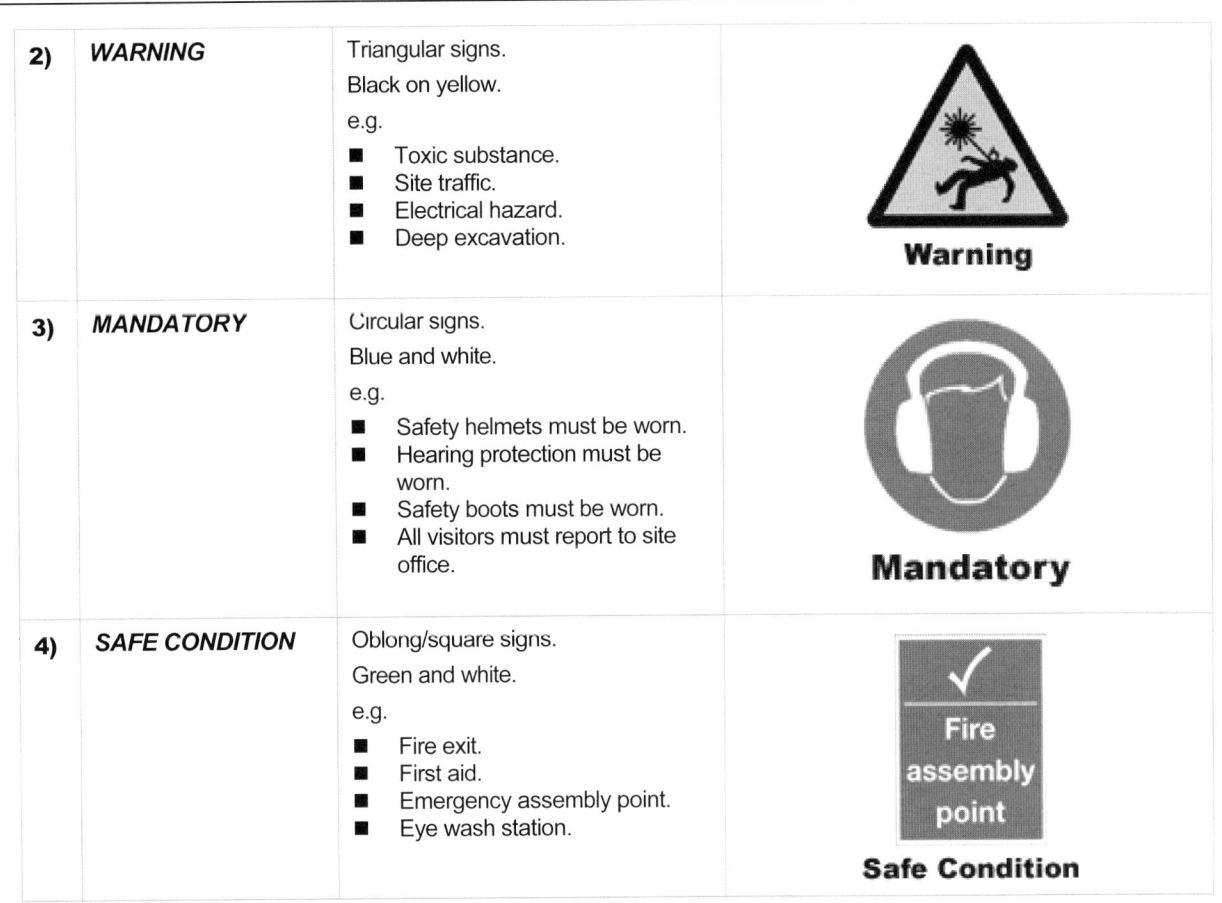

2)	WARNING	Triangular signs. Black on yellow. e.g. ■ Toxic substance. ■ Site traffic. ■ Electrical hazard. ■ Deep excavation.	**Warning**
3)	MANDATORY	Circular signs. Blue and white. e.g. ■ Safety helmets must be worn. ■ Hearing protection must be worn. ■ Safety boots must be worn. ■ All visitors must report to site office.	**Mandatory**
4)	SAFE CONDITION	Oblong/square signs. Green and white. e.g. ■ Fire exit. ■ First aid. ■ Emergency assembly point. ■ Eye wash station.	**Safe Condition**

Figure 1-6-2: Categories of safety signs. *Source: ACT.*

Supplementary signs provide additional information. For example where a noise hazard is identified by a warning sign - 'hearing protection available on request' may be added as supplementary information.

Figure 1-6-3: Prohibition signs. *Source: ACT.*

Figure 1-6-4: Warning and mandatory sign. *Source: ACT.*

Figure 1-6-5: Mandatory sign. *Source: ACT.*

Figure 1-6-6: Safe condition sign. *Source: ACT.*

Supplementary safety signs can be used to mark obstacles e.g. the edge of a raised platform and dangerous locations e.g. an area where objects may fall or an area where work is going on that the public should not access.

These may be yellow and black or red and white - in each case they consist of alternate colour stripes set at 45°. These supplementary signs must not be used as a substitute for other signs as defined above.

Figure 1-6-7: Hazard identification - obstruction.   Source: ACT.

Figure 1-6-8: Hazard identification-restricted width. Source: ACT.

General hierarchy of control

AVOIDING RISKS

Avoiding risk at source is the best option for controlling risk. It means that everyone is protected and there is no residual risk to manage. In many cases this may be a difficult option to achieve, however, it is something that must be considered by designers at the conception stage of a project. For example, in order to avoid the risk of falling it is critical, where possible, to design out the need to work at height.

ELIMINATION/SUBSTITUTION

Removal of the hazard in total from the working environment where possible, but this is not always practical. Reducing the hazard to an acceptable level by substituting something less hazardous/or reducing the strength of the hazardous material/or reducing the quantity in use/etc.

REDUCING/TIME LIMITING EXPOSURE

Reduction of exposure may be achieved by keeping the numbers at risk to a minimum by timing certain work so that other tasks are not taking place nearby. Rotating work to minimise the exposure to any one person, for example, by reducing the frequency and duration of exposure to radiation, noise or vibration.

ISOLATION/SEGREGATION

Enclose the hazard so there is a controlled barrier between people and the hazard, for example, fitting fixed guards around dangerous parts of a machine, provision of guard rails on scaffolds or barriers round street works.

ENGINEERING CONTROL

Control the numbers at risk by systems of working or by engineering methods, for example, provision of an overload or over run device on a crane or hoist, control dust / fumes released into the atmosphere by local exhaust ventilation, or to limit the noise level emitted by use of sound insulation.

SAFE SYSTEMS OF WORK

A safe system of work is a formal procedure which results from systematic examination of a task in order to identify all the hazards. It defines safe methods of working, to ensure that hazards are eliminated or risks minimised. In some cases the system of work is controlled by the use of structured checklists that ensure steps in the system of work are carried out. This is often called a permit to work.

TRAINING AND INFORMATION

Relevant information and training on risks and on protective and preventive measures should be limited to what workers need to know to ensure their own health and safety and not put others at risk.

PERSONAL PROTECTIVE EQUIPMENT

Requirements

Personal protective equipment (PPE) is a low level control. It is often in the form of a simple barrier between the user and the risk, for example, gloves and acid, and as such its effectiveness is subject to correct fit or adjustment. PPE is best used for low risk protection or as additional protection to safeguard against engineering control failure, for example, breathing apparatus to protect against fume extraction failure when dealing with volatile toxic substances. It is critical to determine the limitations of particular PPE before use. The main benefits include low cost and portability when considered against engineering strategies.

- Ensure PPE is suitable for hazard and person.
- No PPE should be issued without adequate training/instruction.
- Issue, obtain signature and record.
- Set-up monitoring systems.
- Provide suitable storage.
- Organise routine exchange systems.
- Implement cleaning/sterilisation.
- Issue written/verbal instructions, define when and where to use.

Training and instruction will include both:

- **Theoretical** - provision of a clear understanding of the reasons for wearing the PPE, factors which may affect the performance, the cleaning, maintenance and identification of defects.
- **Practical** - practising the wearing, adjusting, removing, cleaning, maintenance and testing of PPE.

Benefits and limitations

> "Whatever PPE is chosen, it should be remembered that, although some types of equipment do provide very high levels of protection, none provides 100%"

Figure 1-6-9: PPE quote. *Source: Guidance on the Personal Protection Equipment Regulations 1992.*

PPE includes the following when worn for health and safety reasons at work:

- Aprons.
- Adverse weather gear.
- High visibility clothing.
- Gloves.
- Safety footwear.
- Safety helmets.
- Eye protection.
- Life-jackets.
- Respirators.
- Safety harness.
- Underwater breathing gear.

There are numerous reasons why personal protective equipment (PPE) should be considered only after other possibilities have been exhausted:

- PPE may not provide adequate protection because of such factors as poor selection, poor fit, incompatibility with other types of PPE, contamination, and misuse or non-use by workers.
- PPE is likely to be uncomfortable and relies for its effectiveness on a conscious action by the user.
- In certain circumstances, its use can actually create additional risks (for instance, warning sounds masked by hearing protection).
- PPE only protects the wearer and not others who may be in the area and also at risk.
- The introduction of PPE may bring another hazard such as impaired vision, impaired movement or fatigue.
- PPE may only be capable of minimising injury rather than preventing it.
- If PPE fails to give 100% protection, it is impossible to measure actual exposure to hazards such as dust, vapours and noise.

Protection will depend upon fit in many cases, e.g. with respirators, breathing apparatus, noise protection devices. Factors that can influence fit are whether adequate training and instruction have been given and certain other individual conditions such as:

- Long hair.
- Wearing of spectacles.
- Male facial hair growth during a shift may necessitate the progressive adjustment of respiratory protection during the work period.

PPE will not be suitable unless:

- It is appropriate to the risk involved and the prevailing conditions of the workplace.
- It is ergonomic (user-friendly) in design and takes account of the state of health of the user.
- It fits the wearer correctly, perhaps after adjustment.
- It is effective in preventing or controlling the risk(s) [without increasing the overall risk], so far as is practicable.
- It must comply with EU directives or other specific local standards.
- It must be compatible with other equipment where there is more than one risk to guard against.

WELFARE

The provision of adequate welfare facilities is intended to reduce the likelihood of ill health and skin disease. Promoting good personal hygiene through the provision of suitable and sufficient toilets, washbasins and changing rooms.

MONITORING AND SUPERVISION

Monitoring of the success or limitations of a selected control in the hierarchy is critical and enables improved control to be put in place. For example, this can include monitoring of the controls for noise or vibration by conducting medical surveillance.

The supervisor has a crucial part to play in controlling hazard and risk. It is critical to balance the amount and timing of supervision against the work being done. Supervision helps to ensure that workers understand the risks associated with their work and that the necessary safety precautions are carried out.

6.2 - Safe systems of work

Responsibility of the employer to provide safe system of work

In the United Kingdom, in criminal law the **Health and Safety at Work etc. Act (HASAWA) 1974** clearly requires the provision and maintenance of plant and systems of work that are, so far as is reasonably practicable, safe and without risks to health. The employer should also provide **safe systems of work** in order to fulfil his common law duty of care established in principles of negligence.

Definition of safe system of work (SSW):

> **"the integration of P eople, E quipment and M aterials in the correct E nvironment to produce the safest possible conditions in a specific work area"**

This means that all work must be conducted in a safe way, but does not require that all work has to be prescribed in a written form. It is perfectly acceptable that a safe system of work be established and communicated orally at the time of the need to conduct the work e.g. work for using a ladder to inspect a pipe joint. In contrast it does not mean that all systems of work can be specified orally.

The higher the risks the more appropriate it is to specify safe systems of work in writing. This is reflected in the more formal approach to specifying a safe system of work for entry into a confined space, where the safe system of work is accompanied by a permit to work to provide higher assurance that it is followed correctly.

COMPONENTS OF THE SYSTEM (PEME)

People

Safe behaviour - sound knowledge, skills (both mental and physical), risk and control aware, willingness to conform with the system (motivation), resistance to pressures to behave unsafely, adequately trained, with job experience and supervised, working in harmony with each other.

Equipment

Good design and safety specification of plant, machinery and equipment - taking into account the work that it is to do, the environment and ergonomic factors, inspection and maintenance requirements.

Materials

Safe and healthy in both the raw state and as the finished product - appropriate purchasing and quality standards; consideration of use, handling, storage, transport and safe disposal of waste.

Environment

Establishing critical elements in the workplace that surround the workforce - effective control of heating, lighting and ventilation; safe levels of noise and vibration; effective control of dust, fumes, radiation, chemicals and biological hazards; effective means of access and egress and a good standards of welfare amenity provision (sanitation, hand washing, showers, clothing storage, catering, drinking water, and first aid).

The role of competent persons in the development of safe systems

It is critical that those involved in the development process gain a perspective on the acceptability of the standards of proposed systems of work. This will mean consideration of the proposed safe system of work by people competent to provide a perspective. In a general sense this could be a health and safety practitioner who would be able to provide a general review of the proposed system of work against legal, where appropriate, and practical requirements.

In addition, depending on the technical complexity and the risks associated with the task, it may be necessary to get a perspective from someone that is competent in the technical health and safety issues involved, for example, an electrical specialist. Care should be taken not to presume the health and safety competence of specialist engineers or similar, and this should be confirmed before involvement in the development process. The onus is on the employer to determine the competence of people who may be involved in, for example, development of safe systems of work, carrying out risk assessments, inspections, or issuing permits to work. Broadly, a competent person should have knowledge (practical and theoretical) and skill, as well as experience.

Importance of involvement in the development of safe systems

Worker involvement in the development of safe systems is essential to ensure their safe behaviour when working to the system. The worker knows all the practical difficulties in working to theoretical systems of work, such as the absence of equipment specified or requirements that mean more people to do the task than are available. They have frequently encountered circumstances that make the work difficult and how they get round them, such as poor access/egress. By discussing proposed systems of work with workers it is possible to learn these practicalities and ensure the system of work takes account of them. Involvement in this way often ensures that the agreed system of work is followed.

Importance and relevance of written procedures

Where the safe system of work is complex or the risks of not working to it are high it is critical to define what must be done in written procedures. This does not mean that written procedures have to be complicated or wordy; some of the most effective are those that are clear, simple and easily understood.

The importance of creating written procedures is that they serve as a clear setting of standards of work, including how the risks of the work are to be combated. This is particularly relevant when communicating to a client how a contractor is going to conduct work safely.

Written procedures may relate to specific work to be done, such as carrying out a cutting operation or to general health and safety matters such as reporting accidents. The construction industry makes particular use of written procedures in the form of method statements. As the name suggests they are documents that express how work is to be conducted, the order of events, the health and safety considerations and the measures that will make it safe and healthy for those that might be affected.

It is critical that procedures express how the work is done, not just how it should be done in theory. If there is a poor match between the procedure and what can be done in practice it will devalue that and other procedures and cause confusion. If a good match is achieved, in a manner that is clear to workers and supervisors, there is a higher chance that it will be complied with and the supervisor is more able to enforce it.

Job / task analysis is not only necessary to identify the hazards and controls, but is essential for preparing written procedures. These can then be translated into comprehensive training plans to ensure the correct skill and knowledge content for the work to be carried out safely.

The distinction between technical, procedural and behavioural controls

In the workplace we use a variety of controls. In order to give emphasis to them and to help identify how complete our approach is to health and safety we group controls into a number of categories. The categories tend to reflect the main strategies used to improve health and safety. The categories reflect the strategies referred to in 6.1 above but use slightly different words.

It is critical to note that in order to deal effectively with a hazard we will need to use all three forms of control, to a greater or lesser degree, for example, with the use of a hard hat for the control of a hazard of falling materials. A hard hat is a technical control that will afford a quantity of protection - the technical aspects of this come into play when we consider how long a hard hat lasts, what type is suitable for what work / person. Purchasing hard hats will not be effective if procedures are not in place to enable issue and replacement. These controls will be immediately undermined if we do not provide education and training to those that wear and enforce the wearing of hard hats in order to ensure the correct behaviour of the wearer.

Risk control measures:

technical	(place)	(job)
procedural	(system)	(organisation)
behavioural	(person)	(person)

TECHNICAL CONTROLS INCLUDE:
- Equipment - design (e.g. guarding) and maintenance.
- Access/egress - provision of wide aisles, access kept clear of storage items.
- Materials (substances and articles) - choice of packaging to make handling easier.
- Environment (temperature, light, dust, noise) - local exhaust ventilation (LEV).

PROCEDURAL CONTROLS INCLUDE:
- Policy and standards.
- Rules.
- Procedures.
- Permit to work.
- Authorisation and co-ordination of actions.
- Purchasing controls.
- Accident investigation and analysis.
- Emergency preparedness.

BEHAVIOURAL CONTROLS INCLUDE:
- Awareness, knowledge, skill, competence.
- Attitude, perception, motivation, communication.
- Supervision.
- Health surveillance.
- Personal protective equipment.

In practice, the most successful organisations use a combination of the three strategies, with the emphasis on making the place safe/healthy (providing technical controls) and supporting this with procedures and paying attention to the person. Many organisations that feel they have done all that is necessary to get the place and procedures correct are taking a fresh look at the actions necessary to ensure the person's behaviour is also correct. Studies have shown that this too is a critical aspect of effective management of health and safety.

Development of a safe system of work

ANALYSING THE TASK

Assessment of the task must consider not only the job to be done, but the environment where it is to be done, to allow a full consideration of the hazards to be made. This may involve a detailed review known as Job or Task Analysis. Job/task safety analysis consists of a formal step by step review of the work to be carried out. All aspects of the task should be considered and recorded in writing to ensure that nothing is overlooked. Typical considerations would be:

- The task to be done.
- Where the task is done.
- That which is used.
- The current controls.
- Adequacy of controls.
- Correct use by operators of the controls.
- Behavioural factors operators/supervisors (error considerations).

The objective is to establish the hazards and controls at each stage of the procedure to ensure a safe result. How the progress of work, in particular safety arrangements, will be monitored should be considered. Any special requirements for monitoring should be specified during the planning stage, e.g. gas testing, temperature or pressure levels, measurement of emissions.

HAZARD IDENTIFICATION AND RISK ASSESSMENT

The identification of hazards and the assessment of risks are key factors arising from the task analysis step of developing safe systems of work. From this we can build in appropriate controls to the system of work and plan to warn workers of the risks considered and how to prevent or minimise such risks identified to them. A suitable and sufficient risk assessment should be made of all risks to which workers and others who may be affected are exposed. Where a significant risk is identified through the general risk assessments a more formal detailed analysis is often required to develop a safe system of work e.g. work to inspect the lifting equipment of an office passenger lift. Considerations should be given to who does what, when and how.

Introducing controls and formulating procedures

Define the safe methods

1) Where possible, hazards should be eliminated at source. Residual hazards should be evaluated and controlled.
2) Specific responsibilities at various stages and the person in control of work should be clearly identified.
3) The need for protective or special equipment should also be identified, as should the need for the provision of temporary protection, guards or barriers.
4) Adequate emergency procedures should be in place, or developed, to control likely incidents e.g. fire, spillage.
5) If there is a possibility that injury could result during the task rescue methods should be identified.
6) The system should be checked against three main criteria:
   - It should adequately control hazards associated with the task.
   - It should comply with company standards.
   - It should comply with relevant legal standards.

Implementation

Once the system has been developed and agreed, preparation for implementation can proceed. Provision for the communication of relevant information to all involved or affected should be an essential requirement to any system of work. It is critical that care be taken to ensure that controls referred to when the system of work was being developed are available to the workers when the procedure is implemented. If they are not they will devalue the procedure and cause the workers to have to work outside of the arrangement, possibly in an unsafe way.

The process of implementation will involve:

- The person in charge of work must ensure that elements outlined in the Planning and Organisation stages are clearly understood and implemented.
- If problems arise which necessitate modification to the system, formal approval and documentation should be made.
- Any permanent record of any monitoring must be kept and regularly checked by a member of the management team.

Instruction and training in the operation of the system

Many organisations may be tempted to issue procedures without instruction and training; this can lead to a great deal of misunderstanding about what the system of work is and will often lead to people not being motivated to work to the system. This is particularly the case when the system is a change from the usual way that workers may have worked. Workers and supervisors can have a naturally high resistance to change.

Simply providing information will not usually be sufficient to change behaviour. A more assured way to introduce the system would be to utilise such things as 'tool box' talks, which provide practical opportunity to develop the workers' understanding of the operation of the system and if these are done as part of a cascade training method the supervisor or similar person will have received training from someone committed to the new system and will be better placed to get over the resistance of workers to change.

When the system of work relates to work equipment it is essential to ensure that training takes place. For example, supervisors should be adequately trained to enable them to identify the hazards and control strategies associated with work equipment under their control.

Job / task analysis is not only useful to identify the hazards and controls, but is essential for preparing written procedures and specifying the skill and knowledge content of the work to be carried out. The analysis will not only identify the sequence of work but often the work rate expected - sometimes timeliness is an important consideration, particularly in relation to certain chemical manufacturing processes. The analysis is then incorporated into job training programmes.

- For certain high risk tasks this will often involve a training course to develop knowledge and understanding. This is then followed by practical application either utilising a work simulator (e.g. train driver / aircraft pilot) or close one to one supervision while on the job (e.g. forklift truck driver).
- Where training requirements have been identified, a record of those affected should be made. The required training should be confirmed as successful and recorded.

Monitoring the system

All safe systems should be formally monitored and records kept of compliance and effectiveness. This can be done by direct observation or by discussion at team meetings or safety committee meetings.

Safe Systems of Work should not be simply imposed upon the people responsible for their operation. A system of monitoring and feedback should be implemented to ensure it is effective. Audits and accidents that occur can provide a valuable insight into whether systems of work are effective.

Confined spaces

A failure to appreciate the dangers associated with confined spaces has led not only to the deaths of many workers, but also to the demise of some of those who have attempted to rescue them. A confined space is not only a space which is small and difficult to enter, exit or work in; it can also be a large space, but with limited/restricted access. It can also be a space that is badly ventilated e.g. a tank or a large tunnel.

PRINCIPLES OF CONTROL - ELEMENT 6 - UNIT IGC1

Figure 1-6-10: Confined space - chamber.   *Source: ACT.*

Figure 1-6-11: Confined space - sewer.   *Source: ACT.*

Figure 1-6-12: Confined space - tank.   *Source: ACT.*

Figure 1-6-13: Confined space - open tank.   *Source: ACT.*

For example a confined space may be any of the following:

Chamber	caisson, cofferdam, or interception chamber for water
Tank	storage tanks for solid or liquid chemicals
Vat	process vessel which may be open, but by its depth confines a person
Silo	may be an above the ground structure for storing cereal, crops
Pit	Below ground, such as a chamber for a pump
Pipe	concrete, plastic steel etc, fabrication used to carry liquids or gases
Sewer	brick or concrete structure for the carrying of liquid waste
Flue	exhaust chimney for disposal of waste gases
Well	deep source of water

or other similar space, in which, by virtue of its enclosed nature, there is a foreseeable risk of a 'specified occurrence'.

A "specified occurrence"

Is defined as:

a) Fire or explosion.
b) Loss of consciousness or asphyxiation of any person at work arising from gas, fumes, vapour or lack of oxygen.
c) Drowning of any person at work.
d) Asphyxiation of any person at work arising from a free flowing solid.
e) Loss of consciousness of any person arising from a high ambient temperature.

Work in confined spaces

- No person should work in a confined space if it is practicable for that work to be carried out without entering the space.
- No person at work shall enter, leave or carry out work in a confined space other than in accordance with a safe system of work.
- Before working in a confined space consideration should be given to carrying out the work without entering the confined space. Before entry is carried out, the employer (or self-employed) should complete a risk assessment to identify the precautions necessary to ensure a safe system of work.

The risk assessment will in particular help to identify the need for a formal Permit to Work system which will typically involve procedures for:

- Testing the atmosphere.
- Respiratory protective equipment and other personal protective equipment for those risks which cannot be controlled by other means.
- Equipment for safe access and exit.
- Suitable and sufficient emergency rescue arrangements.

UNIT IGC1 - ELEMENT 6 - PRINCIPLES OF CONTROL

Testing the atmosphere
- Testing of the atmosphere may be needed where the atmosphere might be contaminated or abnormal.
- The appropriate choice of testing equipment will depend on particular circumstances. For example, when testing for toxic atmospheres, chemical detector tubes or portable atmospheric monitoring equipment is appropriate. However there may be cases requiring monitoring equipment specifically designed to measure for flammable atmospheres.
- Only persons experienced and competent in the practice should carry out testing and records should be kept. Personal gas detectors should be worn whenever appropriate to mitigate the hazard of local pockets of contaminant.

Safe access to and egress from confined spaces
- Openings need to be sufficiently large and free from obstruction to allow the passage of persons wearing the necessary protective clothing and equipment and to allow access for rescue purposes.
- Practice drills will help to check that the size of openings and entry procedures are satisfactory.
- Where entry to a confined space is necessary, employers will need to ensure that the necessary safety features are followed. For example, alongside openings which allow for safe access these might include a safety sign warning against unauthorised entry and platforms to enable safe working within the confined space.

Respiratory Protective Equipment (RPE)
Where RPE is provided or used in connection with confined space entry (including emergency rescue), it must be suitable. Other equipment - ropes, harnesses, lifelines, resuscitating apparatus, first aid equipment, protective clothing and other special equipment will usually need to be provided.

Figure 1-6-14: Entrance to a confined space. *Source: ACT.*

Here a worker wearing full breathing apparatus is also wearing a harness with a lanyard connected to a winch so that he can be hauled to the surface in an emergency without others having to enter the manhole to rescue him.

Figure 1-6-15: Access to a confined space. *Source: HSG150, HSE.*

Emergency arrangements
No person should enter or carry out work in a confined space unless there are suitable and sufficient rescue arrangements in place. Emergency arrangements shall be suitable and sufficient provided they:
- Require the provision and maintenance of resuscitation equipment.
- Require the provision and maintenance of such equipment as is necessary to enable the emergency rescue to be carried out effectively.
- Restrict, so far as is reasonably practicable, the risks to health and safety of any rescuer.
- Shall immediately be put into operation when circumstances arise requiring a rescue.

The arrangements for emergency rescue will depend on the nature of the confined space, the risks identified and consequently the likely nature of an emergency rescue. The arrangements might need to cover:

1) Rescue and resuscitation equipment.
2) Special arrangements with local hospitals (e.g. for foreseeable poisoning).
3) Raising the alarm and rescue.
4) Safeguarding the rescuers.
5) Safeguarding the third parties.
6) Fire fighting.
7) Control of plant.
8) First aid.
9) Public emergency services.

Summary of main points for confined spaces

Identify the hazards e.g.
- Flammable substances.
- Oxygen deficiency or enrichment.
- Toxic gas, fume or vapour.
- Ingress or presence of liquids.
- Solid materials which can flow e.g. flour, grain, sugar.
- Excessive heat.

Prevent the need for entry by:
- Use of portholes for inspection.
- Clean from outside using water jets, long handled tools.
- Use vibrators to clear blockages.

Develop safe working practice
- Based on a permit to work.

Develop emergency procedures to include
- Means of raising the alarm.
- Safeguarding the rescuers.
- Fire safety.
- Notifying public emergency services.

Provide training to include
- Need to avoid entry.
- Hazards and precautions.
- How emergencies arise.
- Emergency arrangements.

Lone working

Lone workers are those who work by themselves without close or direct supervision. They are found in a wide range of situations and some examples are given below.

People in fixed establishments where:
- Only one person works on the premises e.g. petrol stations, kiosks, shops and also home workers.
- People work separately from others e.g. in factories, warehouses, leisure centres or fairgrounds.
- People work outside normal hours e.g. cleaners, security, facilities management staff or contractors conducting special tasks better done at this time.

Mobile workers working away from their fixed base:
- On construction, plant installation, maintenance and cleaning work, electrical repairs, painting and decorating.
- Agricultural and forestry workers.
- Service workers e.g. rent collectors, postal staff, home helps, drivers, district nurses.

Control measures may include instruction, training, supervision, protective equipment etc. When the risk assessment shows that it is not possible for the work to be done safely by a lone worker, arrangements for providing help or back-up should be put in place. Where a lone worker is working at another employer's workplace, that employer should inform the lone worker's employer of any risks and the control measures that should be taken. This helps the lone worker's employer to assess the risks.

Risk assessment should help decide the correct level of supervision. There are some high-risk activities where at least one other person may need to be present. Examples include some high-risk confined space working where a supervisor may need to be present, as well as someone dedicated to the rescue role, and electrical work at or near exposed live conductors where at least two people are sometimes required.

Employers need to be aware of any specific law on lone working applying in their industry; examples include supervision in diving operations, vehicles carrying explosives, fumigation work.

Establishing safe working for lone workers is no different from organising the safety of other workers. Employers need to know the law if appropriate and standards which apply to their work activities and then assess whether the requirements can be met by people working alone.

Consider
- Any special risks associated with the workplace.
- Safe access and egress for one person.
- Ease of handling of temporary access equipment such as portable ladders or trestles.
- All plant, substances and goods involved in the work can be safely handled within the capability of one person.
- Requirements for one person to operate essential controls for the safe running of equipment.
- A risk of violence.
- Female special risks.
- Young workers special risks.

Importance of training
- Where there is limited supervision.
- Experienced enough to understand the risks and precautions of lone working fully and to avoid panic reactions in unusual situations.
- Competent to deal with circumstances which are new, unusual or beyond the scope of training e.g. when to stop work and seek advice from a supervisor. How to handle aggression.
- Able to respond correctly to emergencies, also given information on established emergency procedures and danger areas.
- Able to administer first aid.

Supervision
- To ensure that workers understand the risks associated with their work and that the necessary safety precautions are carried out.
- To provide guidance in situations of uncertainty.
- Supervision can be carried out when checking the progress and quality of the work. May take the form of periodic site visits combined with discussions in which health and safety issues are raised.
- Should be increased when an employee is new to a job, undergoing training, doing a job which presents special risks, or dealing with new situations and may need to be accompanied at first.
- Level of supervision required should be based on the findings of a risk assessment.

Procedures for monitoring purposes
- Supervisors' periodically visiting and observing people working alone.
- Regular contact using either a telephone or radio.
- Use of automatic warning devices which operate if specific signals are not received periodically from the lone worker e.g. systems for security staff.
- Other devices designed to raise the alarm in the event of an emergency and which are operated manually or automatically by the absence of activity.
- Check returned to their base or home on completion of a task.

UNIT IGC1 - ELEMENT 6 - PRINCIPLES OF CONTROL

Medical considerations
- Check that lone workers have no medical conditions making them unsuitable for working alone.
- Consider both routine work and foreseeable emergencies which may impose additional physical and mental burdens on the individual.
- Ensure they have access to first-aid facilities and mobile workers should carry a first-aid kit suitable for treating minor injuries.

WORKING AND TRAVELLING ABROAD IN RELATION TO SYSTEMS OF WORK

When sending workers abroad, a safe system of work should be adopted, these should include:

- Visas/Work Permits - requirements should be checked with the country's regulations.
- Health requirements - insurance and inoculations i.e. hepatitis - these can be verified with country's embassy or website.
- Travel - arrangements should be made to minimise the effects of long haul flights i.e. deep vain thrombosis (DVT).
- Personal Safety - security / terrorism issues should be checked prior to departure with your country's Government, either by telephone or by using an official website.
- Equipment / Plant - some countries restrict the import of certain pieces of equipment - checks should be made prior to departure.

6.3 - Permit to work systems

OPERATION AND APPLICATION

Main elements
- A description of the task to be performed.
- An indication of the duration of the validity of the permit.
- The isolations that have been made and the additional precautions required.
- Details and signature of the person authorising the work.
- An acknowledgement of acceptance by the worker carrying out the task, who would then need to indicate on the permit that the work has been completed and the area made safe in order for the permit to be cancelled.

Permit to work document
- Sets out the work to be done and the precautions to be taken.
- Predetermines a safe drill.
- Is a clear record that:
  - All foreseeable hazards have been considered.
  - All precautions are defined and taken in the correct sequence.

Requirements of the system
- Must be formal.
- Simple to operate.
- Have commitment of those who operate and are affected by it.

Operation
- Permit must provide concise and accurate information.
- Overrides any other instructions until cancelled.
- Excludes work not described within the permit.
- In the event of a change to programme must be amended or cancelled and a new permit issued.
- Only the originator may amend or cancel.
- Acceptor assumes responsibility for safe conduct of work.
- Liaison with controllers of other plant or work areas whose activities may be affected by the permit to work.
- Boundary or limits of work area must be clearly marked or defined.
- Contractors undertaking specific tasks must be included in the permit to work system, including any briefing prior to commencement.

TYPICAL PERMITS AND CIRCUMSTANCES IN WHICH THEY MAY BE APPROPRIATE

A permit to work system is a formal safety control system designed to prevent accidental injury to personnel, damage to plant, premises and product, particularly when work with a foreseeable high hazard content is undertaken and the precautions required are numerous and complex.

Hot work

Typically involving welding operations, such as pipe work where the risk of sparks may ignite nearby flammable materials. Elimination or protection of such items will need to be considered. The provision of fire fighting equipment and trained personnel to deal with ignition is also critical.

Work on electrical systems

Work on electrical equipment, such as a transformer, will require safe isolation, access and egress, work at a height and heavy lifting to be considered.

Machinery maintenance

Machinery / plant maintenance sometimes requires workers with different disciplines to work on large complex plant at the same time. This is aggravated by the fact that the plant may be spread over a number of floors in a building, such as power generation plant, flour mills or lift systems in an office block.

PRINCIPLES OF CONTROL - **ELEMENT 6 - UNIT IGC1**

This sort of work involves many risks - related to a variety of services and energy sources, dangerous parts of the equipment, problems with access, risk of falling or being trapped inside the plant. These risks are best controlled by a well established system of work, supported by a permit to work.

HOT WORK PERMIT
APPLIES ONLY TO AREA SPECIFIED BELOW

Part 1

Site:………………………………………………..…… Floor:…………………………………………………..

Nature of the job (including exact location) ……………………………………………………………………

……….

The above location has been examined and the precautions listed on the reverse side have been taken.

Date:……………………………………………………….

Time of issue:…………………………………………….. Time of expiry:………………………………………..

NB. This permit is only valid on the day of issue.

Signature of person issuing permit: ……………………………………………………………………………….

Part 2

Signature of person receiving permit:……………………………………………………………………………..

Time work started:………………………………………………………………….

Time work finished and cleared up:………………………………………………………………………………..

Part 3   **FINAL CHECK UP**

Work areas and all adjacent areas to which sparks and heat might spread (such as floors above and below and opposite side of walls) were inspected one hour after the work finished and were found fire safe.

Signature of person carrying out final check: …………………………………………………………………...

After signing return permit to person who issued it.

Figure 1-6-16: Hot work permit - front of form.   *Source: Lincsafe.*

HOT WORK PERMIT
PRECAUTIONS

Hot Work Area

☐   Loose combustible material cleared

☐   Non moveable combustible material covered

☐   Suitable extinguishers to hand

☐   Gas cylinders fitted with a regulator and flashback arrester

☐   Other personnel who may be affected by the work removed from the area

Work on walls, ceilings or partitions

☐   Opposite side checked and combustibles moved away

Welding, cutting or grinding work

☐   Work area screened to contain sparks

Bitumen boilers, lead heaters etc.

☐   Gas cylinders at least 3m from burner

☐   If sited on roof, heat insulating base provided

Figure 1-6-17: Hot work permit - reverse of form.   *Source: Lincsafe.*

EXAMPLE

ENTRY INTO CONFINED SPACES

Possible Lay-Out For A Permit-To-Work Certificate

Permit-To-Work Certificate

PLANT DETAILS (Location, identifying number, etc)		ACCEPTANCE OF CERTIFICATE Accepts all conditions of certificate	
WORK TO BE DONE			Signed Date Time
WITHDRAWAL FROM SERVICE	Signed Date Time	COMPLETION OF WORK All work completed - equipment returned for use	Signed Date Time
ISOLATION Dangerous fumes Electrical supply Sources of heat	Signed Date Time		
CLEANING AND PURGING Of all dangerous materials	Signed Date Time	EXTENSION	Signed Date Time
TESTING For contamination	Contaminations tested Results Signed Date Time		
I CERTIFY THAT I HAVE PERSONALLY EXAMINED THE PLANT DETAILED ABOVE AND SATISFIED MYSELF THAT THE ABOVE PARTICULARS ARE CORRECT (1) THE PLANT IS SAFE FOR ENTRY WITHOUT BREATHING APPARATUS (2) BREATHING APPARATUS MUST BE WORN Other precautions necessary: Time of expiry of certificate: Signed Delete (1) or (2) Date Time		THIS PERMIT TO WORK IS NOW CANCELLED. A NEW PERMIT WILL BE REQUIRED IF WORK IS TO CONTINUE Signed Date Time	
		RETURN TO SERVICE	I accept the above plant back into service Signed Date Time

Figure 1-6-18: Example of a permit to work for entry into confined spaces.

Source: HSE Guidance note on permits to work.

6.4 - Emergency procedures

THE IMPORTANCE OF DEVELOPING EMERGENCY PROCEDURES

Adequate emergency procedures should be in place, or developed, to control likely incidents e.g. fire, spillage, exposure to poisoning and pathogens etc. Fire is a specific risk which will need regular review throughout a major build or modification project. The exit routes may need to be redefined and signed and those affected trained and drilled. Similarly, assembly points may change. Local arrangements should consider the provision of fire suppression equipment, such as extinguishers, whenever contractors use equipment which may present a source of ignition.

Procedures should be in writing and regularly tested through drills and exercises. The results of such exercises should be recorded and the procedures amended as necessary. For identified high-risk activities, arrangements should be formalised with local Accident and Emergency services (A&E), for example, where there may be a need to have available special anti toxins or isolation facilities.

ARRANGEMENTS FOR CONTACTING EMERGENCY AND RESCUE SERVICES

The employer should consider the risks arising from their undertaking and the related emergencies that could result. It may be necessary before work is started to contact the external emergency and rescue services if complex hazardous work is to be carried out. This can include alerting them to the timing of special, high hazard tasks such as work in a confined space or where there is a significant risk that people may need to be rescued. In some cases it will mean contacting services and agreeing the boundary of what support can be expected from external services and what must be arranged by the employer.

The employer must identify and assess the nature of any injury likely to occur and consider the distance to emergency hospital facilities. It may be necessary to provide a first aid room and to train staff in specific emergency techniques, for example, resuscitation or to engage more capable staff with medical qualifications.

Part of the arrangements must ensure the means to contact the appropriate services at the time of the emergency - by telephone, radio or suitable other means.

6.5 - First aid

FIRST-AID REQUIREMENTS

To ensure adequate first aid provision, an employer must make an assessment to determine the needs. Consideration should be given to the following:

- Different work activities - some, such as offices, have relatively few hazards and low levels of risk; others have more or more specific hazards (construction or chemical sites). Requirements will depend on the type of work being done.
- Difficult access to treatment - an equipped first-aid room may be required if ambulance access is difficult or likely to be delayed.
- Workers working away from employer's premises - the nature of the work and its risk will need to be considered.
- Workers of more than one employer working together - agreement can be made to share adequate facilities, with one employer responsible for their provision.
- Provisions for non-employees - employers do not usually make first-aid provisions for any person other than their own workers.
- Having made this assessment, the employer will then be able to work out the number and size of first-aid boxes required.
- Additional facilities such as a stretcher or first-aid room may also be appropriate.

Role of first aiders

The role of first aiders is to:

- Give immediate assistance to casualties with workplace injuries or illness.
- To summon an ambulance or other professional help.

Appointed person

In appropriate, often low risk circumstances, an employer may choose to provide an "appointed person" instead of a first-aider. The "appointed person" is someone appointed by the employer to take charge of the situation (for example, to call an ambulance) if a serious injury occurs in the absence of a first-aider. It is recommended that the "appointed person" be able to administer emergency first-aid and be responsible for the equipment provided. An appointed person is unlikely to be adequate for most construction activities, where the risk of injury may be major.

The following training requirements should be considered:

- What to do in an emergency.
- Cardio-pulmonary resuscitation.
- First aid for the unconscious casualty.
- First aid for the wounded or bleeding.

COVERAGE IN RELATION TO SHIFT WORK AND GEOGRAPHICAL LOCATION

Additional staff will be necessary to cover for out of hours, shift working or overtime. In particular where there is a specific legal duty to provide such coverage - e.g. first aid provisions in the UK. The person with overall control of the site must ensure that coverage remains in place throughout the period work is going on.

Particular care must be paid to high risk work being conducted outside normal working hours. It may be possible to maintain good emergency cover for these times by ensuring, where there is permanent security staff, that these are appropriately trained.

If the area of work is geographically large, for example, gas, electrical or telecommunication field work all staff may need to be trained and equipped with first aid equipment in order that they may administer self first aid. This may be by means of a full first aid kit in a vehicle or a personal provision in a pouch. Particular attention should be given to the likelihood and type of injuries when equipping people in this way.

Shared facilities and arrangements

Where a site has multiple occupancy or a group of contracting employers exist within a site, arrangements need to be in place to identify and inform people of where first aid equipment is and who might be responsible for performing first aid duties. It is possible for an agreement to be made such that each occupier or employer does not have to make separate arrangements. This can be particularly useful in providing cover for each other's first aiders and will avoid the need for small contractors to provide their own first aid if they can obtain it from a main contractor's facilities.

Where small works are going on in a host's premises the contractor may find an acceptable agreement may be made with the host to provide first aid and other facilities. It is critical that such agreements be made formally, preferably with a written agreement that will substantiate the existence of such an arrangement if it is challenged or people change their mind as the work unfolds.

This page is intentionally blank

Element 7

Monitoring, review and audit

Learning outcomes

On completion of this element, candidates should be able to demonstrate understanding of the content through the application of knowledge to familiar and unfamiliar situations. In particular they should be able to:

7.1 Outline and differentiate between active (pro-active) monitoring procedures, including inspections, sampling, tours and reactive monitoring procedures, explaining their role within a monitoring regime.

7.2 Outline the role of work place inspections, and communicate findings in the form of an effective and persuasive report.

7.3 Explain the purpose of regular reviews of health and safety performance, the means by which reviews might be undertaken and the criteria that will influence the frequency of such reviews.

7.4 Explain the meaning of the term 'health and safety audit' and describe the preparations that may be needed prior to an audit and the information that may be needed during an audit.

Content

7.1 - Active and reactive monitoring..81
    Active monitoring measures..81
    Use of safety inspections, sampling and tours..82
    Reactive monitoring measures 82
7.2 - Workplace inspections..83
    Role of workplace inspections..83
7.3 - Review of health and safety performance 85
    Gathering information to review health and safety performance 85
    Reporting on health and safety performance...86
    Role of senior management team 86
    Feeding into action and development plans as part of continuous improvement 87
7.4 - Auditing 87
    Scope and purpose of auditing health and safety management systems...87
    Pre-audit preparations 87
    Responsibility for audits..87
    Advantages and disadvantages of external and internal audits...88

Sources of reference

Guidelines on Occupational Safety and Health Management Systems (ILO-OSH 2001) ISBN 0-580-37805-5

Occupational Health and Safety Assessment Series (OHSAS 18000): Occupational Health and Safety Management Systems OHSAS 18001:1999 (ISBN 0-580-28298-8), OHSAS 18002:2000 (ISBN: 0-580-33123-7), BSI

7.1 - Active and reactive monitoring

Active monitoring measures

OBJECTIVES OF ACTIVE MONITORING

The primary objectives of active (sometimes referred to as "proactive") monitoring are to:

- Check that health and safety plans have been implemented.
- Monitor the extent of compliance with the organisation's systems/procedures, and with its legislative/technical standards.

The assessment of the appropriateness, implementation and effectiveness of health and safety standards (in the form of objectives and arrangements, including Risk Control Systems (RCSs)) includes the operation of the current management systems.

Organisations need to know:

- Where they are.
- Where they want to be.
- What is the difference - and why.

Active monitoring will tell the organisation about the reliability and effectiveness of its systems. This provides a good basis from which decisions and recommendations for maintenance and improvement may be made.

Active monitoring also provides an opportunity for management to confirm commitment to health and safety objectives. In addition it also reinforces a positive health and safety culture by recognising success and positive actions, instead of 'punishing' failure after an undesired event.

Organisations must see active monitoring as an integral (and normal) part of the management (work) function. As such it must take place at all levels and opportunities in the organisation. Managers should be given responsibility for the monitoring of objectives and compliance with standards for which they and their subordinates are responsible. The actual method of monitoring will depend on the situation and the position held by the person monitoring.

METHODS OF ACTIVE MONITORING

The various methods and levels of active monitoring include the following:

- Routine procedures to monitor specific objectives, e.g. quarterly or monthly reports or returns.
- Periodic examination of documents to check that systems relating to the promotion of the health and safety culture are complied with, e.g. the way objectives for managers are established or appraised, assessment of records of training needs and delivery of training.
- Systematic inspection of premises, plant, and equipment by supervisors, maintenance staff, management, safety representatives and other workers to ensure continued effective operation of workplace precautions.
- Environmental monitoring and health surveillance to check on the effectiveness of health control measures and to detect early signs of harm to health.
- Systematic direct observation of work and behaviour by first-line supervisors to assess compliance with risk control systems (RCSs) and associated procedures and rules, particularly those concerned with risk control.
- The operation of audit systems.
- Consideration of regular reports on health and safety performance by the board of directors.

Active monitoring effort should be applied on a risk basis. Monitoring of workplace precautions would typically be more detailed and frequent than management system activities that carry a low risk if misapplied.

(Source: HSG 65)

MONITORING PERFORMANCE STANDARDS

Health and safety performance in organisations that manage health and safety effectively is measured against established standards. This enables confirmation of compliance with standards and where improvement is required. By establishing standards of expectation it enables deficiencies to be quickly translated into improvement actions.

The success of action to manage risks is assessed through active monitoring involving a range of techniques. This includes techniques which examine technical measures (equipment, premises and substances), procedural measures (systems of work, method statements, safety cases, and permits to work), and behavioural measures (motivation, attitudes, and competencies).

Deficiencies in control measures are assessed through reactive monitoring which requires the thorough investigation of accidents, ill health or events with the potential to cause harm or loss.

In both active and reactive monitoring, the objectives are not only to determine the immediate causes of sub-standard (at risk) performance but, more importantly, to identify the underlying causes and the implications for the structure and operation of the health and safety management system.

SYSTEMATIC INSPECTION OF PLANT AND PREMISES

The systematic inspection of plant and premises can identify health and safety conditions, providing an indication of the effectiveness of controls used to prevent sub-standard conditions, for example, planned maintenance or cleaning operations. If inspections are done on a timely basis it is possible to limit the harmful effects that can arise from sub-standard conditions. Periodic inspection provides a monitoring method that gives early indication of standards (declining or improving) by comparison with the previous results of inspections over time.

Use of safety inspections, sampling and tours

SAFETY INSPECTIONS

Inspections involve examination of the workplace or equipment in order to identify hazards and determine if they are effectively controlled. Four different types of inspections are:

- General workplace inspections - carried out by local first-line managers and worker's representatives.
- Statutory inspections (thorough examination) of equipment, e.g. boilers, lifting equipment, pressured tanks/containers - carried out by specialist Competent Persons.
- Preventive maintenance inspections of specific (critical) items - carried out by maintenance staff.
- Pre-use 'checks' of equipment, e.g. vehicles, fork lift trucks, access equipment - carried out by the user.

SAFETY SAMPLING

Sampling is where only a partial amount of a potential group/area is examined to establish facts that can indicate the standard of compliance of the whole.

A very small sample, such as the examination of three pieces of lifting tackle, may only give a rough, but acceptable, indication of the situation relating to lifting tackle as a whole.

When a representative sample is taken this may be considered to reasonably represent the situation for the whole group.

Sampling is conducted relating to the following:

- Specific hazards - such as noise or dust - typically conducted by workers trained in appropriate hygiene techniques.
- Good practice - such as the wearing of personal protective equipment - typically conducted by first-line managers.
- General workplace hazards - such as those identified during a defined walk through a work area - typically conducted by first-line managers, employee representatives and workers.

TOURS

Tours provide opportunity for management to explore the effectiveness of risk control measures through planned visits to the workplace to observe and discuss the controls in use.

It is critical, when developing a positive health and safety culture, that management commitment is visible. The conducting of planned tours to workplaces to meet work groups is one effective way of achieving this. As such it is a monitoring method that senior and middle managers would find useful. It has the advantage of enabling direct contact and communication between workers and senior management. This gives an accurate picture of work conditions and the understanding of workers. It can indicate deficiencies or success in managers carrying the organisation's objectives through to action. It also provides a forum for gaining the viewpoint of workers directly, without the translation that takes place through formal management channels.

In order to be planned there must be an intended outcome e.g. to communicate or review a topic, even if this includes some free time for other comment. Details of the tour and outcomes, including improvement actions, must be recorded to be effective.

Reactive monitoring measures

OBJECTIVES OF REACTIVE MONITORING

The primary objectives of reactive monitoring are to analyse data relating to:

- Accidents/Near-misses.
- Ill-health.
- Other downgrading events.

In order to carry out reactive monitoring effectively systems must be in place to identify the event, record it and report it. Without this nothing may be learnt. Indeed, what little data that is communicated might serve to reinforce that there is no need to put in a great deal of health and safety effort. If reporting etc. is planned and encouraged it is not uncommon to find a large increase in recorded events. This does not necessarily mean an increase in events, merely an increase in reporting.

Events contribute to the 'corporate memory', helping to prevent a repeat in another part of the organisation or at a later time. Though it should be remembered that the 'corporate memory' is said to be short, in the average organisation (one undergoing some change) it is said to be 4 years.

Data may be gained from other organisations to reinforce or extend experience of events and the hazards involved.

REACTIVE MONITORING MEASURES

These methods are deemed to be after the event and are therefore reactive monitoring measures:

- Identification.
- Reporting.
- Investigation.
- Collation of data and statistics, on the events.

The events monitored include those resulting in:

- Injuries.
- Cases of illness (including sickness absence).
- Property damage.
- Near misses.
- Dangerous occurrences.
- Complaints by the workforce.
- Enforcement actions.

Figure 1-7-1: Accident statistics.   Source: ACT.

It is critical to identify, in each case, why performance was sub-standard. Trends and common features may be identified, such as when, where and how these events occur. This provides an opportunity to learn and put into place improvements to the overall management system and to specific risk controls.

ACCIDENT STATISTICS

Many organisations spend considerable time developing data on their health and safety performance based on the accidents, dangerous occurrences, near misses, ill-health, complaints by workforce and enforcement actions they have. Whilst there is value in doing so it has the limitation of being after the event (reactive). Accidents must occur to get the data, thus tending to reflect what is done to prevent a recurrence rather than what was being done prior to the event. A more complete approach to monitoring will tend to include 'before the event' actions (proactive) such as audits and inspections to indicate what is currently being done to prevent accidents.

A low injury accident rate is not a guarantee that risks are being effectively controlled. In some cases this might be a matter of good fortune, or the fact that incidents e.g. near-misses are not being reported rather than effective management.

If organisations wait until an event occurs to determine where health and safety effort is required then some sort of loss must have occurred. In order to gain sufficient management attention this could be an event resulting in personal injury to someone. Clearly this is an undesirable way of learning, particularly as, with an amount of effort, planning and thought, the event could have been foreseen and prevented. The more mature organisation seeks to learn most from activities (e.g. risk assessment) before the event or, at the very least, learn from those events that result in no personal injury, e.g. near misses.

The obvious use of accident data is to identify specific problem areas by recording instances where control measures have failed. However, analysis of the data allows general trends to be shown in order perhaps to identify common root causes, as well as comparisons to be made with others in order to learn from successes elsewhere. Accident data can also help to raise awareness in the minds of both managers and workers of health and safety in general, and of specific problems in particular. In addition, collection of data allows costs to be calculated, which can increase the likelihood of resources being allocated.

Examples of statistical analysis in common usage by workplace organisations are:

$$\text{Frequency rate} = \frac{\text{Number of accidents in the period}}{\text{Total hours worked during the period}} \times 100\,000$$

$$\text{Incidence rate} = \frac{\text{Number of accidents in the period}}{\text{Average number employed during the period}} \times 1\,000$$

For statistics derived to be of value their limitations have to be understood. Variables in work methods, hours of work, hazard controls and management system effort make it difficult to make comparisons outside the organisation deriving the data. Indices such as these are best suited to comparison of performance of the same organisation over similar periods of time, for example, yearly. In this way trends may be observed and conclusions drawn. If comparisons are to be made outside the organisation, it should be remembered that other organisations might have a different understanding of the following:

- Definition of an accident (lost time or reportable).
- Hours worked may not be actual (contracted minimum hours - easier to work out).
- Who is included (are contractors included or excluded?).
- What multiplier is used (International Labour Office and the Health and Safety Executive (UK) use 1,000,000 for the frequency rate, USA use 200,000).

DANGEROUS OCCURRENCES

'an accident not resulting in personal injury Reportable to an enforcing authority'

In some territories significant adverse events must be reported to local enforcement agencies. Where such an obligation is not required it may still be beneficial for organisations to investigate property loss or damage to prevent a reoccurrence. Typical dangerous occurrences might include:

- A collapse in a scaffold over 5 metres.
- The failure of any load bearing part of any lift, hoist, crane or derrick.

ILL-HEALTH

'harm to a worker's health caused by their work'

This term refers to harm to a worker's health caused by their work and will include harm to health in a physical or mental capacity. This will include types of harm, as in a notified disease e.g., dermatitis.

COMPLAINTS BY WORKFORCE

These complaints made by workers or others may be done informally (verbally) or in writing to supervisors or management. There may be supporting evidence available to support these claims through accident data, recorded near-misses or slip/trips/falls. These complaints should be considered carefully as they may be an indicator of ineffective/dangerous working practices/procedures, and risk assessments should be formally reviewed.

ENFORCEMENT ACTION

'the legal enforcement of improvement or prohibition notices of dangerous machinery OR equipment'

These legal enforcement notices imposed by local health and safety inspectors normally occur following the reporting of a major accident or reportable incident.

7.2 - Workplace inspections

Role of workplace inspections

The role of health and safety inspections is to identify the health and safety status of what is being inspected and what improvements are needed. They are particularly well suited to identifying workplace hazards and determining if they are under satisfactory control or not. Conducting workplace inspections may also affect the organisational health and safety culture, particularly where workers' views are sought as part of the inspection. In this way, the employer's commitment to health and safety can be demonstrated, ownership of health and safety can be shared and workers' morale can be increased by simple improvements being implemented at the time of the inspection.

A critical aid used by anyone carrying out an inspection is a checklist, i.e. a list of "the way things ought to be". When a work area or item of equipment fails this test it is considered substandard and represents a hazard. Each substandard condition should be assessed and corrective action carried out and details recorded. Issues to be considered when creating a checklist should include: substances or materials being used, condition of traffic routes and means of access and egress, work equipment, work practices i.e. manual handling, work environment, electricity, fire precautions, welfare provision including first aid arrangements and workstation ergonomics.

Inspections will not improve health and safety performance unless corrective measures are set out (where a deficiency is identified) and fully implemented. This will not happen on its own or by default, indeed, the opposite is likely to occur. Standards will continue to deteriorate where workers/managers find their inspection efforts, which identify improvement needs, are not followed through and actions are not implemented. They may quickly regard their efforts as "a waste of time". It is, however, equally critical to avoid putting in a substandard or inadequate solution as this is bound to result in a waste of company resources (time, equipment, money, for example.). To get the correct solution implemented will usually take a quantity of management time and effort. If the risk is significant clearly this is warranted. Whenever a sub-standard (at risk) situation is identified two critical steps must be taken:

- Each situation must be evaluated as to its risk potential.
- The underlying cause(s) of the situation must be identified.

The first step ensures that resources are prioritised and allocated on a worst first basis, and the second step ensures that the appropriate corrective action will reduce the risk and prevent its return to the same level.

A simple approach to risk evaluation levels (rating) and allocation of time for actions may follow the method below:
- High risk (likely to cause a major loss) - complete within 24 hours.
- Moderate risk (likely to cause a serious loss) - complete within 7 days (1 month if preferred).
- Low risk (will possibly cause a minor loss) - complete within 30 days (3 months if preferred).

A common approach is to refer to the three categories above as Class A, Class B and Class C risks respectively, with Class A being the highest.

Once situations that require most urgent attention are identified and corrective actions have been determined, the maximum time period by which the action is to be completed (tied to the risk rating) can be agreed. A structured approach is necessary to ensure that the actions needed are initiated and followed up (monitored) in such a way that they are not simply forgotten.

FACTORS GOVERNING FREQUENCY AND TYPE OF INSPECTION

The frequency of inspections should be established using data gathered from several sources i.e. risk assessments, accidents/near-misses, plant breakdowns or failure. Once this information has been obtained, then a frequency for inspection can be established. However, the frequency might be increased or even decreased if any of the following occur:

- Changes in legislation.
- Modifications are made to existing plant/machinery.
- Re-location of equipment or changes in environment.
- Equipment fails the test.
- Accident data / near-misses recorded by workers.

Inspections fall into two main categories:

- Mandatory, as stated within legislation or local rules, for example, for safe maintenance of lifting equipment.
- Routine, conducted by a competent person.

COMPETENCE OF INSPECTOR

Inspectors must have relevant qualifications and experience, knowledge of the specified plant / machinery and they should also be trained in risk assessments. Resources should be available relating to any Government, EU or International legislation.

USE OF CHECKLISTS

These can be useful aids, especially when information/data is incorporated from plant designers/ and manufacturers; however, these may also limit what is inspected.

THE REQUIREMENTS FOR EFFECTIVE REPORT WRITING

Style

Use clear and concise wording, try not to use any ambiguous phrases or words and use plain language where possible.

Structure

A simple structure is best, use simple headings, which make it easier to read and understand.

Emphasis

Emphasis should be prioritised to any weaknesses found, with clear recommendations. Try to grade any risks i.e. high, medium, low. Strengths should also be included.

Persuasiveness

Highlight any potential changes and indicate any benefits i.e. fewer days' sickness, therefore an increase in productivity. Do not go into great detail - this should be done when a correct action plan is implemented.

The primary purpose of written information is to communicate. The writer should, therefore, always bear the reader in mind when producing the text. The use of plain language must be encouraged; this is particularly critical for safety related material.

To increase persuasiveness, one simple structure is as follows:

- Introduction and background.
- Summary.
- Main body of the report.
- Recommendations.
- Conclusions.

Introduction and background

This section includes the title page which should clearly identify the writer and the document. It should contain a brief explanation of the subject described in the document title and the reason for the document. Consider the aim of the report and inform the reader of the problems it intends to address.

Summary

Most reports benefit from a summary, which seeks to provide the reader with an overview of the strengths and weaknesses of the subject being reported on. It should be sufficient to motivate the reader to read the rest of the report with an idea of what it is going to cover.

Main body of the report

This section deals with details, facts and findings. The style should be kept simple and to the point, avoiding the use of jargon or embellishment. Inaccuracy, inadequate and poor presentation can distract the reader and lessen the impact.

Recommendations

These should flow logically from the main body of the report. Recommendations should consist of a plain statement of action without repeating the arguments of the preceding section. In short, in simple reports the recommendation may follow each of the findings and therefore appear in the main body of the report.

Conclusions

This section should contain a summary of the main findings and inferences. Ideally, the writer should end on a positive note. The report should also be signed and dated.

7.3 - Review of health and safety performance

Gathering information to review health and safety performance

Learning from all relevant experience (including that of the organisation and of other organisations) needs to be done systematically, through regular reviews of performance. The review draws on data from monitoring activities and from independent audits. These form the basis of continuous improvement, necessary to maintain compliance and effectiveness. This helps to maintain a management system that is fresh, dynamic, appropriate and effective.

For example, it is a well established principle that things like health and safety policy and risk assessments are reviewed. This is done when something it is believed may affect them has changed. For example, legislation may change and cause a review, or an accident may occur leading to a review to determine if the arrangements and controls in place are effective.

ACCIDENT AND INCIDENT DATA

Whilst accident data trend analysis is critical it should be remembered it is after the event. Any analysis should consider the potential for each occurrence to have resulted in a more significant outcome. Two elements to consider here are:

- Quality of planning before the event.
- Failure of controls. This will often result in the need to review the current risk assessment.

INSPECTIONS

The primary purpose of workplace planned general inspections is to identify general workplace hazards that are out of control before they result in any harmful outcome. Other inspections similarly are necessary to forestall harmful outcomes for specific hazards, for example, inspections of scaffolds, excavations, lifting equipment and pressure systems. The presence of hazards or substandard condition of equipment identified at inspection might illustrate a need to review maintenance or use regimes.

5/02	Chains Ropes and Lifting Tackle Does the organisation ensure that statutory inspections are carried out? *Notes:*	Consider: • Examined by a competent person • Examined every period of six months • Register of examination • Certificate of test and examination • Distinguishing number or mark • Safe working load (SWL) - displayed • Fault procedure • Monitoring

Figure 1-7-2: Extract from Audit 123 Level 2 Vol 1 of 2 Auditor's Guidance [ISBN 1 900420 83 X].   Source: RMS Publishing.

ABSENCES AND SICKNESS

Whilst physical injury will be recorded in the accident book and may have resulted in some investigation it should be remembered that some workplace hazards or working environments may result in sickness absence or ill health. Sickness or general absence data should be collected and analysed to determine if it has resulted from work or working environment issues. Such analysis may determine causes such as shift working, overwork or poor environmental conditions, including inadequate ventilation or extremes of temperature or humidity.

UNIT IGC1 - ELEMENT 7 - MONITORING, REVIEW AND AUDIT

SURVEYS, TOURS AND SAMPLING

A survey is an identification of need, for example, a noise survey may identify where it is necessary to carry out a formal assessment of noise level and frequency.

Tours are best carried out by the most senior managers of an organisation, to identify success or gaps in health, safety and environmental (board level) funding that are visible at the workers' level. This will ensure that senior managers are kept up to date with progress on implementation strategies and day to day problems affecting those at greatest risk. It often cuts through the "glue" which sometimes occurs in pyramid management structures, where key issues at the employee level are not always passed up the line management structure to the board.

Sampling is a technique used to identify a 'representative portion to illustrate the whole', for example, we may sample the use of a specific item of personal protective equipment (PPE) or lifting tackle. Sampling techniques may rely either on professional judgement or statistical methods to identify the sample size.

OBSERVATIONS OF PHYSICAL CONDITIONS

Category	Number Checked (C)	Number Standard (S)	% Meeting Standard $\frac{S}{C} \times 100$	Comments
EQUIPMENT *For Guidance Notes consider Audit 123 Level 1 - Sections 4 and 7*				
Guarding				
Hand tools				
Power tools				
Electrics (visual)				
Electrics (technical inspection)				
Pressure systems				
Ladders and mobile towers				
Personal protective equipment				
Total Score				Total % Compliance $\frac{Total\ S}{Total\ C} \times 100$

Figure 1-7-3: Sampling - extract from Audit 123 Level 3 Section 1 Workbook [ISBN 1 900420 50 3]. *Source: RMS Publishing.*

QUALITY ASSURANCE REPORTS, AUDITS, MONITORING DATA / RECORDS/ REPORTS, COMPLAINTS

Quality assurance techniques are useful because they will identify the "normal or abnormal" features of a process and as such may be a useful indicator of the wellbeing of the workers involved.

Audits are designed to determine the effectiveness of the management system and in particular the degree of management control. Audits will examine all types of data, documents and records to determine the degree of system compliance and their suitability with the passage of time. Quality assurance audits may identify system non-compliance that can have an effect on health and safety, particularly where the organisation provides a service or product to an end user outside the organisation, for example, the defective manufacture of an electric drill intended for sale.

A system should be in place to enable all workers to bring to the management's attention any issues of concern. This can provide valuable feedback on how systems affect workers in practice. Such concerns should be documented and actioned within an agreed time frame with appropriate feedback, in much the same way as customers complaints might be dealt with.

Quality assurance performance information, in its various forms, can provide a useful confirmation on the effectiveness of health and safety systems that work in parallel with quality. This is particularly useful in contributing to the process of health and safety performance review.

Reporting on health and safety performance

Health and safety performance should be reported at board level and it is customary to include a statement, along with other risks, within the annual report. Such reports should be available to all workers and other stakeholders.

Role of senior management team

The role of the management team is to treat health, safety and the environment as equal partners to other business issues such as production (service) and quality. To this end, goals should be stated and clear measurable objectives to achieve such goals must be established and implemented.

> "Safety is an integral part of business excellence and, together with product and service quality, and corporate health and profitability, is the foundation for our future success".

Figure 1-7-4: Policy Statement abstract. *Source: Standard Wire Corporation circa. 1996.*

Ref No.	Validation Material	Evaluation
1/1/05	**Health and safety as an equal partnership** Do managers readily accept that health and safety is a manageable item and should be seen to have equal standing with production and quality?	**Consider:** • Board commitment e.g. policy statement • Appointment of a Director for health and safety • Included in job descriptions/responsibility statements • Accepted as a line management responsibility

Notes:	• Included fully in all technical, procedural and behavioural standards of performance
	• Identified in appraisal documents
	• Planned allocation of time to health and safety issues
	• Health and safety performance measured and reported on equal basis with other management objectives

Figure 1-7-5: Extract from Audit 123 Level 3 Section 1 Auditor's Guidance [ISBN 1 900420 14 7]. Source: RMS Publishing.

The senior managers of an organisation should conduct a formal periodic, at least once per year, strategic review of health and safety. This would usually draw on the review data described earlier and reports from other reviews conducted for specific reasons, for example, due to re-organisation, changes in legislation or changes in technology.

Involvement in periodic reviews provides an opportunity for senior management to refresh their commitment to health and safety and to confirm the degree to which the organisation is being effective in managing health and safety risks. This in turn enables senior management to take action and meet their responsibilities for health and safety.

Feeding into action and development plans as part of continuous improvement

It is critical that health and safety reviews take place in an analytical way, questioning if actions taken to date have been appropriate, effective and completed. From this review process objectives and actions to improve health and safety may be identified and fed into development/improvement plans. The strategic level plans enable the production of local level plans through information cascade. In this way health and safety in an organisation is maintained dynamically, leading to continuous improvement.

Health and safety objectives should be established for all development/improvement plans and be subject to key performance indicators (KPI's) in the same way as KPI's are established for the other key business objectives such as production or quality. For example, proactive reporting at meetings should be established for health and safety items such as the status of inspections and risk assessments. It is critical not to limit the meeting to considering the number or absence of accidents since the last meeting. Whilst many may regard the safety committee to be the place for such considerations, the frequency of safety committees will always be less than the frequency of production (service) meetings and reserving consideration to committee meetings can remove 'safety' from the day to day consideration and concern of line managers.

7.4 - Auditing

Scope and purpose of auditing health and safety management systems

DISTINCTION BETWEEN AUDITS AND INSPECTIONS

An audit is a systematic, critical examination of an organisation's systems to determine the extent of compliance with a set of agreed standards.

The entire health and safety management system should be subjected to a comprehensive audit from time to time. Individual elements of the health and safety programme can, of course, be subjected to individual audits, for example:

- Evaluation of compliance with health and safety programme procedures.
- Evaluation of compliance with set occupational health standards.
- Evaluation of compliance with physical safeguards (health and safety hardware).
- Evaluation of compliance with fire prevention/control standards.

Workplace inspections help prevent injuries and illnesses. Through critical examination of the workplace, inspections identify and record hazards for corrective action. Joint occupational health and safety committees plan, conduct, report and monitor inspections. Regular workplace inspections are a critical part of the overall occupational health and safety programme.

Pre-audit preparations

The audit must be structured and co-ordinated in its assessment of the systems. This is best achieved by utilising audit checklists developed or obtained before the audit. The audit involves assessment of documents, interview of people and observations in the workplace.

In order to prepare for an audit it is necessary to decide who needs to be interviewed and organise a timetable in order to meet them on a planned and organised basis. It is critical that people involved in the audit are informed of what type of documents they need to make available. In this way there is a better chance that they will be provided at the time of audit.

Interviews should be structured to provide the interviewee with opportunity to express what they are doing to meet the requirements being audited.

The outcome from an audit should be a detailed report of findings and recommendations to improve or maintain the health and safety management system. A structure and approach to the report should be agreed at the pre-audit stage.

Responsibility for audits

The responsibility to ensure audits take place rests within the organisation. Conducting audits will assist the organisation in complying with local legislative requirements and to have in place arrangements to monitor. Audits should be conducted by people that are both independent and competent. Health and safety specialists that have received specific training in health and safety auditing techniques would usually be able to carry out this function.

Audits can be carried out by the management of the organisation, provided that the managers do not audit their own efforts directly (bias must be eliminated) and that the managers concerned have been trained in audit technique. Often a small team will be commissioned to conduct the exercise, in order to widen the experience base and establish some degree of independence. A team may comprise three essential groups of people:

- A manager.
- A representative from the workforce.
- A health and safety professional.

Extra individuals with specific skills may join the team when specific topics are under assessment. A more independent approach would be to conduct an audit using auditors from outside the organisation or location.

Advantages and disadvantages of external and internal audits

	Advantages	Disadvantages
Internal audits	Internal audits ensure local acceptance to implement recommendations and actions. The auditor often has intimate knowledge of the hazards and existing work practices. An awareness of what might be appropriate for the industry. Familiarity with the workforce including their strengths and weaknesses. Relatively low cost and easier to arrange.	May not possess auditing skills. May not be up to date with current legislation and best practice. The auditor may also be responsible for implementation of any proposed changes and this might inhibit recommendations because of the effect on workload. May be subject to pressure from management and time constraints.
External audits	External audits are usually impartial, auditors will have a range of experience of different types of work practices. May be able to offer solutions to what might be considered unsolvable problems within. Not inhibited by criticism. Will see the organisation's performance without prior bias.	Need to plan well to identify nature and scope of the organisation. Individuals may not be forthcoming, be nervous or resistant to discussing their workplace with an outsider. May seek unrealistic targets.

(Sample) Overall Compliance ACT AUDIT 1 2 3
(Single Location)

These marks are obtained from totalling the (total achieved marks and total maximum mark) from audit check list matrix (by location) for each section heading or directly from audit check list (whole organisation) for each section heading, depending on which is used.

Enter the totalled achieved marks in column 1 for each section heading (total achieved marks). Enter the totalled maximum obtainable marks in column 2 for each section heading (total maximum marks).

This compliance matrix is used to show the overall compliance of the organisation by section headings only.

Determine the percentage: $\dfrac{\text{Total Achieved Marks}}{\text{Maximum Obtainable Marks}} \times 100$

and enter in column 3 (Percentage).

Main Section Heading	Column 1 Total Achieved Marks	Column 2 Maximum Obtainable Marks	Column 3 Percentage
Administration and Procedures	78	160	49
Legislation Compliance	90	210	75
Environment	58	110	53
Equipment	60	120	50
Materials Handling	80	100	80
Facilities	88	90	98
Special Risks	75	100	75
External	76	120	63
Environment - Office	70	90	78
Facilities - Office	60	110	55
Special Risks - Office	N/A	N/A	N/A
Totals	735	1210	
	Organisation Compliance		61

Figure 1-7-6: Sample page from the ACT / RMS Audit 123 system.   Source: ACT.

Element 8

Occupational incident and accident investigation, recording and reporting

Learning outcomes

On completion of this element, candidates should be able to demonstrate understanding of the content through the application of knowledge to familiar and unfamiliar situations. In particular they should be able to:

8.1 Explain the purpose of, and procedures for, investigating occupational incidents (accidents, cases of work-related ill-health and other occurrences).

8.2 Describe the organisational requirements for recording and reporting such incidents.

Content

8.1 - The process and purpose of investigating occupational incidents 91
    Role and function of investigation of accidents 91
    Different types of incident 91
    Basic accident investigation procedures 92
    Interviews, plans, photographs, relevant records and checklists 93
    Identifying immediate and (root) underlying causes 94
    Identifying remedial actions 96
8.2 - The organisational requirements for recording and reporting occupational incidents...............................96
    Internal systems for collecting, analysing and communicating data..96
    Organisational requirements for recording and reporting incidents...97
    Typical examples of major injuries, diseases and dangerous occurrences that might be reportable to external agencies..97

Sources of reference

Recording and Notification of Occupational Accidents and Diseases, ILO ISBN 92-2-108784-0

8.1 - The process and purpose of investigating occupational incidents

Role and function of investigation of accidents

WHY INVESTIGATE?

The reasons for investigating accidents are the same as for accident prevention, i.e.

- Humane.
- Economic.
- Legal.

In some countries there is a specific requirement to report accidents to external organisations such as enforcement agencies, insurance institutions and worker compensation organisations. The information needed for the report will cause an investigation into the circumstances leading up to an accident. The findings should be applied to prevent recurrence by improving work place standards, procedures and training requirements.

ROLE OF INVESTIGATION

The role of investigation includes:

- Establish what happened.
- Identify measures to prevent a recurrence.
- Establish legal and/or worker compensation liability.
- Data gathering.
- Identification of trends.
- Determine the causes of what happened, including underlying causes.

FUNCTION OF INVESTIGATION

Ideally all accidents should be investigated. A study of minor injuries and near misses can often reveal a major hazard, as the occurrence and severity of injury is a random happening. The degree of investigation may well vary with the degree of injury or damage, but should be based on the worst possible case of injury which is reasonably foreseeable as a result of the accident in question.

The objectives of any investigation will vary according to the circumstances, but it will always include the following points:

- The need to establish the causes of an accident, both immediate and underlying, in order that appropriate preventative action can be taken.
- Identify weaknesses in current systems so that standards can be improved.
- Determine economic losses.
- Recommend actions to prevent a recurrence.
- Determine compliance with statutory requirements or with company regulations.
- Improve staff relations by demonstrating commitment to health and safety.
- Acquire statistics.
- Prepare for criminal/civil action and provide insurance/worker compensation data.

The role and directive for the investigation of this nature should **never** seek to blame any individual or group of individuals.

If human error is believed to be a significant cause, the reasons for this must be investigated. Lack of knowledge, training or unsuitability for the job may be the causes of this error. These are **management** and not operator **failings**. Only when these have been evaluated can the conclusion of wilful and intentional acts or omissions be considered.

Different types of incident

OUTCOME

Outcome can be defined as an effect following an unplanned, uncontrolled event. This may include such things as injury, ill health, near miss or property damage.

INJURY

"physical harm or damage done to or suffered by a person"

The term refers to physical harm to an individual. Typically, injuries are classified in broad groups such as major, serious and minor. Major injuries include amputations, loss of sight and loss of consciousness. A serious injury is where a person is unable to do their normal work activities typically for more than three consecutive days. The remainder are classified as minor injuries, where the incapacity lasts for typically less than three days.

ILL-HEALTH

"harm to a person's health caused by their work"

The term refers to harm to a person's health caused by their work and will include harm to health in a physiological or psychological way.

DANGEROUS OCCURRENCE

"Readily identifiable event as defined under national laws and regulations, with potential to cause an injury or disease to persons at work or the public."

Figure 1-8-1: Definition of a dangerous occurrence. *Source: International Labour Office (ILO) - Recording and Notifying of Occupational Accidents and Diseases (RNOAD) - Code of Practice.*

In practice, a dangerous occurrence is an event that does not result in personal injury but has the potential to cause major personal injury and as such might need to be notified and reported to the appropriate competent / enforcing authority (e.g. explosion of a pressure vessel or collapse of a scaffold of five metres high or more).

NEAR-MISS

"an accident that results in no apparent loss"

The term 'near-miss' refers to an event (accident) which did not result in personal injury, equipment damage or some other loss, but under slightly different circumstances could have done (e.g. building block falling off a scaffold and landing on the floor).

DAMAGE ONLY

'Damage only' describes damage to property, equipment, the environment or production losses.

INCIDENT

> "An unsafe occurrence arising out of or in connection with work where no personal injury is caused, or where personal injury only requires first aid".

Figure 1-8-2: Definition of an incident.
Source: International Labour Office (ILO).

Basic accident investigation procedures

The ILO Code of Practice for Recording and Notifying of Occupational Accidents and Diseases (COP-RNOAD) sets out requirements at 'enterprise level' that each organisation should follow. This begins with the requirement for employers to investigate reported occupational accidents, commuting accidents, occupational diseases, dangerous occurrences and incidents. The Code of Practice proposes that if the employer does not have the expertise to conduct an investigation that they should call upon the services of a person that does, even if this is from outside the enterprise. It further requires that arrangements be in place to enable the immediate investigation of occupational accidents, occupational diseases, dangerous occurrences and incidents.

APPROACH TO INVESTIGATION

Step 1: Gathering the information - the where, when and who of the adverse event. The information gathered will include results of interviews, photographs of the equipment involved and the area in which it was positioned at the time, sketches of the workplace layout, weather conditions, etc.

Step 2: Analysing the information - the "what happened and why" stage. Analysing the information to find the immediate, underlying and root causes. At this stage it should be considered if human error is a contributory factor. Job factors, human factors and organisational factors can all influence human behaviour and will all need to be considered in the analysis.

Step 3: Identifying suitable risk control measures. Possible solutions can be identified. This will involve looking at the technical, procedural and behavioural controls, with the technical or engineering risk control measures being more reliable than those that rely on human behaviour.

Step 4: The action plan and its implementation - which risk control measures should be implemented in the short and long term? This is the risk control action plan, which should have **'smart'** objectives, i.e. Specific, Measurable, Agreed and Realistic, with Timescales. This will also state which risk assessments need to be reviewed and which procedures need to be updated; any trends that need further investigation; and the adverse event cost.

PREPARING FOR THE INVESTIGATION

- Determine who should be involved to ensure the investigation team has all the necessary skills and expertise:
  - A senior manager from another department who could act as an independent chairman.
  - A health and safety practitioner to advise on specific health and safety issues.
  - An engineer or technical expert to provide any technical information required.
  - A senior manager from the department where the accident occurred, whose responsibilities would include ensuring that the recommendations of the investigating team were actioned.
  - A local manager or supervisor with detailed knowledge of the site of the accident and of the systems of work in place.
  - A worker safety representative who, apart from having the statutory right to be involved if trade union-appointed, could represent the injured worker and his/her co-workers.
- Ensure that the accident scene remains undisturbed insofar as it is reasonable and safe to do so (COP-RNOAD - 10.2).
- Collate all relevant existing documents such as previous incident reports, maintenance records, risk assessments etc.
- Identify the persons (witnesses) who will need to be interviewed during the investigation.
- Check that legal reporting requirements have been met.
- Ascertain the equipment that will be needed e.g. measuring tape, camera.
- Determine the style and depth of the investigation.

TRAINING FOR THE REPORTING OF ACCIDENTS/INCIDENTS

To ensure that the investigation team has all the necessary information, training in some of these areas may be required for some workers:

- The importance of reporting accidents and incidents for legal, investigative and monitoring reasons.
- The types of event that the organisation requires to be reported.
- The lines of reporting.
- How to complete internal documents and forms.
- How to report to external organisations, where appropriate.

SCOPE AND DEPTH OF INVESTIGATION

Ideally all accidents should be investigated. A study of minor injuries and near misses can often reveal a major hazard, as the occurrence and severity of injury is a random happening. The depth of investigation should depend on the severity of actual or potential loss, whichever is the greater.

TYPES OF INVESTIGATIONS

Supervisory investigations

As the person in immediate operating control of an area or activity it is logical to expect the supervisor to gather information on all accidents that happen in their sphere of responsibility. This investigation is normally all that is necessary for the majority of accidents. It should result in swift remedial actions being implemented, and underlines the supervisor's responsibility for safety on a day to day basis.

Formal investigation

In some cases a formal investigation will be convened to carry out the functions described above.

The committee should include the following people:

- A senior manager to sit as chairperson.
- A manager at a lower level than the chairperson e.g. supervisor/team leader.
- A person competent to give technical advice e.g. an electrical engineer in the case of electrocution.
- The safety professional, who may sometimes act as secretary.
- A worker representative.

Any person whose responsibilities or actions may have been involved in the incident being investigated should be excluded from sitting on the committee, but would, of course, be valuable witnesses.

INVESTIGATION GUIDELINES

- The scene of the accident may still be highly hazardous. Anyone wishing to assist the injured party must take care, so that they too do not become victims.
- The investigation must begin as soon as possible after the accident.
- Keep the objective clearly in mind - to discover the causes in order to initiate remedial action, not only to find someone to blame.
- Witnesses must be interviewed one at a time and not in the presence of any other witnesses to avoid influencing subsequent statements.
- Identify the root causes of the accident, not just immediate ones.
- Ask probing questions - to avoid leading the witnesses.
- Avoid making early assumptions.
- Approach the witness without bias or pre conceptions.
- Notes should be taken so that the investigator is not relying on memory.
- Interviews are of critical importance. The witnesses may be very defensive, feeling that blame could be directed their way, so it is critical to put the person being interviewed at ease - state that the purpose of the interview is to help determine the facts to prevent a re-occurrence.

SUMMARY OF ACTIONS TO TAKEN

- Isolating services and making the area safe.
- Administering first-aid treatment and summoning the emergency services.
- Informing the next of kin.
- Notifying the enforcement authority by the quickest practicable means, where appropriate.
- Collecting initial evidence such as photographs and sketches and the names of witnesses.
- Setting up the accident investigation.

Interviews, plans, photographs, relevant records and checklists

The ILO Code of Practice for Recording and Notifying of Occupational Accidents and Diseases (COP-RNOAD) - 10.2 requires the employer to arrange that the site of an accident be left undisturbed before the start of an investigation, unless first aid provision or a further risk is presented. If it is necessary to disturb the site, the employer should arrange for a competent person to make a record of the site, including photographs, plans and the identification of witnesses, before intervention.

INTERVIEWS

Good interview technique will include:

- Recording the details: names of the interviewers, interviewee and anyone accompanying interviewees; place, data and time of the interview; and any significant comments or actions during the interview.
- Conducting the interview in private with no interruptions.
- Interviewing more than one person at a time.
- Protecting the reputation of the people interviewed.
- Setting a casual, informal tone during the interview to put the individual at ease.
- Summarising your understanding of the matter.
- Expressing appreciation for the witnesses' information.
- Translating conclusions into effective action.

PLANS

Plans can be used to provide a clear indication of the accident scene including position of any injured person, witnesses, plant and equipment. The use of a sketch plan by the investigator, as well as any service or layout plans can assist in determining root causes of the event.

PHOTOGRAPHS

Cameras can be used to record and preserve images of accident scenes or resulting injuries. This can be especially useful if the situation changes with time through corrective actions, healing process, changes in environmental conditions etc.

RELEVANT RECORDS

The amount of time and effort spent on information gathering should be proportionate to the level of the investigation, but should include all available and relevant information such as opinions, experiences, observations, measurements, check sheets, work permits, risk assessments, method statements and training records.

CHECKLISTS

Investigation report forms vary in design, layout and content. Many organisations recognise that a different report form may be necessary for first line managers' initial investigations (a level 1 report) and those done by other managers and health and safety professionals (a level 2 report), the main difference being in the section relating to causes of the accident. The version used by other managers and professionals often has more analysis in this area and causes greater investigation of underlying causes. In the same way, reports prepared by an investigation team would not tend to be on a pre-printed format, but would be designed around agreed headings and the content/extent of the report would depend on the matter being investigated and findings (a level 3 report).

Common structure of a report tends to determine:

- What happened   -   the loss.
- How it happened   -   the event.
- Why it happened   -   the causes.
- Recommendations   -   remedial (and preventive) action.

Drawings and photographs and statements as appendices usually support the report.

Identifying immediate and (root) underlying causes

The ILO Code of Practice for Recording and Notifying of Occupational Accidents and Diseases (COP-RNOAD) - 10.2 requires the employer to, as far as possible:

- Establish what happened.
- Determine the causes of what happened.
- Identify measures to prevention a recurrence.

IDENTIFYING IMMEDIATE CAUSES

The cause of injury should be identified. Injuries are caused by:

Unsafe acts by individuals e.g. not wearing the correct personal protective equipment such as goggles to prevent an eye injury.

Unsafe conditions in the workplace e.g. an electrical cable, supplying energy to a power tool, trailing across a busy walkway and presenting a trip hazard.

ROOT OR UNDERLYING CAUSES

The cause of the accident is often the result of many underlying or root causal failures.

Typical root or underlying causes result:

- When people lack understanding or training, they are in a hurry and they are poorly supervised.
- When the wrong equipment is provided or the equipment is inadequate, not maintained or regularly inspected.

These are known as **management system failures** and occur when the organisation does not establish an adequate safety policy, incorporating an appropriate approach to risk identification and control for the organisation's activities.

Research by Frank Bird and others into accident causation has led them to put forward an accident causation model based on a row of dominoes standing on one end. If any of the earlier dominoes fall, a chain reaction follows which results in a loss.

Figure 1-8-3: Domino theory of accident causation.   Source: Frank Bird.

Considering each stage separately:

"Loss"

This is the consequence of the accident and can be measured in terms of people (injuries), property (damage) or loss to the process (failed telecommunication) and hence loss of profit.

"Event (accident or incident)"

The event producing the loss involving contact with a substance or source of energy above the threshold limits of the body or structure.

"Immediate (direct) causes"

These are the substandard (unsafe) **acts** (e.g. using tools and equipment for tasks they were not designed to do) and substandard (unsafe) **conditions** (e.g. a trailing telephone cable in an office) which gives rise to an accident. These are physical symptoms which can be seen or sensed. Whilst these symptoms cannot be ignored, action solely at this level will not, by itself, ensure that recurrence is not prevented. Unsafe acts and conditions may be considered as workplace **hazards.**

"Indirect (root or underlying) causes"

These are the underlying or root causes of accidents. Identifying the root causes will explain why the substandard act happened or the condition arose. They are not always easy to identify. Indirect causes fall into three major categories:

1) Organisational Factors.
2) Job Factors.
3) Personal Factors.

Organisational factors:
- Work standards and procedures.
- Communication.
- Co-ordination.
- Supervision.

Personal Factors include:
- Physical capability.
- Mental capability.
- Physical stress.
- Mental stress.

Job Factors:
- Design of equipment and layouts.
- Maintenance.
- Purchase of materials and equipment.

- Knowledge.
- Skill.
- Motivation.
- Information.

"Lack of management control"

This is the initial stage, centred on the management functions of:

- Policy.
- Planning.
- Organising.
- Controlling.
- Monitoring.
- Reviewing.

It should be remembered that accident investigation experience confirms that there is usually more than one causative factor. Therefore each of the multiple causation factors may be seen as one domino in its own line of dominoes [just as the **roots** of a tree branch out].

EXAMPLES

An accident involving an operator coming into contact with dangerous machinery could be the result of any of the following:

Immediate cause	*Root (underlying) cause*
Inadequate or non-existent safety devices.	Inadequate training, instruction and / or supervision.
Poor housekeeping.	Poor maintenance.
Loose clothing.	Inadequate risk assessment.
Machine malfunction.	A range of personal factors i.e. stress, fatigue, influence of drugs and alcohol.
Operator error.	Poor design of guard.

A worker slipped on a patch of oil on a warehouse floor and was admitted to hospital where the person remained for several days. The oil was found close to a stack of pallets that had been left abandoned on the designated pedestrian walkway.

Immediate cause	*Root (underlying) cause*
Oil leaking onto the floor from equipment or being spilled by a worker.	The absence of adequate risk assessments and safe systems of work.
The floor remaining in a slippery condition because the spillage was not cleaned up.	A failure to introduce procedures for routine maintenance of equipment and for cleaning up spillages.
The abandoned pallets blocking the walkway causing the injured person to make a detour.	Poor warehouse design with inadequate walkways.
Inadequate lighting at the scene of the accident.	Failure by management to monitor working conditions in the warehouse to ensure workers were not exposed to risks to their health and safety.
The worker wearing unsuitable footwear and not paying sufficient attention to the placing of their feet.	Little training or instruction of workers in those procedures that might have been introduced.

Identifying remedial actions

ACTION FOLLOWING A SERIOUS ACCIDENT

Immediately after an accident:
- Attend to the victim.
- Secure the scene of the accident.
- Notify the next of kin.
- Report to enforcing authority if necessary.

Longer-term actions will include:
- Identifying witnesses.
- Undertaking an investigation.
- Reviewing work procedures.

Reporting a death at work following an accident should include informing:
- Next of kin.
- The senior manager.
- Health and safety specialist.
- Coroner or law enforcement agency where appropriate.
- Enforcing authority or law enforcement agency where appropriate.
- Worker representatives.
- Other workers.
- Insurance company, where appropriate.

REPORTS AND FOLLOW-UP

The report should include a summarised version of the facts and recommendations together with discussion of controversial points, and if necessary appendices containing specialist reports (medical and technical), photographs and diagrams.

This virtually finishes the work of the investigator, but management is still responsible for seeing that the necessary remedial actions are implemented and monitored to ensure that the causes are satisfactorily controlled. The line manager, health and safety professional and health and safety committee/members will monitor these actions.

SUMMARY

Throughout the process of investigation it must be clearly borne in mind that the object is to prevent a recurrence of the accident, not to apportion blame. It is critical to identify the true causes of the accident, not superficial ones. This cannot be achieved without the full commitment and assistance of witnesses and other persons who work in that area.

It follows that recommendations must be put into action and this itself may be a protracted business. However, if this is thoroughly carried out it may identify further measures of inspection and training or other positive measures that will substantiate the effort spent in trying to extract some degree of improvement from the occurrence.

8.2 - The organisational requirements for recording and reporting occupational incidents

Internal systems for collecting, analysing and communicating data

COLLECTING DATA

Report form types

A number of report forms are utilised to identify and inform that accidents and ill-health have occurred. These include:

- Initial record of the accident, e.g. 'Accident book'.
- First aid treatment reports.
- Medical treatment reports.
- Medical (doctor) reports of ill-health.
- Sickness absence reports.
- Event (accident) reports.
- Event (dangerous occurrence / near miss) reports.
- Maintenance/repair reports.
- If required by external organisations, external reports.
- Insurance reports.

The ILO Code of Practice for Recording and Notifying of Occupational Accidents and Diseases (RNOAD) sets out requirements that the employer should make arrangements, in accordance with national legislation, to record occupational accidents, commuting accidents, occupational disease, dangerous occurrences and incidents. The employer should ensure that records are prepared in accordance with national requirements, and in any case within 6 days. Records should be available and retrievable at any reasonable time.

Whilst a number of countries have requirements to report to external organisations few have requirements to make and retain internal records. Among those that do are the Philippines, South Africa, United States and Vietnam. Here the requirement extends to all occupational accidents and disease. In some countries, for example the United Kingdom, there is a requirement to maintain a record of accidents in an 'accident book' and record those accidents that have been reported to an external enforcing agency. Records which should be maintained for a suitable period, this could be 3 years for an injury accident and 40 years for events that might lead to an occupational disease. It is useful to maintain a statistical record of the number of accidents as well as a descriptive record/report. This is a specific requirement in some countries, such as Vietnam.

Reporting routes

Internal reporting of an accident or ill-health may be by a number of means and includes:

- Person receiving harm.
- Person causing harm.
- Person discovering harm.

Person receiving harm

This person is often the source of first reporting of less serious events. The reporting system must make available to them the means to make a report. This might be fulfilled by using first aid/medical treatment documents or event (e.g. accident) report forms or log books. These reports should be under the control of a responsible person who would then initiate an investigation.

Person causing loss

This person would be expected to bring the loss to the attention of a line manager who would fill in the appropriate event (e.g. accident) report and initiate an investigation to complete the remainder of the report that the person reporting the loss may not be able to do.

Person discovering the loss

If this person were not the manager responsible for the location in which the loss took place they would have to bring the loss to the attention of a line manager, as above. If the person were the line manager they would initiate an investigation and report on the appropriate event form.

ANALYSING AND COMMUNICATING DATA

Reports from first line managers may be copied to the next line manager (middle manager), health and safety professional, worker representative. It is critical that the originator retains a copy until action to prevent is complete, to encourage ownership and continued involvement.

The copy passed to the next line manager is usually seen as the primary document. The manager confirms/adds to the investigation, retains a copy and passes the report to a central record point.

Clearly this may be done in part or whole as a computer or paper system.

Records held by the line manager/health and safety professional may be held for varying periods depending on their role. Central records are usually maintained in accordance with the organisation's own practices.

Organisational requirements for recording and reporting incidents

National practices vary considerably regarding the terms and definitions used for occupational accidents and injuries. Some countries do not have a definition, with a simple reference in legislation to accidents occurring in the workplace, for example, Botswana, Myanmar and the United Kingdom, or to injuries occurring during the performance of work, for example, Norway. Others, such as the United States, have a definition which includes explicit reference to a sudden or unexpected event, as well as violent acts.

The definitions of what is to be recorded and notified have huge implications on the data to be collected and analysed. The following definitions are provided in the ILO Code of Practice for Recording and Notification of Occupational Accidents and Diseases (RNOAD):

Occupational accident

An occurrence arising out of or in the course of work which results in:

(a) Fatal occupational injury.

(b) Non-fatal occupational injury.

Occupational disease

A disease contracted as a result of an exposure to risk factors arising from work activity.

Commuting accident:

An accident occurring on the direct way between the place of work and

(a) The worker's principal or secondary residence.

(b) The place where the worker usually takes their meals.

(c) The place where the worker usually receives their remuneration, which results in death or personal injury involving loss of
working time.

Dangerous occurrence

Readily identifiable event as defined under national laws and regulations, with potential to cause an injury or disease to persons at work or the public.

Incidents

An unsafe occurrence arising out of or in the course of work where no personal injury is caused, or where personal injury requires only first-aid treatment.

Reporting requirements may include reporting to an enforcement agency, insurance institutions, worker compensation organisations or a doctor, depending on the event being reported and local requirements. The ILO Code of Practice for Recording and Notifying of Occupational Accidents and Diseases (RNOAD) sets out requirements that occupational accidents resulting in death should be reported immediately and other accidents within a prescribed period of time set out by national legislation.

Typical examples of major injuries, diseases and dangerous occurrences that might be reportable to external agencies

MAJOR INJURIES

The ILO Code of Practice for Recording and Notifying of Occupational Accidents and Diseases (RNOAD) does not specify types of major injury resulting from accidents that should be reported. This is left to national legislation.

One country that has set out categories of major injury selected for particular attention for reporting purposes is the United Kingdom and the following list is based on those specified by that country.

UNIT IGC1 - ELEMENT 08 - OCCUPATIONAL INCIDENT AND ACCIDENT INVESTIGATION

A list of major injuries that might be reportable includes:

- Any fracture, other than the finger or thumbs or toes.
- Any amputation.
- Dislocation of the shoulder, hip, knee or spine.
- Permanent or temporary loss of sight.
- Chemical, hot metal or penetrating eye injury.
- Electrical shock, electrical burn leading to unconsciousness or resuscitation or admittance to hospital for more than 24 hours.
- Loss of consciousness caused by asphyxia or exposure to a harmful substance or biological agent.
- Acute illness or loss of consciousness requiring medical attention due to any entry of substance by inhalation, ingestion or through the skin.
- Acute illness where there is a reason to believe that this resulted from exposure to a biological agent or its toxins or infected material.
- Any other injury leading to hypothermia, heat-induced illness or unconsciousness requiring resuscitation, hospitalisation greater than 24 hours.

DISEASES

The Employment Injury Benefits Convention, 1964 (No. 121), established by the International Labour Office (ILO), provides for the competent authority of a country to define occupational accidents and diseases for which certain compensation benefits will be provided. Schedule I of the Convention lists those diseases that are common and well recognised. This ILO list plays a key role in harmonising the development of policy on occupational diseases and in promoting their prevention and it provides a clear statement of diseases or disorders that can and should be prevented. This includes the employer recording and reporting such diseases to external agencies.

The ILO list of occupational diseases includes the following examples.

Diseases caused by agents

Diseases caused by physical agents, e.g.
- Impairment caused by noise.
- Diseases caused by ionising radiation.
- Diseases caused by work in compressed air.
- Diseases due to extremes of temperature.
- Diseases caused by vibration (Hand-arm vibration syndrome).

Diseases caused by chemical agents, e.g.
- Caused by lead.
- Caused by asphyxiants: e.g. carbon monoxide.
- Caused by vanadium or its toxic compounds.
- Caused by carbon disulphide.
- Caused by mercury.
- Due to phosgene.
- Due to thallium.
- Caused by benzene

Biological agents, e.g.

Infections and parasitic diseases contracted in an operation where there is a particular risk of contamination e.g.
- Anthrax.
- Hepatitis.

Diseases by target organ systems

Respiratory diseases, e.g.
- Occupational asthma.
- Siderosis.
- Bronchopulmonary diseases e.g. caused by cotton.
- Pneumoconioses e.g. asbestosis, silicosis.

Skin diseases, e.g.
- Occupational vitiligo.
- Caused by physical, chemical and biological agents.

Musculo-skeletal disorders, e.g.

Caused by specific work activities or environment e.g.
- Awkward or non-neutral postures.
- Rapid repetitive motion.
- Forceful exertion.

Occupational cancer

Cancer caused by agents, e.g.
- Asbestos.
- Mineral oil.
- Benzene.
- Wood dust.

DANGEROUS OCCURRENCES

Dangerous occurrences are events that have the potential to cause death or serious injury and so should be reported, even though no one is injured. The ILO Code of Practice for Recording and Notifying of Occupational Accidents and Diseases (RNOAD) does not specify classes of dangerous occurrences that should be reported. Examples of dangerous occurrences that may be required to be reported under national laws are:

- Failure of lifting equipment.
- Fire.
- Collapse of a building.
- Failure of a pressurised closed vessel.
- Explosion.

Element 1

Movement of people and vehicles - hazards and control

Learning outcomes

On completion of this element, candidates should be able to demonstrate understanding of the content through the application of knowledge to familiar and unfamiliar situations. In particular they should be able to:

1.1 Identify the hazards that may cause injuries to pedestrians in the workplace and the control measures to reduce the risk of such injuries.

1.2 Identify the hazards presented by the movement of vehicles in the workplace and the control measures to reduce the risks they present.

Content

1.1 - Movement of people	101
Hazards to pedestrians	101
Control strategies for pedestrian hazards	102
1.2 - Movement of vehicles	106
Hazards in vehicle operations	106
Control strategies for safe vehicle operations	107

Sources of reference

Workplace Transport Safety - Guidance for Employers (HSG136), HSE Books ISBN 0-7176-0935-9

Other sources of reference

Department of Transport Safety of Loads on Vehicles Code of Practice, The Stationery Office Ltd 2002 ISBN 0-1155-2547-5

Workplace transport safety - An overview INDG199 (rev1) Reprinted 09/06, HSE Books ISBN 0-7176-2821-3

1.1 - Movement of people

Hazards to pedestrians

TYPICAL HAZARDS

Slips, trips and falls on the same level

Slips, trips and falls on the same level are the most common causes of major injuries. Broken bones are the usual result when the following conditions are present.

- Poorly maintained surfaces - e.g. highly polished surfaces, damaged floor tiles, holes in roads, site debris, insecure ducting or grates, poor re-instatements of roads or walk ways.
- Changes in level caused by ramps, slopes, kerbs, or steps not clearly marked.
- Slippery surfaces caused by water, oils, fuels, silt, mud, or mixed compounds such as plaster.
- Inappropriate footwear.
- Rules not followed - e.g. running or not taking care when walking.
- General obstructions in walkways such as trailing cables, pipes and air hoses.

Figure 2-1-1: Trip hazard. Source: ACT.

Figure 2-1-2: Slip hazards. Source: ACT.

Falls from a height

- Inadequate access to and from the workplace.
- Fragile roofs.
- Inadequate barriers e.g. hand rails, edge protection boards.
- Trenches - barriers / fences.

Figure 2-1-3: Falls from a height. Source: ACT.

Figure 2-1-4: Fall from a height - roof used for storage. Source: ACT.

Collisions with moving vehicles

- Restricted space to allow for manoeuvring and passing - e.g. where there is a high volume of mobile plant and materials.
- Undefined routes to segregate site traffic - e.g. workers with vehicles such as fork lift trucks or heavy goods vehicles.
- Traffic routes not defined.
- Vehicles reversing into loading bays without anyone providing assistance.
- Disregard for rules concerning vehicles - e.g. speed restrictions, competent operators.
- No or insufficient warning devices fitted to vehicles and a general lack of maintenance.

Striking by moving, flying or falling materials

It is also critical to consider precautions to prevent workers being struck by moving, flying or falling objects. Situations that increase the likelihood of this hazard are:

- Stacking raw materials, finished products (sacks and drums) too high.
- Use of damaged or unsuitable pallets.
- Overloading of materials on racking.
- Loose materials stacked at too steep an angle e.g. soil, grain or vegetables.

UNIT IGC2 - ELEMENT 1 - MOVEMENT OF PEOPLE AND VEHICLES - HAZARDS AND CONTROL

- Faulty or inappropriate means of lifting or lowering materials to the workplace.
- Unstable loads on vehicles - e.g. not correctly supported, tied or secured.
- Insecure components or work piece in moving machinery.
- Obstructed designated walkways.
- Products of machining processes not contained - e.g. metal shavings or waste material ejected such as scrap.
- Free dust from work processes or outside areas blown into the eyes of workers.

Figure 2-1-5: Obstructed designated walkway.   Source: ACT.

Figure 2-1-6: Falling materials i.e. unstable Stack. Source: ACT.

Striking against fixed or stationary objects

Whilst bumps and bruises are considered by many as "minor" injuries, they are painful and can be distressing for the sufferer. Therefore, the following situations should be avoided.

- Poorly sited machinery and furniture - avoid sharp corners protruding out.
- Insufficient space for storing tools and materials causing poor access in and out.
- Poor lighting.
- Work in enclosed areas.
- Walking into cranes or lifting devices with hanging hooks / slings.

CONDITIONS AND ENVIRONMENTS IN WHICH HAZARDS MAY ARISE

Conditions that promote hazards include

- Poor standards of housekeeping in the workplace. Allowing rubbish to accumulate also increases the risk of fire, and biological hazards from vermin / pests.
- Adverse weather conditions - e.g. high winds, rain, and snow.
- Outdoor working, warehouses where vehicles operate alongside workers or poorly laid out offices.
- Typical high risk work - maintenance, construction, demolition and excavating.
- Distribution centres, commercial vehicle depots, loading yards where fork lift trucks are used, freight and bus terminals.

Why accidents may occur on staircases

- Poor design of the staircase.
- Not using handrail (e.g. carrying).
- Slippery condition of the stairs (e.g. due to polish or water).
- Inadequate maintenance (e.g. worn or damaged stairs, tiles, carpets).
- Obstructions on the stairs (e.g. boxes of photocopy paper).
- Inadequate standards of lighting.
- Bad practice (carrying loads, inappropriate footwear, non-use of handrails or rushing).
- Too narrow for volume of workers using it.

Control strategies for pedestrian hazards

RISK ASSESSMENT

Some or all of the following issues might affect the hazards faced by pedestrians and should be considered when carrying out a risk assessment:

- Weather conditions - particularly snow and ice.
- Lighting - especially at night.
- Surfaces - the presence of holes to the floor or the presence of mud.
- Unusually high numbers of workers. Consider, for example, busy periods such as holiday sales in department stores causing large numbers of the public to be near streetworks and fluctuations in workloads which could lead to an influx of temporary workers.
- The effectiveness of existing controls - such as barriers.
- Unexpected movements of workers - such as shortcuts, entry into restricted areas, emergency evacuation.
- Special needs for certain groups of workers - such as disabled workers, young persons, pregnant women and elderly workers.

SLIP RESISTANT SURFACES

How slip and trip hazards in the workplace might be controlled:

- Improved work layout with designated walkways.
- Using high grip surface coating.
- Highlighting changes in level with hazard warning strips.
- Providing good lighting.
- Introducing procedures for reporting defects and for dealing with spillage.
- Ensuring high standards of housekeeping to keep floors clear of obstructions, debris or spillage.
- Roughened non-slip concrete walkways on site.
- High grip grit sheets on the edge of steps and stairs.
- Mats at entrance to buildings and cabins.

Design features and/or safe practices intended to reduce the risk of accidents on staircases used as internal pedestrian routes within work premises:

- Adequate width.
- The provision of handrails.
- The dimensions of treads and risers.
- The provision of landings.
- Special provisions for disabled persons.
- Possibility of using a lift as an alternative.
- Avoid the need to carry large or heavy items up or down stairs.
- Appropriate footwear - low heels.
- The provision of non-slip surfaces, together with reflective edging.
- Adequate lighting and effective maintenance.
- The removal of obstructions, with particular attention to escape routes.

Figure 2-1-7: Anti-slip flooring. Source: ACT.

Figure 2-1-8: Slip resistance surface on steps. Source: ACT.

SPILLAGE CONTROL AND DRAINAGE

A procedure for spillage response for hazardous liquids should include:

- Raise the alarm and inform emergency services and relevant authorities (e.g. fire and rescue service, water supply authority).
- Evacuate all personnel, seal off access from danger area (if safe to do so without personal risk).
- Quickly assess the nature and extent (if possible) of the incident.
- Do not approach the liquid if you do not know what it is.
- Raise first aid treatment for those who might have been affected.
- Provide a barrier or some other form of spillage containment such as sand or special granules to contain the spillage.
- Isolate any ignition sources.
- Keep workers away.
- For internal spills with no fire risk, ventilate by opening windows and closing doors, that is, ventilate the area but isolate the material.
- For external spills, cover drains to prevent the material going into drains and or watercourses. Do not wash spillage into drains.
- Issue appropriate personal protective equipment to those involved and competent in carrying out the procedure.
- Ensure safe disposal of the spilled substance and any absorbent material used.

DESIGNATED WALKWAYS

Walkways should be clearly marked and free of obstruction and maintenance. An important consideration when considering traffic systems is the safety interface between pedestrians and traffic. The routes that workers use should be clearly defined and marked. Every workplace shall be organised in such a way that pedestrian and vehicles can circulate in a safe manner.

The workplace may be some distance from the ground as with construction workers or several miles underground as with miners. Therefore, such things as approach roads, portable access equipment (ladders, etc.), and support of underground workings must be considered. Particular thought should be given to access and egress for emergency vehicles.

Control of hazards related to floors and gangways

Floors and traffic route surfaces must be constructed so that they are suitable for the purpose for which they are used. This means such things as having no holes or being slippery or uneven. Measures to control hazards related to floors and gangways may include:

- Kept clean and free from obstructions that may hinder passage.
- Good drainage in wet process areas or wet weather conditions.
- Suitable footwear or working platforms provided where necessary.
- Ramps kept dry and with non-skid surfaces.
- Level, even ground without holes or broken boards.
- Floor load capacities posted in lofts and storage areas.
- Salting/sanding and sweeping of outdoor routes during icy or frosty conditions.
- Steps, corners and fixed obstacles clearly marked.
- Excavations and chambers kept covered when not in use and the edges clearly marked.

FENCING AND GUARDING

Suitable and effective measures should be taken to prevent any person falling a distance likely to cause personal injury and any person from being struck by a falling object likely to cause personal injury.

Physical barriers should be erected to ensure that there is adequate protection for pedestrians who may be exposed to falls, falling objects and being struck by a moving object such as a vehicle.

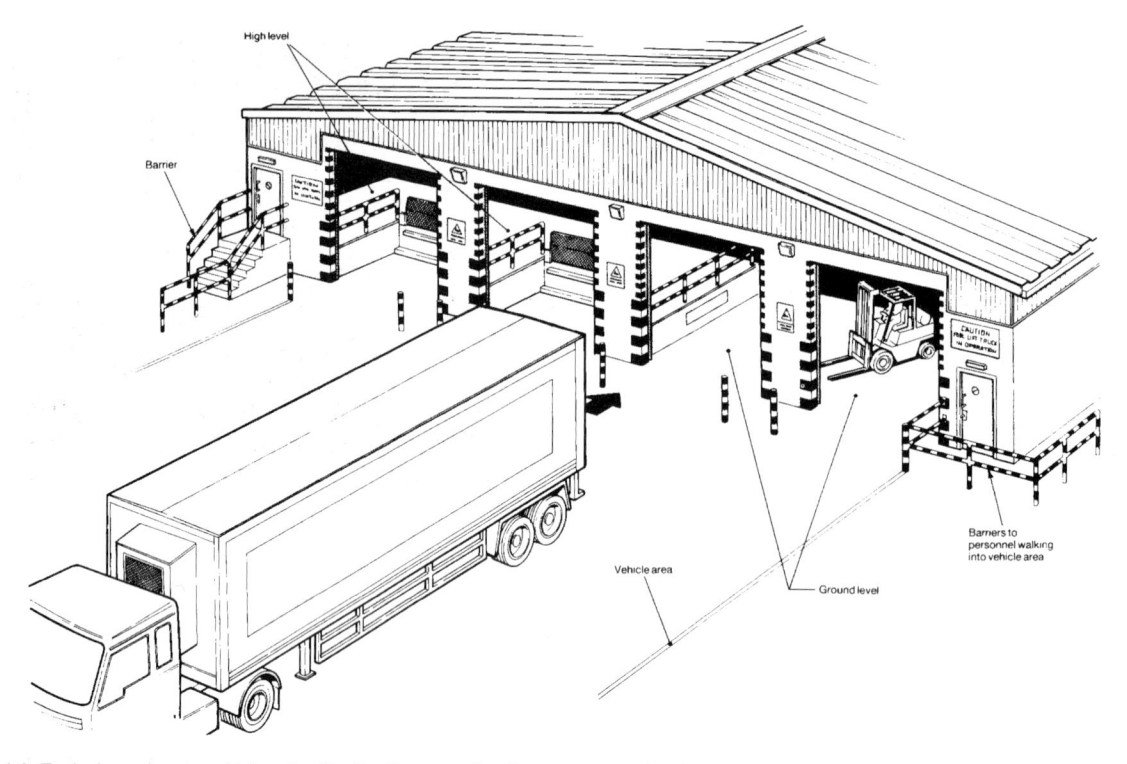

Figure 2-1-9: Typical warehouse vehicle unloading/loading area showing separate pedestrian access. *Source: HSG76.*

USE OF SIGNS AND PERSONAL PROTECTIVE EQUIPMENT

Signs must be clearly visible and be easily understood.

Safety signs should indicate the need to use personal protective equipment, such as hard hats, protective footwear or high visibility clothing, when entering certain work areas even if people are just visiting or passing quickly through. Signs to indicate the presence of a temporary hazard should be used to warn workers who might be affected to keep clear of that area. Hazard signs might be used where excavations are present, a change in height occurs or for the demarcation of a hazard area to assist with the provision of diversionary routes - for example, a vehicle unloading area where pedestrians are prohibited. Edges of steps, overhead obstructions and cables or pipes laid temporarily across walkways should also be clearly identified with hazard markings.

Suitable footwear is critical to avoid slips or trips or puncture wounds in the workplace. The risk assessment process should consider the possibility of slips, trips and sharp material hazards, and where the decided control of this hazard includes the use of specific footwear this should be arranged.

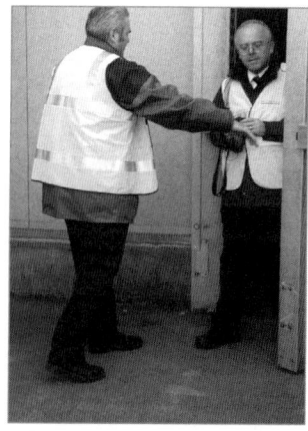

Figure 2-1-10: Correct clothing & footwear. *Source: ACT.*

On sites where vehicles operate and for streetworks it is essential that workers are able to be seen, therefore it is essential that high visibility clothing be used. Though this is not a substitute for the separation of vehicles from workers, for the many situations where workers work in close proximity to vehicles it will provide valuable assistance in preventing contact.

INFORMATION, INSTRUCTION, TRAINING AND SUPERVISION

The employer, through management, should ensure that rules, policies and procedures are followed and that workers do not act irresponsibly. Certain circumstances may require specific information, instruction and training, for example, procedures for climbing ladders or wearing appropriate clothing (e.g. high visibility jackets).

Employers must provide supervision as necessary. This means that the employer must actively supervise the workplace and the work conducted in it, for example, if high visibility clothing is required or walkways are to be kept clear this must be supervised. The concept requires the supervisor to increase the level of supervision on a needs basis, for example, the higher the risk related to the work or workplace hazard or the more persistent the problem, the greater is the supervision necessary. If a large number of the public are to use a route after it has been cleaned the supervisor should make a special effort to ensure that it is safe. If an obstruction of a walk route keeps returning, the supervisor will need to put in extra effort to bring it under control.

MAINTENANCE OF A SAFE WORKPLACE

Cleaning and housekeeping requirements

Maintenance of a safe workplace may be achieved through the development of a housekeeping procedure. Good housekeeping implies "a place for everything and everything in its place". Laid down procedures are necessary for preventing the spread of contamination, reducing the likelihood of accidents resulting in slips, trips, and falls and reducing the chances of unwanted fire caused by careless storage of flammable waste.

Access and egress

- Adequate space for easy movement, and safe plant or equipment use.
- No tripping hazards, e.g. trailing cables or pipes.
- Handholds or guardrails where workers might fall from floor edges.
- Emergency provision, e.g. life belts/jackets for work near water or means of escape from confined spaces.
- Neat and tidy storage of tools, plant and equipment so that they do not present a hazard to passers-by.
- Identify storage areas.
- Mark areas to be kept clear.
- Pay particular attention to emergency routes.
- Vision panels in doors to avoid contact injuries.
- Emergency provision, e.g. life belts/jackets for work near water; means of escape from freezer rooms.

Figure 2-1-11: Vision panels in fire doors. Source: ACT.

Work environment considerations

Heating

Workers can be exposed to a varying degree of conditions and resultant temperatures. The effects of excessive cold or heat can have harmful effects on their health and accidents can result due to fatigue or thermal stress. Areas should be provided to enable workers who work in cold environments to warm themselves.

When work in hot environments or in controlled systems is required, it will be necessary for workers to be acclimatised. Drinks and the provision of refuge from heat may be necessary to reduce body temperatures.

Where the temperatures cannot be maintained, for example, when working outside, areas should be provided to enable workers who work in cold environments to warm themselves. Practical measures and adequate protection must be provided against adverse conditions, for example, workers may be provided with a sheeted area to work in order to protect them from the rain and wind.

Lighting

Lighting plays an important part in health and safety. Factors to consider include:

- Good general illumination with no glare, especially where there are vehicle movements.
- Regular cleaning and maintenance of lights and windows.
- Local lighting for dangerous processes and to reduce eye strain and fatigue.
- No flickering from fluorescent tubes (it can be dangerous with some rotating machinery).
- Adequate emergency lighting which is regularly tested and maintained.
- Specially constructed fittings for flammable or explosive atmospheres e.g. where paint spraying work is carried out.
- Outside areas satisfactorily lit for work and access during hours of darkness - for security as well as safety.
- Light coloured wall finishes improving brightness, or darker colours to reduce glare, for example, arc welding flash.

Care should be taken, in particular where temporary lighting is rigged, to ensure that glare and shadows are minimised. Particular attention should be paid to changes in level, corners and where workers pass between the outside and inside of buildings when darkness occurs.

Factors to consider when assessing the adequacy of lighting within an open plan office:

- The types of task being undertaken (in particular the use of display screen equipment).
- The availability of natural light and emergency lighting, and the problems caused by glare.
- The effect of office layout (in terms of shadows cast, etc.) and the appropriateness of general lighting (its type, colour and intensity in relation to, for instance, the floor area), and the suitability and adjustability of local lighting in relation to specific tasks.

Suitable and sufficient lighting should be provided in order for workers to conduct their work safely. If there is a potential danger due to failure of artificial lighting then the provision of emergency lighting may be required. This would be particularly relevant where it was necessary for workers to move away from machinery or to take or use a complex route of exit.

Noise

Noise can produce a number of types of damage to the ear. Noise levels should be assessed and appropriate controls established. Noise can cause an environmental nuisance to surrounding areas, and can have negative effects on communities in general and wildlife. Controls implemented may include barriers and screens around site boundaries to contain noise produced, the use of equipment that produces lower noise levels and restrictions on operating times to reduce the nuisance dependant upon the sensitivity of the area.

Dust

Dust is a common hazard with many processes or operations and because it enters the atmosphere can easily escape past site boundaries and then have adverse effects on the environment. The health hazards associated with dusts can vary but usually result in an attack on the respiratory system on humans and other living creatures.

Dust can also present significant risk of eye injury and general discomfort. Other problems are layers of dust settling within the environment, causing damage to vegetation, wildlife habitats and private property. Activities creating dust include venting of processes, loading and off loading of open top vehicles and demolition.

The area where dust may be created can be watered down to minimise dust transfer into neighbouring premises. Stockpiles of material should be damped down or otherwise suitably treated to prevent the emission of dust from the site. Stockpiles should be planned and sited to minimise the potential for dust generation. The handling of material should be kept to a minimum and when deposited onto a stockpile it should be from the minimum possible height.

1.2 - Movement of vehicles

Hazards in vehicle operations

Many workers die each year because of works transport related accidents. There is also a high incidence of accidents causing serious injury, e.g. spinal damage, amputation and crush injuries. Very few accidents involving traffic result in minor injury. In addition, transport accidents cause damage to plant, infrastructure and vehicles.

TYPICAL HAZARDS CAUSING LOSS OF CONTROL AND OVERTURNING OF VEHICLES

Various circumstances that may cause such a vehicle to overturn are insecure and unstable loads, manoeuvring with the load elevated, colliding with kerbs and other obstructions, cornering at speed, braking harshly, driving on uneven or soft ground, and mechanical failure.

Possible causes of a dumper truck overturning
- Overloading or uneven loading of the bucket.
- Cornering at excessive speed.
- Hitting obstructions.
- Driving too close to the edges of embankments or excavations.
- Mechanical defects.
- Inappropriate tyre pressures.
- Driving across slopes.

Possible causes of a fork lift truck overturning
- Driving too fast.
- Sudden braking.
- Driving on slopes.
- Driving over debris.
- Under-inflated tyres.
- Driving over holes in floor, such as drains.
- Driving with load elevated.
- Overloading - exceeding maximum capacity.
- Collisions with buildings or other vehicles.
- Incorrect choices of fork lift truck type when used for the wrong application, e.g. the use of a warehouse truck in a rough terrain environment.

COLLISIONS WITH OTHER VEHICLES, PEDESTRIANS OR FIXED OBJECTS

Workers may unexpectedly appear from a part of a building structure or workers intent on the work they are doing may step away into a danger area from where they are working to collect materials or tools.

CONDITIONS AND ENVIRONMENTS IN WHICH EACH HAZARD MAY ARISE

Other factors are:
- Inadequate lighting.
- Inadequate direction signs.
- Inadequate signs or signals to identify the presence of vehicles.
- Drivers unfamiliar with site.
- Need to reverse.
- Poor visibility e.g. sharp bends, mirror / windscreen misted up.
- Poor identification of fixed objects e.g. overhead pipes, doorways, storage tanks, corners of buildings.
- Lack of separation of pedestrians and vehicles.
- Lack of safe crossing points on roads and vehicle routes.
- Lack of separate entrance / exit for vehicles and pedestrians.
- Pedestrians using doors provided for sole vehicle use.
- Lack of barriers to prevent pedestrians suddenly stepping from an exit/entrance into a vehicle's path.
- Poor maintenance of vehicles e.g. tyres or brakes.
- Excessive speed of vehicles.
- Lack of vehicle management e.g. use of traffic control, 'signaller'.
- Environmental conditions e.g. poor lighting, rain, snow or ice.

Figure 2-1-12: Collision - lack of vehicle management.   *Source: ACT.*

Figure 2-1-13: Risk of collision between people / vehicles.   *Source: ACT.*

Control strategies for safe vehicle operations

GENERAL SITE STRATEGIES
Design features of the vehicle intended to minimise the consequences of an overturn include rollover protection and seat belts. In addition, features designed to prevent overturning include the width of the wheelbase and the position of the centre of gravity of the vehicles.

RISK ASSESSMENT
The employer, through management, needs to consider the safe movement of vehicles and their loads as part of the overall safety policy. This includes the use of vehicles such as dumper trucks, lift trucks, and those used for delivery. Consideration should be given to the following.

SUITABILITY AND SUFFICIENCY OF TRAFFIC ROUTES
- Clearly marked and signed. These should incorporate speed limits, one way systems, priorities and other factors normal to public roads. Vehicles, which are visiting the premises, should be made aware of any local rules and conditions.
- Consideration should be given to adequate lighting on routes and particularly in loading/unloading and operating areas.
- Separate routes, designated crossing places and suitable barriers at recognised danger spots. As far as is practicable pedestrians should be kept clear of vehicle operating areas and/or a notice displayed warning pedestrians that they are entering an operating area.
- Clear direction signs and marking of storage areas and buildings can help to avoid unnecessary movement, such as reversing.
- Sharp bends and overhead obstructions should be avoided where possible. Hazards that cannot be removed should be clearly marked with black and yellow diagonal stripes i.e. loading bay edges, stacks, pits etc. If reasonably practicable barriers should be installed.
- Consideration to vehicle weight and height restriction on routes - signs, barriers and weight checks may be necessary.

MANAGEMENT OF VEHICLE MOVEMENTS
Many sites are complex in nature and require the careful management of vehicles in order to ensure that they are brought onto, move around and leave the site safely. Where materials are brought to site it may be necessary to manage deliveries to prevent too many vehicles arriving at the site at the same time causing them to back up into the public highway. Site security arrangements play a significant part in the management of vehicles on site and will assist with controlling vehicles so that they are routed correctly and safely. It is not uncommon for vehicles to be sent to a site that are too big or too heavy to access the roadways. Site security workers should be trained to identify these to prevent them accessing the site and causing harm.

Safe operation
- Appoint someone on site to be responsible for transport.
- Drivers properly trained.
- Ensure unauthorised workers are not allowed to drive.
- Make sure visiting drivers are aware of site rules.
- Check vehicles daily and have faults rectified promptly.
- Keep keys secure when vehicles are not in use.
- Ensure safe movements - particularly when reversing.
- Keep roadways/gangways properly maintained and lit.
- Separate vehicles and pedestrians where practicable.
- Use of horns before entering doorways or at blind corners.

Factors that should be taken into account when planning traffic routes for internal transport
- The purpose of the routes, the types of vehicle using the routes.
- The likely volume of traffic, the layout of the area.
- The possible need for one-way systems.
- Speed limits.
- Markings.
- Crossing points and signs.
- The importance of separating pedestrians and vehicles possibly by the use of physical barriers.
- Suitability of floors as well as environmental issues such as lighting levels and ventilation when diesel-powered transport is to be used inside a building.

ENVIRONMENTAL CONSIDERATIONS

Where vehicles operate, environmental conditions such as lighting and adverse weather will make a significant impact on their safe operation by affecting **visibility**. Where reasonably practicable a suitable standard of lighting must be maintained so that operators of vehicles can see to operate and their vehicle can be seen by others. It is critical to avoid areas of glare or shadow that could mask the presence of a person or vehicle. Similarly if vehicles travel from within buildings to the outside it is critical that the light level is maintained at a roughly even level in order to give the driver's eyes time to adjust to the change in light. Fixed structure hazards should be made as visible as possible with additional lighting and/or reflective strips.

Roads, gangways and aisles should have sufficient width and overhead clearance for the largest vehicle. Attention should be paid to areas where they might meet other traffic, e.g. the entrance to the site. If ramps (sleeping policemen) are used a by-pass for trolleys and shallow draft vehicles should be provided. A one-way traffic system should be considered to reduce the risk of collision.

Gradients and changes in ground level, such as ramps, represent a specific hazard to plant and vehicle operation. Vehicles have a limit of stability dependent on loading and their wheelbase. These conditions could put them at risk of overturning or cause damage to articulated vehicle couplings. Any gradient in a vehicle operating area should be kept as gentle as possible.

Where **changes in level** are at an edge that a vehicle might approach, and there is risk of falling, it must be provided with a robust barrier or similar means to demarcate the edge. Particular care must be taken at points where loading and unloading is conducted.

In some workplaces, such as factories or chemical plants, process products may contaminate the **surface condition** of the road making it difficult for vehicles to brake effectively.

It is critical to have a programme that anticipates this with regular cleaning or renewal of the surface as well as means of dealing with spills. The floor surface should be in good condition, free of litter and obstructions.

Excessive background noise levels can mask the sound of vehicles working in the area; additional visual warning e.g. flashing lights should be used. Sufficient and suitable parking areas should be provided away from the main work area and located where the risk of unauthorised use of the vehicles will be reduced.

MAINTENANCE OF VEHICLES

All vehicles should be well maintained and 'roadworthy' with a formal system of checks and maintenance in place. A vehicle, such as one used for moving trailers in a transport yard, that does not usually go outside the site would be expected to be kept to the same good standard as one that was used on public roads for such critical items as tyres and brakes. Vehicle maintenance should be planned for at regular intervals and vehicles taken out of use if critical items are at an acceptable standard. In addition, it is critical to conduct a pre-use check of the vehicle. This is usually done by the driver as part of their taking it over for a period of use such as a work shift or day. This would identify the condition of critical items and provide a formal system to identify and consider problems that may affect the safety of the vehicle. If there is no nominated driver and the vehicle is for general use someone should be nominated to make these checks. A record book or card would usually be used to record the checks and the findings.

DRIVER PROTECTION AND RESTRAINT SYSTEMS

In many work vehicle accidents the driver is injured because the vehicle does not offer protection when it rolls over or it does not restrain the driver to prevent them falling out of the vehicle and being injured by the fall or the vehicle falling on them. Vehicles such as dumper trucks, road rollers and forklift trucks are examples of equipment that may present this risk. New equipment must be provided with protection and restraint systems, where relevant.

Figure 2-1-14: Roll bar and seat restraint.   *Source: ACT.*

Figure 2-1-15: Falling materials.   *Source: ACT.*

Protection from falling materials

There is a risk of material falling on a vehicle driver where the vehicle is used to provide materials at a height or to remove materials from delivery vehicles. It is critical that suitable protection of the driver be provided by the structure of the vehicle. Protection should also be provided where vehicles work in close proximity to areas where there is a risk from falling materials. This may be by the provision of a frame and mesh above it or by the provision of a totally enclosing cab. Safety helmets alone are unlikely to provide sufficient protection but may be a useful addition where a mesh structure is provided.

SEGREGATING PEDESTRIANS AND VEHICLES

Means of segregation

Clearly defined and marked routes should be provided for workers going about their business at work. These should be provided for access and egress points to the workplace, car parks, and vehicle delivery routes. Safe crossing places should be provided where people have to cross main traffic routes. In buildings where vehicles operate, separate doors and walkways should be provided for pedestrians to get from building to building. Meshed handrails can be used to channel people into the pedestrian route. Where it is not possible to have a pedestrian route with a safe clearance from vehicle movement, because of building and plant design, then a raised pedestrian walkway could be considered to help in segregation.

Figure 2-1-16: Segregating pedestrians & vehicles. *Source: ACT.*

- Accidents can be caused where vehicles are unsafely parked as they can be an obstruction and restrict visibility. There should be clear entrance and exit routes in parking areas and designated parking areas to allow the load and sheeting of outgoing transport to be checked safely before leaving the site.
- There should be clear, well-marked and signposted vehicle traffic routes, which avoid steep gradients where possible, especially where fork lift trucks operate. It is critical to have speed limits that are practicable and effective. Speed limit signs should be posted and traffic slowing measures such as speed bumps and ramps may be necessary in certain situations. Monitoring speed limit compliance is necessary, along with some kind of action against persistent offenders.
- Speed limits of 10 or 15 mph are usually considered appropriate, although 5 mph may be necessary in certain situations.
- Transport requires clear routes to be designated, marked with painted lines and preferably fenced off from pedestrians. Accidents can occur when plant and people collide: the pedestrian may be injured by contact and the driver injured if the vehicle overturns.
- Separate gates/doorways should be provided for vehicles' entry, and blind spots (where vision of the driver / pedestrian is restricted) should be dealt with by the careful positioning of mirrors on walls, plant or storage. Routes should be wide enough to allow manoeuvrability and passing.
- Where it is unavoidable that pedestrians will come into proximity with transport, people should be reminded of the hazards by briefings, site induction and signs, so they are aware at all times.

Any traffic route which is used by both pedestrians and vehicles should be wide enough to enable any vehicle likely to use the route to pass pedestrians safely. Where it is not practical to make the route wide enough, passing places or traffic management systems should be provided as necessary. In buildings, lines should be drawn on the floor to indicate routes followed by vehicles such as fork lift trucks.

On routes used by automatic, driverless vehicles that are also used by pedestrians, steps should be taken to ensure that vehicles do not trap pedestrians. The vehicles should be fitted with safeguards to minimize the risk of injury, sufficient clearance should be provided between the vehicles and pedestrians, and care should be taken that fixtures along the route do not create trapping hazards.

MEASURES TO BE TAKEN WHEN SEGREGATION IS NOT PRACTICABLE

Where pedestrians and vehicle routes cross, appropriate crossing points should be provided and used. Where necessary, barriers or rails should be provided to prevent pedestrians crossing at particularly dangerous points and to guide them to designated crossing places. At crossing places where volumes of traffic are particularly heavy, the provision of suitable bridges or subways should be considered. At crossing points there should be adequate visibility and open space for the pedestrian where the pedestrian route joins the vehicle route.

Where segregation is not practicable and vehicles share the same workplace as pedestrians it is critical to mark the work areas as being separate from vehicle routes to warn drivers to adjust their approach and be more aware of pedestrians. Audible and visual warnings of the presence of the vehicle would also assist. Where vehicles are dominant but pedestrians need to access, similar means may be used but for the opposite reason. In this situation the added use of personal protective equipment that increases the ability to see the pedestrian, and safety footwear, are usually needed. High visibility clothing is mandatory on the majority of construction projects. The reversing of large vehicles that have a restricted view should be controlled by the use of a signaller to guide them.

Figure 2-1-17 No segregation - high visibility clothing. *Source: ACT.*

Figure 2-1-18: Control of vehicle movement. *Source: ACT.*

Summary of methods
- Defined traffic routes.
- One-way systems.
- Provision of refuges.
- Speed control.
- Mirrors / cameras.
- Good lighting.
- High visibility clothing.
- A good standard of housekeeping.
- Audible warnings on vehicles.
- Training and supervision of drivers.
- Drawing up and enforcement of site rules.

PROTECTIVE MEASURES FOR PEOPLE AND STRUCTURES

It is critical to anticipate that drivers of vehicles might misjudge a situation and collide with structures whilst operating. For this reason vulnerable plant and parts of the building should be provided with barriers that continuously surround the plant or alternatively posts can be provided at key positions. Clearly, critical plant and structures that are at the same level of the vehicle should be protected. Care should also be taken of structures at a height, such as a pipe bridge, roof truss or door lintel. All of these could be damaged by tall vehicles or those that have tipping mechanisms that raise their effective height. Though it may not always be possible to protect all structures, such as a doorway, it is critical to apply **markings** to make them more visible. In addition, **signs** warning of overhead structures or the presence of vehicles in the area will help increase awareness and avoid collisions. There is a need to alert people to the hazard when working in or near a vehicle operating area. Signs might help and these can be supplemented by **visual and audible warning systems** that confirm the presence of the vehicle. These may be operated by the driver, such as a horn on a dumper truck or automatically, such as an audible reversing signal on a large road vehicle. Visibility can be improved by mounting mirrors or other suitable visual aides at strategic points. Consideration should be given to the provision of protective clothing - boots, helmets and high visibility clothing - for personnel working within areas where vehicles operate.

Barriers

Moving vehicles, and in particular large plant, have high impact energy when they are in contact with structures or people. It is essential that vehicles be separated from vulnerable people and structures. Because of the high energy involved the barrier used must reflect the type of thing in contact with it. If it is only people that might contact it a simple portable barrier may be adequate, but if it is heavy plant robust barriers including concrete structures may need to be considered. It is critical to identify vulnerable locations that warrant protection, for example storage tanks or bund walls.

Markings

Any structure that represents a height or width restriction should be readily identified for people and vehicle drivers. This will include low beams or doorways, pipe bridges and protruding scaffolds and edges where a risk of falling exists. These markings may be by means of attaching hazard tape or painting the structure to highlight the hazard.

Signs

Signs should be used to provide information, such as height restrictions, and to warn of hazards on site. Signs may direct vehicles around workers at a safe distance.

Figure 2-1-19: Barriers and markings. *Source: ACT.*

Figure 2-1-20: Visual warning on a dumper truck. *Source: ACT.*

Warnings on vehicles

Warnings may be audible or visual or a combination of each. They are used to warn that the vehicle is operating in the area, such as a flashing light on the top of a dumper truck or to warn of a specific movement, such as an audible warning that a large vehicle is reversing. These are designed to alert workers in the area in order that they can place themselves in a position of safety. They do not provide the driver with authority to reverse the vehicle or to proceed in a work area without caution.

Measures to prevent accidents when pedestrians work in vehicle manoeuvring areas
- Segregated systems for vehicular and pedestrian traffic (barriers, separate doors).
- Maintaining good visibility (mirrors, transparent doors, provision of lighting, vehicle reversing cameras).
- Signs indicating where vehicles operate in this area.
- Audible warnings on vehicles and sometimes flashing lights on vehicles.
- Establish and enforcement of site rules.
- The provision of refuges.
- The wearing of high-visibility clothing.
- A good standard of housekeeping.
- Training for, and supervision of, all concerned, competency certificates, refresher training, trained banksmen to direct cranes.
- Provision of parking areas.
- Provision of suitable battery charging or refuelling areas if necessary.
- Careful design of traffic routes.
- Maintenance of traffic routes.
- Traffic control e.g. identification of "no go" areas.

PRECAUTIONARY MEASURES FOR REVERSING VEHICLES WITHIN A WORKPLACE
- Separation of vehicles and pedestrians.
- Warning signs.
- Audible alarms / vehicle cameras.
- Space to allow good visibility / mirrors / refuges / lighting.
- Appropriate site rules adequately enforced.
- Procedural measures such as the use of trained signallers.
- Avoiding the need for vehicles to reverse (by the use of one-way and 'drive-through' systems or turning circles).

SITE RULES

It is critical to establish clear and well understood site rules regarding vehicle operations. These may have to be communicated to drivers by security workers at the time they visit the site. They would often stipulate where the driver should be whilst vehicles are being loaded, where the keys to the vehicle should be, not reversing without permission and what access they have to areas of the site for such things as refreshment. Pedestrians should also know what the site rules are in order to keep themselves safe. Site rules for pedestrians might include such things as using pedestrian exits/entrances or crossing points, not entering hazardous areas or the need to wear personal protective equipment in hazardous areas, and not walking behind a reversing vehicle. Where sites are made up of or join a highway, such as carriageway repairs on a motorway, it is critical to identify who has priority - the vehicle or the worker. Site rules may clarify that once the site boundary is crossed the worker has priority - this has to be clear. The site rules may be reinforced by the provision of additional signs to clarify a speed limit and the nature of the priority of workers. In certain industries, such as the construction industry, it is common practice for a traffic management plan to be devised and displayed in key locations at a construction site. During induction and at each signing in event all workers will sign to say that they have read and understood the traffic management plan which is initially emphasised at the induction stage. The plan will need to be reviewed and updated before the traffic route is to be changed.

SELECTION AND TRAINING OF DRIVERS

Only authorised persons should be permitted to operate plant or vehicles after they have been selected, trained and authorised to do so, or are undergoing properly organised formal training, under supervision.

Selection

The safe usage of plant and vehicles calls for a reasonable physical and mental fitness. The selection procedure should be devised to identify workers who have been shown to be reliable and mature enough to perform their work responsibly and carefully. To avoid wasteful training for workers who lack co-ordination and ability to learn, selection tests should be used.

Consideration must be given to any legal age restrictions that apply to vehicles that operate on the public road. A similar approach may be adopted for similar vehicles used on site though the local law may not be specific on age limitations in such cases.

Potential operators should be medically examined prior to employment/training in order to assess the individual's physical ability to cope with this type of work. They should also be examined every five years in middle age and after sickness or accident.
Points to be considered are:

a) General - Normal agility, having full movement of trunk, neck and limbs.

b) Vision - Good eyesight is critical, as operators are required to have good judgement of space and distance.

c) Hearing - The ability to hear instructions and warning signals with each ear is critical.

Training

It is essential that immediate supervisors receive training in the safe operation of plant and vehicles and that senior management appreciates the risks resulting from the interaction of vehicles and the workplace.

For the operator/driver, safety must constitute an integral part of the skill-training programme and not be treated as a separate subject. The operator/driver should be trained to a level consistent with efficient operation and care for the safety of themselves and other persons. On completion of training they should be issued with a company authority to drive and a record of all basic training, refresher training and tests maintained in the individual's personal documents file. Certification of training by other organisations must be checked. Training should be in accordance with local standards where appropriate.

MANAGEMENT SYSTEMS FOR ASSURING DRIVER COMPETENCE

The trained operator/driver

It should not be assumed that workers who join as trained operators/drivers have received adequate training to operate safely in their new company. The management must ensure that they have the basic skills and receive training in company methods and procedures for the type of work they are to undertake. They should be examined and tested before issue of company driving authority.

Testing

On completion of training, the operator/driver should be examined and tested to ensure that he/she has achieved the required standard. It is recommended that at set intervals or when there is indication of the operator/driver not working to required standards, or following an accident, formal check tests be introduced.

Refresher training

If high standards are to be maintained, periodic refresher training and testing should be considered. A vigorous management policy covering operator training, plant maintenance and sound systems of work, supported by good supervision will reduce personal injury and damage to equipment and materials. This in turn will lead to better vehicle utilisation and increased materials handling efficiency.

Operator/driver identification

Many organisations operate local codes of practice and take great care to evidence the authority they have given to operators/drivers by the provision of a licence for that vehicle and sometimes a visible badge to confirm this. Access to vehicles is supervised and authority checked carefully to confirm that the actual class of vehicle is within the authority given. This is critical with such things as rough terrain lift trucks that operate differently to a standard counterbalance truck. It is essential that access to keys for vehicles is restricted to those that are competent to operate/drive them; this is not just a practical point but enables compliance with local codes of practice.

Element 2

Manual and mechanical handling - hazards and control

Learning outcomes

On completion of this element, candidates should be able to demonstrate understanding of the content through the application of knowledge to familiar and unfamiliar situations. In particular they should be able to:

2.1 Describe the hazards and the risk factors which should be considered when assessing risks from manual handling activities.

2.2 Suggest ways of minimising manual handling risk.

2.3 Identify the hazards and explain the precautions and procedures to ensure safety in the use of lifting and moving equipment with specific reference to fork-lift trucks, manually operated load moving equipment (sack trucks, pallet trucks), lifts, hoists, conveyors and cranes.

Content

2.1 - Manual handling hazards and risks	115
Common types of manual handling hazards and injuries	115
The assessment of manual handling risks	115
2.2 - Minimising manual handling risks	117
Means of minimising the risks from manual handling	117
Techniques for manually lifting loads	121
2.3 - Safety in the use of lifting and moving equipment	122
Forklift trucks	122
Manually operated load moving equipment hazards	125
Lifts and hoists	126
Conveyors	126
Cranes	128
Requirements for lifting operations	130
The need for periodic examination / testing of lifting equipment	133

Sources of reference

ISO 12100 - 1: 2003, Safety of machinery, basic concepts, general principles for design, basic terminology, methodology ISBN 0-580-42922-9

ISO 12100 - 2: 2003, Safety of machinery, basic concepts, general concepts, general principles for design, technical principles ISBN 0-580-42923-7

Manual Handling (Guidance) (L23), HSE Books ISBN 0-7176-2414-3

Safety in Working with Lift Trucks (HSG6), HSE Books ISBN 0-7176-1781-5

Safe Use of Lifting Equipment (L113), HSE Books ISBN 0-7176-1628-2

MANUAL AND MECHANICAL HANDLING - HAZARDS AND CONTROL - ELEMENT 2 - UNIT IGC2

2.1 - Manual handling hazards and risks

Common types of manual handling hazards and injuries

Commonly, around 25% of all workplace injuries have been attributed to the manual lifting and handling of loads. The injuries arise from such **hazards** as stooping while lifting, holding the load away from the body, twisting movements, frequent or prolonged effort, heavy / bulky / unwieldy / unstable loads, sharp / hot / slippery surfaces of loads, space constraints, and lack of capability of the individual.

Manual handling operations can cause many types of **injury**. The most common injuries are:

- Rupture of intervertebral discs ('slipped disc') in the lower spine.
- Muscle strain and sprain.
- Tendons and ligaments can also be over-stretched and torn.
- Rupture of a section of the abdominal wall can cause a hernia.
- Loads with sharp edges can cause cuts.
- Dropped loads can result in bruises, fractures and crushing injuries.

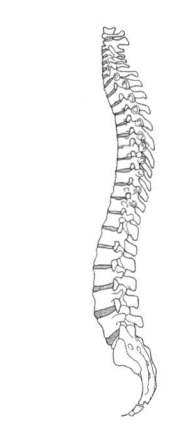

Figure 2-2-1: Manual handling - Spine. *Source: ACT*

The assessment of manual handling risks

FACTORS TO CONSIDER

Four factors to which the employer must have regard, and questions he must consider, when making an assessment of manual handling operations are:

- **L** oad.
- **I** ndividual Capability.
- **T** ask.
- **E** nvironment.

Each factor in turn should be assessed to determine whether there is a risk of injury. When this has been completed the information can then be processed giving a **total** risk assessment.

FACTORS	QUESTIONS	Level of Risk: High	Med	Low
Load	Is it: ■ Heavy? ■ Bulky or Unwieldy? ■ Difficult to grasp? ■ Unstable, or with contents likely to shift? ■ Sharp, hot or otherwise potentially damaging?			
Individual Capability	Does the job: ■ Require unusual strength, height, etc.? ■ Create a hazard to those who have a health problem? ■ Require special knowledge or training for its safe performance?			

Task	Does it involve:
	■ Holding load at distance from central body area?
	■ Unsatisfactory bodily movement or posture?
	  • Twisting the central body area.
	  • Stooping.
	■ Excessive movement of load?
	  • Excessive lifting or lowering distances.
	  • Excessive pushing or pulling distances.
	  • Risk of sudden movement of load.
	  • Frequent or prolonged physical effort.
	  • Insufficient rest or recovery periods.			

Working Environment	Are there: ■ Space constraints preventing good posture? ■ Uneven, slippery or unstable floors? ■ Variations in level of floors or work surfaces? ■ Extremes of temperature, humidity or air movement? ■ Poor lighting conditions?			

Figure 2-2-2: Sample manual handling risk assessment form. *Source: HSE Guidance L23.*

The detailed consideration of each factor is necessary to achieve a suitable and sufficient risk assessment. The process of risk assessing includes observing the task as it is actually done; recording the factors that contribute to risk; assessing the level of risk that each factor represents (taking account of the circumstances and controls in place); and considering if the risks are different at different times and for different workers. The following considerations are offered to assist in making a risk assessment.

The Load

- Consideration should be given to reducing the weight although this may mean increasing the frequency of handling.
- If there is a great variety of weight to be handled it may be possible to sort the loads into weight categories so that precautions can be applied selectively.
- Where the size, surface texture or nature of a load makes it difficult to grasp, consideration should be given to the provision of handles, hand grips, indents etc. to improve the grasp.
- Loads in packages should be such that they cannot shift unexpectedly while being handled.
- Any loads to be handled should not have sharp corners, jagged edges, rough, very hot or very cold surfaces and the like.
- Good practice would include Information on the load packaging to give a general indication of the weight and nature of the loads to be handled should form part of any basic training, so that workers have sufficient information to carry out the operations they are likely to be asked to do.

Figure 2-2-3: Manual handling. Source: ACT.

Individual capability

- The individual's state of health, fitness, height and strength can significantly affect the ability to perform a task safely.
- An individual's physical capacity can also be age-related, typically climbing until the early 20's and declining gradually from the mid 40's. A key high risk group would be expectant mothers or workers with disabilities.
- It is clear then that an individual's condition and age could significantly affect the ability to perform a task safely.

The Task

- Ensure work and components in regular use are stored at waist height. Storage above or below this height should be used for lighter or less frequently used items.
- Layout changes should avoid the necessity for frequent bending, twisting, stooping, reaching, etc. and the lessening of any travel distances.
- Pay attention to the work routine i.e. fixed postures dictated by sustained holding or supporting loads, frequency of handling loads, with particular emphasis on heavy and awkward loads.
- Fixed breaks are generally less effective than those taken voluntary within the constraints of the work organisation.
- Handling while seated also requires careful consideration. Use of the powerful leg muscles is precluded and the weight of the handler's body cannot be used as a counterbalance. For these reasons, the loads that can be handled in safety by a person who is seated are substantially less than can be dealt with while standing.
- In general if a load can be lifted and lowered, it can also be carried without endangering the back. However, if a load is carried for an excessive distance, physical stresses are prolonged, leading to fatigue and increased risk of injury. As a rough guide if a load is carried further than about 10M then the physical demands of carrying the load will tend to predominate over those of lifting and lowering and individual capability will be reduced.

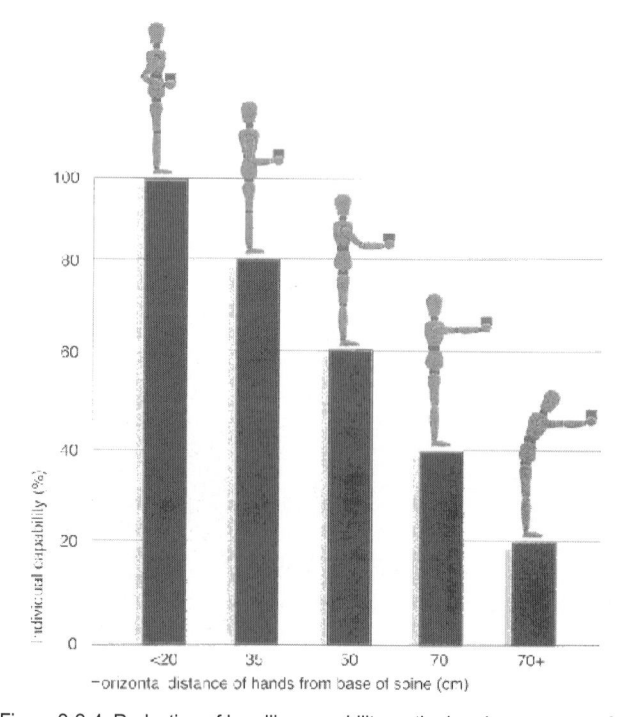

Figure 2-2-4: Reduction of handling capability as the hands move away from the central body area. Source: HSE Guidance L23.

- Be aware of pushing or pulling activities as they are usually introduced as a way of reducing manual handling, for example, eliminating carrying by loading goods onto a trolley. However, lifting, lowering and carrying, pushing or pulling a load can harm the handler.
- When a rate of work is imposed by a process, mild fatigue which might otherwise quickly be relieved by a short pause or a brief spell doing another operation using different muscles, can soon become more pronounced, leading to an increased risk of injury.
- Regardless of the handling techniques used, not keeping the load close to the body will increase the stress. As a rough guide holding a load at arms length imposes about five times the stress experienced when holding the same load very close to the central body area.
- Team handling could be a solution for some tasks that are beyond the capability of one person. However team handling can create additional problems. The proportion of the load carried by each member of the team will vary; therefore, the load that can be handled in safety will be less than the sum of the loads with which an individual could cope.

The working Environment

- Adequate gangways, space and working area should be provided in order to allow room to manoeuvre during handling.
- Lack of headroom could cause stooping and constrictions caused by a poor workstation, adjacent machinery, for example, should also be avoided.
- Floors which are uneven slippery and unstable should be well- maintained i.e. spillages of water, oil soap, food scraps and other substances likely to make the floor slippery should be cleared away promptly.
- When working with weather conditions such as extreme temperatures, high humidity, or gusts of wind the worker should be protected as the risk of injury during manual handling will be increased by extreme thermal conditions. For example, high temperatures or humidity can cause rapid fatigue, and perspiration on the hands may reduce grip. Work at low temperatures may impair dexterity. Any gloves and other protective clothing which may be necessary may also hinder movement, impair dexterity and reduce grip. The influence of air movement on working temperatures - the wind chill factor - should also be considered. Additional strong air movements and gusts of wind can make large loads more difficult to manage safely.
- Whenever possible all manual handling tasks should be carried out on a single level. If tasks are to be carried out on more than one level, access should preferably be by a gentle slope, or failing that, properly positioned and well maintained stairs/steps. Steep slopes should be avoided.
- Workbenches should be of a uniform height, thus reducing the need for raising or lowering loads.
- Finally, look at the general working environment. A comfortable working environment (e.g. heating, ventilating and lighting) will help to reduce the risk of injury.

REVIEWING ASSESSMENTS

The assessment should be kept up to date. It should be reviewed whenever there is a reason to suppose that it is no longer valid, for example, because the working conditions or the personnel carrying out the operations have changed. It should also be reviewed whenever there has been a significant change in the manual handling operations, for example, affecting the nature of the task or load.

2.2 - Minimising manual handling risks

Means of minimising the risks from manual handling

GENERAL APPROACH

Practical measures that can be taken to reduce the risk of injury can also be based on **LITE**. For example:

Load	Changing the load by lightening, reducing in size, provision of handles, elimination of sharp edges etc.
Individual	Address the individual factors such as selection, provision of information and training, provision of appropriate protective equipment and clothing.
Task	Redesign the task so that manual handling is eliminated or reduced by mechanisation, reducing carrying distances, team lifting, job rotation, etc.
Environment	Improving the working environment e.g. optimum heights of surfaces, improving floor conditions, increasing workspace, improving lighting, avoidance of changes in floor level etc.

MINIMISING THE RISK FROM MANUAL HANDLING

Each manual handling operation should be examined and appropriate steps taken to minimise the risk of injury to the lowest level reasonably practicable in order to eliminate the potential of Musculoskeletal Disorder (MSD) degeneration, for example, bad backs, bone, muscle and tissue injury. Wherever reasonably practicable, manual handling should be replaced or reduced by using mechanical handling aids, examples of which are shown below.

Mechanical assistance

This involves the use of handling aids. Although this may retain some elements of manual handling, bodily forces are applied more efficiently.

Examples are:

Levers	Reduces bodily force to move a load. Can avoid trapping fingers.
Hoists	Can support weights, allowing handler to position load.
Trolley, sack truck, truck roller or hoist	Reduces effort to move loads horizontally.
Chutes	A way of using gravity to move loads from one place to another.
Handling devices	Hand-held hooks or suction pads can help when handling a load that is difficult to grasp.

Figure 2-2-5: Mechanical assistance. Source: ACT.

Ergonomic approach (human physical and mental ability)

Emphasis must be given to all the factors involved in manual handling operations, task, load, working environment and individual capability. This should be carried out with a view to fitting the operation to the individual rather than the other way round.

Involving the workforce

Effort should be made to seek contributions from workers and, where applicable, safety representatives or representatives of employee safety.

Training

Employers should ensure that all workers who carry out manual handling operations receive the necessary training to enable them to carry out the task in a safe manner.

A training programme should include:

- How potentially hazardous loads may be recognised.
- How to deal with unfamiliar loads.
- The proper use of handling aids.
- The proper use of personal protective equipment.
- Features of the working environments that contribute to safety.
- The importance of good housekeeping.
- Factors affecting individual capability.
- Good handling techniques.

It should always be remembered that training is not a "one off remedy". For training to be effective it should be on-going to reflect improved techniques developed by experienced workers and be supported by periodic refresher training and supervision.

DESIGN, AUTOMATION / MECHANISATION

Workplace and workstation design

The layout should suit the employee and there should be adequate room to perform the task safely. In general, working levels should be waist high with tools, plant and equipment to be handled, placed in front of the employee and within easy reach. Tools should be appropriate and well designed.

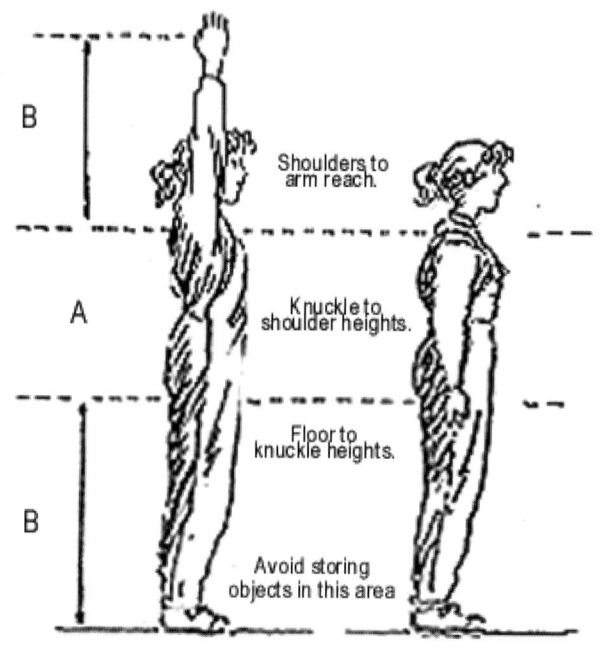

Figure 2-2-6: Frequently used objects should be stored in the 'A' zone. *Source: www.comcare.gov.au.*

Consider if the workplace:

- Suits the employee.
- Has adequate space.
- Work heights are matched or adjustable.
- Has back support and leg room.

Prevent excessive bending of the back

Many jobs have combinations of risky movements. For example, loading a machine from a bin on the floor combines sidestepping, twisting, low lifting and reaching.

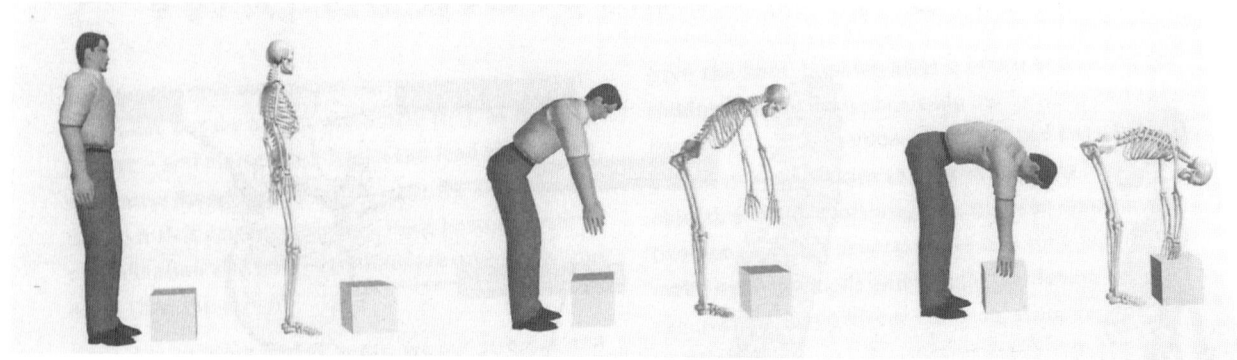

Figure 2-2-7: Kinetic lifting - How not to do it! *Source: Ambiguous.*

Figure 2-2-8: Kinetic lifting - How not to do it! Source: Manual handling, major workplace hazards, Government of South Australia.

The above figures show how **not** to lift a load. As for the second image it is better to redesign by changing the work layout and providing a spring loaded table to minimise extreme bending.

Remember:

- Pulling is more efficient than pushing where body weight is used.
- Pulling up is stronger than pushing down when standing.
- Pulling/pushing is more efficient if applied at or around waist level.
- Pulling/pushing capacity is significantly reduced when the limbs are in extreme positions.
- Controls requiring large forces should be operated by foot or by power aided hand controls.

- Precision Work: bench just above elbow height.
- Light Work: bench just below elbow height.
- Heavy Work: bench near hip height.

This prevents workers having to sustain a bent back posture greater than 20 degrees.

Work surface heights should be appropriate to the job and the individual employee. In an employee-shared work area it is advisable to have work benches at more than one height or provide adjustable benches.

Figure 2-2-9: Work bench heights. Source: www.comcare.gov.au.

Figure 2-2-10: Work bench heights. Source: www.comcare.gov.au.

Avoid twisting or side bending of the spine.

Twisting and side bending or the combination of the two are considered to be particularly bad for the spine. You can eliminate these movements by moving the load closer and placing it directly in front of the employee.

MECHANICAL AIDS

Manual handling aids or equipment can be introduced if redesign is not possible or as a short term/temporary measure. Such equipment reduces the risk by replacing the employee as the main source of force in the manual handling task. Forklift trucks, cranes and conveyors are all examples of mechanical aids or equipment.

Figure 2-2-11: Using a forklift to move a drum eliminates the Manual Handling required. *Source: www.comcare.gov.au.*

Figure 2-2-12: An electrically operated vacuum lifter eliminates the heavy lifting. The mechanical arm is guided by the employee.

Figure 2-2-13: Ingredients can be put into a hopper then lifted by a hoist.

Source: www.comcare.gov.au.

Techniques for manually lifting loads

LIFTING TECHNIQUES USING KINETIC HANDLING PRINCIPLES

In order to avoid musculoskeletal disorders due to lifting, poor posture and repetitive awkward loads it is critical to use recognised techniques. Many of these techniques use a kinetic handling approach, which seeks to use the body's natural movement to the advantage of lifting.

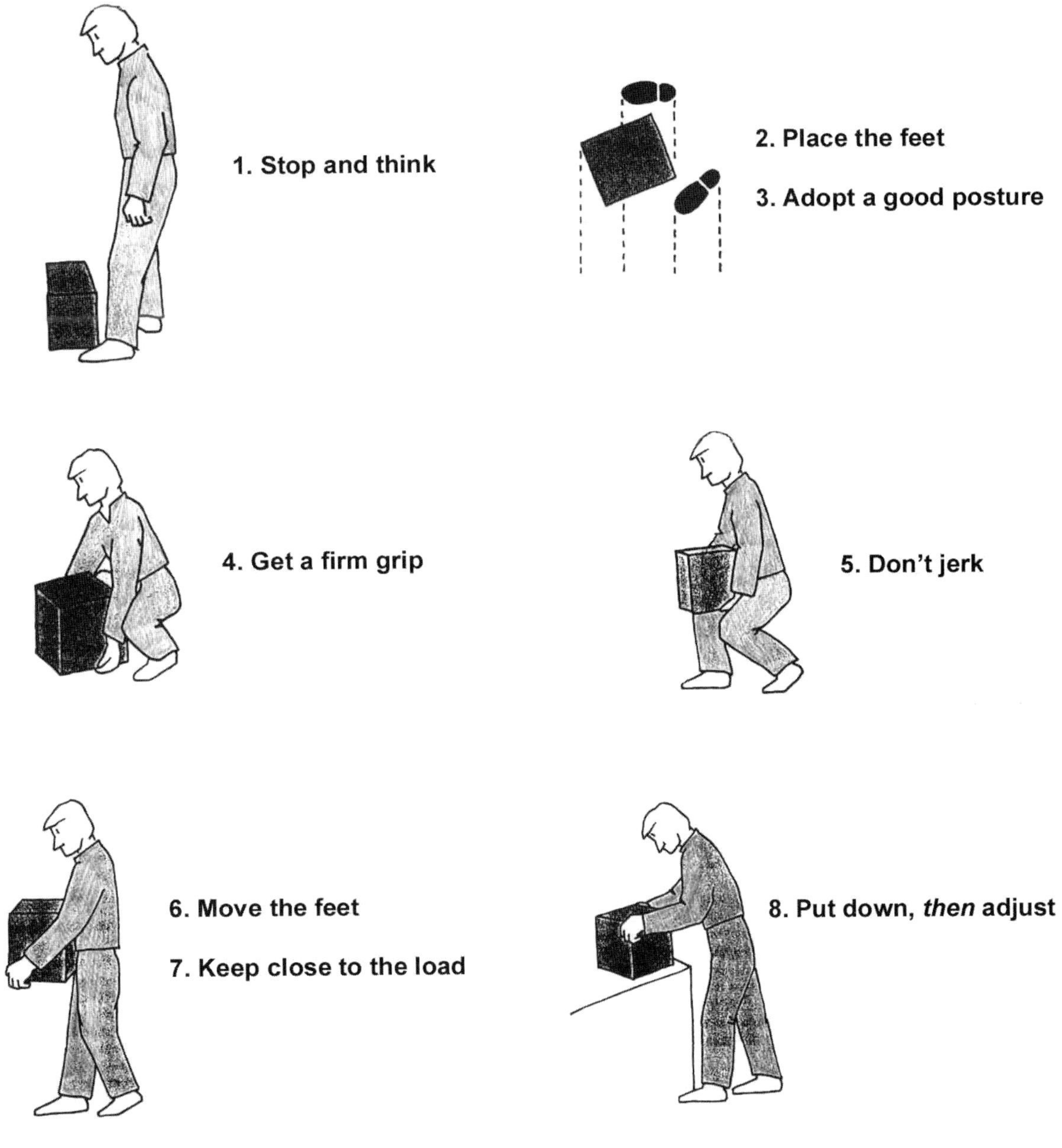

1. Stop and think
2. Place the feet
3. Adopt a good posture
4. Get a firm grip
5. Don't jerk
6. Move the feet
7. Keep close to the load
8. Put down, *then* adjust

Figure 2-2-14: Basic lifting principles.

Source: Ambiguous.

Putting it all into practice

a) Begin with the **load between the feet**, the leading foot should be in line with the side of the load, pointing in the direction of movement.

b) Bend your knees, tuck your chin in **and keep your back straight** (not vertical).

c) Generally grip the load at the upper outer corner on the side of the leading foot, tilt it slightly and grip the opposite corner with the other hand. *(Ensure the palm, not fingers, take the weight)*.

d) Keep your **arms close to your body**, move rear hand forward along the lower edge of the load. Stand up in one movement, keeping the load in contact with the body at all times.

e) To lower the load, reverse the procedure, **bending your knees** whilst tilting the load to avoid trapping fingers.

Always remember:
- Assess the Load.
- Lift the load smoothly - do not jerk.
- Avoid twisting and stretching.

Poor posture

Injuries that are received as a result of carrying out activities that include manual handling operations need not necessarily arise solely from lifting large, awkward or heavy items. Poor posture can greatly increase the likelihood of suffering manual handling injuries. Examples of poor posture can include over-stretching, twisting, lifting with the spine (in bending position) or lifting whilst seated. Many construction tasks can encourage the worker to take up a poor posture so they are bent over for a period of time, for example laying a floor. Training should be given in correct manual handling techniques, adoption of the correct posture and ensuring that the 'kinetic' lifting method is used (feet slightly apart, straight back and use of the leg muscles to lift).

For example, there is guidance that is published in the UK by the Health & Safety Executive (HSE), which indicates the values of weights and ideal positions for these given weight values that should be adopted when manually handling *(see also - Figure 2-2-4: Guideline figures - earlier in this element)*. It can be seen from the guidance that the ideal position for manually handling is waist height whilst standing; also to be noted are the different values given for the male and female gender. These figures are not strict and are quoted as maximum under guidance only and allowances must be made for individual differences in capability.

Whilst standing is seen to give the more suitable posture for lifting, it should also be noted that movements made in the standing position can also reduce individual weight values and lifting zones significantly. A twisting motion of the spine of 45 degrees will result in a 10% reduction in lifting capability, whilst a twisting motion of 90 degrees will result in a 20% reduction.

Manually handling whilst seated also reduces individual weight values and lifting zones significantly, with guidance stating 5kg for a male and 3kg for a female as maximum weights whilst seated. Sitting, something done more frequently during work activities can result in back injuries. Research has found that pressure exerted on the spine and discs of the spine are increased by approximately 40% whilst seated. This pressure increases to 90% when leaning forward.

Repetitive movements

The aim of assessment should be to reduce the risk of injury from manual handling operations. One of the main methods used to reduce the load being manually lifted is to package smaller weights or break the bulk load down into smaller batches. This solution avoids the need to lift heavy items, however it will introduce increased frequency.

Injuries received from manual handling operations can either be immediate, resulting from over exertion and poor posture or also occur over time as a result of performing the manual handling task repeatedly, for example, digging an excavation or laying bricks. Whilst acute, painful injuries are typically more immediately noticeable, long-term effects from cumulative muscle strain can prove equally detrimental to individual health.

Where frequency is increased, in addition to training in the correct lifting method, regular breaks or job rotation must be introduced in order to share the workload suitably throughout the workforce. Mechanical assistance may also be introduced to prevent twisting or bending under strain (rollers, conveyors, air suction devices, and waist height benches).

Awkward movements

Training should be given in the correct lifting method (the kinetic method), that if used correctly, should eliminate incorrect posture and provide a means for lifting safely in most positions (floor level, waist height, but not stretching). Awkward movements that should be avoided include, stretching, bending at the waist using the spine, twisting, lifting whilst seated, sudden movements, over exertion whilst pushing or pulling. It should be remembered that many construction tasks require a person to hold awkward positions for a period of time, for example the fitting of overhead lights or tiles. These awkward movements can lead to cumulative strain and it is critical that there are sufficient rest periods or work rotation built into the work activity to allow relief of the muscles likely to be affected.

2.3 - Safety in the use of lifting and moving equipment

Forklift trucks

FORKLIFT TRUCK HAZARDS

Although the forklift truck (FLT) is a very useful machine for moving materials in many industries, it features prominently in industrial accidents. In the United Kingdom (UK) alone, every year about 20 deaths and 5,000 injuries can be attributed to forklift trucks and these can be analysed as follows:

- Injuries to driver.   40%
- Injuries to assistant.   20%
- Injuries to pedestrians. 40%

- Fractures.   80%
- Injury to ankles & feet. 60%

Unless preventative action is taken these accidents are likely to increase as forklift trucks are increasingly used in industry.

As about 45% of the accidents can be wholly or partly attributed to operator error, the need for proper operator training is underlined. There are, however, many other causes of accident including inadequate premises, gangways, poor truck maintenance, lighting etc.

- Overturning:
  - Driving too fast.
  - Sudden braking.
  - Driving on slopes.
  - Driving with load elevated.
- Collisions:
  - With buildings.
  - With pedestrians.
  - With other vehicles.
- Loss of load:
  - Insecure load.
  - Poor floor surface.
  - Passengers should not be carried.
- Overloading:
  - Exceeding maximum capacity.
- Failure:
  - Load bearing part (e.g. chain).

SAFE USE AND MAINTENANCE

Selection of equipment

There are many types of truck available for a range of activities. There are many situations when specialist trucks such as reach trucks, overhead telescopic or rough terrain trucks are required. Many accidents happen due to the incorrect selection and/or use of forklift trucks.

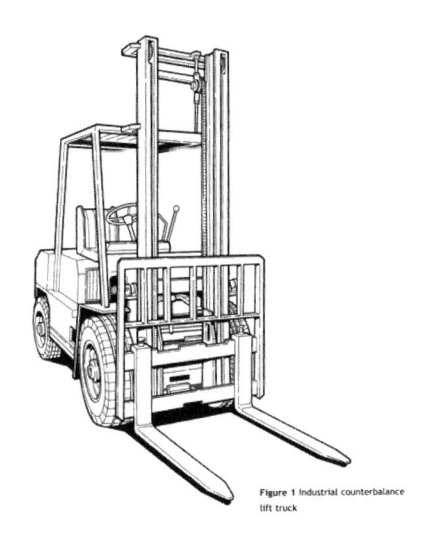

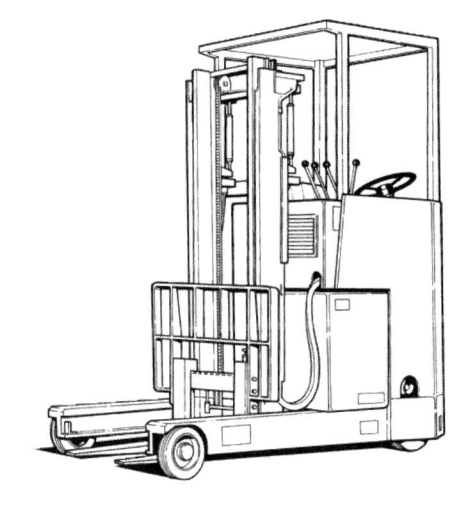

Figure 2-2-15: Industrial counter balance lift truck.

Figure 2-2-16: Industrial reach truck. *Source: HSE Guidance HSG6.*

Industrial counterbalance lift truck

This has a counterweight to balance the load on the fork arms. The fork arms and load project out from the front of the machine. Loads can be raised or lowered vertically and the mast maybe tilted forwards or backwards up to 150 (but in practice more usually about 50). This type of lift truck is only suitable for use on substantially firm, smooth, level and prepared surfaces. A wide range of attachments is available.

Industrial reach truck

This is so called because the mast is moved forwards or reached out to pick up the load. For travelling, the load is reached back and carried within the wheelbase. This allows greater manoeuvrability in areas where space is restricted. This type of lift truck is only suitable for use on substantially firm, smooth, level and prepared surfaces and is particularly used in warehouses.

Figure 2-2-17: Rough-terrain counter balance lift truck.

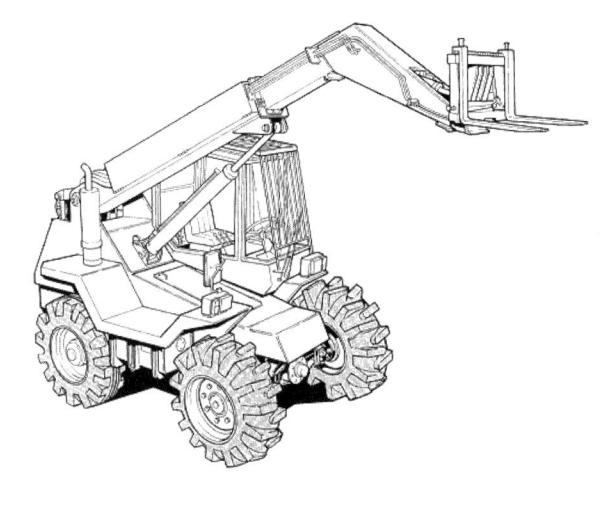

Figure 2-2-18: Telescopic materials handler.
Source: HSE Guidance HSG6.

Rough-terrain counterbalance lift truck

This is similar in design to the industrial counterbalanced lift truck but is equipped with larger wheels and pneumatic tyres, giving it greater ground clearance. It has greater ability to operate on uneven and soft ground and is mainly used in the construction industry and in agriculture. It may be used with a range of attachments.

Telescopic materials handler

This is fitted with a boom that is pivoted at the rear of the machine. The boom is raised and lowered by hydraulic rams. In addition, the boom can be extended or retracted (telescoped) to give extra reach or height.

UNIT IGC2 - ELEMENT 2 - MANUAL AND MECHANICAL HANDLING - HAZARDS AND CONTROL

These machines may be two or four-wheel drive, and have two-wheel, four-wheel or crab steering. They are used mainly in agriculture and the construction industry. A range of attachments may be used with them.

Side-loading lift truck

The operator is positioned at the front and to one side of the lift truck. The load is carried on the deck, the mast being traversed out sideways to pick up or set down the load. This type of lift truck is used for stacking and moving long loads such as bales of timber and pipes, and may be fitted with stabilisers for use when picking up or setting down loads.

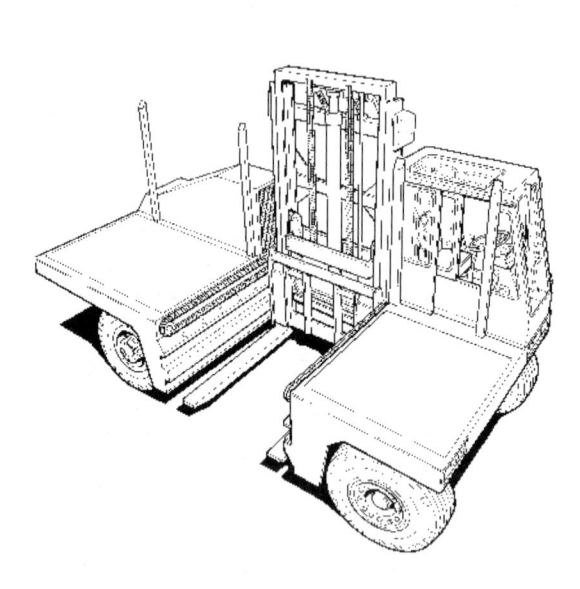

Figure 2-2-19: Side loading lift truck.

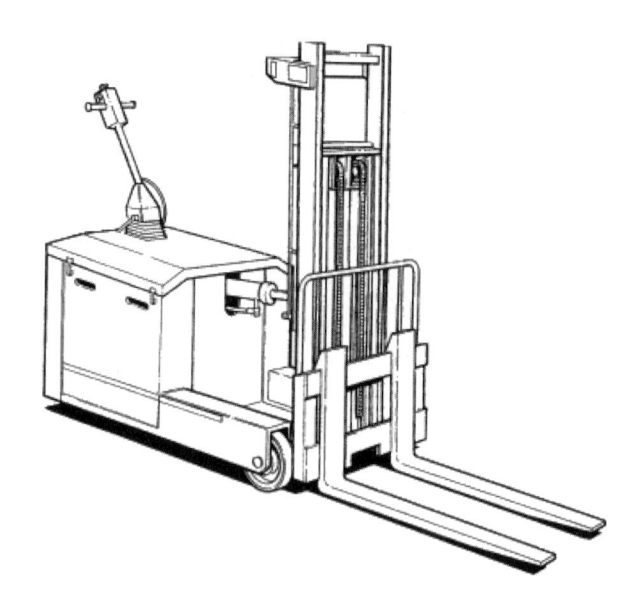

Figure 2-2-20: Pedestrian controlled lift truck.
Source: HSE Guidance HSG6.

Pedestrian-controlled lift truck

This has a limited lift height, usually not greater than two metres. It may be electrically or manually powered for lifting and for traction. The operator walks with the machine and controls it with a handle.

Large lift truck

This may be either masted or telescopic, and is often fitted with a spreader for lifting freight containers. The spreader may attach to the side or top of the container. These are specialist lift trucks used mainly in container terminals.

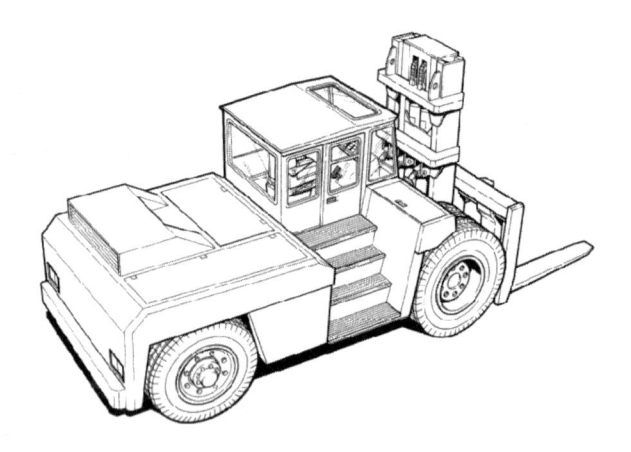

When choosing the correct truck for the job the following factors should be taken into account:

- Power source - the choice of battery or diesel will depend on whether the truck is to be used indoors (battery) or outdoors (diesel).
- Tyres - solid or pneumatic depending on the terrain.
- Size and capacity - dependent on the size and nature of loads to be moved.
- Height of the mast.
- Audible and/or visual warning systems fitted according to the proximity of pedestrians.
- Protection provided for the operator dependent on rough terrain which might increase the likelihood of overturning or the possibility of falling objects resulting, for example, from insecure racking.
- Training given to operators must be related specifically to the type of truck.

Figure 2-2-21: Large lift truck. *Source: HSE Guidance HSG6.*

MECHANICAL HANDLING EQUIPMENT OPERATORS

No person should be permitted to drive a forklift truck or mobile plant unless they have been selected, trained and authorised to do so, or have had properly organised formal training.

Selection of personnel

The safe use of forklift trucks calls for a reasonable degree of both physical and mental fitness and of intelligence. The selection procedure should be devised to identify workers who have shown themselves reliable and mature during their early years at work.

Training

Training should consist of three stages, the last being the one in which the operator is introduced to his future work environment. This is illustrated by the stages of training of a fork lift truck operator.

Stage one - should contain the basic skills and knowledge required to operate the forklift truck safely, to understand the basic mechanics and balance of the machine, and to carry out routine daily checks.

Stage two - under strict training conditions closed to other personnel. This stage should include:
- Knowledge of the operating principles and controls.
- Use of the forklift truck in gangways, slopes, cold-stores, confined spaces and bad weather conditions, etc.
- The work to be undertaken e.g. loading and unloading vehicles.

Stage three - after successfully completing the first two stages, the operator should be given further instruction in the place of work.

Testing - on completion of training, the operator should be examined and tested to ensure that he/she has achieved the required standard.

Refresher training - if high standards are to be maintained, periodic refresher training and testing is essential good practice.

Figure 2-2-22: Width of traffic route.   Source: ACT.

Figure 2-2-23: Keys not secure.   Source: ACT.

Manually operated load moving equipment hazards

SACK TRUCK

A sack truck is a simple, 'low-tech' fabrication fitted with two wheels on which the load is pivoted and supported when the truck is tilted back and pushed manually. A risk assessment must be made of manual handling operations associated with using equipment of this type. As with the wheelbarrow there is still a need to manually handle materials when using a sack truck.

Hazard and control

Sack trucks are typically manually driven and like the wheelbarrow the hazards arising from their use are generally of an ergonomic nature relating to posture and over exertion through manual handling. Mechanical hazards are restricted to the wheels of the truck that only move when moved by the operator. Other associated hazards are tripping and falling whilst using the equipment and manual handling back and strain injuries. Control measures include indicating a safe working load for the equipment and the provision of information / instruction in the safe loading and use of the equipment for the operator. A manual handling assessment may be required when using this equipment.

THE PALLET TRUCK

This truck has two elevating fingers for insertion below the top deck of a pallet. When the 'forks' are raised the load is moved clear of the ground to allow movement. This truck may be designed for pedestrian or rider control. It has no mast and cannot be used for stacking. Pallet trucks may be powered or non-powered.

Hazard and control

Pallet trucks can be driven both manually or by quiet running electric motor. Hazards include crush from moving loads or momentum of the equipment when stopping, crush and trap in the forks of the equipment, manual handling strain injuries and electricity hazards from battery power points. In addition, some pallet trucks have a lifting mechanism to raise and lower the load. Control measures should include trained and authorised operatives; identification of safe working loads; inspection and maintenance; and designated areas for parking the equipment.

UNIT IGC2 - ELEMENT 2 - MANUAL AND MECHANICAL HANDLING - HAZARDS AND CONTROL

Figure 2-2-24: Hand operated pallet truck. Source: ACT.

Figure 2-2-25: Sack truck. Source: ACT.

Lifts and hoists

HAZARDS

In general, the hazards associated with lifts and hoists are the same as with any other lifting equipment.

- The lift / hoist may overturn or collapse.
- The lift / hoist can strike persons, during normal operations, who may be near or under the platform or cage.
- The supporting ropes may fail and the platform/cage fall to the ground.
- The load or part of the load may fall.
- The lift / hoist may fail in a high position.
- Persons being lifted may become stranded if the lift or hoist fails.

SAFE USE AND MAINTENANCE

Lifts and hoists for movement of goods require:

- Statutory safety devices.
- Holdback gears (for rope failure).
- Overrun tip systems.
- Guards on hoist machinery.
- Landing gates (securely closed down during operation).

In addition, passenger hoists require more sophisticated controls:

- Operating controls inside the cage.
- Electromagnetic interlocks on the cage doors.
- The enclosing shaft must be of fire-proof construction, if within a building.

Safe use of lifts and hoists depends on:

- Adequate design.
- Competent operation.
- Construction of suitable strength.
- Regular inspection.
- Correct selection.
- Adequate maintenance.
- Correct installation.

For further details see later in this element.

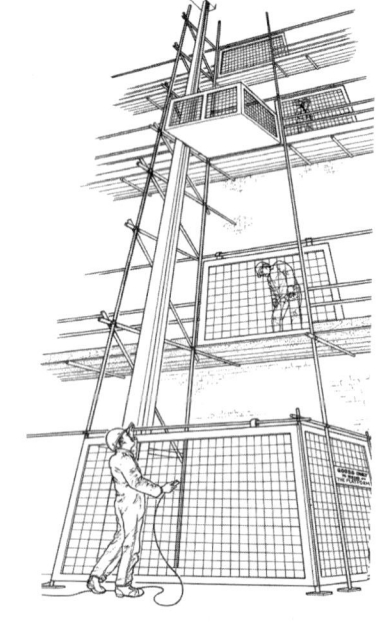

Figure 2-2-26: Lift / hoist. Source: HSG150, HSE books.

Conveyors

HAZARDS

- Drawing in   -   Clothing or limbs being drawn in to in-running pinching points (nips) caused by moving parts.
- Contact   -   With moving parts (cut and abrasion).
- Entanglement   -   With rollers.
- Striking   -   Falling objects, especially from overhead conveyors.
- Manual Handling -   Loading and unloading components / packages.
- Noise   -   From mechanical movement.

TYPES OF CONVEYOR

The three basic types of conveyor are belt, roller and screw.

Belt

Materials are transported on a moving belt. Trapping points are created between the belt and the rotating drum. The 'head and tails' pulleys create the main risks. Guards can be fitted enclosing the sides or at each drawing in point (in-running nip).

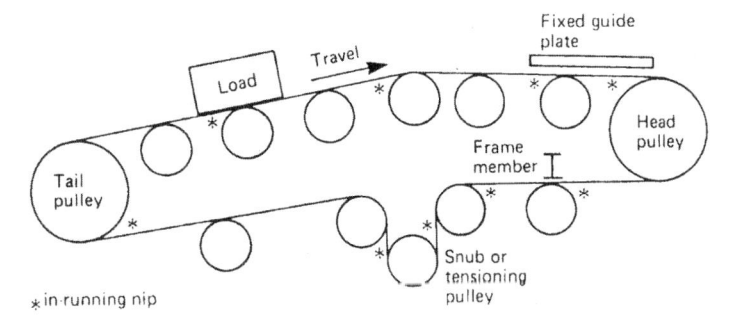

Figure 2-2-27: Diagrammatic layout of belt conveyor showing in-running nips.
Source: J Ridley; Safety at Work; Fourth Edition.

Roller

- Power Driven Rollers: guards are required on power drives and in-running nips.
- Powered and Free Running Rollers: guards are required between each pair of powered and free running rollers.
- Free Running Rollers: no nips occur on these, but injuries can occur when workers try to walk across them. Providing walkways can solve this problem.

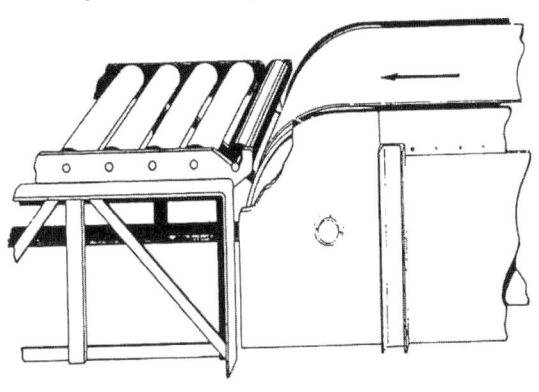

Figure 2-2-28: Preventing free running roller trap.
Source: J Ridley; Safety at Work; Fourth Edition - Courtesy HSE.

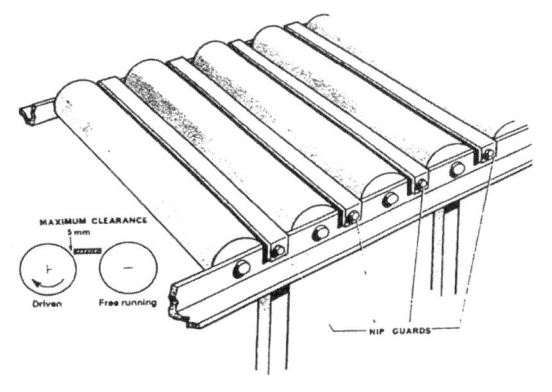

Figure 2-2-29: Guards between alternative drive-rollers.
Source: J Ridley; Safety at Work; Fourth Edition - Courtesy HSE.

Figure 2-2-30: Roller conveyor.
Source: ACT.

Figure 2-2-31: Belt conveyor guard.
Source: ACT.

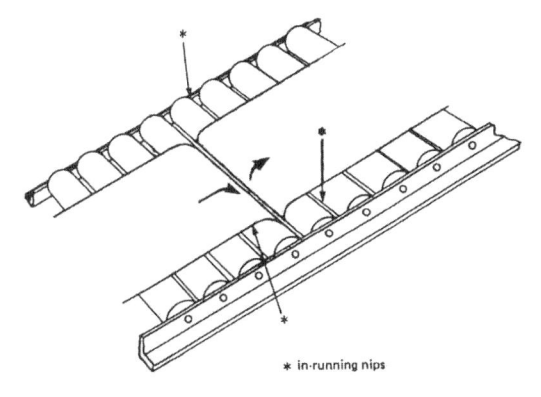

Figure 2-2-32: Nip points on roller conveyor with belts.
Source: J Ridley; Safety at Work; Fourth Edition - Courtesy HSE.

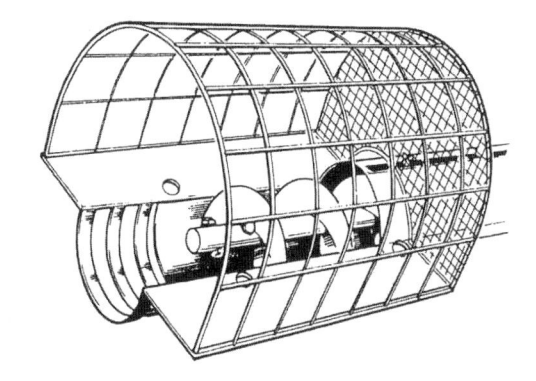

Figure 2-2-33: Screw conveyor guarding.
Source: J Ridley; Safety at Work; Fourth Edition - Courtesy HSE.

Screw

Materials are pushed forward by a rotating screw. Screw conveyors can cause terrible injuries and should be guarded or covered at all times. A locking-off system is required for maintenance and repairs.

SAFE USE AND MAINTENANCE

- Fixed guards on drums.
- Enclosure of conveyed items by side guards.
- Trip wires, if necessary, along the full length of the conveyor.
- Emergency stop buttons
- Safe access at regular intervals.
- Avoid loose clothing.
- Restrict access.
- Wearing bump caps.
- Regular maintenance by competent workers.

Cranes

CRANE HAZARDS

The principal hazards associated with any lifting operation are:

- **Overturning** which can be caused by weak support, operating outside the capabilities (range, strength) of the machine and by striking obstructions.
- **Overloading** by exceeding the operating capacity or operating radii, or by failure of safety devices.
- **Collision** with other cranes, overhead cables or structures.
- **Failure of load bearing part** - structural components of the crane itself siting over cellars and drains, made-up or not solid ground, outriggers not extended.,
- **Loss of load** from failure of lifting tackle or slinging procedure.

Factors which will affect all cranes:

- Ground condition
  - Capable of bearing the load.
  - Level.
  - Underground voids or cellars.
- Erecting dismantling
  - Use of other cranes.
- Load
  - Sufficient capacity for the lift.
- Position of the crane
  - Sufficient room for light.
  - No overhead obstructing e.g. power lines.
  - Proximity to buildings or often cranes.
  - Worker and members of the public access restrictions.
  - Tower cranes (construction) near or in an aircraft flight path
- Adverse weather conditions
  - Rain, wind, temperature.
  - Corrosion of key parts.

Figure 2-2-34: Safety latch on hook. *Source: Corel Clipart.*

SAFE USE AND MAINTENANCE

General requirements for cranes

Lifting operations must be properly planned by a competent person, appropriately supervised and carried out in a safe manner.

There are a number of common measures for safe operation that apply to all cranes, including crane identification and capacity marking i.e. safe working load (SWL), and maintenance (preventative maintenance, as well as statutory implications). The main safety measures that should be incorporated for the safe operation of a crane include:

- Pre-use check by operator.
- Lifting equipment must be of adequate strength and stability for the load. Stresses induced at mounting or fixing points must be taken into account. Similarly every part of a load, anything attached to it and used in lifting must be of adequate strength.
- The safe working load (SWL) must be clearly marked on lifting machinery, equipment and accessories in order to ensure safe use. Where the SWL depends on the configuration of the machinery, it must be clearly marked for each configuration used and kept with the machinery. Equipment which is not designed for lifting persons, but which might be used as such, must have appropriate markings to the effect that it is not to be used for passengers.
- Load indicators - two types - a requirement with jib cranes (a crane with a projecting arm), but beneficial if fitted to all cranes.
  - ✓ Load/radius indicator - shows the radius the crane is working at and the safe load for that radius. Must be visible to the driver.
  - ✓ Automatic safe load indicator - providing visible warning when SWL is approached and audible warning when SWL is exceeded.
- Controls - should be clearly identified and of the "hold to run" type.
- Over travel switches - limit switches to prevent the hook or sheave block being wound up to the cable drum.
- Access - safe access should be provided for the operator and for use during inspection and maintenance/emergency.
- Operating position - should provide clear visibility of hook and load, with the controls easily reached.
- Passengers - should not be carried without authorisation, and never on lifting tackle.

- Lifting tackle - chains, slings, wire ropes, eyebolts and shackles should be tested / examined.

Accessories

Lifting accessories include slings, hooks, chains eyes and cradles. This equipment is designed with the aim of assisting in lifting items without the need for manual force. Because these accessories are in a constantly changing environment and are in and out of use they need to be protected from damage - a failure of any one item could result in a fatality. For example, lifting eyes need to be correctly fitted, slings have to be used with the correct technique and all equipment must be stored when not in use to prevent damage. Accessories must be attached correctly and safely to the load by a competent person, and then the lifting equipment takes over the task of providing the necessary required power to perform the lift. As with all lifting equipment, accessories must be regularly inspected and certificated and only used by trained authorised persons.

Figure 2-2-35: Lifting operation. *Source: ACT.*

Figure 2-2-36: Lifting points on load. *Source: ACT.*

Figure 2-2-37: Safety latch on hook. *Source: ACT.*

Figure 2-2-38: Accessories. *Source: ACT.*

Operator training and practices

Crane operators and slingers should be fit and strong enough for the work. Training should be provided for the safe operation of the particular equipment.

A safe system of work should be developed and communicated to all those involved. The planning should involve selecting competent persons including the mobile crane driver and appointed person who will supervise the lifting operation. Circumstances will differ from site to site and additional rules should be inserted to cover individual circumstances and conditions.

Site rules should apply before use, for example, before taking over a mobile crane the driver must always check around the crane, and check the pressure of tyres, the engine for fuel, lubrication oil, water and the compressed air system. All controls, such as clutches, brakes and safe load indicator, should be tested to see that all ropes run smoothly and check limit switches, operate where fitted.

The driver of a ***mobile crane*** should carry out the following:

- Before travelling unladen, lower jib onto its rest (if fitted) or to the lowest operating position and point in the direction of travel, but beware of steep hills.
- Understand the signalling system and observe the signals of the appointed signaller (lifting operations coordinator).
- Do not permit unauthorised persons to travel on the crane.
- Do not use the crane to replace normal means of transport, or as a towing tractor.
- Before lifting, check that the crane is on firm and level ground, and that spring locks and out-riggers (extended stabilisers) are properly in position
- Keep a constant watch on the load radius indicator. Do not lift any suspected overload. Overloads are forbidden.
- Ensure movements are made with caution. Violent handling produces excess loading on the crane structure and machinery.
- Make allowances for adverse weather conditions.
- Do not attempt to drag loads or cause loads to swing. Always position the crane so that the pull on the hoist rope is vertical.
- Ensure that the load is properly slung. A load considered unsafe should not be lifted.
- Ensure that all persons are in a safe position before any movement is carried out.
- Make certain before hoisting that the hook is not attached to any anchored load or fixed object.
- Do not drag slings when travelling.

UNIT IGC2 - ELEMENT 2 - MANUAL AND MECHANICAL HANDLING - HAZARDS AND CONTROL

- If the crane is slewing (swinging in a sideways or circular motion), the jib (crane arm), hook or load must be in a position to clear any obstruction, but the load must not be lifted unnecessarily high.
- Be on a constant lookout for overhead obstructions, particularly electric cables.
- Never tamper with or disconnect safe load indicators.
- If the hoist or jib ropes become slack or out of their grooves, stop the crane and report the condition.
- Report all defects to the supervisor and never attempt to use a crane with a suspected serious defect until rectified and certified by a competent person that it is not dangerous.
- When leaving a crane unattended, ensure that the power is off, the engine stopped, the load unhooked, and the hook is raised up to a safe position.
- Where using special devices; e.g. magnets, grabs, for example, ensure they are used only for the purpose intended and in accordance with the instruction given.
- Keep the crane clean and tidy.
- When parking a crane after use, remember to apply all brakes, slew locks, and secure rail clamps when fitted. Some cranes, however, particularly tower cranes, must be left to weather vane and the manufacturer's instructions must be clearly adhered to. Park the crane where the weather vaning jib will not strike any object. Lock the cabin before leaving the crane.
- When it is necessary to make a report this must be done promptly through supervision.
- Drive smoothly - drive safely. Remember that cranes are safe only when they are used as recommended by the makers. This applies in particular to speciality cranes.

Rules for safe operation of a crane

Always	Ensure operators/slingers are trained and competent.
Always	Select the correct appliance and tackle for the job.
Always	Ensure the appliance is stable when lifting - e.g. not outside lifting radius, firm, level ground, outriggers.
Always	Use correct slinging methods.
Always	Protect sling from sharp edges - pack out and lower onto spacers.
Always	Ensure the sling is securely attached to the hook.
Always	Ensure load is lifted to correct height and moved at an appropriate speed.
Always	Use standard signals - which are relevant to local or national legislation.
Never	Drag a load or allow sudden shock loading.
Never	Use equipment if damaged (check before use) - e.g. stretched or not free movement, worn or corroded, outside inspection date.
Never	Exceed the safe working load.
Never	Lift with sling angles greater than 120^0.
Never	Lift a load over workers.

Figure 2-2-39: Crane operation. Source: ACT.

Requirements for lifting operations

CONTROL OF LIFTING OPERATIONS

Employers should ensure that every lifting operation involving lifting equipment for the purposes of lifting or lowering of a load is organised safely. This will include ensuring the following:

a) Lifting operations to be properly planned by a competent person.
b) Provision of appropriate supervision.
c) Work is to be carried out in a safe manner.

Figure 2-2-40: Lifting operations. Source: ACT.

Figure 2-2-41: Lifting operations. Source: ACT.

STRONG, STABLE AND SUITABLE EQUIPMENT

Strength

The Employer should ensure that:

- Lifting equipment is of adequate strength and stability for each load, having regard in particular to the stress induced at its mounting or fixing point.
- Every part of a load and anything attached to it and used in lifting it is of adequate strength.

When assessing whether lifting equipment has adequate strength for the proposed use, the combined weight of the load and lifting accessories should be taken into account. It is important to consider the load, task and environment in order to match the strength of the lifting equipment to the circumstances of use. For example, if the environment is hot or cold this can affect the lifting capacity of the lifting equipment. In order to counteract this effect equipment with a higher rated safe working load may be needed. If the load to be lifted is a person, equipment with a generous capacity above the person's weight should be selected to provide an increased factor for safety. If the load is likely to move unexpectedly, such as an animal or liquids in a container, this sudden movement can put additional forces on the equipment and may necessitate equipment with increased strength to be selected. When conducting the lifting task the lifting accessories may be used in such a way that may reduce its lifting capacity below its stated safe working load; sharp corners on a load and 'back hooking' can have this effect. In these circumstances accessories with a higher rated safe working load may be required. It is essential to remember that in a lifting operation the equipment only has an overall lifting capacity equivalent to the item with the lowest strength. For example, in a situation where a crane with a lifting capacity of 50 tonnes is used with a hook of 10 tonnes capacity and a wire rope sling of 5 tonnes capacity this would give an overall maximum lifting strength/capacity of 5 tonnes.

Stability

A number of factors can affect the stability of lifting equipment, for example wind conditions, slopes/cambers, stability of ground conditions and how the load is to be lifted.

Lifting equipment must be positioned and installed so that it does not tip over when in use. Anchoring can be achieved by securing with guy ropes, bolting the structure to a foundation, using ballast as counterweights or using outriggers to bring the centre of gravity down to the base area.

Mobile lifting equipment should be sited on firm ground with the wheels or outrigger feet having their weight distributed over a large surface area. Care should be taken that the equipment is not positioned over cellars, drains or underground cavities, or positioned near excavations.

Sloping ground should be avoided as this can shift the load radius out or in, away from the safe working position. In the uphill position, the greatest danger occurs when the load is set down. This can cause the mobile lifting equipment to tip over. In the downhill position, the load moves out of the radius and may cause the equipment to tip forwards.

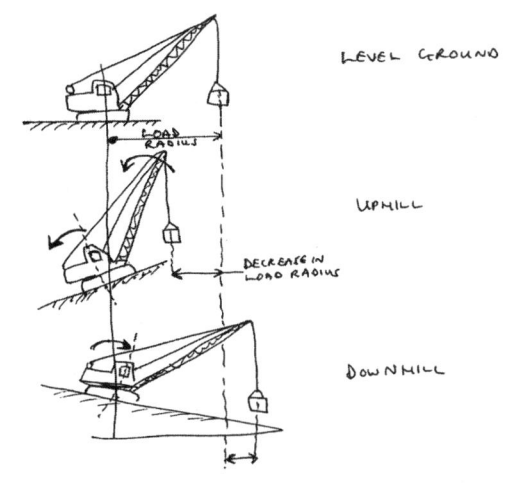

Figure 2-2-42: Stability of cranes (hand drawn example).

Source: ACT.

Suitability

The employer should ensure that work equipment is used only for operations for which it has been designed, including consideration of the working conditions for each lifting operation.

In order for lifting equipment to be suitable it must be of the correct type for the task, have a safe working load limit in excess of the load being lifted, and have the correct type and combination of lifting accessories attached.

Lifting equipment used within industry varies and includes mobile cranes, static tower cranes and overhead travelling cranes. The type of lifting equipment selected will depend on a number of factors including the weight of the load to be lifted, the radius of operation, the height of the lift, the time available, and the frequency of the lifting activities. This equipment is often very heavy, which means its weight can cause the ground underneath the equipment to sink or collapse. Other factors like height and size may have to be considered as there may be limitations in site roads that are located between structures or where overhead restrictions exist.

These considerations should be made when selecting the correct crane. Selecting lifting equipment to carry out a lifting activity should be done at the planning stage, where the most suitable equipment can be identified that is able to meet all of the lifting requirements and the limitations of the location. In the construction industry it is common practice to have specific drawings and lifting plans constructed for all types of work with particular attention focused on high risk and complicated lifting operations.

POSITIONED AND INSTALLED CORRECTLY

Lifting equipment must be positioned or installed so that the risk of the equipment striking a person is low. Similarly, the risk of a load drifting, falling freely or being unintentionally released must also be considered and equipment positioned to take account of this.

All nearby hazards, including overhead cables and uninsulated power supply conductors, should be identified and removed or covered by safe working procedures such as locking-off and permit systems. The possibility of striking other lifting equipment or structures should also be examined.

Detailed consideration must be given to the location of any heavy piece of lifting equipment due to the fact that additional weight is distributed to the ground through the loading of the equipment when performing a lift.

Surveys must be carried out to determine the nature of the ground, whether soft or firm, and what underground hazards are present such as buried services or hollow voids.

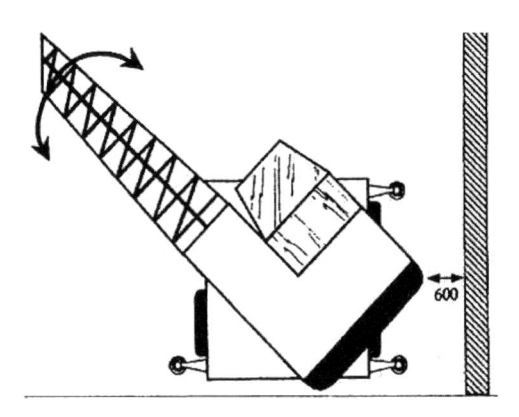

Figure 2-2-43: Danger zone - crane & fixed item viewed from above.
Source: ACT.

Figure 2-2-44: Siting and stability.   Source: ACT.

If the ground proves to be soft, then this can be covered in timber, digger mats or hard core to prevent the equipment or its outriggers sinking when under load. The surrounding environment must also be taken into consideration and factors may include highways, railways, electricity cables, areas of public interest. The area around where lifting equipment is sited should be securely fenced, including the extremes of the lift radius, with an additional factor of safety to allow for emergency arrangements such as emergency vehicle access or safety in the event of a collapse or fall.

Where practicable, lifting equipment should be positioned and installed such that loads are not carried or suspended over areas occupied by workers. Where this is necessary appropriate systems of work should be used to ensure it is done safely.

If the operator cannot observe the full path of the load an appointed person (and assistants as appropriate) should be used to communicate the position of the load and provide directions to avoid striking anything or anyone.

VISIBLY MARKED

The safe working load (SWL) should be clearly marked on lifting machinery, equipment and accessories in order to ensure safe use. Where the SWL depends on the configuration of the machinery, it must be clearly marked for each configuration used and kept with the machinery. Accessories should be marked with supplementary information that indicates the characteristics for its safe use, for example, safe angles of lift. Equipment designed for lifting workers should be clearly marked as such and equipment which is not designed for lifting persons, but which might be used as such, should have appropriate markings to the effect that it is not to be used for lifting workers.

PLANNED, SUPERVISED AND CARRIED OUT IN SAFE MANNER BY COMPETENT WORKERS

The employer should ensure that every lifting operation involving lifting equipment is:

- Properly planned by a competent person.
- Appropriately supervised.
- Carried out in a safe manner.

The type of lifting equipment that is to be used and the complexity of the lifting operations will dictate the degree of planning required for the lifting operation.

Planning combines two parts:

1) Initial planning to ensure that lifting equipment is provided which is suitable for the range of tasks that it will have to carry out.

2) Planning of individual lifting operations so that they can be carried out safely with the lifting equipment provided.

Factors that should be considered when formulating a plan include:

- The load that is being lifted - weight, shape, centres of gravity, surface condition, lifting points.
- The equipment and accessories being used for the operation and suitability - certification validity.
- The proposed route that the load will take including the destination and checks for obstructions.
- The team required to carry out the lift - competencies and numbers required.
- Production of a safe system of work, risk assessments, permits to work.
- The environment in which the lift will take place - ground conditions, weather, local population.
- Securing areas below the lift - information, restrictions, demarcation and barriers.
- Construction of specific lifting plan diagrams.
- A suitable trial to determine the reaction of the lifting equipment prior to full lift.
- Completion of the operation and any dismantling required.

It is critical that someone takes supervisory control of lifting operations at the time they are being conducted. Though the operator may be skilled in lifting techniques this may not be enough to ensure safety as other factors may influence whether the overall operation is conducted safely, for example, workers may stray into the area. The supervisor of the lifting operation must remain in control and stop the operation if it is not carried out satisfactorily. Lifting equipment and accessories should be subject to a pre-use check in order to determine their condition and suitability. In addition, care should be taken to ensure the lifting accessories used are compatible with the task and that the load is protected or supported such that it does not disintegrate when lifted.

Lifting operations should not be carried on where adverse weather conditions occur, such as fog, poor lightning, strong wind or where heavy rainfall makes ground conditions unstable. It is critical that measures be used to prevent lifting equipment overturning and that there is sufficient room for it to operate without contacting other objects. Lifting equipment should not be used to drag loads and should not be overloaded.

Special arrangements need to be in place when lifting equipment not normally used for lifting workers is used for that purpose, for example, de-rating the working load limit, ensuring communication is in place between the workers being lifted and the operator, and ensuring the operation controls are manned at all times.

Employers should ensure that any person who uses a piece of work equipment has received adequate training for purposes of health and safety, including training in the methods which may be adopted when using work equipment, any risks which such use may entail and precautions to be taken.

Drivers / operators of cranes and other lifting appliances, including others involved in lifting operations (e.g. those that direct the movement of the load), must be adequately trained and experienced. The only exception is when under the direct supervision of a competent person for training requirements.

There are various appointments with specified responsibilities in order to ensure the safety of lifting operations on site. These are as follows:

- Competent person   -   Appointed to plan the operation.
- Load handler   -   Attaches and detaches the load.
- Authorised person   -   Ensures the load safely attached.
- Operator   -   Appointed to operate the equipment.
- Responsible person   -   Appointed to communicate the position of the load (signaller).
- Assistants   -   Appointed to relay communications.

SPECIAL REQUIREMENTS FOR LIFTING EQUIPMENT FOR LIFTING PERSONS

The employer should ensure that lifting equipment for lifting persons:

- Is such as to prevent a person using it being crushed, trapped or struck or falling from the carrier.
- Is such as to prevent so far as is reasonably practicable a person using it, while carrying out activities from the carrier, being crushed, trapped or struck or falling from the carrier.
- Has suitable devices to prevent the risk of a carrier falling.
- Is such that a person trapped in any carrier is not thereby exposed to danger and can be freed.

In addition, the employer should ensure that if the risk described above cannot be prevented for reasons inherent in the site and height differences:

- The carrier has an enhanced safety coefficient suspension rope or chain.
- The rope or chain is inspected by a competent person every working day.

Special arrangements need to be in place when lifting equipment not normally used for workers is used for that purpose, e.g. de-rating the working load limit, ensuring communication is in place between the workers and operator, and ensuring the operation controls are manned at all times. Lifting equipment for lifting workers is subject to specific requirements for statutory examination - *see below for details*.

The need for periodic examination / testing of lifting equipment

To ensure that damaged or dangerously worn equipment does not remain in service, all items of lifting equipment must periodically be examined by a "competent person". Where the safety of lifting equipment depends on the installation conditions it must be thoroughly examined prior to first use, after assembly and on change of location in order to ensure that it has been installed correctly and is safe to operate.

Lifting equipment exposed to conditions causing deterioration that is liable to result in dangerous situations is to be thoroughly examined regularly. Where appropriate to ensure health and safety, inspections must be carried out at suitable intervals between thorough examinations. Examinations and inspections must ensure that the good condition of equipment is maintained and that any deterioration can be detected and remedied in good time.

The term "competent" is generally taken to mean someone who is qualified and experienced in carrying out such examinations.

This page is intentionally blank

Element 3

Work equipment - hazards and control

Learning outcomes

On completion of this element, candidates should be able to demonstrate understanding of the content through the application of knowledge to familiar and unfamiliar situations. In particular they should be able to:

3.1 Outline general principles for selection, use and maintenance of work equipment.

3.2 Outline the hazards and controls for hand tools.

3.3 Describe the main mechanical and non-mechanical hazards of machinery.

3.4 Describe the main methods of protection from machinery hazards.

Content

3.1 - General principles for selection, use and maintenance of work equipment	137
Types of work equipment	137
Suitability for the task	137
Requirement to restrict the use and maintenance of equipment	138
Information, instruction and training	138
Requirement for equipment to be maintained and maintenance to be conducted safely	138
The need for periodic examination and testing of pressure systems	140
Importance of operation and emergency controls	141
What is expected of operators	142
3.2 - Hand-held tools	142
Hazards and misuse of hand tools and controls for safe use	142
Hazards of portable power tools and the means of control	143
3.3 - Machinery hazards	144
Main mechanical and non-mechanical hazards	144
Hazards presented by a range of equipment	147
3.4 - Protection from machinery hazards	150
The principles, merits and limitations of protection methods	151
Application of protection methods to a range of equipment listed	156
Basic requirements for guards and safety devices	157

Sources of reference

Safe Use of Work Equipment (ACOP) (L22), HSE Books ISBN 0-7176-1626-6

ISO 12100 - 1: 2003, Safety of machinery, basic concepts, general principles for design, basic terminology, methodology ISBN 0-580-42922-9

ISO 12100 - 2: 2003, Safety of machinery, basic concepts, general principles for design, technical principles ISBN 0-580-42923-7

Ambient Factors in the Workplace (ILO Code of Practice), ILO ISBN 92-2-11628-X

3.1 - General principles for selection, use and maintenance of work equipment

Types of work equipment

Work equipment may be defined as any machinery, appliance, apparatus, tool or assembly of components which are arranged so that they function as a whole. Clearly the term embraces many hand tools, power tools and types of machinery.

Suitability for the task

Suitability of work equipment

(1) Work equipment should be constructed or adapted as to be suitable for the purpose for which it is used or provided.

(2) When selecting equipment, consideration should be given to the working conditions and to the risks to the health and safety of workers and others who may be affected by the work to be done.

(3) Care should be taken to select the correct equipment for the work to be done, taking into consideration the working conditions to ensure that work equipment is used only for operations for which, and under conditions for which, it is suitable.

Suitability should consider:

- Its initial integrity.
- The place where it will be used.
- The purpose for which it will be used.

Integrity - is equipment safe through its design, construction or adaptation? - sharp edges removed from equipment casings, tools modified or made by workers to enable them to do their tasks, equipment adapted to do a specific task.

Place - is equipment suitable for different environments (risks)? - wet or explosive. Account must be taken of the equipment causing a problem - a petrol generator used in a confined space, a hydraulic access platform used in a location with a low roof.

Use - is equipment suitable for the specific task? - a hacksaw being used to cut metal straps used to secure goods to a pallet (instead of a purpose designed tool); the use of a ladder to do work at a height (instead of a scaffold or other access platform); exceeding the safe working load of a crane or fork lift truck, a swivel chair used as a means of access to a shelf.

CONFORMITY WITH RELEVANT STANDARDS, CE MARKING

Those involved in the supply (including design and manufacture) of equipment to ensure that it is safe and healthy, so far as is reasonably practicable. This will require them to take account of all relevant standards.

What is CE Marking (CE Mark)?

It is a protocol which establishes a common standard throughout the European Union.

The letters "CE" are the abbreviation of French phrase "Conformité Européene" which literally means "European Conformity". "CE Marking" is applied to the entire European Union for health and safety in design and maintenance of equipment.

CE Marking on a product is a manufacturer's declaration that the product complies with the essential requirements of the relevant European health, safety and environmental protection legislation, in practice by many of the Product Directives.

Product Directives contain the "essential requirements" and/or "performance levels" and "Harmonised Standards" to which the products must conform. Harmonised Standards are the technical specifications (European Standards or Harmonisation Documents) which are established by several European standards agencies (CEN, CENELEC, etc). CEN stands for European Committee for Standardisation and CENELEC stands for European Committee for Electrotechnical Standardisation.

WHAT 'INTERNATIONAL STANDARDISATION' MEANS

When the large majority of products or services in a particular business or industry sector conform to International Standards, a state of industry-wide standardization can be said to exist. This is achieved through consensus agreements between national delegations representing all the economic stakeholders concerned - suppliers, users, Government regulators and other interest groups, such as consumers. They agree on specifications and criteria to be applied consistently in the classification of materials, in the manufacture and supply of products, in testing and analysis, in terminology and in the provision of services. In this way, International Standards provide a reference framework, or a common technological language, between suppliers and their customers - which facilitates trade and the transfer of technology.

HOW ISO STANDARDS BENEFIT SOCIETY

For businesses, the widespread adoption of International Standards means that suppliers can base the development of their products and services on specifications that have wide acceptance in their sectors. This, in turn, means that businesses using International Standards are increasingly free to compete in many more markets around the world.

For customers, the worldwide compatibility of technology which is achieved when products and services are based on International Standards brings them an increasingly wide choice of offers, and they also benefit from the effects of competition among suppliers.

Source: http://www.iso.org/iso.

FIT FOR PURPOSE

Equipment used for any activity must be suitable to fulfil the exact requirements of the task. This means considering the ergonomic requirements *(see paragraph below)*, strength, durability, power source, portability, protection against the environment, range of tasks to be carried out and the frequency and duration of use. Equipment that is designed to perform a specific task must only be used for that task and not adapted for other tasks not considered in the manufacturer's design and instructions.

An example of this is where a portable battery operated drill is rotated by hand or the back / butt of the drill is used as a hammer, clearly a task not meant for this equipment. Equipment used in these types of situation identifies a lack of forethought in the planning stage of a project when the correct equipment should have been sought and used.

The equipment may be used indoors or outdoors where consideration must be given to the dangers of damp, water and electricity or explosive atmospheres within confined spaces. The grade of equipment should be industrial or commercial type for work activities and not the type of equipment designed for use at home. Whenever equipment is required, the full capacity and limitation requirements should be identified and it should be confirmed that the equipment provided can cope with the demands/limitations placed upon it. For example, construction sites use 110 volt supply and it is critical that workers only use equipment that suits this power supply.

ERGONOMIC CONSIDERATIONS

Ergonomic considerations involve the study of person-equipment interface, with an emphasis on adjustability of the machinery and equipment. The aim is to suit a variety of individual sizes and positions in order to provide the most comfortable position possible. In considering the ergonomic factors of a task that requires equipment to be used, it is essential to include the operator's individual attributes, and how they affect and may be affected by the process. Factors might include posture when seated or standing, height of the work station, how the equipment may be adjusted and frequency of the task being performed. It is essential that ergonomic considerations form an active part at the planning stage of a process to ensure the correct equipment is obtained and the reactive effects of poor ergonomics eliminated.

MEETING BASIC SAFETY STANDARDS

Work equipment should be designed and manufactured such that it conforms to all relevant standards. Historically this will have been British Standards. Though many British Standards remain in place today many new standards for work equipment are produced in conjunction with European and international standards organisations. Those that have been agreed at a European level will carry the letters 'EN' in addition to the familiar BS, for example, BS EN 60974 - Arc welding equipment. Those that have been agreed at an international level carry the letters 'ISO', for example, BS EN ISO 12100 Safety of machinery Part 1 - Basic terminology and methodology.

Requirement to restrict the use and maintenance of equipment

SPECIFIC RISKS TO APPROPRIATE PERSONS

It would be appropriate to restrict the use of a nail gun, circular saw or mobile elevated work platform to those competent and authorised to use it. In the same way maintenance (replacement of a grinding wheel) of an abrasive wheel or (replacement of load bearing components) of a rough terrain fork lift truck should be restricted.

Maintenance regimes should be carefully considered before selecting equipment. Maintenance workers may not have the specific expertise or skill to work on new equipment, leading to increased risk to themselves and others. It is essential that operation and maintenance of equipment with specific risks be restricted to those that have appropriate skill and expertise.

Information, instruction and training

INFORMATION AND INSTRUCTION

Whenever equipment is provided and used in the workplace, the employer should ensure that all operators are given adequate information and instruction in order that they can use the equipment safely. The issues covered should include the safe operation of the equipment and also the capacities and limitations of the equipment. Specific information must be given on the particular hazards of equipment and instruction and training given on how to implement, use and maintain control measures correctly.

Supervisors or managers should have adequate health and safety information and, where appropriate, written instructions on:

a) The conditions in which and the methods by which the work equipment may be used.
b) Abnormal situations and the action to be taken if such a situation were to occur.
c) Any conclusions to be drawn from experience in using the work equipment.

TRAINING

Training may be needed for existing workers as well as inexperienced workers or new starters (do not forget temporary workers), particularly if they have to use powered machinery. The greater the danger, the better the training needs to be. For some high risk work such as driving forklift trucks, using a chainsaw and operating a crane, training should be carried out by specialist instructors. Remember that younger workers can be quite skillful when moving and handling powered equipment, but they may lack experience and judgment and may require closer supervision to begin with.

Examples:

Routine workers - How to carry out pre-use checks, report defects, only to use equipment for the purpose designed.

Maintenance workers - Safe isolation, recommended spares and adjustments in accordance with manufacturer's manuals.

Managers - Be aware of the hazards and controls and maintain effective supervision.

Requirement for equipment to be maintained and maintenance to be conducted safely

EQUIPMENT TO BE MAINTAINED

Equipment must be maintained in efficient working order and good repair. In order to achieve this, a system of maintenance should be in place which involves regular inspection, adjustment and testing. Maintenance logs, where they exist, must be kept up to date.

MAINTENANCE TO BE CONDUCTED SAFELY

No one should be exposed to undue risk during maintenance operations. In order to achieve this equipment should be stopped and isolated as appropriate before work starts. If it is necessary to keep equipment running then the risks must be adequately controlled. This may take the form of controlling running speed, range of movement or providing temporary guards.

Maintenance hazards

The principal sources of hazards are associated with maintenance work on:

- Conveyors.
- Elevators.
- Cranes.
- Concrete pumps.
- Storage tanks.
- Hoppers.
- Chemical and degreasing plant.

Typical hazards associated with maintenance operations

Mechanical	-	Entanglement, machinery traps, contact; shearing traps, in-running nips (pinching points), ejection, unexpected start up.
Electrical	-	Electrocution, shock, burns.
Pressure	-	Unexpected pressure releases, explosion.
Physical	-	Extremes of temperature, noise, vibration, dust.
Chemical	-	Gases, vapours, mists, fumes, etc.
Structural	-	Obstructions and floor openings.
Access	-	Work at heights, confined spaces.

Typical accidents

- Crushing by moving machinery.
- Falls.
- Burns.
- Asphyxiation.
- Electrocution.

One or more of the following factors causes maintenance accidents:

- Lack of perception of risk by managers/supervisors, often because of lack of necessary training.
- Unsafe or no system of work devised, for example, no permit-to-work system in operation, no facility to lock off machinery and electricity supply before work starts and until work has finished.
- No co-ordination between workers, and communication with other supervisors or managers.
- Lack of perception of risk by workers, including failure to wear protective clothing or equipment.
- Inadequacy of design, installation, siting of plant and equipment.
- Use of contractors with no health and safety systems or who are inadequately briefed on health and safety aspects.

Figure 2-3-1: Conveyor.   *Source: ACT.*

Figure 2-3-2: Electrical isolator with hole for padlock.   *Source: ACT.*

Maintenance control measures

Isolation

This does not simply mean switching off the equipment using the stop button. It includes switching the equipment off at the start button and switching off the isolator for the equipment

In new workplaces, individual isolators should be used; i.e. each piece of equipment has its own isolator near to it. In the past, one isolator often governed several items of equipment making it impossible to isolate a single piece of equipment on its own.

Lock out and tag out

Isolation alone does not afford adequate protection because there is nothing to prevent the isolator being switched back on, or removed fuses being replaced inadvertently, while the person who isolated the item in the first place is still working on the equipment (and still in danger).

To ensure that this does not happen, the isolator needs to be physically locked in the off position (typically using a padlock, the key to be held by the person in danger). Multiple lock out devices that can carry a number of padlocks for the different workers working on the equipment are also available. It is also a good idea to sign **"Do not switch on..."** or tag the equipment.

UNIT IGC2 - ELEMENT 3 - WORK EQUIPMENT - HAZARDS AND CONTROL

Summary of control measures
- Plan work in advance - provide safe access, support parts of equipment which could fail.
- Use written safe systems of work, method statements or permit to work systems as appropriate.
- Plan specific operations using method statements.
- Use physical means of isolating or locking off plant.
- Systems of working should incorporate two-man working for high risk operations.
- Integrate safety requirements in the planning of specific high risk tasks.
- Prevent unauthorised access to the work area by using barriers and signs.
- Ensure the competence of those carrying out the work.
- Ensure the availability and use of appropriate personal protective equipment (PPE) - gloves, eye protection.
- Prevent fire or explosion - thoroughly clean vessels that have contained flammable solids or liquids, gases or dusts and check them thoroughly before hot work is carried out.

Procedures for defective equipment

Workers should notify any shortcomings in the health and safety arrangements, even when no immediate danger exists, so that employers can take remedial action if needed.

Work equipment should be maintained in an efficient state, in efficient working order and in good repair. Defective work equipment should be removed from use.

The need for periodic examination and testing of pressure systems

INSPECTION AND EXAMINATION

Inspection

Work equipment exposed to conditions causing deterioration which is liable to result in dangerous situations should be inspected:

a) At suitable intervals.
b) Each time that exceptional circumstances which are liable to jeopardise the safety of the work equipment have occurred, to ensure that health and safety conditions are maintained and that any deterioration can be detected and remedied in good time.
c) Records of inspection results should be kept.

Every employer should ensure that the result of an inspection is recorded and kept until the next inspection is recorded.

Figure 2-3-3: Inspection and examination. Source: ACT.

Equipment should be inspected on a regular basis in order to confirm the condition that it is in. The inspection required is more than a simple daily pre-use check carried out by the operator. The person using equipment, who should be confirmed as competent, should carry out operator checks prior to the use of any equipment. Operator checks should include guards, cables, casing integrity, cutting or machine parts and safety devices such as cut-outs. The inspection required should be significant and address a list of identifiable health and safety critical parts. The purpose of an inspection sheet is to record deterioration of specific parts, abuse and misuse and also to ensure that all items are considered at the time of inspection, by serving as a reminder. The results of the inspection will confirm whether or not a piece of equipment is in a safe enough condition to use.

A pressure system is defined as follows:
- A system comprising one or more pressure vessels of rigid construction, and any associated pipework and protective devices.
- The pipework with its protective devices to which a transportable gas container is or is intended to be connected.
- A pipeline and its protective devices.

A pressure vessel is generally considered one which operates at a pressure greater than atmospheric pressure, e.g. steam boilers, receivers and air receivers.

Figure 2-3-4: Air compressor. Source: ACT.

Figure 2-3-5: Air receiver. Source: ACT.

Schemes of examination

Examination means a careful and critical scrutiny of a pressure system or part of a pressure system, in or out of service as appropriate. It means using suitable techniques, including testing where appropriate, to assess its actual condition and whether, for the period up to the next examination, it will not cause danger when properly used if normal maintenance is carried out.

Normal maintenance means such maintenance as it is reasonable to expect the user (in the case of an installed system) or owner (in the case of a mobile system) to ensure is carried out independently of any advice from the competent person making the examination.

A written scheme of examination must be available before any system is used. This should be established by a competent person and include:

- Pressure vessels.
- Pipe work and valves.
- Protective devices.
- Pumps and compressors.

Examination intervals should be specified, though these may be different for different parts of the system, so that, for example, deterioration can be detected before danger arises. An initial examination should be done before use. Any repairs or modifications should be controlled. Factors to be taken into account when deciding upon the frequency of examination will include:

- Previous intervals and system records.
- Standards of supervision and routine checks.
- Type and quality of fluids in the system.
- The likelihood of creep, fatigue, etc. failures.
- Corrosion potential and effect.
- Presence of heat sources etc.

The type of examination should also be specified.

Examinations should be carried out in accordance with the written scheme and the system adequately assessed for fitness for continued use. Appropriate preparations for and precautions during examination should be arranged for by the user. A report with any conditions or limitations on use should be prepared on completion of the examination.

Where the competent person's examination identifies imminent danger then a report must be made to the user.

Anyone operating a pressure system must be given adequate and suitable instructions for safe operation and emergency action. This instruction should form part of the operating instructions for the plant and should include information on start-up, shutdown, normal operation, functions of controls and emergency procedures. Doors providing routine access should be dealt with by specific instructions covering interlocking checks, opening and closing precautions and failure signs. Precautions must be taken to prevent unintentional pressurisation of parts of any system not designed for pressure.

Routine and regular maintenance should be carried out including periodic checks and inspections of critical parts or components.

Adequate records of examinations, repairs, modifications etc., should be kept at the premises where the system is used.

Importance of operation and emergency controls

OPERATION AND EMERGENCY CONTROLS

Any change in the operating conditions should only be possible by the use of a control, except if the change does not increase risk to health or safety. Examples of operating conditions include speed, pressure, temperature and power.

The controls provided should be designed and positioned so as to prevent inadvertent or accidental operation. Buttons and levers should be of appropriate design, for example, including a shroud or locking facility. It should not be possible for the control to automatically start due to the effects of gravity, vibration, or failure of a spring mechanism.

It should be possible to identify easily what each control does and on which equipment it takes effect. Both the controls and their markings should be clearly visible. As well as having legible wording or symbols, factors such as the colour, shape and position of controls are critical.

Warnings should be given sufficiently in advance of the equipment actually starting to give those at risk time to get clear. As well as time, suitable means of avoiding the risk should be provided. This may take the form of a device by means of which the person at risk can prevent start-up or warn the operator of their presence. Otherwise, there must be adequate provision to enable workers at risk to withdraw, e.g. sufficient space or exits. Circumstances will affect the type of warning chosen.

Stop controls

The action of the control should bring the equipment to a safe condition in a safe manner. This acknowledges that it is not always desirable to bring all items of work equipment immediately to a complete or instantaneous stop, for example, to prevent the unsafe build-up of heat or pressure or to allow a controlled run-down of large rotating parts. Similarly, stopping the mixing mechanism of a reactor during certain chemical reactions could lead to a dangerous exothermic reaction.

Accessible dangerous parts must be rendered stationary. However, parts of equipment which do not present a risk, such as suitably guarded cooling fans, do not need to be positively stopped and may be allowed to idle.

Emergency stop controls

Emergency stops are intended to effect a rapid response to potentially dangerous situations and they should not be used as functional stops during normal operation.

Emergency stop controls should be easily reached and actuated. Common types are mushroom-headed buttons, bars, levers, kick plates, or pressure-sensitive cables.

UNIT IGC2 - ELEMENT 3 - WORK EQUIPMENT - HAZARDS AND CONTROL

Figure 2-3-6: Controls and emergency stop.   Source: ACT.

Figure 2-3-7: Controls.   Source: ACT.

STABILITY

Employers should ensure that work equipment or any part of work equipment is stabilised by clamping or otherwise where necessary for purposes of health or safety.

Most machines used in a fixed position should be bolted or otherwise fastened down so that they do not move or rock during use. It has long been recognised that woodworking and other machines (except those specifically designed for portable use) should be bolted to the floor or similarly secured to prevent unexpected movement.

LIGHTING

Any workplace where a person is using work equipment must have adequate lighting. Local lighting may be needed to give sufficient view of a dangerous process or to reduce visual fatigue. Operations such as maintenance work may not have sufficient general lighting and equipment such as overhead cranes may temporarily obscure lighting.

MARKINGS

Certain markings may also serve as a warning, e.g. the maximum working speed, maximum working load, speed and direction of rotation, contents and direction of movement in pipework or the contents being of a hazardous nature (e.g. colour coded gas bottles or service mains).

WARNINGS

Warnings and warning devices are introduced following the implementation of markings and other physical measures but where appropriate risks to health and safety remain. Warnings are usually in the form of a notice, sign or similar. Examples of warnings are positive instructions (hard hats **MUST** be worn), prohibitions (no smoking) and restrictions (do not heat above 60 degrees Celsius). Warning devices are active units that give out either an audible or visual signal, usually connected to the equipment in order that it operates only when a hazard exists.

CLEAR UNOBSTRUCTED WORKSPACE

Workrooms should have enough free space to allow workers to get to and from workstations and to move within the room with ease. Workrooms should be of sufficient height (from floor to ceiling) over most of the room to enable safe access to workstations. In older buildings with obstructions such as low beams, the obstruction should be clearly marked.

The work space which is necessary for the tasks to be carried out should be determined and provided to ensure safe working.

Where work equipment, such as a circular saw, is used in a workplace care should be taken to ensure that adequate space is around the equipment to ensure it is not overcrowded and does not cause risk to operators and those passing by the equipment when it is operating.

What is expected of operators

Operators should use any machinery or equipment in accordance with any training or instruction that they have received. Furthermore, operators should be expected to report any faults or defects in their machinery or equipment which, if not rectified, could lead to the development of hazardous situations.

3.2 - Hand-held tools

Hazards and misuse of hand tools and controls for safe use

Hand tools are tools powered manually, i.e. axes, hammers, screwdrivers; therefore the biggest hazard would arise from errors made by the user e.g. striking a finger whilst using a hammer or cuts from a saw.

REQUIREMENTS FOR SAFE USE

Hammers	Avoid split, broken or loose shafts (handles) and worn or chipped heads. Heads should be properly secured to the shafts.
Files	These should have a proper handle. Never use them as levers.
Chisels	The cutting edge should be sharpened to the correct angle. Do not allow the head of cold chisels to spread to a mushroom shape - grind off the sides regularly. Use a hand guard on the chisel.

Screwdrivers Never use them as chisels, and never use hammers on them. Use the correct size and type of screwdriver for the screw. Split handles are dangerous.

Spanners Avoid splayed jaws. Scrap any which show signs of slipping. Have enough spanners of the right size. Do not improvise by using pipes, etc., as extensions to the handle.

Examples of misuse of hand tools are shown below:

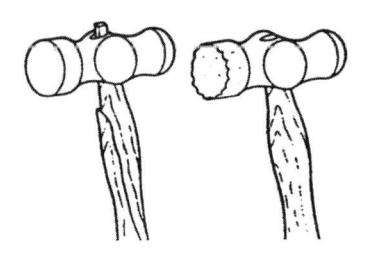

Figure 2-3-8: Hammer shaft split with peg holding on head and very worn hammer head. *Source: ACT.*

Figure 2-3-9: Mushroom shape head. *Source: ACT.*

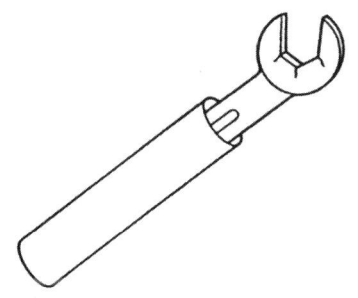

Figure 2-3-10: Piece of tube used as an extension. *Source: ACT.*

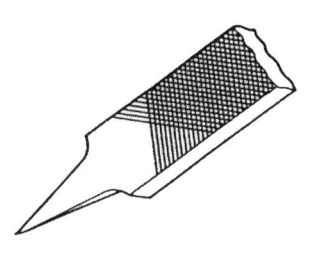

Figure 2-3-11: Broken file. *Source: ACT.*

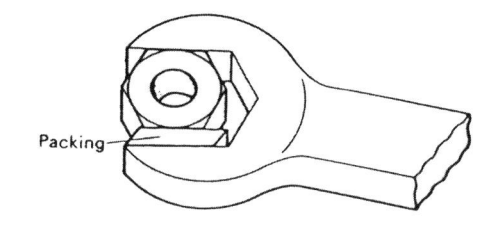

Figure 2-3-12: Packing material used in spanner head. *Source: ACT.*

Figure 2-3-13: File used as a lever. *Source: ACT.*

SUITABILITY FOR PURPOSE AND LOCATION

Use of alloy or bronze hammers or spanners to prevent sparks, and damping with water, in areas where there is a flammable atmosphere.

Hazards of portable power tools and the means of control

ELECTRIC DRILL

Electric drills are used for penetrating various materials and in construction are usually of a medium to heavy-duty nature. This equipment involves rotating shafts and tool bits, sharp tools, electricity and flying debris.

Hazards

Obvious hazards include shock and electrocution leading to possible fatalities - however this potential is reduced by using 110 volt or battery operated equipment. Other hazards include puncture, entanglement hazards, noise and dust.

Control

Control measures include using only equipment that is suitable for the task, ensuring equipment is tested and inspected as safe to use, suitable shut off and isolation measures, goggles, hearing protection. Care should be taken to ensure the drill bits are kept sharp as injuries can occur when the rotating drill bit gets stuck in material and the drill is caused to kick and rotate in the operator's hands.

SANDER

Hazards

Sanding equipment is available in a variety of sizes from hand held equipment to large industrial machines. Sanders are used to provide a smooth finished surface, using a mechanical abrasive action. Sanding operations are carried out on a wide variety of materials including wood, minerals such as marble and man-made fibres. The main hazards associated with the sanding process are vibration and noise. Also, harm can be caused by the inhalation of respirable particles from dust. Where organic materials such as wood are being processed, fire may result from overheated surfaces or explosion from dust by-products. Associated hazards may include electrocution and if supply cables are damaged by hand held sanders, particularly if the sander is placed on the ground whilst still rotating. Other risks include trips from training leads, cuts from sharp surfaces and strains or sprains from manual handling of process materials.

Control

When using sanding equipment, suitable personal respiratory protective equipment (RPE) is required to protect the user from the dust exposure. Where possible, local exhaust ventilation equipment should be used to minimise dust in the atmosphere.

UNIT IGC2 - ELEMENT 3 - WORK EQUIPMENT - HAZARDS AND CONTROL

In order to protect against vibration injuries, the operator should be given regular breaks and the equipment maintained at intervals, including the renewal of sanding media to prevent the need for over exertion by the operator. Where hand-held tools are used suitable hand protection will also reduce injuries from vibration, cuts and manual handling. Pre-use inspections by the operator and regular thorough examinations should be carried out to identify potential electrical problems. Care should be taken to ensure that power leads do not create tripping hazards and they are positioned so that the likelihood of mechanical damage is minimised.

3.3 - Machinery hazards

Main mechanical and non-mechanical hazards

MECHANICAL HAZARDS

Entanglement

The mere fact that a machine part is revolving can in itself constitute a very real hazard. Loose clothing, jewellery, long hair, etc. increase the risk of entanglement. Examples of rotating action hazards include: couplings, drill chucks/ bits, flywheels, spindles and shafts (especially those with keys/bolts).

Figure 2-3-14: Auger drill - entanglement. *Source: STIHL.*

Figure 2-3-15: Grinder - entanglement, eye injury & abrasion. *Source: ACT.*

Friction and abrasion

Friction burns and encountering rough surfaces moving at high speed, e.g. sanding machine, grinding wheel etc., can cause abrasion injuries.

Figure 2-3-16: Chop saw - cutting. *Source: Speedy Hire plc.*

Figure 2-3-17: Abrasive wheel - abrasion. *Source: ACT.*

Cutting

Saw blades, knives and even rough edges, especially when moving at high speed, can result in serious cuts and even amputation injuries. The dangerous part can appear stationary! Examples of cutting action hazards include saws, slicing machines, abrasive cutting discs, chains (especially chainsaws) etc.

Shear

When two or more machine parts move towards/past, one another a "trap" is created. This can result in a crush injury or even an amputation. Examples of shearing/crushing action hazards include: scissor lifts, power presses, guillotines etc.

Stabbing and puncture

The body may be penetrated by sharp pieces of equipment, or material contained in the equipment, e.g. fixing materials such as nails fired into a part of the body, or a drill bit puncturing the hand.

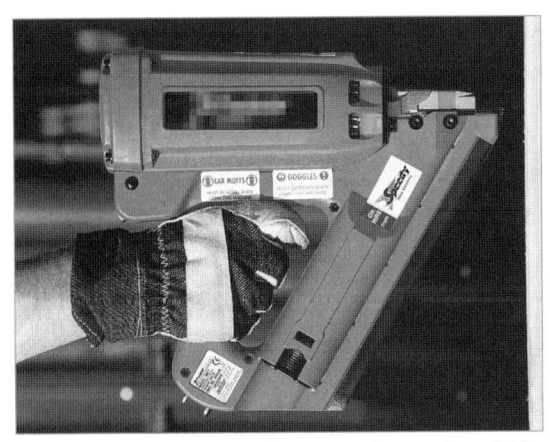

Figure 2-3-18: Nail gun - stabbing & puncture. *Source: Speedy Hire plc.*

Figure 2-3-19: Mobile elevated work platform - shear. *Source: ACT.*

Impact

Impact is caused by objects that strike the body, but do not penetrate it. They may cause the person or part of the person to be moved, sometimes violently, resulting in injury e.g. struck by the jib of a crane/excavator or materials on a hoist or the moving platter of a machine like a surface grinder.

Figure 2-3-20: Elevated work platform - crushing. *Source: ACT.*

Figure 2-3-21: Digger and dumper truck - impact. *Source: ACT.*

Crushing

Caused when part of the body is caught between either two moving parts of machinery or a moving part and a stationary object, e.g. the platform of hoist closing together with the ground or an overhead beam; moving parts of piling equipment or the callipers of a spot welding machine.

Drawing-in

When a belt runs round a roller an in-running nip (pinch point) is created between them (in the direction of travel); this inward movement draws in any part of the body presented to it. Examples of drawing-in (in-running / nip) hazards are V-belts - such as on the drive from a motor to the drum of a cement mixer, meshing gears and conveyors.

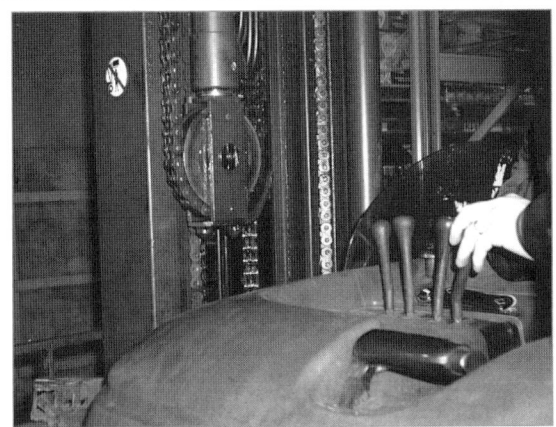

Figure 2-3-22: Lift mast - drawing-in. *Source: ACT.*

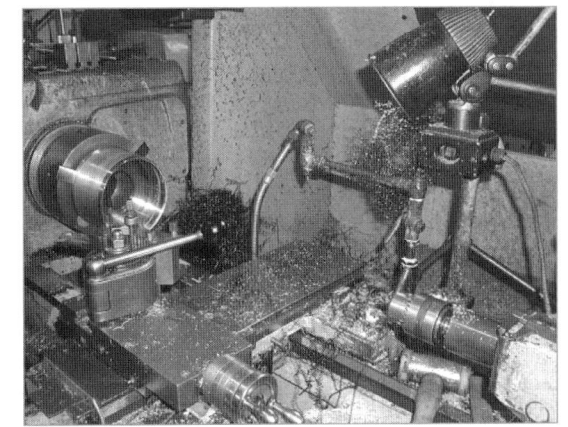

Figure 2-3-23: Lathe - ejection. *Source: ACT.*

Ejection

When pieces of the material being worked on or components of the machinery are thrown or fired out of the equipment during operation they represent an ejection hazard. For example, parts of a shattered grinding wheel, sparks, swarf (waste metal shavings) or a nail from a nail gun.

UNIT IGC2 - ELEMENT 3 - WORK EQUIPMENT - HAZARDS AND CONTROL

Injury by compressed air or high pressure fluid injection

Injection of fluids through the skin may lead to soft tissue injuries similar to crushing. Air entering the blood stream through the skin may be fatal. Examples are diesel injectors, spray painting, compressed air jets for blast cleaning the outside of a building and a high pressure lance for cutting concrete.

Figure 2-3-24: Disc saw - ejection. *Source: Water Active, Nov 06.*

Figure 2-3-25: Fluid injection. *Source: ACT.*

Check your understanding

Identify the mechanical hazards sketched in figure 2-3-26. Answers are given in figure 2-3-33.

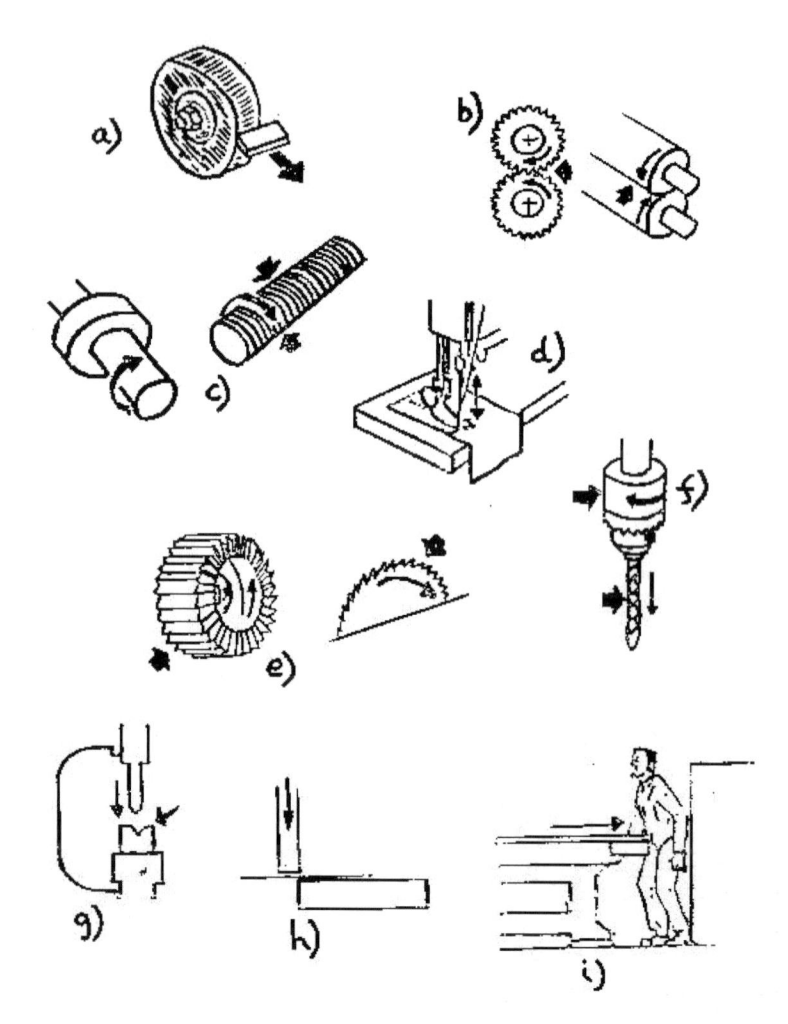

Figure 2-3-26: Examples of mechanical machinery hazards (Questions). *Source: ACT.*

146

NON MECHANICAL HAZARDS

Machinery may also present other hazards. The nature of the hazard will determine the measures taken to protect workers from them.

The various sources of non-mechanical hazards include the following:

- Electricity - shock and burns.
- Hot surfaces / fire.
- Noise and vibration.
- Biological - viral and bacterial.
- High/low temperatures.
- Chemicals that are toxic, irritant, flammable, corrosive, explosive.
- Ionising and non ionising radiation.
- Access - slips, trips and falls; obstructions and projections.
- Manual handling.

SUMMARY - MACHINERY HAZARDS

Mechanical		Non -mechanical
Entanglement	e.g. Auger drill, drilling machine	Electricity
Friction and abrasion	e.g. Grinding wheel	Hot surfaces / fire
Cutting	e.g. Sharp edges of circular saw	Noise
Shear	e.g. Scissor lift mechanism	Vibration

Mechanical		Non -mechanical
Stabbing and Puncture	e.g. Nail gun	Extremes of temperature
Impact	e.g. Moving arm of an excavator	Chemicals
Crushing	e.g. Platform of a hoist, ram of a forge hammer	Radiation
Drawing in	e.g. Conveyor belt	Access
Injection	e.g. High pressure hydraulic oil system	Manual handling
Ejection	e.g. Grinding wheel - sparks	

Hazards presented by a range of equipment

OFFICE MACHINERY

Photocopier

Hazards are drawing-in, hot surfaces, fumes, toner, electrical, manual handling, noise and glare.

Document shredder

Main hazards are drawing-in, cutting or crushing and also cuts from paper handling and electrical dangers.

Figure 2-3-27: Abrasive wheel (grinder). *Source: ACT.*

Figure 2-3-28: Document shredder. *Source: www.axminster.co.uk.*

MANUFACTURING / MAINTENANCE MACHINERY

Bench-top grinder

Bench top grinders are typically found in workshops (indoor use) and operators are required to be trained, competent and formally appointed in order to dress (re-surface) or change grinding wheels. Positioning of grinders should be at a suitable height to avoid poor posture whilst using them and they must be permanently fixed or bolted in position. Grinders may be used on construction sites when installed in a site mobile workshop. Tasks involve sharpening of tool bits (drills, chisels, blades), shaping steel, and de burring cut steel components lead to hazards including friction and abrasion from contact with the spinning wheel which can revolve at speeds in excess of 2,900 revolutions per minute, entanglement or drawing in (of fingers, gloves or other items being pulled between the rotating parts of the abrasive wheel and rest) and possible ejection when parts of the wheel or work piece break and sparks are thrown off. Other hazards are electricity, heat and noise. Control measures include an adjustable fixed guard that is fitted and in good working order, trained and competent operatives, grade1 (EN166: 2002) impact resistant goggles, respiratory protective equipment (depending on task) and personal hearing protection.

Pedestal drill

Hazards in setting up the equipment include failure to remove chuck-key (which will be thrown off in use) and failure to secure guard to drive pulleys.

Hazards when the equipment is in use include entanglement, puncture and flying swarf.

AGRICULTURAL / HORTICULTURAL MACHINERY

Cylinder mower

Hazards are:

- Contact with revolving blades.
- Potential for the machine to overturn when on inclines.
- Noise.
- Collision with road traffic or pedestrians.
- Fumes.
- Dust.
- Possibility of being struck by stones ejected from the machine.
- Exposure to sun.
- Attacks by insects.
- Flammability dangers associated with fuel.

Petrol-driven strimmer / brush-cutter

Hazards are:

- Exposure to fumes.
- Possibility of fire or explosion.
- Contact with the moving parts of the strimmer.
- Stuck by flying stones and fragments.
- Noise and vibration.
- Manual handling.
- Slips, trips and falls.
- Possibility of being struck by traffic.
- Exposure to extreme weather conditions.

Figure 2-3-29: Brushcutter.   Source: www.kawasaki.co.uk.

Chain-saw

Despite safety improvements, chainsaws can be dangerous, and injuries can arise from their use. The most common accident arises from "kickback," when a chain tooth at the upper quadrant of the guide bar tip cuts into wood without cutting through it. The chain cannot continue moving, and the bar is driven in an upward arc toward the operator. Kickback can result in serious injuries or death. Another dangerous situation occurs when heavy timber begins to fall or shift when a cut is nearly complete - the chainsaw operator can be trapped or crushed. Operation of chainsaws can also cause vibration white finger, tinnitus or industrial deafness. The risks associated with chainsaw use mean that protective clothing and hearing protectors should be worn while operating them, and many jurisdictions require that operators be certified or licensed to work with chainsaws. Injury can also result if the chain breaks during operation due to poor maintenance or attempting to cut inappropriate materials.

Source: wikipedia.org.

RETAIL MACHINERY

Compactor

Compactors are used to reduce waste volume for transport and disposal. Hazards include crushing and impact injuries, also fumes and noxious substances.

Checkout conveyor system

Hazards include trapping and drawing-in between the rollers and belt and also crushing between the load and conveyor. Ergonomic hazards due to the working position of the operator, may also be present.

CONSTRUCTION SITE MACHINERY

Cement mixer

Cement mixers are portable construction plant used for mixing a variety of aggregates and cement used in the construction process. The main benefit of this equipment is removing a significant volume of the manual labour aspect of the mixing process although a significant amount of labour intensive activities remain.

The equipment consists of a motor (electric, petrol or diesel) linked through a gear box and drive shaft to a rotating drum that incorporates internal mixing blades to aid the mixing process. The assembly may vary from a complete unit that pivots on a central bar or a two part system where the mixer is seated onto a plinth or stand and pivots forward to enable emptying of the drum when the mixture is complete.

Hazards arise from the source of power when electricity is combined with the water used in the mixing process.

Figure 2-3-30: Cement mixer. Source: ACT.

In order to control this risk, a low voltage power supply should be used, with suitable heavy duty cable and cable covers when there is a risk of running over them with vehicles or plant. Used with a residual current protection device a good level of protection can be obtained. When the fuel source is diesel or petrol there is a risk of fire, which increases during refuelling operations when the exhaust system may still be hot or workers may be smoking in the close vicinity of the equipment.

The rotating drum and drive shaft poses an entanglement risk with personal protective equipment and other tools. If covers are removed they can expose drive belts or gearing with the associated risk of drawing in. Operatives loading mixers should be warned of the dangers of shovels and trowels becoming caught in the mixer blades and snatching the hand tool out of the operatives hand with force, which may result in personal injury to limbs and muscles. Loading the mixer is a manual task which can result in injury from repetitive, twisting motion when emptying shovels or gauging buckets into the mixer. Job rotation should be planned. Risk assessments may be required for the fumes and dusts involved in the mixing process. Often the mixing activity is a slow process, and operatives may tend to leave the mixer running alone until the mix is ready. The equipment when running should, at all times, be attended to prevent unauthorised access and injuries to third parties. As the mixing process proceeds there is a likelihood of build up of materials on the floor, leading to a risk of slips and trips and a possibility of falling onto the moving equipment.

Bench-mounted circular saw

Cutting is the main hazard together with electricity, noise and sawdust.

Figure 2-3-31: Bench cross-cut circular saw. Source: ACT.

Figure 2-3-32: Pedestal drill. Source: ACT.

Reference to examples of machinery hazards (Questions), check your understanding page 146.

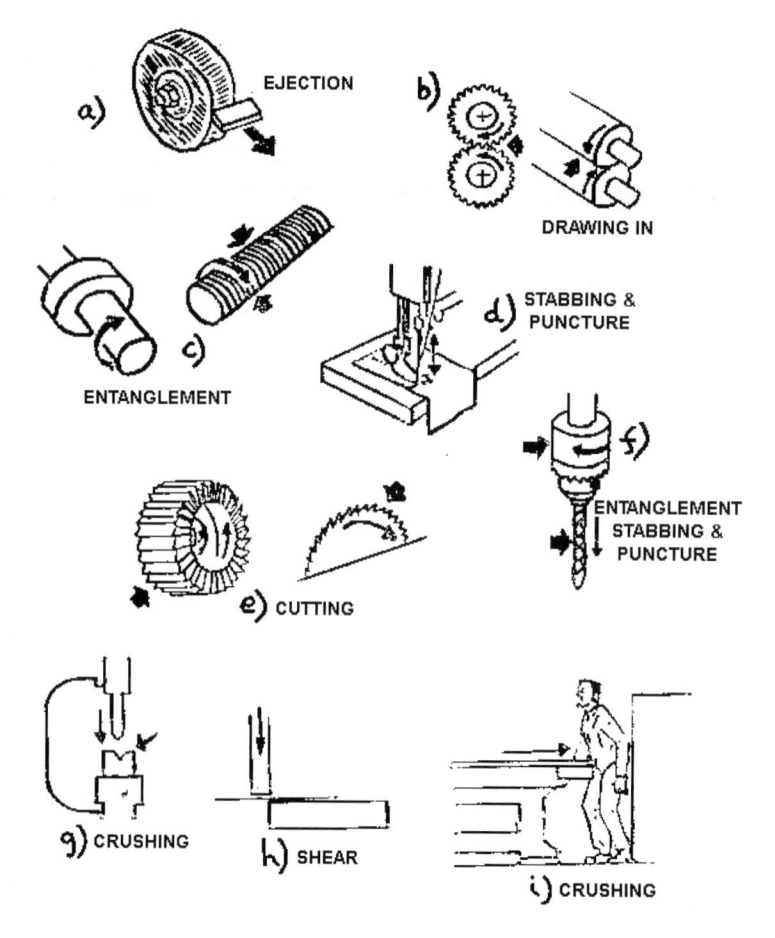

Figure 2-3-33: Examples of mechanical machinery hazards (Answers). Source: ACT.

3.4 - Protection from machinery hazards

MACHINERY GUARDING

Objective of machinery guarding
- To prevent workers from coming into contact with dangerous parts of machinery.
- To prevent physical injury from power driven and manually operated machines.
- To enable machines to be operated safely without interference with production.

Dangerous parts of machinery

Measures should be taken to prevent access to any dangerous part of machinery or to any rotating part; or to stop the movement of any dangerous part of the machinery before any part of a person enters a danger zone. Effective measures for guards are as follows:

- Whenever possible, the provision of fixed guards enclosing every dangerous part.
- The provision of other guards or protection devices where access is required for the functional use of the equipment.
- The provision of jigs, holders, push-sticks or similar protection appliances used in conjunction with the machinery.
- The provision of information, instruction, training and supervision.

All guards and protection devices provided should:

- Be suitable for the purpose for which they are provided.
- Be of good construction, sound material and adequate strength.
- Be maintained in an efficient state, in efficient working order and in good repair.
- Not give rise to any increased risk to health or safety.
- Not be easily bypassed or disabled.
- Be situated at sufficient distance from the danger zone.
- Not unduly restrict the view of the operating cycle of the machinery, where such a view is necessary.
- Be so constructed or adapted that they allow operations necessary to fit or replace parts and for maintenance work, restricting access so that it is allowed only to the area where the work is to be carried out and, if possible, without having to dismantle the guard or protection device.

Notes:

- When deciding on the appropriate level of safeguarding, risk assessment criteria i.e. likelihood of injury, potential severity of injury, numbers at risk, need to be considered both in relation to the normal operation of the machinery and also other operations such as maintenance, repair, setting, tuning, adjustment etc. Further information is given in machine-specific and sector-specific guidance.

- Where guards, protection devices and jigs are not effective in preventing access and a significant residual risk of injury remains, supervision is of paramount importance.
- When considering the maintenance of guards and protection devices additional consideration should be given to include those which are not attached to the machine itself, e.g. perimeter fences and also particularly when relevant to CE marked equipment.

The principles, merits and limitations of protection methods

HIERARCHY OF MEASURES FOR DANGEROUS PARTS OF MACHINERY

- Prevent access to dangerous parts by means of **F**ixed guard (preferably fully enclosing).
- When the above is not practicable protect by other guards (**I**nterlock, **A**utomatic) or safety devices (e.g. **T**rip device).
- When the above is not practicable protect by using safety appliances (e.g. push stick or jig).
- When the above is not practicable protect by information, instruction and training.
- The various guards and safety devices can be summarised as follows:

    Fixed

    Interlock

    Automatic

    Trip devices

FIXED GUARDS

A fixed guard/fence must be fitted such that it cannot be removed other than by the use of specialist tools which are not available to operators of the equipment. A fixed guard may be designed to enable access by authorised personnel for maintenance or inspection, but only when the dangerous parts of the machine have been isolated. A common example of a fixed guard is shown in figure 9-31. The holes in the mesh guard are of sufficient size to allow air circulation to cool the drive belt, but small enough to prevent the finger of the hand from penetrating the mesh and result in injury from the belt.

Distance (fixed) guard

Fixed guards do not completely cover the danger point but place it out of normal reach. The larger the opening (to feed in material) the greater must be the distance from the opening to the danger point. A tree shredding machine uses a fixed distance guard design to prevent operators reaching the dangerous part of a machine when in use.

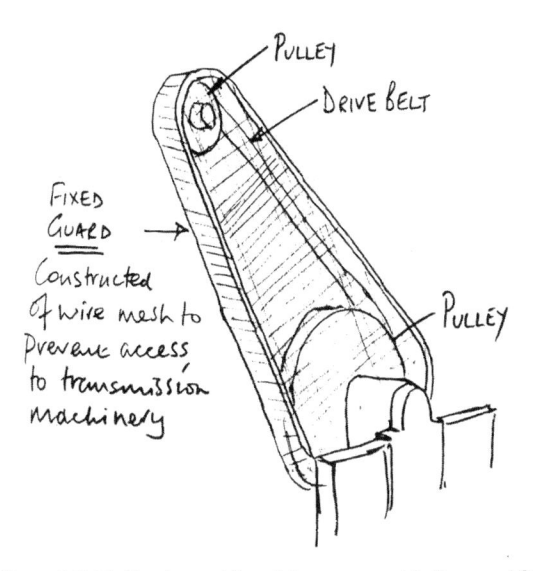

Figure 2-3-34: Fixed guard (hand drawn example). *Source: ACT.*

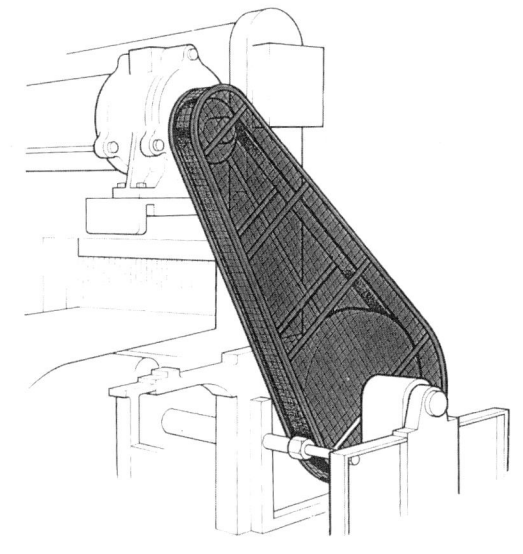

Figure 2-3-35: Total enclosure fixed guard. *Source: BS EN ISO 12100.*

Figure 2-3-36: Fixed guard - panel removed. *Source: ACT.*

Figure 2-3-37: Fixed guard over fan - mesh too big. *Source: ACT.*

Merits of fixed guards
- Create a physical barrier.
- Require a tool to remove.
- Can protect against non-mechanical hazards such as dust and fluids which may be ejected.
- No moving parts - therefore they require very little maintenance.

Limitations of fixed guards
- Do not disconnect power when not in place, therefore, machine can still be operated without guard.
- May cause problems with visibility for inspection.
- If enclosed, may create problems with heat.

INTERLOCKING GUARDS

An interlocking guard is similar to a fixed guard, but has a movable (usually hinged) part, so connected to the machine controls that if the movable part is in the open/lifted position the dangerous moving part at the work point cannot operate. This can be arranged so that the act of closing the guard activates the working part (to speed up work efficiently), e.g. the front panel of a photocopier. Interlocked guards are useful if operators need regular access to the danger area.

Merits of interlocking guards
- Connected to power source, therefore machine cannot be operated with guard open.
- Allow regular access.

Limitations of interlocking guards
- Have moving parts therefore need regular maintenance.
- Can be over-ridden.
- If interlock is in the form of a gate, a person can step inside and close gate behind them (someone else could re-activate machine).
- Dangerous parts of machinery may not stop immediately the guard is opened. A delay timer or brake might need to be fitted as well, e.g. the drum on a spin drier does not stop instantly when the door is opened.

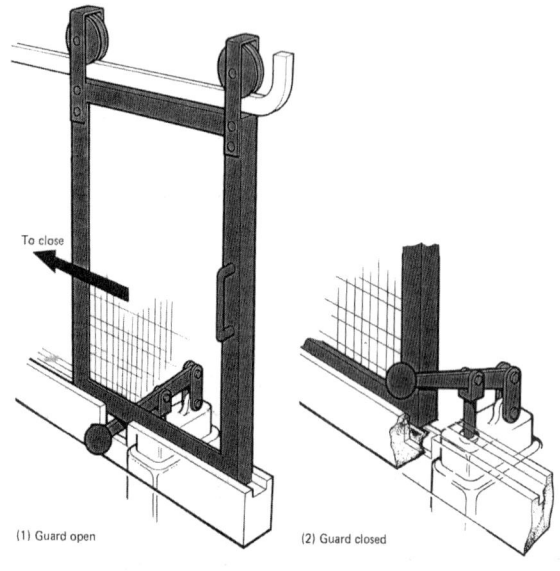

Figure 2-3-38: Open & closed interlock guard.
Source: BS EN ISO 12100.

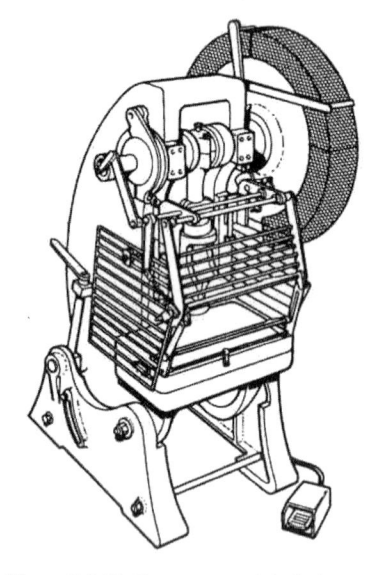

Figure 2-3-39: Power press - interlock guard.
Source: BS EN ISO 12100.

Automatic guard

A guard which operates as the machine goes through its cycle. In some cases it physically moves the operator away from danger and is therefore only suitable for slow cycling equipment, e.g. on a guillotine or large panel press.

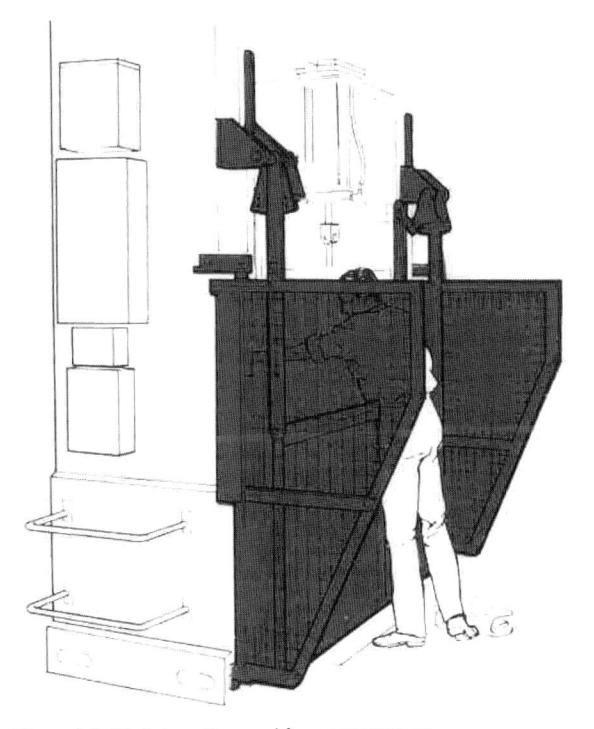

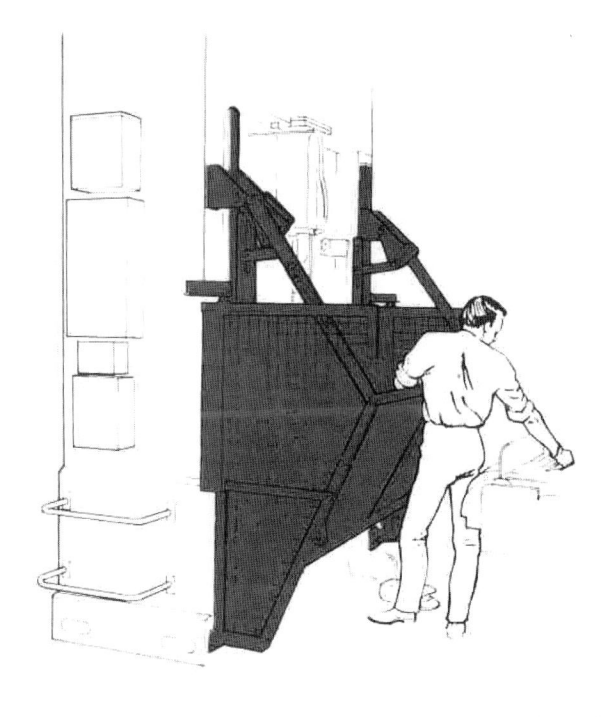

Figure 2-3-40: Automatic guard for a power press. *Source: BS EN ISO 12100.*

Merits of automatic guards
- Guard becomes effective as part of the normal cycle of the equipment. Does not have to rely on human intervention.

Limitations of automatic guards
- Usually restricted to slow cycling machinery.

TRIP DEVICES

A sensitive rod, cable or other mechanism, which causes the device to activate a further mechanism which either stops or reverses the machine. It is critical to note that this is not classed as a guard. A guard is something that physically prevents access to the hazard whereas a trip device detects the person in the danger zone and responds to this - e.g. pressure sensitive mats.

Merits of trip devices
- Can used as an additional risk control measure.
- Can minimise the severity of injury.

Limitations of trip devices
- Can be over-ridden.
- May not prevent harm from occurring.
- May cause production delays and increase stress in users with false 'trips'.

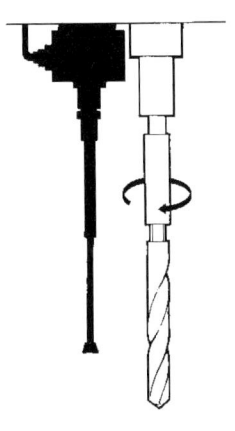

Figure 2-3-41: Trip device. *Source: BS EN ISO 12100.*

Figure 2-3-42: Trip device on radial drill. *Source: ACT.*

UNIT IGC2 - ELEMENT 3 - WORK EQUIPMENT - HAZARDS AND CONTROL

ADJUSTABLE GUARD

A fixed guard which incorporates an adjustable element (which remains fixed for the duration of a particular operation).

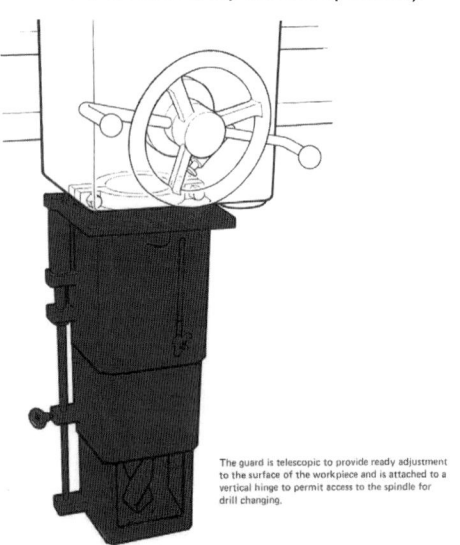

The guard is telescopic to provide ready adjustment to the surface of the workpiece and is attached to a vertical hinge to permit access to the spindle for drill changing.

Figure 2-3-43: Adjustable (fixed) guard.   Source: BS EN ISO 12100.

SELF ADJUSTING GUARD

Guards which prevent accidental access by the operator, but allow entry of the material to the machine in such a way that the material actually forms part of the guarding arrangement itself. For example, a hand held circular saw.

Figure 2-3-44: Self adjusting (fixed) guard.   Source: ACT.

Merits of adjustable guards
- Can be adjusted by operator to provide protection.

Limitations of adjustable guards
- Are reliant on the operator to adjust to the correct position.
- May obscure visibility when in use.

TWO-HAND CONTROL (2HC) DEVICE

They provide a level of protection where other methods are not practicable, helping to ensure the operators' hands remain outside the danger area. A two handed control is a device that requires both hands to operate it. Note that '2HC' devices protect only the operator and then, only provided the assistance of a colleague is not solicited to activate one control e.g. hedge trimmer, garment press.

Merits of two hand control devices
- Ensures both of the operator's hands are out of danger area when machine is operated.

Limitations of two hand control devices
- Only protects the operator from harm.
- May limit speed of operation with delays if controls are not pressed at exactly same time.

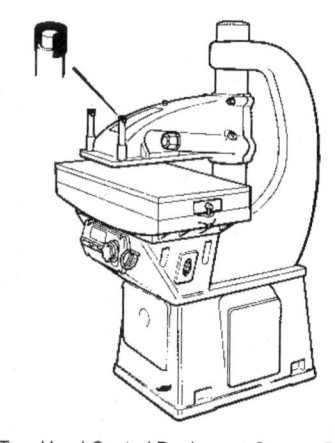

Figure 2-3-45: Two-Hand Control Device.   Source: BS EN ISO 12100.

Figure 2-3-46: Fixed guard and push stick.   Source: Lincsafe.

PROTECTION APPLIANCES

When the methods of safeguarding mentioned above are not practicable then protection appliances such as jigs, holders and push-sticks must be provided. They will help to keep the operator's hands at a safe distance from the danger area. There is no physical restraint to prevent the operator from placing their hands in danger.

Merits of protection appliances
- Provide distance between operator and hazard.

Limitations of protection appliances
- Harm may still occur from other non-mechanical hazards.
- Failure of protection appliance (e.g. breaking or kickback) may present additional hazard to operator.

EMERGENCY STOP CONTROLS

Emergency stops are intended to effect a rapid response to potentially dangerous situations and they should not be used as functional stops during normal operation.

Emergency stop controls should be easily reached and actuated. Common types are mushroom-headed buttons, bars, levers, kick plates, or pressure-sensitive cables.

Merits
- Removes power immediately.
- Equipment has to be reset after use.
- Prevents accidental restarting of the equipment.

Limitations
- Does not prevent access to the danger area.
- May be incorrectly positioned.

PERSONAL PROTECTIVE EQUIPMENT (PPE)

PPE is as a last resort and should only be relied upon when other controls do not adequately control risks. The use of machinery presents a number of mechanical hazards and care has to be taken that PPE is not used in situations where they present an increased risk of entanglement or drawing in to machinery, such as might happen with loose overalls and gloves.

Main examples are:

- Eye protection (safety spectacles / glasses, goggles and face shields) - protection for the eyes and the head from flying particles, welding glare, dust, fumes and splashes.
- Head protection (safety helmets or scalp protectors i.e. bump caps) - protection from falling objects, or striking fixed objects.
- Protective clothing for the body (overalls) - protection from a wide range of hazards.
- High Visibility clothing - enables an operative who may work in or around a dangerous area to be better seen by others working in that area, for example, operatives working where there are plant and machinery movements.
- Gloves (chain mail gloves and sleeves) - protection against cuts and abrasions when handling machined components, raw material or machinery cutters.
- Footwear (steel in-soles and toe-caps) - protection against sharp objects that might be stood on or objects dropped while handling them.
- Ear protection for noisy machine operations.

Merits
- Easy to see if it is being worn.
- Provides protection against a variety of hazards.

Limitations
- Only protects the user.
- May not give adequate protection.
- May pose additional hazards e.g. gloves becoming entangled.

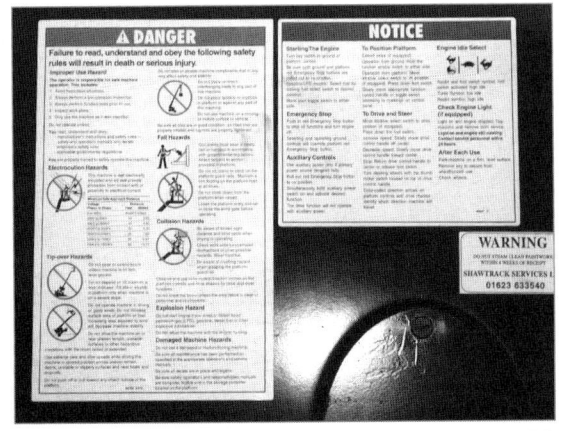

Figure 2-3-47: Information and instruction. *Source: ACT.*

Figure 2-3-48: PPE and supervision. *Source: ACT.*

INFORMATION, INSTRUCTION, TRAINING AND SUPERVISION

The employer should ensure that all persons who use work equipment and any of the other workers who supervise or manage the use of work equipment have available to them adequate health and safety information and, where appropriate, written instructions relevant to the use of the work equipment.

This includes information and, where appropriate, written instructions that are comprehensible to those concerned on:

- The conditions in which and the methods by which the work equipment may be used.
- Foreseeable abnormal situations and the action to be taken if such a situation were to occur.
- Any conclusions to be drawn from experience in using the work equipment.

Merits
- Easy to reach a wide audience on a variety of subjects.

Limitations
- Relies entirely on the person concerned to follow the instruction.
- May be misunderstood.

Application of protection methods to a range of equipment listed

OFFICE MACHINERY

Photocopier
Appropriate precautions are to avoid loose clothing i.e. ties, signage for hot components, well ventilated / suitable extraction, gloves, isolate from power source, training in good practice when removing paper jams, etc.

Shredder
Appropriate precautions are interlocked guards and trip wires.

MANUFACTURING / MAINTENANCE MACHINERY

Bench grinder
Appropriate precautions are fixed and adjustable guards together with PPE.

Pedestal drill

Appropriate precautions for pre-use are:
- Drive pulley entanglement prevented by isolation from power.
- Check that chuck key is removed before use.

Appropriate precautions during use are:
- Prevent entanglement - close fitting clothing, control of long hair and removal of jewellery.
- Puncture prevented by jigs or clamping devices.
- Adjustable guard, face shield / goggles for protection from flying swarf.

AGRICULTURAL / HORTICULTURAL MACHINERY

Cylinder mower
Appropriate precautions are:
- Fitting of guards to protect the blades.
- Provision of personal protective equipment (e.g. ear defenders, eye protection and high visibility clothing).
- Coning off areas in close proximity to moving traffic.
- Training drivers in the operation of the machine on sloping ground and on re-fuelling procedures.

Petrol-driven strimmer / brush-cutter
Appropriate precautions are fixed guards and PPE.

RETAIL MACHINERY

Compactor
Appropriate precautions are interlocked guards.

Checkout conveyor system
Appropriate precautions are interlocked guards and trip devices.

CONSTRUCTION MACHINERY

Cement mixer
Appropriate precautions are interlocked and adjustable guards.

Bench-mounted circular saw
Appropriate precautions are self adjusting guards and PPE.

Basic requirements for guards and safety devices

EFFECTIVE GUARDS AND DEVICES

All guards and protection devices provided should:

a) Be *suitable* for the purpose for which they are provided.
b) Be of *good construction*, sound material and adequate strength.
c) Be *maintained* in an efficient state, in efficient working order and in good repair.
d) Not give rise to any *increased risk* to health or safety.
e) Not be *easily bypassed* or disabled.
f) Be situated at *sufficient distance* from the danger zone.
g) Not unduly *restrict the view* of the operating cycle of the machinery, where such a view is necessary.
h) Be so constructed or adapted that they allow operations necessary to fit or replace parts and for maintenance work, restricting access so that it is allowed only to the area where the work is to be carried out and, if possible, without having to dismantle the guard or protection device.

COMPATIBLE WITH PROCESS

Compatibility with the material being processed - this is particularly important in the food processing industry where the guard material should not constitute a source of contamination of the product. Its ability to maintain its physical and mechanical properties after coming into contact with potential contaminants such as cutting fluids used in machining operations or cleaning and sterilising agents used in food processing machinery is also very important. In selecting an appropriate safeguard for a particular type of machinery or danger area, it should be borne in mind that a fixed guard is simple, and should be used where access to the danger area is not required during operation of the machinery or for cleaning, setting or other activities. As the need for access arises and increases in frequency, the importance of safety procedures for removal of a fixed guard increases until the frequency is such that interlocking should be used.

ADEQUATE STRENGTH

Guard mounting should be compatible with the strength and duty of the guard. In selecting the material to be used for the construction of a guard, consideration should be given to the following:

- Its ability to withstand the force of ejection of parts of the machinery or material being processed, where this is a foreseeable danger.
- Its ability to provide protection against hazards identified. In many cases, the guard may fulfil a combination of functions such as prevention of access and containment of hazards. This may apply where the hazards include ejected particles, liquids, dust, fumes, radiation, noise, etc. and one or more of these considerations may govern the selection of guard materials.

MAINTAINED

All guards must be maintained in effective order to perform their function. This will require a planned approach to checks on guards and work such as checking the security of fixed guards.

ALLOW MAINTENANCE WITHOUT REMOVAL

Its weight and size are factors to be considered in relation to the need to remove and replace it for routine maintenance.

NOT INCREASE RISK OR RESTRICT VIEW

Any guard selected should not itself present a hazard such as trapping or shear points, rough or sharp edges or other hazards likely to cause injury or restrict the view of the process or machine by the operator.

Power operated guards should be designed and constructed so that a hazard is not created or restrict the view of the process or machine by the operator.

NOT EASILY BY-PASSED

Guards or their components must not be easily by-passed, in particular by operators. There is always a temptation to do so when under production or similar pressures. When siting such things as interlock switches it is best to locate them away from the operator and preferably within the guard.

This page is intentionally blank

Element 4

Electrical - hazards and control

Learning outcomes

On completion of this element, candidates should be able to demonstrate understanding of the content through the application of knowledge to familiar and unfamiliar situations. In particular they should be able to:

4.1 Identify the hazards and evaluate the consequential risks from the use of electricity in the workplace.

4.2 Describe the control measures that should be taken when working with electrical systems or using electrical equipment.

Content

4.1 - Hazards and risks associated with electricity at work	161
Electric shock and its effect on the body	162
Electrical burns	164
Electrical fires	164
Portable electrical equipment	165
4.2 - Control measures	166
Selection and suitability of equipment	166
Inspection and maintenance strategies	168

Sources of reference

Electricity at Work - Safe Working Practices (HSG85), HSE Books ISBN 0-717-62164-2

Maintaining Portable and Transportable Electrical Equipment (HSG107), HSE Books ISBN 0-7176-2805-1

Other sources of reference

Electricity and You INDG231 HSE Books 1998 ISBN 0-7176-1207-4

Maintaining Portable Electrical Equipment in Offices and Other Low-Risk Environments INDG236 HSE Books 1996 ISBN 0-7176-1272-4

Maintaining Portable Electrical Equipment in Hotels and Tourist Accommodation INDG237 HSE Books 1996 ISBN 0-7176-1273-2

Electrical Test Equipment for Use by Electricians GS38 (rev) HSE Books 1995 ISBN 0-7176-0845 X

BS 7671: 2001 Requirements for Electrical Installations, IEE Wiring Regulations 16th edition

ELECTRICAL - HAZARDS AND CONTROL - ELEMENT 4 - UNIT IGC2

4.1 - Hazards and risks associated with electricity at work

Principles of electricity

Electricity is a facility that we have all come to take for granted, whether for lighting, heating, as a source of motive power or as the driving force behind the computer. Used properly it can be of great benefit to us, but misused it can be very dangerous and often fatal.

Electricity is used in most industries, offices and homes and our modern society could now not easily function without it. Despite its convenience to the user, it has a major danger. The normal senses of sight, hearing and smell will not detect electricity. Making contact with exposed conductors at the supply voltage of 110V, 240V can be potentially lethal.

Unlike many other workplace accidents, the actual number of electrical notifiable accidents is small. However, with a reported 10-20 fatalities each year in the UK alone, the severity is high. Accidents are often caused by complacency, not just by the normally assumed ignorance. It must be recognised by everyone working with electricity that over half of all electrical fatal accidents are to skilled/competent persons. In order to avoid the causes of electric injury, it is necessary to understand the basic principles of electricity, what it does to the body and what controls are necessary.

BASIC CIRCUITRY

The flow of electrons through a conductor is known as a current. Electric current flows due to differences in electrical "pressure" (or potential difference as it is often known), just as water flows through a pipe because of the pressure behind it. Differences in electrical potential are measured in volts.

In some systems the current flows continually in the same direction. This is known as direct current (DC). However the current may also constantly reverse its direction of flow. This is known as alternating current (AC). Most public electricity supplies are AC. The UK system reverses its direction 50 times per second and it is said to have a frequency of 50 cycles per second or 50 Hertz (50Hz). DC is little used in standard distribution systems but is sometimes used in industry for specialist applications. Although there are slight differences in the effects under fault and shock conditions between AC and DC it is a safe approach to apply the same rules of safety for the treatment and prevention of electric shock.

As a current passes round a circuit under the action of an applied voltage it is impeded in its flow. This may be due to the presence in the circuit of resistance, inductance or capacitance, the combined effect of which is called impedance and is measured in ohms.

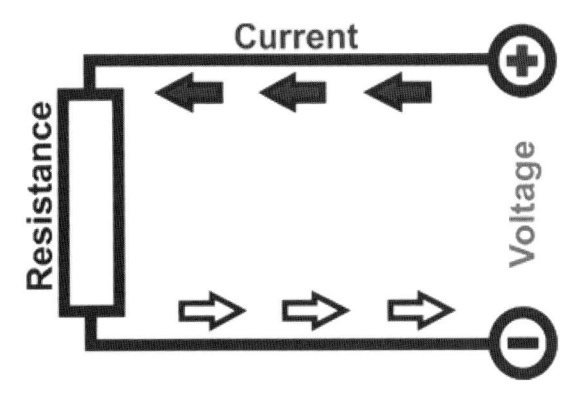

Figure 2-4-1: A basic electrical circuit.   Source: ACT.

RELATIONSHIP BETWEEN VOLTAGE, CURRENT AND RESISTANCE

There is a simple relationship between electrical pressure (Volts), current (measured in Amperes or milliamperes) and resistance (measured in Ohms) represented by Ohm's Law:

Voltage **(V)** = current **(I)** multiplied by the circuit resistance **(R)**. $V = I \times R$ or $I = \dfrac{V}{R}$

Hence, given any two values the third can be calculated. Also, if one value changes the other two values will change accordingly.

This basic electrical equation can be used to calculate the current that flows in a circuit of a given resistance.

This will need to be done to determine, for example, the fuse or cable rating needed for a particular circuit. Similarly, the current that will flow through a person who touches a live conductor can be calculated.

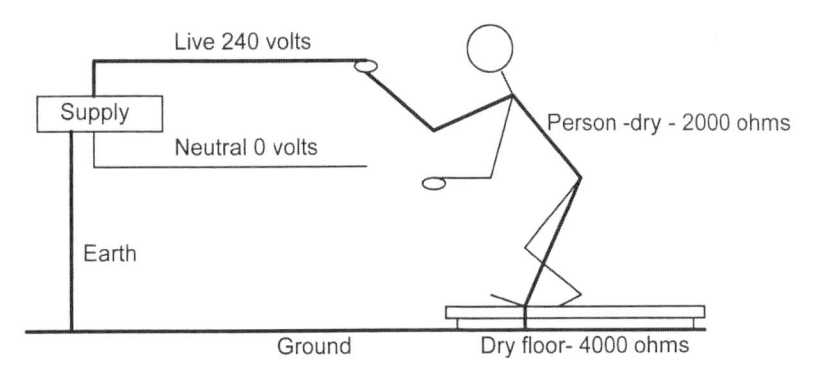

Figure 2-4-2: An electric circuit under fault conditions showing resistances in the path of a fault current.   Source: R. Gilmour.

By Ohm's law:

Current = $\dfrac{\text{Voltage}}{\text{Resistance}}$ or $I = \dfrac{V}{R}$

Resistance in a circuit is dependent on many factors. Most metals, particularly precious metals (silver, gold, platinum), allow current to pass very easily. These have a low resistance and are used as conductors. Other materials such as plastics, rubber and textiles have a high resistance and are used as insulators.

If the person is on, say, a dry concrete floor, resistance in the body will only be about 2,000 Ohms and the resistance in the floor about 4,000 Ohms, therefore the combined resistance would be 6,000 Ohms. Presuming the person is in contact with a live electrical supply at 240 Volts the current flowing through the person in this fault condition can be calculated.

$$I = \frac{V}{R} = \frac{240 \text{ Volts}}{2000 + 4000 \text{ Ohms}} = 0.04 \text{ Amperes}$$

The current flowing through the operator will be about 0.04 Amperes or 40mA (40 milliAmperes). This could result in a fatal shock.

FREQUENCY

In Europe the frequency of the alternating current is 50 Hz, with 230 V of rated voltage. In North America the frequency of the alternating current is 60 Hz, with 117 V of rated voltage.

Hazards of electricity

The consequences of contact with electricity are:

- *Shock* - resulting from the current flowing through the body interfering with muscle and central nervous system functions.
- *Electrical burns* - resulting from the heating effect of the current which burns the body tissue.
- *Electrical fires* - caused by overheating or arcing apparatus in contact with a fuel.
- *Explosions* - from sparks in a flammable atmosphere.
- *Secondary injuries* - falling from a ladder.

Electric shock and its effect on the body

EFFECTS OF CURRENT FLOWING IN THE HUMAN BODY

Current (mA)	Length of time	Likely effects [mA = milliAmperes mS = milliseconds]
0-1	Not Critical	Threshold of feeling. Undetected by person.
1-15	Not Critical	Threshold of cramp. Independent loosening of the hands no longer possible.
15-30	Minutes	Cramp-like pulling together of the arms, breathing difficult. Limit of tolerance
30-50	Seconds to minutes	Strong cramp-like effects, loss of consciousness due to restricted breathing. Longer time may lead to fibrillation.
50-500	Less than one heart period (70 mS)	No fibrillation. Strong shock effects.
	Greater than one heart period	Fibrillation. Loss of consciousness. Burn marks.
Over 500	Less than one heart period	Fibrillation. Loss of consciousness. Burn marks.

Figure 2-4-3: Effects of current flowing in the human body.   Source: ACT.

FACTORS INFLUENCING SEVERITY

The severity of electric shock or the amount of current which flows for a given voltage will depend on the frequency of the supply voltage, on the level of the voltage which is applied and on the state of the point of contact with the body, particularly the moisture condition.

Voltage

Voltage is the driving force behind the flow of electricity, somewhat like pressure in a water pipe. The correct name for this term is potential difference as a voltage is the measure of the difference in electrical energy between two points. Any electrical charge that is free to move about will move from the higher energy to the lower one, taking a bit of that energy difference with it.

Frequency

The frequency of current flow in an alternating current supply, such as the mains supply in an office block, operates at 50 cycles per second. This frequency is close to that of the heart when functioning normally. It can have the effect of disrupting the operation of the heart causing it to beat in a discordant manner, to fibrillate.

Duration

For an electric shock to have an effect a person needs to be in contact with the current for sufficient time. At low current levels the body tolerates the current so the time is not material, however at higher current levels, e.g. 50Ma, the person has to remain in contact for sufficient time to affect the heart, in the order of milliseconds. In general, the longer a person is in contact with the current the more harm may be caused.

Resistance

The amount of resistance in a circuit influences the amount of current that is allowed to flow, as explained above by Ohm's law. It is possible for a person to be in contact with a circuit and to present sufficiently high resistance so that very little current is allowed to flow through their body. The example shown above illustrates this. It should be noted that the level of current is also dependent on the voltage; at high voltages an enormous amount of resistance is needed to ensure current flow will remain at a safe level. The human body contributes part of the resistance of a circuit, the amount it contributes depends on the current path taken and other factors such as personal chemical make-up (a large portion of the body is water), dryness and thickness of skin, and any clothing that is being worn, such as shoes and gloves.

Current Path

The effect of an electric shock on a body is particularly dependent on the current path through the body. Current has to flow through from one point to another as part of a circuit. If the flow was between two points on a finger the effect on the body would be concentrated between the two points. If the current path is between one hand and another across the chest this means the flow will pass through major parts of the body, such as the heart, and may have a specific effect on it. In a similar way a contact between hand and foot (feet) can have serious effects on a great many parts of the body, including the heart. These latter current paths tend to be the ones leading to fatal injuries. Workers should be reminded that, although many may experience shock from 240 volts this may not be fatal if they were, for example, standing on or wearing some insulating material. This may be a matter of fortune and should not be relied on.

FIRST AID TREATMENT FOR ELECTRIC SHOCK

With electricity, of the typically reported accidents each year, 75 per year are thought to be fatal in the UK. The severity of accidents involving electricity therefore merits detailed study of their causes and development in order to prevent them. The first aid treatment points listed in this section are for guidance only and are not a substitute for a qualified first-aider with knowledge of the workplace.

Figure 2-4-4: Risk of electric shock due to damage to cable. *Source: ACT.*

Figure 2-4-5: Work on live circuits. *Source: ACT.*

In case of electrical shock:

Do
- Switch off or remove the plug.
- Check that there is no remaining connection to the supply and, if possible, prove that the system is discharged and dead.
- Assess the situation and any remaining danger to yourself or the casualty.
- Call for qualified support which may be the emergency services.
- If safe, check the casualty's response (What is the degree of consciousness?).

Check

A - Airway   -   Is it open?

B - Breathing   -   Is the casualty breathing normally?

C - Circulation -   Does the casualty have a normal pulse?

Action

If airway obstructed by teeth, food etc., remove; if tongue tilt head back to clear, and then provide cardio pulmonary resuscitation (CPR).

If trained, place in the recovery position and/or apply resuscitation as required. Cool any burns with cold water.

Keep the casualty under observation for secondary effects until you hand over to a medically qualified person.

Do not

Do not go near the casualty until the electricity supply is proven to be off. This is especially critical with overhead high voltage lines: keep yourself and others at least 18 metres away until the electricity supply company personnel advise otherwise.

Do not delay - after 3 minutes without blood circulation irreversible damage can be done to the casualty.

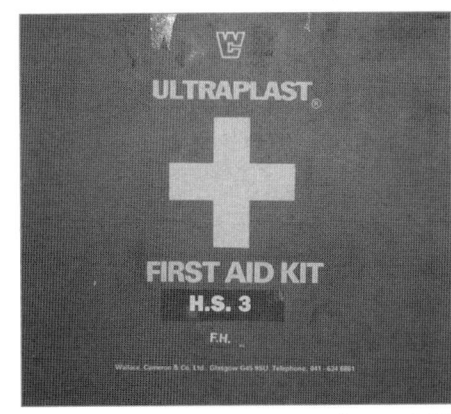

Figure 2-4-6: First aid sign. *Source: ACT.*

Do not wait for an accident to happen - train in emergency procedures and first aid now, plan procedures for an emergency (calling for help, from the emergency services, meeting ambulances and leading them to the casualty) as seconds saved may save a life. Hold emergency drills.

Electrical burns

DIRECT

There will be a heating effect along the route taken by electric current as it passes through body tissue. Whilst there are likely to be burn marks on the skin at the point of contact there may also be a deep seated burning within the body which is painful and slow to heal. As the outer layer of skin is burnt the resistance decreases and so the current will increase. The current flowing through the body can cause major injury to internal organs and bone marrow as it passes through them.

INDIRECT

If while working on live equipment the system is short-circuited by, for example, an un-insulated spanner touching live and neutral this will result in a large and sudden current flow through the spanner. This current will cause the spanner to melt and may throw molten metal out from the points of contact. When this molten metal contacts the parts of a person in the vicinity of the spanner, for example the hands or face, serious burns can take place as the molten metal hits and sticks to the person. With high voltages and the very low resistance of the spanner very large currents can flow. This rapid discharge of energy that follows contact with high voltages not only causes the rapid melting of the spanner but does so with such violent force that the molten particles of metal are thrown off with huge velocity. It is not necessary to have high voltages to melt a spanner in this way - it can also occur with batteries with sufficient stored energy, such as those on a fork lift truck. There are many experiences of people suffering injury in this way when servicing lift truck batteries as a spanner falls out of their overall top pocket.

Electrical fires

COMMON CAUSES

Much electrical equipment generates heat or produces sparks and this equipment should not be placed where this could lead to the uncontrolled ignition of any substance.

The principal causes of electrical fires are:

- Wiring with defects such as insulation failure due to age or poor maintenance.
- Overheating of cables or other electrical equipment through overloading with currents above their design capacity.
- Incorrect fuse rating.
- Poor connections due to lack of maintenance or unskilled personnel.

Electrical equipment may itself explode or arc violently and it may also act as a source of ignition of flammable vapours, gases, liquids or dust through electric sparks, arcs or high surface temperatures of equipment. Other causes are heat created by poorly maintained or defective motors, heaters and lighting.

Figure 2-4-7: Used coiled up - risk of overheating. *Source: ACT.*

Figure 2-4-8: Max current capacity exceeded. *Source: ACT.*

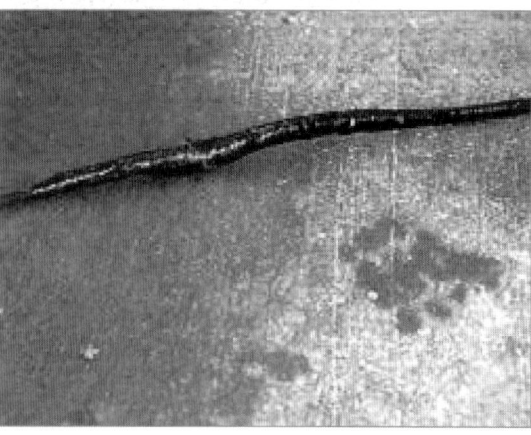

Figure 2-4-9: Worn cable - risk of electrical fire. *Source: ACT.*

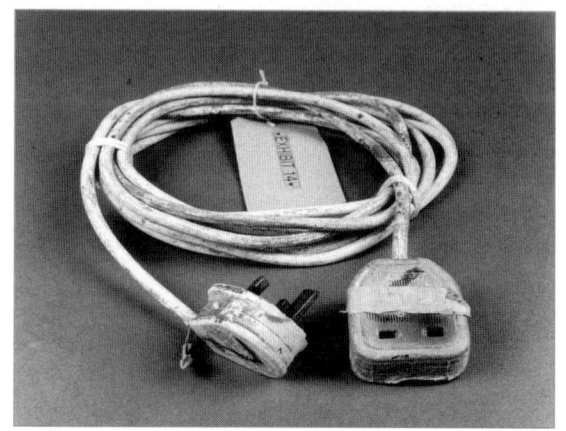

Figure 2-4-10: Evidence of overheating. *Source: ACT.*

Portable electrical equipment

CONDITIONS AND PRACTICES LIKELY TO LEAD TO ACCIDENTS

Unsuitable equipment
- Unsuitable apparatus for the duty or the conditions.
- Misuse.
- Failure to follow operating instructions.
- Wrong connection of system - supply phase, neutral or earth reversed.
- Wrong voltage or rating of equipment.

Inadequate maintenance
- Inadequate maintenance of the installation and the equipment.
- Wrong or broken connection to portable apparatus.
- Inadequate earthing.
- Poor maintenance and testing.
- No defect reporting system.

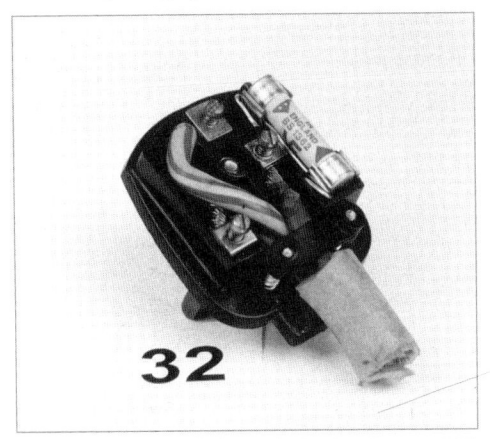

Figure 2-4-11: Hazard - fuse wired out.   Source: ACT.

Figure 2-4-12: Continued use of defective equipment.   Source: ACT.

Use of defective apparatus
- Faulty cables, notably extension leads.
- Plugs and sockets.
- Damaged plug or socket.
- Protection devices, such as fuses or circuit breaker, incorrect rating, damaged or missing.
- Overloaded leading to damage or over-heating.
- Short circuit leading to damage, overheating or movement.
- Isolation procedures or systems of work wrong.
- Bad circuit connections.

Figure 2-4-13: Hazard - damaged cable.   Source: ACT.

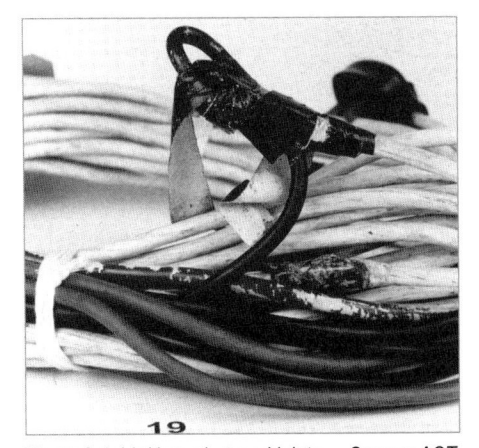

Figure 2-4-14: Hazard - taped joints.   Source: ACT.

Secondary hazards

These occur where the injury results from the flow of electricity through the body's nerves, muscles and organs and causes abnormal function to occur. Muscular spasm may be severe, particularly if the leg muscles are affected, causing a person to be thrown several metres. Injuries may result from dislocation, impact with surrounding objects or fall from a height. In addition, a tool may be dropped causing such injuries as burns or impact injury to the user or others near by.

4.2 - Control measures

Selection and suitability of equipment

It is critical to ensure that all electrical equipment is suitable. For example, if it is to be used for outdoor work on a construction site in conditions that it might get wet, equipment providing protection from the ingress of water must be selected. Many tools are designed and provided for use in a domestic situation and they may not be suitable for use in the more arduous conditions of a construction site, for example, cable entry grips may be more secure and outer protection of cables thicker on equipment designed for construction work. Part of the selection process is to determine situations where low voltage, such as 110 volt systems, can be used in preference to 240 volts.

Advantages and limitations of protective systems

FUSE

This is a device designed to automatically cut off the power supply to a circuit within a given time when the current flow in that circuit exceeds a given value. A fuse may be a rewirable tinned copper wire in a suitable carrier or a wire or wires in an enclosed cartridge.

In effect it is a weak link in the circuit that melts when heat is created by too high a current passing through the thin wire in the fuse case. When this happens the circuit is broken and no more current flows. Fuses tend to have rating in the order of Amperes rather than mA which means it has *limited usefulness in protecting people from electric shock.* The fuse may also operate slowly if the current is just above the fuse rating. Using too high a fuse means that the circuit will remain intact and the equipment will draw power. This may cause it to overheat leading to a fire or if a fault exists the circuit will remain live and the fault current may pass through the user of the equipment when they touch or operate it.

The following formula should be used to calculate the correct rating for a fuse:

$$\text{Current (Amperes)} = \frac{\text{Power (watts)}}{\text{Voltage (volts)}}$$

For example, the correct fuse current rating for a 2-kilowatt kettle on a 240-volt supply would be:

$$\frac{2000\ W}{240\ V} = 8.33A$$

Typical fuses for domestic supply voltages of 240V are 3, 5, 10 and 13 Ampere ratings.

The nearest fuse just above this current level is 10A.

	Typical examples of power ratings are:	Suitable fuses at 240 Volts:
Computer processor.	350 Watts.	3 Amperes.
Electric kettle.	1,850-2,200 Watts.	10 - 13 Amperes.
Dishwasher.	1,380 Watts.	10 Amperes.
Refrigerator.	90 Watts.	3 Amperes.

Summary

- A weak link in the circuit that melts slowly when heat is created by a fault condition. However, this usually happens too slowly to protect people.
- Easy to replace with wrong rating.
- Needs tools to replace.
- Easy to override by replacing a fuse with one of a higher rating or putting in an improvised 'fuse', such as a nail, that has a high rating.

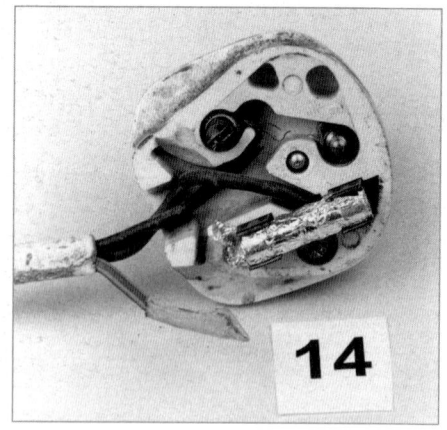

Figure 2-4-15: Plug-foil fuse no earth. *Source: ACT.*

Figure 2-4-16: Earthing. *Source: ACT.*

EARTHING

A conductor called an earth wire is fitted to the system; it is connected at one end to a plate buried in the ground and the other end connected to the metal casing of the equipment. If for any reason a conductor touches the casing so that the equipment casing becomes 'live' the current will flow to the point of lowest potential, the earth. The path to this point (earth) is made easier as the wire is designed to have very little resistance. This *may prevent electric shock* provided it is used in association with a correctly rated fuse, or better still a residual current device (RCD), and no one is in contact with the equipment at the time the fault occurs.

It should be remembered that earthing is provided where the casing can become live. If the equipment is designed so that this cannot be the case, such as double insulated equipment where the user touches non-conducting surfaces, earthing of the equipment is no advantage. In summary, earthing provides a path of least resistance for "stray" current and provides protection against indirect shock.

ISOLATION

Isolation of an electrical system is an excellent way of achieving safety for those that need to work on or near the system; for example, isolation of a power supply into a building that is to be refurbished or isolation of plant that is to be maintained. In its simplest form it can mean switching off and unplugging a portable appliance at times it is not in use. Care must be taken to check that the isolation has been adequate and effective before work starts; this can include tests on the system. It is also critical to ensure the isolation is secure; 'lock off' and 'tag out' systems will assist with this.

REDUCED LOW VOLTAGE SYSTEMS

One of the best ways to reduce the risk from electricity is to reduce the voltage. This is frequently achieved by the use of a transformer (step down) which will reduce the voltage. A common reduction is from the supply mains voltage of 240V to 110V. Normally, transformers that are used to reduce voltage are described as "centre tapped to earth". In practice this means that any voltage involved in an electrical shock will be 55V.

Using the earlier example of Ohms Law, if the voltage is 240V then:

$$I = \frac{V}{R} = \frac{240 \text{ Volts}}{2000+4000 \text{ Ohms}} = 0.04 \text{ Amperes or 40 mA}$$

However, if a centre tapped to earth transformer is used then,

$$I = \frac{V}{R} = \frac{55 \text{ Volts}}{2000+4000 \text{ Ohms}} = 0.009 \text{ Amperes or 9 mA}$$

Reference to figures 2-4-2 and 2-4-3 will clearly show how this **reduces the effects of electric shock** on the body.

An alternative to reduction in voltage by means of a transformer is to provide battery-powered equipment; this will commonly run on 12V-24V but voltages may be higher. The common method is to use a rechargeable battery to power the equipment which eliminates the need for a cable to feed power to the equipment and gives a greater flexibility of use for the user, e.g. for drills and power drivers.

Figure 2-4-17: 110V centre tapped earth transformer. *Source: ACT.*

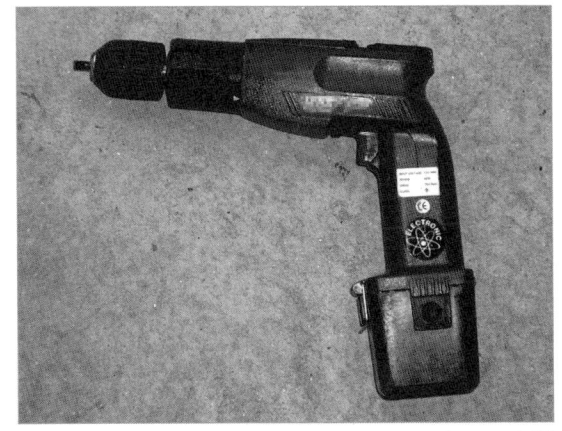

Figure 2-4-18: Battery powered drill - 12V. *Source: ACT.*

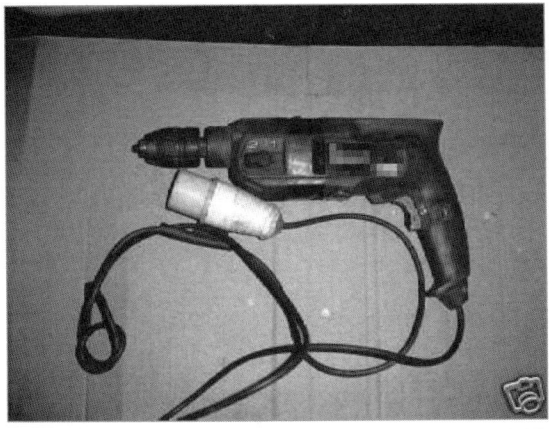

Figure 2-4-19: 110V powered drill. *Source: ACT.*

Figure 2-4-20: 110V powered drill. *Source: ACT.*

RESIDUAL CURRENT DEVICE (RCD)

An electro-mechanical switching device is used to automatically isolate the supply when there is a difference between the current flowing into a device and the current flowing from the device. Such a difference might result from a fault causing current leakage, with possible fire risks or the risk of shock current when a person touches a system and provides a path to earth for the current. RCDs can be designed to operate at low currents and fast response times (usually 30 mA and 30 seconds) and thus they **reduce the effect of an electric shock.** Though they do not prevent the person receiving an electric shock they are very sensitive and operate very quickly and reduce some of the primary effects of the shock.

UNIT IGC2 - ELEMENT 4 - ELECTRICAL - HAZARDS AND CONTROL

It is still possible for a person to receive injury from the shock, not least some of the secondary injuries referred to earlier. But the use of this type of device means the fault current should be isolated before sustained shock, and therefore fibrillation, occurs. The equipment needs to be de-energised from time to time in order to be confident it will work properly when needed. This can easily be done by a simple test routine before use, as equipment is plugged into the RCD.

Summary

- Rapid and sensitive.
- Difficult to defeat.
- Easy and safe to test and reset.
- Does not prevent shock, but reduces the effect of a shock.

Figure 2-4-21: Residual current device.   *Source: ACT.*

Figure 2-4-22: Plug-in residual current device.   *Source: ACT.*

Figure 2-4-23: Double insulated 240V drill.   *Source: ACT.*

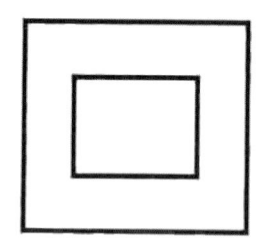

Figure 2-4-24: Double insulation symbol.   *Source: HSG107.*

DOUBLE INSULATION

This is a common protection device and consists of a layer of insulation around the live electrical parts of the equipment and a second layer of insulated material around this, commonly the casing of the equipment. Since the casing material is an insulator and does not conduct electricity, equipment having this type of protection does not normally have an earth wire.

Each layer of insulation must be sufficient in its own right to give adequate protection against shock.

Equipment, which is double insulated, will carry the symbol shown above.

Double insulated equipment has two layers of insulating material between the live parts of the equipment and the user. If a fault occurs with the live parts and a conductor touches the insulating material surrounding it no current can pass to the user, therefore *no shock occurs.*

Inspection and maintenance strategies

USER CHECKS

The user of electrical equipment should be encouraged, after basic training, to look critically at apparatus and the source of power. If any defects are found, the apparatus should be marked and not be used again before examination by a competent person. Obviously, there must be a procedure by which the user brings faults to the attention of a supervisor and/or a competent person who might rectify the fault.

Checks by the user are the first line of defence but should never be the only line taken. Such inspections should be aimed at identifying the following:

- Damaged cable sheaths.
- Damaged plugs. Cracked casing or bent pins.
- Taped or other inadequate cable joints.
- Outer cable insulation not secured into plugs or equipment.
- Faulty or ineffective switches.
- Burn marks or discolouration.

- Damaged casing.
- Loose parts or screws.
- Wet or contaminated equipment.
- Loose or damaged sockets or switches.

FORMAL INSPECTON AND TESTS

Inspection

The maintenance system should always include formal visual inspection of all portable electrical equipment and electrical tests.

The frequency depends on the type of equipment and where it is used. The inspection can be done by a member of staff who has been trained in what to look for and has basic electrical knowledge. They should know enough to avoid danger to themselves or others. Visual inspections are likely to need to look for the same types of defects as user checks but should also include the following:

Opening plugs of portable equipment to check for:

- Use of correctly rated fuse.
- Effective cord grip.
- Secure and correct cable terminations.

Inspection of fixed installations for:

- Damaged or loose conduit, trunking or cabling.
- Missing broken or inadequately secured covers.
- Loose or faulty joints.
- Loose earth connections.
- Moisture, corrosion or contamination.
- Burn marks or discolouration.
- Open or inadequately secured panel doors.
- Ease of access to switches and isolators.
- Presence of temporary wiring.

User checks and a programme of formal visual inspections are found to pick up some 95% of faults.

Testing

Faults such as loss of earth or broken wires inside an installation or cable cannot be found by visual inspection, so some apparatus needs to have a combined inspection and test. This is particularly important for all earthed equipment and leads and plugs connected to hand held or hand operated equipment.

The system should be tested regularly in accordance with any specific requirements in the UK, for example, Institute of Electrical Engineers (IEE) requirements; tests may include earth continuity and impedance tests and tests of insulation material.

FREQUENCY OF INSPECTION AND TESTING

Deciding the frequency

Many approaches to establishing frequency suggest that they should be done regularly. As can be seen above, the word 'regularly' is not specified in terms of fixed time intervals for all systems; a management judgment must be made to specify an appropriate timetable. In effect, the frequency will depend on the condition the system is used in; for example, a test of office portable equipment may be sufficient if conducted every 3 years, whereas equipment used on a construction site may need to be tested every 3 months. The system as a whole rather that just portable equipment must also be tested periodically and again this will depend on the conditions of use and may vary from 10 years to 6 months. Factors to be considered when deciding the frequency include:

- Type of equipment.
- Whether it is hand held.
- Manufacturer's recommendations.
- Its initial integrity and soundness.
- Age.
- Working environment.
- Likelihood of mechanical damage.
- Frequency of use.
- Duration of use.
- Foreseeable use.
- Who uses it.
- Modifications or repairs.
- Past experience.

RECORDS OF INSPECTION AND TESTING

In order to identify what systems and equipment will need inspection and testing they should be listed. This same listing can be used as a checklist recording that the appropriate checks, inspections and tests have been done. It would be usual to include details of the type of the equipment, its location and its age. It is critical that a cumulative record of equipment and its status is held available to those that are responsible for using the equipment as well as those that are conducting the inspection or test.

In addition, it is common practice to add a label to the system or part of the system (e.g. portable appliances) to indicate that an inspection and / or test has taken place and its status following this. Some labels show the date that this took place; others prefer to show the date of next inspection or test.

Figure 2-4-25: PAT labels. *Source: ACT.*

There is a growing trend, especially in offices, for workers to bring to work their own electrically powered equipment including calculators, radios, kettles and coffee makers. The number of electrical accidents has grown accordingly and fires from calculator chargers left on overnight are growing in number. All such equipment should be recorded, inspected and tested by a competent person before use and at regular intervals, as if it were company property.

ADVANTAGES AND LIMITATIONS OF PORTABLE APPLIANCE TESTING (PAT)

The purpose of portable appliance testing is to periodically confirm the critical aspects of the electrical integrity of portable appliances. Three levels of inspection should be included in a maintenance and inspection strategy for portable electrical appliances:

- The first level of inspection would be that carried out by the operator before the appliance is used and would consist of an informal check of the condition of the appliance and its cable and plug.
- The second check would be supplemented by a more formal visual inspection by an appointed person which would follow a set down procedure and include other matters such as the correctness of the rating of the fuses fitted, security of cable grips, earth continuity, impedance and insulation.
- The third strategy would include the periodic combined inspection and testing of the appliance by a competent person.

It is critical to keep centralised records of the results of portable appliance testing within an organisation. Such records can then be used for setting the frequency for appliance testing, to verify whether unlabelled equipment had been tested or had merely lost its label and to provide a record of past faults on all appliances that had been recorded. This approach will demonstrate that the employer is in compliance with the regulations

The limitation with portable appliance testing is that people may have an over-reliance on the apparent assurance that the test indicates. They may be tempted to see it as a permanent assurance that the equipment is safe. This can lead to users not making their own pre-use checks of the appliance. In effect it is only a test, and therefore assurance, at a point in time. It does not assure that someone has not, for example, altered the fuse and put one in with an incorrect rating or that the cable grip has not come loose.

It must also be recognised that there is little benefit in having a perfect portable appliance if it is plugged into a defective socket which may be without proper insulation, with a switch that does not work properly, with the polarity reversed or with a high resistance earth connection.

Element 5

Fire - hazards and control

Learning outcomes

On completion of this element, candidates should be able to demonstrate understanding of the content through the application of knowledge to familiar and unfamiliar situations. In particular they should be able to:

5.1 Identify fire hazards and evaluate main fire risks in a workplace.

5.2 Explain the basic principles of fire prevention and the prevention of fire spread in buildings.

5.3 Identify the appropriate fire alarm system and fire-fighting equipment for a simple workplace.

5.4 Outline the requirements for an adequate and properly maintained means of escape for a simple workplace.

5.5 Outline the factors which should be considered when implementing a successful evacuation of a workplace in the event of a fire.

Content

5.1 - Basic fire principles, hazards and risks in the workplace	173
Basic principles of fire	173
Classification of fires	174
Methods of heat transmission and fire spread	174
Common causes and consequences of fires in workplaces	174
Assessment of fire risks	176
5.2 - Fire prevention and prevention of fire spread	178
Control measures to minimise the risk of fire in a workplace	178
Safe storage and use of flammable liquids	181
Structural measures to prevent spread of fire and smoke	182
5.3 - Fire alarm and fire fighting equipment	184
Fire detection, fire warning and fire fighting equipment	184
5.4 - Means of escape	189
Requirements for fire plans for means of escape	189
5.5 - Evacuation of the workplace	190
Emergency evacuation procedures	190

Sources of reference

Safety in the Use of Chemicals at Work - sections 6 and 7 (ILO Code of Practice), ILO ISBN 9-2210-8006-4

Fire Safety: an Employer's Guide (HSE, Home office, Scottish Executive, DoE Northern Ireland), The Stationery Office ISBN 0-113-41229-0

Other sources of reference

Fire Safety Risk Assessment - Offices and Shops ISBN: 978 1 85112 815 0

Fire Safety Risk Assessment - Factories and Warehouses ISBN: 978 1 85112 816 7

Fire Safety Risk Assessment - Sleeping Accommodation ISBN: 978 1 85112 817 4

Fire Safety Risk Assessment - Residential Care Premises ISBN: 978 1 85112 818 1

Fire Safety Risk Assessment - Educational Premises ISBN: 978 1 85112 819 8

Fire Safety Risk Assessment - Small and Medium Places of Assembly ISBN: 978 1 85112 820 4

Fire Safety Risk Assessment - Large Places of Assembly ISBN: 978 1 85112 821 1

Fire Safety Risk Assessment - Theatres, Cinemas and Similar Premises ISBN: 978 1 85112 822 8

Fire Safety Risk Assessment - Open Air Events and Venues ISBN: 978 1 85112 823 5

Fire Safety Risk Assessment - Healthcare premises ISBN: 978 1 85112 824 2

Fire Safety Risk Assessment - Transport Premises and Facilities ISBN: 978 1 85112 825 9

Fire Safety Risk Assessment - Means of Escape for Disabled People (Supplementary Guide) ISBN: 978 1 85112 873 7

Fire Service Features of Buildings and Fire Protection Systems Occupational Safety and Health Administration U.S. Department of Labor OSHA 3256-07N 2006

5.1 - Basic fire principles, hazards and risks in the workplace

Basic principles of fire

DEFINITIONS

Fire precautions

The measures taken and the fire protection provided in a building to minimise the risk to occupants, contents and structure from an outbreak of fire.

Fire prevention

The concept of preventing outbreaks of fire or reducing the risk of fire spread and avoiding danger from fire to people or property.

Fire protection

Design features, systems or equipment in a building provided to reduce the danger to persons and property by detecting, extinguishing or containing fires.

THE FIRE TRIANGLE

In order for combustion to take place the three essential elements of a fire have to be brought together - fuel, oxygen and source of ignition (heat) - this is called the fire triangle.

In order to prevent fires these elements, particularly the fuel and ignition sources, are kept apart. When they are brought together in the correct proportions combustion takes place. It should be noted that it is only the vapour from a fuel that burns. A solid or liquid must be heated to a temperature where the vapour given off can ignite before combustion takes place.

This principle is critical when considering combustible dusts as this combustion process happens so quickly it becomes an explosion. This explosion can be caused by just a source of ignition, for example, a spark; a small **dust explosion** can often disturb more dust and create bigger explosions.

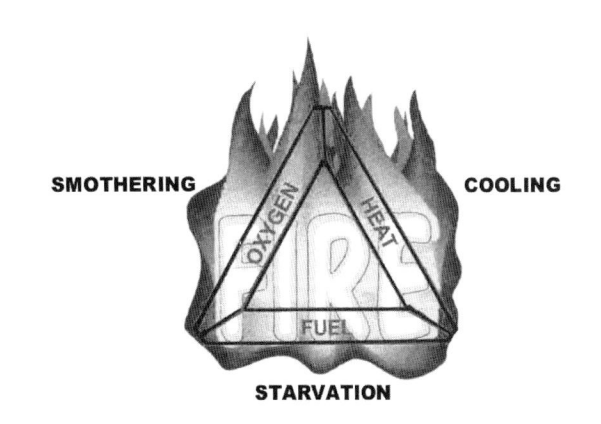

Figure 2-5-1: Fire triangle. *Source: Corel.*

The other critical aspect of this combustion principle is that if one or more of these elements of the fire is removed the fire will be extinguished.

This can be done by:

Cooling - the fire to remove the heat - by applying water to the fire.

Starving - the fire of fuel - by moving material from the area of a fire or closing off an area of combustible material from the fire.

Smothering - the fire by limiting its oxygen supply - by closing a lid on a metal bin that contained a fire, covering a fire with a fire blanket or applying an extinguishing medium such as foam.

SOURCES OF IGNITION

Any source of heat is a possible ignition source. Examples could be:

- Smokers' materials.
- Naked flames.
- Fixed or portable heaters.
- Hot processes e.g. welding.
- Cooking.
- Electrical equipment or machinery.
- Static electricity.

Figure 2-5-2: Smoking materials. *Source: ACT.*

Figure 2-5-3: Combustible materials - waste. *Source: ACT.*

SOURCES OF FUEL

Anything that burns is a fuel for a fire:

- Flammable liquids. e.g. petrol and diesel storage areas, refill containers.
- Flammable gases. e.g. butane LPG heater cylinder.
- Flammable chemicals, paints and solvents.
- Wood. e.g. furniture, dust form manufacturing processes.
- Paper and card, e.g. stationary cupboards and waste paper bins.
- Plastics, rubber and foam. e.g. furniture.
- Insulating materials, e.g. wall and partition insulation.
- Waste materials. Used waste chemicals, general waste, waste papers.

SOURCES OF OXYGEN

- Oxygen supplies e.g. cylinders or piped supply.
- Ventilation systems e.g. windows, doors, vents, air conditioning.
- Chemicals e.g. oxidising agents.

FIRE HAZARDS AND RISKS

The hazards relating to the radiant heat of a fire and contact with flames can give rise to the risk of heat stroke or burns. The degree of exposure to the heat or flames will influence greatly the effect on the body each will have. Significant exposure to heat or flames could quickly lead to shock, coma or death.

Both the hot gases and smoke involved in fires represent separate hazards to a person involved in a fire. The hot gases and smoke can present a direct effect on the lungs causing restriction in breathing. In addition, toxic gases may be liberated as part of a fire; these may include carbon monoxide, which if breathed in sufficient quantities can lead to asphyxiation (suffocation). Other toxic products of combustion can include hydrogen cyanide and chlorine.

Furthermore, fires will cause the release of substances that can be harmful to the environment.

Classification of fires

A basic understanding of the classes of fire needs to be achieved because many fire extinguishers state the classes of fire on which they may be used. Common classifications include:

Class A	-	Fire involving solids - wood, paper or plastics (usually material of an organic nature).
Class B	-	Fires involving liquids or liquefiable solids - petrol, oil, paint, fat or wax.
Class C	-	Fires involving gases - liquefied petroleum gas, natural gas or acetylene.
Class D	-	Fires involving metals - sodium, magnesium, aluminium and many metal powders.
Class E	-	fires involving electrical apparatus. In many cases, electricity is a source of heat.
Class F or K	-	Fires involving cooking oils and fats.

Methods of heat transmission and fire spread

There are four methods by which heat may be transmitted:

Convection	-	The movement of hotter gases up through the air (hot air rises).
		e.g. Smoke and hot gases rising up a staircase through an open door.
Control measure	-	Protection of openings by fire doors and the creation of fire resistant compartments in buildings.
Conduction	-	The movement of heat through a material (usually solid).
		e.g. A metal beam or pipe transmitting heat through a solid wall.
Control measure	-	Insulating the surface of a beam or pipe with heat resistant materials.
Radiation	-	Transfer of heat as invisible waves through the air (the air or gas is not heated but solids and liquids in contact with the heat are).
		e.g. Items or waste containers stored too near to a building may provide enough radiant heat to transfer the fire to the building if they are ignited.
Control measure	-	Separation distances or fire resistant barriers.
Direct Burning	-	Combustible materials in direct contact with naked flame.
		e.g. Curtains or carpet tiles may be consumed by combustion and enable fire to be transferred along them to other parts of a building.
Control measure	-	The use of fire retardant materials.

Common causes and consequences of fires in workplaces

CAUSES

Causes may be split into four main groups. These are:

Careless actions and accidents

e.g. hot works, discarded lighted cigarette end or match, smouldering waste, unattended burning or poor electrical connections.

Misusing equipment

e.g. overloading electrical circuits and using fuses of too high a rating, failure to follow servicing instructions, failure to repair faulty machinery/equipment promptly.

Defective machinery or equipment

e.g. electrical short circuits, electrical earth fault can cause local overheating and electrical insulation failure may occur when affected by heat, damp or chemicals.

Deliberate ignition

e.g. insurance fraud, aggrieved persons, concealment of another crime, political activists or vandalism.

Figure 2-5-4: Careless action - waste paper & smoking materials.　　Source: ACT.

Figure 2-5-5: Misusing equipment - overloaded electrical sockets.　　Source: ACT.

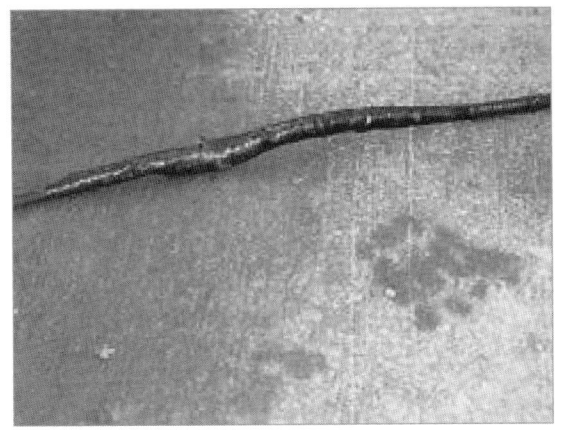

Figure 2-5-6: Defective electrical equipment.　　Source: ACT.

Figure 2-5-7: Potential for deliberate ignition.　　Source: ACT.

CONSEQUENCES

Consequences may be split into three main groups. These are:

Human harm

Fire has the potential for major loss of life due to direct contact with heat and flame or from the effects of smoke and toxic gases. The Düsseldorf airport fire in 1996 caused 17 deaths and 62 injuries.

Economic effects

Commercial losses from fire are substantial, even though recent workplace injury and death has been low. When fires do occur in the workplace the organisation is usually so badly affected it does not resume business again. The Düsseldorf airport fire in 1996 caused approximately €339 million worth of damage.

REASONS WHY FIRES SPREAD

Failure of early detection

- No detection system or patrols.
- No alarm system in place.
- People not knowing or confusing the sound of an alarm.
- Not promptly extinguished due to no hoses or extinguishers.
- Fire starts in unoccupied area.
- Fire starts out of normal work hours.
- Building material waste may be being burnt as a normal routine and smoke and other signs of fire may not be seen as unusual.
- Numerous hot working tasks conducted - therefore smells of burning ignored.
- Frequent occurrence of small, local fires caused by hot work, and not seen as significant.

Absence of compartments in building structure
- Open plan office.
- False ceilings.
- The structure under construction or alteration is incomplete and has reduced separation between levels and/or sections on a level.

Compartments undermined
- Fire doors wedged open.
- Poor maintenance of door structure.
- Holes may be designed to pass through compartments and are waiting fitment of services and subsequent sealing.
- Holes cut for ducts or doorways or to provide temporary access to locate/remove equipment.
- Compartments may be progressively created in buildings under alteration, thus increasing the risk of fire spread.

Materials inappropriately stored
- Flammable liquids not controlled - too much or in unsuitable containers.
- Boxes in corridors.
- Off cuts of wood and sawdust left in the areas where work has taken place.
- Packing materials used in the process, such as shredded paper, polystyrene, bubble wrap etc.
- Pallets and plastic covering left near to ignition sources.

Figure 2-5-8: Compartment undermined-holes cut. *Source: ACT.*

Figure 2-5-9: Fire door held open. *Source: ACT.*

Figure 2-5-10: Materials inappropriately stored. *Source: ACT.*

Assessment of fire risks

CARRYING OUT A FIRE RISK ASSESSMENT

Step 1 - Identify fire hazards
- *Identify sources of ignition* - Smokers' materials, naked flames, heaters, hot processes, cooking, machinery, boilers, faulty or misused electrical equipment, lighting equipment, hot surfaces, blocked vents, friction, static electricity, metal impact and arson.
- *Identify sources of fuel* - Flammable liquids, flammable chemicals, wood, paper and card, plastics, foam, flammable gases, furniture, textiles, packaging materials, waste materials including shavings, off cuts and dust.
- *Identify sources of oxygen* - Natural ventilation, doors, windows, forced ventilation systems, air conditioning, oxidising materials, oxygen cylinders or piped oxygen systems.

Step 2 - Identify people at risk
- Consider people in the premises - workers, visitors, contractors, public, old, young, disabled, and their level of discipline and training.
- How could fire, heat or smoke spread to areas that people occupy? - convection, conduction, radiation or direct burning.
- Who and where are the people that may be at risk? - people carrying out noisy tasks, placed high at the top of a building or in confined spaces conducting work, nearby workers or the public.
- Identify people who are especially at risk.
- How will people be warned of fire and could people be trapped by fire?

Step 3 - Evaluate, remove, or reduce and protect from risk

Risk reduction by prevention
- *Reduce sources of ignition* - Remove unnecessary sources of heat or replace with safer alternatives, ensure electrical fuses etc are of the correct rating, ensure safe and correct use of electrical equipment, enforcing a 'hot work' permit system, safe smoking policy, arson reduction measures.

- **Minimise potential fuel for a fire** - Remove or reduce amount of flammable materials, replace materials with safer alternatives, ensure safe handling, storage and use of materials, safe separation distances between flammable materials and separation from corrosive materials and their containers, use of fire resisting storage, repair or replace damaged or unsuitable furniture, control and removal of flammable waste, care of external storage due to arson, good housekeeping.
- **Reduce sources of oxygen** - Close all doors and windows not required for ventilation particularly out of working hours, shutting down non essential ventilation systems, not storing oxidising materials near heat sources or flammable materials, controlling the use of oxygen cylinders and ensuring ventilation to areas where they are used.

Risk reduction by protection

Consider existing fire safety measures, risk reduction by protection (controls), in the workplace and consider possible improvements.

- Reducing unsatisfactory structural features.
    - Remove, cover or treat large areas of combustible wall and ceiling linings, improve fire resistance of workplace, install fire breaks into open voids.
- Fire detection and warning.
    - Can fire be detected quickly enough to allow people to escape?
    - Can means of warning be recognised and understood?
    - Do workers know how to operate the system?
    - Will workers know what to do if the alarm operates?
    - Are fire notices posted around workplace?
- Means of escape.
    - How long will it take for people to escape once they are aware of a fire?
    - Is this time reasonable?
    - Are there enough exits?
    - Are exits in the correct places?
    - Are there suitable means of escape for all people, including disabled?
    - Could a fire happen that would affect all escape routes?
    - Are escape routes easily identifiable?
    - Are exit routes free from obstructions and blockages?
    - Are exit routes suitably lit at all times?
    - Have workers been trained in the use of the escape routes?
- Means of fighting fire.
    - Is the fire fighting equipment suitable for the risk?
    - Is it suitably located?
    - Is it signed where necessary?
    - Have workers been trained to use equipment where necessary?
- Maintenance and testing
    - Check all fire doors, escape routes, lighting and signs.
    - Check all fire fighting equipment.
    - Check all fire detectors and alarms.
    - Check any other equipment provided to help means of escape arrangements.
    - Are there relevant instructions to workers regarding maintenance and testing?
    - Are those who carry out maintenance and testing competent?
- Fire procedures and training.
    - Is there an emergency plan?
    - Does the emergency plan take account of all reasonably foreseeable circumstances?
    - Are all workers familiar with the plan, trained in its use, and involved in testing it?
    - Is the emergency plan made available to workers?
    - Are fire procedures clearly indicated throughout the workplace?
    - Have all people likely to be present, been considered?

Step 4 - Record, plan, inform, instruct and train

A record must be kept of the assessment in keeping with national legislative requirements. It is advisable that where the organisation is a significant sized undertaking, often where 5 or more workers regularly work at the premises, a record of the significant findings of the assessment and any group of people identified by it as being especially at risk should be made.

A record should also be kept of measures that have been or will be taken by the responsible person for the premises in order to minimise risk. Suitable headings for a record would be:

Significant Hazard	People at risk	Existing control measures	Further action needed	Projected completion date	Responsible person

Emergency plans

Following completion of the fire risk assessment, an emergency plan should be devised. The plan should include the following:

- Action on discovery of fire.
- Action on hearing alarm.
- Details of the fire warning system.
- Details of the evacuation process.
- Means of escape - travel distances.
- Location of assembly points.
- Identification of escape routes - signs, emergency lighting.
- Details of fire fighting equipment.
- Specific workers' duties.
- Safe evacuation of people who need assistance to escape.
- Safe working practices in high risk areas.
- Procedures for calling the Fire Service.
- Workers' training needs and arrangements for providing training.

Step 5 - Review and monitor

The fire risk assessment and the fire safety measures should be reviewed on a regular basis.

In addition a review should be done if:

- Changes to workplace are proposed, e.g. increased storage of flammable materials.
- Changes to work process / activity are proposed, e.g. introducing a new night shift.
- Changes to number or type of people present are proposed, e.g. public are invited on site to buy goods.
- A near miss or a fire occurs.

See also - Unit IGC1 - Element 6 - Principles of control - for more details on risk assessment technique.

5.2 - Fire prevention and prevention of fire spread

Control measures to minimise the risk of fire in a workplace

USE AND STORAGE OF FLAMMABLE AND COMBUSTIBLE MATERIALS

Where possible we should seek to **eliminate** the use of flammable materials in the workplace, for example, replacing adhesives that have a flammable content with those that are water based. Where this is not possible the amount used should be **reduced** and kept to the minimum. Quantities of material stored in the workplace must be in suitable containers and controlled to the minimum for immediate work needs. Flammable materials not in use should be removed to a purpose designed store in a well ventilated area, preferably outside the building but in a secure area. Lids should be kept on containers at all times when they are not in immediate use. Any waste containers, contaminated tools or materials should be treated in the same way and removed to a store in fresh air, until dealt with. Containers and contaminated materials need to be disposed of in a controlled manner so that they do not present a risk of fire.

Care has to be taken to control the delivery and therefore the storage of flammable and combustible materials to site. There is a temptation to have large quantities all delivered at the same time, but where possible deliveries should be staggered to reflect the rate of use in order to minimise the amount stored on site.

Terms used with flammable and combustible materials

Flashpoint

'Flashpoint' is defined as the lowest temperature at which, in a specific test apparatus, sufficient vapour is produced from a liquid sample for momentary or flash ignition to occur. It must not be confused with ignition temperature which can be considerably lower.

Flammable

Flammability (or inflammability) is the ease with which the vapours of a substance will ignite, causing fire or combustion. Substances with vapours that will ignite at temperatures commonly encountered are considered flammable, with various national specific definitions that give a temperature requirement relating to flammability. The flash point of a substance is the critical characteristic when deciding flammability. For example, flash points below 100 °F (37.8 °C) are regulated in the United States by the Occupational Health and Safety Administration (OSHA) and are considered to be potential workplace hazards *(source: www.wikipedia.org)*. Whereas, in the United Kingdom liquids with a flash point between $32°C$ and $55°C$ are classified as flammable and liquids with a flashpoint below $32°C$ are classified as highly flammable.

General principles for storage and use of flammable liquids

When considering the storage or use of flammable liquids, the following safety principles should be applied:

V   Ventilation - plenty of fresh air.

I   Ignition - control of ignition sources.

C   Containment - suitable containers and spillage control.

E   Exchange - try to use a less flammable product to do task.

S   Separation - keep storage away from process areas, by distance or a physical barrier e.g. a wall or partition.

CONTROL OF IGNITION SOURCES

Welding
- Only use competent trained workers.
- Regulators should be of a recognised standard.
- Clearly identify, by colour code the different hoses for oxygen, acetylene, propane.
- Fit non-return valves at blowpipe/torch inlet on both gas lines.
- Fit flashback arrestors incorporating cut-off valves and flame arrestors fitted to outlet of both gas regulators.
- Use crimped hose connections not jubilee clips.
- Do not let oil or grease contaminate oxygen supply due to explosion hazard.
- Check equipment visually before use, and check new connections with soapy water for leaks.
- Secure cylinders in upright position.
- Keep hose lengths to a minimum.

Figure 2-5-11: Welding equipment. *Source: ACT.*

Hot work
Hot work has been responsible for causing many fires. One of the most tragic fires due to hot work was Dusseldorf Airport Fire in 1996. The fire was started by welding on an open roadway which caused 17 deaths, incurred 62 injuries, and resulted in damage in excess of €339 million,

It is imperative that good safe working practices are utilised. Combustible materials must be removed from the area or covered up. Thought must be given to the effects of heat on the surrounding structure, and where sparks, flames, hot residue or heat will travel to. It is often necessary to have a fire watcher to spot any fires that may be started. Fire extinguishers need to be immediately available and operatives must know how to use them. The work area must be checked thoroughly for some time after the completion of work to ensure there are no smouldering fires.

Smoking
Prohibition of smoking may be unreasonable and will lead to illicit smoking, but prohibition is essential where hazardous materials are dealt with, or processes are carried on which involve the release of ignitable or explosive dusts or vapours or the production of readily combustible waste. Smoking should be prohibited in stock rooms and other rooms not under continuous supervision. Any area where 'no smoking' is imposed should have the rule strictly enforced. Where smoking is allowed, easily accessible, non-combustible receptacles for cigarette ends and other smoking material should be provided and empty daily. Smoking should cease half an hour before closing down. In many countries now smoking bans have been imposed in all public and work places.

Arson
Simple but effective ways to deter the arsonist are by giving attention to security, both external and internal, which should encompass the following:

External security
- Control of people having access to the building/site.
- Use of patrol guards.
- Lighting the premises at night.
- Safety of keys.
- Structural protection.
- Siting of rubbish bins / skips at least 8m from buildings.

Internal security
- Good housekeeping.
- Inspections.
- Clear access routes.
- Visitor supervision.
- Control of sub-contractors.
- Audits.

Figure 2-5-12: Control arson by external security. *Source: ACT.*

Figure 2-5-13: Control arson by internal security. *Source: ACT.*

SYSTEMS OF WORK

Systems of work combine people, equipment, materials and the environment to produce the safest possible climate in which to work. In order to produce a safe system of work, it is essential to make an assessment of the area to determine where the hazards and risks arise and how best to control them.

The requirement to carry out a risk assessment should address the following:

- Identify potential fire hazards.
- Decide who may be in danger, and note their locations.
- Evaluate the risks and carry out any necessary improvement measures.
- Record findings and action taken.
- Keep assessment under review.

In addition to the risk assessment carried out, other measures may include implementing the following strategies.

1) A safe place

A safe place begins with ensuring that the fabric of the building is designed or planned in a way that will prevent ignition, suppress fire spread and allow for safe, speedy unobstructed evacuation with signs to direct people. Factors to consider will include compartmentalisation, fire resistant materials, proper and suitable means of storage, means of detection, means of raising the alarm good housekeeping and regular monitoring and review.

2) Safe person

A safe person begins with raising awareness to individuals of any risk of loss resulting from outbreak of fire. Information can be provided that will identify where to raise the alarm, what the alarm sounds like, how to evacuate and where to muster (assemble), responsibility for signing in and out of the site register, fire drill procedures, trained authorised fire appointed persons, use and storage of flammable materials, good housekeeping and use of equipment producing heat or ignition (including hot processes i.e. welding).

3) Safe materials

Safe materials begin with providing information and ensuring safe segregation and storage for materials and sources of ignition / heat. In addition, this will involve providing information on the correct way to handle materials and substances and details of methods of tackling a fire involving hazardous substances.

4) Safe equipment

Safe equipment begins with user information and maintenance to ensure good working and efficient order. Information should also provide the user with a safe method for use and the limitations of and risks from the equipment. Supervision may be necessary to ensure correct use and prevent misuse that may lead to short circuiting or overheating that could result in fire. Where work involves hot processes by nature (welding, grinding, casting, etc) then permit-to-work procedures may be necessary in order to tightly control the operations.

Other equipment required in relation to fire hazards and control may include smoke or heat detection equipment, alarm sounders / bells, alarm call points and appropriate fire extinguishing apparatus. It should be noted that in the event of a fire alarm, all the passenger lifts should not be used. Under normal circumstances the lift will drop to the ground floor and remain in that position with the doors locked in the open position. All equipment should be regularly tested to ensure its conformity and be accompanied with a suitable certificate of validity.

Safe systems must also include consideration of who is at risk, including those persons with special needs such as the young, elderly, infirm or disabled. There may be a requirement to prevent smoking in the workplace or employ appointed persons to take control of the situation and co-ordinate emergency responses in the event of an alarm. If the building relies solely on internal artificial lighting, then the requirement to install emergency back-up lighting will be needed. All systems must be regularly monitored in order to reflect changes to the environment and put remedies in place to ensure full preparedness in the event of a fire.

GOOD HOUSEKEEPING

Housekeeping

By 'housekeeping' we mean the general tidiness and order of the building. At first sight, this may seem a strange matter to discuss when considering fire safety, but as housekeeping affects so many different aspects of this subject, it cannot be ignored.

Housekeeping and its effect on fire safety

Fires need fuel. A build up of redundant combustible materials, rubbish and stacks of waste materials provide that fuel. We cannot eliminate all combustible materials, but we can control them. Any unnecessary build-up of rubbish and waste should be avoided. If a fire starts in a neatly stacked pile of timber pallets, around which there is a clear space, the fire may be spotted and extinguished before it can spread. However, if the same pile were strewn around in an untidy heap, along with adjacent rubbish, the likelihood is that fire would spread over a larger area and involve other combustible materials.

Bad housekeeping

- Can lead to:
- Blocked fire exits.
- Obstructed escape routes.
- Difficult access to fire alarm call points / extinguishers / hose reels.
- Obstruction of vital signs and notices.
- A reduction in the effectiveness of automatic fire detectors and sprinklers.

Checklists

Fire Prevention is a matter of good routine and the checklists shown below are a guide as to what to look out for:

List A Routine checks

Daily at the start of business - including:

- Doors which may be used for escape purposes - unlocked and escape routes unobstructed.
- Free access to hydrants, extinguishers and fire alarm call points.
- No deposits on electric motors.

List B Routine checks

Daily at close-down - including:

- Inspection of whole area for which you are responsible - to detect any incipient smouldering fires.
- Fire doors and shutters closed.
- All unnecessary plant and equipment safely shut down.
- Waste bins emptied.
- No accumulation of combustible process waste, packaging materials or dust deposits.
- Safe disposal of waste.
- Premises left secure from unauthorised access.

List C Periodic inspection

During working hours - weekly/monthly/quarterly as decided:

- Goods neatly stored so as not to impede fire fighting.
- Clear spaces around stacks of stored materials.
- Gangways kept unobstructed.
- No non-essential storage in production areas.
- Materials clear of light fittings.
- Company smoking rules known and enforced.

Safe storage and use of flammable liquids

SMALL QUANTITIES OF HIGHLY FLAMMABLE OR FLAMMABLE LIQUIDS

The objective in controlling the risk from these materials is to remove all unnecessary quantities from the workplace to a recognised storage area outside the building. This may be done as part of a close down routine at the end of the day. It is accepted that quantities of this material may need to be available in a workplace during normal working. This should be kept to the minimum quantity allowed by national legislation. In the absence of national legislation local small scale storage of **up to** 50 litres of highly flammable **or up to** 250 litres of flammable liquids may be kept within the workplace provided it is controlled and placed in a suitable store container. If greater quantities are required a store specifically designed for this purpose must be used. Highly flammable or flammable liquids removed from storage must be in suitable containers to prevent spills and loss of vapours.

Storage in the workplace

- In a suitable sealed container.
- In a suitable cabinet, bin or other store container.
- In a designated area of the workplace.
- Away from ignition sources, working or process areas.
- Capable of containing any spillage.
- Workplace must be fire resistant structure.
- Provided with hazard warning signs to illustrate the flammability of the contents.
- Prohibition signs for smoking and naked flame.
- Not contain other substances or items.

Storage in open air

- Formal storage area on a concrete pad, with a sump for spills.
- Bunded all around to take content of largest drum plus an allowance of 10%.
- Away from other buildings.
- Marked by signs warning of flammability.
- Signs prohibiting smoking or other naked flames.
- Protection from sunlight.
- If lighting is provided within store it must be flameproof.
- Provision for spill containment materials.
- Fire extinguishers located nearby - consider powder type.
- Full and empty containers separated.
- Clear identification of contents.

Figure 2-5-14: Poor storage of flammable liquids. *Source: ACT.*

Figure 2-5-15: Storage of flammable materials. *Source: ACT.*

UNIT IGC2 - ELEMENT 05 - FIRE - HAZARDS AND CONTROL

LIQUEFIED PETROLEUM AND OTHER GASES IN CYLINDERS

Liquefied Petroleum Gas (LPG) is a term that relates to gas stored in a liquefied state under pressure; common examples are propane and butane. LPG and other gas cylinders should be stored in line with the principles detailed below:

Storage
- Storage area should preferably be in clear open area outside.
- Stored in a secure compound, usually at least a 2m high fence.
- Safe distance from toxic, corrosive, combustible materials, flammable liquids or general waste.
- Stored safe distance from any building.
- If stored inside building, keep away from exit routes, consider fire resisting storage.
- Well ventilated area.
- Oxygen cylinders kept well segregated and away from flammable gas cylinders, usually at least 3m.
- Control access to stores to prevent LPG etc being distributed all around site & keep locked.
- More than one exit (unlocked) may need to be available from any secure storage compound where distance to an exit is excessive (greater than 12m will usually be considered to be excessive).
- Storage compound to be locked when not in use.
- Protection from sunlight.
- Flameproof lighting.
- Empty containers stored separate from full.
- Fire extinguishers located nearby - consider powder and water types.

Transport
- Upright position.
- Secured to prevent falling over.
- Protection in event of accident e.g. position on vehicle.
- Transport in open vehicle preferably.
- Avoid overnight parking while loaded.
- Park in secure areas.
- Driver training.
- Fire fighting equipment.

Use

General use
- Only cylinders for use, should be stored in the workplace, additional cylinders should be kept in a purpose built store.
- Cylinder connected for use plus spare in building if necessary - no more unless in a formal purpose built store.
- Fixed position to prevent falling over, or on wheeled trolley - chained.
- Well ventilated area.
- Away from combustibles.
- Keep upright unless used on equipment specifically designed for horizontal use - e.g. gas powered lift truck.
- Handle carefully - don't drop.
- Allow to settle after transport and before use.
- Consider manual handling and injury prevention.
- Turn off cylinder before connecting, disconnecting equipment.
- Check equipment before use.
- Any smell of gas during use, turn off cylinder and investigate.
- Use correct gas regulator for equipment/task.
- Use equipment in line with manufacturers' instructions.

Figure 2-5-16: Gas cylinders for huts. *Source: ACT.*

Use in huts
- Only allow cylinders in a hut if it is part of authorised equipment.
- Pipe into site huts from cylinder located outside where possible.
- If cylinder is outside the hut use the shortest connecting hose as possible.
- Hut to be adequately ventilated high and low.
- Equipment fitted with flame failure devices.
- Turn off heater and cylinder after use and overnight.
- Be aware of danger of leaks inside huts, especially overnight as a severe risk of fire or explosion may occur.
- Keep heaters/cookers away from clothing and other combustibles.

Structural measures to prevent spread of fire and smoke

COMMON BUILDING MATERIALS

Brickwork / blockwork

Both brickwork and blockwork perform well in fires. Dependent upon the materials, workmanship, thickness, and the load carried, fire resistance of 30 minutes to 2 hours may be achieved.

Steelwork

Steel and other metals are extensively used in modern building structures. Generally they can be affected by fire at relatively low temperatures unless they are protected from the effects of the fire by some form of fire retardant materials. This may be done by encasing in concrete, fire retardant boards or spray coatings.

Timber

Timber performs very well in fires as long as it is of sufficient size that, as its outer coat burns away, there is still sufficient strength to do its task. Generally timber does not fail rapidly in a fire, unlike steel.

Glass

Glass generally performs poorly in a fire unless it is fire resistant glass. At high temperatures glass will melt and sag, which is why the traditional fire resistant glass has wire within it.

OPENINGS AND VOIDS

Consideration should be given to the protection of openings and voids by the use of fire barriers such as fire shutters, cavity barriers and fire curtains. It is critical that construction work be managed to minimise the effect on the structure being worked on to keep fire precautions intact as much as possible. This will involve planning for the prompt re-instatement of protection of openings and voids as soon after their breach to do work as is possible. The temptation to leave all breaches to the end of work and then re-instate them should be avoided - the longer that breaches are left open the higher the risk from fires. Where openings or voids are created as part of the construction process they should be considered as part of the fire risk assessment and consideration be given to the timeliness of their protection. If cavity barriers made from vulnerable or delicate material are to be used they may have to have temporary covering to protect them. This is a good example of the sort of thing that a designer should be considering and making arrangements for as part of the construction design.

STRATEGIC APPROACH TO FIRE PRECAUTIONS

The principles used for the control of fire spread within buildings have undergone dramatic changes within the last few years.

Traditional means

- Fire resisting structures.
- Fire stopping of ducts, flues and holes in fire resistant structures.
- Fire resisting doors.
- Smoke seals and intumescent (a material which expands when heat is applied) materials on doors.
- Compartmentalisation to confine the fire to a predetermined size.
- Sprinklers in large compartments.

New concepts in fire safety

Modern systems now revolve around 3 aspects:

- Early and rapid detection of a fire by use of 'intelligent' fire alarm systems.
- Limitation of the size of fire by use of 'rapid response' sprinkler system.
- Control of smoke and toxic fumes by ventilation systems, so that clear air is maintained at head height level, to enable persons to escape.

Figure 2-5-17: Magnetic door holder linked to alarm. *Source: ACT.*

Figure 2-5-18: Door stop with automatic release. *Source: ACT.*

5.3 - Fire alarm and fire fighting equipment

Fire detection, fire warning and fire fighting equipment

COMMON FIRE DETECTION AND ALARM SYSTEMS

Fire detection

Heat detection
Sensors operate by the melting of a metal (fusion detectors) or expansion of a solid, liquid or gas (thermal expansion detectors).

Radiation detection
Photoelectric cells detect the emission of infra-red/ultra-violet radiation from the fire.

Smoke detection
Using ionising radiations, light scatter (smoke scatters beams of light), obscuration (smoke entering a detector prevents light from reaching a photoelectric cell).

Flammable gas detection
Measures the amount of flammable gas in the atmosphere and compares the value with a reference value

Figure 2-5-19: Smoke detector. *Source: ACT.*

Alarm systems

The purpose of a fire alarm is to give an early warning of a fire in a building for two reasons:

- To increase the safety of occupants by encouraging them to escape to a place of safety.
- To increase the possibility of early extinction of the fire thus reducing the loss of or damage to the property.

Types of fire alarms

Voice	-	Simplest and most effective type but very limited because it is dependent upon the size of the workplace and background noise levels.
Manual alarms	-	Rotary gong, hand bell or triangle and sounder but limited by the scale of the building.
Call points with sounders	-	Standard system, operation of one call point sounds alarm throughout workplace.
Automatic system	-	System as above, with added fire detection to initiate the alarm.

Single-stage alarm
The alarm sounds throughout the whole of the building and calls for total evacuation.

Two-stage alarm
In certain large / high rise buildings it may be better to evacuate the areas of high risk first, usually those closest to the fire or immediately above it. In this case, an evacuation signal is given in the affected area, together with an alert signal in other areas.

Nominated worker alarms
In some premises, an immediate total evacuation may not be desirable, e.g. nightclubs, shops, theatres, cinemas. A controlled evacuation by the nominated workers may be preferred, to prevent distress and panic to the occupants. If such a system is used, the alarm must be restricted to the nominated workers and only used where there are sufficient nominated workers and they have been fully trained in the action of what to do in case of fire.

Alarms must make a distinctive sound, audible in all parts of the workplace (sound levels should be sufficiently above any ambient noise in the area). The meaning of the alarm sound must be understood by all. They may be manually or automatically operated.

Figure 2-5-20: Easy operation alarm call point. *Source: ACT.*

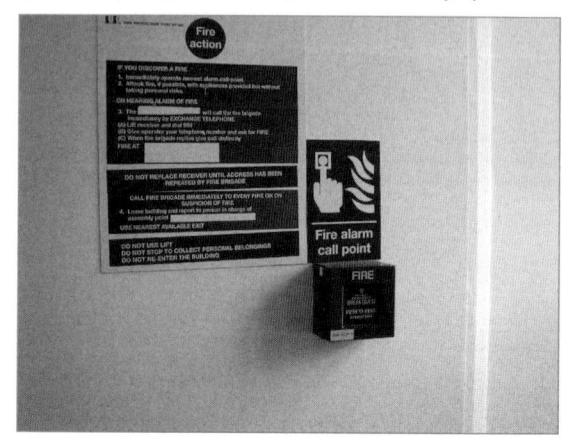

Figure 2-5-21: Alarm point identified & well located. *Source: ACT.*

PORTABLE FIRE FIGHTING EQUIPMENT

Siting

Portable fire extinguishers should always be sited:

- On the line of escape routes.
- Near, but not too near, to danger points.
- Near to room exits inside or outside according to occupancy and/or risk.
- In multi-storey buildings, at the same position on each floor e.g. top of stair flights or at corners in corridors.
- Where possible in groups forming fire points.
- So that no person need travel an excessive distance to reach an extinguisher, 30m will usually be considered to be excessive.
- With the carrying handle about one metre from the floor to facilitate ease of handling, removal from wall bracket, or on purpose designed floor stand.
- Away from excesses of heat or cold.

Maintenance and inspection

Fire fighting equipment provided must be properly maintained and subject to examination and test at intervals such that it remains effective.

Maintenance

This means service of the fire extinguisher by a competent person. It involves thorough examination of the extinguisher, and is usually done annually.

Inspection

A regular check, meeting national legal requirements or in the absence of this typically monthly, should be carried out to ensure that extinguishers are in their proper place and have not been discharged, lost pressure or suffered obvious damage. It may be necessary to increase the frequency of checks made for fire extinguishers on a construction site. This is due to the less structured or controlled work environment that they are sited in which could mean that there is a higher risk of them being damaged or used without notification.

Fire fighting equipment training

It is good practice to make sure that those that may need to take a lead in operating fire extinguishers can do this competently and for most people this would mean practising how to use them in a situation that reproduces the circumstances of a fire. Training should include:

- Understanding of principles of combustion and classification of fires.
- Identification of the various types of fire extinguisher available to them.
- Principles of use and limitations of extinguishers.
- Considerations for personal safety and the safety of others.
- How to identify if the extinguisher is appropriate to the fire and ready to use.
- How to attack fires with the appropriate extinguisher(s).
- Any specific considerations related to the environment the extinguishers are kept or used in.

Training has to clarify the general and specific rules for use of extinguishers:

General - aim at the seat of the fire and move the extinguisher across the fire to extinguish it - this is particularly appropriate for class A fires.

Specific - if using a foam extinguisher for class B fires the foam is allowed to drop onto the fire by aiming just above it. If this is for a flammable liquid fire contained in an open tank it is possible to get good results by this process or aiming it to the back of the tank and allowing the foam to float over the liquid. For other specific limitations or approaches to the use of individual types of extinguisher see section below.

EXTINGUISHING MEDIA

Fire extinguishers

Water

Water extinguishers should only be used on Class A fires - those involving solids like paper and wood. Water works by cooling the burning material to below its ignition temperature, therefore removing the heat part of the fire triangle, and so the fire goes out. Water is the most common form of extinguishing media and can be used on the majority of fires involving solid materials.

Must not be used on liquid fires or in the vicinity of live electrical equipment.

Advantages

- Refill facilities usually readily available.
- Excellent cooling properties.
- Best choice for Class A.

Disadvantages

- **Not to be used** on Electrical Fires.
- Can spread Class B fires.
- Damages/destroys equipment.

Figure 2-5-22: Colour coding by label and sign. *Source: ACT.*

Foam

Foam is especially useful for extinguishing Class B fires - those involving burning liquids and solids which melt and turn to liquids as they burn. Foam works in several ways to extinguish the fire, the main way being to smother the burning liquid, i.e. to stop the oxygen reaching the combustion zone. Foam can also be used to prevent flammable vapours escaping from spilled volatile liquids and also on Class A fires. It is worth noting that the modern spray foams are more efficient than water on a Class A fire.

Must not be used in the vicinity of live electrical equipment, unless electrically rated.

Advantages
- Forms air-tight blanket over burning liquids.
- Minimal chance of re-flash (fire restarting).
- Can be used from distance-around corners and from elevated areas.

Disadvantages
- **Not to be used** on Electrical Fires.
- Damages/destroys equipment.

Dry powder

Designed for Class A, B and C fires but may only subdue Class A fires for a short while. One of the main ways in which powder works to extinguish a fire is the smothering effect, whereby it forms a thin film of powder on the burning liquid, thus excluding air. The extinguisher is also excellent for the rapid knock down (flame suppression) of flammable liquid spills.

Powders generally provide extinction faster than foam, but there is a greater risk of re-ignition and this should always be borne in mind. If used indoors, a powder extinguisher can cause problems for the operator due to the inhalation of the powder and obscuration of vision. This type of extinguisher may be used on live electrical equipment.

Advantages
- Knocks down flames.
- Fast and effective.
- Enables a large coverage range.
- Rated for Class A, B and C fires.

Disadvantages
- Minimal Protection against re-flash (fire restarting).
- Can form a crust when applied which can smoulder and allow the fire to break back through the crust.
- Highly corrosive to electronic equipment.
- Agent can harden and solidify in container.

Vapourising liquids

Vapourising liquids, for example, halogenated hydrocarbon fire extinguishing agents (Halons), are recognised to have desirable properties for many fire fighting applications. They possess a relatively high degree of fire fighting effectiveness per unit weight of agent, and are easily stored as dense liquids. They vaporise either before or during application to leave no particulate residue, i.e. they are 'clean' agents. These properties make them particularly useful for dealing with small scale vehicle engine fires or similar.

However when halogenated hydrocarbons (Halons) are used they release vapours to the atmosphere that are harmful to the environment. As such many countries have banned their use and some have prohibited their possession.

Advantages
- Safe for Class C.
- Non-corrosive, non-damaging to equipment.
- Minimal chance of re-flash in sealed space.
- Effective on small Class A & B fires in open spaces.

Disadvantages
- No re-flash protection in open spaces.
- In very hot fires, can generate deadly phosgene gas.
- Its use in many countries is now illegal.
- No longer available in the UK after 2000.

Gaseous - Carbon Dioxide (CO_2)

Carbon dioxide (CO_2) extinguishers are safe and excellent for use on live electrical equipment. CO_2 may also be used for small Class B fires in their early stages, indoors or outdoors with little air movement. CO_2 replaces the oxygen in the atmosphere surrounding the fuel and the fire is extinguished. As most carbon dioxide extinguishers last only a few seconds, only small fires should be tackled with this type of extinguisher. CO_2 is an asphyxiant and should not be used in confined spaces. It does not remove the heat - therefore beware of the possibility of re-ignition. CO_2 extinguishers are very noisy due to the rapid expansion of gas as it is released; this can surprise people when they operate the extinguisher. This expansion causes severe cooling around the discharge horn and can freeze the skin if the operator's hand is in contact with the horn.

Advantages
- Safe for Class C.
- Non-corrosive, non-damaging to equipment.
- Minimal chance of re-flash in sealed space.
- Effective on small Class A & B fires in open spaces, with little air movement.

Disadvantages
- Displaces oxygen - can kill firefighters.
- No re-flash protection in open spaces.
- Can get frost burn if the nozzle is not an insulated type and the user holds the nozzle whilst discharging onto a fire.

Special fires

Gas fires
Except in very small occurrences, a Class C fire involving gas should not normally be extinguished. If a gas fire is to be extinguished, then isolation of the gas supply must also take place.

Metal fires
Class D metal fires are a specialist type of fire and they cannot be extinguished by the use of any of the traditional fire extinguishers. In fact, it may be dangerous to attempt to fight a metal fire with such an extinguisher as an explosion of the metal may take place or toxic fumes may be produced. Metal fires can be extinguished by smothering them with dry sand. However, the sand must be absolutely dry or an explosion may occur. Extinguishers specifically designed for metal fires are produced; the extinguishing agents used may be pyromet, graphite, talc or salt. All of these extinguishers basically operate by the smothering principle.

Cooking oil fires
New style wet chemical extinguishers have been designed to specifically deal with Class F (Class K in the USA) **cooking oil** fires. This type of extinguisher congeals on top of the oil and excludes the oxygen. They may also be used on Class A fires depending upon the manufacturer's instructions.

Summary matrix - fire extinguishers

	METHOD	Solids	Liquids	Gas	Metals	Electric	Cooking Oils'
WATER	Cools	Yes	No	No	No	No	No
SPRAY FOAM	Smothers	Yes	Yes	No	No	No	No
WET CHEMICAL	Chemical	No	No	No	No	No	Yes
DRY POWDER	Smothers & Chemical	Yes	Yes	Yes & Isolate	Special Powders	Yes - Low Voltage	No
HALON	Chemical & Smothers	Its use in many countries is now illegal					
CARBON DIOXIDE	Smothers	No	Yes - Small Fires	No	No	Yes	No

Figure 2-5-23: Types and use of fire extinguishers - summary.   Source: ACT.

International classifications
Internationally there are several accepted classification methods for hand-held fire extinguishers. Each classification is useful in fighting fires with a particular group of fuel.

Australia

Type	Colour Code	Class
Water	Solid red	A
Foam	Red with a blue band	A, B
Powder	Red with a white band	A, B, C, E
Carbon dioxide	Red with a black band	A (limited), B, C, E, F
Vapourising liquid (not halon)	Red with a yellow band	A, B, C, E
Wet chemical	Red with an oatmeal band	A, F

Figure 2-5-24: Fire extinguisher colour codes and classifications - Australia.   Source: www.wikipedia.org.

In Australia, halon fire extinguishers are illegal to own or use on a fire, unless an essential use exemption has been granted.

United Kingdom (UK)
According to the standard BS EN 3, fire extinguishers in the United Kingdom are predominantly red, and a band or circle of a second colour covering at least 5% of the surface area of the extinguisher indicates the contents. Before 1997, the entire body of the fire extinguisher was colour coded according to the type of extinguishing agent.

Type	Colour Code	Class
Water	Red	A
Foam	Red with Cream as a secondary colour	A, B and sometimes E
Dry Powder	Red with Blue as a secondary colour	A, B, C, E / B, C,E
Carbon Dioxide CO_2	Red with Black as a secondary colour	A (limited), B, E
Wet Chemical	Red with Canary Yellow as a secondary colour	A, F
Class D Powder	Red with a Blue as a secondary colour	D

Figure 2-5-25: Fire extinguisher colour codes and classifications - United Kingdom.   Source: www.wikipedia.org.

The UK recognises six classes of fire. Class A fires involve organic solids such as paper and wood. Class B fires involve flammable liquids. Class C fires involve flammable gases. Class D fires involve metals, Class E fires involve live electrical items and Class F fires involve cooking fat and oil.

Continental Europe

No colour coding is imposed. All extinguishers are red (RAL 3000). Recently, some voluntary colour coding has appeared. However, it is different from the UK National Addendum to EN 3 which provides for the secondary colour code shown above.

United States

There is no official standard in the United States for the colour of fire extinguishers, though they are typically red, except for Class D (combustible metals) extinguishers, which are usually yellow. Extinguishers are marked with pictograms depicting the types of fires that the extinguisher is approved to fight. In the past, extinguishers were marked with coloured geometric symbols, and some extinguishers still use both symbols. No official pictogram exists for Class D extinguishers, though training manuals sometimes show a drill press with shavings burning underneath. The types of fires and additional standards are described in NFPA 10: Standard for Portable Fire Extinguishers.

Intended use	Symbol	Pictogram	Class
Ordinary combustibles	Green Triangle	Garbage can and wood pile burning	A
Flammable liquids	Red Square	Gasoline can with a burning puddle	B
Energized electrical equipment	Blue Circle	Electric plug with a burning outlet	C
Combustible metals	Yellow Star	N/A	D
Cooking oils	Black Hexagon	Pan burning	K

Figure 2-5-26: Fire extinguisher symbols and classifications - United States. *Source: www.wikipedia.org.*

Hosereels

Hose reels are designed for use on Class A - Carbonaceous fires. The hose reel acts as a replacement for water fire extinguishers and it is said that one hose reel equates to 4 x 9 litre water extinguishers. Modern hose reels have an adjustable nozzle and can be adjusted to give a jet of water, water spray or a combination of both. The water jet is normally used for its "striking power" in attacking the seat of a fire. The jet of water should be "played" across the fire surface and into the heart of the fire to extinguish embers, for example. The water spray can be used if the burning material is easily disturbed with the possibility of spreading the fire. The spray pattern produced allows larger areas to be covered in one go than if the water jet has been used and, as it has less pressure behind it, it does not spread materials such as dusts or paper as easily.

Advantages

- Continuous supply of water - no time constraint.
- Greater quantity of water is delivered than from an extinguisher, and this has a better effect at extinguishing the fire.
- The person who is attempting to extinguish the fire does not need to get as close as when using extinguishers.
- A radical spray pattern can be produced to protect the user from radiated heat.

Disadvantages

- Considerable physical effort may be required to pull the hose reel to the fire, especially if the route is twisting and has lots of obstructions.
- Any doors through which the hose reel is pulled will become wedged open by the reel.
- The user may stay in the vicinity of the fire too long.
- The extended hose reel may create an additional tripping hazard.

Limitations

- Hose reels should be connected to a permanent water supply so they are not limited by discharge time factors as are extinguishers.
- Hose reels are often limited to 30 metres in length. This limits the use of a hosereel by virtue of the distance that it is located from a fire that might occur.
- Considerable physical strength is required to pull the full length of hose, and for this reason consideration should be given to shorter lengths of hosereel being provided in more frequent locations.
- A limiting factor is the likely route through which the hosereel will need to pass. If this route includes a lot of corners, turns or doors, then hosereels may not be the most suitable fire equipment to be provided.

5.4 - Means of escape

Requirements for fire plans for means of escape

TRAVEL DISTANCES

Travel distance is a significant component of a successful means of escape plan. Travel distances are judged on the basis of distance to a place of safety in the open air and away from the building; the distance needs to be kept to the minimum. The distance includes travel around obstructions in the workplace and may be greatly affected by any work in progress on a construction site. If someone is outside on a scaffold it is unlikely to be considered as a place of safety and the distance would usually be taken as that to reach the ground away from the building (for example, at an assembly point).

- The route must be sufficiently wide and of sufficiently short distance to allow speedy and safe evacuation.
- There should normally be alternative routes leading in different directions.
- Everyone should be able to escape unaided (if able bodied).
- The distance between work stations and the nearest fire exit should be minimised.

STAIRS

Staircases form an integral part of the means of escape from fire in most buildings. If they are to be part of the escape route, the following points must be ensured:

Figure 2-5-27: Fire escape - hazard. *Source: ACT.*

- Fire resistant structure.
- Fitted with fire doors.
- Doors must not be wedged open.
- Wide enough to take the required number of people.
- Must lead direct to fresh air, or to two totally separate routes of escape.
- Non slip/trip and in good condition.
- No combustible storage within staircase.

PASSAGEWAYS

- The route should lead directly to the open air via a protected route (where necessary).
- Route to be kept unobstructed.

DOORS

- Exit doors are to open outwards easily (unless small numbers of people involved).
- Provide fire doors along the escape route.
- Fire doors along with fire resistant structures serve two purposes:
  - Prevent the spread of fire.
  - Ensure that there is means of escape for persons using the building.
- They should not be wedged open.
- Lead to open air - safety.

EMERGENCY LIGHTING

Emergency lighting should be considered if escape is likely to be required in dark conditions. This could mean late afternoon in winter time, not just at night time.

EXIT AND DIRECTIONAL SIGNS

The escape route should be adequately signposted and easy to follow (see also - Unit IGC1 - Element 6 - Principles of control - Safety Signs).

ASSEMBLY POINTS

The assembly point is a place of safety where people affected by the fire wait whilst any incident is investigated, and where confirmation can be made that all persons have evacuated the premises. The main factors to consider are:

- Safe distance from building.
- Sited in a safe position.
- Not sited so that people will be in the way of the Fire Service / fire fighting team.
- Must be able to walk away from assembly point and back to a public road.
- Clearly signed.
- More than one provided to suit numbers and groups of people.
- Communications should be provided between assembly points.
- Measures provided to decide if evacuation successful.
- Person must be in charge of assembly point and identified.
- Person to meet / brief the Fire Service / fire fighting team clear and identified.

Figure 2-5-28: Assembly point. *Source: ACT.*

NEED FOR CONTINUAL REVIEW AS WORK PROGRESSES

In all workplaces there is a need to actively review and revise the fire risk assessment, the fire safety measures that apply and the fire/emergency plans. This aspect of fire safety is absolutely vital in construction sites or any other workplace where layout changes are constantly taking place.

Dependant upon the state of the build, fire safety may need to be inspected on a weekly or even daily. Checks and assessment should be made to ensure that the fire plan for means of escape is still appropriate and that the following fire safety measures are not being compromised:

- Escape routes.
- Access to fire alarms.
- Audibility of fire alarm systems.
- Access and availability of fire fighting equipment.
- Suitability of fire safety signage.
- Need for and suitability of escape lighting.
- Fire protection / fire resistant structures within the building.
- Introduction of new fire hazards e.g. hot works.
- Correct storage / use of flammable materials.
- Site security / arson prevention.
- New workers and the need for 'fire induction'.

If, as a result of any works that need to be carried out, fire safety standards will be reduced then additional compensating factors may need to be introduced. For example, if detector heads need to be covered to prevent false alarms a fire watch system of patrols may be introduced to compensate. As can be seen, fire safety is a constantly changing factor which must be integral to the everyday management of site safety.

5.5 - Evacuation of the workplace

Emergency evacuation procedures

The danger which may threaten persons if an emergency occurs at work depends on many different factors; consequently it is not possible to construct one model procedure for action in the event of fire and emergency for all premises. Evacuation procedures need to reflect the type of emergency, the people affected and the premises involved. Many of the different issues to consider for different emergencies have common factors, for example, evacuation in an efficient / effective manner, an agreed assembly location (which may be different for different emergencies) and checks to ensure people are safe. These factors are considered below with regard to fire emergencies.

APPOINTMENT OF FIRE MARSHALS

In all premises a person should be nominated to be responsible for co-ordinating the fire evacuation plan. This may be the same person that organises fire instruction and training and drills and co-ordinates the evacuation at the time of the fire. They may appoint persons such as fire marshals to assist them in fulfilling the role. This involves the appointment of certain workers to act as fire marshals to assist with evacuation. The way in which they assist will vary between organisations; for example, some will check areas of the building in the event of a fire to ensure no person is still inside and others will lead the evacuation to show where to go. The fire marshals' appointment should be made known to workers and they should be clearly identifiable at the time of emergency so that those that are asked to evacuate understand the authority of the person requiring them to do so. The appointment of fire marshals contributes to an employer's compliance with the requirement to establish competent persons to assist with health and safety.

FIRE INSTRUCTION NOTICES

At conspicuous positions in all parts of the location, and adjacent to all fire alarm actuating points (e.g. break glass operated call points), printed notices should be exhibited stating, in concise terms, the essentials of the action to be taken upon discovering a fire and on hearing the fire alarm. It is usual to also state what someone must do when they discover a fire.

Fire action

The action in the event of a fire and upon discovery needs to be immediate, and a simple fire action plan should be put into effect. A good plan of action would include the following points.

On discovering a fire:

- Sound the fire alarm (to warn others).
- Call the fire service.
- Go to the assembly point.

On hearing the alarm:

- Leave the building by the nearest exit.
- Close doors behind you.
- Go to the assembly point.
- Get out of the building and stay out.

On evacuation:

- Do not take risks.
- Do not stop for personal belongings.
- Do not use lifts.
- Do not return to the building unless authorised to do so.
- Report to assembly point.

Figure 2-5-29: Fire instruction notice. *Source: ACT.*

Note: You must consider the wording on notices that are posted and ensure that workers are instructed and trained to do what is required.

FIRE TRAINING

Typical issues to be included in a fire training programme relating to emergency action are:

- Fire prevention.
- Recognition of fire alarms and the actions to be taken.
- Understanding the emergency signs.
- Location of fire escape routes and assembly points.
- Requirements for safe evacuation (e.g. non-use of lifts, do not run etc.).
- Location and operation of call points and other means of raising the alarm.
- How the fire service is called.
- Location, use and limitations of fire fighting equipment.
- Consideration of people with special needs.
- Identity and role of fire marshals.

FIRE DRILLS

A fire drill is intended to ensure, by means of training and rehearsal, that in the event of fire:

- The people who may be in danger act in a calm, orderly and efficient manner.
- Those designated with specific duties carry them out in an organised and effective manner.
- The means of escape are used in accordance with a predetermined and practised plan.
- An opportunity for management leadership.

The fire drill enables all people involved in the evacuation to practice and learn under as near realistic circumstances as possible. This can identify what works well in the evacuation procedure and what does not. Practice in the form of a drill helps people to respond quickly to the alarm and, because they have done it before, to make their way efficiently to the assembly point. At least once a year a practice fire drill should normally be carried out simulating conditions in which one or more of the escape routes from the building are obstructed. This will assist in developing an awareness of the alternative exits that can be taken and assist in ensuring people understand the unpredictability of fires.

ROLL CALLS

The traditional method of undertaking a roll call is by use of a checklist of names. Very few workplaces can now operate this system as they do not have such a static workforce as this system requires. Where they can operate they will provide a speedy and efficient means of identifying who has arrived at the assembly point and who has not. Where strict security control to a construction site is used, with signing in and out, this may make this process more viable. This requires people on site to report to their allocated assembly point and for someone (e.g. a Fire Marshal) to confirm that they have arrived safely and determine if anyone is missing.

If it is not known exactly who is in a building a system of Fire Marshals who can make a check of the building at the time of their own evacuation (without endangering their own safety) may be employed. This can assist with the process and may identify people that have not evacuated. However, this system may not be able to provide an absolute confirmation that everyone has evacuated as there may be limited opportunity for the Fire Marshal to check the whole of the area allocated to them. Any doubt or confirmed missing persons should be reported to the person nominated to report to the fire service, who in turn will provide a report to the fire service as soon as they arrive.

PROVISIONS FOR THE INFIRM AND DISABLED

When planning a fire evacuation system we need to consider who may be in the workplace, their abilities and capabilities. Any disability e.g. hearing, vision, mental or mobility impairment must be catered for. Some of the arrangements may be to provide the person with a nominated assistant(s) to support their speedy escape, for example, with the use of a specially designed evacuation chair to enable them to make their way out of a building down emergency exit stairs. Part of the provision is to make sure they are capable of knowing that an emergency exists. This may mean providing them with special alarm arrangements that cater for their disability, for example, a visual and or vibrating alert for the hearing impaired.

This page is intentionally blank

Element 6

Chemical and biological health hazards and control

Learning outcomes

On completion of this element, candidates should be able to demonstrate understanding of the content through the application of knowledge to familiar and unfamiliar situations. In particular they should be able to:

6.1 Recognise the forms of, and classification of, substances hazardous to health.

6.2 Explain the factors to be considered when undertaking a preliminary assessment of the health risks from substances commonly encountered in the workplace.

6.3 Describe the use and limitations of Occupational Exposure Limits including the purpose of long term and short term exposure limits.

6.4 Distinguish between acute and chronic health effects.

6.5 Outline control measures that should be used to reduce the risk of ill-health from exposure to hazardous substances.

6.6 Outline the basic requirements related to disposal of waste and effluent (and the control of atmospheric pollution).

Content

6.1 - Forms and classification of hazardous substances	195
Forms of chemical agents	195
Forms of biological agents	195
General classification of chemical substances hazardous to health	195
The health hazards of specific agents	197
6.2 - Risks associated with hazardous substances	198
Routes of entry of hazardous substances into the body	198
Body response to agents and protective mechanisms	200
Sources of information	202
Basic surveys	203
Basic surveys for health risks	204
6.3 - Occupational exposure limits	206
Application of relevant limits	206
Long-term and short-term exposure limits	206
Limitations of exposure limits	207
International variations and attempts at harmonisation (e.g. EU indicative limit values)	207
6.4 - Acute and chronic health effects	207
Difference between acute and chronic health effects	207
6.5 - Control measures	208
Duty to prevent exposure or, where this is not reasonably practicable, adequately control it	208
Ensuring occupational exposure limits are not exceeded	208
Methods of control	208
Further controls of substances that can cause cancer, asthma or damage to genes	215
6.6 - Waste disposal and control of pollution	216
Key concepts of environmental issues relating to waste disposal and effluent	216

Sources of reference

Safety in the Use of Chemicals at Work (ILO Code of Practice), ILO ISBN 9-2210-80064

Step by Step Guide to COSHH Assessment (HSG97), HSE Books ISBN 0-7176-2785-3

An Introduction to Local Exhaust Ventilation (HSG37), HSE Books ISBN 0-7176-1001-2

Respiratory Protective Equipment at Work - A Practical Guide (HSG53), HSE Books ISBN 0-7176-2904-X

Ambient Factors in the Workplace (ILO Code of Practice), ILO ISBN 92-2-111628-X

Other sources of reference

Personal Protective Equipment at Work Regulations 1992. Guidance on Regulations L25 HSE Books 2005 ISBN-0-7176-6139-3

COSHH a brief guide to the Regulations: What you need to know about the Control of Substances Hazardous to Health Regulations 2002 (COSHH) Leaflet

INDG136 (rev3) HSE Books 2005 (single copy free or priced packs of 10 ISBN 0-7176-2982-1)

Noise at Work: Advice for Employers Leaflet INDG362 HSE Books 2002 (single copy free or priced packs of 10 ISBN-0-7176-2539-7)

Selecting protective gloves for work with chemicals: Guidance for employers and health and safety specialists Leaflet INDG330 HSE Books 2000 (single copy free or priced packs of 15 ISBN 0-7176-1827-7)

A short guide to the Personal Protective Equipment at Work Regulations 1992 INDG174 (rev1) HSE Books, ISBN-0-7176-6141-5.

Biological monitoring in the workplace: A guide to its practical application to chemical exposure HSG167 HSE Books 1997 ISBN 0-7176-1279-1

Breathe freely: A workers' information card on respiratory sensitisers. Pocket card INDG172 HSE Books 1994 ISBN-0-7176-0771-2)

COSHH a brief guide to the Regulations: What you need to know about the Control of Substances Hazardous to Health Regulations 2002 (COSHH) Leaflet INDG136 (rev3) HSE Books 2003 ISBN 0-7176-2982-1

EH40/2005 Workplace exposure limits: Containing the list of workplace exposure limits for use with the Control of Substances Hazardous to Health Regulations 2002 (as amended) Environmental Hygiene Guidance Note EH40 HSE Books 2005 ISBN 0-7176-2977-5

A matter of life and breath: Occupational asthma - the causes, the effects and how to prevent it Video HSE Books 1994 ISBN 0-7176-1859

6.1 - Forms and classification of hazardous substances

Forms of chemical agents

A chemical substance is any material with a definite chemical ratio of elements in its composition. For example, water has the ratio of two hydrogen atoms (small particles) to one of oxygen, and will always exhibit the same chemical properties, for example, boiling at 100ºC.

A chemical substance that cannot be broken down by ordinary chemical processes into a different substance is called an element. There are around 110 known elements, about 80 of which are stable, that is, they do not change by radioactive decay into other elements.

Two or more elements combined into one substance form a chemical compound (chemically combined), which consists of atoms bonded together in molecules (groups of two or more atoms), giving rise to an enormous number of different chemical compounds.

These chemical substances and compounds can be found in different physical forms, such as a solid, liquid or gas. The form taken by a hazardous substance is a contributory factor to its potential for harm. Principally the form affects how easily a substance gains entry to the body, how it is absorbed into the body and how it reaches a susceptible site.

Chemical agents take many forms, the most common being as follows:

Dusts	These are solid airborne particles, often created by operations such as grinding, crushing, milling, sanding or demolition - e.g. silica.
Fumes	Are solid particles formed by condensation from the gaseous state - e.g. lead fume, welding fume.
Gases	Formless fluids usually produced by chemical processes involving combustion or by the interaction of chemical substance. A gas will normally seek to fill the space completely into which it is liberated - e.g. chlorine gas.
Mists	Are finely dispersed liquid droplets suspended in air. Mists are mainly created by spraying, foaming, pickling and electro-plating - e.g. mist from a water pressure washer.
Vapours	Is the gaseous form of a material normally encountered in a liquid or solid state at normal room temperature and pressure; typical examples are solvents - e.g. trichloroethylene which releases vapours when the container is opened.
Liquids	Substances which are liquid at normal temperature and pressure.

Forms of biological agents

FUNGI

Fungi are a variety of organisms that act in a parasitic manner, feeding on organic matter. Most are either harmless or positively beneficial to health; however a number cause harm to humans and may be fatal. An example of a fungi organism is the mould from rotten hay called Aspergilla, which causes aspergillosis (Farmer's lung). Farmer's lung is an allergic reaction to the mould. This occurs deep in the lungs in the alveoli region. It leads to shortness of breath, which gets progressively worse at each exposure. The resulting attack is similar to asthma. Aspergilla can also cause short-term effects of irritation to the eyes and nose and coughing. Moulds from the same family can cause ringworm and athlete's foot.

BACTERIA

Bacteria are single cell organisms. Most bacteria are harmless to humans and many are beneficial. The bacteria that can cause disease are called pathogens. Examples of harmful bacteria are leptospira (causing Weil's disease), bacillus anthracis (causing anthrax), and legionella pneumophila (causing legionnaires disease).

VIRUSES

Viruses are the smallest known type of infectious agent. They invade the cells of other organisms, which they take over and make copies of themselves and while not all cause disease many of them do. Examples of viruses are hepatitis which can cause liver damage and the Human Immunodeficiency Virus (HIV) which causes acquired immune deficiency syndrome (AIDS).

General classification of chemical substances hazardous to health

The Globally Harmonised System of Classification and Labelling of Chemicals or GHS has replaced the various different labelling standards for chemicals used in different countries. Its development began at the United Nations Rio summit in 1992, when ILO (International Labour Organisation), OECD (Organisation for Economic and Cooperation and Development) and various Governments and stakeholders came together at the United Nations. It supersedes the relevant European Union and United States standards.

The hazard classification and labelling process is an essential tool for establishing an effective information transfer so that the degree of the hazard the chemical represents for man and the environment can be recognised, the correct preventive actions be chosen, and safe use achieved.

The (ILO) has adopted the Convention No. 170 and Recommendation No. 177 on `Safety in the use of chemicals at work' in 1990.

Indication of danger	EU Symbol (orange background)	Category of danger	Characteristic properties and body responses
Irritant	X	Irritant	A non-corrosive substance which, through immediate, prolonged or repeated contact with the skin or mucous membrane, can cause inflammation e.g. butyl ester, a severe irritant which can cause abdominal pain, vomiting and burning of the skin and eyes.
		Sensitising (by contact)	May cause an allergic skin reaction which will worsen on further exposures (allergic dermatitis), e.g. nickel or epoxy resin.
Corrosive	(corrosive symbol)	Corrosive	May destroy living tissues on contact e.g. sulphuric (battery) acid or sodium hydroxide (caustic soda).
Harmful	X	Harmful	If inhaled or ingested or it penetrates the skin, has an adverse effect on health e.g. some solvents causing narcosis or central nervous system failure.
		Sensitising (by inhalation)	May cause an allergic respiratory reaction, which will progressively worsen on further exposures (asthma), e.g. flour dust, isocyanates.
		Carcinogenic (category 3)	Only evidence is from animals, which is of doubtful relevance to humans, e.g. benzyl chloride.
		Mutagenic (category 3)	Evidence of mutation in Ames Test and possible somatic cell mutation. properties can lead to heritable mutations or damage which in the long-term can cause cancer or harm to reproduction
		Toxic to reproduction (category 3)	Animal data, not necessarily relevant.
Toxic	(skull & crossbones)	Toxic	If inhaled or ingested or it penetrates the skin, may involve serious acute or chronic health risks and even death e.g. arsenic, a systemic poison.
		Mutagenic (categories 1 & 2)	May cause genetic defects, e.g. 2-Ethoxyethanol may impair fertility.
		Toxic to reproduction (categories 1 & 2)	May cause harm to the unborn child, e.g. lead suspected of causing restricted development of the brain of the foetus.
Very Toxic	(skull & crossbones)		If inhaled or ingested or it penetrates the skin, may involve extremely serious acute or chronic health risks and even death e.g. cyanide, a severe irritant and systemic poison. *Source: The Chemicals (Hazard Information & Packaging for Supply) Regulations (CHIP 3) 2002.*
Carcinogenic	(skull & crossbones)	Category 1 carcinogens	Chemicals that may cause cancer or increase its incidence.

Figure 2-6-1: Harmful, toxic. Source: ACT.

Category 2 carcinogens

Category 3 carcinogens

The health hazards of specific agents

AMMONIA

Ammonia is a gas used extensively as a refrigerant or as an aqueous solution used in cleaning materials. It is a gas usually stored under pressure.

Contact with liquid - it has a corrosive action that will damage or destroy the skin cells on contact and it will severely irritate or damage the cornea (the transparent convex membrane that covers the pupil and iris of the eye).

Gas - it is lighter than air and has a local effect on the lungs. In small concentrations it is an acute irritant but is recoverable; in larger concentrations it can result in pneumonia and pulmonary failure.

Aqueous - (alkaline liquor) can cause skin damage on contact and the vapours from the liquor are an acute respiratory irritant.

CHLORINE

It is usually stored under pressure in its liquid state. If a leak occurs a small amount of liquid will give rise to a large amount of gas. It is an acute respiratory irritant; small quantities may lead to chronic lung disease, large quantities result in pneumonia and pulmonary failure. It is a highly reactive chemical gas which supports violent combustion. It is used extensively in water treatment processes, for example, where water is required for human consumption. Compounds of chlorine include sodium hypochlorite e.g. domestic bleach. These compounds liberate chlorine gas readily when mixed with acids, therefore creating a risk to workers who use mixtures of bleaches and acid cleaners.

ORGANIC SOLVENTS

Include highly volatile / flammable cleaning agents such as acetone, organo chlorides such as trichloroethylene (used for commercial degreasing) or carbon tetrachloride used in dry cleaning processes. In the construction industry they may be encountered as residual contents of storage tanks or may be used as convenient cleaning substances to remove adhesives. Trichloroethylene is capable of absorption through the skin and it is a narcotic - classified "Harmful". If the vapours are inhaled, it can cause drowsiness very quickly, depress the central nervous system and lead to liver failure and death if exposure is for prolonged periods.

CARBON DIOXIDE

A simple asphyxiant (suffocation) produced as a by-product of the brewing processes. As a simple asphyxiant it displaces oxygen in the air that we breathe and means insufficient oxygen goes to the brain, leading to collapse and death. Available commercially as a frozen solid 'dry ice' used as a refrigerant or to generate 'smoke' in theatre productions. Provides the constituent part of a carbon dioxide fire extinguisher and may be encountered in fixed fire fighting installations in buildings. It may be encountered in confined spaces, such as trenches, in areas with chalky soil as carbon dioxide is evolved naturally; it is heavier than air and tends to gather in low areas.

CARBON MONOXIDE

Is a chemical asphyxiant produced as a by-product of incomplete combustion of carbon fuels e.g. gas water heaters, compressors, pumps, dumper trucks or generators. It is a particular risk when such equipment is operated in poorly ventilated confined areas where workers are likely to inhale the gas. Carbon monoxide has a great affinity (200 times that of oxygen) for the haemoglobin red blood cells which means it will inhibit oxygen uptake by red blood cells resulting in chemical asphyxiation, leading to collapse and death.

ISOCYANATES

Isocyanates are used in the manufacture of resins and urethane foams; common compounds are toluene di-isocyanate (TDI) and methylene bisphenyl di-isocyanate (MDI). TDI is an extremely volatile vapour and is evolved during the manufacture of foams. TDI and MDI are highly toxic in very small amounts (parts per billion) and inhalation will result in a severe respiratory reaction. Isocyanates are sensitising agents; in particular they sensitise the lungs.

LEAD

Lead poisoning results from the inhalation of fumes produced from the heating of lead, or certain solders containing lead, at temperatures above 5000C. In construction activities this will include exposure to lead by oxyacetylene cutting of metal coated with paint containing lead. In addition, lead poisoning may result from the inhalation of organic lead compounds e.g. tetraethyl lead. Chronic (cumulative) lead poisoning may result in anaemia, mental dullness and is often accompanied by the presence of a blue line around the gums. Acute lead poisoning is often fatal; symptoms include muscular twitch, hallucinations and violent behaviour.

ASBESTOS

Asbestos is a general term used to describe a range of mineral fibres (commonly referred to by colour i.e. white Chrysotile, brown Amosite and blue Crocidolite). Asbestos was mainly used as an insulating and fire resisting material. Asbestos fibres readily become air borne when disturbed and may enter the lungs, where they cause fibrosis (scarring and thickening) of the lung tissue, asbestosis or mesothelioma (thickening of the pleural lining). Asbestosis typically takes more than 10 years to develop. Research suggests that 50 per cent of asbestos sufferers will also develop cancer of the lung or bronchus.

SILICA

Silica exists naturally as crystalline minerals (tridymite, cristobalite). A common variety is quartz. Industrially silica is used in the morphous (after heating) form e.g. fumed silica, silica gel. In construction activities it may be encountered in stone work or work with quartz based tiles. Inhalation of silica can result in silicosis, a fibrosis of the lung. Nodular lesions are formed which ultimately destroy lung structure reducing the capacity of the lungs.

LEPTOSPIRA

The bacteria leptospira, spiral shaped bacteria, penetrates the skin and causes leptospirosis (Weil's disease). Rodents represent the most important reservoir of infections, especially rats (also gerbils, voles, and field mice). Other sources of infection are dogs, hedgehogs, foxes, pigs, and cattle. These animals are not necessarily ill, but carry leptospires in their kidneys and excrete it in their urine. Infection can be transmitted directly via direct contact with blood, tissues, organs or urine of one of the host animals or indirectly by contaminated environment.

Infection enters through broken skin or mucous membrane. Symptoms vary but include flu-like illness, conjunctivitis, liver damage (including jaundice), kidney failure and meningitis. If untreated infection may be fatal.

Construction workers most at risk are those who work where rats prevail and will include water and sewage work, demolition or refurbishment of old unoccupied buildings, and those working on sites adjoining rivers and other watercourses. The bacteria's survival depends on protection from direct sunlight, so it survives well in water courses and ditches protected by vegetation.

LEGIONNELLOSIS / LEGIONNAIRES DISEASE

Legionnellosis / Legionnaires' Disease is a type of pneumonia caused by Legionella Pneumophila, a bacterium. The organism is ubiquitous in water and frequently present in water cooling systems and domestic hot water systems. Large workplace buildings are therefore susceptible to infected water systems, especially hotels and hospitals.

The organism is widespread in the environment, but needs certain conditions to multiply, for example the presence of sludge, scale, algae, rust and organic material plus a temperature of 20 - 500 C. Transmission is from inhalation of the organism in contaminated aerosols. Smoking, age and alcohol may increase susceptibility. Symptoms are aching muscles, headaches and fever followed by a cough. Confusion, emotional disturbance and delirium may follow the acute phase. The fatality rate in the UK is about 12%.

Greatest risk areas are from showers, air conditioning sprays, water cooling towers and recirculating water cooling systems. The hazard can be controlled by proper design of water systems, disinfection/chlorination of water or heating water to 55-600C.

HEPATITIS

Hepatitis is inflammation of the liver; there are a number of types of hepatitis the B variety being the most serious. Hepatitis is caused by a virus and is passed from human to human. Hepatitis A is spread by ingesting the virus from the faeces of an infected person, from food or water contaminated by the faeces of a contaminated person or from eating raw or undercooked shellfish harvested from contaminated water. The hepatitis B virus, which is very resilient in that it remains viable for weeks in the environment outside the human body, is resistant to common antiseptics and is not affected by boiling for less than thirty minutes.

Symptoms vary, but typically the sequence is: flu-like illness with aches and pains in the joints, general tiredness, anorexia, nausea and high fever, jaundice and the liver enlarged and tender.

Workers most at risk are: those in health care: hospital personnel, dentists, laboratory workers, domestic workers, teachers, prison officers, ambulance workers, police and customs officers. Intravenous drug abusers are also seriously at risk; therefore workers who are responsible for keeping streets, parks and toilets clean are at risk from discarded needles. Construction workers carrying out work on old derelict property and those clearing ground that may have been used by intravenous drug users are particularly at risk.

The C variety causes inflammation of the liver. It is carried and passed to others through blood or sexual contact. Also, infants born to infected mothers may become infected with the virus.

6.2 - Risks associated with hazardous substances

Routes of entry of hazardous substances into the body

INHALATION

The most significant industrial entry route is inhalation. It has been estimated that at least 90% of industrial poisons are absorbed through the lungs. Harmful substances can directly attack the lung tissue causing a local effect or pass through to the blood system, to be carried round the body and affect target organs such as the liver. Examples of substances which have been mentioned above would be ammonia,

Typical effects of entry are:

Local effect - Silicosis

Dust causes scarring of the lung leading to inelastic fibrous tissue developing, thus reducing lung capacity.

Systemic effect - Anoxia

Carbon monoxide replaces oxygen in the bloodstream affecting the nervous system.

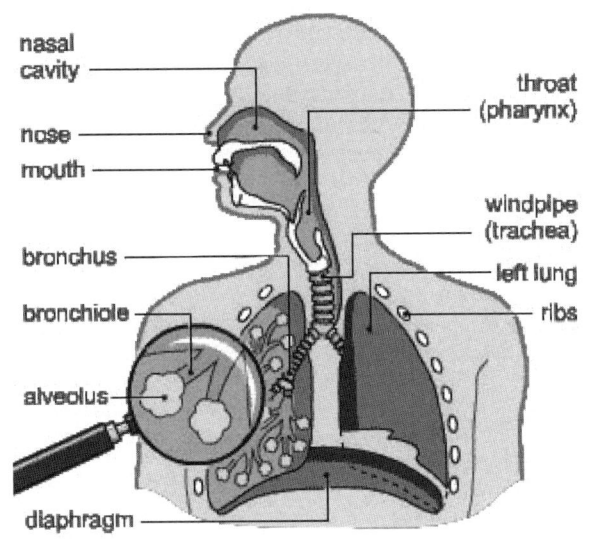

Figure 2-6-2: Respiratory system. *Source: BBC.*

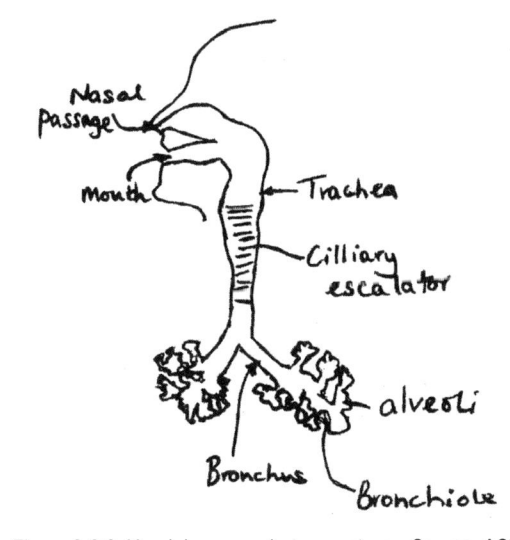

Figure 2-6-3: Hand drawn respiratory system. *Source: ACT.*

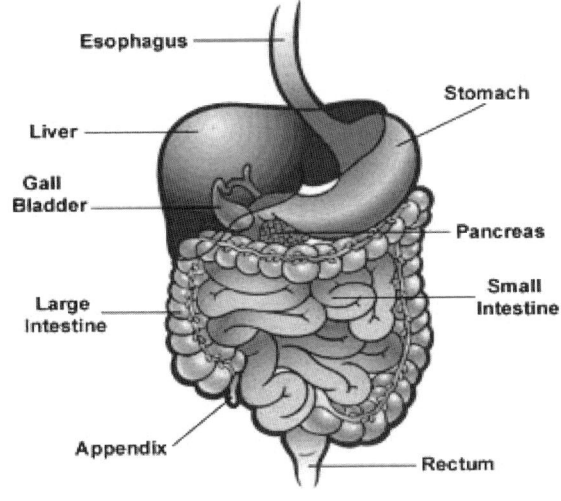

Figure 2-6-4: Digestive system. *Source: STEM.*

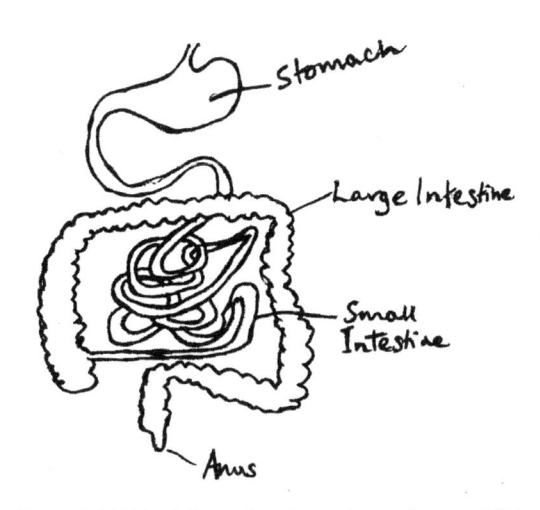

Figure 2-6-5: Hand drawn digestive system. *Source: ACT.*

INGESTION

This route normally presents the least problem as it is unlikely that any significant quantity of harmful liquid or solid will be swallowed without deliberate intent. However, accidents will occur where small amounts of contaminant are transferred from the fingers to the mouth if eating, drinking or smoking in chemical areas is allowed or where a substance has been decanted into a container normally used for drinking. The sense of taste will often be a defence if chemicals are taken in through this route, causing the person to spit it out. If the substance is taken in, vomiting and/or excretion may mean the substance does not cause a systemic problem, though a direct effect, for example, ingestion of an acid, may destroy cells in the mouth, oesophagus or stomach.

ABSORPTION (SKIN CONTACT)

Substances can enter through the skin, cuts or abrasions and conjunctiva of the eye. Solvents such as organic solvents, e.g. toluene and trichloroethylene, can enter either accidentally or if used for washing. The substance may have a local effect, such as de-fatting of the skin resulting in inflammation and cracking of the horny layer, or pass through into the blood system causing damage to the brain, bone marrow and liver.

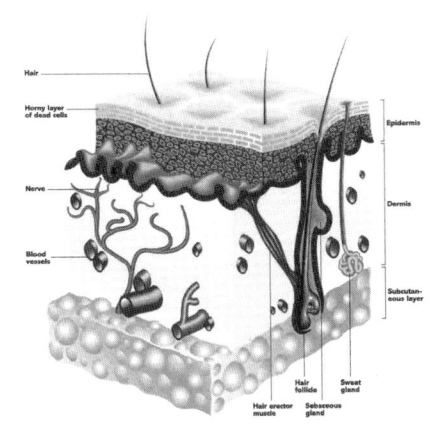

Figure 2-6-6: Skin layer. *Source: SHP.*

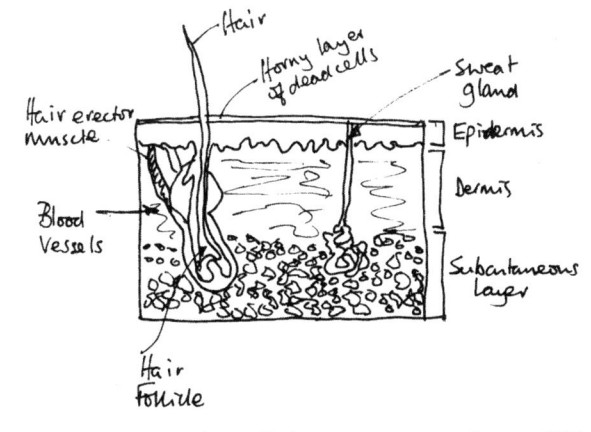

Figure 2-6-7: Hand drawn skin layer. *Source: ACT.*

Contact dermatitis

Caused by contact with substances which interfere with normal skin physiology leading to inflammation of skin, usually on the hands, wrists and forearms. The skin turns red and in some cases may be itchy. Small blisters may occur and the condition may take the form of dry and cracked skin. There are many chemicals which may irritate the skin; including cement, soaps, detergents, industrial chemicals, some metals, cosmetics and plants. For babies, contact with urine causes nappy rash. Removal from exposure allows normal cell repair. A similar level of repeat exposure results in the same response. This class of dermatitis is called contact dermatitis.

Sensitisation dermatitis

A second form of dermatitis is called sensitisation dermatitis. In this case a person exposed to the substance develops dermatitis.

Tissue inflammation and cell damage. When taken away the dermatitis repairs, but the body gets ready for later exposures by preparing the body's defence mechanisms. A subsequent small exposure is enough to cause a major response by the immune system. The person will have become sensitised and will no longer be able to tolerate exposure to the substance without a reaction occurring.

Dermatitis can be prevented by:
- Clean working conditions and properly planned work systems.
- Careful attention to skin hygiene principles.
- Prompt attention to cuts, abrasions and spillages onto the skin.
- Use of protective equipment.
- Barrier cream can help.
- Pre-employment screening for sensitive individuals.

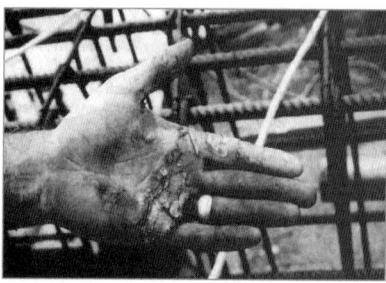

Figure 2-6-8: Dermatitis.   Source: SHP.

INJECTION

A forceful breach of the skin, perhaps as a result of injury, can carry harmful substances through the skin barrier; for example handling broken glass which cuts the skin and transfers a biological or chemical agent. On construction sites there are quite a few items that present a hazard of penetration, such as nails in broken up false work that might be trodden on and penetrate the foot presenting a risk of infection from tetanus. In addition, some land or buildings being worked on may have been used by intravenous drug users and their needles may present a risk of injection of a virus, such as hepatitis. The forced injection of an agent into the body provides an easy route past the skin, which usually acts as the body's defence mechanism and protects people from the effects of many agents that do not have the ability to penetrate.

Body response to agents and protective mechanisms

The body's response against the invasion of substances likely to cause damage can be divided into external or superficial defences and internal or cellular defences.

SUPERFICIAL DEFENCE MECHANISMS

Respiratory (inhalation):

Nose — On inhalation many substances and minor organisms are successfully trapped by nasal hairs, for example, the larger wood dust particles.

Respiratory tract — The next line of defence against inhalation or substances harmful to health begin here, where a series of reflexes activate the coughing and sneezing mechanisms to forcibly expel the triggering substances.

Ciliary escalator — The passages of the respiratory system are also lined with mucus and well supplied with fine hair cells which sweep rhythmically towards the outside and pass along large particles. The respiratory system narrows as it enters the lungs where the ciliary escalator assumes more and more importance as the effective defence. Smaller particles of agents, such as some lead particles, are dealt with at this stage. The smallest particles, such as organic solvent vapours, reach the alveoli and are either deposited or exhaled.

Gastrointestinal (ingestion):

Mouth — For ingestion of substances. Saliva in the mouth provides a useful defence to substances which are not excessively acid or alkaline or in large quantities.

Gastrointestinal tract — Acid in the stomach also provides a useful defence similar to saliva. Vomiting and diarrhoea are additional reflex mechanisms which act to remove substances or quantities that the body is not equipped to deal with.

Skin (absorption):

Skin — The body's largest organ provides a useful barrier against the absorption of many foreign organisms and chemicals (but not against all of them). Its effect is, however, limited by its physical characteristics. The outer part of the skin is covered in an oily layer and substances have to overcome this before they can damage the skin or enter the body. The outer part of the epidermis is made up of dead skin cells. These are readily sacrificed to substances without harm to the newer cells underneath. Repeated or prolonged exposure could defeat this. The skin, when attacked by substances, may blister in order to protect the layers beneath. Openings in the skin such as sweat pores, hair follicles and cuts can allow entry and the skin itself may be permeable to some chemicals, e.g. toluene.

CELLULAR DEFENCE MECHANISMS

The cells of the body possess their own defence systems.

Scavenging action

A type of white blood cell called macrophages attack invading particles in order to destroy them and remove them from the body. This process is known as phagocytosis.

Secretion of defensive substances

Is done by some specialised cells. Histamine release and heparin, which promotes availability of blood sugar, are examples.

Prevention of excessive blood loss

Reduced circulation through blood clotting and coagulation prevents excessive bleeding and slows or prevents the entry of germs.

Repair of damaged tissues

Is a necessary defence mechanism which includes removal of dead cells, increased availability of defender cells and replacement of tissue strength, e.g. scar tissue caused by silica.

The lymphatic system

Acts as a 'form of drainage system' throughout the body for the removal of foreign bodies. Lymphatic glands or nodes at specific points in the system act as selective filters preventing infection from entering the blood system. In many cases a localised inflammation occurs in the node at this time.

THE USE OF ABOVE TO ASSESS HEALTH RISKS

A superficial consideration suggests that extrapolations (to use known facts as the starting point from which to draw inferences or draw conclusions about something unknown) from the oral to inhalation or dermal routes are straightforward, provided that adequate toxicity data are available using the oral route, and that data are also available on the extent of absorption through the lungs or skin.

However, this is not the case, as there are a number of other factors to be considered before assuming that any toxicity seen following oral administration is representative of that likely by the other routes provided that the compound is absorbed to the same extent. There have been a number of reviews that consider the difficulties in such route-to-route extrapolations, and which emphasise the need to consider chemicals on a case-by-case basis with expert judgement. In all cases the desirability of having some toxicokinetic data is critical to assess health risks. The key factors that need to be considered are briefly summarized.

Is the toxicity of concern a local or systemic effect?

Clearly compounds that have been shown to, or might be predicted to, act locally at the initial site of contact will express route-specific toxicity, and thus route-to-route extrapolation is not appropriate. This particularly applies to the case where irritancy is the concern and the effects are often dependent on the concentration present at the site of action rather than the systemic dose. Another area that presents difficulties is sensitisation of the immune system, where reactions are often route-specific.

Furthermore, exposure by the oral route can sometimes lead to tolerance developing, resulting in reduced susceptibility to sensitisation by other routes of exposure.

For route-to-route extrapolation to be appropriate, the toxicological concern has to relate to systemic toxicity, that is, toxicity expressed in tissues/organs distant from the site of administration.

Target organ dose

Systemic toxicity is determined to a large extent both by the concentration of the toxic compound which may be the parent compound or a metabolite) that reaches the target organ (i.e. the site of the toxic action) in the body and by the length of time over which the target organ is exposed to the toxic compound. This is dependent both on the extent of absorption and on the balance between any activation (where appropriate) and detoxification mechanisms. Thus the systemic toxicity may be the result of complex interactions, some of which could be route-specific.

Information as to whether the toxicity is due to the parent compound, or a metabolite, is valuable together with as much information as possible on toxicokinetics for all relevant routes.

Eight key steps for a assessing the health risks posed by exposure to chemicals, which are considered in most countries are as follows keys steps:

Step 1 Assess the risks

Assess the risks to health from hazardous substances used in or created by workplace activities.

Step 2 Decide what precautions are needed

Work should not be carried out which could expose workers to hazardous substances without first considering the risks and the necessary precautions, and what else would be needed to do to control substances hazardous to health..

Step 3 Prevent or adequately control exposure

Employees should be prevented from being exposed to hazardous substances. Where preventing exposure is not reasonably practicable, then exposure should be adequately controlled.

Step 4 Ensure that control measures are used and maintained

The employer should ensure that control measures are used and maintained properly and that safety procedures are followed.

Step 5 Monitor the exposure

The exposure of workers to hazardous substances, should be monitored if necessary.

Step 6 Carry out appropriate health surveillance

Appropriate health surveillance should be conducted where your assessment has shown this is necessary.

Step 7 Prepare plans and procedures to deal with accidents, incidents and emergencies

Plans and procedures to deal with accidents, incidents and emergencies involving hazardous substances, should be prepared where necessary.

Step 8 Ensure workers are properly informed, trained and supervised

Employees should be provided with suitable and sufficient information, instruction and training.

Sources of information

PRODUCT LABELS

All chemicals, both substances and preparations, should have a clear marking to indicate their identity. The packages and containers of dangerous substances and preparations should, in addition to marking only, have a label with required information. The label should draw attention to the inherent danger to persons handling or using the chemical. Symbols and pictograms have been established for each hazard category listed above. The symbol forms an integral part of the label and gives an immediate idea of the types of hazards that the substance or the preparation may cause. To specify the type of danger relevant standard risk phrases should also be included in the label. Advice on the precautions necessary in the handling of chemicals are given with standard safety phrases also included in the label.

Source: www.ilo.org

EUROPEAN UNION LIST OF INDICATIVE LIMIT VALUES

Indicative Occupational Exposure Limit Values, previously known as Indicative Limit Values (ILVs), are European legal limits which are set to protect the health of workers in the European Union from the ill health effects of hazardous substances in the workplace. IOELVs are therefore broadly the same as the Occupational Exposure Standard element of the British system of limits to protect workers against ill-health. The European Commission (EC) made proposals for IOELVs for 63 substances and these have been agreed by Member States.

HSE LIST OF WORKPLACE EXPOSURE LIMITS (WELs) (UK)

WELs are occupational exposure limits set under the Control of Substances Hazardous to Health Regulations (COSHH) 2002 to protect the health of persons in the workplace. They are concentrations of airborne substances averaged over a period of time known as a Time Weighted Average (TWA). The two periods that are used are 8-hours and 15-minutes. The 8-hour TWA is known as an LTEL (long-term exposure limit), used to help protect against chronic ill-health effects. 15-minute STELs (short-term exposure limits) are to protect against acute ill-health effects such as eye irritation, which may happen in minutes or even within seconds of exposure.

AMERICAN CONFERENCE OF GOVERNMENTAL INDUSTRIAL HYGIENISTS (ACGIH) LIST OF THRESHOLD LIMIT VALUES (US)

The ACGIH TLVs and most other OELs used in the United States and some other countries are limits which refer to airborne concentrations of substances and represent conditions under which "it is believed that nearly all workers may be repeatedly exposed day after day without adverse health effects" (ACGIH 1994).

MANUFACTURERS' HEALTH AND SAFETY DATA SHEETS AND RESPONSIBILITY FOR THEIR PROVISION

Manufacturers, importers and suppliers should provide information on substances for use at work; this is usually provided in the form of a material safety data sheet. The content of material in the safety data sheets for substances should include the following:

- Identification of the substance/preparation and the company.
- Composition / information on ingredients.
- Hazards identification.
- First-aid measures.
- Fire fighting measures.
- Accidental release measures.
- Handling and storage.
- Exposure controls / personal protection.
- Physical and chemical properties.
- Stability and reactivity.
- Toxicological information.
- Ecological information.
- Disposal considerations.
- Transport information.
- Regulatory information.

INFORMATION TYPICALLY TO BE INCLUDED BY THE SUPPLIER

Providing hazard information

After deciding what the classification is, suppliers have to tell their customers about the hazards; and tell them, as far as possible, how their customers can use the supplier's chemicals safely.

Suppliers do this by a label and a material safety data sheet which is critical if the suppliers customers use their chemical at work. Other equally good measures may be used for consumers.

Labelling

If suppliers supply a dangerous chemical in a package, the package must be labelled. If the chemical is not supplied in a package (e.g. if the chemical is supplied from a tanker or down a pipeline), then the supplier does not have to provide a label since this would not be practical.

The aim of the label is to inform anyone handling the package or using the chemicals about its hazards, and give brief advice on what precautions are needed. Labels usually possess information such as the chemical's name and how packages should be labelled (e.g. the size of the label).

Material Safety Data Sheets (MSDS)

Material safety data sheets (MSDS) are needed if a chemical is not classified as dangerous, but contains small amounts of a dangerous substance.

If a supplier is selling to someone who is going to use the chemical for their work then a MSDS must be provided, but suppliers can use different (but equally good) methods for other customers, e.g. information on the package. The responsibility is placed on the supplier to ensure that the information provided is sufficient, i.e. enough to allow the user to decide how to protect:

- Workers at work.
- The environment.

This will usually include information on:

- The hazards of the chemical.
- Handling and storage.
- Its environmental effects.
- Exposure controls / personal protection.

LIMITATIONS OF INFORMATION IN ASSESSING RISKS TO HEALTH

Information provided by manufacturers and contained within the HSE Guidance Note EH40 (UK for example) may be very technical and require a specialist to explain its relevance to a given activity. Some substances have good toxicological information, usually gained from past experience of harm; many others have a limited amount of useful toxicological information available to guide the user as to the harm it may produce. This can lead to a reliance on data that is only accurate at the time and this may have to be revised as knowledge on the substance changes. Individual susceptibility of workers differs by, for example, age, gender or ethnic origin. Exposure history varies over the working life of an individual and current exposure may not indicate that the individual may suffer due to a cumulative effect from the earlier exposures. For example, an individual may have been or be engaged in a number of processes within a variety of workplaces or personal pastimes.

Basic surveys

As discussed previously, the health effects of exposure to toxic substances can be acute or chronic. It will therefore be necessary to distinguish appropriate methods of measurement. When embarking upon a monitoring campaign to assess the risk to which an individual may be exposed, it is necessary to ask several questions.

1) What to sample?

This involves a review of the materials, processes and operating procedures being used within a plant, coupled with discussions with management and health and safety personnel. A brief 'walk-through' survey can also be useful as a guide to the extent of monitoring that may be necessary.

Hazard data sheets are also of use. When the background work has been completed it can then be decided what is to be measured.

2) On whom?

This depends on the size and diversity of the group that the survey relates to. From the group of workers being surveyed the sample to be monitored should be selected; this must be representative of the group and the work undertaken. Selecting the individual with the highest exposure can be a reasonable starting point. If the group is large then random sampling may have to be employed, but care has to be exercised with this approach. The group should also be aware of the reason for sampling.

3) How long do we sample for?

There are many considerations when answering this question: what are the control limits; is the hazard acute or chronic; what is the limit of detection; or simply what resources are available?

4) How do we monitor?

The particular sampling strategy, based on the hazard presented, is outlined in the following table:

Measurements to determine	Suitable types of measurement
Chronic hazard	Continuous personal dose measurement.
	Continuous measurements of average background levels.
	Short term readings of containment levels at selected positions and times.
Acute hazard	Continuous personal monitoring with rapid response.
	Continuous background monitoring with rapid response.
	Short term readings of background contaminant levels at selected positions and times.
Environmental control status	Continuous background monitoring.
	Short term readings of background contaminant levels at selected positions and times.
Whether area is safe to enter	Direct reading instruments.

Basic surveys for health risks

SHORT TERM SAMPLERS

Stain tube detectors (multi-gas/vapour)

These are simple devices for the measurement of contamination on a grab (short term) sampling basis. They incorporate a glass detector tube, filled with inert material. The material is impregnated with a chemical reagent which changes colour ('stains') in proportion to the quantity of contaminant as a known quantity of air is drawn through the tube.

There are several different manufacturers of detector tubes including Dräger and Gastec.

It is critical that the literature provided with the pumps and tubes is followed.

These provide a quick and easy way to detect the presence of a particular airborne contaminant. However, they possess inherent inaccuracies and tube manufacturers claim a relative standard deviation of 20% or less (i.e. 1ppm in 5ppm).

Types of tube construction
- Commonest is the simple stain length tube, but it may contain filter layers, drying layers, or oxidation layers.
- Double tube or tube containing separate ampoules (A small glass vial that is sealed after filling and used chiefly as a container), avoids incompatibility or reaction during storage.
- Comparison tube.
- Narrow tube to achieve better resolution at low concentrations.

The above illustrates the main types of tubes; however there are more variations and therefore it can only be re-emphasised that the manufacturer's operating instructions must be read and fully understood before tubes are used.

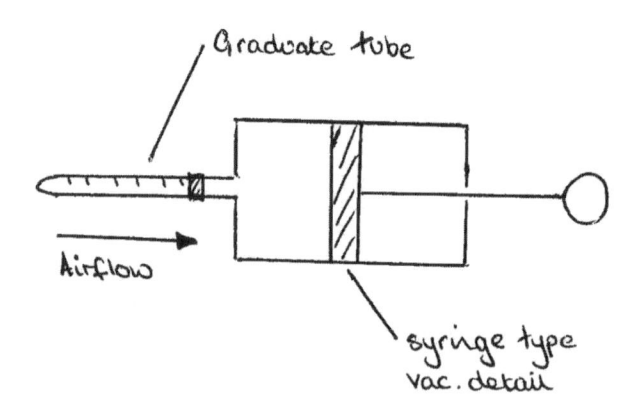

Figure 2-6-9: Detector tube example (hand drawn). Source: ACT.

Pumps

There are four types:
- Bellows pump.
- Piston pump.
- Ball pump.
- Battery operated pump.

Pumps and tubes of different manufacturers should not be mixed.

How to use tubes
- Choose tube to measure material of interest and expected range.
- Check tubes are in date.
- Check leak tightness of pump.
- Read instructions to ensure there are no limitations due to temperature, pressure, humidity or interfering substances.
- Break off tips of tube, prepare tube if necessary and insert correctly into pump. Arrows normally indicate the direction of air flow.
- Draw the requisite number of strokes, to cause the given quantity of air to pass through the tube.
- Immediately, unless operating instructions say otherwise, evaluate the amount of contaminant by examining the stain and comparing it against the graduations on the tube. If there is any doubt when reading the tube, always aim towards the safest option.
- Remove tube and discard according to instructions.
- Purge (a cleaning process) pump to remove any contaminants from inside the pump.

Figure 2-6-10: Gas detector pump. Source: Drager.

Advantages of short term samplers:
- Quick and easy to use.
- Instant reading without further analysis.
- Does not require much expertise to use.
- Relatively inexpensive.

Disadvantages / Limitations of short term samplers:
- Tubes can be cross sensitive to other contaminants.
- Accuracy varies - some are only useful as an indication of the presence of contaminants.
- Is only a grab sample.
- Relies on operator to accurately count pump strokes (manual versions).
- Only suitable for gases and vapours (not dusts).

Direct reading dust sampler (E.g. Tyndall lamp)

Simple methods are by direct observation of the effect of the dust on a strong beam of light e.g. using a Tyndall lamp. High levels of small particles of dust show up under this strong beam of light. Other ways are by means of a direct reading instrument. This establishes the level of dust by, for example, scattering of light. Some also collect the dust sample. The advantages and disadvantages are:

Advantages of direct reading dust samplers:
- Instant reading.
- Continuous monitoring.
- Can record electronically.
- Can be linked to an alarm.
- Suitable for clean room environments.

Disadvantages / Limitation of direct reading dust samplers:
- Some direct reading instruments can be expensive.
- Does not differentiate between dusts of different types.
- Most effective on dusts of a spherical nature.

LONG TERM SAMPLERS

Personal samplers

Passive personal samplers

Passive samplers are so described to illustrate the fact that they have no mechanism to draw in a sample of the contaminant but instead rely on passive means to sample. As such they take a time to perform this function, for example, acting as an absorber taking in contaminant vapours over a period of a working day. Some passive samplers, like gas badges, are generally fitted to the lapel and change colour to indicate contamination.

Active personal samplers

Filtration devices are used for dusts, mists and fumes. A known volume of air is pumped through a sampling head and the contaminant filtered out. By comparing the quantity of air with the amount of contaminant a measurement is made. The filter is either weighed or an actual count of particles is done to establish the amount, as with asbestos. The type of dust can be determined by further laboratory analysis. Active samplers are used in two forms, for personal sampling and for static sampling.

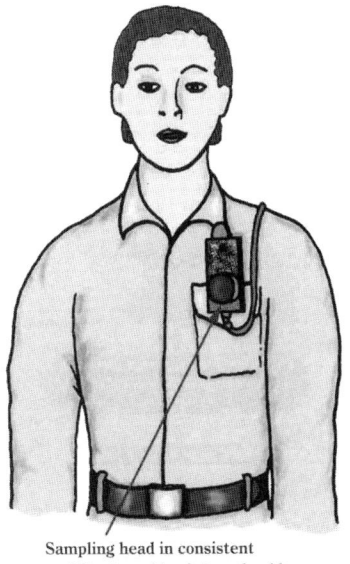

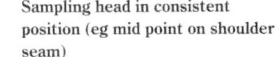

Figure 2-6-11: Personal sampling equipment.

Source: ROSPA OS&H Apr 98.

Static sampling

These devices are stationed in the working area. They sample continuously over the length of a shift, or longer period if necessary. Mains or battery-operated pumps are used. Very small quantities of contaminant may be detected. The techniques employed include absorption, bubblers, and filtration; they are similar in principle to personal samplers, but the equipment is tailored to suit static use.

Advantages of long term samplers:
- Will monitor the workplace over a long period of time.
- Will accurately identify 8 hour time weighted average.

Disadvantages / Limitations of long term samplers:
- Will not generally identify a specific type of contaminant.
- Will not identify multiple exposure i.e. more than one contaminant.
- Does not identify personal exposure.
- Unless very sophisticated, will not read peaks and troughs.

SMOKE TUBES

Smoke tubes are simple devices that generate a 'smoke' by means of a chemical reaction. A tube similar in type to those used in stain tube detectors is selected, its ends broken (which starts the chemical reaction) and it is inserted into a small hand bellows. By gently pumping the bellows smoke is emitted. By watching the smoke air flow can be studied. This can be used to survey extraction and ventilation arrangements to determine their extent of influence.

DUST MONITORING EQUIPMENT

Direct reading dust sampler (E.g. Tyndall lamp)

Simple methods are by direct observation of the effect of the dust on a strong beam of light e.g. using a Tyndall lamp. High levels of small particles of dust show up under this strong beam of light. Other ways are by means of a direct reading instrument. This establishes the level of dust by, for example, scattering of light. Some also collect the dust sample. The advantages and disadvantages are:

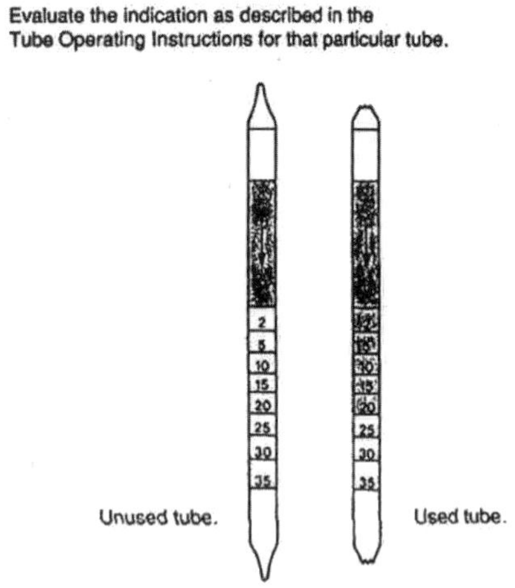

Advantages of direct reading dust samplers:
- Instant reading.
- Continuous monitoring.
- Can record electronically.
- Can be linked to an alarm.
- Suitable for clean room environments.

Disadvantages of direct reading dust samplers:
- Some direct reading instruments can be expensive.
- Does not differentiate between dusts of different types.
- Most effective on dusts of a spherical nature.

Figure 2-6-12: Stain tube detector operating instructions.
Source: Reproduced by kind permission of Drager.

6.3 - Occupational exposure limits

Application of relevant limits

Threshold limit values

TLV's are the maximum concentration of a chemical recommended by the American Conference of Government Industrial Hygienists for repeated exposure without adverse health effects on workers.

Workplace exposure limits

Workplace Exposure Limits are concentrations of airborne substances averaged over a period of time known as a Time Weighted Average (TWA). The two periods that are used are 8-hours and 15-minutes. The 8-hour TWA is known as an LTEL (long-term exposure limit), used to help protect against chronic ill-health effects. 15-minute STELs (short-term exposure limits) are to protect against acute ill-health effects such as eye irritation, which may happen in minutes or even seconds of exposure.

Exposure to hazardous substances should be prevented where it is reasonably practicable. Where this cannot be done by, for example, changing the process, substituting it for something safer or enclosing the process, exposure should be reduced by other methods.

Maximum allowable concentrations

The **M**aximum **A**llowable **C**oncentration of a gas, vapour, spray or substance, is the concentration in the air at the place of work, which in general remains without harmful effects on the health of both workers and their offspring, even after repeated exposure, during a longer period of time up to an entire working life.

The MAC applies to healthy adults who work up to eight hours a day, interrupted by periods of rest in a non-contaminated atmosphere. Their working week does not exceed 40 hours and the nature of the work is not physically exhausting. Additional protective measures must be taken in the case of substances that are easily absorbed through the skin, and no other toxic substances must be present in the same room.

MAC values are regularly adapted as a result of new insights. Although you cannot determine the concentration of a particular substance at the place of work, the MAC does indicate how a particular substance should be handled. The concentrations of the substances that are used in laboratory settings should remain far below the MAC values. Nevertheless, the way chemicals are handled should be in accordance with the data found.

Long-term and short-term exposure limits

Long-term exposure limits

LTEL   Concerned with the total intake averaged over a reference period (usually 8 hours) and is therefore appropriate for protecting against the effects of long term exposure (chronic effects).

Short-term exposure limits

STEL Aimed primarily at avoiding the acute effects or at least reducing the risk of occurrence. They are averaged over a 15 minute reference period.

Limitations of exposure limits

There are many reasons why control of exposure should not be based solely on WELs:

- **Inhalation only.** Many substances (e.g. trichloroethylene) have the ability to absorb through the skin. WELs do not account for these compound routes of entry.
- **Personal susceptibility (vulnerability).** The majority of the work has been based on the average male physiology from the countries in which studies were conducted. Some work has been done where specific health related effects have been noted amongst females e.g. exposure to lead compounds.
- **Adopted from American TLV.** Work done to date has been based upon exposure to individuals in the developed countries e.g. Europe and USA.
- **Variations in control.**
- **Errors in monitoring.** Measuring microscopic amounts of contamination requires very accurate and sensitive equipment. Lack of maintenance and misuse can lead to inaccuracies in monitoring.
- **Synergistic (Connected) effects.** The standards that are available relate to single substances and the effects of multiple substances in the workplace need to be considered.

International variations and attempts at harmonisation (e.g. EU indicative limit values)

Occupational exposure limits (OELs) for hazardous substances provide critical information for risk assessment and management. However, OELs have only been set for a limited number of the substances currently used in the workplace. Binding and indicative limit values are laid down in European Directives.

Each Member State in the European Union establishes their own national OELs, usually including more substances than the directive. National OELs can be binding (which means that they must be met), or indicative limits (as an indication of what should be achieved). Employers should ensure that the exposure of the workers does not exceed the national limits.

6.4 - Acute and chronic health effects

Difference between acute and chronic health effects

The effect of a substance on the body depends not only on the substance, but also on the dose, and the susceptibility of the individual. No substance can be considered non-toxic; there are only differences in degree of effect.

Toxicology	Is the study of the body's responses to substances. In order to interpret toxicological data and information, the meaning of the following terms should be understood.
Toxicity	The ability of a chemical substance to produce injury once it reaches a susceptible site in or on the body. A poisonous substance (e.g. organic lead), which causes harm to biological systems and interferes with the normal functions of the body. The effects may be acute or chronic, local or systemic.
Dose	Is the level of environmental contamination multiplied by the length of time (duration) of exposure to the contaminant.
Acute effect	Is an immediate or rapidly produced, adverse effect, following a single or short term exposure to an offending agent, which is usually reversible.
Chronic effect	Is an adverse health effect produced as a result of prolonged or repeated exposure, with a gradual or latent, and often irreversible, effect that may often go unrecognised for a number of years.
Local effect	Is usually confined to the initial point of contact. Possible sites affected include the skin, mucous membranes or the eyes, nose or throat. Examples are burns to the skin by corrosive substances (acids and alkalis), asbestos scarring lung tissue.
Systemic effect	Occurs in parts of the body other than at the point of initial contact. Frequently the circulatory system provides a means to distribute the substance round the body to a target organ/system.
Target organs	An organ within the human body on which a specified toxic material exerts its effects e.g. lungs, liver, brain, skin, bladder or eyes.
Target systems	Central nervous system, circulatory system, and reproductive system. Examples of substances that have a systemic effect and their target organs are:

        Alcohol   -   central nervous system, liver.
        Lead   -   bone marrow and brain damage.
        Mercury   -   central nervous system.

6.5 - Control measures

Duty to prevent exposure or, where this is not reasonably practicable, adequately control it

The *eight* principles of good practice for the control of exposure to substances hazardous to health are:
- Design and operate processes and activities to minimise emission, release and spread of substances hazardous to health.
- Take into account all relevant routes of exposure - inhalation, skin absorption and ingestion - when developing control measures.
- Control exposure by measures that are proportionate to the health risk.
- Choose the most effective and reliable control options which minimise the escape and spread of the substances hazardous to health.
- Where adequate control of exposure cannot be achieved by other means, provide, in combination with other control measures, suitable personable protective equipment.
- Check and review regularly all elements of control measures for their continuing effectiveness.
- Inform and train all workers on the hazards and risks from the substances with which they work and the use of control measures developed to minimise the risks.
- Ensure that the introduction of control measures does not increase the overall risk to health and safety.

Ensuring occupational exposure limits are not exceeded

OELs define a maximum permissible exposure, but exposure must also be reduced as far as reasonably practicable. (This is a legally defined concept which means that exposures must be reduced to a level where further reduction would involve a cost grossly disproportionate to the benefit achieved.)

In the control of occupational health hazards many approaches are available, the use of which depends upon the severity and nature of the hazard. The principal control strategies are outlined below and follow the general strategy:
- Elimination or substitution.
- Process change.
- Reduced time exposure.
- Enclosure of hazards, process or workers.
- Local exhaust ventilation.
- Dilution ventilation.
- Respiratory protective equipment.
- Other personal protective equipment.
- Personal hygiene.
- Health surveillance.

Methods of control

With reference to the hierarchy of control contained in Unit IGC1 - Element 6.

ELIMINATION OR SUBSTITUTION OF HAZARDOUS SUBSTANCES OR FORM OF SUBSTANCE

Elimination

This represents an extreme form of control and is appropriately used where high risk is present from such things as carcinogens (cancer forming substances). It is usually achieved through the prohibition of use of these substances. Care must be taken to ensure that all stock is safely disposed of and that controls are in place to prevent their re-entry, even as a sample or for research. If this level of control is not achievable then another must be selected.

Reduction

By substitution

The substitution of a less toxic substance in place of a more highly toxic one, e.g. toluene for benzene, glass fibre for asbestos, or water based adhesives for solvent based adhesives is a frequently used technique. It is also possible to substitute the form of the substance in that a substance that requires mixing from dry products, such as cement, may be ordered pre-prepared thus avoiding the additional contact with the substance in the mixing process and in the dry state where dust may be liberated. In the same way dust generated in a demolition process may be watered down so that the dust becomes liquid slurry.

Quantity

A useful approach is to reduce the actual quantity of the substance presenting the hazard. This may be achieved by limiting the amount used or stored. It may be possible to use a more dilute form than is presently being used, for example, with acids. In the case of disposal it is possible to reduce the quantity by neutralisation.

PROCESS CHANGES

The role of the occupational hygienist is to identify peaks in exposure to operators during their normal working day e.g. when charging or discharging process equipment - at this time higher than normal background levels of contamination may occur in the general work area.

Whenever process changes occur through plant failure or maintenance, consideration needs to be given to exposure to those affected at these times. It may be necessary to re-assess the process / maintenance arrangements to ensure adequacy of health controls.

Figure 2-6-13: Reduced exposure - bulk supply.   Source: ACT.

REDUCED TIME EXPOSURE AND SIGNIFICANCE OF TIME WEIGHTED AVERAGES

There is a close relationship between exposure and time. At a fixed level of contamination the effect will be proportional to the time exposed. This is the basis of occupational exposure limits, i.e. long-term exposure limits (8 hours time weighted average value) and short-term exposure limits (15 minutes weighted average value). The strategy is also encompassed in the approach to control noise exposure whereby the total noise dose over an eight hour day, 5-day week, must not exceed 85 dB(A). It may be possible to organise work so that exposure to any one person is controlled by means of job/task rotation.

ENCLOSURE OF HAZARDS

In its simplest sense this can mean putting lids on substances that have volatile vapours, such as tins of solvent based products. In this way the strategy is to enclose the hazard so that vapours are not given off. In this case, this is best done when the substance is not in use, this does not just mean at the end of the day but at intervals when the substance is not actually in use. It makes a very simple and effective control of exposure to hazards.

SEGREGATION OF PROCESS

This strategy is based on the containment of an offending substance or agent to prevent its free movement in the working environment. It may take a number of forms, e.g. acoustic enclosures, pipelines, closed conveyors, laboratory fume cupboards. In construction situations this is used in processes such as asbestos removal where the work being done is enclosed in plastic sheeting in order to segregate the work from the surrounding areas. In a similar way this may be for building cleaning processes using shot or for spray protection being applied to a structure.

SEGREGATION OF PEOPLE

Segregation is a method of controlling the risks from toxic substances and physical hazards such as noise and radiation. It can take a number of forms:

By distance

This is a relatively simple method where the minimum number or workers working with biological or toxic hazards are distanced (segregated) from the general workforce.

By age

The protection of young workers in certain trades is still valid today, a good example being lead. In this case in some countries relevant legislations excludes the employment of young persons in lead processes.

By time

This involves the restriction of certain hazardous operations to periods when the number of persons present is at its smallest, for instance at weekends. An example might be the radiation of an item for non-destructive test.

By gender

There remains the possibility of gender linked vulnerability to certain toxic substances such as the exposure of females to lead; segregation affords a high level of control in these circumstances.

LOCAL EXHAUST VENTILATION

General applications and principles of capture and removal of hazardous substances

Various local exhaust ventilation (LEV) systems are in use in the workplace, for example:

- Receptor hoods such as are used in fume cupboards and kilns.
- Captor hoods (used for welding and milling operations).
- High velocity low volume flow systems e.g. as used on a grinding tool.

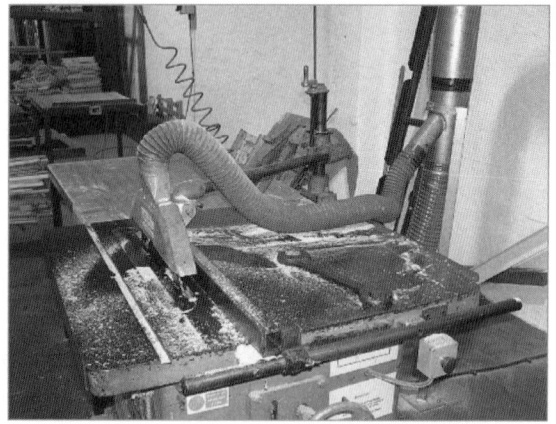

UNIT IGC2 - ELEMENT 6 - CHEMICAL AND BIOLOGICAL HEALTH HAZARDS AND CONTROL

Figure 2-6-14: Captor system on circular saw. Clearly shows the fixed captor hood, flexible hose and rigid duct. *Source: ACT.*

Figure 2-6-15: Shows the size of fan and motor required for industrial scale LEV. *Source: ACT.*

Figure 2-6-16: Flexible hose showing how captor hood can be repositioned to suit the work activity. *Source: ACT.*

Figure 2-6-17: Self contained unit which can be moved around the workplace. *Source: ACT.*

COMPONENTS OF A BASIC SYSTEM

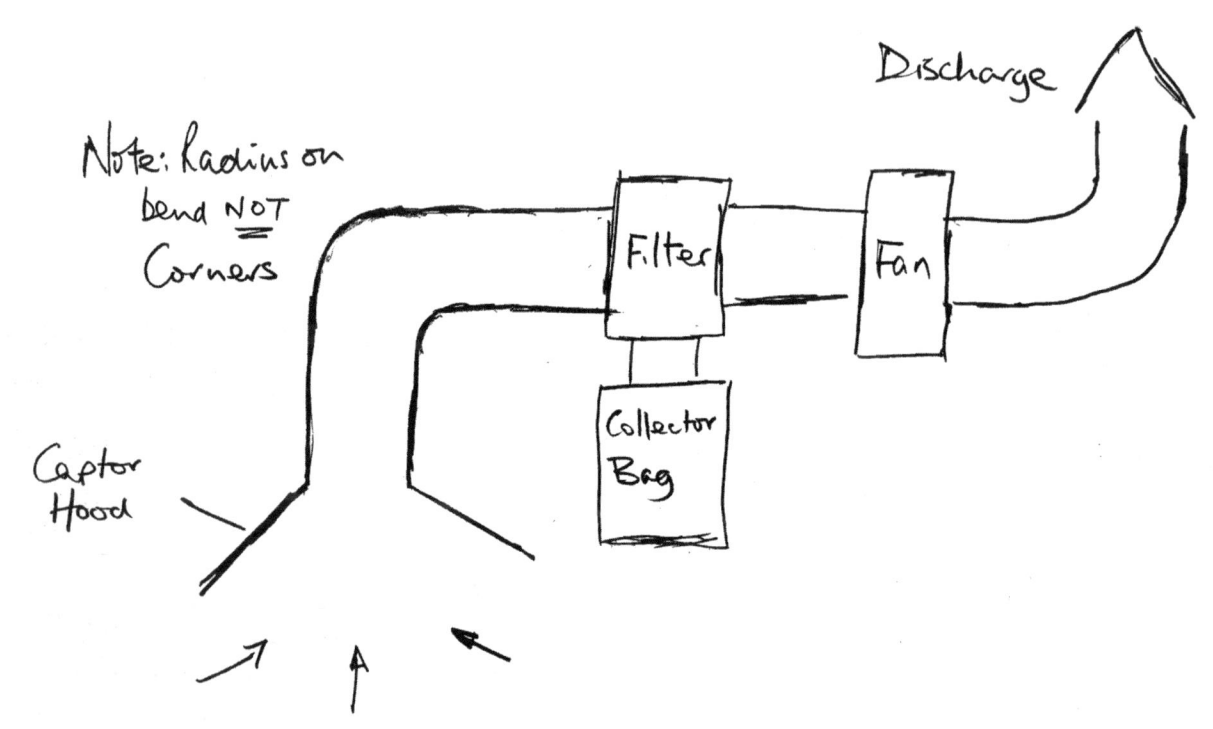

Figure 2-6-18: Components of a basic system (basic sketch). *Source: ACT.*

FACTORS THAT REDUCE A LEV SYSTEM'S EFFECTIVENESS

The efficiency of LEV systems can be affected by many factors including the following:

- Damaged ducting.
- Unauthorised alterations.
- Process changes leading to overwhelming amounts of contamination.
- Incorrect hood location.
- Fan strength or incorrect adjustment of fan.
- Too many bends in ducts.
- Blocked or defective filters.
- Leaving too many ports open.
- The cost of heating make up air may encourage employers to reduce flow rates.

It is vital that the pre and post ventilation contamination levels are determined and the required reduction should be part of the commissioning contract.

REQUIREMENTS FOR INSPECTION

In the UK for example the law sets out requirements for inspection of LEV systems. A thorough examination and test must take place once every 14 months. Records must be kept available for at least 5 years from the date on which it was made. In other countries the national legislation related to test and inspection may differ.

The majority of ventilation systems, although effective in protecting workers' health from airborne contaminants, can create other hazards. One of the main hazards that needs to be considered when designing LEV systems is that of noise. Even if it has been considered as a design feature when establishing LEV systems, it should be monitored on a periodic basis.

USE AND LIMITATIONS OF DILUTION VENTILATION

Dilution ventilation is a system designed to induce a general flow of clean air into a work area. This may be done by driving air into a work area, causing air flow around the work area, dilution of contaminants in the work area and then out of the work area through general leakage or through ventilation ducts to the open air.

A variation on this is where air may be forcibly removed from the work area, but not associated with a particular contaminant source, and air is allowed in through ventilation ducts to dilute the air in the work area. Sometimes a combination of these two approaches is used, an example may be general air conditioning provided into an office environment.

A particularly simple approach to providing dilution ventilation is to open a window and door and allow natural air flow to dilute the workplace air. This is not a reliable means of dealing with toxic contaminants and may be over-relied on in the construction industry. On its own it may prove inadequate but supported by respiratory protection equipment it may be acceptable for some substances.

Because it does not target any specific source and it relies on dispersal and dilution instead of specific removal, it can only be used with nuisance contaminants that are themselves fairly mobile in air. Dilution ventilation systems will only deal with general contamination and will not prevent contaminants entering a person's breathing zone. Local exhaust ventilation is the preferred means of controlling a person's exposure to substances.

Dilution ventilation may only be used as the sole means of control in circumstances where there is:

- Non toxic contaminant or vapour (not dusts).
- Contaminant which is uniformly produced in small, known quantities.
- No discrete point of release.
- No other practical means of reducing levels.

RESPIRATORY PROTECTIVE EQUIPMENT

This equipment includes two main categories of respiratory protection:

1) Respirators.
2) Breathing apparatus.

Respirators

Respirators filter the air breathed but do not provide additional oxygen. There are a number of types of respirator that provide a variety of degrees of protection from dealing with nuisance dusts to high efficiency respirators for solvents or asbestos. Some respirators may be nominated as providing non-specific protection from contaminants whereas others will be designed to protect from a very specific contaminant such as solvent vapours.

There are five main types of respirators:

1) Filtering face piece.
2) Half mask respirator.
3) Full face respirator.
4) Powered air purifying respirator.
5) Powered visor respirator.

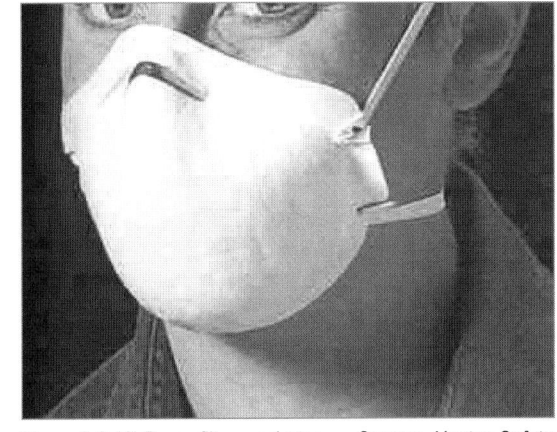

Figure 2-6-19: Paper filter respirator.   *Source: Haxton Safety.*

UNIT IGC2 - ELEMENT 6 - CHEMICAL AND BIOLOGICAL HEALTH HAZARDS AND CONTROL

Advantages
- Unrestricted movement.
- Often lightweight and comfortable.
- Can be worn for long periods.

Limitations
- Purify the air by drawing it through a filter to remove contaminants. Therefore, can only be used when there is sufficient oxygen in the atmosphere.
- Requires careful selection by a competent person.
- Requires regular maintenance.
- Knowing when a cartridge is at the end of its useful life.
- Requires correct storage facilities.
- Can give a 'closed in' / claustrophobic feeling.
- Relies on user for correct fit/use etc.
- Incompatible with other forms of personal protective equipment (PPE).
- Performance can be affected by beards and long hair.
- Interferes with other senses, e.g. sense of smell.

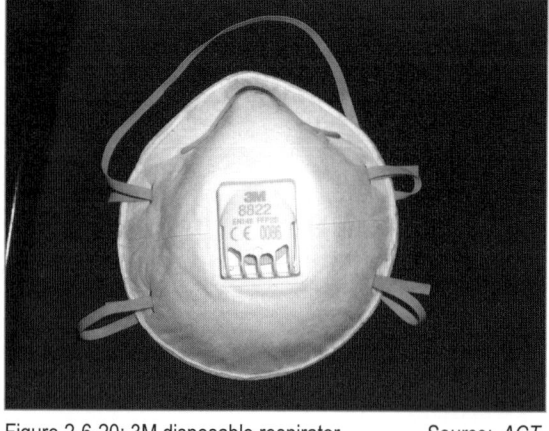

Figure 2-6-20: 3M disposable respirator.   Source: ACT.

Breathing apparatus

Breathing Apparatus provides a separate source of supply of air (including oxygen) to that which surrounds the person. Because of the self-contained nature of breathing apparatus it may be used to provide a high degree of protection from a variety of toxic contaminants and may be used in situations where the actual contaminant is not known or there is more than one contaminant.

There are three types of breathing apparatus:

1) Fresh air hose apparatus - clean air from uncontaminated source.
2) Compressed air line apparatus from compressed air source.
3) Self-contained breathing apparatus - from cylinder.

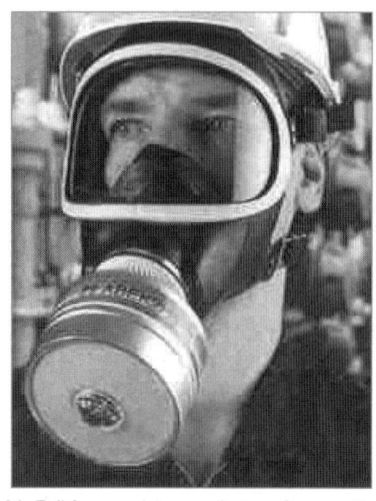

Figure 2-6-21: Full face canister respirator. *Source: Haxton Safety.*

Figure 2-6-22: Breathing apparatus. *Source: Haxton Safety.*

Advantages
- Supplies clean air from an uncontaminated source. Therefore can be worn in oxygen deficient atmospheres.
- Has high assigned protection factor (APF). Therefore may be used in an atmosphere with high levels of toxic substance.
- Can be worn for long periods if connected to a permanent supply of air.

Limitations
- Can be heavy and cumbersome which restricts movement.
- Requires careful selection by competent person.
- Requires special training.
- Requires arrangements to monitor / supervise user and for emergencies.
- Requires regular maintenance.
- Requires correct storage facilities.
- Can give a 'closed in' / claustrophobic feeling.
- Relies on user for correct fit/use etc.
- Incompatible with other forms of PPE.
- Performance can be affected by e.g. long hair.
- Interferes with other senses, e.g. sense of smell.

Figure 2-6-23: Mis-use of respirator.   Source: ACT.

Selection

There are a number of issues to consider in the selection of respiratory protective equipment (RPE), not least the advantages and limitations shown above. A general approach must not only take account of the needs derived from the work to be done and the contaminant to be protected from but must include suitability for the person. This will include issues such as face fit and the ability of the person to use the equipment for a sustained period, if this is required. One of the important factors is to ensure that the equipment will provide the level of protection required. This is indicated by the assigned protection factor given to the equipment by the manufacturers - the higher the factor the more protection provided. With a little knowledge it is possible to work out what APF is needed using the following formula.

$$APF = \frac{\text{Concentration of contaminant in the workplace}}{\text{Concentration of contaminant in the face-piece}}$$

It is critical to understand that this factor is only an indication of what the equipment will provide. Actual protection may be different due to fit and the task being conducted.

Use

Every employee must use any personal protective equipment provided in accordance with the training and instructions that they have received.

Maintenance

Where respiratory protective equipment (other than disposable respiratory protective equipment) is provided the employer must ensure that thorough examination and, where appropriate, testing of that equipment is carried out at suitable intervals.

OTHER PROTECTIVE EQUIPMENT AND CLOTHING

Eye protection

When selecting suitable eye protection some of the factors to be considered are:

Type and nature of hazard (impact, chemical, ultra violet (UV) light, etc.), type/standard/quality of protection, comfort and user acceptability issues, compatibility, maintenance requirements, training requirements and cost.

Figure 2-6-24: Eye and ear protection. *Source: Speedy Hire plc.*

Figure 2-6-25: Arc welding visor - UV reactive. *Source: ACT.*

Figure 2-6-26: Goggles. *Source: ACT.*

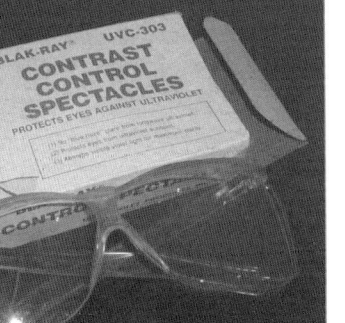

Figure 2-6-27: Spectacles. *Source: ACT.*

Types	Advantages	Limitations
Spectacles	■ Lightweight, easy to wear. ■ Can incorporate prescription lenses. ■ Do not 'mist up'.	■ Do not give all round protection. ■ Relies on the wearer for use.
Goggles	■ Give all round protection. ■ Can be worn over prescription lenses. ■ Capable of high impact protection. ■ Can protect against other hazards e.g. dust, molten metal.	■ Tendency to 'mist up'. ■ Uncomfortable when worn for long periods. ■ Can affect peripheral vision.
Face shields (visors)	■ Gives full face protection against splashes. ■ Can incorporate a fan which creates air movement for comfort and protection against low level contaminants. ■ Can be integrated into other PPE e.g. head protection.	■ Require care in use, otherwise can become dirty and scratched. ■ Can affect peripheral vision. ■ Unless the visor is provided with extra sealing gusset around the visor, substances may go underneath the visor to the face.

Protective clothing

1) Head protection - safety helmets or scalp protectors (bump caps) - scalp protectors give limited protection and are unsuitable for confined spaces. Safety helmets have a useful life of three years and this can be shortened by prolonged exposure to ultra-violet light. There is specific legal requirement in the UK to wear head protection on construction sites where there is risk of injury from falling objects.

2) Protective outer clothing - normally PVC, often high visibility to alert traffic.

3) Protective inner clothing - overalls, aprons.

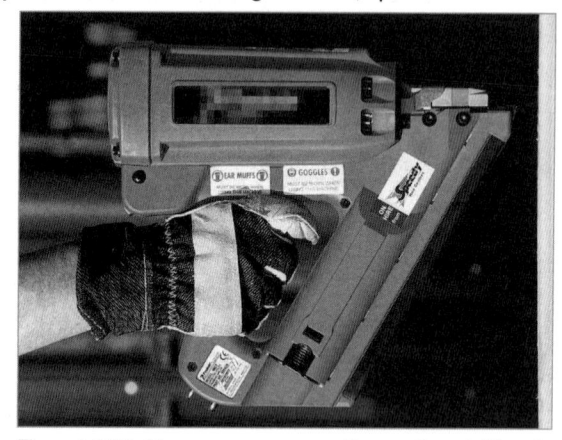

Figure 2-6-28: Gloves.　　Source: Speedy Hire plc.

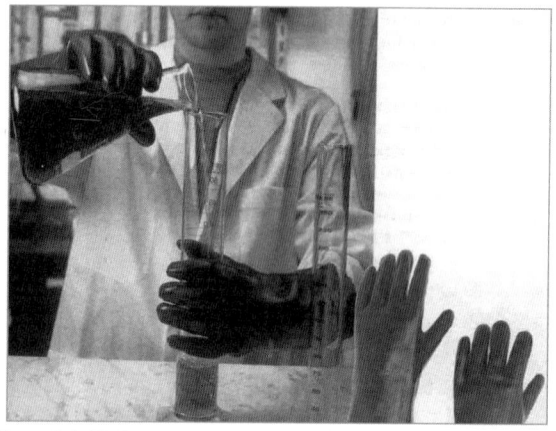

Figure 2-6-29: Protective clothing - gloves.　Source: Haxton Safety.

Hand / arm protection (Gloves)

This area of protection is vast. There are numerous types of glove and gauntlets available that offer protection from hazards:

- Chemical hazards such as acids, alkalis etc.
- Thermal hazards such as hot and cold surfaces.
- Mechanical hazards in the form of splinters and sharp edges.

The materials used in the manufacture of these products are an essential feature to consider when making the selection. There are several types of rubber (latex, nitrile, PVC, butyl) all giving different levels of protection against aqueous chemicals; leather affords protection against heat, splinters and cuts; space age technology in the form of Kevlar (a tough, lightweight material) protects against cuts from knife blades and is used in the sleeves of jackets for those using chainsaws.

Footwear - safety boots / shoes

The importance of foot protection is illustrated by the fact that around 21,000 foot and ankle injuries are reported annually in the UK. Inadequate protection and a lack of discipline on the part of the wearer commonly cause these. There are many types of safety footwear on the market, many of them offering different types of protection. It is vital that the nature of the hazard is considered when selecting appropriate footwear. Here are some common examples:

- Falling objects   - steel toe-caps.
- Sharp objects   - steel in-soles.
- Flammable atmospheres - anti-static footwear.
- Spread of contamination - washable boots.
- Electricity   - rubber soles.
- Wet environments   - impermeable Wellingtons.
- Slippery surfaces   - non-slip soles.
- Cold environments   - thermally insulated soles.

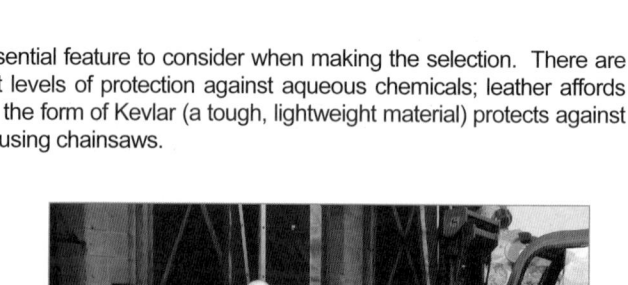

Figure 2-6-30: Personal protective equipment.　Source: ACT.

Ear protection
See also - Physical and psychological health hazards and control - Unit IGC2 - Element 7 for details of ear protection.

PERSONAL HYGIENE AND PROTECTION REGIMES

Personal hygiene and good housekeeping have an important role in the protection of the health and safety of the people at work. Laid down procedures and standards are necessary for preventing the spread of contamination. The provision of adequate washing / showering facilities is critical to remove contamination from the body.

The provision of laundry facilities for overalls and PPE reduces the effect of contamination. Barrier creams and suitable hand protection are important considerations for chemical and biological risks.

Where personal hygiene is critical, for example, when stripping asbestos, a 'three room system' is employed. Workers enter the 'clean end' and put work clothes on, leaving by means of the 'dirty end'. When work has been completed they return by means of the 'dirty end', carry out personal hygiene and leave by means of the 'clean end'.

Vaccination

Certain occupations, such as water treatment / sewage workers, medical profession, have a higher than average risk from some biological hazards. Workers from these occupations may need to be immunised against common high risks e.g. hepatitis B. Whilst vaccination can be an effective way of preventing ill health as a result of exposure to biological agents, it is critical that employers are aware of problems that can arise. In the first instance, vaccination is intrusive.

Employers need the permission of workers before adopting this method - this may not always be forthcoming. Secondly, it is possible that some workers will suffer adverse effects from the vaccination. Finally, not all diseases are treatable by vaccination and, for those that are, vaccination might not be available.

HEALTH AND MEDICAL SURVEILLANCE

Surveillance may be appropriate where exposure to hazardous substances is such that an identifiable disease or adverse health effect may be linked to the exposure. There must be a reasonable likelihood that the disease or effect may occur under the particular conditions of work prevailing and that valid techniques exist to detect such conditions and effects.

It is good practice for the employer to keep records of surveillance in respect of each employee for at least 40 years. This requirement still applies where companies cease to trade, in which case the records must be offered to the national health and safety governing body as applicable.

Further controls of substances that can cause cancer, asthma or damage to genes

Carcinogens are substances that have been identified as having the ability to cause cancer. Examples of these include arsenic, hardwood dusts and used engine oils. Additionally, substances known as mutagens have been identified that cause changes to DNA, increasing the number of genetic mutations above natural background levels. These changes can lead to cancer in the individual affected or be passed to their offspring's genetic material.

Due to the serious and irreversible nature of cancer and genetic changes, an employer's first objective must be to prevent exposure to carcinogens and mutagens. These substances should not be used or processes carried out with them, if a safer alternative less hazardous substance can be used instead.

Where this is not feasible suitable control measures should include:

- Totally enclosed systems.
- Where total enclosure is not possible, exposure to these substances must kept to as low level as possible through the use of appropriate plant and process control measures such as handling systems and local exhaust ventilation (these measures should not produce other risks in the workplace).
- Storage of carcinogens/mutagens must be kept to the minimum needed for the process, in closed, labelled containers with warning and hazard signs, including waste products until safe disposal.
- Areas where carcinogens/mutagens are present must be identified and segregated to prevent spread to other areas.
- The number of workers exposed and the duration of exposure must be kept to the minimum necessary to do the work.
- Personal protective equipment is considered a secondary protection measure used in combination with other control measures.
- Measures should be in place for monitoring of workplace exposure and health surveillance for work involving carcinogens and mutagens.

Occupational asthma is caused by substances in the workplace that triggers a state of specific airway hyper-responsiveness in an individual, resulting in breathlessness, chest tightness or wheezing. These substances are known as asthmagens and respiratory sensitisers. Exposure to these substances should be prevented, but where that is not possible, kept as low as reasonably practicable. Control measures used should take account of long term time weighted averages and short term peak exposures to the substance. If an individual develops occupational asthma, their exposure must be controlled to prevent any further attacks. Workers who work with asthmagens must have regular health surveillance to detect any changes in respiratory function.

6.6 - Waste disposal and control of pollution

Key concepts of environmental issues relating to waste disposal and effluent

Environmental pollution is a major issue today with the industrialised countries of the world concerned about the long term effects on Earth's resources and on plant, animal and human life. Major concerns on health are often blamed on pollution and there are many pressure groups that focus on environmental issues, particularly pollution.

The problem of pollution is not new, it has been with us since Roman times and the land around old lead mines is still contaminated with the heavy metal today. Since the industrial revolution industry has relied on the capacity of the environment to dilute and disperse pollutants by discharging them to the ground, water and air. This has left a legacy of polluted areas, land pollution being the most persistent, but the discharges to air and water are more global in their effect.

An example of an intentional release of pollution is the emission of sulphur dioxide (SO_2) and nitrogen oxides (NO_x) into the atmosphere by coal-fired power stations. This example also illustrates the global, as well as local, impact that such emissions have which, in this case, results in acid rain falling in Scandinavia, a country which emits very little sulphur dioxide itself. A further impact by such power stations is caused by the carbon dioxide emissions that lead to global warming.

The local effects of the emission of particulates and sulphur dioxide is illustrated by the London smogs of the 1950s, and more recently by the increase in road traffic - many cities in Britain now have pollutants above recommended limits, especially in warm, still conditions. Other countries such as Mexico Japan and North America, for example, have regular smog warnings at peak high activities periods such as work commuter rush hours.

Plant failure and accidents can lead to abnormal releases following higher than expected temperatures and pressures. This has led to a loss of process control with uncontrolled venting to the environment. Lack of control can lead to losses e.g. overfilling.

A definition of pollution

"The introduction into the environment of substance or energy liable to cause hazards to human health, harm to living resources and to ecological systems, damage to structures or amenity or interference with the legitimate use of the environment".

AIR POLLUTION

The atmospheric system

The atmosphere of the planet is a complex fluid system of gases and suspended particles. Five gases - nitrogen, oxygen, argon, carbon dioxide and water vapour make up 99.9% of the total volume of the atmosphere. The balance is made up of suspended particles such as water droplets, dust and soot, and the minor gases. Into this system a range of pollutants are released.

Common sources of air pollutants

Many sources of air pollution are introduced to the atmosphere as a deliberate release from local exhaust extraction and ventilation stacks due to combustion and other industrial processes.

Sulphur dioxide. The major source of sulphur dioxide is the combustion of fossil fuels containing sulphur. These are predominantly coal and fuel oil, since natural gas, petrol and diesel fuels have a relatively low sulphur content.

Suspended particulate matter. The main source of primary man-made particulate pollutants is combustion of fossil fuels, especially coal. Power stations use large tonnages of coal. There has been a massive decrease in urban concentrations of smoke. The main source of black smoke in urban air in the UK is diesel engine road vehicles.

Oxides of nitrogen. The most abundant nitrogen oxide in the atmosphere is nitrous oxide, N_2O, and this is formed by natural microbiological processes in the soil. It is not normally considered as a pollutant, although it does have an effect upon stratospheric ozone concentrations and there is concern that use of nitrogenous fertilisers may be increasing atmospheric levels of nitrous oxide. The main concerns are nitric oxide, NO, and nitrogen dioxide, N_2O, which together is called NOx. The major source of NOx is in high temperature combustion processes.

Carbon monoxide. The main source of this pollutant is petrol engine road vehicles. Car exhaust gases contain several per cent carbon monoxide under normal running conditions, and greater amounts when cold and choked.

Hydrocarbons. The major sources of hydrocarbons in air are the evaporation of solvents and fuels, and the partial combustion of fuels.

Carbon dioxide. Increasingly CO_2 is viewed as an air pollutant because of its importance as a "greenhouse gas". Its source lies in animal and plant respiration, and anoxic decomposition processes. It may be both absorbed and released by the oceans. Fossil fuel combustion receives a lot of attention but it is a minor source. However a small imbalance in the CO_2 cycle is leading to a steady increase in atmospheric concentration.

Ozone. Ozone is a naturally occurring gas in the atmosphere and is critical in the upper reaches because it forms a protective layer (the ozone layer) to filter out potentially harmful rays from the sun.

"Holes" in the ozone layer have been discovered at both North and South poles and severe thinning over large parts of North America and Europe - people living in these areas suffer from a greater risk of skin cancer due to increased ultra violet exposure. In addition plant and aquatic life can be affected with corresponding problems for the whole food chain. A range of chemicals containing chlorine or bromine primarily causes the ozone depletion. *Chlorofluorocarbons (CFCs)* are in this group and, when they react with radiation from the sun, release chlorine that reacts with and destroys ozone. However the chlorine is not destroyed and can go on to repeat the process up to 100,000 times. Other ozone depleting gases include halons and carbon tetrachloride.

WATER POLLUTION

Water is present on the planet in all three of its phases; that is, as a solid, liquid and gas. Most water vapour is found within the atmosphere; the oceans store most of the water in its liquid phase and the poles and high alpine regions store water in the form of ice. Water moves between each of these three states by processes such as evaporation, condensation, melting and freezing. Operating together these are known as the hydrological cycle and these processes make a major contribution to the weather of the planet. Over 97% of all water on Earth is salt water. Of the 3% that is fresh water 77.5% is locked up in the ice caps and glaciers. The atmosphere, rivers, lakes and underground stores hold less than 1%. The largest volumes of freshwater are held in the Great Lakes of North America.

In terms of water pollution it is the water in its liquid phase that is of most interest. This water appears in the oceans of the world, rivers, lakes, streams and lochs. Water is also stored in its liquid phase in the ground and is referred to as **groundwater**. It is defined as water which occupies the earth's mantle and which forms the sub surface section of the hydrological cycle. An aquifer is a layer of permeable rock, sand or gravel that absorbs water and allows it free passage through the interstices of the rock.

Common sources of water pollution

One way of thinking about pollution is too much of something in the wrong place and therefore there are many potential water pollutants. This fact is recognised within the European Community by the listing of **black** and **grey list** materials, sometimes called List I and List II substances. Black List or List I substances are considered to be so toxic, persistent or bio accumulative in the environment that priority should be given to eliminating pollution by them. This includes waste substances such as organohalogens, organophosphorus, cyanide, cadmium and mercury and their compounds. Sheep-dip and solvents are included in this list. The Grey List or List II covers those substances considered less harmful when discharged to water. Included here are metals such as zinc, nickel, chromium, lead, arsenic and copper. Also included are various biocides such as those used in cooling towers or humidifiers and substances such as phosphorus and its compounds (detergents), and ammonia (present in sewage effluent).

Diffuse and point sources

A diffuse source of pollution is one which is spread over a wide area, an example of which is the use of fertilisers over wide areas. Nitrate pollution from fertilisers represents a significant pollutant to rivers, coastal areas and seas. A discharge from an industrial sewer represents an example of a point source. Pollution from diffuse sources is more significant than from point sources and is much more difficult to control.

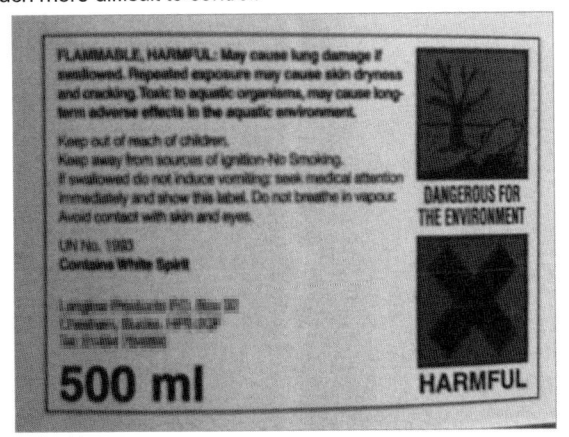

Figure 2-6-31: Hazard label - environment.   Source: ACT.

Figure 2-6-32: Environmental hazard oil spill.   Source: ACT.

Principles of protection against accidental release

Leaking and spillage can result from a number of sources: faulty valves or connectors to pipework; containers such as tins, drums or bags; loss from tanks (typically one tonne) of solids and liquids; road or rail freight containers; cargo vessels etc.

Typical techniques to contain spillage include: curbed areas for drum storage, tanker loading of liquids, bunded (walled containment perimeters) areas to contain sited tanks, drip trays at decanting points (piped systems and 45 gallon [205 litre] drums).

Portable tanks are available with two skins (a tank within a tank) to contain any spillage from the internal tank, often used where there is a need for portability such as with construction sites, to minimise the impact of spillage on the environment when storing materials such as fuel oils. Similarly cargo vessels may have double skinned tanks or hulls.

Bunding

A bund often consists of an area contained by a rectangular wall built upon a concrete slab. The bund floor and walls should be treated to be impervious to any spillage. Storage tanks are located within this confined area. It is necessary to consider the potential escape of any spillage beyond the bund area in the event of the tank developing a hole (known as jetting). The risk of this can be minimised by:

- Keeping the primary container as low as possible.
- Increasing the height of the bund wall.
- Leaving sufficient space between the tank and bund walls.
- Not sitting one tank above another.
- Providing screens or curtains.

The bund should be impermeable to the stored liquid and water which is likely to be present from rainfall. And there should be no direct uncontrolled outlet:

- Connecting the bund to any drain, sewer or watercourse.
- Discharging onto a yard or unmade ground.

Ideally, pipework should not pass through the bund wall. If unavoidable, seal the pipe into the bund with a material that is resistant to attack by the substance stored to ensure the bund remains leak-proof.

It is good practice for the secondary containment system to provide storage of at least 110% of the tank's maximum capacity. If more than one container is stored, the system should be capable of storing 110% of the biggest container's capacity or 25% of the total tank capacity within the bund, whichever is the greater.

Source: Environment Agency: Above Ground Oil Storage Tanks.

WASTE DISPOSAL

The surface of the planet is made up of materials including rocks, gravels, sands, clays and soils, which are present in many combinations. Superimposed on these are the various ecosystems (a localized group of interdependent organisms together with the environment that they inhabit and depend on) which combine to produce a complex system which is therefore not easy to characterise. Glacial action has formed the landscape as the ice age retreated. Rivers, floods, earthquakes, volcanoes, winds, and all forms of life shape the surface of the planet. Each country has unique forms and habitats which provide for the great diversity of life on the planet. Human life results in waste being generated and depending on how these are deposited pollution of the land can occur. As we have mainly populated the land masses, it is these that have traces of pollution dating back to ancient times. Some typical pollutants and their effects include the following:

Contaminant	*Hazard pathway*	*Harmful effects*
Heavy metals	Ingestion	May cause respiratory cancers, emphysema and other lung disorders, kidney dysfunction and birth defects (teratogenicity).
Zinc, copper, nickel	Phytotoxicity	Can stunt plant growth, cause discoloration, shallow root system and die back.
Sulphate and sulphides	Contact with buildings	Can corrode and accelerate the weathering of services and structural components.

Waste and the duty of care (UK Legalisation example)

Waste is defined in the Act as:
- Scrap material.
- Effluent or unwanted substances.
- Something that is broken or worn out.
- Something contaminated or spoilt.
- Something discarded as if it is waste.

The Act introduces the common law concept of duty of care to waste management and applies it to anyone involved in producing, handling or disposing of waste.

Agents or 'brokers' who arrange for waste disposal also have a duty of care under the Act. The producer of the waste retains this duty of care until their waste loses its identity - e.g. it is mixed with other waste at a waste transfer station.

This duty does not apply to domestic producers. Their local authority assumes this responsibility.

The Act requires that the duty holder must:
- Store waste securely and prevent its escape.
- Ensure that waste is only transferred to a licensed carrier and eventually to a licensed site. This should involve the producer carrying out 'duty of care audits' on carriers and waste processors.
- Provide a description of the waste to anyone involved in handling it (Transfer Note). The Transfer Note should contain information including:
  - The identity of the waste.
  - The quantity.
  - The type of containers used.
  - Times and dates of transfer.
  - Names and addresses of producer, carrier etc.
  - Relevant license numbers.

Some **carriers** are exempt from the requirement for a waste carriers licence, such as charities and voluntary organisations. Some **businesses** are exempt from the need for a waste management licence, such as scrap metal recyclers or car dismantlers.

The penalty for a breach of the duty of care can be unlimited fines.

Hazardous waste

In the UK hazardous waste is given an extra level of consideration and enforcement of the regime for this type of waste is as follows:
- Waste producers must register annually with the Environment Agency.
- Producers must issue a consignment note describing Hazardous Waste.
- The waste description must include a code obtained with reference to 14 hazardous properties described in the *European Waste Catalogue*.

Non-hazardous waste

Non-hazardous waste does not have dangerous properties e.g. paper, wood, which degrade without producing harmful decomposition products.

Controlled waste

This category covers the main waste streams from:
- *Household* - includes households, campsites, prisons, churches, schools.
- *Industrial* - includes factories, laboratories, workshops, bus depots, some hospital waste.
- *Commercial* - includes offices, showrooms, hotels, sports centres.

Consignment notes

When hazardous waste is moved from premises then consignment notes must be used. A consignment note must be completed prior to the movement and contains information on:

- Current location and destination.
- The waste producer.
- The waste description including process which gave rise to the waste.
- Chemical properties of the waste, including hazardous characteristics.

Registration of sites

Additional information required for the consignment is a unique reference number for the premises known as the 'Hazardous Waste Generator Number'. This is obtained by registering with the Environment Agency.

The storage of incompatible materials and their segregation

In addition to general safe storage practices, segregated storage of incompatible materials is a must. As a minimum, wastes should be segregated according to similar hazards, such as flammability, corrosivity, sensitivity to water or air, and toxicity.

When establishing a storage scheme, the main consideration should be the flammability characteristics of the material. If the material will contribute significantly to a fire (i.e. oxidisers), it should be isolated from the flammables. If a fire were to occur, the response to the fire with water would exacerbate the situation.

Consider the toxicity of the material, with particular attention paid to regulated materials. In some cases, this may mean that certain wastes will be isolated within a storage area, for instance, a material that is an extreme poison but is also flammable, should be locked away in the flammable storage area to protect it against accidental release. There will always be some chemicals that will not fit neatly in one category or another, but with careful consideration of the hazards involved, most of these cases can be handled in a reasonable fashion. For the safety of all personnel and to protect the integrity of the facilities, hazardous materials must be segregated.

Minimising pollution from waste

Organisations should use the following hierarchy in reducing waste in their processes:

- Reduce the amount of raw materials and energy involved in their processes.
- Re-use materials or recover energy.
- Recycle materials - make a useful product from materials unusable in the original process.
- Convert waste to energy - by incineration and use of the heat for industrial heating or electricity generation.
- Dispose to landfill or land raising.

Physical and chemical waste treatment

The aim of physical and chemical treatment of wastes is to minimise the environmental impact. Physical treatment techniques include settling, sedimentation, filtration, flotation, evaporation and distillation (e.g. the separation of oil and water using settlement lagoons or the recovery of solvents by distillation). Chemical conversion processes, such as flue gas desulphurisation (FGD), change the chemical make-up of the substance making it more compatible with the environment. In this latter case, the conversion of sulphur dioxide into gypsum can render the waste inert with little or no environmental impact. Other techniques include:

- Making soluble wastes insoluble.
- Destroying toxicity (e.g. oxidation of cyanides).
- Neutralisation of acids and alkalis.

The majority of waste techniques of this type relate to waterborne contamination and particularly the Water Industry. It should be noted that treated wastes will still require final disposal of solid residues (e.g. water treatment residues).

Landfill and land raising sites

Landfill sites play a crucial role in waste management alongside other methods such as incineration, waste minimisation and recycling techniques. A landfill site is a complex engineering, technical and commercial project that requires thorough planning and high standards of management to ensure that it is successful throughout its lifetime, which may be up to 50 years or more. A land-raising site involves the filling of a natural geographical feature such as a flood plain. The raised site may then be used for industrial or domestic development. Land raising sites can have all the problems, which are discussed below, as can occur with a landfill site.

Legislation relating to landfill/land raising sites

In most countries any person wishing to operate a site must comply with the relevant national legislation and also obtain a waste management licence from the national environment enforcing agency.

The objective of the waste management licensing system is to ensure that waste management facilities do not cause pollution of the environment, do not cause harm to human health and do not become seriously detrimental to the amenities of the locality. The effect of this legislation has been to reduce dramatically the number of sites that will accept hazardous waste.

Incineration

Incineration falls under two main categories; the burning of:
1. Municipal solid wastes (MSW).
2. Hazardous wastes.

The principle of incineration of MSW is to reduce the volume of waste by burning it under controlled conditions in order to reduce volume/mass for final disposal. The heat produced can also be used as an energy source (as a fuel MSW wastes are about 30-40% that of industrial bituminous coal). Incineration is the only really secure environmental option for most pathogens (something that can cause disease, such as a bacterium or a virus), inflammable liquids and carcinogens (a substance or agent that can cause cancer, some chemicals and viruses are carcinogens.) such as PCBs (a compound derived from biphenyl and containing chlorine that is used in electrical insulators, flame retardants, and plasticisers.) or dioxins (any derivative of dibenzo-p-dioxin, produced as a toxic by-product of combustion processes, the manufacture of some herbicides and bactericides, and in chlorine bleaching of paper.) Thus this option represents a suitable treatment/disposal for a waste stream if combustion or application of high temperature destroys or transforms it. Thus its potential as an environmental hazard is reduced. About 2% of controlled waste destined for disposal in the UK is incinerated. There are two main types of incinerator - thermal and catalytic (involving or causing an increase in the rate of a chemical reaction by the use of a catalyst).

Recycling or composting

The waste collection authorities in the UK draw up plans for recycling household and commercial waste and empowers waste disposal authorities to pay recycling credits as a result of waste collected for recycling by waste collection authorities.

Element 7

Physical and psychological health hazards and control

Learning outcomes

On completion of this element, candidates should be able to demonstrate understanding of the content through the application of knowledge to familiar and unfamiliar situations. In particular they should be able to:

7.1 Identify work processes and practices that may give rise to musculoskeletal health problems (in particular work-related upper limb disorders - WRULD) and suggest practical control measures.

7.2 Identify common welfare and work environment requirements in the workplace.

7.3 Describe the health effects associated with exposure to noise and suggest appropriate control measures.

7.4 Describe the health effects associated with exposure to vibration and suggest appropriate control measures.

7.5 Describe the principal health effects associated with ionising and non-ionising radiation and outline basic protection techniques.

7.6 Explain the causes and effects of stress at work and suggest appropriate control actions.

7.7 Describe the situations that present a risk of violence towards employees and suggest ways of minimising such risk.

7.8 Describe the effects on health and safety of alcohol and drugs and suggest appropriate control actions.

Content

7.1 - Musculoskeletal health	223
The principles of ergonomics as applied to the workplace	223
The ill-health effects of poorly designed tasks and workstations	223
The factors giving rise to ill-health conditions	224
Risk activities giving rise to ill-health conditions	225
Preventative and precautionary measures	225
7.2 - Welfare and work environment issues	226
Principal expectations	226
7.3 - Noise	228
The effects on hearing of exposure to noise	228
The meaning of common sound measurement terms	229
The decibel scale	229
Acceptable and unacceptable levels of noise	230
Simple noise measurement techniques	230
Basic noise control techniques	231
Personal hearing protection	232
Health surveillance	233
7.4 - Vibration	233
Effects of exposure to vibration	233
Acceptable and unacceptable levels of vibration	234
Basic vibration control measures	235
Health surveillance	235
7.5 - Heat and radiation	236
Temperature	236
Ionising and non-ionising radiation	237
International Commission on Radiological Protection (ICRP) recommendations on dose limits	238
Typical occupational sources of ionising and non-ionising radiation	239
Basic radiation protection and control strategies	239
7.6 - Stress	240
Causes of stress	240
Effects of stress	241
Prevention strategies	241
7.7 - Violence at work	241
Risk factors	241
Prevention strategies	242
7.8 - Effects on health and safety of alcohol and drugs	242
Health and safety of alcohol and drugs	242

Sources of reference

Ambient factors in the workplace (ILO Code of Practice), ISBN 92-2-11628-X
A Pain in Your Workplace? Ergonomic Problems and Solutions (HSG121), HSE Books ISBN 0-7176-0668-6
Display Screen Equipment Work (Guidance) (L26), HSE Books ISBN 0-7176-2582-6
Lighting at Work (HSG38), HSE Books
Personal Protective Equipment at Work (Guidance) (L25), HSE Books ISBN 0-7176-1232-5
Seating at Work (HSG57), HSE Books ISBN 0-7176-1231-7
Ergonomic Checkpoints, ILO ISBN 92-2-109442-1
Work Organisation and Ergonomics, ILO ISBN 92-2-109518-5
Real Solutions, real people: A managers guide to tackling work-related stress, HSE Books ISBN 0-7176-2767-5
HSE Stress Management Standards www.hse.gov.uk/stress/standards

7.1 - Musculoskeletal health

The principles of ergonomics as applied to the workplace

Ergonomics, often referred to as human factors in the United States, is the 'application of scientific information concerning humans to the design of objects, systems and environment for human use' (Definition adopted by the International Ergonomics Association in 2007). Ergonomics comes into everything which involves people.

The study of ergonomics is essential to good job design. It is the applied science of equipment design intended to maximise productivity by reducing worker fatigue and discomfort. It can be defined as 'the study of the relationship between human beings, the equipment with which they work and the physical environment in which this worker-machine system operates'.

It is a broad area of study that includes the disciplines of psychology, physiology, anatomy and design engineering. Ergonomics has the human being at the centre of the study where individual capabilities and fallibilities are considered in order to, ultimately, eliminate the potential for human error. It is also the study of ways to prevent the so-called 'ergonomic illnesses' - work-related musculoskeletal disorders. These areas of ill health may lead to disability. They stem from poorly designed machines, tools, task and workplace.

Figure 2-7-1: Workstation design.   Source: ACT.

Human beings work within certain boundaries, which must be recognised for all situations. However, even when human beings work within their limitations, there will still be degradation in performance. Why, when and how degradation occurs needs to be understood in order to make allowances for or to remedy the situation.

The aims of ergonomics, therefore, are to design the equipment and the working environment to fit the needs and capabilities of the individual, i.e. fitting the task to the individual, and to ensure that the physical and mental well-being of the individual are being met. This involves a consideration of psychological and physical factors, including the work system, training, body dimensions, intelligence, noise, temperature and lighting.

The design of the human body is basically uniform, allowing for differences of gender. The spine, joints, tendons and muscles work in the same way and will suffer also the same abuse, although to a varying extent. Individuals, therefore, have different physical capabilities due to height, weight, age and levels of fitness. They also have different mental capabilities, memory retention and personalities.

The ill-health effects of poorly designed tasks and workstations

MUSCLOSKELETAL DISORDERS

Musculoskeletal disorders (MSDs) can affect the body's muscles, joints, tendons, ligaments and nerves. Most-work related MSDs develop over time and are caused either by the work itself or by the workers' working environment. Usually, MSDs affect the back, neck, shoulders and upper limbs. The lower limbs are affected less frequently. The health problems range from discomfort, minor aches and pains, to more serious medical conditions requiring time off work and even medical treatment. In more chronic cases, treatment and recovery are often unsatisfactory - the result could be permanent disability and loss of employment. MSDs are an increasing problem. For the worker, they cause personal suffering and loss of income; for the employer, they reduce business efficiency; and for Government, which operate social benefit schemes costs are increased. The EU has made MSDs a priority in its Community strategy on Occupational Health and Safety. Reducing the musculoskeletal load of work is part of the 'Lisbon objective', which aims to create 'quality jobs' by:
- Enabling workers to stay in employment.
- Ensuring that work and workplaces are suitable for a diverse population.

Back pain can arise in many work situations. The exact cause is often unclear, but back pain is more common in tasks that involve:
- Heavy manual labour.
- Manual handling; in awkward places, like delivery work.
- Long periods in the same posture (sitting at a workstation or on board a vehicle).

WORK RELATED UPPER LIMB DISORDERS [WRULD]

Work related upper limb disorders (WRULD's) were first defined in medical literature as long ago as the 19th century as a condition caused by forceful, frequent, twisting and repetitive movements. The body will be affected to a varying degree by tasks which involve bending, reaching, twisting, repetitive movements and poor posture. WRULD covers well-known conditions such as tennis elbow, flexor tenosynovitis and carpal tunnel syndrome. It is usually caused by the tasks and movements detailed above and aggravated by excessive workloads, inadequate rest periods and sustained or constrained postures, the result of which is pain, soreness or inflammatory conditions of muscles and the synovial lining of the tendon sheath. Present approaches to treatment are largely effective, provided the condition is treated in its early stages. Clinical signs and symptoms are local aching pain, tenderness, swelling, crepitus (a grating sensation in the joint).

Some common WRULD's are:

Carpal Tunnel Syndrome	Carpal tunnel syndrome (CTS) occurs when tendons or ligaments in the wrist become enlarged, often from inflammation, after being aggravated. The narrowed tunnel of bones and ligaments in the wrist pinches the nerves that reach the fingers and the muscles at the base of the thumb. The first symptoms usually appear at night. Symptoms range from a burning, tingling numbness in the fingers, especially the thumb and the index and middle fingers, to difficulty gripping or making a fist, to dropping things.

Tenosynovitis	An irritation of the tendon sheath. It occurs when the repetitive activity becomes excessive and the tendon sheath can no longer lubricate the tendon. As a result, the tendon sheath thickens and becomes aggravated.
Tendinitis	Tendinitis involves inflammation of a tendon, the fibrous cord that attaches muscle to bone. It usually affects only one part of the body at a time, and usually lasts a short time, unless involved tissues are continuously irritated. It can result from an injury, activity or exercise that repeats the same movement.
Peritendinitis	Inflammation of the area where the tendon joins the muscle.
Epicondylitis	Tennis Elbow or Lateral Epicondylitis is a condition when the outer part of the elbow becomes painful and tender, usually because of a specific strain, overuse, or a direct bang. Sometimes no specific cause is found. Tennis Elbow is similar to Golfer's Elbow (Medial Epicondolytis) which affects the other side of the elbow.

The aches, pains and fatigue suffered doing certain tasks will eventually impair the operator's ability and lead to degradation in performance. It is therefore essential to consider the task in order to match it to the individual so the level of general comfort is maximised. For example, when carrying out manual handling assessments it is critical to look at the relationship between the individual, the task, the load and the environment.

HAND-ARM VIBRATION SYNDROME

Prolonged intense vibration transmitted to the hands and arms by vibrating tools and equipment can lead to a condition known as *hand-arm vibration syndrome (HAV's).* These are a range of conditions relating to long term damage to the circulatory system, nerves, soft tissues, bones and joints. Probably the best known of these conditions is known as *vibration white finger (VWF).* Here the fingers go white and numb (known as *Raynaud's phenomenon*), leading to sharp tingling pains in the affected area and an often painful deep red flush. This seems to occur in response to a change in metabolic demand in the fingers induced, for example, by temperature change. It seems that the blood vessels are unable to dilate either at all or rapidly enough because of the thickened tissues that then become anoxic (lacking in oxygen).

The factors giving rise to ill-health conditions

TASKS

Tasks should be assessed to determine the health risk factors.

If the task is *repetitive* in nature, i.e. the same series of operations are repeated in a short period of time, such as ten or more times per minute, then injury may occur to the muscles and ligaments affected. Similarly, work of a *strenuous* nature, such as moving heavy or difficult shaped objects, perhaps in limited space or hot environments, will cause fatigue, strains and sprains.

ENVIRONMENT

Poor working environments. Working in *extremes of temperature* or handling hot or cold items will make simple work more strenuous. Long hours of work in cold conditions causes problems with blood circulation which, in turn, may increase the likelihood of hand arm vibration syndrome. Fatigue will also occur to the eyes if the *lighting* levels are low, typically below 100-200 lux. or bright, typically greater than 800 lux Other lighting factors may need to be considered such as the stroboscopic effects associated with moving machinery, which may appear to be stationary when viewed under fluorescent light powered by alternating current.

The risk of injury increases with the *length of time* that a task is carried out. However, injury may occur over a short period if the work requires a lot of effort.

Working in *uncomfortable positions* such as working above head height or holding something in the same place for a long period of time increases the risk of injury. These factors will often be reduced if the worker is able to adjust the conditions to their personal needs.

There is robust scientific evidence of an association of increases in selected respiratory health effects with building dampness or visible mould. These health effects are asthma exacerbation in sensitized individuals, and cough, wheeze, and upper respiratory symptoms in otherwise healthy individuals.

Dampness in buildings is a concern because it often leads to growth of moulds and bacteria and to increased emissions of chemicals. In addition, dampness causes structural degradation on buildings. Building dampness problems have a number of causes. The way to reduce these problems and the risk of associated health effects is to improve the design, construction, operation, and maintenance of buildings.

Poor posture. The position of the body and the way it has to move to carry out a particular function. This can be affected by such things as: badly designed work methods (e.g. the need for regular bending or twisting), and poor layout of the workplace (e.g. having to kneel or stretch to put articles in a cupboard).

Figure 2-7-2: Poor posture. Source: Speedy Hire Plc.

EQUIPMENT

All work factors that influence health issues should be under the influence of the operator as much as possible, such as the ability to adjust temperature and lighting, and the opportunity to take rest breaks.

If this is not possible with continuous automated lines, such as with car assembly, then work should be designed to provide facilities for operators' work patterns to be rotated to reduce these effects. Consideration to automation should be given whenever possible.

Equipment design should take into account the ergonomic requirements of the operator and, where possible, allow the user to adjust any settings to suit their needs. Such things as workbench height and positioning of switches and buttons should be in the operator's control.

Risk activities giving rise to ill-health conditions

ASSEMBLY OF SMALL COMPONENTS

Many light assembly tasks have a high risk of causing WRULD's. Typical are repetitive assembly tasks e.g. inserting a spring into a car radiator cap using one's thumb; operating a hand power press to insert ball bearings into a component. Each task should be reviewed to determine the best technique is used to reduce fatigue or strain. In the case of the radiator cap, an example of a change following review would be - providing a tool to replace the use of the thumb.

KEYBOARD OPERATION

Some or all of the above factors may affect keyboard operators. In addition, over the years there has been some concern regarding conditions such as:

- Common WRULD's associated with key board / mouse operation are:
  - Carpal Tunnel Syndrome - painful inflammation of the nerves and tendons passing through the carpal bone in the wrist area, which affects the whole hand.
  - Tenosynovitis - inflammation of the synovial lining of the tendon sheath.
- Photosensitive epilepsy - a very rare form of epilepsy. Sufferers will usually know about the condition and not put themselves at risk.
- Facial dermatitis - evidence suggests that this condition is usually caused by other environmental factors such as low humidity.

Figure 2-7-3: Position of screen, reflective desk surface. *Source: ACT.*

Figure 2-7-4: Basic office chair, glare & space. *Source: ACT.*

ANALYSIS OF A DSE WORKSTATION

Should take account of:

Equipment:	Screen -	positioning, character definition, character stability.
	Keyboard -	tiltable, character legibility.
	Desk -	size, matt surface.
	Chair -	adjustable back and height, footrest available.
Environment:	Noise -	levels of noise not distractive.
	Humidity -	low humidity, less 40% Relative Humidity (RH), may cause sore eyes, facial acne.
	Lighting -	levels appropriate, contrast between surroundings balanced.
	Space -	adequate for work conducted.
Person/software interface:	Software -	easy to use.
	Work rate -	not governed by software.
	Monitoring -	operator/user informed.

Preventative and precautionary measures

PREVENTATIVE

Control measures

- Improved design or working areas.
- Provision of special tools.

PRECAUTIONARY

General

- Better training and supervision.
- Adjustment of workloads and rest periods.
- Health surveillance aimed at early detection.

Following risk assessment of the task, actions involving the workers and their representatives should be identified and prioritised. These should be focused on preventive measures (to stop the injury or ill health occurring in the first place), but consideration should also be given to precautionary measures to minimise the seriousness of any injury sustained. The risk management strategy must ensure that all workers receive appropriate information and training, consideration should be given to:

- **Workplace** - layout improvements to avoid tasks requiring high force applications in awkward, static working postures.

- **Work equipment** - ergonomic design to tools. For example, the use of powered tools to reduce the force required for a task. Will the use of such tools increase exposure to hand-arm vibration?
- **Workers** - training to increase worker awareness of ergonomic factors, and to recognise and avoid unsafe working conditions. In addition, workers must understand what might happen if the preventative measures are ignored or not used. They should also be made aware of the benefits of adopting good practices and work methods.
- **Work tasks** - reduction in the physical demands of the job by decreasing levels of force required, repetition, awkward postures and / or vibration exposure.
- **Work management** - planning of the work or implementation of safe systems of work. Consider the reallocation of tasks between workers to reduce repeated motions, forceful hand exertion, and prolonged bending and twisting.
- **Organisation** - precautionary solutions include establishing appropriate work/rest ratios to reduce the build-up of fatigue, organising breaks, and providing job rotation.
- **Corporate** - precautionary solutions include promotion of a positive safety culture, including stakeholder involvement in identifying and controlling WRULD's risk factors and improving safety and surveillance measures.

Information and training

Should include:

- Risks to health.
- How to recognise problems.
- Precautions in place (e.g. the need for regular breaks).
- How to report problems.

7.2 - Welfare and work environment issues

Principal expectations

DRINKING WATER

An adequate supply of wholesome drinking water must be provided. The supply needs to be accessible. If not provided in the form of a fountain, then drinking vessels must also be provided. The supply outlet from taps should be labelled, 'suitable for drinking', or 'Unsuitable for drinking' as appropriate.

WASHING FACILITIES

Suitable and sufficient washing facilities, including showers where necessary for the nature of the work or for health reasons, provided at readily accessible places. The supply of clean, hot and cold or warm water, preferably clean running water, soap or other means of cleaning, towels or other means of drying. The rooms that contain these facilities must be kept clean, ventilated, lit and maintained.

SANITARY CONVENIENCES

Readily accessible suitable and sufficient sanitary conveniences must be provided. The conveniences must be adequate for the numbers and gender employed, lit, kept clean and maintained in an orderly fashion. Separate conveniences for male and female workers must be provided except where the convenience is in a separate room and the door of which is capable of being locked from the inside.

ACCOMMODATION FOR CLOTHING

Suitable and sufficient accommodation must be provided for personal clothing not worn at work and clothing worn at work but not taken home. Such clothing accommodation must: be secure when personal clothing not worn at work is being stored; separate storage for work clothing and other clothing where necessary to avoid health risks or damage due to cross contamination; be in a suitable location and where necessary include drying facilities.

FACILITIES FOR CHANGING CLOTHING

Where special clothing must be worn at work, or for reasons of health or propriety a person cannot change in another room then suitable and sufficient changing facilities must be provided. Separate facilities or separate use of facilities for male and female workers must be taken into account. Changing facilities should be readily accessible to workrooms (and eating facilities if provided) and should contain adequate seating arrangements. The facilities provided should be sufficiently large to enable the maximum number of workers to use them comfortably and quickly at any one time.

REST AND EATING FACILITIES

Readily accessible, suitable and sufficient rest facilities should be provided. Such rest facilities should be provided in one or more rest rooms (new and modified, etc. workplaces) or in rest rooms or rest areas (existing workplaces). Where meals are regularly eaten in the workplace suitable and sufficient facilities must be provided for their consumption. Where food eaten in the workplace and is liable to become contaminated, suitable facilities for eating meals must be included in the rest facilities. Some countries have banned smoking within the public buildings and workplace where this has not happened, rest rooms and eating areas must include suitable arrangements for protecting non-smokers from the discomfort of tobacco smoke. Suitable rest facilities must also be provided for pregnant women and nursing mothers.

Rest facilities should include suitable and sufficient seats and tables for the number of workers likely to use them at any one time. Work seats in offices or other clean environments may be acceptable as rest facilities provided workers are not subjected to excessive disturbance during rest periods. Eating facilities should include a facility for preparing or obtaining a hot drink, and where hot food cannot be readily obtained, means should be provided to enable workers to heat their own food. Work canteens, eateries, and restaurants may be used as rest facilities providing there is no obligation to buy food.

Figure 2-7-5: Accommodation for clothing.   Source: ACT.

Figure 2-7-6: Facilities for rest and to eat meals.   Source: ACT.

SEATING

Suitable seats should be provided for workers who have to stand to carry out their work and occasionally have the opportunity to sit down. Seats should be provided for use during breaks. Rest areas should have sufficient seats with backrests for the number of workers who may use them at one time. Seats in the work area can be counted as eating facilities provided the place is clean and there is a suitable surface to place food. There should also be facilities for pregnant and nursing mothers to lie down if required.

VENTILATION

The principal features of a ventilation system are:

- Provision and maintenance of the circulation of fresh air in every occupied part of a workplace.
- The rendering harmless of all potentially injurious airborne contaminants e.g. dusts, fumes, vapours and gases.

HEATING

The level of heating should be appropriate to provide physical comfort. The nature of the work and the working environment will need to be assessed to achieve the correct level. Whenever possible, the individual should be able to adjust their workplace to achieve this objective.

Workplaces can vary greatly:

- Very cold and exposed, such as an oil rig in the Sea or a frozen food storage warehouse.
- General warehousing at ambient temperature.
- General office where the nature of the work is sedentary.
- High temperature processing such as a laundry.
- High temperature manufacturing such as with glass, steel or ceramics production.

Several factors should be considered such as personal capability, degree of hot or cold, wind speed and humidity. *These factors are covered in more depth in the section 'Heat and Radiation'.*

LIGHTING

Lighting the task and workstation

In general, for each visual task we require a certain minimum quantity of light arriving on each unit area of the object in view (i.e. a minimum 'planar' illuminance). The value of this minimum illuminance depends primarily on the size of the detail which must be perceived, but will also depend on the visual contrast that the task makes with the background against which it is seen, the duration of the task, whether or not errors may have serious consequences and the presence or absence of daylight.

Ideally the workstation should be designed in such a way as to make the task the brightest part of the field of view. Research has shown that favourable conditions exist when the task has a luminance, which is about three times that of its immediate surrounds, and when the immediate surrounds, again, have about three times the luminance of the general surrounds to the workstation. These conditions can be achieved by a combination of general and local lighting used to illuminate the work surfaces, which have appropriately chosen reflectance's. For example, when a desk lamp provides local lighting for white paper seen against a grey-blotting pad placed on a desktop served by a general installation of ceiling-mounted fluorescent lighting, an approximation to these desirable conditions is then obtained.

Not all problems caused by poor lighting can be overcome simply by the provision of more light. When tasks are visually demanding, the quality of the available light is at least as critical as its quantity.

Daylight has qualities which are difficult to imitate artificially. Moreover the provision of a distant view seen through a window will provide welcome relief to eyes which must focus at their 'near point' while work is in progress. Aspects of lighting quality, which should receive attention when lighting the workstation, are the control of glare, the provision of adequate modelling *(see also - 'Lighting the interior of the workplace')* and, where necessary, good colour rendering.

Figure 2-7-7: Reflected light from window. *Source: ACT.*

Figure 2-7-8: Light from windows controlled by blinds. *Source: ACT.*

Lighting the interior of the workplace

The basic need is to provide sufficient and suitable light in the circulation areas to allow movement of personnel, materials and equipment between workstations to take place conveniently and in safety. The aim should be to provide conditions which remain comfortable to the eye as it passes from one zone of the workplace to another, and to make available all information relevant to the well being and safety of the workforce which can be received through the sense of sight. All the aspects of quantity and quality considered under task lighting would assume some significance in this larger scale application and so contribute to the achievement of these desirable conditions.

Attention should be given to accident high risk areas, such as changes in floor level or flights of stairs, with increased levels of illuminance served by luminaires which are carefully positioned to provide good three-dimensional modelling, while preventing any direct sight of the unshielded source, so as to avoid disabling glare. Machinery which makes fast cyclic movements should be carefully illuminated to prevent the occurrence of stroboscopic effects.

Sudden changes in lighting levels should not occur between neighbouring zones of the workplace. Levels should be graded to allow time for the eye to adapt. The processes of dark adaptation can take several minutes (more than half an hour in extreme cases) during which time the efficiency of the eye is severely reduced, making accidents more likely.

Differences in the colour characteristics of so-called 'white light' sources are sometimes apparent to the eye and although its ability to colour-adapt is considerable, the occurrence of frequent noticeable changes due to the use of various kinds of sources in the same interior may accelerate the onset of fatigue as well as making fine colour judgements impossible.

7.3 - Noise

The effects on hearing of exposure to noise

The ear senses **sound**, which is transmitted in the form of pressure waves travelling through a substance, e.g., air, water, metals etc. Unwanted sound is generally known as **noise.**

The ear has 3 basic regions *(see - Figure 2-7-9)*:

a) The **outer** ear channels the sound pressure waves through to the eardrum.

b) In the **middle** ear, the vibrations of the eardrum are transmitted through three small bones (hammer, anvil and stirrup) to the inner ear.

c) The cochlea in the **inner** ear is filled with fluid and contains tiny hairs (nerves) which respond to the sound. Signals are then sent to the brain via the acoustic nerve.

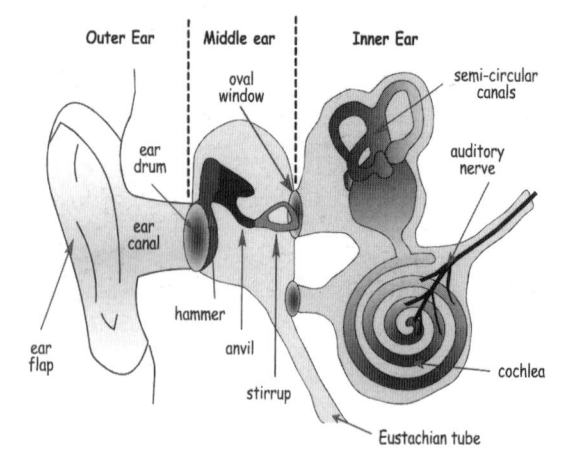

Figure 2-7-9: Inner ear diagram. *Source: www.echalk.co.uk.*

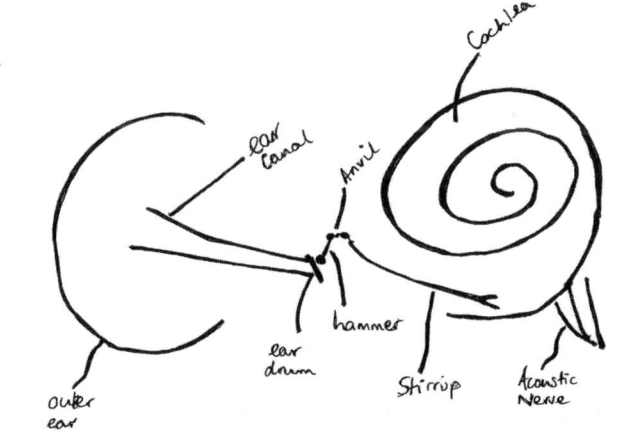

Figure 2-7-10: The ear (hand drawn). *Source: ACT.*

Excessive noise over long periods of time can cause damage to the hairs (nerves) in the cochlea of the ear. This results in **noise induced hearing loss (deafness)**, which can be of a temporary or permanent nature. Also, a single high pressure event can damage the ear by dislocation of a bone or rupturing the ear drum. It has been shown that high levels of noise can cause, or increase the onset of, *tinnitus* ('ringing in the ears').

Noise induced hearing loss is considered the main risk from sustained exposure to excessive noise, causing permanent hearing damage. Historically this has been in heavy industry, but noise is hazardous to worker safety and health in many places of employment. High noise levels have been identified as a potential causal factor in work accidents, both by masking hazards and warning signals, and by impairing concentration. Also, noise can act as a causal factor for stress and raise systolic blood pressure. In addition, there is a risk of ototoxicity (damage to the ear) where noise acts synergistically with certain solvents.

The meaning of common sound measurement terms

SOUND POWER AND PRESSURE

For noise to occur power must be available. It is the sound power of a source (measured in Watts) which causes the sound pressure (measured in Pascals) to occur at a specific point.

INTENSITY AND FREQUENCY

The amplitude of a sound wave represents the intensity of the sound pressure. When measuring the **amplitude** of sound there are two main parameters of interest - *as shown in Figure 2-7-11*. One is related to the energy in the sound pressure wave and is known as the 'root mean square' (*rms*) value, and the other is the 'peak' level. We use the *rms* sound pressure for the majority of noise measurements, apart from some impulsive types of noise when the peak value is also measured.

Sound (noise) waves travel through air at the *'speed of sound'* which is approximately equal to 344 m/s. A sound can have a *'frequency'* or *'pitch'*, which is measured in cycles per second (Hz).

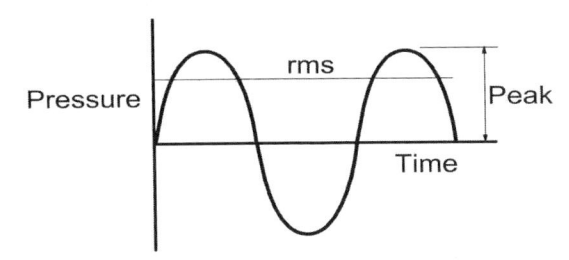

Figure 2-7-11: Rms and peak levels of a sound wave.   Source: ACT.

The decibel scale

The ear can detect pressures over a very wide range, from 20 µPa to 20 Pa (Pascals). To help deal with this wide range, the **deciBel (dB)** is used to measure noise. A decibel is a unit of sound pressure (intensity) measured on a logarithmic scale from a base level taken to be the threshold of hearing (0dB). Typical noise levels include:

Source	dB	Source	dB
Disco / night club	110	Radio in average room	70
Smoke detector at 1 metre	105	Library	30
Machine Shop	90	Threshold of Hearing	0

A problem with decibels is that they are based on a logarithmic scale and cannot be added together in the conventional way, for example:

2 dB + 2 dB = 5 dB   (deciBel Arithmetic) and

85 dB + 85 dB = 88 dB   (deciBel Arithmetic)

Weighting scales - the terms dB(A) and dB(C)

The human ear can hear sound over a range of frequencies, from 20 Hz up to approximately 20,000 Hz (20 kHz). However, the ear does not hear the same at all frequencies; it naturally reduces (attenuates) low frequencies and very high frequencies to the range of speech. To take account of the response of the human ear sound level meters use weighting scales or filters. The most widely used sound level filter is the A scale. Using this filter, the sound level meter is thus less sensitive to very high and very low frequencies. Measurements made on this scale are expressed as dB(A) or referred to as *'A weighted'*. The majority of measurements are made in terms of dB(A), although there are other weightings that are used in some circumstances. One of these is the C scale which is suitable for subjective measurements only for very high sound levels. Measurements made on this scale are expressed as dB(C). There is also a (rarely used) B weighting scale, intermediate between A and C.

The range of frequencies that we encounter is often divided into **Octave Bands**. A noise can be measured in each octave band and these levels can be used when assessing the attenuation of hearing protectors, or when diagnosing noise problems.

Other noise units

In most situations the noise level varies with time. When measuring noise we need to determine the average, or 'equivalent continuous level', over a period of time. This is known as the **Leq**. Not all noise meters include a **Leq** function. Other noise units commonly encountered are also listed below:

L_{eq} the average, or 'equivalent continuous level'.

$L_{EP,d}$ daily personal exposure level, dB(A). This is equivalent to the L_{eq} over an 8-hour working day. The $L_{EP,d}$ is directly related to the risk of hearing damage.

L_{peak} peak pressure - pascals or dB (C). For a single instant exposure.

Acceptable and unacceptable levels of noise

Standards concerning noise exposure limits are usually based on an 8-hour work shift and also provide exposure limits for shorter and longer working days. Many regulatory agencies recommended a time-weighted average (TWA) sound level of 85 dB(A) to 90 dB(A) as a noise exposure limit for 8-hour work day. However, following the implementation of the Noise directive in 2003 in the EU, these action levels have been reduced by 5 dB(A) to the action values outlined below. It is assumed that other countries still using 85 dB (A) as the first action level will reduce to the lower value in time. Weekly noise exposure level means the average of daily noise exposure levels over a week and normalised to five working days.

	Lower exposure action values	Upper exposure action values	Exposure limit values
Daily or weekly personal noise exposure (A-weighted).	80 dB	85 dB	87 dB
Peak sound pressure (C-weighted).	135 dB	137 dB	140 dB

If the noise levels in the workplace vary greatly, then the employer can choose to use weekly noise exposure levels instead of daily noise exposure levels. The exposure can take into account personal hearing protection provided to the employee.

Lower exposure action value

Where the daily or weekly exposure level of 80dB(A) or a peak sound pressure level of 135 dB(C) is likely to be exceeded the employer must make hearing protection available upon request and provide the workers and their representatives with suitable and sufficient information, instruction and training. This shall include:

- Nature of risks from exposure to noise.
- Organisational and technical measures taken in order to comply.
- Exposure limit values and upper and lower exposure action values.
- Significant findings of the risk assessment, including any measurements taken, with an explanation of those findings.
- Availability and provision of personal hearing protectors and their correct use.
- Why and how to detect and report signs of hearing damage.
- Entitlement to health surveillance.
- Safe working practices to minimise exposure to noise.
- The collective results of any health surveillance in a form calculated to prevent those results from being identified as relating to a particular person.

Figure 2-7-12: Noise hazard sign. Source: ACT.

Figure 2-7-13: Mandatory signs. Source: Stocksigns.

Upper exposure action value

Where the daily or weekly exposure level of 85dB(A) or a peak sound pressure level of 137 dB(C) is likely to be exceeded the employer shall:

- Provide workers with hearing protection. In addition the employer will:
  - Ensure that the area is designated a hearing protection zone, fitted with mandatory hearing protection signs.
  - Ensure access to the area is restricted where practicable.
  - So far as reasonably practicable, ensure those workers entering the area wear hearing protection.

The employer must ensure that workers are not exposed to levels above an exposure limit value or if one is exceeded immediately reduce exposure below that level, investigate the reasons and modify measures to prevent a reoccurrence.

Simple noise measurement techniques

REGULATION REQUIREMENTS FOR NOISE ASSESSMENT

Any employer that carries out work which is likely to expose any workers to noise should make a suitable and sufficient assessment of the risk to health and safety created by noise at the workplace. In conducting the risk assessment the employer should assess the level of noise the workers are exposed to by:

- Observation.
- Reference to information on expected levels for work conditions and equipment.
- If necessary by measurement of the level of noise to which the workers may be exposed.

The risk assessment shall include consideration of:

- Level, type and duration of exposure, including any exposure to peak sound pressure.
- Effects of exposure to *noise* on workers or groups of workers whose health is at particular risk from such exposure.
- So far as is practicable, any effects on the health and safety of workers resulting from the interaction between *noise* and the use of toxic substances at *work*, or between *noise* and vibration.

- Indirect effects on the health and safety of workers resulting from the interaction between *noise* and audible warning signals or other sounds that need to be audible in order to reduce risk at *work*.
- Information provided by the manufacturers of *work* equipment.
- Availability of alternative equipment designed to reduce the emission of *noise*.
- Any extension of exposure to *noise* at the workplace beyond normal *working* hours, including exposure in rest facilities supervised by the employer.
- Appropriate information obtained following health surveillance, including, where possible, published information.
- Availability of personal hearing protectors with adequate attenuation characteristics.

Workers or their representatives should be consulted, significant findings and measures taken or planned to comply with the requirements should be recorded.

MEASUREMENT TECHNIQUES

Noise is measured using a sound level meter, which works in simple terms by converting pressure variations into an electric signal. This is achieved by capturing the sound with a microphone, pre-amplification of the resultant voltage signal and then processing the signal into the information required dependent on the type of meter (e.g. 'A' weighting, integrating levels, fast or slow response). The microphone is the most critical component within the meter as its sensitivity and accuracy will determine the accuracy of the final reading. Meters can be set to fast or slow response depending on the characteristics of the noise level. Where levels are rapidly fluctuating, rapid measurements are required and the meter should be set to fast time weighting.

Sound level meters should be calibrated using a portable acoustic calibrator and batteries checked before, during and after each measurement session. Laboratory calibration should be carried out annually or according to the manufacturer's instructions. Meters are used to measure the:

- Sound pressure level (L_p) - the intensity of sound at a given moment in time at a given position (i.e. the instantaneous level): an unweighted linear measurement dB (L_{in}).
- Equivalent continuous sound level (L_{eq}) - an average measure of intensity of sound over a reference period, usually the period of time over which the measurement was taken. Measured in dB(A). As the intensity and spacing of the noise levels usually vary with time, an integrating meter is used. This meter automatically calculates the L_{eq} by summing or integrating the sound level over the measurement period.
- Peak pressure level - some sound level meters produce peak pressure values for impulsive noise or where a fast time weighting reading exceeds 125 dB(A).

The expense and time consuming nature of personal dosimetry means that they should only be used when other techniques are unsuitable. It is used in situations where the task of the worker involves movement around the workplace and exposure is likely to vary.

Basic noise control techniques

Employers must ensure that risk from the exposure of the workers to noise is either eliminated at source or, where this is not reasonably practicable, reduced to as low as is reasonably practicable. Consideration should be made to:

- Other *working* methods which reduce exposure to *noise*.
- Choice of appropriate *work* equipment emitting the least possible *noise*, taking account of the *work* to be done.
- Design and layout of workplaces, *work* stations and rest facilities.
- Suitable and sufficient information and training for workers, such that *work* equipment may be used correctly, in order to minimise their exposure to *noise*.
- Reduction of *noise* by technical means.
- Appropriate maintenance programmes for *work* equipment, the workplace and workplace systems.
- Limitation of the duration and intensity of exposure to *noise*.
- Appropriate *work* schedules with adequate rest periods.

The employer should take care that noise levels in rest facilities are suitable for their purpose. The employer should adapt measures provided to suit a group or individual workers whose health is likely to be of particular risk from exposure to noise at work. Workers or their representatives should be consulted on the measures used.

NOISE CONTROL TECHNIQUES

Noise can be controlled at different points in the following 'chain':

1) The source (e.g., a noisy machine).
2) The path (e.g., through the air).
3) The receiver (e.g., the operator of a machine).

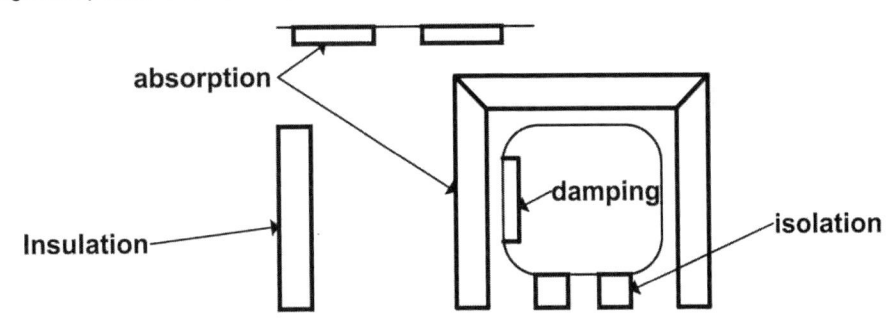

Figure 2-7-14: Basic layout of the main control methods.

Source: ACT

UNIT IGC2 - ELEMENT 7 - PHYSICAL AND PSYCHOLOGICAL HEALTH HAZARDS AND CONTROL

The main methods of noise control are listed below:

Isolation Positioning an elastic element (e.g. rubber mount etc.) in the path of vibration can isolate a noise radiating area from a vibration input.

Absorption When noise passes through porous materials (e.g. foam, mineral, wool etc.) some of its energy is absorbed.

Insulation Imposing a barrier (e.g., a brick wall, lead sheet etc.) between the noise source and the receivers will provide noise insulation.

Damping Mechanical vibration can be converted into heat by damping materials (e.g. metal/plastic/metal panels).

Silencers Pipe/boxes can be designed to reduce air/gas noise (e.g. engine exhaust silencers, duct silencers, etc.).

Other specialist control methods:

Force Reduction - Reduce impacts by using rubber pads or lower drop heights.

Air exhaust and jet silencers - Proprietary silencers can be used.

Active - Equal but opposite phase noise can cancel a problem noise.

In addition to controlling the amplitude of noise the **exposure level** can be reduced by minimising the amount of time an employee is exposed to noise, for example, by job rotation. Increasing the distance between noisy equipment and a work location can reduce the noise to which an employee is exposed. When buying new plant and equipment employers should adopt a purchasing policy which results in the quietest machines being purchased.

Figure 2-7-15: Cover to reduce noise. Source: ACT.

Personal hearing protection

All types of personal ear protector should carry a CE marking within the European Union. They should aim to reduce the noise level to achieve 85 dB or below at the ear.

PURPOSE

The purpose of personal hearing protection is to protect the worker from the adverse effects on hearing caused by exposure to high levels of noise. All hearing protection must be capable of reducing exposure to below the second level or lower exposure action value.

APPLICATION AND LIMITATIONS OF VARIOUS TYPES

Earmuffs:
1) Banded.
2) Helmet mounted.
3) Communication muffs.

Advantages:
- Worn on the outside of the ear so less chance of infection.
- Clearly visible therefore easy to monitor.
- Can be integrated into other forms of PPE e.g. head protection.

Limitations:
- Can be uncomfortable when worn for long periods.
- Incompatibility with other forms of PPE.
- Effectiveness may be compromised by e.g. long hair, spectacles etc.
- Requires correct storage facilities and regular maintenance.

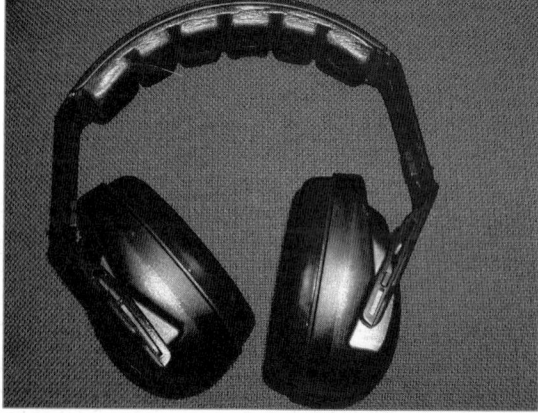

Figure 2-7-16: Ear defenders. Source: ACT.

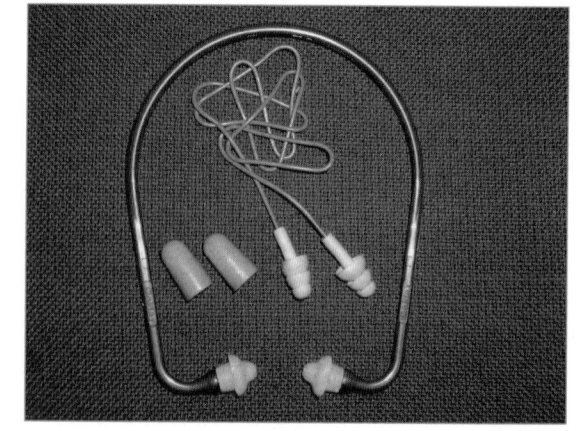

Figure 2-7-17: Disposable ear plugs. Source: ACT.

Ear plugs:
1) Pre-moulded.
2) User formable.
3) Custom moulded.
4) Banded plugs.

Advantages:
- Easy to use and store - but must be inserted correctly.
- Available in many materials and designs, disposable.
- Relatively lightweight and comfortable.

Limitations:
- They are subject to hygiene problems unless care is taken to keep them clean.
- Correct size may be required. Should be determined by a competent person.
- Interferes with communication.

- Can be worn for long periods.
- Worn inside the ear, difficult to monitor.

SELECTION

When selecting personal hearing protectors, employers must take into consideration several factors, including:

- Provision of information and training.
- Readily available.
- Comfort and personal choice.
- Issue to visitors.
- Care and maintenance.
- Noise reduction.

USE

All PPE should be used in accordance with employer's instructions, which should be based on manufacturer's instructions for use. PPE should only be used after adequate training has been given. Also, adequate supervision must be provided to ensure that training and instructions are being followed. Personal ear protection may not provide adequate protection due to any of the following reasons:

a) Long hair, spectacles, earrings etc, may cause a poor seal to occur.
b) Ear protectors are damaged, e.g., cracked.
c) Not fitted properly - due to lack of training.
d) Not wearing ear protectors all of the time.
e) Specification of protectors does not provide sufficient attenuation.

MAINTENANCE

Employers have a legal duty to ensure that any PPE is maintained in an efficient state, efficient working order and good repair. Simple maintenance can be carried out by the trained wearer, but more intricate repairs should only be done by specialist personnel.

ATTENUATION FACTORS

The attenuation (noise reduction) associated with personal ear protectors must be supplied with the product. The information required is in terms of:

1) Octave band mean attenuation and the standard deviation.
2) HML (High, Medium and Low) values.
3) SNR (Single Number Rating) values.

Health surveillance

If a risk assessment indicates a risk to the health and safety of workers who are, or are liable to be, exposed to noise, then they must be put under suitable health surveillance (including testing of their hearing). The employer must keep and maintain a suitable health record. The employer will, providing reasonable notice is provided, allow the worker access to their health record.

Where, as a result of health surveillance, a worker is found to have identifiable hearing damage the employer shall ensure that the worker is examined by a doctor. If the doctor, or any specialist to whom the doctor considers it necessary to refer the worker, considers that the damage is likely to be the result of exposure to *noise*, the employer shall:

- Ensure that a suitably qualified person informs the worker accordingly.
- Review the risk assessment.
- Review any measure taken to comply with the regulations.
- Consider assigning the employee to alternative *work*.
- Ensure continued health surveillance.
- Provide for a review of the health of any other worker who has been similarly exposed.

Workers must, when required by the employer and at the cost of the employer, present themselves during *working* hours for health surveillance procedures.

7.4 - Vibration

Effects of exposure to vibration

HARM TO HEALTH

Occupational exposure to vibration may arise in a number of ways, often reaching workers at intensity levels disturbing to comfort, efficiency and health and safety. Long-term, regular exposure to vibration is known to lead to permanent and debilitating health effects such as vibration white finger, loss of sensation, pain, and numbness in the hands, arms, spine and joints. These effects are collectively known as hand-arm or whole body vibration syndrome.

In the case of whole body vibration it is transmitted to the worker through a contacting or supporting structure which is itself vibrating, e.g. a ship's deck, the seat or floor of a vehicle (tractor or tank), or a whole structure shaken by machinery (e.g. in the processing of coal, iron ore or concrete), where the vibration is intentionally generated for impacting. By far the most common route of harm to the human body is through the hands, wrists and arms of the subject - so called **segmental vibration**, where there is actual contact with the vibrating source.

Figure 2-7-18: Use of road drill - vibration. *Source: ACT.*

Prolonged intense vibration transmitted to the hands and arms by vibrating tools and equipment can lead to a condition known as **hand-arm vibration syndrome (HAVs).** These are a range of conditions relating to long term damage to the circulatory system, nerves, soft tissues, bones and joints. Probably the best known of these conditions is known as vibration white finger (VWF). Here the fingers go white and numb (known as **Raynaud's phenomenon**), leading to 'pins and needles' and an often painful deep red flush. This seems to occur in response to a change in metabolic demand in the fingers induced, for example, by temperature change. It seems that the blood vessels are unable to dilate either at all or rapidly enough because of the thickened tissues that then become anoxic (lacking in oxygen).

CONTRIBUTORY FACTORS

As with all work-related ill health there are a number of factors which when combined result in the problem occurring. These include:-

- Vibration frequency - frequencies ranging from 2- 1,500 Hz are potentially damaging but the most serious is the 5-20 Hz range.
- Duration of exposure - this is the length of time the individual is exposed to the vibration.
- Contact Force - this is the amount of grip or push used to guide or apply the tools or work piece. The tighter the grip the greater the vibration to the hand.
- Factors affecting circulation - including temperature and smoking, which reduce the blood flow.
- Individual susceptibility.

EXAMPLES OF RISK ACTIVITIES

- The use of hand-held chain saws in forestry.
- The use of hand-held rotary tools in grinding or in the sanding or polishing of metal, or the holding of material being ground, or metal being sanded or polished by rotary tools.
- The use of hand-held percussive metal-working tools, or the holding of metal being worked upon by percussive tools in riveting, caulking, chipping, hammering, fettling or swaging.
- The use of hand-held powered percussive drills or hand-held powered percussive hammers in demolition, or on roads or footpaths, including road construction.

The medical effects are in the main more serious and permanent and are summarised below:

a) Vascular changes in the blood vessels of the fingers.
b) Neurological changes in the peripheral nerves.
c) Muscle and tendon damage in the fingers, hands, wrists and forearms.
d) Suspected bone and joint changes.
e) Damage to the autonomic centres of the central nervous system in the brain influencing the endocrine, cardiac, vestibular and cochlear functions (not proven).

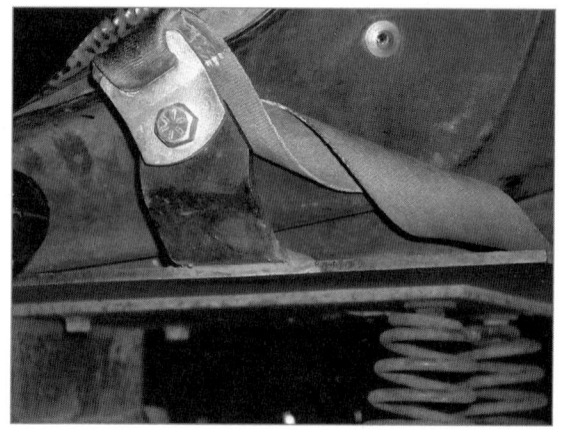

Figure 2-7-19: Dumper truck seat.   Source: ACT.

HAND-ARM VIBRATION

Prolonged intense vibration transmitted to the hands and arms by vibrating tools and equipment can lead to a condition known as hand-arm vibration syndrome (HAVs). These are a range of conditions relating to long term damage to the circulatory system, nerves, soft tissues, bones and joints. Probably the best known of these conditions is known as vibration white finger (VWF).

WHOLE BODY VIBRATION (WBV)

Whole body vibration (WBV) is caused by machinery vibration passing through the buttocks of seated people or the feet of standing people. The most widely reported WBV injury is back pain. Prolonged exposure can lead to considerable pain and time off work and may result in permanent injury and having to give up work. High-risk activities include driving site vehicles (e.g. dumper trucks) and the prolonged use of compactors.

Acceptable and unacceptable levels of vibration

Worker's vibration exposure is assessed in terms of acceleration amplitude and duration. The duration of use of the tool or trigger time is defined as the period when the worker actually has their finger on the trigger to make the tool operate (hours per day). Vibration amplitude is quoted in metres per second squared and can vary significantly with tool design, condition and style of use.

The main purpose of local legislative limits on vibration is intended to ensure employers provide better-designed, better-maintained tools, and to train workers appropriately. In addition, tool designers and manufacturers must actively seek to improve vibration levels in new machines.

ACTION LEVELS

An EU Directive ratified in 2005, gives rise to local legislative vibration limits in European states. These state the personal daily exposure limits and daily exposure action values, normalised over an 8-hour reference period.

	Daily exposure action values	Daily exposure limits
Hand arm vibration	2.5 m/s^2	5 m/s^2
Whole body vibration	0.5 m/s^2	1.15 m/s^2

RISK ASSESSMENT

The employer should make a suitable and sufficient assessment of the risk created by work that is liable to expose workers to risk from vibration. The assessment must observe work practices, make reference to information regarding the magnitude of vibration from equipment and, if necessary, measurement of the magnitude of the vibration.

Consideration must also be given to the type, duration, effects of exposure, exposures limit / action values, effects on workers at particular risk, the effects of vibration on equipment and the ability to use it, manufacturers' information, availability of replacement equipment, and extension of exposure at the workplace (e.g. rest facilities), temperature and information on health surveillance. The risk assessment should be recorded as soon as is practicable after the risk assessment is made and reviewed regularly.

Basic vibration control measures

PREVENTIVE AND PRECAUTIONARY MEASURES

The employer must seek to eliminate the risk of vibration at source or, if not reasonably practicable, reduce it to as low a level as is reasonably practicable. Where the personal daily exposure limit is exceeded the employer must reduce exposure by implementing a programme of organisational and technical measures. Measures include the use of other methods of work, ergonomics, maintenance of equipment, design and layout, rest facilities, information, instruction and training, limitation by schedules and breaks and the provision of personal protective equipment to protect from cold and damp.

Measures must be adapted to take account of any group or individual worker whose health may be of particular risk from exposure to vibration.

Protective measures are the only means of protecting people who work with vibrating machinery. The following controls should be considered.

Prevention
- The need for such machinery should be reviewed so as to eliminate unnecessary operations.
- Consideration should be given to the automation of processes.
- Wearing gloves is recommended for safety and for retaining heat. They will not absorb a significant fraction of the vibration energy which lies within the 30-300Hz range. Care needs to be taken to select appropriate gloves, as the absorbent material in some gloves for thermal insulation may introduce a resonance frequency which may increase the total energy input to the hands (early work, Bednall, Health and Safety Executive).
- Many manufacturers claim to use composite materials that, when moulded into hand-grips and fitted onto vibrating power tools, reduce vibration by up to 45%.
- The greater the coupling (hand and tool interface), the more energy enters the hand. Increasing grip force increases the coupling. There are good working techniques for all tools and the expertise developed over time justifies an initial training period for new workers.
- Operators with established HAVS should avoid exposure to cold and thus minimise the number of blanching attacks. Workers with advanced HAVS who are deteriorating (as measured by annual medical checks) should be removed from further exposure. The medical priority is to prevent finger tip ulceration (tissue necrosis).

Precautionary
- The vibration characteristics of the hand tools should be assessed and reference made to the BSI and ISO Guidelines.
- The work schedule should be examined to reduce vibration exposure either by alternating with non-vibration work or avoiding continuous vibration by, for example, scheduling ten minute breaks every hour.
- A detailed ergonomic assessment of hazardous tasks (e.g. breaking asphalt with a road breaker) should be done. This should include duration and frequency of the task.
- A purchasing policy to include consideration of vibration and, where necessary, vibration isolating devices should be established.
- All exposed workers should be trained in the proper use of tools and techniques to minimise exposure.
- A routine health surveillance programme should be established. Workers should be trained to recognise the early symptoms of HAVS and WBV and how to report them.
- Tools should be maintained to their optimum performance thereby reducing vibration to a minimum (e.g. the bearings of grinders).
- A continuous review with regard to the redesigning of tools, rescheduling work methods, or automating the process until such time as the risks associated with vibration are under control.
- As with any management system, the controls in place for vibration should include audit and review.

Employers must provide information, instruction and training to all workers who are exposed to risk from vibration and their representatives. This includes any organisational and technical measures taken, exposure limits and values, risk assessment findings, why and how to detect injury, entitlement to and collective results of health surveillance and safe working practices. Information, instruction and training shall be updated to take account of changes in the employer's work or methods. The employer should ensure all persons, whether or not a worker, who carries out work in connection with the employer's duties have been provided with information, instruction and training.

Health surveillance

Health surveillance must be carried out if there is a risk to the health of workers liable to be exposed to vibration. This is in order to prevent or diagnose any health effect linked with exposure to vibration. A record of health should be kept of any worker who undergoes health surveillance. The employer should, providing reasonable notice is given, provide the worker with access to their health records and provide copies to an enforcing officer on request.

If health surveillance identifies a disease or adverse health effect, considered by a doctor or other occupational health professional to be a result of exposure to vibration, the employer should ensure that a qualified person informs the worker and provides information and advice. The employer should ensure workers are kept informed of any significant findings from health surveillance, taking into account any medical confidentiality. In addition the employer should also:

- Review risk assessments.
- Review the measures taken to comply.
- Consider assigning the worker to other work.
- Review the health of any other worker who has been similarly exposed and consider alternative work.

7.5 - Heat and radiation

Temperature

The body generates heat energy by the conversion of foodstuffs; energy is generated through muscle action. At rest, typically 80 watts of energy is produced, whereas during heavy physical exercise perhaps 500 watts is produced. The body loses (exchanges) heat energy by the process of sweat evaporation, conduction contact of the feet with the floor and by radiation (infra red energy loss).

EXTREMES OF TEMPERATURE

Exposure to the effects of cold temperature relies on high calorie diet, physical exercise and suitable protective clothing. Clothing should have a high tog rating of 20 - 25 tog, and prevent absorption of water and be suitably fastened to reduce the effects of wind chill.

The feet should be insulated to avoid loss through conduction. The head should be covered to the maximum extent to avoid excessive heat loss. Clothing should be light and white in colour to prevent heat loss through radiation.

Exposure to the effects of heat may be minimised by suitable clothing, such as light and loose or reflective clothing if working with very hot sources of heat. Issues such as conduction from hot surfaces and movement of heat will need to be considered. Consideration will also need to be given to humidity levels and workload.

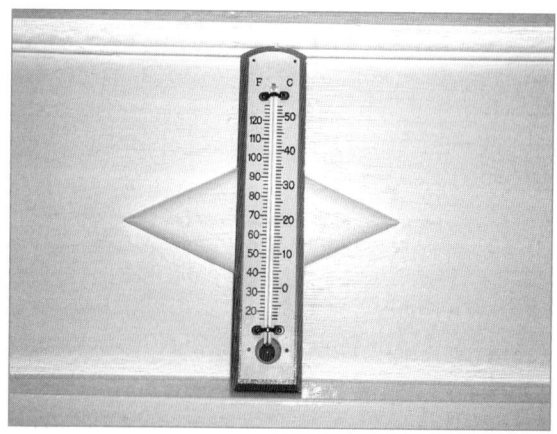

Figure 2-7-20: Workplace temperature.   Source: ACT.

EFFECTS

People working outside their thermal comfort range can suffer a dramatic loss of efficiency e.g. hot metal process working, working in refrigerated warehouses, working outdoors. The precise effects will depend upon the type of work being carried out, the rate of air movement (wind chill) and temperature and humidity. The main effects of working at high and low temperatures are outlined as follows:

General effects

Cold
- Loss of concentration in mental work.
- Reduced manipulative powers in manual work.
- Discomfort caused by shivering.

Hot
- Loss of concentration.
- Reduced activity rate.
- Discomfort caused by sweating.

Heat stress

Heat syncope	-	fainting due to vasodilatation.
Heat rash or 'prickly heat'	-	skin disorder.
Heat exhaustion	-	fatigue, nausea, headache, giddiness.
Anhidrotic heat exhaustion	-	insufficient moisture to sweat.
Heat cramps	-	painful spasms of muscles - insufficient salt.
Heat stroke	-	breakdown of control mechanisms, body temperatures soar, immediate cooling of body temperature required, otherwise death ensues.

Cold

- Hypothermia.
- Frost bite.
- Trench foot.
- Violent shivering.

RELEVANT FACTORS

One of the fundamental mechanisms by which the body regulates its temperature is by perspiration. Key factors which aid or hinder this process are airflow and humidity. Humidity relates to the moisture content in the air. Air with a relatively high humidity has little capacity to cool the body by 'wicking' away sweat whereas low relative humidity can cause dry skin and has been identified as a possible factor in facial dermatitis (occasional itching or reddened skin) reported by some Display Screen Equipment (DSE) users. Industries and occupations particularly susceptible to extremes of temperature include foundries, cold stores, those who carry out hot work (e.g. burning and welding) or work in confined spaces where temperatures are often uncomfortably high. Likewise, those who work outdoors can be subject to extreme weather conditions. In winter the strength of the wind can significantly effect the temperature (wind-chill).

PREVENTIVE MEASURES

Steps that workers should consider to reduce the effects of extremes of temperature should include: regular work breaks with fluid intake. Improved ventilation and humidity control, screening, suitable clothing. In the case of cold stores, removal of ice, improved lighting and the provision of anti-locking devices.

Ionising and non-ionising radiation

IONISING RADIATION

Radiation is emitted by a wide range of sources and appliances used throughout industry, medicine and research. It is also a naturally occurring part of the environment.

All matter is composed of **atoms**. Different atomic structures give rise to unique **elements**. Examples of common elements, which form the basic structure of life, are hydrogen, oxygen and carbon.

Atoms form the building blocks of nature and cannot be further sub divided by chemical means. The centre of the atom is called the **nucleus**, which consists of **protons** and **neutrons**. Electrons take up orbit around the nucleus.

Protons   -   Have a unit of mass and carry a positive electrical charge.

Neutrons -   These also have mass but no charge.

Electrons   -   Have a mass about 2,000 times less than that of protons and carry a negative charge.

In an electrically neutral atom the number of electrons equals the number of protons (the positive and negative charges cancel out each other). If the atom loses an electron then a positively charged atom is created. The process of losing or gaining electrons is called *ionisation*. If the matter which is ionised is a human cell, the cell chemistry will change and this will lead to functional changes in the body tissue. Some cells can repair radiation damage, others cannot. The cell's sensitivity to radiation is directly proportional to its rate of cell production; bone marrow, and reproductive organs with a high rate of cell production are the most vulnerable.

"Ionising radiation is that radiation which has sufficient energy to produce ions by interacting with matter".

Figure 2-7-21: Ionising radiation. Source: ACT.

Ionising radiations found in industry are alpha, beta and gamma, and X-rays. Whilst X-rays may occur in nature generally they are created in the work place either with knowledge, e.g. X-ray machines or sometimes without knowledge from high voltage equipment. The human body absorbs radiation readily from a wide variety of sources, mostly with adverse effects.

Types of ionising radiation

(**Note**. For the purpose of the NEBOSH International General Certificate you do not need to understand the differences between types of ionising radiation).

There are a number of different types of ionising radiation each with their different powers of penetration and effects on the body. Therefore, the type of radiation will determine the type and level of protection.

Alpha particles

Are comparatively large. Alpha particles travel short distances in dense materials, and can only just penetrate the skin. The principal risk is through ingestion or inhalation of a source e.g. radon gas an alpha particles emitter which might place the material close to vulnerable tissue; when this happens the high localised energy effect will destroy adjacent tissue of the organ/s affected.

Beta particles

Are much faster moving than alpha particles. They are smaller in mass than alpha particles, but have longer range, so they can damage and penetrate the skin. Whilst they have greater penetrating power than alpha particles, beta particles are less ionising and take longer to effect the same degree of damage.

Gamma rays

Have great penetrating power. Gamma radiation passing through a normal atom will sometimes force the loss of an electron, leaving the atom positively charged; this is called an *ion*.

X-rays

Are very similar in their effects to gamma rays. X-rays are produced by sudden acceleration or deceleration of a charged particle, usually when high-speed electrons strike a suitable target under controlled conditions. The electrical potential required to accelerate electrons to speeds where X-ray production will occur is a minimum of **15,000 volts**. X-rays and gamma rays have **high energy**, and **high penetration** power through fairly dense material. In low density substances, including air, they may travel long distances.

Potential health effects

The effects on the body of exposure to ionising radiation will depend on the type of radiation, the frequency and duration of exposure. Acute effects will include nausea, vomiting, diarrhoea and burns (either superficial skin burns or deep, penetrating burns causing cell damage). Long term (chronic) effects such as dermatitis, skin ulcers, cataracts and cancers can also be expected.

NON IONISING RADIATION

Generally, non-ionising radiation does not possess sufficient energy to cause the ionisation of matter. Radiation of this type includes ultraviolet, visible, infra-red, micro and radio waves. Artificially produced laser beams are a special case.

Types of non-ionising radiation

Ultraviolet

Possible sources

There are many possible sources of Ultra Violet (UV) radiation to which people may be exposed at work:

- The sun.
- Electric arc welding.
- Insect killers.
- Forgery detectors.
- Some lasers.
- Mercury vapour lamps.

- Sunbeds and sunlamps.
- Crack detection equipment.
- Tanning and curing equipment.
- Tungsten halogen lamps.

Potential effects

Much of the natural ultraviolet in the atmosphere is filtered out by the ozone layer. Sufficient penetrates to cause sunburn and even blindness.

Its effect is thermal and photochemical, producing burns and skin thickening, and eventually skin cancer. Electric arcs and ultraviolet lamps can produce an effect by absorption on the conjunctiva of the eyes, resulting in photo-kerititis ("arc-eye") and cataract formation.

Visible light (including lasers)

Possible sources

Any high intensity source of visible light can cause problems. Lasers are an obvious danger but so are light beams, powerful light bulbs and the sun. The danger is always due to direct or reflected radiation.

Potential health effects

Light in the visible frequency range can cause damage if it is present in sufficiently intense form. The eyes are particularly vulnerable but skin tissue may also be damaged. Indirect danger may also be created by workers being temporarily dazzled.

Figure 2-7-22: UV - from welding. *Source: Speedy Hire Plc.*

Infra-red

Possible sources

Anything that glows is likely to be a source of IR radiation, for example:
- Furnaces or fires.
- Molten metal or glass.
- Burning or welding.
- Heat lamps.
- Some lasers.
- The sun.

Potential health effects

Exposure results in a thermal effect such as skin burning and loss of body fluids (heat exhaustion and dehydration). The eyes can be damaged in the cornea and lens which may become opaque (cataract). Retinal damage may also occur if the radiation is focused.

Radio-frequency and microwaves

Possible sources

This type of radiation is produced by radio/television transmitters. It is used industrially for induction heating of metals and is often found in intruder detectors.

Potential health effects

Burns can be caused if persons using this type of equipment allow parts of the body which carry jewellery to enter the radio frequency field. Intense fields at the source of transmitters will damage the body and particular precautions need to be taken to isolate radio/television transmitters to protect maintenance workers. Microwaves can produce the same deep heating effect in live tissue as they can produce in cooking.

Figure 2-7-23: Radio mast. *Source: ACT.*

International Commission on Radiological Protection (ICRP) recommendations on dose limits

Recommendations made by the International Commission on Radiological Protection (ICRP) take account of current biological and physical information and trends in the setting of radiation standards. The three basic principles of radiological protection are still justification of activities that could cause or affect radiation exposures, optimisation of protection in order to keep doses as low as reasonably achievable, and the use of dose limits. The recommendations give emphasis to protection of the environment, and provide a platform for developing an updated strategy for handling emergency situations and situations of pre-existing radiation exposures.

Typical occupational sources of ionising and non-ionising radiation

SOURCES OF IONISING RADIATION

The most familiar examples of ionising radiation in the workplace are in hospitals, dentist surgeries and veterinary surgeries where X-rays are used extensively. X-ray machines are used for security purposes at baggage handling points in airports. In addition, Gamma rays are used in non-destructive testing of metals, for example, site radiography of welds in pipelines.

In other industries ionising radiation is used for measurement, for example, in the paper industry for measuring the thickness of paper, and in the food processing industry for measuring the contents of sealed tins.

SOURCES OF NON-IONISING RADIATION

- Ultra-violet.
    - The sun.
    - Arc welding and cutting.
    - Adhesive curing processes.
    - Water treatment.
- Microwave.
    - Telecommunications.
    - Cooking equipment.
- Visible radiation.
    - Lasers, for example, in surveying or level alignment equipment.
    - Other high intensity lights such as photocopiers and printers.
- Radio frequency.
    - Overhead power lines.
    - Plastic welding.
    - High powered transmitters.

Basic radiation protection and control strategies

CONTROLS FOR IONISING RADIATION

Preventive measures

Reduced time

Reducing the duration of exposure through redesigning work patterns. Giving consideration to shift working, job rotation etc. The dose received will depend upon the time of the exposure. These factors must be taken into account when devising suitable operator controls.

Increased distance

Radiation intensity is subject to the inverse square law. Energy received *(dose)* is inversely proportional to the square of the distance from the source.

Shielding

The type of shielding required to give adequate protection will depend on the penetration power of the radiation involved. For example, it may vary from thin sheets of silver paper to protect from Beta particles through to several centimetres of concrete and lead for protection against Gamma or X-rays. In addition to the previous specific controls, the following general principles must be observed:

- Radiation should only be introduced to the work place if there is a positive benefit.
- Safety information must be obtained from suppliers about the type(s) of radiation emitted or likely to be emitted by their equipment.
- Safety procedures must be reviewed regularly.
- Protective equipment provided must be suitable and appropriate, as required by relevant Regulations. It must be checked and maintained regularly.
- Emergency plans must cover the potential radiation emergency.
- Written authorisation by permit should be used to account for all purchase/use, storage, transport and disposal of radioactive substances.

Precautionary measures

Basic radiation protection strategies include the application of the principles of time, distance and shielding. Exposure should be limited to as few as possible and those individuals should be monitored and exposure levels maintained within limits. Where possible only sealed sources should be used and a system developed to minimise dose levels to individuals. This work must be under the control of the radiation protection advisor.

Figure 2-7-24: Personal dose monitor. *Source: ACT.*

Figure 2-7-25: Contamination monitoring. *Source: ACT.*

CONTROLS FOR NON-IONISING RADIATION

Ultra-violet

Protection is relatively simple; outdoor workers may use simple barrier creams. That emitted from industrial processes can be isolated by physical shielding such as partitions or plastic curtains; some plastic materials differ in their absorption abilities and care needs to be taken in selection. Users of emitting equipment, such as welders, can protect themselves by the use of goggles and protective clothing - the latter to avoid similar effects to "sunburn". Welding assistants often fail to appreciate the extent of their own exposure, and require similar protection.

Visible light

Is detected by the eye which has two protective control mechanisms, the eyelid and the iris. These are normally sufficient, as the eyelid has a reaction of 150 milliseconds. There are numerous sources of high-intensity light in workplaces which could produce damage or damaging distraction, and sustained glare may also cause eye fatigue and headaches. Basic precautions include confinement of high-intensity sources, matt finishes to nearby paint-work, and provision of optically-correct protective glasses for outdoor workers in snow, sand or near large bodies of water.

Infra-red

Radiation problems derive from thermal effects and include burning to the skin, sweating and loss of body salts leading to cramps, exhaustion and heat stroke. Clothing and gloves will protect the skin, but the hazard should be recognised so that effects can be minimised without recourse to personal protective equipment.

Radio-frequency and microwaves

Radiation can usually be shielded to protect the users. If size and function prohibits this, restrictions on entry and working near an energised microwave device will be needed. Metals, tools, flammable and explosive materials should not be left in the electromagnetic field generated by microwave equipment. Appropriate warning devices should be part of the controls for each such appliance.

7.6 - Stress

When individuals experience too much work load without the opportunity to recover they start to experience stress. Employers have a duty to assess the risk to their workers from work-related stress to protect their health, safety and welfare.

Causes of stress

Six key risk factors that can be the causes of work related stress have been identified. Dealing with each factor forms the basis of management standards introduced to help employers devise prevention strategies.

Demand

This includes issues like workload and work patterns - where an individual cannot cope with the demands of the job, and the work environment itself. Typical environmental stressors are:

- Bodily injury.
- Noise.
- Extremes of temperature.
- Poor lighting.

Control

If an individual worker has little control over the pace and manner of their work stress may result as a consequence of anxiety from perceived poor performance. For example, undertaking new or difficult work without first achieving the appropriate skills to complete the task successfully or safely.

Support

If an individual worker perceives a lack of encouragement, sponsorship or resources provided by the organisation, line management and colleagues, a feeling of remoteness and low esteem can be created.

Relationships

This includes issues with conflict and unacceptable behaviour between individuals, such as bullying at work or harassment.

Role

If individuals do not understand their role within the organisation or have been allocated conflicting roles then this can increase the potential for stress.

Change

If the management of organisational change in an organisation is not conducted or communicated well, individuals can be confused and concerned for their future employment.

Effects of stress

Being exposed to stressful situations brings about changes in behaviour and also physical well being,

Physical effects
- Increased heart rate.
- Increased sweating.
- Headache.
- Dizziness.
- Blurred vision.
- Aching neck and shoulders.
- Skin rashes.
- Lowered resistance to infection.

Behavioural effects
- Increased anxiety.
- Irritability.
- Increased alcohol intake.
- Increased smoking.
- Erratic sleep patterns.
- Poor concentration.
- Feeling of inability to cope with everyday tasks.

This can result in
- Lack of motivation.
- Lack of commitment.
- Poor timekeeping.
- Increase in mistakes.
- Increase in sickness absence.
- Poor decision making.
- Poor planning.

Stress is reflected in relationships at work as
- Tension between colleagues/supervisors.
- Poor service to clients.
- Deterioration in industrial relations.
- Increase in disciplinary problems.

Prevention strategies

GENERAL MANAGEMENT AND CULTURE

The organisation should ensure:

- Workers are provided with adequate and achievable demands in relation to the hours of work and breaks.
- Workers are consulted over their work patterns.
- Workers' concerns about their work environment are addressed.
- Where deficient, workers are encouraged to develop their skills.
- Policies and procedures to adequately support workers.
- Workers are aware of the probable impact of any changes to their jobs and if necessary, workers are given training to support any changes in their jobs.

Job design

The organisation should ensure:

- Jobs are designed to be within the capabilities of workers.
- Individual skills, abilities and capabilities are matched to the job demands.
- Workers know how to access the required resources to do their job.

Relationships at work

The organisation should ensure that:

- Positive behaviour at work is promoted to avoid conflict and ensure fairness.
- Workers share information relevant to their work.
- Policies and procedures to prevent or resolve unacceptable behaviour are in place.
- Different requirements it places upon workers are compatible.

7.7 - Violence at work

Risk factors

People who deal directly with the public may face aggressive or violent behaviour. They may be verbally abused, threatened or even physically attacked. In addition, it is necessary to consider possible violence between workers. Construction activities can carry quite a lot of pressure to conduct work within strict, often pressured, timetables. This can lead to increased tension that might result in violence.

> "any incident in which a person is abused, threatened or assaulted in circumstances relating to their work".

Figure 2-7-26: Definition of work related violence. Source: HSE.

Verbal abuse and threats are the most common types of incident. Physical attacks are comparatively rare. Those most at risk are employed in caring, education, cash handling, representing authority.

Find out if you have a problem
- Ask staff informally through managers and safety representatives.
- Keep detailed records.
- Classify all incidents according to their severity of outcome.
- Try to predict what might happen.

Prevention strategies

Decide what action to take
- Decide who might be harmed and how. Who is most vulnerable? Where appropriate identify potentially violent people in advance.
- Evaluate the risk. Check existing arrangements. Train your workers to recognise early signs of violence.
- Provide information - case histories, etc.
- Improve the environment - better seating, lighting, etc.
- Improve security - video cameras, coded locks, wider/higher counters.
- Redesign the job - use credit cards rather than cash, bank money more frequently, check arrangements for lone workers.
- Arrange safe transport or secure car parking for people who work late at night.

Take action
The policy for dealing with violence should be written into the safety policy statement so that all workers are aware of it. This will encourage workers to co-operate with the policy and report further incidents.

Check what you have done
Check regularly to see if the arrangements are working by consulting workers and safety representatives. If violence is still a problem, go back to stages one and two.

What about the victims
If there is a violent incident involving your workplace you might like to consider the following:

- Debriefing   - victims might need to talk through their experience as soon as possible.
- Time off work   - individuals may need differing times to recover. In some cases they might need counselling.
- Legal help   - legal assistance may be appropriate in serious cases.
- Other workers   - may need guidance or counselling to help them react appropriately.

Source: HSE INDG69 (rev).

7.8 - Effects on health and safety of alcohol and drugs

Health and safety of alcohol and drugs

EFFECTS

Alcohol and drugs are becoming increasingly commonplace in society. People who start consuming alcohol or drugs usually have a nil or low dependency and do so for recreational reasons. This however can escalate quickly into abuse when larger quantities of alcohol are consumed more frequently and become habitual. The effects of alcohol or drugs can vary dependant upon the individual's state of health and fitness, and resilience to the chemicals. Alcohol and drugs can remain in the body for a considerable time after consumption and its effects still be present the next day when at work. Effects on health and safety include:

- Poor co-ordination and balance.
- Perception ability reduced.
- Overall state of poor health including fatigue, poor concentration and stress.
- Poor attitude, lack of adherence to rules, violence to fellow workers.

CONTROL STRATEGIES

The use of alcohol and drugs is a personal choice over which workers usually have little or no control. However employers should have a policy to deal with the issue should it start to impact on the workers' performance at work.

Control strategies often start with the identification of safety critical work, where the influence of drugs and alcohol would have a significant effect. It is usual that strategies do not presume use or non-use of drugs and alcohol for those that conduct safety critical work, treating them all equally. In a simple approach all workers that come on to a construction site might be considered to be in safety critical work. All would work to the same rules banning them being under the influence while at work and offering them opportunities to talk to someone about how this affects them, coupled with carrying out random drugs and alcohol tests. When accidents occur it is common to consider drugs and alcohol as factors. It may not always be possible to test an injured party for causing their own accident by being under the influence of drugs and alcohol, but it may be possible to test a driver of a dumper truck that ran into someone for example.

Element 8

Construction activities - hazards and control

Learning outcomes

On completion of this element, candidates should be able to demonstrate understanding of the content through the application of knowledge to familiar and unfamiliar situations. In particular they should be able to:

8.1 Identify the main hazards of construction and demolition work and outline the general requirements necessary to control them.

8.2 Identify the hazards of work at height, outline the general requirements necessary to control them and describe the safe working practices for common forms of access equipment.

8.3 Identify the hazards of excavations and outline the general requirements necessary to control them.

8.4 Identify the hazards to health commonly encountered in small construction activities and explain how risks might be reduced.

Content

8.1 - General construction hazards and control	245
Scope of the term construction	245
Safe stacking and storage of materials and flammable substances	245
Main construction and demolition hazards and controls	246
Management controls for significant construction projects	249
8.2 - Working above ground level	251
Typical activities and injuries associated with falls from height	251
Basic hazards of work above ground level	251
Methods of avoiding working at height	252
Main precautions necessary to prevent falls and falling material	252
Requirements for head protection	254
Safe working practices for common forms of access equipment	255
Inspection requirements for work equipment	263
8.3 - Excavations	264
The hazards of work in and around excavations	264
Precautions for working in and around excavations	265
Inspection requirements for excavations	268
8.4 - Health hazards commonly encountered in construction activities	269
Identification and control of common health hazards	269
Health surveillance	272

Sources of reference

Safety and Health in Construction Convention (C167), ILO
Safety and Health in Construction Recommendation (R175), ILO
Safety and Health in Construction (ILO Code of Practice), ILO ISBN 92-2-107104-9
Health and Safety in Construction (HSG150), 3rd Edition HSE Books ISBN 0-7176-2106-5

8.1 - General construction hazards and control

Scope of the term construction

CONSTRUCTION WORK

The term **"construction work"** is quite wide ranging and involves the carrying out of any **building**, civil engineering or engineering construction work and includes the following:

- The **construction**, alteration, conversion, fitting out, commissioning, renovation, repair, upkeep, redecoration or other **maintenance** (including cleaning which involves the use of water or an abrasive at high pressure or the use of substances classified as corrosive or toxic, de-commissioning, **demolition** or dismantling of a *structure*).
- The preparation for an intended *structure*, including site clearance, exploration, investigation (but not site survey) and excavation and laying the foundations of the *structure*.
- The assembly of prefabricated (pre-built) elements to form a *structure* or the disassembly of prefabricated elements which, immediately before such disassembly, formed a *structure*.
- The removal of a *structure* or part of a *structure*, or of any product or waste resulting from demolition or dismantling of a *structure* or from disassembly of prefabricated elements which, immediately before such disassembly, formed a *structure*.
- The installation, commissioning, maintenance, repair or removal of mechanical, electrical, gas, compressed air, hydraulic, telecommunications, computer or similar services which are normally fixed within or to a *structure*.

Safe stacking and storage of materials and flammable substances

A construction site is continually changing with a variety of activities being conducted at once as well as workers and materials being moved around. For this reason, it is critical that the site is kept tidy. Safe stacking and storage of materials used in construction can help to keep the vehicle and pedestrian routes clear and keep the materials themselves from causing harm, e.g. prevent tripping over bricks, or chemical burns from spilt cement.

STACKING

Stacking should not be so high or leaning that it poses a risk of toppling over and crushing someone. A number of workers have been killed on construction sites in this way.

Generally, stacking should be kept small with the goods on pallets that are in good repair. Boxes that can be crushed and bags of free-flowing solid should **never** be stacked on each other and should always be palletised. Different types of container should be stacked separately.

The stack should not be placed so that it blocks fire points, extinguishers or blocks out the light. It should not be placed on soft ground or floors that may not be strong enough to support it.

The stack should not be placed near vehicle routes to avoid vehicles hitting them as they pass or turn.

Workers should be trained on the correct way to remove items from the stack and the dangers associated with leaving an unsafe stack. They should be instructed to never climb up the stack or stand on the top of it.

Figure 2-8-1: Storage of materials. *Source: ACT.*

Figure 2-8-2: Poor storage of ladder and scaffold. *Source: ACT.*

STORAGE

The storage of materials is dependent on the type of material to be stored.

Different contents should be stored apart as a liquid may spill and contaminate a powder, or worse, it may set off a chemical reaction. Even if mixed storage is possible, different materials should be kept apart for ease of access.

The storage area should be designed to allow access by fork lift trucks (FLTs) as well as workers. It should be kept tidy and suitably lit and ventilated. There should be suitable fire precautions, e.g. appropriate extinguisher.

It should not be used for any other purposes such as mixing or as a rest room or smoking room.

The storage area should be protected against unauthorised use and should have the correct signage, e.g. warning of any dangers or the mandatory wearing of personal protective equipment (PPE).

STORAGE OF FLAMMABLE SUBSTANCES

Substances should be stored in such a way that they cannot

1) Escape and contaminate personnel or the environment.
2) Interact with other substances causing explosion, fire or dangerous fumes.

Requirements for storage

1) Store small quantities only in the workplace.
2) Small quantities of flammables should be stored in clearly marked flameproof metal containers.
3) Non-compatible chemicals should be stored apart.
4) Chemicals giving off fumes should be stored and used in a fume cupboard.
5) Chemicals should be stored away from sources of heat, possibly refrigerated.
6) Bulk storage should be outside away from other buildings and sources of heat, including sunlight.

Features of a bulk flammable substance store

1) Single storey, light construction in non-combustible materials.
2) Flame proof electrics.
3) Door sill (seal) and perimeter bunding (retaining perimeter wall) for containment of up to 110% of the chemical. It is good practice for the secondary containment system to provide storage of at least 110% of the tank's maximum capacity. If more than one container is stored, the system should be capable of storing 110% of the biggest container's capacity or 25% of the total tank capacity within the bund, whichever is the greater.
4) Interceptor pits (multi level weir or filter system for separating and capturing pollutants) for spillage.

Main hazards and controls relating to construction and demolition

MACHINERY AND VEHICLES

Machinery can vary in size and can range from a small circular saw to large earthmovers. Hazards include the mechanical type: impact with the machine, entanglement with moving parts, cuts and amputation from blades, and the non-mechanical type: dust, vibration, electricity and noise.

Machinery on a construction site may have to withstand rough treatment and therefore needs to be robust in construction and well maintained. It must be suitable for use and not used for a task for which it was not intended, e.g. the misuse of a circular saw for cross cutting. All dangerous parts of the machine must be guarded so far as is practicable. Work on a machine that produces dust or noise should be isolated and where this is not possible, ear defenders and respiratory protective equipment should be used.

Anyone using machinery must be competent in its use and therefore know when not to use and how to report any defect.

Plant such as cranes, dumper trucks and diggers and vehicles such as lorries, fork lift trucks and cement mixers are hazards mostly because of their size. They operate on uneven and sometimes soft terrain where space to manoeuvre is limited. Lifting machines may overbalance and fall over, vehicles may collide with other vehicles, workers or structures and they are usually difficult to park and store.

The site should be organised and clearly marked so that there is a clear segregation of workers and vehicles. There should be space for parking and care taken so that the vehicle cannot move once parked up, (brakes should be on), vehicles should not be moved by an unauthorised person, (key control system). Banksmen or traffic marshals should be employed to help with the movement of the plant or vehicles when visibility is poor or manoeuvring space is limited.

All plant and vehicles must be properly maintained and operators trained and licensed in their use.

There should be site rules for the movement, use and parking of vehicles which should be strictly adhered to.

Figure 2-8-3: Unauthorised access. *Source: ACT.*

Figure 2-8-4: Perimeter fencing and signs. *Source: ACT.*

SITE SECURITY

Perimeter fencing

Construction sites must be contained within a perimeter fence. The main purpose of fencing is to keep out unauthorised persons (e.g. members of the public and children) and to prevent injury or death. Perimeter fencing also provides security against theft of materials, plant or equipment from the site. Fences should be adequate and suitable and installed at a reasonable distance from the structure to allow unrestricted movement on site of workers and mobile plant, and prevent any activities being undertaken affecting the environment outside the fence. The fence should be regularly inspected to ensure there is no damage, breaks or gaps to allow unauthorised entry.

Signs

Signs should be fixed at regular intervals on the perimeter fence to warn of the dangers within the site and instruct people to 'keep out'. Quite often, the name of the security company that is responsible for 'out of hours' security will also be displayed with a telephone number for emergency contact or to report any trespass.

Safe viewing points

Members of the public are quite often intrigued by construction sites and can be attracted to the perimeter fence to see for themselves what is going on. This may result in injury from flying particles, dust, fumes or splashes, even though the person is outside the perimeter fence. This can be avoided by arranging for a pre-planned viewing point that consists of a wire mesh panel integrated into the fence that allows members of the public to view the site's activities. The viewing point will be planned and situated in an area that is not exposed to hazards.

Means of securing plant, materials and chemicals

Plant, equipment, materials and chemicals should be suitably secured to prevent injury by unauthorised access. Plant should be locked up at all times when not in use and keys held in a secure location (site office, safe). It may be practical to house plant in an additional internal site compound. In order to improve security certain items of heavy mobile plant are provided with steel sheets or shutters fitted around the cab and padlocked in position.

Means of controlling environmental dangers on public highways

Areas that surround a construction site are subject to mud and debris from the tyres and chassis of vehicles that frequent the site, which creates additional hazards to other road users as highway surfaces become slippery and create skid hazards. This can be controlled by the implementation of regular highway cleaning with road sweeper vehicles. Action can also be taken at site exits prior to vehicles leaving the site by routing site traffic through a tyre and undercarriage cleaning system, which assists in preventing mud and debris leaving the site.

ELECTRICITY

Electric shock and burns can occur from using unsafe equipment or contact with overhead electric lines and buried cables.

Overhead power lines - controls

- Isolate the supply (usually conducted by the electricity provider).
- Erect 'goal-post' barriers to define clearance distances.
- Clearly mark danger zones with signs and/or bunting (demarcation streamer).
- Ensure safe access under lines.
- Use banksmen or marshals where appropriate.
- Restrict the use of metal equipment such as ladders and scaffolds (temporary building and worker support structures).

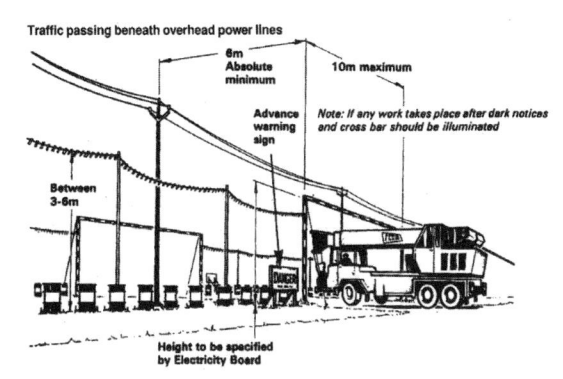

Figure 2-8-5: Traffic passing beneath power lines.   *Source: HSG 144.*

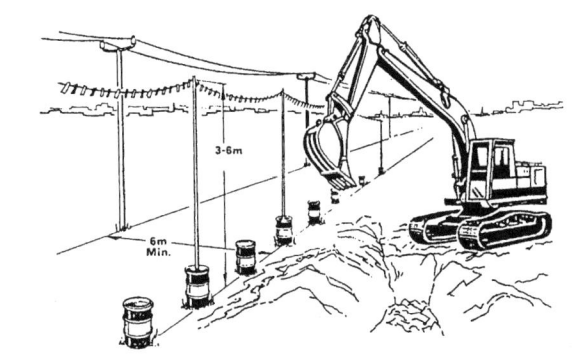

Figure 2-8-6: Working near power lines.   *Source: HSG 144.*

UNIT IGC2 - ELEMENT 8 - CONSTRUCTION ACTIVITIES - HAZARDS AND CONTROL

WORKING AT A HEIGHT

Falling objects
- Poor housekeeping of workers working above.
- Absence of toe boards or edge protection.
- Incorrect hooking and slinging.
- Incorrect assembly of pulley wheels (sometimes known as gin wheels or jenny wheels) for raising materials.
- Surplus materials incorrectly stacked.
- Open, unprotected edges.
- Deterioration of structures causing crumbling masonry.

Falls from height
- Pitched roofs that are wet or covered in moss growth.
- Failure to cover openings (e.g. skylights).
- Roof unable to support person and/or equipment.
- Wrong footwear.
- Extreme weather conditions such as high winds.
- Insufficient or inappropriate edge protection.

Figure 2-8-7: Risk of falling objects.   Source: ACT.

Figure 2-8-8: Risk of workers falling.   Source: ACT.

Ladders
- Slipping outwards at base.
- Defective or rotten wooden ladders.
- Overreaching when working at the top of a ladder.
- Insecurely tied to structure.
- Lack of handholds to alight from ladder to landing.
- Too close or too far away from wall (incorrect angle).
- Overhead obstructions. Pay special attention to electricity when using aluminium or ladders.
- Unsound ground conditions.

EXCAVATIONS
- Adverse weather (flooding).
- Gas accumulation.
- Collapse.
- Instability of adjacent buildings.
- Underground services.
- Falling objects (e.g. spoil).
- Traffic.

Figure 2-8-9: Ladder too long.   Source: ACT.

DEMOLITION

Hazards

Demolition is probably the most hazardous operation undertaken in the construction industry. The principal hazards are:

- Falls of workers, falls of materials, flying materials, dust and debris, resulting in a wide range of injuries and conditions, some of which are of a fatal nature.
- Collapse of a building or structure, either deliberately or unplanned.
- Overloading of floors or the structure with debris, resulting in floor and/or building collapse.
- Explosions in tanks or other confined spaces.
- Presence of live electric cable or gas mains.
- Presence of dusty, corrosive and poisonous materials and/or atmospheres.
- Projecting nails in timber, for example, broken glass and cast iron fragments, which can penetrate the hands, feet and parts of the body.

Figure 2-8-10: Excavation hazards.   Source: ACT.

Controls

Prior to demolition commencing
- A safe system of work must be established. In most cases, this would be done through a written method statement.

248   © ACT

- A pre-demolition survey which should identify:
  - Nature and method of construction of the building.
  - Arrangement of adjacent buildings.
  - Locations of underground services e.g. water mains, electricity cables for example.
  - Presence of dangerous substances inherent in the structure e.g. asbestos, or stored internally.
  - System of shoring or the provision of other support necessary during demolition.
- Local authorities and owners of adjacent properties must be notified and consulted.
- Services such as gas, water and electricity, must be isolated.
- A competent supervisor must be appointed.
- All dangerous areas, particularly those affecting members of the public, must be fenced off.
- Operators must be briefed that personal protective equipment, including safety helmets with chin straps, goggles, heavy duty gloves and safety boots with steel insoles, must be provided and worn. Adequate training must also be provided in the correct use of this equipment.

Figure 2-8-11: Pre-demolition survey required.   Source: ACT.

Figure 2-8-12: Site Signs.   Source: ACT.

During the demolition process
- Demolition should be carried out in the reverse order of erection of the building.
- No freestanding wall should be left on its own unless considered to be secure by the competent person.
- Scaffold working platforms should be used.
- Entrances, passages, stairs and ladder runs should be kept clear of all material.
- Disturbed staircases, particularly stone staircases, should not be used.
- Timber with protruding nails should have the nails removed.
- Glass in partitions, doors, roofs and windows should be removed separately.
- Adequate and suitable lighting should be provided.

Management controls for significant construction projects

(Measures should be taken to ensure that there is cooperation between employers and workers, in accordance with arrangements to be defined by national laws or regulations, in order to promote safety and health at construction sites).

National laws or regulations may also require that employers and self-employed persons have a duty to comply with the prescribed safety and health measures at the workplace.

GENERAL REQUIREMENTS

Contractors carrying out maintenance works are one of the main causes of accidents in industry. In general, visiting contractors are less familiar with the workplace and associated risks than the indigenous / local workforce yet often carry out operations more hazardous than those normally occurring there. In order to minimise the risk potential of such activities and to ensure that all concerned are made aware of their health and safety responsibilities, a detailed knowledge of relevant legislation is essential, risks must be identified and effective control methods introduced.

ASSESSMENT, SELECTION AND CONTROL OF CONTRACTORS

A control strategy for contractors

The main elements to a control strategy are:

Assessment
- Checking of the health and safety aspects / requirements of bids and selection of contractor.

Selection
- Contractor agrees to be subject to client's rules.

Control
- Control of the contractor on site.
- Checking after completion of contract.

The extent to which each element is relevant will depend upon the degree of risk and nature of work to be contracted.

Assessment

Acquiring the services of a competent contractor with relevant professional qualifications and a proven safety record is fundamental to any risk control programme. This should be a proactive exercise. As far as is possible the types of works and activities that are likely to involve contractors working in the premises should be identified, e.g. electrical, mechanical, gas, maintenance, for example. It will be possible from this to draw up a list of professionally suitably qualified contractors and carry out an investigation into their safety policies and their safety performance at previous locations. Employers should additionally check out their qualification to do the required works.

The employer should produce a pre-qualification questionnaire which should be completed by each contractor to assist in the vetting process. This could include the following:

- A copy of contractor's health and safety policy document.
- Details of any previous works carried out by the contractor.
- Details of any risk assessments which have been carried out and the risk control measures that have been introduced.
- References from previous employers of the contractor.
- Details of the contractor's emergency procedures for their workers, e.g. fire, accident, injury and first aid.
- The effect of contractor's works on the employer's workers and premises.
- The appointment of 'competent persons' to assist in health and safety matters.
- Details of health and safety training provided.
- Brief details of safe systems of work (e.g. permit-to-work).
- Brief details of how the contractor controls their sub-contractors.

Following the above exercise, a 'short-list' of competent contractors can be produced. This procedure could prove to be invaluable, as often the services of contractors are needed in emergency situations when sufficient time is not available to carry out these vetting procedures.

A checklist should be followed in order to define a specification for the contract; this will give a pointer to most if not all the common health and safety problems which may arise during the work. These should be communicated to the contractor in the specification before the bid is made, and the received bid checked against them to ensure that proper provision is being made for the control of risk and that the contractor has identified the hazards. Suitable headings for the checklist could include:

- Special hazards and applicable national or local Regulations and Codes of practice (asbestos, noise, permits to work).
- Safe access/egress to, from, on the site, and to places of work within the site.
- Buried and overhead services.
- Confined space entry.
- First-aid/emergency rescue.
- Welfare amenities.

Selection

When the bids are returned, it should be possible to distinguish the potentially competent at this stage. An 'approved list' of contractors, scrutinised at intervals, can save the need for carrying out a complete selection process as described on every occasion.

Before any contract work is commenced, a responsible person representing the main contractor must discuss with the occupier the health and safety precautions necessary as far as the contractor's workforce is concerned and any other parties on site.

A basic principle of control is that as much as possible should be set down in detail in the contract. A critical condition should be that the contractor agrees to abide by all the provisions of the client's safety policy, which may affect the contractor's workers or the work, including compliance with site health and safety rules.

Areas of concern, which should be covered by general site rules and within the client's safety policy, should be communicated to the contractor in the form of site rules.

They include:

- Materials storage, handling, disposal.
- Use of equipment which could cause fires.
- Noise and vibration.
- Scaffolding and ladders, access.
- Cartridge-powered fixing tools.
- Welding equipment - and use of client's electricity supply, for example.

Control

- Appointment/nomination of a person or team to co-ordinate all aspects of the contract, including health and safety matters.
- A pre-contract commencement meeting held with the contractor to review all safety aspects of the work.
- Control access to contractor work area.
- Arrangement of regular progress meetings between all parties, where health and safety is the first agenda item.
- Regular (at least weekly) inspections of the contractor's operations by the client.
- Participation in safety committees on site by contractors should be a condition of the contract.
- Provision by the contractor of risk assessments and/or written method statements in advance of undertaking particular work, as agreed.
- The formal reporting to the client by the contractor of all lost-time accidents and dangerous occurrences, including those to sub-contractors.
- The contractor should leave the work site clean and tidy, removing all waste, materials, tools and equipment. This should be checked.

8.2 - Working at height

Typical activities and injuries associated with falls from height

Falls are the most common cause of fatal injuries in the construction industry. They account for more than half of those accidentally killed each year. Much of the work carried out on a building site is done above ground at height, commonly more than 2 metres. Typical activities that involve working at height are:

- Steel erecting.
- Fixing of cladding, roof work.
- Painting and decorating.
- Demolition and dismantling.
- Bricklaying.
- Scaffold erection.
- Electrical installation and maintenance.

The risks of falls from height are substantial however long or short the work. Risks related to work activities at height are increased by the presence of fragile roofs, roof lights, voids, deteriorating materials and the weather. Some workers though, only rarely work at height. Such as:

- Welders.
- Inspectors.
- Machinery maintenance personnel.

This means that, workers with little or no experience may find themselves exposed to the dangers of working above ground level.

Basic hazards of work above ground level

VERTICAL DISTANCE

Though some construction work involves work activities to be carried out at a significant height, for example on a roof or scaffold it should not be assumed that work at less significant heights is without risk. Major injuries can occur if a fall results whilst carrying out tasks at a height of less than 2 metres, for example fitting false ceilings or installing utilities inside buildings. Above ground floor working, but below 2 metres represents significant risk and many injuries result each year as a result of such work.

ROOFS

Working on roofs carries a high risk of accidents, unless proper procedures and precautions are taken. The danger of workers or materials falling affects the safety of those working at height and those working beneath.

Particular danger arises from two types of roof - fragile roofs and sloping roofs.

Fragile roofs

Materials such as asbestos, cement, glass or plastic are likely to be unable to hold the weight of a person. Asbestos sheet deteriorates over time leaving the remaining material in a particularly fragile state. Though the sheet looks intact it will only have a small fraction of its original strength. In a similar way plastic roof material, such as may be used in roof lights, will be affected by exposure to sunlight leaving it brittle. It should not be assumed that it is safe to walk on newly installed roof material though it will have its original strength but this may not be enough to hold the weight of a worker. All fragile roofs and/or access routes to them should be marked with an appropriate warning sign, with guard rails or other means of fall protection in place.

Sloping roofs

Sloping roofs are those that exceed that prescribed by national laws or regulations for example a pitch greater than 10 degrees. Falls from the edge of sloping roofs can cause serious injury even when the eaves are relatively low. The hazard of sloping roofs is less obvious when the pitch is small causing workers to underestimate the possibility of workers sliding off the edge. The material and therefore the surface of the roof have a significant influence on the hazard, for example, a smooth sheet metal surface can present a significant hazard even when the pitch is small. The chances of an accident are increased when working on roofs that are wet or covered in moss growth and in extreme weather conditions such as high winds. The other significant influencing issue is the footwear used by the worker; smooth flat soled footwear may seem suitable in dry conditions but may not provide sufficient grip to deal with surface water in wet conditions. A build up of dry particles or grit on a roof can present a surface that leads to a high risk of slipping as the particles become free to move and form a mobile layer between the roof and the worker's foot.

DETERIORATION OF MATERIALS

The condition of the structure on which workers are working can deteriorate with time. The rate of deterioration will accelerate if the structure is exposed to adverse weather conditions (including extremes of temperature) or attack by chemicals, animals, insects, for example. It may be obvious that deterioration has occurred and is a factor to be considered at the time of pre work assessment.

UNPROTECTED EDGES

Roofs, scaffolds, unfinished steel work and access platforms may sometimes have open sides. This increases the likelihood of someone or something falling, particularly if workers have to approach them, work at them or pass by them repeatedly. It is very easy in these circumstances to lose perception of the hazard and forget that it is there. Errors, such as stepping back over an edge, overreaching, or being pushed over the edge whilst manoeuvring materials can easily lead to fatal falls.

UNSTABLE / POORLY MAINTAINED ACCESS EQUIPMENT

An employer having committed to providing access to a height by the provision of work equipment might yet have workers using it who are at risk from basic hazards relating to its stability and maintenance. Working with mobile elevated work platforms (MEWPs), ladders and scaffolds have their own specific stability and maintenance issues, the hazard of falling from a height whilst using them being the common theme. Each is influenced by the problem of the stability of the ground conditions they are placed on and the height they are used at compared to their stability base.

All equipment, access equipment being no exception, can fail if not properly maintained. Cracks may occur in the sides of ladders and loose rungs can lead to failure. They may warp or rot if left exposed to the elements. Defects in ladders may be hidden if they are painted or covered in plaster.

The effective working of the hydraulics of a MEWP is critical and failure to maintain this could lead to a sudden and catastrophic failure of the MEWP whilst it is extended. Scaffolds need periodic maintenance to ensure load bearing parts are still secured and those critical items such as brakes on mobile scaffolds are in place and effective. Failure to maintain them can quickly undermine the strength, integrity and stability of the scaffold leading to collapse or overturning.

WEATHER

Adverse weather can have a significant effect on the safety of those working at a height. Rain, snow and ice increase the risk of slips and falling from a roof. When handling large objects, such as roof panels, high winds can be a serious problem and may cause the person to be blown off the roof. Extremely cold temperatures can increase the likelihood of brittle failure of materials and therefore increase the likelihood of failure of roof supports, scaffold components and plastic roof lights.

In addition, moisture can freeze, increasing the slipperiness of surfaces and on many occasions the presence of ice is not easily visible. Workers exposed to the cold can lose their dexterity (feeling and grip) and when hot, sweat perspiration may cause them to lose their grip.

FALLING MATERIALS

Caused by:

- Poor housekeeping of workers working above.
- Absence of toe boards or edge protection.
- Incorrect hooking and slinging.
- Incorrect assembly of gin wheels for raising materials.
- Surplus materials incorrectly stacked.
- Open, unprotected edges.
- Deterioration of structures causing crumbling masonry.

Figure 2-8-13: Working above ground level.   Source: ACT.

The risk of falling materials causing injury should be minimised by keeping platforms clear of loose materials. In addition, methods provided should prevent materials or other objects rolling, or being kicked off the edges of platforms. This may be done with toe boards, solid barriers, brick guards, or similar being positioned at open edges. If working in a public place, nets, fans or covered walkways may be needed to give extra protection for people who may be passing below. High-visibility barrier netting is not suitable for use as a fall prevention device.

Materials such as old slates, tiles, for example. should not be thrown from the roof or scaffold - passers-by may be at risk of being injured. Enclosed debris chutes should be used or debris should be lowered in containers.

Methods of avoiding working at height

Where possible, work at height should be avoided by conducting the work at ground level. This could be achieved by using different equipment or method of work, for example the pre-assembly of roof trusses (roof support structures sometimes referred to as "A" frames), either before delivery or on the ground on site, instead of assembly at a height.

Good planning arrangements, considering how fixtures / fittings, plant and services can be designed or installed can be utilised to avoid the need to work at height both during construction and in ongoing cleaning or maintenance.

Main precautions necessary to prevent falls and falling material

PROPER PLANNING AND SUPERVISION OF WORK

Where work cannot safely be done from the ground or from the building or structure being worked on, there should always be suitable and sufficient scaffolding. This must be properly constructed of sound material which is of adequate strength to provide a safe means of access and a safe place of work.

Scaffolds should be erected, altered or dismantled only by competent persons.

After erection, scaffolds should be inspected at least once a week and a written report of each inspection kept.

Fall of people

Organisations should review work done to determine a response to the above requirements. This may affect those that fill equipment hoppers (bulk storage delivery vessels) located at height manually, requiring consideration of bulk delivery and automatic feed systems. Where workers have to lubricate or adjust equipment set at height by hand, options to automate or route the lubrication/adjustment mechanisms to ground level should be considered. If materials are pre-painted or pre-drilled this can greatly reduce the work needed to be done at height. Long reach handling devices can be used to allow cleaning or other tasks to be conducted from the ground. Where equipment, such as light units, requires maintenance, an option may be to lower it sufficiently to enable bulbs to be changed and cleaning to be conducted from the ground.

Fall of materials

Employers should take reasonably practicable steps to prevent injury to any person from the fall of any material or object; and where it is not reasonably practicable to do so, to take similar steps to prevent any person being struck by any falling material or object which is liable to cause personal injury. Also, that no material is thrown or tipped from height in circumstances where it is liable to cause injury to any person. Materials and objects must be stored in such a way as to prevent risk to any person arising from the collapse, overturning or unintended movement of the materials or objects.

Employers must ensure that where an area presents a risk of falling from height or being struck from an item falling at height, the area is equipped with devices preventing unauthorised persons from entering such areas and the area is clearly indicated.

AVOIDING WORKING IN ADVERSE WEATHER CONDITIONS

Adverse weather can include wind, rain, sun, cold, snow and ice. Each of these conditions, particularly in extreme cases, can present a significant hazard to construction work. When long term projects are planned methods are often adjusted to minimise the effects. For example, road and walk routes that could quickly be affected by rain are made up into formal structures by the use of hardcore, concrete and tarmac. Work areas can be covered over at an early stage to enable work to be conducted in relative comfort. In some cases it may be that work is organised in an order that predicts expected adverse weather, allowing tasks to be adjusted until short term weather conditions improve. In some cases adverse weather must be considered formally and work may have to cease until conditions improve, for example, work on a roof in icy conditions or high winds. Similar approaches may have to be taken for operating a mobile elevating work platform (MEWP) in windy conditions or another example may be when entering a sewer during a rain storm.

GUARDRAILS, FENCING AND TOEBOARDS

Guardrails are designed to prevent workers falling whilst toeboards prevent materials falling. Toeboards are usually planks laid on their edge to create a ledge which prevents rubble, tools and other materials from being kicked or knocked over the edge of the working platform. Brick guards, a form of fencing, provide more substantial protection to prevent larger amounts of material from falling and have the added advantage of providing protection for people or workers. It is advisable that these means of protection must:

- Be of sufficient dimensions, of sufficient strength and rigidity for the purposes for which they are being used, and otherwise suitable.
- Be so placed, secured and used as to ensure, so far as is reasonably practicable, that they do not become accidentally displaced.
- Be so placed as to prevent, so far as is practicable, the fall of any person, or of any material or object, from any place of work.

WORKING PLATFORMS

Any platform used as a place of work or as a means of access to or egress from a place of work may include any scaffold, suspended scaffold, cradle, mobile platform, trestle (a supporting framework consisting of a horizontal beam held up by a pair of splayed legs at each end), gangway, gantry and stairway which is so used.

Safety requirements that work platforms must fulfil are:

- Condition of surfaces on which the work platform rests.
- Stability of supporting structures.
- Stability of working platforms.
- Safety on working platforms.
- Safe loading of platforms.

The following practical precautions should also be considered:

- Wide enough - at least 2 feet (approximately 600 mm) wide - to allow workers to pass back and forth safely and to use any equipment or material necessary for their work at that place.
- Free of openings and traps through which worker's feet could pass and cause them to trip, fall or be injured in any other way.
- Constructed to prevent materials from falling. As well as toe boards or similar protection at the edge of the platform, the platform itself should be constructed to prevent any object which may be used on the platform from falling through gaps or holes, causing injury to workers working below. For scaffolds, a close-boarded platform would suffice, although for work over public areas, a double-boarded platform sandwiching a polythene sheet may be needed. If a Mobile Elevated Work Platform (MEWP) or cradle is used and it has meshed platform floors, the mesh should be fine enough to prevent materials, especially nails and bolts, from slipping through.
- Kept free of tripping and slipping hazards. Where necessary, handholds and footholds should be provided. Platforms should be clean, tidy and mud should not be allowed to build up on platforms.

ACCESS BOARDS

Roof ladders (or crawling boards) spread across the supporting structures distribute the weight over a greater area so that the load can be sustained by the roof. They also provide hand and foot holds and may be equipped with guard rails and toe boards.

PERSONAL PROTECTION SYSTEMS

Fall arrest harnesses are useful when other means of fall protection are not reasonably practicable, such as work where open edges exist during steel erection. The harness itself may cause injury when the person comes to a sudden stop, therefore inertia reel harnesses (the same principle as a car seat belt) may be preferable. When using harnesses in a mobile elevating work platform (MEWP), the harness should always be fixed to the *inside* of the cradle.

Personal fall protection system shall be used only if:

- A risk assessment has demonstrated that:
    - Work can, so far as is reasonably practicable, be performed safely while using that system.
    - Use of other safer work equipment is not reasonably practicable.
- The user and a sufficient number of available persons have received adequate training specific to the operations envisaged, including rescue procedures.

In addition a personal fall protection system shall:
- Be suitable and of sufficient strength for the purposes for which it is being used, having regard to the work being carried out and any foreseeable loading.
- Where necessary, fit the user.
- Be correctly fitted.
- Be designed to minimise injury to the user and, where necessary, be adjusted to prevent the user falling or slipping from it, should a fall occur.
- Be so designed, installed and used as to prevent unplanned or uncontrolled movement of the user.

FALL ARRESTING SYSTEMS

A fall arresting safeguard shall be used only if:
- A risk assessment has demonstrated that the work activity can, so far as is reasonably practicable, be performed safely while using it and without affecting its effectiveness.
- Use of other, safer work equipment is not reasonably practicable.
- A sufficient number of available persons have received adequate training specific to the safeguard, including rescue procedures.

A fall arresting safeguard must be suitable and of sufficient strength to arrest safely the fall of any person who is liable to fall. In addition it must:
- In the case of a safeguard which is designed to be attached, be securely attached to all the required anchor points.
- The anchors and the means of attachment must be suitable and of sufficient strength and stability for the purpose of supporting the foreseeable loading in arresting the fall and during any subsequent rescue.
- In the case of an airbag, landing mat or similar safeguard, be stable.
- In the case of a safeguard which distorts in arresting a fall, afford sufficient clearance.

Suitable and sufficient steps must be taken to ensure, so far as practicable, that in the event of a fall by any person the safeguard does not itself cause injury to that person.

Fall arresting systems such as safety nets, air / bean bags or crash mats can be used to minimise the impact of falls through the gaps created within a structure. Safety netting is the preferred fall arrest option since it provides collective protection and, unlike a fall arrest harness, does not rely on individual user discipline to guarantee acceptable safety standards. They can simplify systems of work and can protect not only roof workers, but others such as supervisors. Where safety nets are used, they must be installed as close as possible beneath the roof surface, securely attached and able to withstand a person falling onto them. These must be installed and maintained by competent personnel.

Ladder hoops are attached to vertical ladders to create a "tunnel" for safe climbing. There is a risk of fatigue when climbing vertical ladders because the climber needs to physically pull and step their body up the ladder. The ladder hoops are designed to prevent workers falling away from the ladder but do not prevent sliding down the ladder. Hoops should be used in conjunction with rest platforms, at intervals of 9 metres, to allow the climber to rest and recover from fatigue. Construction workers may make use of them to gain access to a roof or similar areas.

Figure 2-8-14: Ladder hoop. *Source: http://www.demuth.com.*

EMERGENCY RESCUE

Where an individual has fallen from height but has been protected by personal fall arrest equipment such as a harness, significant health effects known as suspension trauma may be experienced if they are not rescued quickly. This is mainly due to blood pooling in the legs, reducing the amount circulating through the rest of the body which has consequential effects for vital organs such as the brain, heart and kidneys. Unless the individual is rescued very quickly the lack of oxygenated blood to vital organs can be fatal. Therefore a rescue procedure and equipment must be available and practiced. The procedure should also take into account that a sudden transition from a vertical to a horizontal position when rescued and laid down, can lead to a massive amount of deoxygenated blood entering the heart, causing cardiac arrest. Steps must be taken to minimise the risk of injury due to the fall or contact with the safeguard. Even a short fall onto a net or other fall arresting safeguard could cause minor injuries or fractures. This should be anticipated and workers taught how to minimise the likelihood of injury.

The need for head protection

Hard hats are required where there is a foreseeable risk of injury to the head other than by falling e.g. struck by falling materials or where workers might hit their heads.

Hazards to consider:
- Loose material kicked into an excavation.
- Material falling from a scaffold platform.
- Material falling off a load being lifted by a crane or goods hoist or carried on a site dumper or truck.
- Dropping a fitting while erecting or dismantling a scaffold.

Action to be taken include:
- Decide on which areas of the site where hats have to be worn.
- Make site rules and tell everyone in the area.
- Provide workers with hard hats.
- Make sure hats are worn and worn correctly.

A wide range of hats is available. Let workers try a few and decide which is most suitable for the job and for them. Some hats have extra features including a sweatband for the forehead and a soft, or webbing harness. Although these hats are slightly more expensive, they are much more comfortable and therefore more likely to be worn.

Safe working practices for common forms of access equipment

SCAFFOLDING

General points

Many accidents are due to simple faults, such as misuse of tools, a ladder left unfixed, a missing toeboard. Regrettably, some accidents are caused by failure to take due regard of good practice and basic faults such as using a board which is seen to be defective, or using a board over an excessive span.

Reasons why scaffolds collapse
- Incorrect erection.
- Overloading.
- Uneven distribution of loads.
- Poor ground conditions.
- Adverse weather.
- Insufficient or inappropriate ties.
- Interference with ties.
- Vehicle collision.
- Incompatible components.
- Unauthorised alteration.

Common misuse
- Removal of bracings and ties.
- Unsecured or removal of scaffold boards.
- Removal of handrails or toeboards.
- Excavations near the scaffold.
- Use of the scaffold for propping shuttering (a structure generally made of timber in which liquid concrete is placed, compacted, and allowed to harden.) when it was not designed for that purpose.

Scaffolding terms

Base Plate	Distribute the load from a standard.
Reveal Pin	A screw Jack, fitting in the end of a tube.
Brace	A tube fixed diagonally across two or more members in a scaffold for stability.
Guard - Rail	A member incorporated in the structure to prevent personnel from falling.
Ledger	A tube spanning horizontally and tying the scaffold longitudinally. It may act as a support for putlogs or transoms.
Putlog	A tube with a flattened end, spanning from a horizontal member to a bearing in or on a brick wall. It may support scaffold boards.
Reveal Pin	A tube wedged by means of a reveal screw between two opposite surfaces (e.g. window reveals) to make a friction anchorage for tying a scaffold.
Standard / Column	A vertical or near vertical supporting member.
Tie	A member used for fixing the scaffold to the building or other structure for stability.
Transom	A tube spanning across ledgers to tie a scaffold transversely. It may also support boards.

Independent tied

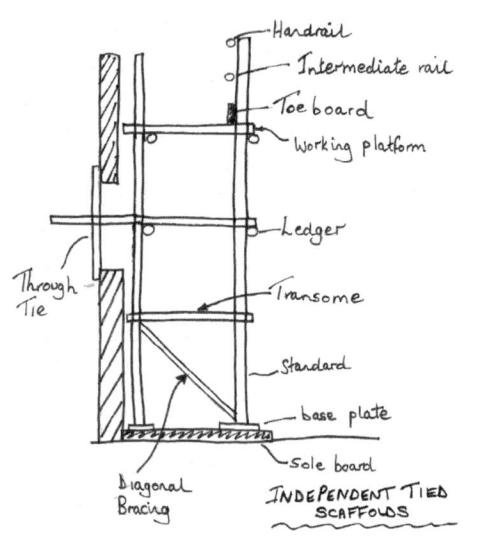

Figure 2-8-15: Independent tied scaffold (hand drawn). *Source: ACT.*

Figure 2-8-16: Independent tied scaffold. *Source: ACT*

This type of scaffold typically uses two sets of standards; one near to the structure and the other set at the width of the work platform. It is erected so that it is independent from the structure and does not rely on it for its primary stability. However, as the name suggests, it is usual to tie the scaffold to the structure in order to prevent the scaffold falling towards or away from the structure.

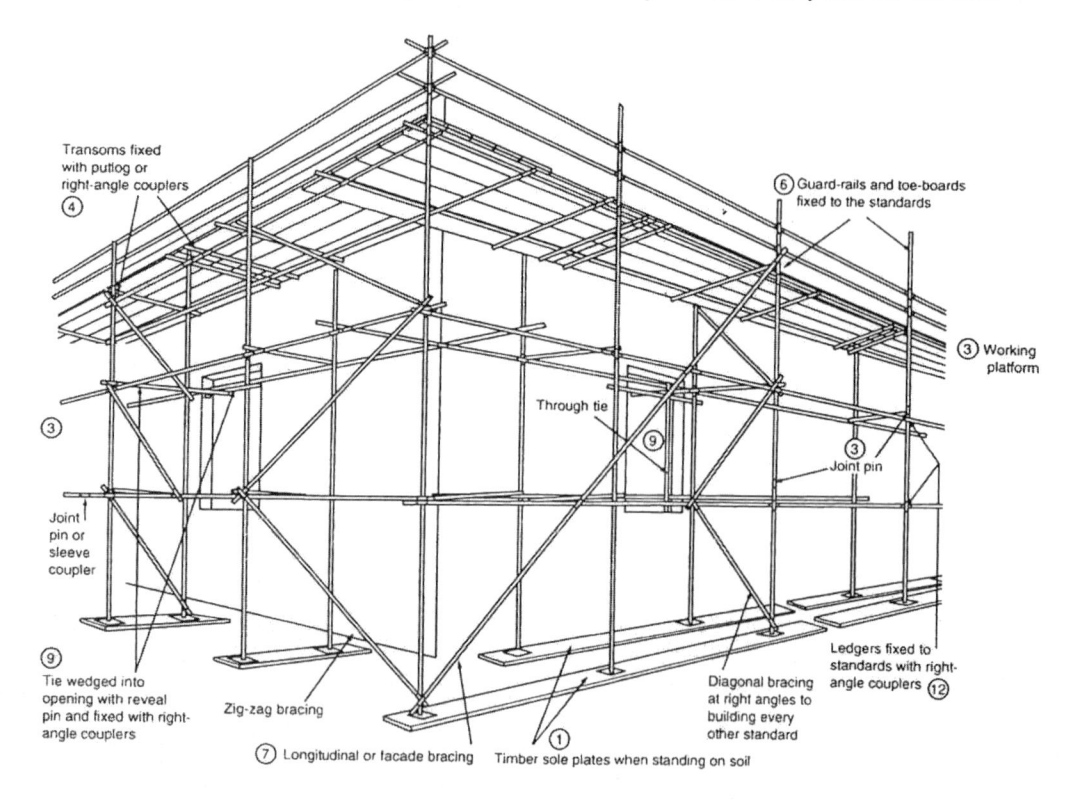

Figure 2-8-17: Independent tied scaffold. *Source: HSG150 Safety in Construction.*

Mobile tower

Figure 2-8-18: Mobile tower scaffold. *Source: ACT.*

Figure 2-8-19: Tower scaffold. *Source: ACT.*

Mobile scaffold towers are widely used as they are convenient for work which involves frequent access to a height over a short period of time in a number of locations that are spaced apart. However, they are often incorrectly erected or misused and accidents occur due to workers / materials falling or the tower overturning / collapsing. They must be erected and dismantled by trained, competent personnel, strictly in accordance with the supplier's instructions. All parts must be sound and from the same manufacturer.

- The height of an untied, independent tower must never exceed the manufacturer's recommendations. A good practice may be:
  - Outdoor use - 3 times the minimum base width.
  - Indoor use - 3.5 times the minimum base width.
- If the height of the tower is to exceed these maximum figures then the scaffold **must** be secured (tied) to the structure or outriggers used.
- Working platforms must only be accessed by safe means. Use internal stairs or fixed ladders only and never climb on the outside.
- Before climbing a tower the wheels must be turned outwards, the wheel brakes "on", locked and kept locked.
- Never move a tower unless the platform is clear of workers, materials, tools, for example.
- Towers must only be moved by pushing them at base level. Instruct operators not to pull the tower along whilst on it. Pay careful attention to obstructions at base level and overhead.
- Never use a tower near live overhead power lines or cables.
- Working platforms must always be fully boarded out. Guard rails and toe boards must be fitted if there is a risk of a fall as determined via a risk assessment. Inspections must be carried out by a competent person and documented - before first use, after substantial alteration and after any event likely to have affected its stability. A safe maximum working load must also be stated.

Base plates and sole boards

- A base plate must be used under every standard - it spreads the load and helps to keep the standard vertical.
- Sole boards are used to spread the weight of the scaffold and to provide a firm surface on which to erect a scaffold, particularly on soft ground. Sole boards must be sound and sufficient, and should run under at least two standards at a time.

Figure 2-8-20: Base plates and sole boards. *Source: Lincsafe.*

Figure 2-8-21: Base plate and protection. *Source: ACT.*

Standards

- All standards must be truly plumb (straight / vertical), or leaning only a little **towards** the structure. One standard out of plumb will "bow" and push the others.
- Any joints in standards must be staggered.

Ledgers

- These must be truly horizontal, and not more than 2.7 metres above the ground or the ledgers below, on **any** scaffold.

- Any joints in ledgers must be made with sleeve couplers, and the joints must be staggered.
- Ledger bracings must be fixed to alternate standards, on every platform. They must *not* be fixed to the handrail.

Boards
- Boards supported by transoms or putlogs must be close fitting, free from cracks or splits or large knots, and must not be damaged in any way, which could cause weakness.

Working platforms
- However wide a working platform may be, if its height above ground or floor level is 2 metres or more, then it must be fitted with guardrails and toeboards. If it is also to carry materials, then the space between guardrails and toeboards must be reduced to a maximum 470 mm. This can be done with an intermediate rail, mesh or similar material.
- General access must not be allowed to any scaffold until its erection has been fully completed. Access must be blocked off to any section of any scaffold which is not yet finished.
- If a gap or opening is created in a platform for any reason, then it must immediately be blocked off and a warning notice displayed.
- Where a ladder passes through a working platform, the access must be as small as practicable.
- Any access point through a working platform must be covered when it is not being used, and clearly marked to show its purpose.
- Trestles *must not* be put up on any working platform.
- If a working platform becomes covered with ice, snow, grease or any other slippery material, then suitable action must be taken to reduce the hazard, by sprinkling sand, salt, sawdust, for example, to absorb/remove the slippery material/substances.
- Rubbish or unused materials must not be left on working platforms.
- Platforms must not be used for "storing" materials. All materials placed on a platform must be for immediate use only.
- Loadings must be evenly spread out over working platforms to the fullest extent possible.
- Where loadings cannot be distributed evenly (as with bricklayers' materials) then the larger weights should be kept nearest to the standards.
- Any platform near to fragile items should be sheeted out to the full height of the guardrail.
- Everything loose must be taken off the working platforms before any start is made on dismantling.

Toe boards
These are scaffold boards placed against the standards at correct angles to the surface of the working platform. They help prevent materials from falling from the scaffold and workers slipping under rails.
- The toe boards should be fixed to the inside of the standards with toe board clips.
- Minimum height of 150 mm.
- Joints must be as near as possible to a standard.
- Continuous around the platform where a guard-rail is required.
- Any toe board which is removed temporarily for access or for any other reason must be replaced as soon as possible.

Guardrails
These are horizontal scaffold tubes which help to prevent workers falling from a scaffold.
- They must be fitted to any working platform which have been identified via a risk assessment or more above ground level.
- They must be fixed to the *inside* of the standards, at least 950 mm from the platform.
- An intermediate guardrail must be positioned such that the gap between it and the top guardrail and the toe boards is no more than 470 mm.
- Guardrails must always be fitted with load-bearing couplers.
- Joints in guardrails must be near to a standard.
- Must be secured with sleeve couplers.
- Guardrail must go all round the work platform.
- Where there is a gap between the structures then a guardrail must be fitted to the inside of the working platform as well as the outside.
- Guardrails must always be carried round the end of a scaffold, to make a "stop end".

Figure 2-8-22: Scaffold boards - some defective. *Source: ACT.*

Brick guards

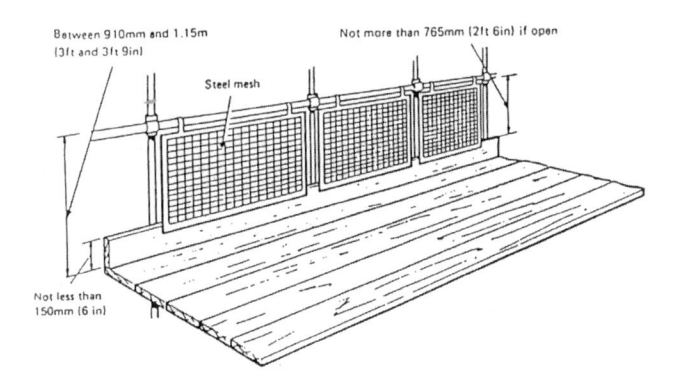

Figure 2-8-23: Brick guards. *Source: HSG150 Safety in Construction.*

Ties and bracing

Ensuring stability of a scaffold is critical. In the case of an independent tied scaffold the scaffold is set a small distance away from the structure and ties connect it to the structure and prevent the scaffold falling away from or towards the structure. One of the ways to do this is to use a 'through tie' which is set into place through an opening in the structure such as a window. In addition to this it is critical that the scaffold is a rigid structure. A scaffold comprising of standards, transoms and ledgers alone may not be rigid enough, particularly in the case of tall scaffolds. In order to improve rigidity a system of braces, scaffold poles set at a diagonal angle, is used. They are placed at the ends, in opposite diagonals for each level of scaffold, at intervals along the scaffold. In addition bracing is placed diagonally across the front of the scaffold.

Figure 2-8-24: Tie through window.   *Source: ACT.*    Figure 2-8-25: Ladder access.   *Source: ACT.*

Debris netting

Debris netting is often fixed to the sides of a scaffold to limit the amount of debris escaping from the scaffold that may come from work being done on it. It provides a tough, durable and inexpensive method of helping to provide protection from the danger of falling debris and windblown waste. It allows good light transmission and reduces the effects of adverse weather. Debris netting may also be slung underneath steelwork or where roof work is being conducted to catch items that may fall. In this situation it should not be assumed that the debris netting is sufficient to hold the weight of a person who might fall.

Figure 2-8-26: Side nets and sheets.   *Source: ACT.*    Figure 2-8-27: Safety nets.   *Source: ACT.*

Signs

Safety signs are used to provide people with information relating to the works being carried out, to control or divert people and most importantly of any dangers or hazards. Signs may be situated at a location in advance of the work area to give prior warning in addition to the works perimeter and actual work location.

Marking

Where equipment used to gain access to a height may be collided with it should carry hazard marking. For example, the standards of a scaffold at ground level on a street may be marked with hazard tape.

Lighting

Suitable and adequate lighting should be provided to allow the works being carried out and any possible hazards to be seen clearly in advance and allow people to take the required actions to avoid interference with the site. Scaffolds located near roads may be fitted with lighting to warn traffic of its presence.

Fans

Fans are scaffold boards fixed on scaffold tubes set at an upward angle out from a scaffold in order to catch debris that may fall from the scaffold. They may be provided at the entrances to buildings to protect persons entering and leaving the building that the scaffold is erected against. They are also used where a scaffold is erected alongside a pedestrian walkway where there is a need to have an increased confidence that materials that might fall cannot contact people below. In some cases it may be necessary for horizontal barriers to be erected to direct pedestrians under the fan.

Figure 2-8-28: Signs. *Source: ACT.*

Figure 2-8-29: Marking. *Source: ACT.*

Figure 2-8-30: Fans. *Source: ACT.*

Figure 2-8-31: Wheels with brakes *Source: ACT.*

MOBILE ELEVATING WORK PLATFORMS

A mobile elevating work platform (MEWP) is, as the name suggests, a means of providing a work platform at a height. The equipment is designed to be movable, under its own power or by being towed, so that it can easily be set up in a location where it is needed. Various mechanical and hydraulic means are used to elevate the work platform to the desired height, including telescopic arms and scissor lifts. The versatility of this equipment, enabling the easy placement of a platform at a height, makes it a popular piece of access equipment. Often, to do similar work by other means would take a lot of time or be very difficult. They are now widely available and, like other equipment such as fork lift trucks, there is a tendency for employers to oversimplify their use and allow workers to operate them without prior training and experience. This places users and others at high risk of serious injury.

Some MEWPs can be used on rough terrain. This usually means that they are safe to use on uneven or undulating ground. Always check their limitations in the manufacturer's handbook before moving on to unprepared or sloping ground and operate within the defined stability working area. Wearing a harness with a lanyard attached to the platform provides extra protection against falls especially when the platform is being raised or lowered.

MEWPs and similar equipment used in poor lighting conditions on or near roads and walkways must use standard vehicle lighting.

USE OF MOBILE ELEVATING WORK PLATFORM

Mobile Elevating Work Platforms (MEWPs) can provide excellent safe access to high level work. When using a MEWP make sure:

- Whoever is operating it is fully trained and competent.
- The work platform is fitted with guard rails and toe boards.
- It is used on suitable firm and level ground. The ground may have to be prepared in advance.
- Tyres are properly inflated.
- The work area is cordoned off to prevent access below the work platform.
- That it is well lit if being used on a public highway in poor lighting.
- Outriggers are extended and chocked as necessary before raising the platform.
- All involved know what to do if the machine fails with the platform in the raised position.

Figure 2-8-32: Mobile elevated work platform (MEWPs). *Source: ACT.*

Figure 2-8-33: Mobile elevated work platform (MEWPs). *Source: ACT.*

Figure 2-8-34: Use of harness with a MEWP. *Source: HSG150.*

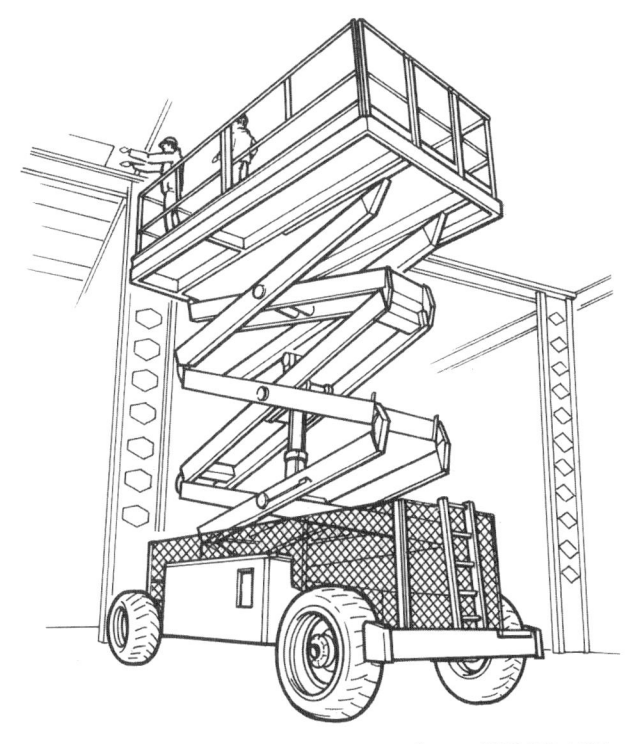

Do not attach harnesses to a point outside platform!

Figure 2-8-35: Scissor lift. *Source: HSG150, HSE.*

Figure 2-8-36: Scissor lift. *Source: ACT.*

Do not

- Operate MEWPs close to overhead cables or dangerous machinery.
- Allow a knuckle, or elbow, of the arm to protrude into a traffic route when working near vehicles.
- Move the equipment with the platform in the raised position unless the equipment is especially designed to allow this to be done safely (check the manufacturer's instructions).
- Overload or overreach from the platform.

LADDERS

Ladders are primarily a means of vertical access to a workplace. However, they are often used to carry out work and this frequently results in accidents. Many accidents involving ladders happen during work lasting 30 minutes or less. Ladders are often used for short jobs when it would be safer to use other equipment, e.g. mobile scaffold towers or MEWPs. Generally, ladders should be considered as access equipment and use of a ladder as a work platform should be discouraged.

There are situations when working from a ladder would be inappropriate, for example:

- When two hands are needed or the work area is large.
- Where the equipment or materials used are large or awkward.
- Excessive height.
- Work of long duration.
- Where the ladder cannot be secured or made stable.
- Where the ladder cannot be protected from vehicles, for example.
- Adverse weather conditions.

Figure 2-8-37: Ladder as access and workplace. *Source: ACT.*

Figure 2-8-38: Improper use. *Source: ACT.*

Before using a ladder to work from, consider whether it is the correct equipment for the job. Ladders are only suitable as a workplace for light work of short duration, and for a large majority of activities a scaffold, mobile tower or mobile elevating work platform (MEWP) is likely to be more suitable and safer.

Selection of ladders

Before using a ladder it is critical that the correct one with suitable strength be selected and used for the job or activity to be undertaken. Taking the UK as an example, there are three categories of ladder strength:

1. Industrial Duty (Class 1) ladders are designed for a Maximum Static Vertical Load 175kg (27.5 stones). This will sometimes be referred to as "safe working load".
2. Trade Duty (previously Class 2, but now EN131) ladders are designed for a Maximum Static Vertical Load 150kg (23.5 stones).
3. Domestic Duty (Class 3) ladders are designed for a Maximum Static Vertical Load 125kg (19.5 stones).

Confusion frequently arises from the use of the term "Duty Rating" on some ladders, where Class 1 ladders are designated a Duty Rating 130kg and Class 3 ladders are designated a Duty Rating 95kg. These figures were arrived at by British Standards from a consideration of the frequency and general conditions of use. They are not an accurate guide to the Safe Working Load. The "Maximum Static Vertical Load" is a more useful measure and gives a more accurate guide to relative strengths.

The British Standards for UK ladders are:

1. BS 2037 - applies to metal ladders (Class 1 and Class 3).
2. BS EN131 - applies to metal and timber ladders.
3. BS 1129 - applies to timber ladders.
4. BS EN131 has been recently adopted as a European-wide standard (ladders manufactured in most of Europe will be known simply as EN131). In the UK it has replaced the old Trade Duty (Class 2) of BS 2037.

- Pre-use inspection. Make sure the ladder is in good condition. Check the rungs and stiles for warping, cracking or splintering, the condition of the feet, and for any other defects. Do not use defective or painted ladders.
- Position the ladder properly for safe access and out of the way of vehicles.
- Ladders must stand on a firm, level base, be positioned approximately at an angle of 75^0 (1 unit horizontally to 4 units vertically) and extend about 1 metre above the landing place. Do not rest ladders against fragile surfaces.
- Ladders must be properly tied near the top, even if only in use for a short time, while being tied a ladder must be footed. If not tied ladders must be secured near the bottom, footed or weighted.
- Keep both hands free to grip the ladder when climbing or descending, with only one person on the ladder at any time. Beware of wet, greasy or icy rungs and make sure soles of footwear are clean.

Figure 2-8-39: Poor storage. *Source: Lincsafe.*

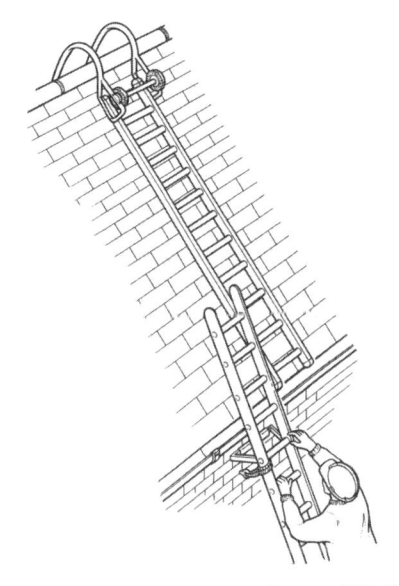

Figure 2-8-40: Use of roof ladders. *Source: HSG150, HSE.*

Step ladders

Stepladders require careful use. They are subject to the same general health and safety rules as ladders. However, in addition, they will not withstand any degree of side loading and overturn very easily. Over-reaching is to be avoided at all costs. The top step of a stepladder should not be used as a working platform unless it has been specifically designed for that purpose. Ladder stays must be 'locked out' properly before use.

Inspection requirements for work equipment

Inspection requirements for work equipment specified for use for work at height are:

- Where safety depends on how it is installed or assembled in any position - before used in that position.
- Where exposed to conditions causing deterioration which is liable to result in dangerous situations, to ensure that health and safety conditions are maintained and that any deterioration can be detected and remedied in good time - at suitable intervals and each time that exceptional circumstances which are liable to jeopardise the safety of the work equipment have occurred.
- Work platforms used for construction work in which a person could fall 2 metres or more - inspected in position, or if a mobile work platform inspected on the site, within the previous 7 days.

Results of an inspection must be recorded and kept until the next inspection. An inspection report containing the particulars set out below must be prepared before the end of the working period within which the inspection is completed and, within 24 hours of completing the inspection, and be provided to the person it was carried out for. The report must be kept at the site where the inspection was carried out until the construction work is completed and afterwards at an office of the person it was carried out for 3 months, or as prescribed by national laws or regulations (UK typically).

Reports on inspections must include the following particulars:

Figure 2-8-41: Stepladder. *Source: ACT.*

1) Name and address of person for whom the inspection is carried out.
2) Location of the work equipment.
3) Description of the work equipment.
4) Date and time of inspection.
5) Details of any matter identified that could give rise to a risk to the health and safety of any person.
6) Details of any action taken as a result of 5 above.
7) Details of any further action considered necessary.
8) Name and position of the person making the report.

8.3 - Excavations

The hazards of work in and around excavations

Work in excavations and trenches, basements, underground tanks, sewers, manholes, for example, can involve high risks and each year construction workers are killed with some buried alive or asphyxiated.

Figure 2-8-42: Buried services.　　Source: ACT.

Figure 2-8-43: Excavation hazards.　　Source: ACT.

FALLS OF EQUIPMENT, MATERIALS AND PERSONS FALLING INTO THE EXCAVATION

When workers are working below ground in excavations, the problems are very similar to those faced when workers are working at a height - falls and falling objects. Particular problems arise when:

- Materials, including spoil (ground which has been excavated), are stored too close to the edge of the excavation.
- The excavation is close to another building and the foundations may be undermined.
- The edge of the excavation is not clear, especially if the excavation is in a public area.
- Absence of barriers or lighting.
- Poor positioning or the absence of access ladders allowing workers to fall.
- Absence of organised crossing points.
- Badly constructed ramps for vehicle access which can cause the vehicle to topple.
- No stop blocks for back filling.
- Routing of vehicles too close to the excavation.

COLLAPSE OF THE EXCAVATION

Often, the soil and earth that make up the sides of the excavation cannot be relied upon to support their own weight, leading to the possibility of collapse. The risk can be made worse if:

- The soil structure is loose or made unstable by water logging.
- Heavy plant or materials are too close to the edge of the excavation.
- Machinery or vehicles cause vibration.
- There is inadequate support for the sides.

The consequences of even a minor collapse can be very serious. A minor fall of earth can happen at high speed and bring with it anything (plant and machinery) that may be at the edge. Even if the arms and head of a person are not trapped in the soil, the material pressing on the person can lead to severe crush injuries to the lower body and asphyxiation due to restriction of movement of the chest.

COLLAPSE OF STRUCTURES NEARBY

Excavations that are carried out within close proximity to existing buildings or structures may result in their foundations becoming undermined and create the potential for significant settling damage to occur or worse still, collapse. Consideration should be given to the effects that excavation work might have on foundations of neighbouring buildings or structures, and control measures implemented to ensure that foundations are not disturbed or undermined. Building foundations that are at a distance of less than twice the excavation depth from the face of the excavation are more likely to be affected by ground movement; underpinning (the process of strengthening and stabilising the foundation of an existing building or other structure) or shoring (the process of supporting a structure in order to prevent collapse so that construction can proceed) of such structures may be required to prevent structural damage.

BURIED SERVICES

Although electricity cables provide the most obvious risk, gas pipes, water mains, drains and sewers can all release dangerous substances. Gas is particularly dangerous if there is a potential ignition source close by. Fibre-optic cables may carry layers presenting a risk to sight if damaged they are also very expensive to repair.

Buried services (electricity, gas, water, etc) are not obvious upon site survey and so the likelihood of striking a service when excavating, drilling or piling is increased. The results of striking an underground service are varied, and the potential to cause injury or fatality is high. As with overhead power lines, any underground service should be treated as live until confirmed dead by an authority. Incidents can include shock, electrocution, explosion and burns from power cables, explosion, burns or unconsciousness from gas or power cables, impact injury from dislodged stones or flooding from ruptured water mains. Before groundwork is due to commence it is common and good practice to check for presence of any of the previously mentioned services or hazards by using a detection device.

A common device used regularly is a cable avoidance tool more commonly known as a CAT scanner when utilised as a detection device in a particular area.

FLOOD

Unless a major watercourse is breached, leading to a massive ingress of water, drowning is not likely to be an issue. However, heavy rainfall, breaking into drains and digging below the natural water table can all lead to flooding. In deep excavations, where access is not readily available, the combined effect of water and mud could lead to difficulty in escape and risk of drowning. In addition, this can lead to the sides of the trench becoming soft and the integrity of the supports can be undermined.

HAZARDOUS SUBSTANCES

Digging may uncover buried materials that have the potential to be hazardous to health. The history of the site should be examined to try to identify if substances have been buried on the site during its previous use. Sites that once were used as steel works may contain arsenic and cyanide dating back many years; farmyards may have been used as graves for animals and to dispose of pesticides and organo-phosphates. There is always the presence of vermin to consider - this can increase the risk of diseases such as leptospirosis.

Excavations can under different circumstances be subject to toxic, asphyxiating or explosive fumes/gases/vapours. Chalk or limestone deposits when in contact with acidic groundwater can release carbon dioxide, and gases such as methane or hydrogen sulphide can seep into excavations from contaminated ground or damaged services in built-up areas. These atmospheres can accumulate at the bottom of an excavation and result in asphyxiation, poisoning, explosion or potential fatalities.

Precautions necessary when working in and around excavations

BASIC METHODS OF SHORING AND BATTERING

Precautions must be taken to prevent collapse. The methods of supporting (shoring) the sides of excavations vary widely in design depending on:

- The nature of the subsoil - for example wet may require close shoring with sheets.
- Projected life of the excavation - a trench box may give ready made access where it is only needed for short duration.
- Work to be undertaken, including equipment used - for example the use of a trench box for shoring where pipe joints are made.
- The possibility of flooding from ground water and heavy rain - close shoring would be required.
- The depth of the excavation - a shallow excavation may use battering instead of shoring, particularly where shoring may impede access.
- The number of workers using the excavation at any one time - a lot of space may be required so cantilever sheet piling may be preferred.

In order to ensure satisfactory support for excavations:

- Prevent collapse by battering (see below) the sides to a safe angle or supporting them with sheeting or proprietary support systems.
- Use experienced workers for the erection and dismantling of timbering and other supports.
- Adequate material must be used to prevent danger from falls or falling objects.

An alternative precaution to the use of shoring is where soil and material is removed from the sides of the excavation so that steps or a shallow slope is created in the sides; this is called battering. Battering relies on the material in the steps or slopes of the sides of the excavation creating minimal downward/sideways pressure, reducing the likelihood and effect of collapse.

Figure 2-8-44: Battering. *Source: ACT.*

Figure 2-8-45: Trench box - for shoring. *Source: ACT.*

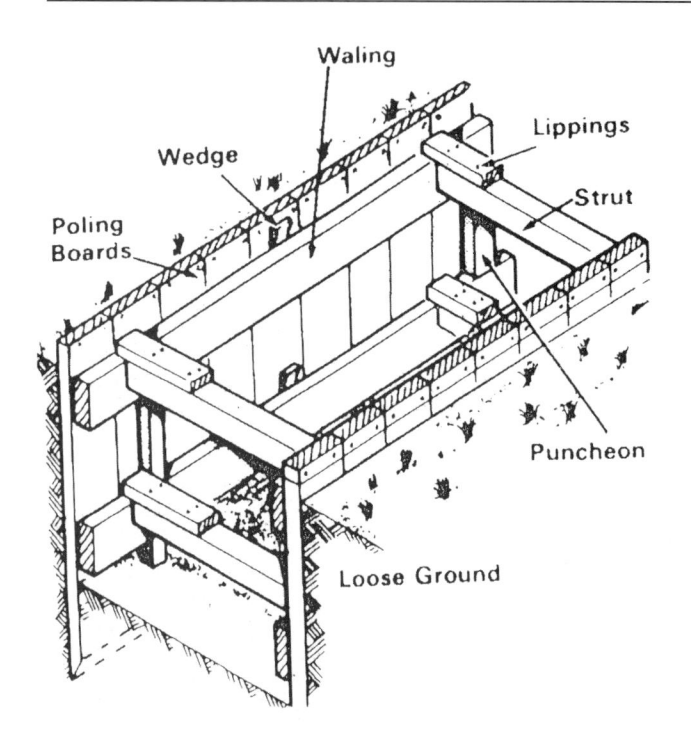

Figure 2-8-46: Close boarded excavation. Source: BS6031.

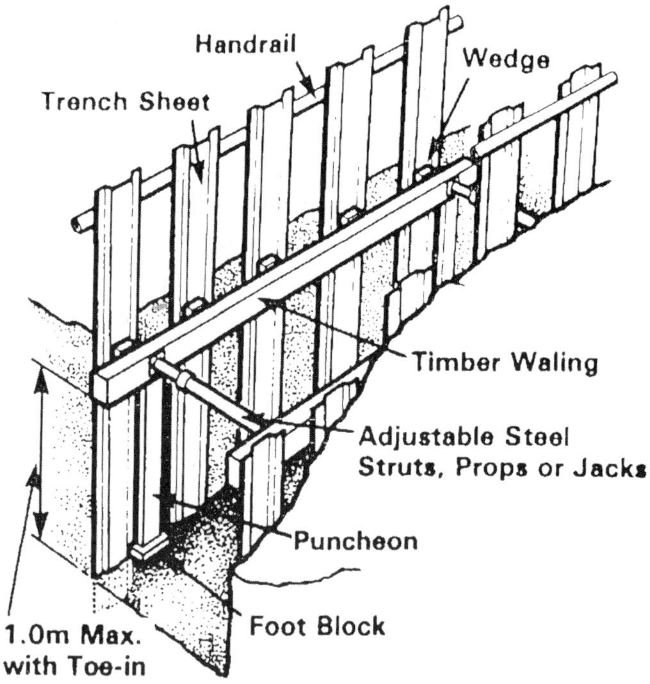

Figure 2-8-47: Open sheeting. Source: BS6031.

Figure 2-8-48: Close sheeting. Source: ACT.

Figure 2-8-49: Open sheeting. Source: ACT.

BARRIERS

Where workers or materials can fall from height edge protection must be considered. In some cases the shoring method used can provide this barrier by ensuring the top of the shoring extends sufficiently above the edge of the excavation. It is also good practice to cover shallow trenches when they are left unattended. Guardrails must meet the same standards as those provided for working platforms. Concrete or wooden blocks (usually old railway sleepers) can be placed some distance from the edge to prevent vehicles from getting too close, particularly when the excavation is being 'back filled'. In this case the wooden blocks provide a 'stop block'.

Large pieces of mobile plant and equipment that are commonly used on construction sites have the potential to cause serious harm to site workers and members of the public. In order to keep people and vehicles apart exclusion zones identified by barriers, warning signs and lights should be provided.

ACCESS LADDERS

Ladders are the usual means of access and egress to excavations. They must be properly secured, in good condition and inspected regularly. The ladder should extend about 1 metre or three rungs above ground level to give a good handhold. To allow for emergency egress it is recommended that a ladder is placed, on average, every 15 metres.

CROSSING POINTS

Crossing excavations should only be allowed at predetermined points. The crossing point should be able to withstand the maximum foreseeable load and be provided with guard rails and toe boards. The spacing or location of crossing points should be such that workers and others are encouraged to use them, rather than to attempt other means of crossing the excavation.

LIGHTING AND WARNING SIGNS

Appropriate lighting should be provided; it must provide sufficient illumination for those at work but should not create glare or other distractions for passers by, especially motorists. Battery operated headlamps (to avoid trailing cables) may be considered for individual use. If excavations are present in dark conditions they must be suitably lit to prevent vehicles or people colliding or falling into them. If working on a public highway, the police or the local authority must be consulted over the positioning of traffic lights. Signs should be displayed to warn people of the excavation and any special measures to be taken.

PERSONAL PROTECTIVE EQUIPMENT

As well as the need for hard hats to limit the risks from falling materials, other personal protective equipment (PPE) may be necessary, such as:

- Breathing apparatus.
- Safety harnesses.
- Hearing protection.
- Clothing to protect from the rays of the sun.
- Masks and respirators.
- Face masks and gloves for welding and grinding.
- Footwear.

CHECKS FOR BURIED SERVICES

Excavation operations should not begin until all available service location drawings have been identified and thoroughly examined. Record plans and location drawings should not be considered as totally accurate but serve only as an indication of the likelihood of the presence of services, their location and depth. It is possible for the position of an electricity supply cable to alter if previous works have been carried out in the location due to the flexibility of the cable and movement of surrounding features since original installation of the cable. In addition, plans often show a proposed position for the services that does not translate to the ground, such that services are placed in position only approximately where the plan says.

It is critical that 'service location devices' such as a cable avoidance tool (CAT) are used by competent, trained operatives to assist in the identification and marking of the actual location and position of buried services. When identified it is essential that physical markings be placed on the ground to show where these services are located.

Figure 2-8-50: Marking of services. *Source: ACT.*

NOT WORKING CLOSE TO EXCAVATORS

Large pieces of equipment have great potential for causing serious harm to not only site workers but also members of the public if work is carried out on a busy thoroughfare. To keep people and vehicles apart, the following need to be considered:

- Exclusion zones identified by barriers.
- Warning signs and lights.
- Excavator cabs should have good visibility and operators properly trained.
- Workers should wear high visibility clothing.
- Work should be done under close supervision.

POSITION AND ROUTES FOR EQUIPMENT

A critical consideration when developing safe positions and routes for equipment is a traffic management system which is the safety interface between pedestrians and traffic. The routes that workers use should be clearly defined and marked. Every workplace should be organised in such a way that pedestrian and vehicles can circulate in a safe manner. There should be clear, well-marked and signposted vehicle traffic routes, which avoid steep gradients where possible, especially where fork lift trucks operate. It is critical to have speed limits that are practicable and effective. Speed limit signs should be posted and traffic slowing measures such as speed bumps and ramps may be necessary in certain situations. Monitoring speed limit compliance is necessary, along with some kind of action against persistent offenders.

Speed limits of 10 or 15 mph are usually considered appropriate, although 5 mph may be necessary in certain situations.

Transport requires clear routes to be designated and preferably fenced off from pedestrians. Accidents can occur when plant and people collide: the pedestrian may be injured by contact and the driver injured if the vehicle overturns.

Separate site gates should be provided for vehicles' entry and blind spots (where vision of the driver / pedestrian is restricted) should be dealt with by the careful positioning of mirrors on walls, plant or storage. Routes should be wide enough to allow manoeuvrability and passing.

Where it is unavoidable that pedestrians will come into proximity with transport, workers should be reminded of the hazards by briefings, site induction and signs, so they are aware at all times.

Any traffic route which is used by both pedestrians and vehicles should be wide enough to enable any vehicle likely to use the route to pass pedestrians safely. Where it is not practical to make the route wide enough, passing places or traffic management systems should be provided as necessary.

The vehicles should be fitted with safeguards to minimize the risk of injury, sufficient clearance should be provided between the vehicles and pedestrians, and care should be taken that fixtures along the route do not create trapping hazards.

It is common practice for a traffic management plan to be devised and displayed in key locations at a construction site. During induction and at each signing in event all workers will sign to say that they have read and understood the traffic management plan which is initially emphasised at the induction stage. The plan will need to be reviewed and updated before the traffic route is to be changed.

Routes should be clearly marked and signed. Signs should incorporate speed limits, one way systems, priorities and other factors normal to public roads. Vehicles, which are visiting the premises, should be made aware of any local rules and conditions.

Consideration should be given to adequate lighting on routes and particularly in loading/unloading and operating areas.

Separate routes, designated crossing places and suitable barriers at recognised danger spots. As far as is practicable pedestrians should be kept clear of vehicle operating areas and/or a notice displayed warning pedestrians that they are entering an operating area.

Clear direction signs and marking of storage areas and buildings can help to avoid unnecessary movement, such as reversing.

Sharp bends and overhead obstructions should be avoided where possible. Hazards that cannot be removed should be clearly marked with black and yellow diagonal stripes i.e. loading bay edges, stacks, pits, for example. If reasonably practicable barriers should be installed.

Consideration to vehicle weight and height restriction on routes - signs, barriers and weight checks may be necessary.

MATERIALS AND VEHICLES

Excavated material (spoil), other materials, plant and vehicles should never be stored or parked close to the sides of any excavation. The additional pressure distributed on the ground from spoil, vehicles, etc significantly increases the likelihood of collapse occurring at the sides of the excavation. Though it will depend on the weight of the material it would normally be kept a minimum of 1 metre from the edge of the excavation. In addition, spoil heaps consist of loose materials that have the risk of spilling into the excavation. A means of preventing spillage of spoil into an excavation is by positioning scaffold boards as toe boards, fixed along the outside of trench sheets. This provides additional protection to combat the risk of loose materials spilling into the excavation. An alternative to this is to allow boards or sheeting to protrude above the top of the excavation sufficient to act as toe boards and prevent materials falling.

Unless sufficient control is implemented, workers can suffer injury from spoil or stored materials falling from ground level into an excavation. Head protection must be worn and this will provide protection for those working in the excavation from small pieces of materials falling either from above or from the sides of the excavation. If stored at a suitable distance away from an excavation and at a suitable height, spoil heaps can form an effective barrier against vehicles travelling around the construction site and assist in preventing falls of vehicles and plant into an excavation and onto workers.

Figure 2-8-51: Materials storage. Source: ACT.

Figure 2-8-52: Preventing water ingress. Source: ACT.

To prevent objects falling into excavations, the following precautions should be taken:

- Spoil and building materials must not be stacked near to the edge.
- The weight of stacks should not be enough to cause the sides to collapse.
- Designated operating areas for vehicles and machinery must be routed away from the excavation.
- Where vehicles have to approach, stop blocks must be provided to prevent overrunning.

CARE FILLING IN

On completion of use of the excavation experienced workers should remove support materials. A competent person should inspect the site to ensure that all workers and materials have been removed. The excavation may need water pumping from it before filling. Where vehicles approach the excavation to add materials it is essential that stop barriers are used at the edge of the excavation to avoid vehicles falling into it. Materials added to the excavation must be sufficiently compacted to allow for the next use of the area, for example, as part of a roadway or to allow a scaffold to be placed on top of it.

Only appropriate materials must be used. Uncontrolled tipping is an offence.

The need for a system of inspections for excavations

A competent person must inspect excavations:

- At the start of each shift before work begins.
- After any event likely to have affected the strength or stability of the excavation.
- After any accidental fall of rock, earth or other material.

The competent person must:

- Complete the inspection report before the end of the working period.
- Provide the report or a copy to the person for whom the inspection was carried out within 24 hours.

A copy of the reports must be kept on site until the work is complete. Reports should then be kept for three months at an office of the person for whom the inspections were carried out or as prescribed by national laws or regulations.

Where the person carrying out the inspection is not satisfied that it is safe to work in the excavation they must inform the person who they are doing the inspection for and work must not continue until the matters identified by the inspection have been remedied.

The inspection record must include the following information:

- Name and address of person on whose behalf the inspection was carried out.
- Location of the workplace inspected.
- Description of workplace or part of workplace inspected (including any plant and equipment and materials, if any).
- Date and time of inspection.
- Details of any matter identified that could lead to a risk to the health and safety of anyone.
- Details of any action taken as a result of any matter identified in the last point.
- Details of any more action considered necessary.
- The name and position of the person making the report.

8.4 - Health hazards commonly encountered in construction activities

Identification and control of common health hazards

There are many causes of ill health associated with construction activities, some of them associated with outside work and others with the plant and materials used. Examples include:

- Exposure (heat/cold).
- Sun (e.g. skin damage; skin cancer).
- Zoonooses (e.g. leptospirosis).
- Noise.
- Musculo-skeletal (e.g. sprains and strains).
- Chemical.

The inhalation of, and contact with dust in its many forms is a construction hazard. Dust is generated from activities such as the chasing out of grooves in walls, the cutting of concrete and mixing cement. The latter is particularly associated with dermatitis. In addition to these hazards, the ever-present risk of asbestos inhalation must be considered. It is particularly critical that the presence or otherwise of asbestos should be assessed in any pre-demolition survey undertaken.

NOISE AND VIBRATION

Loud noise at work can cause irreversible hearing damage. It accelerates the normal hearing loss, which occurs as we grow older. It can cause other problems such as tinnitus ('ringing in the ears'), interference with communication, and stress.

Vibration is often associated with noise, but is difficult to measure. Excessive exposure through the use of hand-held power tools and machinery such as chipping hammers, grinders and chain-saws can cause hand-arm vibration syndrome (HAVS) - a painful condition affecting blood circulation, nerves, muscles and bones in the hands and arms. Its best known effect is vibration white finger (VWF). Whole body vibration (WBV) mainly affects drivers of vehicles such as dumpers, tractors and lift trucks, and causes low back pain and spinal damage.

DUST

Dust is a hazard that can affect adjacent land users as well as workers working on the site. Brick and cement dust are common problems on both construction and demolition sites. However, other dusts need special consideration:

- Asbestos - **see below**.
- Bird droppings in roof spaces.
- Chemicals - on land where processes have been involved cadmium, zinc or lead.

ASBESTOS

Use and possible exposure

There are three critical types of asbestos:

Crocidolite - *Blue* asbestos, liable to produce particularly high dust levels. Blue asbestos, like all other forms, cannot be identified by colour. Laboratory analysis is necessary. Blue asbestos was once quite common in Britain particularly for fire protection, heat or noise insulation. Although no longer used in Britain it can still be found in older buildings and those that have been refurbished in the past.

Amosite - *Brown* asbestos, used to strengthen asbestos insulation and other building products. It also has very good insulation qualities, therefore it will often be found on pipe lagging.

Chrysotile - *White* asbestos, the most common type, found in asbestos cement sheeting, roofing sheets, rainwater goods and a far wider range of applications.

Asbestos minerals may occur in natural mineral products as well as compounded or manufactured materials. Their presence may not always be clearly identifiable from appearance, the trade name or trade literature. All asbestos materials, or products containing asbestos, (including used protective clothing) must be labelled as such. In the case of a product containing crocidolite, the words 'contains asbestos' must be replaced by the words 'contains crocidolite/blue asbestos', on the standard asbestos label.

Asbestos is not a single chemical but a family of compound chemicals that have crystallised in nature as long thin separable fibres with some useful mechanical properties in common. The biological effects are due partly to the chemical constitution of the material and partly to the physical configuration of the fibres, both of which vary with the type of asbestos that is used.

Asbestos is commonly mixed with other materials and is typically used in the following applications:

- As yarn or cloth - for protective clothing, for example.
- Insulation boards - for protection of buildings against fire.
- Asbestos cement products - for construction of buildings and pipes.
- Asbestos resins - for clutch faces and brake linings.
- Various other applications - in gaskets, filters, floor tiles and decorative plasterwork in old buildings.
- Asbestos spraying for thermal and acoustic insulation of buildings and plant, and for fire resistance in structural steelwork, is no longer carried out, although it is encountered as a problem when being removed.
- Atmospheric contamination of workplace and neighbourhoods may occur during building work involving asbestos products or during work to repair or remove such products. Slow disintegration of materials containing asbestos may also cause contamination. There is a hazard whenever airborne fibres are released.

Type of fibre

Crocidolite and amosite are more hazardous than chrysotile and extra precautions need to be taken when exposure to them cannot be avoided.

Effects of asbestos

Knowledge of the medical effects of asbestos has accumulated slowly since the early 1900's and it is now universally agreed that the exposure of men and women to asbestos fibres can, in certain circumstances, lead to three diseases: asbestosis, lung cancer, and mesothelioma of the pleura (an exceedingly delicate serous membrane, the pleura, which is arranged in the form of a closed invaginated sac. A portion of the serous membrane covers the surface of the lung and dips into the fissures between its lobes; it is called the *pulmonary pleura* or *visceral pleura*.) or peritoneum (the *peritoneum* is the serous membrane that forms the lining of the abdominal cavity - it covers most of the intra-abdominal organs. It is composed of a layer of mesothelium supported by a thin layer of connective tissue.).

Asbestosis

The signs and symptoms attributable to asbestosis (that is, fibrosis of the lungs caused by asbestos) can be produced by other conditions and diagnosis during life is a matter of judgment. The early stages of the disease produce symptoms of breathlessness, tiredness and persistent cough. Later, the person may experience severe breathing difficulties, cough up blood, experience disturbance of sleep and pain in the chest and develop congestive heart failure. Therefore, diagnosis is seldom difficult with advanced disease and a clear history, but may be difficult otherwise, as there is no sharp point at which a change in state from healthy to diseased can be said to have occurred. There is a serious risk of the development of *lung cancer* or *mesothelioma*, which also produce these symptoms.

Asbestosis develops slowly and even the gross exposure of the past seldom caused death in less than 10 years. With decreased exposure, no person with otherwise healthy lungs should die of it. In the presence of other diseases the marginal effects of minor fibrosis may aggravate symptoms and hasten death.

Lung cancer

An uncontrolled growth of malignant cells in the lung.

Symptoms and indications of this incurable disease are severe, permanent cough producing sputum (matter that is coughed up from the respiratory tract, such as mucus or phlegm, mixed with saliva and then expectorated from the mouth) that may be specked with blood. Wheezing, pain in the chest and abnormal tiredness. Unexplained weight loss. Any person with a persistent cough or other symptoms of lung cancer should seek medical treatment as soon as possible.

In almost all cases of lung cancer the cause is smoking - usually direct smoking of cigarettes but also 'passive smoking'. It may be caused by breathing in airborne pollutants, especially asbestos dust, but smoking is widely recognised as the main preventable reason for this disease. Hence, the most obvious preventative measure is not to take up, or stop smoking. A smoker who gives up the habit immediately reduces their chance of developing the disease.

Lung cancer attributable to asbestos usually occurs more than 10 years after first exposure. The risk can be reduced by reducing exposure, but there is not thought to be a threshold dose below which no risk is produced.

Mesotheliomas

Usually a malignant tumour occurring in the pleura (a membrane that covers the lungs and inside of the chest wall). They may also affect the peritoneum (the membrane lining the abdominal cavity) or the pericardium (the membrane surrounding the heart). These sites are inoperable.

Early indications include breathlessness on exercise, there may be chest pain and cough and the symptoms of bronchitis. The breathlessness continues to get worse, ultimately leading to respiratory failure and death as the cancer spreads.

Most mesotheliomas are attributable to asbestos, especially crocidolite. Even a brief period of exposure of as little as six months to two years may be enough to cause problems later in life. The risk of developing all forms of lung cancer is greatly increased by smoking.

When caused by asbestos, mesotheliomas seldom occur within 15 years of first exposure and possibly never within 10 years. The risk is unaffected by smoking, but varies with the amount and type of asbestos to which exposure occurs.

CEMENT

Cement is used extensively in the construction industry as part of the mix for mortar and concrete. It is mildly corrosive and can cause harm in the following ways:

- Skin contact - causing contact dermatitis. If it is trapped inside a worker's boot or glove then it can cause severe chemical burns.
- Eye contact - causing irritation and inflammation.
- Inhalation - causing irritation of the nose and throat. Possible long term respiratory problems.

Gloves and masks should always be worn. Wash skin thoroughly after use.

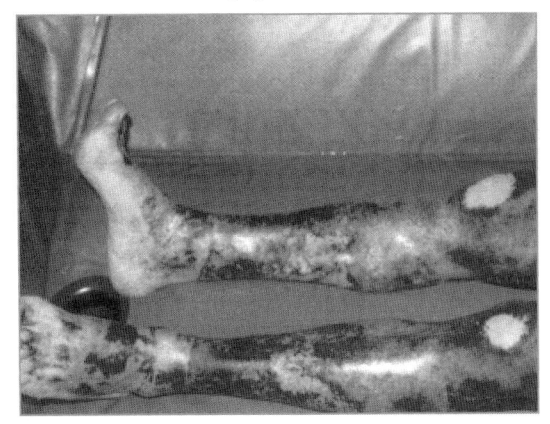

Figure 2-8:53: This man's right leg had to be amputated owing to the severe burns he sustained from kneeling in wet cement for three hours.

Source: The Safety & Health Practitioner (Aug 2003)

SOLVENTS

Many chemical substances which are used to dissolve or dilute other substances or materials are called solvents. Industrial solvents are often a mixture of several industrial substances. They can be found under a number of trade names.

Some of the more commonly used chemicals are trichloroethylene, benzene, toluene and carbon disulphide. They are used extensively in the following industries:

- Engineering.
- Chemicals.
- Printing.
- Rubber.
- Plastics.
- Pharmaceutical manufacture.
- Footwear.
- Textiles.
- Foodstuffs.
- Woodworking.
- Dry cleaning.
- Paint manufacture.
- Ink manufacture.

It should therefore be anticipated that construction activities taking place in premises relating to these industries may expose workers to solvents.

Solvents are used in a variety of construction activities, particularly those relating to the application of adhesives or sealants. They are also found in a variety of products such as:

- Cleaning and degreasing materials.
- Paints, lacquers and varnishes.
- Pesticides.

All organic solvents have a vapour density greater than one, which means that their vapours are heavier than air and will therefore settle at ground level, which is an important point when considering ventilation. With the exception of chlorinated hydrocarbons (e.g. trichloroethylene) they tend to be flammable and explosive. In liquid form, they have a specific gravity less than one so will float on water.

Effects of solvents

Different solvents affect the body in different ways. The effects will vary according to such things as breathing pattern, activity, obesity and thickness of skin.

Typical acute effects:

Most solvents have an anaesthetic effect and are therefore dangerous in confined spaces. Headaches, dizziness, lack of concentration and eventually unconsciousness will result. Vapours may cause irritation of eyes and skin. If ingested they can cause abdominal pain, diarrhoea and vomiting. Occasional cases of cardiac arrest have also been reported following gross short-term over-exposure.

Chronic effects

The main problem from repeated exposure is dermatitis caused by the removal of the natural oils from the skin. The toxic effect of solvents will also cause damage to internal organs, notably the kidneys and liver.

Precautions for solvents

- Avoid skin contact by wearing suitable protective clothing (gloves, apron, goggles or face shield) where necessary.
- Prohibit eating and smoking where there are solvents.
- Prohibit hot work in areas which may contain vapours. Chlorinated solvents can decompose if exposed to naked flames and create acidic fumes, which may also contain phosgene, which are harmful to the lungs.
- Encourage good personal hygiene; wash thoroughly before eating or smoking. Do not use solvents to remove oil or paint from the skin.
- Ensure a well-ventilated area using local exhaust ventilation if necessary.
- Encourage good housekeeping; do not leave solvent contaminated rags lying around.
- Prevent unnecessary evaporation by keeping quantities to a minimum, keeping lids on containers, using sealed containers, for example.

CLEANERS

Numerous cleaning fluids used in industry contain solvents (dealt with earlier in this element), acids or alkalis. These can cause injury by coming into direct contact with the skin - the corrosive nature of acids and alkalis can cause serious chemical burns leading to permanent scarring, or respiratory trach/lung damage through inhaling fumes or mists.

BIOLOGICAL AGENTS

Tetanus

A life-threatening disease caused by toxins produced by the bacterium Clostridium tetani, which often grow at the site of a cut or wound. Muscles first become stiff, then rigidly fixed (lockjaw). Vaccination against tetanus should be done every 10 years or at the time of injury.

Leptospira

The bacteria Leptospira, spiral shaped bacteria, penetrates the skin and causes leptospirosis (Weil's Disease). Rodents represent the most important reservoir of infections, especially rats (also gerbils, voles, and field mice). Other sources of infection are dogs, hedgehogs, foxes, pigs, and cattle. These animals are not necessarily ill, but carry leptospires in their kidneys and excrete it in their urine. Infection can be transmitted directly via direct contact with blood, tissues, organs or urine of one of the host animals or indirectly by contaminated environment.

Infection enters through broken skin or mucous membrane. Symptoms vary but include flu-like illness, conjunctivitis, liver damage (including jaundice), kidney failure and meningitis. If untreated infection may be fatal.

Construction workers most at risk are those who work where rats prevail and will include water and sewage work, demolition or refurbishment of old unoccupied buildings, and those working on sites adjoining rivers and other watercourses. The bacteria's survival depends on protection from direct sunlight, so it survives well in water courses and ditches protected by vegetation.

Hepatitis

Hepatitis is inflammation of the liver; there are a number of types of hepatitis, the B variety being the most serious. Hepatitis is caused by a virus and is passed from human to human. Hepatitis A is spread by ingesting the virus from the faeces of an infected person, from food or water contaminated by the faeces of a contaminated person or from eating raw or undercooked shellfish harvested from contaminated water. The hepatitis B virus, which is very resilient in that it remains viable for weeks in the environment outside the human body, is resistant to common antiseptics and is not affected by boiling for less than thirty minutes.

Symptoms vary, but typically the sequence is: flu-like illness with aches and pains in the joints, general tiredness, anorexia, nausea and high fever, jaundice and the liver enlarged and tender.

Construction workers carrying out work on old derelict property and those clearing ground that may have been used by intravenous drug users are particularly at risk.

Health surveillance

Health surveillance may be appropriate where exposure to hazardous substances is such that an identifiable disease or adverse health effect may be linked to the exposure. There must be a reasonable likelihood that the disease or effect may occur under the particular conditions of work prevailing and that valid techniques exist to detect such conditions and effects.

The employer must keep records of surveillance in respect of each employee for at least 40 years.

Active health surveillance means preventative action can be taken early to protect the individual and it can also highlight problems with equipment that can be corrected before any other workers are affected.

Assessment

Content

Written assessments - Papers IGC1 and IGC2 274
NEBOSH sample questions 275
International health and safety practical application - Unit IGC3 280
Sample practical assessment 281
NEBOSH sample questions - Answers 289

QUESTIONS ARE REPRODUCED BY THE KIND PERMISSION OF NEBOSH

Please note that some words may have been changed to reflect the international nature of the examination

ASSESSMENT

Written assessments - Papers IGC1 and IGC2

At every examination a number of candidates - including some good ones - perform less well than they might because of poor examination technique. It is essential that candidates practice answering both essay-type and short answer questions and learn to allocate their time according to the number of marks allocated to questions (and parts of questions) as shown on the paper.

Each written paper is 2 hours duration and contains 2 sections:

Section 1 has one question carrying 20 marks requiring quite an 'in-depth' answer. This question should be allocated 30 minutes in total. If time (e.g. 5 minutes) is given to reading, planning and checking, the time available for writing is 25 minutes. Two pages are allowed for this answer; candidates should produce approximately 1½ sides for an average answer.

Section 2 has 10 questions each carrying 8 marks. If time (e.g. 10 minutes) is allowed for reading, planning and checking then there are 8 minutes to answer each question. One page is allowed for each of these answers, candidates should produce approximately ½ a side for an average answer.

A common fault is that candidates may fail to pay attention to the action verb in each question. The most common 'action verbs' used in Certificate examination questions are:

Define	provide a generally recognised or accepted definition
State	a less demanding form of 'define', or where there is no generally recognised definition
Sketch	provide a simple line drawing using labels to call attention to specific features
Explain	give a clear account of, or reasons for
Describe	give a word picture
Outline	give the most important features of (less depth than either 'explain' or 'describe', but more depth than 'list'.)
List	provide a list without explanation
Give	provide without explanation (used normally with the instruction 'give an example [or examples] of…')
Identify	select and name

Other questions may start with 'what, when, how' etc. In such cases the examiners are expecting candidates to give their own explanations.

NEBOSH questions have progressively changed to reflect practical issues that need to be managed in the workplace. Questions have increasingly reflected more than one element of knowledge, for example "electrical fires" which could require an understanding of Unit IGC2 - Elements 4 and 5 to answer adequately. We have chosen example questions of this type to enable you to better apply your knowledge and approach to meet the future requirements.

The need to understand the meaning of the 'action verb' and to read the question carefully is emphasised in the comments below that are taken from some recent examiner's reports:

"… many answers were too brief to satisfy the requirement for an outline or description. Points made should have been supported by sufficient reasoning to show their relevance to the question."

"Some candidates, even though they identified many of the relevant factors, could not be awarded the full range of marks available because they produced a truncated list that did not properly outline the relationship between each factor and the corresponding risks."

"It was disappointing to note that some candidates again misread the question and provided outlines of the duties of employers rather than employees."

"While answers to this question were generally to a reasonable standard, many were too brief to attract all the marks that were available."

"In answering questions on Paper IGC2, practical issues should be addressed. It is not sufficient in questions such as this merely to refer to generic issues such as risk assessment and safe systems of work without providing further detail of the controls that a risk assessment might show to be necessary or the elements of a safe system of work."

"Weaker answers tended to be those that provided insufficient detail - for example, mention of "PPE" or "edge protection" should have been accompanied by some examples of what might be required and reference to the purpose that they serve."

"Some answers were extremely brief and candidates should remember that one-fifth of the marks for the entire paper are available for answers to this question (question 1). Answers are expected to be proportionate to the marks available."

ASSESSMENT

NEBOSH sample questions

IGC1 - Management of international health and safety

ELEMENT 1

1. Replacement or repair of damaged plant and equipment is a cost that an organisation may face following a workplace accident.

    List **EIGHT** possible costs to the organisation following a workplace accident. **(8)**

    Mar 2005 Paper A1 Question 11

ELEMENT 2

1. Outline the key areas that should be addressed in the 'arrangements' section of a health and safety policy document. **(8)**

    Guide to the NEBOSH International General Certificate in Occupational Health and Safety, Unit IGC1 Sample Paper 1, Question 4

ELEMENT 3

1. (a) **Outline** the benefits to an organisation of having a health and safety committee. **(4)**

    (b) **Outline** the reasons why a health and safety committee may prove to be ineffective in practice. **(8)**

    (c) **Identify** a range of methods that an employer can use to provide health and safety information directly to individual workers. **(8)**

    Jun 2005 Paper A1 Question 1

2. **Outline** the topics that may typically be included on the agenda of a safety committee meeting. **(8)**

    Sep 2001 Paper A2 Question 8

3. **List** the factors that could be considered when assessing the health and safety competence of a contractor. **(8)**

    Dec 2002 Paper A1 Question 11

4. Following a significant increase in accidents, a health and safety campaign is to be launched within an organisation to encourage safer working by employees.

    (i) Outline how the organisation might ensure that the nature of the campaign is effectively communicated to, and understood by, the employees. **(8)**

    (ii) Other than poor communication, describe the organisational factors that could limit the effectiveness of the campaign. **(12)**

    Guide to the NEBOSH International General Certificate in Occupational Health and Safety, Unit IGC1 Sample Paper 1, Question 1

5. Outline reasons for maintaining good standards of health and safety within an organisation. **(8)**

    Guide to the NEBOSH International General Certificate in Occupational Health and Safety, Unit IGC1 Sample Paper 1, Question 2

ELEMENT 4

1. An investigation has identified the two key underlying causes of a workplace accident as ineffective verbal communication between employees and shortcomings in the quality of health and safety training.

    (a) **Identify** the barriers to effective verbal communication. **(8)**

    (b) **Outline** the means by which communication could be improved. **(6)**

    (c) **Describe** the variety of training methods a trainer could use to improve the effectiveness of worker training in health and safety. **(6)**

    Jun 2000 Paper A2 Question 1

2. **Outline** the main health and safety issues to be included in an induction training programme for new workers. **(8)**

    Guide to the NEBOSH International General Certificate in Occupational Health and Safety, Unit IGC1 Sample Paper 1, Question 6

3. An independent audit of an organisation has concluded that employees have received insufficient health and safety training.

    (i) **Describe** the factors that should be considered when developing an extensive programme of health and safety training within the organisation. **(12)**

    (ii) **Outline** the various measures that might be used to assess the effectiveness of such training. **(4)**

ASSESSMENT

    (iii)   Give **FOUR** reasons why it is important for an employer to keep a record of the training provided to each worker. **(4)**

Mar 2005 Paper A1 Question 1

4. Outline ways in which the health and safety culture of an organisation might be improved. **(8)**

Guide to the NEBOSH International General Certificate in Occupational Health and Safety, Unit IGC1 Sample Paper 1, Question 7

ELEMENT 5

1. **Outline** the factors to be considered when assessing the risks to a long distance transport vehicle driver. **(8)**

Mar 2005 Paper A1 Question 2

2. (a)   **Explain**, using an example, the meaning of the term 'risk'. **(2)**

   (b)   **Outline** the factors that should be considered when selecting individuals to assist in carrying out risk assessments in the workplace. **(6)**

Sep 2000 Paper A2 Question 10

3. **Outline** the key stages of a general risk assessment. **(8)**

Dec 2002 Paper A1 Question 8

ELEMENT 6

1. **Identify EIGHT** sources of information that might usefully be consulted when developing a safe system of work. **(8)**

Jun 2001 Paper A2 Question 11

2. **Outline** the precautions to ensure the health and safety of persons engaged in paint-spraying in a motor vehicle repair workshop. **(8)**

Dec 2002 Paper A2 Question 5

3. With respect to the management of risk within the workplace:

   (i)   Explain the meaning of the term 'hierarchy of control'. **(2)**

   (ii)   Outline, with examples, the standard hierarchy that should be applied with respect to controlling health and safety risks in the workplace. **(6)**

Guide to the NEBOSH International General Certificate in Occupational Health and Safety, Unit IGC1 Sample Paper 1, Question 8

ELEMENT 7

1. **Identify FOUR** active and **FOUR** reactive means by which an organisation can monitor its health and safety performance. **(8)**

Mar 2006 Paper A1 Question 11

2. **Identify** the advantages **AND** disadvantages of carrying out a health and safety audit of an organisation's activities by:

   (i)   an internal auditor. **(4)**

   (ii)   an external auditor. **(4)**

Jun 2006 Paper A1 Question 2

ELEMENT 8

1. (a)   A worker has been seriously injured after being struck by a reversing vehicle in a loading bay.

      (i)   Give **FOUR** reasons why the accident should be investigated by the person's employer. **(4)**

      (ii)   **Outline** the information that should be included in the investigation report. **(8)**

   (b)   Outline **FOUR** possible immediate causes and **FOUR** possible underlying (root) causes of the accident. **(8)**

Dec 2001 Paper A2 Question 1

2. (a)   **Identify FOUR** reasons why accidents should be reported and recorded within a workplace. **(4)**

   (b)   **Outline** factors that might discourage workers from reporting workplace accidents. **(4)**

Sep 2001 Paper A1 Question 9

3. Outline the immediate and longer term actions that should be taken following a serious injury accident at work. **(8)**

Guide to the NEBOSH International General Certificate in Occupational Health and Safety, Unit IGC1 Sample Paper 1, Question 10

ASSESSMENT

IGC2 - Control of international workplace hazards

ELEMENT 1

1. **List EIGHT** design features and/or safe practices intended to reduce the risk of accidents on staircases used as internal pedestrian routes within work premises. **(8)**

    Mar 2000 Paper A1 Question 6

2. Outline the precautions that might be needed to ensure the safety of pedestrians in vehicle manoeuvring areas. **(8)**

    Guide to the NEBOSH International General Certificate in Occupational Health and Safety, Unit IGC2 Sample Paper 2, Question 2

3. **Outline** the means by which the risk of accidents from reversing vehicles within a workplace can be reduced. **(8)**

    Dec 2002 Paper A2 Question 2

4. (a) Identify the types of hazard that may cause slips or trips at work. **(4)**
   (b) Outline how slip and trip hazards in the workplace might be controlled. **(4)**

    Guide to the NEBOSH International General Certificate in Occupational Health and Safety, Unit IGC2 Sample Paper 2, Question 3

ELEMENT 2

1. **Identify EIGHT** rules to follow when a fork-lift truck is left unattended during a driver's work break. **(8)**

    Jun 2006 Paper A2 Question 11

2. **Outline** the precautions to be taken when using a mobile elevating work platform (MEWP) to reach a high point such as a streetlight. **(8)**

    Dec 2002 Paper A2 Question 8

3. (a) List **FOUR** specific types of injury that may be caused by the incorrect manual handling of loads. **(4)**
   (b) Outline the factors in relation to the load that will affect the risk of injury. **(4)**

    Guide to the NEBOSH International General Certificate in Occupational Health and Safety, Unit IGC2 Sample Paper 2, Question 4

ELEMENT 3

1. A public services worker uses a petrol-driven strimmer to maintain roadside grass verges.
   (i) **Describe** the possible hazards faced by the worker in carrying out this task. **(10)**
   (ii) **List FIVE** items of personal protective equipment that should be provided to, and used by, the workers. **(5)**
   (iii) **Outline** measures other than the use of personal protective equipment that might be necessary to ensure the health and safety of the worker. **(5)**

    Dec 2000 Paper A1 Question 1

2. **Outline** the sources and possible effects of **FOUR** non-mechanical hazards commonly encountered in a woodworking shop. **(8)**

    Mar 2001 Paper A1 Question 6

ELEMENT 4

1. **Outline** a range of checks that should be made to ensure electrical safety in an office environment. **(8)**

    Dec 2001 Paper A1 Question 7

2. In relation to the use of electrical cables and plugs in the workplace:
   (i) **Identify FOUR** examples of faults and bad practices that could contribute to electrical accidents **(4)**
   (ii) **Outline** the corresponding precautions that should be taken for **EACH** of the examples identified in (i). **(4)**

    Mar 2000 Paper A1 Question 10

3. In relation to electrical safety, **explain** the meaning of the following terms:
   (i) 'isolation' **(2)**
   (ii) 'earthing' **(2)**
   (iii) 'reduced low voltage' **(2)**

© ACT

ASSESSMENT

(iv) 'overcurrent protection'. **(2)**

Dec 2002 Paper A2 Question 4

ELEMENT 5

1. **List EIGHT** ways of reducing the risk of a fire starting in a workplace. **(8)**

Jun 2001 Paper A1 Question 11

2. (a) **Explain**, using a suitable sketch, the significance of the 'fire triangle'. **(4)**

   (b) **Identify TWO** methods of heat transfer and **explain** how **EACH** method can contribute to the spread of fire in work premises. **(4)**

Dec 2005 Paper A2 Question 3

ELEMENT 6

1. (a) **Identify** possible routes of entry of biological organisms into the body. **(4)**

   (b) **Outline** control measures that could be used to reduce the risk of infection from biological organisms. **(4)**

Dec 2001 Paper A1 Question 10

2. A worker is engaged in general cleaning activities in a large veterinary practice.

   (i) **Identify FOUR** specific types of hazard that the cleaner might face when undertaking the cleaning. **(4)**

   (ii) **Outline** the precautions that could be taken to minimise the risk of harm from these hazards. **(4)**

Mar 2001 Paper A1 Question 8

3. A company produces a range of solid and liquid wastes, both hazardous and non-hazardous. **Outline** the arrangements that should be in place to ensure the safe storage of the wastes prior to their collection and disposal. **(8)**

Dec 2004 Paper A2 Question 4

4. For each of the following agents, **outline** the principal health and safety effects **AND identify** a typical workplace situation in which a person might be exposed:

   (i) Isocyanates **(2)**

   (ii) Asbestos **(2)**

   (iii) Leptospira bacteria **(2)**

   (iv) Lead **(2)**

Mar 2005 Paper A2 Question 3

5. (a) Define the term 'acute health effect'. **(2)**

   (b) An airborne corrosive chemical contaminant has been released into the atmosphere of a workplace.

   (i) Give an example of a corrosive chemical. **(1)**

   (ii) Describe the typical health effects resulting from exposure to this contaminant. **(4)**

   (c) State a suitable environmental monitoring method for a corrosive airborne compound. **(1)**

Guide to the NEBOSH International General Certificate in Occupational Health and Safety, Unit IGC2 Sample Paper 2, Question 10

ELEMENT 7

1. In relation to the ill-health effects from the use of vibrating hand-held tools:

   (i) **Identify** the typical symptoms that might be shown by affected individuals. **(4)**

   (ii) **Outline** the control measures that may be used to minimise the risk of such effects. (4)

Mar 2006 Paper A2 Question 5

2. (a) For **EACH** of the following types of non-ionising radiation, **identify** a source and state the possible ill-health effects on exposed individuals:

   (i) Infrared radiation **(2)**

   (ii) Ultraviolet radiation. **(2)**

(b) **Identify** the general methods for protecting people against exposure to non-ionising radiation. **(4)**

Jun 2001 Paper A1 Question 4

3. An office building is about to be occupied by new owners.

   (i) **Outline** the factors that should be considered by the new owners when assessing the suitability of lighting within the building. **(8)**

   (ii) **Describe FOUR** effects on health and safety that might result from inadequate lighting. **(4)**

   (iii) **Outline** the welfare facilities that should be provided in the building. **(8)**

Jun 2001 Paper A2 Question 1

4. (a) **Explain** the following terms in relation to noise exposure at work:

   (i) 'noise-induced hearing loss' **(2)**

   (ii) 'tinnitus'. **(2)**

   (b) **Identify** FOUR limitations of personal hearing protection as a means of protecting against the effects of noise. **(4)**

Dec 2002 Paper A2 Question 10

ELEMENT 8

1. The water main supplying a school is to be repaired. The work will be carried out in a 1.5 metre deep excavation, which will be supported in order to ensure the safety of those working in the excavation.

   (i) **Identify** when **THREE** main inspections of the supported excavation should be carried out by a competent person. **(3)**

   (ii) **State** the information that should be recorded in the excavation inspection report. **(5)**

   (iii) Other than the provision of supports for the excavation, **outline** additional precautions to be taken during the repair work in order to reduce the risk of injury to the employees and others who may be affected by the work. **(12)**

Mar 2006 Paper A2 Question 1

2. **Outline EIGHT** precautions that should be considered to ensure the safety of children who might be tempted to gain access to a construction site. **(8)**

Mar 2000 Paper A1 Question 2

3. **Outline** the particular hazards that may be present during the demolition of a building. **(8)**

Jun 2002 Paper A1 question 3

PLEASE REFER TO BACK OF THIS ASSESSMENT SECTION FOR ANSWERS

ASSESSMENT

International health and safety practical application - Unit IGC3

The practical assessment is intended to test candidates' abilities to apply their knowledge of health and safety to a practical situation, to demonstrate their understanding of key issues and to communicate findings in an effective way. The practical assessment require candidates to carry out unaided a safety inspection of a workplace and then prepare a management report. Completion of study for both IGC1 and IGC2 is recommended in order to undertake the practical application unit.

It should be carried out under the control of the accredited centre and be invigilated (supervised) by a safety professional or a senior manager. The assessment must take place within 14 days of (before or after) the date of the written papers (date of the examination). Please make sure you are clear about when you will carry out the assessment and that your assessment invigilator has set the time aside.

Procedure

Copies of the observation sheet should be used during your inspection. There are four columns on the form; observations, priority / risk, timescales; and brief notes on actions. The forms must be completed during the inspection and must be included with your covering management report for marking by the assessor.

The maximum time allocated to the practical assessment is 1 hour and 45 minutes. You should spend no more than 45 minutes making an assessment of your workplace, covering as wide a range of hazards as possible. The remaining time should be allocated to writing a report to management in your own handwriting, you should use lined paper to produce a report, consulting your own (and only your own) notes made during the inspection.

The whole assessment must be carried out under as near examination conditions as possible and you must not use anything previously prepared or company check lists, nor any other aids which would give you an advantage over other candidates at other centres.

You are expected to recognise physical, health and environmental hazards - good, as well as bad, work practices. While only short notes on each hazard are required, it is important that the assessor is able to subsequently identify the following:

- Where the hazard was located.
- The nature of the hazard.
- In what way, if any, the hazard is being controlled.
- The remedial action, where appropriate.
- Preventative action required.

You should, however, note that the assessment is not intended to be a pure hazard spotting exercise and consideration should be given to other matters such as:

- Availability and standard of washing and toilet facilities.
- Adequacy of heating, lighting and ventilation.
- General condition of floors and gangways.
- Cleanliness of structures.
- If staff are present, are they aware of the actions to take in the event of an emergency?

ASSESSMENT

Sample practical assessment

NEBOSH INTERNATIONAL GENERAL CERTIFICATE
Unit IGC3 – International health and safety practical application

Candidate's observation sheet

Sheet No 1 of 6

Candidates Name: _____ And number: C

Place inspected: Company Offices   Date of Inspection: Mon 4 Dec XX

No	Observations – List hazards, unsafe practices and good practice	Priority /risk (H,M,L)	Action to be taken (if any) – List any immediate or longer-term action required	Timescale (immediate, 1 week, etc.)
1	Risk of slips and trips due to loose and worn carpets in office generally	M	I – Alert staff to hazards and fix/tape down most hazardous areas	Immediate
			M – Replace carpets (worst should be replaced first)	1 Week
			L – Monitor to ensure no recurrence of problem	Monthly
2	Reduce risk of falls due to incorporation of window cleaners fixings at each window	M	I – No immediate action.	
			M – Ensure window cleaners are using harness and fixings	1 Week
			L – Ensure fixings tested regularly.	3 Monthly
3	Increased risk of fire / smoke speed, due to fire doors being wedged open & propped open with fire extinguishers	M	I – Close fire doors (remove wedges, etc.)	Immediate
			M – Inform / train staff	1 day
			L – Monitor and remind staff. Consider installing hold open devices linked to fire alarms	6 Months
4	Risk of falls due to possible failure of loose balustrading (at 2 locations on main staircase)	M	I – Inform staff or risk and effect a temporary repair (boarding fixed across balusters or similar)	Immediate
			M – Effect permanent repair (replacement steel balusters fixed to floor etc)	1 Week
			L – Monitor for recurrence	Monthly

ASSESSMENT

NEBOSH INTERNATIONAL GENERAL CERTIFICATE
Unit IGC3 – International health and safety practical application

Candidate's observation sheet

Sheet No 2 of 6

Candidates Name: _____ And number: C
Place inspected: Company Offices   Date of Inspection: Mon 4 Dec XX

No	Observations — List hazards, unsafe practices and good practice	Priority/risk (H,M,L)	Action to be taken (if any) — List any immediate or longer-term action required	Timescale (immediate, 1 week, etc.)
5	Risk of electric shock due to broken plastic casing on electric fan in project management office	H	I — Isolate from electricity and remove from service M — Replace plastic casing L — Monitor as part of standard procedure	Immediate 1 Week Weekly
6	Reduce risk of injury (cuts, amputation) from guillotine (for paper and card cutting) with fixed guard	M	I — No action required at present M — Maintain on regular basis L — Ensure guard is not removed and inform/train staff	 1 week 1 month
7	Risk of irritation due to use of dry powder fire extinguisher in enclosed areas (small store room) (combustion products toxic)	M	I — Replace with an alternative appropriate extinguisher suited to the risk M — Inform / train staff L — Monitor to ensure correct extinguisher kept in room	1 day 1 Week Weekly
8	Risk of trips and slips due to trailing cables in project management and drawing offices	M	I — Fix cover over cables or tape down M — Re-route cables, re locate desk / drawing boards or provide flexi sockets L — Review office layouts Train staff in awareness of hazards	Immediate 1 Month 3 Monthly

NEBOSH INTERNATIONAL GENERAL CERTIFICATE
Unit IGC3 – International health and safety practical application

Candidate's observation sheet

Sheet No 3 of 6

Candidates Name: _____ And number: C

Place inspected: Company Offices Date of Inspection: Mon 4 Dec XX

No	Observations List hazards, unsafe practices and good practice	Priority /risk (H,M,L)	Action to be taken (if any) List any immediate or longer-term action required	Timescale (immediate, 1 week, etc.)
9	Risk of electric shock due to frayed power cable on draughtsman's hand held erasing machine (in drawing office)	H	I — Isolate electrical supply and remove machine from service L — Replace damaged cable M — Monitor equipment on a regular basis and train staff in awareness	Immediate 1 Week Monthly
10	Risk of injury and damage due to collapse of shelving over drawing boards as a result of loose brackets (faulty fixings) (drawing office)	L	I — Remove shelving L — Refit shelving securely (establishing reason for failure) M — Monitor for possible recurrence	Immediate 1 Week 1 Month
11	Risk of work-related upper limb disorder, back and neck pain, eye strain, fatigue, stress etc, due to poorly laid out work stations with computers, inappropriate chairs, etc (secretarial, computer drafting, etc) Noted generally	M	I — Assess each users workstation M — Adjust layouts and provide appropriate equipment as necessary L — Reassess at regular intervals and monitor Display Screen Equipment Regs	Immediate 1 Week 1 Month
12	Risk of lacerations and / or falls due to low cilled window at bottom of stair flight (quarter landing)	H	I — Fix temporary protection M — Fix permanent protection barrier (metal bar or similar) across window and apply safety film to glazing L — Monitor	Immediate 1 Week 1 Month

ASSESSMENT

NEBOSH INTERNATIONAL GENERAL CERTIFICATE
Unit IGC3 – International health and safety practical application

Candidate's observation sheet

Sheet No 4 of 6

Candidates Name: _____ And number: C

Place inspected: Company Offices Date of Inspection: Mon 4 Dec XX

No	Observations — List hazards, unsafe practices and good practice	Priority /risk (H,M,L)	Action to be taken (if any) — List any immediate or longer-term action required	Timescale (immediate, 1 week, etc.)
13	Risk of confusion etc in the event of fire due to missing fire exit sign at ground floor (people not knowing direction of escape	H	I — Inform staff of escape requirements M — Fix up new fire exit sign as soon as possible L — Train staff and have fire drills	1 week 2 Week Monthly
14	Risk of strains / injury due to moving of large boxes of photocopy paper stored on floor near to photocopier	L	I — Inform staff to move small amounts at a time M — Fix shelves at appropriate height for paper storage. L — Train staff in manual handling and use of shelves	Immediate 1 Week 3 Months
15	Risk of falls and strains due to heavy articles on high shelves, with no adequate means of access (general office)	M	I — Remove articles form high shelves M — Supply means of access (steps etc) and store small items at high level. L — Monitor situation and train staff	Immediate 1 Week 1 Month
16	Risk of fire and possible reduced means of escape due to papers and files stored under fire escape stair at basement level	H	I — Remove papers, etc M — Inform / train staff L — Monitor situation to ensure situation does not recur	Immediate 1 Week On going

NEBOSH INTERNATIONAL GENERAL CERTIFICATE
Unit IGC3 – International health and safety practical application

Candidate's observation sheet

Sheet No 5 of 6

Candidates Name: _____ And number: C

Place inspected: Company Offices Date of Inspection: Mon 4 Dec XX

No	Observations — List hazards, unsafe practices and good practice	Priority /risk (H,M,L)	Action to be taken (if any) — List any immediate or longer-term action required	Timescale (immediate, 1 week, etc.)
17	Location of first aid box and names and locations of appropriate persons (First Aiders) prominently displayed. Risk of delay in first aid treatment reduced / controlled	M	I — No immediate action M — Ensure all staff kept informed (including changes) and monitor	Monthly
18	Risk of injury due to impact of forward opening door into small utility room (sink and kettle immediately behind door)	L	I — Put warning sign on outside of door and inform staff M — Fit inside panel into door (fire resisting) L — Monitor	Immediate 1 Week 1 Month
19	Increased risk of electric shock due to electrical socket (for kettle) within 1M of sink (utility room)	H	I — Inform staff of risk and display prominent warning signs M — Replace socket with residual current circuit breaker (RCCB) type as soon as possible L — Monitor regularly and respectfully remind staff / train	Immediate 1 Month Monthly
20	Risk of laceration due to breakage of glass in glazed screen at entrance reduced / controlled by application of protective clear plastic film	M	I — No immediate action M — Check that appropriate type of film approved L — Monitor condition at regular intervals	1 Week 1 Month

ASSESSMENT

NEBOSH INTERNATIONAL GENERAL CERTIFICATE
Unit IGC3 – International health and safety practical application

Candidate's observation sheet

Sheet No 6 of 6

Candidates Name: _____ And number: _____C_____
Place inspected: _Company Offices_ Date of Inspection: _Mon 4 Dec xx_

No	Observations — List hazards, unsafe practices and good practice	Priority /risk (H,M,L)	Action to be taken (if any) — List any immediate or longer-term action required	Timescale (immediate, 1 week, etc.)
21	Risk of bruising, lacerations etc, due to poor layout in reception rear office, outstanding sharp corners protruding into circulation areas	L	l — Fix padding to sharp corners	3 Days
			M — Remove offending items of furniture	1 Week
			L — Review and amend furniture layout	1 Month
22	Generally poor lighting increased risk of trips, eye strain, etc	L	l — Assess most hazardous areas and provide additional lighting in these areas if possible immediately.	Immediate
			M — Provide task lighting to individuals	1 Week
			L — Assess requirements and provide additional lighting. Monitor Lighting levels	1 Month
23	Poor ventilation to offices fronting onto busy road. Fumes and traffic noise when windows opened	L	l — Keep windows closed and ensure staff take regular breaks	Immediate
			M — Provide ventilation ducted from different areas or through new filtering and alternating ventilator(s) (plus possible secondary glazing)	1 week
			L — Monitor	1 Month
24	Welfare / Sanitary Lack of soap and paper towels plus holders, in a number of toilets. Broken toilet seat in basement toilet	L	l — Supply items where they are missing / broken	Immediate
			M — Fix holders where missing and establish system for regular supply of items	1 Week
			L — Monitor	1 Month

<u>Management Report on Hazards etc Noted
During Inspection of Offices.</u>

1. <u>Introduction</u>

    This report addresses matters noted at an inspection of offices at 120 .... Street, which was carried out on Monday 4th ***ember 20xx. It covers hazards and office related welfare matters. A number are considered in detail and the full observation list is included in the appendix.

2. <u>Summary</u>

    Detailed consideration is given to faulty balustrading and electric fan, fire precautions, and a dangerous window. Urgent repairs/replacement are recommended to balustrade and fan, improved management systems for fire prevention and remedial measures to window. Approximate costs are given.

3. <u>Main Findings</u>

3.1 <u>Observation no. 4 Loose balustrading on main stair</u>

    Two sections of balustrading are loose and likely to fail if leaned against. Locations are 1st and 2nd floor and any fall could be serious/fatal. Apart from the cost in human terms there would also be a loss of professional time because of such an accident. Since the stair is in constant use, I recommend immediate temporary repair using boarding, quickly followed by permanent repair comprising replacement steel balusters fixed to floor and handrail. I assess cost of repairs at £650 + VAT.

    Balustrading must be inspected regularly in future.

3.2 <u>Observation no. 5 Faulty electric fan.</u>

    A section of the plastic cover is broken and electrically conductive parts are possible to touch. Accidental electrocution could easily occur, so the fan should be taken out of service and the cover replaced. If parts are not available, the whole fan should be replaced. Cost off repair is £10 (carried out by our staff) and replacement is £55 (incl.VAT). Action should be taken immediately to avoid a serious/fatal accident, lost time and to comply with current legislation (where applicable).

ASSESSMENT

3.3 <u>Observation no. 16 Basement Fire escape Stair.</u>

Documents are stored under the fire escape stair. This is a fire hazard and in the event of fire the only escape route would be cut off. This could lead to fatalities. The situation is remedied, at almost no cost, by removing the documents. I recommend, this is done immediately and management procedures adopted to prevent reoccurrence. This should include immediate information to staff, staff training and supervision.

3.4 <u>Observation no. 12 Stair windows with low cill.</u>

This 2nd floor window has a very low cill and is unprotected. If someone falls against it, they could break the glass and cut themselves badly and possibly fall through to the outside. To prevent this possibility the glazing should be protected by applying plastic safety film and fixing a bar or hand rail across the opening. Costs would be <u>approx £450 (+VAT).</u>

Whilst the above are the most critical flaws there are a number of items requiring attention and reference should be made to the observation sheets in the appendix.

4. <u>Conclusion</u>

Occupational health and safety is a subject which needs to be managed properly. Failure to do this might result in legal action (where applicable). The attendant costs and adverse publicity could have a significant impact on profitability.

Accidents have to be investigated by management and when time is lost from work, workloads have to be reorganised and sometimes re-training has to take place. These issues also have an economic impact.

Accidents that result in personal injury obviously cause pain and suffering to the victim. More serious accidents affect a wider circle of family and friends. Witnesses to serious accidents may also suffer. It is my belief that people have a right to be protected from the hazards that are present in the workplace and that managers have a duty to ensure this protection is in place.

<u>End</u>

ASSESSMENT

NEBOSH sample questions - Answers

IGC1 - Management of international health and safety

ELEMENT 1

1. Replacement or repair of damaged plant and equipment is a cost that an organisation may face following a workplace accident.

    List **EIGHT** possible costs to the organisation following a workplace accident. **(8)**

    Mar 2005 Paper A1 Question 11

There are many possible responses to this question and a long list of possible costs. They include:

- *Costs associated with lost production.*
- *Damage to materials.*
- *First-aid.*
- *Investigation and remedial action.*
- *Additional administration incurred.*
- *Replacement staff.*
- *Increases in insurance premiums as well as in some territories criminal and civil actions (the imposition of fines, parts of compensation payments not covered by insurance and legal representation).*

There may also be intangible costs following an accident arising from a poor corporate image and a possible detrimental effect on employee morale resulting in reduced productivity.

ELEMENT 2

1. Outline the key areas that should be addressed in the 'arrangements' section of a health and safety policy document. **(8)**

    Guide to the NEBOSH International General Certificate in Occupational Health and Safety, Unit IGC1 Sample Paper 1, Question 4

A number of candidates struggled with this question, for reasons which were not obvious to the examiners. perhaps they were not adequately prepared at being asked to deal with the "arrangements" section of a health and safety policy on its own, as opposed to the three elements of the health and safety policy, or possibly, this being the last question on the paper, they did not have the time to give it the attention it necessary.

Those candidates who did understand what was required and had sufficient time left, outlined a number of items that might be contained within the arrangements section of a policy such as arrangements for: carrying out risk assessments; controlling exposure to specific hazards (e.g. noise, radiation, hazardous substances, manual handling, etc); monitoring procedures; use of personal protective equipment; reporting accidents and unsafe conditions; controlling contractors; ensuring the safety of visitors; maintenance; the provision of welfare facilities; dealing with emergencies; training; consultation with employees and environmental control including dealing with waste, to name a few.

ELEMENT 3

1. (a) **Outline** the benefits to an organisation of having a health and safety committee. **(4)**

    (b) **Outline** the reasons why a health and safety committee may prove to be ineffective in practice. **(8)**

    (c) **Identify** a range of methods that an employer can use to provide health and safety information directly to individual workers. **(8)**

    Jun 2005 Paper A1 Question 1

Benefits which can be outlined include: it demonstrates management commitment and in some territories compliance with the legal requirement to consult with employees; it facilitates consultation and communication with the workforce via employee representatives; it provides a means of recording discussions that have taken place on health and safety matters and it may help to enhance a positive health and safety culture by encouraging employee involvement and ownership. (In error - many candidates concentrated on the 'functions' of a health and safety committee, rather than the 'benefits' to an organisation of having a health and safety committee in place).

Identify reasons such as: a lack of management commitment; no terms of reference for the committee; no agenda and/or minutes of the meetings being produced; an uneven balance between management and employee representatives; poor chairmanship; no access to the decision making processes; infrequent meetings; inappropriate topics for discussion and no access to health and safety expertise.

A range of valid methods such as: notice boards; team briefings; training sessions including induction and tool box talks; news letters and the inclusion of messages with wage/pay slips; posters, competitions and signs; and one to one briefing such as in appraisal sessions.

2. **Outline** the topics that may typically be included on the agenda of a safety committee meeting. **(8)**

    Sep 2001 Paper A2 Question 8

© ACT

ASSESSMENT

These may include, for instance, a review of recent incidents, a review of proactive monitoring strategies such as safety inspections and audits, in some territories reports following visits by enforcement authorities, and the effects on the company of new or impending health and safety legislation. Additionally, the safety committee agenda should include items on possible amendments to the company's health and safety policy and risk assessments, the extent and effectiveness of any health and safety training given to employees, and the introduction of new equipment and processes.

Furthermore, identify that the safety committee is the place for health and safety concerns of employees to be raised by their representatives, as well as for management to raise its concerns about poor safety practices.

Do not spend too much time detailing the administrative items to be included on an agenda, such as welcomes, previous minutes and dates of future meetings. Although these do form part of any agenda, they do not really satisfy the description of 'topics' and therefore do not form an important part of the answer.

3. **List** the factors that could be considered when assessing the health and safety competence of a contractor. **(8)**

Dec 2002 Paper A1 Question 11

Candidates should be able to list a good range of factors that include, amongst many others:
- *The contractor's previous experience with the type of work.*
- *The reputation of the contractor amongst previous or current clients.*
- *The content and quality of the contractor's health and safety policy and risk assessments.*
- *The level of training and qualifications of staff (including those with health and safety responsibilities).*
- *Accident/enforcement history.*
- *Membership of accreditation or certification bodies.*
- *Equipment maintenance and statutory examination records.*
- *The detailed proposals (e.g. method statements) for the work to be carried out.*

4. Following a significant increase in accidents, a health and safety campaign is to be launched within an organisation to encourage safer working by employees.

　　(i)　Outline how the organisation might ensure that the nature of the campaign is effectively communicated to, and understood by, the employees. **(8)**

　　(ii)　Other than poor communication, describe the organisational factors that could limit the effectiveness of the campaign. **(12)**

Guide to the NEBOSH International General Certificate in Occupational Health and Safety, Unit IGC1 Sample Paper 1, Question 1

In answering part (i) of the question, candidates were expected to outline the key requirements to ensure that everybody within an organisation knows the part that they are to play within a health and safety campaign. An important prerequisite is to have clear objectives and targets for the campaign, and to be clear on the means of achieving them. It is also important that key responsibilities for aspects of the campaign are allocated, and accepted with due commitment, in order to avoid mixed messages. While an outline of the different means of communication should have been included in the answer, many candidates concentrated solely on this point and thus restricted the number of marks that they could have gained. In this respect, though, a variety of means (posters, emails, toolbox talks, training sessions, etc) could be used to communicate and reinforce the message with account taken of the language used in order to facilitate understanding (avoidance of jargon, use of plain English. etc). Toolbox talks, suggestion boxes surveys and informal means of consultation can be used to involve employees and to provide a feedback loop to check that employees understand what the campaign is about and to assess the level of support. It is also important to provide feedback to employees on how the campaign is progressing so that focus on the campaign's objectives is maintained.

Many candidates did not read part (ii) of the question with sufficient care and referred to communication problems rather than the range of other organisational factors that might affect the success of a health and safety campaign. Such issues can include: lack of senior management commitment; production or other pressures taking priority over health and safety; insufficient resources allocated to the campaign; and a poor safety culture in general. It should also have been recognised that poor working conditions are likely to induce cynicism towards the campaign amongst employees. In addition poor industrial relations or a lack of confidence in management's ability could mean that the campaign is not given the support of influential members of staff. Work patterns (eg shiftwork) could also mean that some sections of the workforce are not fully considered or supported, possibly due to the non-availability of key staff.

Overall this question was not well answered and many candidates either treated it as a general question on communication or produced an explanation of how accidents could be prevented (ie what a health and safety campaign should comprise). In addition many answers were too brief to satisfy the requirement for an outline or description. Points made should have been supported by sufficient reasoning to show their relevance to the question.

5. Outline reasons for maintaining good standards of health and safety within an organisation. **(8)**

Guide to the NEBOSH International General Certificate in Occupational Health and Safety, Unit IGC1 Sample Paper 1, Question 2

There were some good answers to this question, balanced by a significant number of very weak ones and, again, some non-attempts. Better answers were structured around the moral, economic and in some territories legal arguments for maintaining good standards of health and safety within an organisation.

The moral argument centres on the need to provide a reasonable standard of care and to reduce the injuries, pain and suffering caused to workers by accidents and ill-health, while legal where applicable in some territories arguments are concerned with the desire to avoid enforcement action and civil claims. Economic benefits include: a more motivated workforce resulting in increased production rates; the avoidance of direct costs associated with accidents (e.g. downtime, administrative, investigation and first-aid costs, repair of plant and equipment, employing and training replacement workers, etc); possibly cheaper insurance premiums; the avoidance of costs associated with legal action; and maintaining the image and reputation of the organisation with its various stakeholders.

ELEMENT 4

1. An investigation has identified the two key underlying causes of a workplace accident as ineffective verbal communication between employees and shortcomings in the quality of health and safety training.

    (a) **Identify** the barriers to effective verbal communication. **(8)**

    (b) **Outline** the means by which communication could be improved. **(6)**

    (c) **Describe** the variety of training methods a trainer could use to improve the effectiveness of worker training in health and safety. **(6)**

    Jun 2000 Paper A2 Question 1

For part (a), reference to:
- Background noise.
- Different languages, accents or dialects.
- The complexity of the information.
- Use of technical jargon.
- Interference due to personal protective equipment.
- Distractions.
- Sensory impairment.
- Ambiguity.

For part (b), an outline of a broad range of issues, not restricted to verbal communication:
- Seeking confirmation that the message has been understood.
- Developing the communication skills of key personnel.
- Adopting in-house standards to ensure consistent use of technical terms.
- Ensuring communication is made at appropriate times (e.g. when the recipient is free from distraction).
- Supplementing verbal communication with other means of communication (e.g. written instruction or teaching by example).

For part (c), description of:
- Video.
- Case studies.
- Group exercises.
- Role play.
- Practical exercises.
- Quizzes, etc.

2. **Outline** the main health and safety issues to be included in an induction training programme for new workers. **(8)**

    Dec 2002 Paper A1 Question 9

This question was designed to examine the issues involved in the training of new staff.

Answers should concentrate on the matters to be included in an induction training programme required and not include wider training issues.

Outline the main topics as the organisation's health and safety policy, emergency procedures, hazards specific to the workplace and the need to comply with health and safety requirements, health and safety responsibilities and lines of communication, accident and first-aid arrangements, welfare provision, health surveillance and consultation procedures.

3. An independent audit of an organisation has concluded that employees have received insufficient health and safety training.

    (i) **Describe** the factors that should be considered when developing an extensive programme of health and safety training within the organisation. **(12)**

    (ii) **Outline** the various measures that might be used to assess the effectiveness of such training. **(4)**

    (iii) Give **FOUR** reasons why it is important for an employer to keep a record of the training provided to each worker. **(4)**

    Mar 2005 Paper A1 Question 1

For part (i), the completion of a training needs analysis is an important first step in the development of any programme of training (i.e. comparing what workers need to know with what they already know). In deciding what workers need to know, consideration should be given to their responsibilities, the activities carried out, the risks associated with those activities and the actions required of workers to minimise such risks. It should be recognised in this context that a senior manager, for instance, will have different training needs with respect to health and safety from those of a supervisor or a general labour worker. An assessment should then need to be made of workers' existing knowledge, taking into account their previous experience, the levels and types of training already received and any indications of where efficiencies may lie (e.g. from incident data or by observation). From the training needs analysis would emerge information on the number of workers involved, the types of training needed and the resources (in terms of financial costs, time and facilities) required to carry out the programme. The factors to be considered at this stage would include the competence and expertise

ASSESSMENT

of trainers to provide the required training, the possible need to involve external sources and the means of communicating the programme to workers at all levels in order to seek their commitment to, and their views on, the programme.

Answers to part (ii) outline such measures as: post-training evaluation by trainers, the trainees themselves and their supervisors; accident rates and sickness absences; levels of compliance with laid-down procedures (such as the wearing of personal protective equipment); the results of attitude surveys; and the number and quality of suggestions made, and concerns raised, by employees with respect to health and safety.

In answering part (iii), candidates should cite a number of reasons for keeping individual training records. These might include: to provide proof of an employee's expected level of competence; to identify when additional or refresher training might be needed; to enable a review of the effectiveness of any training to be carried out; to assess the progress of the training programme against targets; and to provide evidence to be used in any future accident investigations or legal actions.

4. Outline ways in which the health and safety culture of an organisation might be improved. **(8)**

Guide to the NEBOSH International General Certificate in Occupational Health and Safety, Unit IGC1 Sample Paper 1, Question 7

The standard of response to this question was reasonable with most candidates outlining ways such as: establishing and implementing a sound health and safety policy; securing the commitment of management and ensuring that managers lead by example; involving and consulting with employees on matters affecting their health and safety; and providing effective supervision and training.

Better candidates referred to such additional factors as the organisation being seen to give equal priority to health and safety as other business objectives (such as production and quality), establishing effective means of communication with the workforce, and providing a pleasant working environment with good welfare facilities.

ELEMENT 5

1. **Outline** the factors to be considered when assessing the risks to a long distance transport vehicle driver. **(8)**

Mar 2005 Paper A1 Question 2

Good answers tend to be structured broadly under the four headings of the job, the individual, the vehicle and the load, with two or three factors outlined for each. Job factors would include the duration of the journey, the demands of the route (complexity, road conditions, etc), means of communication and security issues (e.g. the potential for violence). Individual factors would relate to the physical and psychological capabilities of the driver to cope with the demands of the job, taking into account the level of training provided. For the vehicle, ergonomic factors would relate to the design and layout of the cab but other features of the vehicle, such as tail-lifts, would be particularly important. Lastly, candidates should consider aspects of the load in terms of its nature (e.g. hazardous, heavy, etc), the means of handling materials and any emergency equipment and procedures that are, or should be, in place.

2. (a) **Explain**, using an example, the meaning of the term 'risk'. **(2)**

   (b) **Outline** the factors that should be considered when selecting individuals to assist in carrying out risk assessments in the workplace. **(6)**

Sep 2000 Paper A2 Question 10

Part (a) while 'hazard' refers to the potential of something to cause harm, 'risk' is the likelihood of that harm actually occurring together with the severity of its consequences. A suitable example for risk should be "the chance of someone being killed by coming into contact with electricity".

For part (b) outline factors such as:
- The level of training in health and safety generally, and in carrying out risk assessments in particular.
- Experience of the process/activity.
- The possession of technical knowledge of the plant or equipment involved.
- The ability to interpret standards, regulations and guidance.
- Communication and reporting skins.
- Attention to detail.

Commitment to the task may also be highlighted as an important factor by some candidates, as is the individual's awareness of his/her own limitations.

3. **Outline** the key stages of a general risk assessment. **(8)**

Dec 2002 Paper A1 Question 8

The initial stage in any assessment is to define the task and identify both the hazards associated with the task and the classes of persons at risk of harm. The next stage would be to evaluate the risks arising from the hazards, to assess the effectiveness of existing precautions and to decide whether additional measures are required to eliminate or control the risks. Finally the findings of the assessment need to be recorded and a timescale set for their review and, if necessary, revision.

ELEMENT 6

1. **Identify EIGHT** sources of information that might usefully be consulted when developing a safe system of work. **(8)**

Jun 2001 Paper A2 Question 11

A selection can be made from sources such as:

- *Statutory instruments, ACOPs, HSE guidance in territories where applicable.*
- *Manufacturers' information.*
- *European and international official standards.*
- *Industry or trade literature.*
- *Results of risk assessments.*
- *Accident statistics and health/medical surveillance records, the workers involved, and where applicable enforcement agencies and other experts.*

2. **Outline** the precautions to ensure the health and safety of persons engaged in paint-spraying in a motor vehicle repair workshop. **(8)**

Dec 2002 Paper A2 Question 5

This question presents candidates with a particular scenario and requires them to outline the precautions that should be taken to ensure the health and safety of those involved in the activity described. Examiners are looking to candidates to suggest such precautions as: segregation of the activity, typically by means of a spray booth fitted with local exhaust ventilation and protected electrical equipment; suitable storage and fire precautions for flammable paints and solvents; the provision and use of personal protective equipment (clothing, respiratory protection, etc); monitoring workers exposures to airborne substances; ensuring the examination and maintenance of control measures; providing appropriate training to workers; and maintaining welfare and hygiene facilities.

3. With respect to the management of risk within the workplace:

    (i) Explain the meaning of the term 'hierarchy of control'. **(2)**

    (ii) Outline, with examples, the standard hierarchy that should be applied with respect to controlling health and safety risks in the workplace. **(6)**

Guide to the NEBOSH International General Certificate in Occupational Health and Safety, Unit IGC1 Sample Paper 1, Question 8

For part (i) of the question, an acceptable explanation of the term "hierarchy of control" would have been either a list of measures designed to control risks which are considered in order of importance or effectiveness or measures designed to control risk that normally begin with an extreme measure of control and end with the use of personal protective equipment (PPE) as a last resort.

In answering part (ii) on the application of the standard hierarchy, candidates should have begun with the possibility of eliminating the risks either by designing them out or changing the process. The next step would be the reduction of the risks by, for example, the substitution of hazardous substances with others which were less hazardous. If this were not possible, then isolation would have to be considered, using enclosures, barriers or worker segregation. The application of engineering controls such as guarding, the provision of local exhaust ventilation systems, the use of reduced voltage systems or residual current devices would follow, with the final control measure being the provision of PPE such as ear defenders or respiratory protective equipment.

Answers to this question were generally to a poor standard and some candidates made no attempt at all to provide a response. Examiners were disappointed to note that many candidates had a poor grasp of this important principle in the management of health and safety with some confusing the hierarchy of control with the hierarchy of management within an organisation.

ELEMENT 7

1. **Identify FOUR** active and **FOUR** reactive means by which an organisation can monitor its health and safety performance. **(8)**

Mar 2006 Paper A1 Question 11

Active methods of monitoring might include: safety audits involving comprehensive and independently executed examinations of all aspects of an organisation's health and safety performance against stated objectives; safety surveys focusing on a particular activity such as manual handling, training programmes and workers' attitudes towards health and safety; sampling where specific areas of occupational health and safety are targeted; tours involving unscheduled workplace inspections to check on issues such as wearing of PPE and housekeeping; benchmarking where an organisation's performance in certain areas is compared with that of other organisations with similar processes and risks and health surveillance using techniques such as audiometry.

Reactive methods of monitoring might include: an analysis of statistics on accidents, dangerous occurrences, near misses and cases of occupational ill-health; assessment of the cost of these incidents including damage to property; and where applicable in some territories the number of enforcement actions such as prosecutions and notices taken against the organisation and the number of civil claims for damages persued on behalf of its workers.

Avoid confusion between 'active' and 'reactive' methods of monitoring.

2. **Identify** the advantages **AND** disadvantages of carrying out a health and safety audit of an organisation's activities by:

    (i) an internal auditor. (4)

    (ii) an external auditor. (4)

Jun 2006 Paper A1 Question 2

(Advantages in one type of audit are often mirrored by disadvantages in the other).

ASSESSMENT

The possible advantages of using an *internal auditor* for a safety audit of an organisation would include familiarity with the workplace, its tasks and processes and an awareness of what might be practicable for the industry; familiarity with members of the workforce including knowledge of an individual's qualities and attitude; and an audit which was relatively less costly and easier to arrange. On the other hand, an internal auditor may not be in possession of recognised auditing skills, may not be up to date with legal requirements and be less likely to be aware of best practice in other organisations. They may be subject to pressure from management and the workforce and have time constraints imposed upon him.

Conversely an *external auditor* is more likely to posses the necessary auditing skills and credibility; will not be inhibited from criticising members of management or the workforce; is more likely to be up to date with legal requirements and best practice in other companies and will view the organisation's performance with no personal bias. However, they will be disadvantaged in that they are unlikely to be familiar with the workplace, tasks and processes; may have difficulty in obtaining the full cooperation of the workforce; may be unfamiliar with the industry and seek unrealistic standards and may well be more costly than an internal member of staff.

ELEMENT 8

1. (a) A worker has been seriously injured after being struck by a reversing vehicle in a loading bay.

    (i) Give **FOUR** reasons why the accident should be investigated by the person's employer. **(4)**

    (ii) **Outline** the information that should be included in the investigation report. **(8)**

   (b) Outline **FOUR** possible immediate causes and **FOUR** possible underlying (root) causes of the accident. **(8)**

Dec 2001 Paper A2 Question 1

For part (i), candidates should recognise that the primary purpose of investigating an accident is to identify the immediate and root causes in order to prevent similar accidents occurring in the future. In this respect, the main reasons for investigation relate to the identification of possible weaknesses in risk assessment processes and other aspects of safety management systems. Other reasons relate to:

- *Facilitating compliance with legal obligations (where applicable).*
- *Collecting evidence to defend a civil claim, where applicable.*
- *Determining economic loss.*
- *Demonstrating management commitment to occupational health and safety.*

Part (ii) requires an outline of a sufficient range of information to gain the eight marks available. This should include reference to information such as:

- *The personal details of the injured party.*
- *The date, time and location of the accident.*
- *Environmental conditions, the work activity at the time of the accident.*
- *The control measures in place.*
- *The precise circumstances of the accident.*
- *The type and extent of injury sustained.*
- *Details of witnesses and copies of their statements where taken.*
- *Drawings and photographs.*
- *Immediate and root causes identified.*
- *Possible breaches of the law, where applicable.*
- *The recommendations of the investigation team in relation to remedial action required.*

In answering part (iii), marks are available for outlining possible immediate causes such as:

- *Human error or failure to comply with procedures.*
- *Mechanical failure.*
- *Poor visibility in the loading bay (e.g. absence of lighting).*
- *Restricted view for the driver.*
- *Environmental conditions such as high noise levels.*

Underlying causes could include:

- *Lack of driver and/or other employee training.*
- *Lack of supervision.*
- *Absence of site rules or procedures for the control of reversing vehicles.*
- *Failure to separate vehicular and pedestrian traffic.*
- *Lack of maintenance of vehicles and/or the workplace.*

2. (a) **Identify FOUR** reasons why accidents should be reported and recorded within a workplace. **(4)**

   (b) **Outline** factors that might discourage workers from reporting workplace accidents. **(4)**

Sep 2001 Paper A1 Question 9

For part (a), candidates should identify that accidents should be reported and recorded in order to comply with where applicable legislative requirements, to enable an accident investigation to take place (with the aim of preventing accidents of a similar type) and to identify accident trends from later statistical analysis. Marks are also available for identifying that accident reporting and recording can also lead to a useful review of risk assessments and can assist in the consideration of any civil claims that may arise.

In answering part (b), Examiners are looking to candidates to outline factors such as:

ASSESSMENT

- *Ignorance of the reporting procedures.*
- *The possibility of retribution (particularly within a 'blame culture').*
- *Peer pressure.*
- *A previous lack of management response.*
- *An aversion to form filling.*

Other factors include:

- *A reluctance to lose time from the job in hand.*
- *The trivial nature of any injury sustained.*
- *A desire to preserve the company's, the department's or the individual's personal safety record, particularly where bonus payments are affected by it.*

3. Outline the immediate and longer term actions that should be taken following a serious injury accident at work. **(8)**

Guide to the NEBOSH International General Certificate in Occupational Health and Safety, Unit IGC1 Sample Paper 1, Question 10

Candidates who gained high marks were those who clearly structured their answers into the actions that are required immediately after an accident -such as providing first-aid and medical treatment, informing the next of kin and securing the scene of the accident -and the subsequent actions that are required to satisfy statutory requirements and to determine immediate and root causes. Longer term actions should therefore include where applicable reporting the accident to the enforcing authority, identifying witnesses, undertaking an investigation and, on the basis of the findings, revising work procedures.

Answers to the question were generally to a reasonable standard with candidates perhaps less confident in identifying longer term measures than those required immediate .The question asked for an outline and, as is so often the case, some candidates were much too brief in their answers.

IGC2 - Control of international workplace hazards

ELEMENT 1

1. **List EIGHT** design features and/or safe practices intended to reduce the risk of accidents on staircases used as internal pedestrian routes within work premises. **(8)**

Mar 2000 Paper A1 Question 6

This question calls for practical suggestions on ways of preventing accidents such as slips, trips and falls on staircases. Matters that should spring to mind almost immediately include:

- *The removal of obstructions.*
- *The provision of non-slip surfaces, together with reflective edging.*
- *Adequate lighting and effective maintenance.*

Important design features of a staircase (which are to a large extent defined by building standards) are:

- *Its width.*
- *The provision of handrails.*
- *The dimensions of treads and risers.*
- *The provision of landings.*

Better answers to this question should also refer to the need to make special provision for disabled persons and also to the possibility of using a lift as an alternative, in particular to avoid the need to carry large or heavy items up or down stairs. Site rules should address such issues as well as defining appropriate footwear.

2. Outline the precautions that might be needed to ensure the safety of pedestrians in vehicle manoeuvring areas. **(8)**

Guide to the NEBOSH International General Certificate in Occupational Health and Safety, Unit IGC2 Sample Paper 2, Question 2

Answers should generally include:

- *References to segregated systems for vehicular and pedestrian traffic.*
- *Appropriate road markings.*
- *Maintaining good visibility (mirrors, transparent doors, provision of lighting etc.).*
- *Audible warnings on vehicles.*

Other relevant measures that should be mentioned include:

- *The drawing up and enforcement of site rules.*
- *The provision of refuges.*
- *The wearing of high-visibility clothing.*
- *A good standard of housekeeping.*
- *Training for, and supervision of, all concerned.*

3. **Outline** the means by which the risk of accidents from reversing vehicles within a workplace can be reduced. **(8)**

Dec 2002 Paper A2 Question 2

© ACT

295

ASSESSMENT

Present a hierarchical range, from avoiding the need for vehicles to reverse (one-way and 'drive-through' systems, turning circles, etc), through the separation of vehicles and pedestrians (barriers, signs, etc) and aspects of vehicle and workplace design (audible alarms, mirrors on vehicles and at blind corners, refuges, lighting, etc), to procedural measures (use of banksmen, site rules, driver training, etc).

4. (a) Identify the types of hazard that may cause slips or trips at work. **(4)**

   (b) Outline how slip and trip hazards in the workplace might be controlled. **(4)**

   Guide to the NEBOSH International General Certificate in Occupational Health and Safety, Unit IGC2 Sample Paper 2, Question 3

There are many reasons why people slip or trip, including the floor being poorly maintained, changes in level (with ramps, slopes or kerbs), slippery surfaces caused by oil, water or ice, inappropriate footwear, and general obstructions in walkways such as trailing cables, pipes and air hoses. Some candidates struggled to find a full range of hazards for part (a) and sometimes gave examples that were very similar in nature. Those who, for example, merely gave four different types of obstruction in a walkway had only addressed one type of hazard, which reduced the number of marks that could be awarded.

In answering part (b), candidates should have outlined control measures such as highlighting changes in level with hazard warning strips, providing good lighting, introducing procedures for reporting defects and for spillages, gritting oily and icy surfaces, using non-slip flooring, and ensuring high standards of housekeeping to keep floors free of obstruction. Many answers were restricted to housekeeping issues.

ELEMENT 2

1. **Identify EIGHT** rules to follow when a fork-lift truck is left unattended during a driver's work break. **(8)**

   Jun 2006 Paper A2 Question 11

Examiners expected candidates to identify rules such as the return of the fork-lift truck to a designated area on firm level ground with the mast tilted forward and the forks resting on the floor; the isolation of the power with the ignition key removed and returned to a responsible person; and the need to park the truck away from other vehicles and in a position that did not block emergency exits.

Most candidates achieved a good / reasonable mark for this question even though on occasions Examiners were required to interpret some answers where forks were referred to as "spikes", "blades" or "bars" and the mast as a "boom" or "stack".

2. **Outline** the precautions to be taken when using a mobile elevating work platform (MEWP) to reach a high point such as a streetlight. **(8)**

   Dec 2002 Paper A2 Question 8

Candidates should outline precautions such as:

- *The need to inspect the equipment before use and to ensure it is in a good state of repair.*
- *Using only competent workers.*
- *Using outriggers and brakes.*
- *Erecting warning signs and barriers to avoid collisions.*
- *Ensuring the platform is not overloaded.*
- *Avoiding overhead obstructions.*
- *Wearing a harness.*

3. (a) List **FOUR** specific types of injury that may be caused by the incorrect manual handling of loads. **(4)**

   (b) Outline the factors in relation to the load that will affect the risk of injury. **(4)**

   Guide to the NEBOSH International General Certificate in Occupational Health and Safety, Unit IGC2 Sample Paper 2, Question 4

Part (a) of the question asked for a list of specific injuries that might be caused by the incorrect manual handling of loads. These would include spinal disc compression or slipped discs, torn ligaments or strained or sprained tendons, hernias, dislocations and fractures, muscular strains, cuts and abrasions, and crushing and impact injuries. While there were some good answers to this part of the question, too many candidates referred in vague and general terms to back, muscular and hand injuries when a more specific answer was required.

Part (b) tested candidates' knowledge of how the nature of a load can affect the risk of injury during manual handling activities. They should have identified matters such as the size and weight of the load, the possibility that the contents might move and the load become unbalanced, the weight distribution (the centre of gravity not being in the centre of the load), difficulty in securing a firm grasp of the load, and the presence of sharp edges or very hot or cold surfaces. Again, better candidates were able to provide a focused answer with sufficient detail to demonstrate a clear understanding of the issues. Other answers, however, were extremely brief (sometimes no more than four words) and a few identified controls instead of risk factors.

ELEMENT 3

1. A public services worker uses a petrol-driven strimmer to maintain roadside grass verges.

   (i) **Describe** the possible hazards faced by the worker in carrying out this task. **(10)**

   (ii) **List FIVE** items of personal protective equipment that should be provided to, and used by, the worker. **(5)**

ASSESSMENT

(iii) **Outline** measures other than the use of personal protective equipment that might be necessary to ensure the health and safety of the worker. **(5)**

Dec 2000 Paper A1 Question 1

This question is designed to test the ability of candidates to apply basic principles of health and safety to a practical situation. Part (i) requires candidates to describe the possible hazards faced by workers using a petrol-driven strimmer on grass verges on the roadside. These would include:

- *Contact with the moving parts of the strimmer.*
- *The possibility of being struck by flying stones or other material.*
- *Slips/trips/falls.*
- *Manual handling hazards.*
- *The danger posed by moving traffic, noise and vibration, dust and fumes.*
- *The hazards associated with the storage and transfer of petrol.*

Candidates who provide only a bare list of hazards without further amplification should not expect to be awarded all the marks available since the question clearly asks for a description. For instance, identification of extreme weather conditions as a hazard requires some mention of ultra-violet radiation and the effects on the skin. Other hazards are perhaps a little more obvious and require rather less by way of a description. Nevertheless, some indication should be provided of how each particular hazard presents itself in the situation given. Part (ii), on the other hand, does require candidates to provide a list. This should include reference to:

- *Ear defenders.*
- *Eye protection.*
- *Respiratory protection (dust mask).*
- *Gloves.*
- *Safety footwear.*
- *Gaiters.*
- *High visibility clothing that also afforded protection against the weather.*

For part (iii) outline measures such as:

- *The use of traffic control or barriers.*
- *The selection and maintenance of equipment to reduce to a minimum the levels of noise and vibration.*
- *The provision of information, instruction, training and supervision, and health surveillance.*

Completion of a risk assessment is undoubtedly a useful starting point, but the assessment alone without the further possible action that should follow is not sufficient to ensure the health and safety of workers.

2. **Outline** the sources and possible effects of **FOUR** non-mechanical hazards commonly encountered in a woodworking shop. **(8)**

Mar 2001 Paper A2 Question 6

The key expression in this question is 'non-mechanical'. Candidates should be able to outline hazards such as:

- *Dust from sawing and sanding operations (leading to lung disorders and possibly cancer).*
- *Chemical hazards from varnishes, glues etc (leading to a range of ill-health effects).*
- *Noise from machinery (causing noise-induced hearing loss and other auditory and non-auditory effects).*
- *Sharps and splinters (causing eye injuries, cuts and infections).*
- *Manual handling hazards (resulting in musculoskeletal disorders).*
- *Electricity (causing shock, burns and fire).*

ELEMENT 4

1. **Outline** a range of checks that should be made to ensure electrical safety in an office environment. **(8)**

Dec 2001 Paper A1 Question 7

Answers can include reference to visual inspections for damage to cables, plugs and sockets, the need to ensure that all fuses are of the correct rating, and checking that equipment is sited such that outlets are not overloaded and cables are not in vulnerable positions. The equipment itself should be checked to ensure suitability and conformity with recognised standards (e.g. CE marking) for Europe and a specific testing procedure for portable appliances should be in place, as well as a procedure for reporting defects or damage.

2. In relation to the use of electrical cables and plugs in the workplace:

   (i) **Identify FOUR** examples of faults and bad practices that could contribute to electrical accidents **(4)**

   (ii) **Outline** the corresponding precautions that should be taken for **EACH** of the examples identified in (i). **(4)**

Mar 2000 Paper A1 Question 10

For part (i), examples include:

- *Failure to select the right equipment for the environment (e.g. armoured or heat resistant cable might be required in arduous conditions).*
- *Incorrect rating of fuses.*
- *Ineffective or discontinuous earthing.*
- *Overloading of socket outlets.*
- *Cables unnecessarily long (or short).*
- *The use of coiled extension leads.*

ASSESSMENT

- *Poorly wired plugs (e.g. wires under tension or outer protective sheath not clamped).*
- *The use of defective cables and plugs.*

For part (ii) an outline of relevant precautions for the examples identified are required:

- *Earthing*
- *Calculate correct rating for a fuse.*
- *Residual current device (RCD).*
- *Reduce voltage.*
- *Battery powered.*
- *Double Insulation.*

3. In relation to electrical safety, **explain** the meaning of the following terms:
    (i) 'isolation' **(2)**
    (ii) 'earthing' **(2)**
    (iii) 'reduced low voltage' **(2)**
    (iv) 'overcurrent protection'. **(2)**

Dec 2002 Paper A2 Question 4

The question aimed to test candidates' knowledge of some key electrical terms. 'Isolation' refers to shutting off the electrical supply to an item of equipment or part of an electrical system and preventing inadvertent reconnection in order, for instance, to carry out maintenance work. 'Earthing', on the other hand, is a means whereby electrical equipment and conductive items are connected to earth by a cable or metal pipework such that the route to earth provides the path of least resistance to a current flowing under fault conditions. 'Reduced low voltage', commonly used on construction sites, involves the reduction of local supply voltage by a transformer to a lower, safer voltage - typically 110 or 55 volts; while 'overcurrent protection' is a method of preventing the flow of excess current by cutting the supply under fault conditions by means of a fuse or circuit breaker.

ELEMENT 5

1. **List EIGHT** ways of reducing the risk of a fire starting in a workplace. **(8)**

Jun 2001 Paper A1 Question 11

This question requires candidates to provide a simple list. Candidates can choose from a list including:

- *The control of smoking and smoking materials.*
- *Good housekeeping to prevent the accumulation of waste paper and other combustible materials.*
- *Regular lubrication of machinery.*
- *Frequent inspection of electrical equipment for damage.*
- *Ensuring ventilation outlets on equipment are not obstructed.*
- *Controlling hot work.*
- *The provision of proper storage facilities for flammable liquids and the segregation of incompatible chemicals.*

2. (a) **Explain**, using a suitable sketch, the significance of the 'fire triangle'. **(4)**
   (b) **Identify TWO** methods of heat transfer and **explain** how **EACH** method can contribute to the spread of fire in work premises. **(4)**

Dec 2005 Paper A2 Question 3

Part (a) of this question required candidates to explain, with a clearly labelled diagram, that each side of the fire triangle represents one of the three elements - namely, fuel, oxygen and a source of ignition - that must be present for combustion to occur. This part of the question was generally well answered.

For part (b), candidates could have chosen two methods of heat transfer from the following: conduction (where, for example, heat can travel through metal beams between separate compartments); radiation (where heat is radiated through the air and affects material at a distance); convection (the upward transfer of heat by gases such as air) and contact or direct burning (where a heat source comes into direct contact with combustible material causing ignition).

Whilst many candidates where able to identify two methods of heat transfer, explanations of how each of the two examples quoted spread fire within a work premise varied considerably in quality especially amongst those candidates who had chosen direct burning and conduction. Again, some candidates did not read the question and wasted valuable time by outlining four methods of heat transfer. It is important that candidates read the questions properly to prevent them from answering previously set questions.

ELEMENT 6

1. (a) **Identify** possible routes of entry of biological organisms into the body. **(4)**
   (b) **Outline** control measures that could be used to reduce the risk of infection from biological organisms. **(4)**

Dec 2001 Paper A1 Question 10

For part (a), candidates can choose from a list including:

- *Inhalation.*
- *Injection.*
- *Entry through broken skin.*
- *Exchange of body fluids and ingestion.*

ASSESSMENT

In answering part (b), candidates should bring to mind hospital or laboratory situations. This should include an outline of measures such as:

- *Cleaning and disinfecting.*
- *Personal protective equipment.*
- *Engineering controls (such as containment and the use of microbiological safety cabinets).*
- *Vermin control.*
- *Good personal hygiene.*
- *Immunisation.*

2. A worker is engaged in general cleaning activities in a large veterinary practice.

    (i) **Identify FOUR** specific types of hazard that the cleaner might face when undertaking the cleaning. **(4)**

    (ii) **Outline** the precautions that could be taken to minimise the risk of harm from these hazards. **(4)**

    Mar 2001 Paper 1 Question 8

Hazards that specifically relate to cleaners are:

- *Cleaning fluids.*
- *Manual handling.*
- *Slips/trips/falls.*
- *Sharp objects.*
- *Those associated with the working environment, such as biological hazards, contact with animals and those arising from the use of specialised equipment.*

In answering part (ii), Examiners are looking to candidates to outline precautions such as:

- *The provision and use of personal protective equipment (including overalls and gloves).*
- *The introduction of a procedure for the handling and disposal of sharps.*
- *The need for animals to be kept in secure enclosures.*
- *The possible need for immunisation against diseases known to be transmitted by animals.*
- *Highlighting that the worker would need specific training in the precautions outlined will gain an additional mark.*

3. A company produces a range of solid and liquid wastes, both hazardous and non-hazardous. **Outline** the arrangements that should be in place to ensure the safe storage of the wastes prior to their collection and disposal. **(8)**

    Dec 2004 Paper A2 Question 4

In answering this question, candidates can refer to arrangements such as:

- *The completion of risk assessments that address the nature, properties and quantities of the wastes likely to be stored.*
- *Minimising the quantities stored by organising regular collections.*
- *Ensuring the separation of incompatible wastes.*
- *providing appropriate means for containing the wastes in secure storage facilities (e.g. protected against unauthorised persons, weather, vehicles, etc).*
- *Installing and maintaining fire protection and fire-fighting systems in the case of flammable or combustible wastes.*
- *Installing bunds and drawing up procedures to deal with spillages that might present environmental risks.*
- *Providing safe means of transport and access to the storage site.*
- *Ensuring that wastes are accurately identified and that warning signs are in place where appropriate.*
- *Training employees in the precautions to be taken.*
- *Ensuring that they are provided with, and use, appropriate personal protective equipment, such as gloves, overalls and eye protection.*

4. For each of the following agents, **outline** the principal health and safety effects **AND identify** a typical workplace situation in which a person might be exposed:

    (i) Isocyanates **(2)**

    (ii) Asbestos **(2)**

    (iii) Leptospira bacteria **(2)**

    (iv) Lead **(2)**

    Mar 2005 Paper A2 Question 3

Isocyanates are a respiratory sensitiser and may also cause dermatitis. Persons carrying out work involving the use of isocyanate-based printing inks, adhesives or paints would be at risk.

Exposure to asbestos may cause asbestosis, lung cancer or mesothelioma (a rare cancer that is associated almost exclusively with asbestos). Carrying out maintenance work on, or the demolition of, a building where asbestos is contained in the fabric of the structure could lead to the inhalation of airborne fibres.

An infection caused by exposure to the leptospira bacterium is called leptospirosis, with symptoms that resemble influenza (fever, chills, muscular aches and pains, etc). In rare cases, a severe form of the condition known as Weil's disease can develop and this is characterised by symptoms that include bruising of the skin, anaemia, sore eyes, nose bleeds and jaundice. Serious damage to internal organs can result, which often proves fatal. The bacterium is carried by animals, particularly rats and cattle, and exposure to

ASSESSMENT

the urine of infected animals can put people such as sewer workers, farm workers and vets at particular risk. While there were some good accounts given for this part of the question, Examiners were disturbed to find that many candidates confused 'leptospira' with 'legionella'.

The health effects of exposure to lead are many and varied but principally include anaemia, fertility problems and damage to the kidneys, the nervous and muscular systems and, particularly in children, the brain. Signs and symptoms of lead poisoning include irritability, lethargy, memory and concentration problems, muscle and joint pain, 'wrist drop' and a blue line on the gums. Those engaged in any activity that involves lead and produces fume, vapour or dust (such as in battery manufacture, lead crystal glass-making or the removal of lead paint) are at risk.

ELEMENT 7

1. In relation to the ill-health effects from the use of vibrating hand-held tools:

    (i) **Identify** the typical symptoms that might be shown by affected individuals. **(4)**

    (ii) **Outline** the control measures that may be used to minimise the risk of such effects. **(4)**

    Mar 2006 Paper A2 Question 5

In answering part (i) of the question, Examiners expected candidates to identify symptoms such as numbness and blanching of the fingers and swollen and painful joints in addition to a reduction in dexterity, strength and sensory perception. Many candidates concentrated on diseases and not symptoms and there appeared to be confusion between noise and vibration which was demonstrated in part by references to deafness and ear/eye damage.

For part (ii), candidates should have outlined a hierarchy of control measures such as elimination by mechanisation or automation; substituting the tools with lower vibration producing equipment; reducing the time of vibration exposure to the operatives; introducing a planned maintenance programme for the tools and providing appropriate personal protective equipment such as gloves to keep hands warm. Few candidates were able to produce this hierarchy of control measures with most referring inaccurately to the use of personal protective equipment to protect against vibration.

2. (a) For **EACH** of the following types of non-ionising radiation, **identify** a source and state the possible ill-health effects on exposed individuals:

    (i) Infrared radiation **(2)**

    (ii) Ultraviolet radiation. **(2)**

    (b) **Identify** the general methods for protecting people against exposure to non-ionising radiation. **(4)**

    Jun 2001 Paper A1 Question 4

In answering part (a) typical sources:
- *Infrared radiation - fire or furnaces.*
- *UV light - welding operations.*

Health effects caused are:
- *Burns to the skin and eye damage (common to both types of radiation).*
- *Effects of the sun (sunburn and skin cancers).*

For part (b), these include:
- *Shielding.*
- *Increasing the distance between source and person.*
- *Reducing the duration of exposure.*
- *Appropriate personal protective equipment (such as clothing and eye protection).*
- *The use of barrier creams.*

3. An office building is about to be occupied by new owners.

    (i) **Outline** the factors that should be considered by the new owners when assessing the suitability of lighting within the building. **(8)**

    (ii) **Describe FOUR** effects on health and safety that might result from inadequate lighting. **(4)**

    (iii) **Outline** the welfare facilities that should be provided in the building. **(8)**

    Jun 2001 Paper A2 Question 1

Part (i) of this question requires an outline of the factors to be considered when assessing the suitability of lighting within an office building. With eight marks available, this should have given a clear indication to candidates that a reasonable outline of a range of relevant factors are needed. Examiners expect candidates to outline factors such as:
- *The type of work to be undertaken.*
- *The type of equipment to be used.*
- *The possibility of glare at workstations and on VDU screens.*
- *The availability of natural light during both summer and winter.*
- *The type of artificial light provided.*
- *The requirement for local lighting for specific tasks.*
- *The availability of emergency lighting.*

- The number of lighting units provided in relation both to the floor area and to the amount of light emitted from each one.

Also important is the possibility of shadows being cast and contrasts in lighting levels between one area and another.

In part (ii), there are marks to be gained for descriptions of the possible effects on health from inadequate lighting, such as eyestrain, headaches and increased levels of stress. Additionally, candidates are expected to refer to other relevant health and safety effects - such as trips and falls, and the possibility of errors in performing tasks that might then put others at risk.

A comprehensive answer to part (iii) of the question includes reference to:

- The provision of sanitary conveniences (adequate in number, separate male and female etc).
- Suitable and sufficient washing facilities.
- A supply of drinking water, eating and rest areas.
- Accommodation for clothing.
- First aid facilities.
- Protection for non-smokers against passive smoking.
- Rest facilities for expectant and nursing mothers.

4. (a) **Explain** the following terms in relation to noise exposure at work:

    (i) 'noise-induced hearing loss' **(2)**

    (ii) 'tinnitus'. **(2)**

   (b) **Identify** FOUR limitations of personal hearing protection as a means of protecting against the effects of noise. **(4)**

Dec 2002 Paper A2 Question 10

For part (a), a general understanding of the effects of noise on hearing is required. Noise-induced hearing loss is normally caused by prolonged exposure to high noise levels causing damage to the hair cells of the inner ear and leading to a permanent threshold shift at particular frequencies, which worsens with continued exposure both in terms of the extent of the threshold shift and of the frequencies affected. Tinnitus, on the other hand, is typified by a ringing or similar sound in the ears caused by over-stimulation of the hair cells. It can be acute or chronic, permanent or intermittent.

The main limitations of hearing protection, for part (b), are:

- Poor fit.
- Resistance to use.
- Comfort factors.
- Incompatibility with other protective equipment.
- Costly in terms of replacement and maintenance.
- Interference with communication.
- Hygiene problems.
- The need for constant supervision and attention (unlike some engineering solutions to noise problems).

ELEMENT 8

1. The water main supplying a school is to be repaired. The work will be carried out in a 1.5 metre deep excavation, which will be supported in order to ensure the safety of those working in the excavation.

    (i) **Identify** when **THREE** main inspections of the supported excavation should be carried out by a competent person. **(3)**

    (ii) **State** the information that should be recorded in the excavation inspection report. **(5)**

    (iii) Other than the provision of supports for the excavation, **outline** additional precautions to be taken during the repair work in order to reduce the risk of injury to those and others who may be affected by the work. **(12)**

Mar 2006 Paper A2 Question 1

For part (i), candidates seemed unaware of the specific occasions when inspections must be carried out. These are at the start of every shift before work commences, after any event likely to affect the strength or stability of the excavation, and after any accidental fall of rock or earth or other material. Candidates generally referred to the inspection of the excavation at the start of every shift but not to the other two main inspections.

Part (ii) should have provided candidates with the opportunity to gain marks simply by stating the information that should be contained in an inspection report. The opportunity was not taken by many. What was needed was reference to information such as the name and address of the person for whom the inspection was carried out, the location of the place of work, a description of the place of work inspected, details of any matters identified that could lead to risks to the health or safety of any person, the action taken to reduce the risk, any further action that might be needed, the name and position of the person making the report, and the date and time of the inspection.

For part (iii), precautions that should be taken to reduce the risk of injury to workers include the detection of underground services, safe digging, preferably by hand, near to the services and the provision of adequate support for them once exposed; the isolation of the water supply to reduce the risk of flooding the excavation; ensuring the stability of adjacent buildings if this was thought to be necessary; the provision of safe access in and out of the excavation and placing stop blocks to prevent plant from approaching too close to its edge; and using appropriate personal protective equipment such as head protection, ear defenders and safety footwear. As for the possible risk of injury to others who might be affected by the work, there would initially need to be close liaison between the contractors and the school authorities to ensure, whenever possible, that work in the excavation was carried out outside school hours. Additionally, barriers would need to be erected to provide a safe walkway for teachers and children and other members of the public

ASSESSMENT

and precautions would also have to be taken to ensure that materials and equipment were stored in a safe compound and plant immobilised when not in actual use.

While the standard of response to this part of the question was marginally better than for the first two parts, there were not many candidates who were able to outline a full range of additional precautions for those who would possibly be at risk.

2. **Outline EIGHT** precautions that should be considered to ensure the safety of children who might be tempted to gain access to a construction site. **(8)**

Mar 2000 Paper A1 Question 2

Outline a hierarchy of measures beginning with attempts to prevent entry by the use of fencing and signs, and monitoring by the use of security patrols or closed-circuit television. This is followed by reference to the need, should entry be gained, to make the site itself safe by isolating services, reducing heights of materials, covering or fencing excavations, as well as removing ladders and denying access to scaffolding. Also consider further precautions such as securing tools, chemicals, equipment and vehicles.

3. **Outline** the particular hazards that may be present during the demolition of a building. **(8)**

Jun 2002 Paper A1 question 3

The main hazards associated with this type of work include:
- *Falls from a height.*
- *Falling debris and premature collapse.*
- *Use of explosives.*
- *Contact with and noise from equipment and heavy plant.*
- *Dust (possibly including asbestos).*
- *The possible presence of services such as electricity, gas and water.*

Index

A

Absence data, 12
Absolute, 10
Absorption, 199
Access and egress, 105
Access equipment, 252
Accessories for lifting, 129
Accident and incident investigation
    identifying immediate and (root) underlying causes, 94
    identifying remedial actions, 96
    the process and purpose of, 91
Accident categories as causes of injury, 54
Accident rates, 11
Accident Statistics, 83
Accidents and ill-health costs, 6
Accident / ill-health data, 11
Accidents, 3
    damage only, 50
    dangerous occurrence, 50
    injury accident, 50
    meaning of, 3
    near-miss, 50
    occupational, 3
    types, 49
Acute health effects, 207
Adapting to technical progress, 63
Adapting work to the individual, 63
Age, 39
Agents
    biological, 195
    chemical, 195
    forms, 195
Air receivers - statutory examination of, 140
Alarm systems for fire, 184
Alcohol, 242
Ammonia, 197
Aptitude, 36
Arrangements
    emergency and rescue services, 76
    health and safety, 20
Asbestos, 197, 269
Assembly points, 189
Attitude, 36
Auditing, 87
Avoiding risks, 63

B

Bacterial agents, 195
Base plates, 257
Basic electricity circuitry, 161
Basic surveys, 203
Behaviour
    controls, 69
Biological agents, 195
    bacterial, 195
    fungi, 195
    viruses, 195
Biological hazards, 51
Body response to agents and protective mechanisms, 200
Brick guards, 258
British standards, 13

C

Categories
    accident as causes of injury, 54
    health risks, 54
Causes
    common for fires, 174
    injury, accident categories, 54
CE marking, 137
Chemical agents, 195
Chronic health effects, 207
Classification
    fires, 174
    substances hazardous to health, 195
Cleaners, risk assessment, 65
Client and Contractor, 27
    duties to each other and to the other's employees, 27
    planning and co-ordination of contracted work, 28
    procedures for the selection of contractors, 28
Clothing, 213
Combustible materials, 178
Common building materials, 182
Common terms
    accidents, 3
    dangerous occurrences, 3
    environmental protection, 3
    hazard, 4
    health, 3
    near-misses, 3
    risk, 4
    safety, 3
    welfare, 3
    work-related ill-health, 4
Communication, 41
    barriers, 41
    general principles, 41
    written, 41
    internal influence, 44
Confined spaces, 70
Construction, 245
    hazards and controls, 246
    health hazards, 269
    terms, 245
Construction projects - management controls, 249
Consultation, 29
    duties to consult, 29
    with employees, 29
Contact with overhead power lines, 247
Contractors,
    client relationship, 27
    planning and co-ordination, 28
    procedures for the selection of, 28
    risk assessment, 56
Control measures, 208
    electricity, 165
    elimination or substitution of hazardous substances, 208
    enclosure, 209
    health surveillance, 215
    ignition sources, 173
    lifting operations, 130
    local exhaust ventilation, 209
    other protective equipment and clothing, 213
    pedestrian hazards, 102
    personal hygiene and protection regimes, 215
    process changes, 219
    respiratory protective equipment, 211
    use and limitations of dilution ventilation, 211
Controlling hazards at source, 63
Controls measures technical, procedural and behavioural, 69
Conveyors, 126
Co-ordination and co-operation, 28
Costs of accidents and ill-health, 6
    direct, 6
    indirect, 6
    insured, 7
    uninsured, 7
Cranes, 128
Culture
    communication, 41
    competent personnel, 40
    correlation with performance, 33
    definition, 33
    effecting change, 40
    external influences on, 34
    indicators, 44
    internal influences on, 45
    leadership, 40
    link to health and safety performance, 33
    management commitment, 40
    outputs or indicators, 33
    training, 43
Current, electrical, 161

D

Damage-only accidents, 50
Dangerous, 3

INDEX

Dangerous occurrences, 4
Definition
    fire, 173
    hazard, 49
    health and safety culture, 33
    risk, 49
Demolition, 248
Design
    risk factors, 224
    ill-health effects, 223
    workstation, 223
Designated walkways, 103
Detection of fire, 184
Developing a coherent prevention policy, 63
Development of a safe system of work, 69
    role of competent persons, 68
Dilution ventilation, 211
Direct costs of accidents and ill-health, 6
Directors and senior managers
    legal and organisational responsibilities, 26
Disabled workers, 59
Diseases, 98
Distinction between different types of incident, 50
Double insulation, 168
Drivers
    competence, 111
    protection and restraint systems, 108
    selection and training, 111
Drugs and alcohol, 242
Duties
    absolute and qualified, 10
    to consult, 29

E

Ear protection, 215
Eating, 226
Electric protection systems
    double insulation, 168
    earthing, 166
    fuses, 166
    isolation, 167
    portable appliance testing, 170
    residual current device, 167
Electricity
    protective systems, 166
    basic circuitry, 161
    burns, 164
    control measures, 166
    fires, 164
    hazards, 162
    inspection and maintenance, 168
    overhead power lines, 247
    principles, 161
    secondary hazards, 165
    selection and suitability of equipment, 166
    shock and its effect on the body, 162
Elimination or substitution, 208
Emergency
    developing procedures, 76
    emergency and rescue services, 76
    first-aid, 76
    shift work and geographical location, 77
Employee involvement in safe systems, 68
Employee
    handbooks, 42
Employee representatives, 42, 43, 45
Employer's
    duty to provide safe system of work, 67
Enclosure, 209
Encyclopaedias, 13
Engineering control, 66
Environmental, 216
    protection, 3
Equipment, 137
Ergonomics, 223
Errors, 38
European Union, 7
Evacuation procedures, 190
Evaluating risk
    qualitative, 56
    risk ranking, 56
    semi-qualitative, 56
Evaluating unavoidable risks, 63
Examination of work equipment, 140
Excavations, 248
Expectant and nursing mothers, 59
Experience, 39
External agencies, 13
External influences, 45
Extinguishing media, 185

F

Factors influencing safety related behaviour, 34
    attitude, aptitude and motivation, 36
    effects of age and experience, 39
    errors and violations, 38
    individual, job and organisational factors, 34
    peers, 39
    perception of risk, 37
Falling materials prevention, 252
Falls from a height, 251
Falls prevention, 252
Fans, 259
Fencing and guarding - pedestrian hazards, 104
Fire
    alarm systems, 184
    arson, 179
    assembly points, 189
    basic principles, 173
    classification of fires, 174
    common causes, 174
    conduction, 174
    control measures, 178
    control of ignition sources, 179
    convection, 174
    definitions, 173
    detection systems, 184
    direct burning, 191
    drills, 191
    emergency lighting, 189
    evacuation procedures, 190
    exit and directional signs, 189
    extinguishing media, 185
    flammable and combustible materials, 178
    flashpoint, 178
    good housekeeping, 180
    heat transmission and fire spread, 174
    hosereels, 188
    hot work, 179
    marshalls, 190
    means of escape, 189
    passageway, 189
    plans, 189
    portable fire fighting equipment, 185
    precautions, 183
    provisions for the infirm and disabled, 191
    purpose of fire drills, 191
    radiation, 174
    risk assessment, 176
    roll calls, 191
    smoking, 179
    sources of fuel, 174
    sources of ignition, 173
    sources of oxygen, 174
    spread, 175
    stairs, 189
    systems of work, 180
    travel distances, 189
    triangle, 173
    welding, 179
Fire action, 190
Fire drills, 191
First aid, 77, 163
    appointed person, 77
    boxes, 77
    coverage, 77
    number, 77
    requirements, 77
    role, 77
    selection, 77
    training, 77
Flammable and combustible materials
    fire, 178, 181
    gases in cylinders, 182
Forklift trucks, 122
Forms of agents, 195
Frequency rate, 11
Functions of employee representatives, 29
Fuse, 166

G

Generic risk assessment, 63
Giving priority to collective protective measures, 63
Good housekeeping and fire, 180
Guards and safety devices, 156

H

Hand-held tools, 142
Hazard, 4, 49
    confined spaces, 70

INDEX

equipment, 147
excavations, 248
machinery, 144
manual handling, 115
electricity, 162
pedestrians, 101
site vehicle, 106
work above ground level, 251
Hazardous substances - classification, 195
Head protection, 254
Health and safety
arrangements, 20
culture, 34
external influences, 45
Internal influences, 44
management system key elements, 15
moral, legal and financial reasons, 5
multi-disciplinary nature of, 3
organising, 20
performance, 33
policy, 19
size of the problem, 5
sources of information, 11
Health, 3
construction hazards, 269
hazards of specific agents, 197
surveillance, 215
Health risks
biological hazards, 55
chemical hazards, 54
physical hazards, 55
psychological hazards, 55
surveys, 203
Hearing protection, 232
Heat, 236
Heating, 227
Hepatitis, 198
Hierarchy of control, 66
elimination/substitution, 66
engineering control, 66
isolation/segregation, 66
personal protective equipment, 66
reducing exposure, 66
Hierarchy of measures
machinery, 151
Highly flammable or flammable liquids, 181
Hoists, 126
Housekeeping, 105
HSG65 - Successful Health and Safety Management, 15

I

Ignition sources, 179
Immediate causes, 94
Incidence rate, 11
Incident types, 50
Independent tied scaffolding, 256
Indicators of culture, 33
Indirect costs of accidents and ill-health, 6
Individual factors, 34
Information
work equipment, 138
Information, instruction, training and supervision
work equipment, 138
Ingestion, 199
Inhalation, 198
Injection, 200
Injuries from manual handling, 115
Inspection
electrical equipment, 169
work equipment, 140
workplace, 83
Inspectors' powers under HASWA, 15
Instructions for work equipment, 138
Insured costs, 6
Internal influences on health and safety, 44
Internal audits, 88
Investigation
procedures, 92
Ionising radiation, 237, 239
Isocyanates, 197
Isolation of services, 167
Isolation/segregation, 66

J

Job factors, 35
Joint occupation
co-operation and co-ordination, 28
premises, 28
shared responsibilities, 28

K

Keyboard operation, 225
Key elements of a health and safety management system, 15
Kinetic handling, 121

L

Ladders, 261
Lead, 197
Legal & organisational health & safety roles & responsibilities, 25
Legionnellosis / Legionnaires Disease, 198
Leptospira, 198
Liabilities
Lifting operations
competent people, 132
control, 130
correct position, 131
installed correctly, 131
special requirements, 133
stability, 131
suitability, 131
Lifts, 126
accessories, 129
control of lifting operations, 130
cranes, 128
statutory examination of lifting equipment, 133
Lighting, 227
Liquefied petroleum and other gases in cylinders, 182
Local exhaust ventilation, 209
Lone working, 59, 73
Long-term and short-term exposure limits, 206

M

Machinery guards
automatic, 153
fixed distance, 151
fixed, 151
interlocking, 152
Machinery
application of protection methods, 156
guards and safety devices, 156
hierarchy of measures, 151
mechanical hazards, 144
non-mechanical hazards, 147
protection from hazards, 150
trip device, 153
Maintenance
conducted safely for work equipment, 139
electrical equipment, 168
electricity, 168
equipment, 138
safe workplace, 119
work equipment, 138
Management system
the key elements of a, 15
controls for construction projects, 249
health and safety arrangements, 20
objectives, 19
organising for health and safety, 20
setting targets, 20
auditing, 87
Management systems for driver competence, 111
Manual handling, 115
hazards, 115
injuries, 115
means of minimizing the risks from, 117
risks assessment, 115
techniques for manually lifting loads, 121
Manually operated load moving equipment, 125
Manufacturers' data, 13, 54
Manufacturers' safety data sheets, 202
Mean duration rate, 12
Meanings of common terms, 3
Means of escape, 189
assembly points, 189
doors, 189
emergency lighting, 189
exit and directional signs, 189
passageways, 189
stairs, 189
travel distances, 189
Mechanical handling, 117
Mechanical hazards, 144
Memos / e-mails, 42
Middle manager and supervisors, 26
Minimising
fire risk, 178
manual handling risks, 117
Mobile elevating work platforms (MEWP), 260

© ACT 305

INDEX

Mobile tower scaffolding, 257
Monitoring, 81
    purpose, 81
    reactive measures, 82
    workplace inspections, 83
Motivation, 36
Movement of peoples and vehicles
    conditions and environments, 106
    hazards to pedestrians, 101
Multi-disciplinary nature of health and safety, 3
Musculoskeletal health, 223
    ergonomics, 223
    ill-health effects, 223
    ill-health risk, 224
    keyboard operation, 225
    preventative and precautionary measures, 225
    risk activities, 225

N

Near-misses, 4
Negative health and safety culture, 34
Nets, 259
Noise, 105, 228
    action values, 230
    common terms, 228
    control techniques, 231
    hearing, 228
    measurement techniques, 231
    personal hearing protection, 232
Non-ionising radiation, 237, 239
Non-mechanical hazards, 144
Notice boards, 41

O

Objectives of risk assessment, 49
Opening and voids, 183
Organic solvents, 197
Organisational factors, 35
Organising for health and safety, 20

P

Pedestrian hazards
    movement of people and vehicles, 101
    signs and personal protective equipment, 104
Pedestrians
    control strategies, 102
    hazards, 101
    measures for no segregation from vehicles, 109
    segregating from vehicles, 108
Peers, 39
Performance
    continuous improvement, 87
    gathering information, 85
    reporting, 86
    review, 85
    role of management team, 86
Performance standards, monitoring, 81
Permits to work, 75
    circumstances of use, 74
    electrical, 74
    hot work, 74
    maintenance, 74
    operation and application, 74
    typical permits, 74
Personal hygiene, 215
Personal protective equipment and clothing, 66, 155, 213, 267
    benefits, 66
    legal and organisational, 26
    limitations, 66
    requirements, 66
Policy
    aims, objectives and key elements, 19
    arrangements, 20
    health and safety arrangements, 20
    organising, 20
    reviewing the policy, 21
    role of the health and safety, 19
    setting targets, 20
Portable
    electrical equipment, 165
    fire fighting equipment, 185
    power tools, 143
Power tools, 143
Practicable, 10
Precautions
    adapting to technical progress, 63
    adapting work to the individual, 63
    avoiding risks, 63
    collective protective measures, 63
    controlling hazards at source, 63
    developing a coherent prevention policy, 63
    emergency procedures, 76
    evaluating unavoidable risks, 63
    excavations, 264
    falling materials, 253
    falls, 252
    general hierarchy of control, 66
    general principles of, 63
    permits-to-work, 74
Principles
    fire, 173
    heat transmission and fire spread, 174
    electricity, 161
Procedural
    emergency, 76
    importance, 68
Process changes, 208
Product labels, 202
Projects, construction management controls, 249
Protection
    machinery hazards, 150
Protective electrical systems, 166
Protective measures for people and structures on site, 110
Providing training, information and supervision, 63
    replacing the dangerous by the less / non dangerous, 63
    safe systems of work, 66
Psychological hazards, 55
Public, risk assessment, 55

R

Radiation, 238
    ionising, 238
    means of controlling exposures, 240
    non-ionising, 238
    protection strategies, 240
Reactive monitoring, 82
Reasonably practicable, 10
Reasons why fires spread, 175
Recording and reporting
    collecting, analysing & communicating data, 96
    typical reportable events in the construction industry, 97
Recording risk assessment, 58
Reduced time exposure, 208
Reduced voltage, 167
Reducing exposure, 66
Remedial actions, 96
Replacing the dangerous by the less/non-dangerous, 63
Report writing, 84
Reporting accidents - statutory requirements, 96
Residual current device, 167
Residual risk, 57
Resistance, electrical, 161
Respiratory protective equipment, 211
    client, 27
    contractor, 28
    directors' and senior managers', 26
    employer's, 25
    middle managers and supervisors, 25
    persons in control of premises, 26
    self-employed, 26
    "the supply chain", 27
Restrict the use work equipment, 138
Review, 85
    policy, 19
    risk assessment, 59
Risk assessment
    a general approach to, 55
    evaluating adequacy of current controls, 56
    evaluating risk, 56
    fire, 176
    identifying hazards, 51
    identifying population at risk, 55
    manual handling, 115
    objectives of, 49
    pedestrian hazards, 102
    qualitative and semi-quantitative risk ranking, 56
    recording, 58
    reviewing, 58
    vehicle, 107
Risk, 4
    definition, 49
    perception, 38
Risk ranking
    qualitative, 56
    semi-quantitative, 56
Role
    competent persons in safe systems, 68
Roll calls, 191
Roof work, 251
Root causes, 94

INDEX

Routes of entry, 198

S

Safe maintenance of work equipment, 138
Safe systems of work, 67
    access equipment, 252
    employer's duty to provide, 67
    confined spaces, 70
    development, 69
    fire, 192
    importance of written procedures, 68
    lone working, 73
    permits to work, 74
    role of competent persons in the development, 68
    technical, procedural and behavioural controls, 69
    written procedures, 68
Safety committees, 30
Safety devices and guards, 156
Safety in the use of lifting and moving equipment, 122
    forklift trucks, 122
    hoists, 126
    manually operated load moving equipment, 125
    means of minimising the risks from manual handling, 117
Safety propaganda, 42
Safety signs, 64
Safety, 3
Samplers
    long term, 205
    short term, 204
Sampling, 82
Scaffolding, 255
    base plates, 257
    brick guards, 258
    fans, 259
    guard rails, 258
    independent tied Scaffolding, 256
    inspection, 263
    mobile tower Scaffolding, 257
nets, 259
    sole boards, 257
    toe boards, 258
Segregating pedestrians and vehicles, 108
Selection
    contractors, 28
    drivers, 111
    electrical equipment, 166
Services, 264, 267
Setting targets, 20
Severity rate, 12
Signs, 64, 104, 110
Silica, 198
Slip resistant surfaces, 103
Smoke control, 184
Smoke tubes, 206
Sole boards, 257
Sources of information on health and safety, 11
    internal, 11
    external, 13
Sources of information, 202
Spillage control and drainage, 103
Stacking and storage, 245
Statistics, accidents, 83
Storage of flammable and combustible materials, 178
Stress, 240
Suitability of work equipment, 137
Supply chain, 27

T

Technical controls, 69
Temperature, 236
Time weighted averages, 209
Toolbox talks, 42
Tools, 142
    hand tools, 142
    portable power tools, 143
Tours, 82
Traffic routes, 107
Training, 43
    drivers, 111
    effects and benefits, 44
    fire, 191
    general, 43
    induction, 44
    job change, process change, 44
    manual handling, 188
    refresher, 44
    work equipment, 138
Travel distances, 189

U

Underlying causes, 94
Uninsured costs, 6
Use and limitations of dilution ventilation, 221
Use of flammable and combustible materials, 178
Use of safety inspections, sampling and tours, 82

V

Vehicle operations, 106
    control strategies for safe, 107
    management systems for assuring driver competence, 111
    protective measures for people and structures on site, 110
    selection and training of drivers, 111
    site rules, 111
    vehicle hazards, 106
Vehicles
    collisions, 106
    driver protection, 108
    hazards, 106
    maintenance, 108
    markings, 110
    measures when segregation is not practicable, 109
    movements, 107
    operations, 106
    overturning, 106
    restraint systems, 108
    segregating pedestrians, 108
    segregation, 108
    signs, 110
    warnings, 110
Ventilation, 227
    dilution, 211
    local exhaust, 209
Vibration, 233
    effects of exposure, 233
    preventative and precautionary measures, 235
    risk activities, 234
    whole body, 234
Violations
    exceptional, 39
    routine, 39
    situational, 39
Violence, 241
Viruses, 195
Visitors, risk assessment, 55
Voltage, 161

W

Waste disposal, 216
Welfare, 3
Work above ground level, 251
Work equipment, 137
    hazards and control, 137
    information, instruction and training, 138, 155
    inspection, 140
    maintained 139
    maintenance to be conducted safely, 139
    requirement to restrict the use, 138
    restrict of use and maintenance, 138
    scope of work equipment, 137
    suitability, 137
Work in and around excavations, 264
Working at height
    base plates, 257
    brick guards, 258
    fall arrest equipment, 254
    fans, 259
    guard rails, 259
    hazards, 251
    independent tied Scaffolding, 256
    inspection, 2635
    ladders, 262
    mobile tower scaffolding, 257
    nets, 259
    putlog scaffolding, 255
    roof work, 251
    scaffolding, 255
    sole boards, 257
    toe boards, 258
Working environment
    dust, 105
    heating, 105
    lighting, 105
    noise, 105
Workplace Exposure Limits, 206
Workplace inspections, 83
Work-related ill-health, 3

NOTES